Oliver Goldsmith, William Pinnock

The History of England

From the invasion of Julius Caesar to the death of George II, with a continuation to

the year 1858

Oliver Goldsmith, William Pinnock

The History of England

From the invasion of Julius Caesar to the death of George II, with a continuation to the year 1858

ISBN/EAN: 9783742837837

Manufactured in Europe, USA, Canada, Australia, Japa

Cover: Foto ©ninafisch / pixelio.de

Manufactured and distributed by brebook publishing software (www.brebook.com)

Oliver Goldsmith, William Pinnock

The History of England

This is a reproduction of a book from the McGill University Library collection.

Title:	Pinnock's improved edition of Dr. Goldsmith's History of England : from the invasion of Julius Caesar to the death of George II, with a continuation to the year 1858. With questions for examination at the end of each section, besides a variety of valuable information added throughout the work, consisting of tables of contemporary sovereigns and of eminent persons, copious explanatory notes, remarks on the politics, manners, and literature of the age, an outline of the Constitution, &c., &c. Illustrated with numerous engravings
Author:	Goldsmith, Oliver, 1730?-1774
Edition:	3rd Canadian ed.
Publisher, year:	Montreal : J. Lovell, 1866

The pages were digitized as they were. The original book may have contained pages with poor print. Marks, notations, and other marginalia present in the original volume may also appear. For wider or heavier books, a slight curvature to the text on the inside of pages may be noticeable.

ISBN of reproduction: 978-1-926846-97-2

This reproduction is intended for personal use only, and may not be reproduced, re-published, or re-distributed commercially. For further information on permission regarding the use of this reproduction contact McGill University Library.

McGill University Library
www.mcgill.ca/library

LOVELL'S SERIES OF SCHOOL-BOOKS.

PINNOCK'S
IMPROVED EDITION OF
DR. GOLDSMITH'S
HISTORY OF ENGLAND,
FROM THE INVASION OF
JULIUS CÆSAR TO THE DEATH OF GEORGE II.
WITH A CONTINUATION TO THE YEAR 1858,

WITH

QUESTIONS FOR EXAMINATION
AT THE END OF EACH SECTION,

BESIDES A VARIETY OF VALUABLE INFORMATION ADDED THROUGHOUT THE WORK:

Consisting of Tables of Contemporary Sovereigns and of Eminent Persons; Copious Explanatory Notes; Remarks on the Politics, Manners, and Literature of the Age; an Outline of the Constitution, &c., &c.

ILLUSTRATED WITH NUMEROUS ENGRAVINGS.

BY WM. C. TAYLOR, LL.D.,
OF TRINITY COLLEGE, DUBLIN,
AUTHOR OF MANUAL OF ANCIENT AND MODERN HISTORY, ETC., ETC.

Third Canadian Edition.

Montreal:
JOHN LOVELL, PRINTER AND PUBLISHER,
AND FOR SALE AT THE BOOKSTORES.
1866.

PREFACE TO THE AMERICAN EDITION.

NEXT to our own national history, it is incumbent on American youth to make themselves acquainted with that of the country from which we derive our political existence, and the most valuable of our customs and institutions. The history of England will never cease to be interesting to us. It will never be other than a valuable and important branch of instruction in our schools.

Among all the histories of that country which have been written, none has been so long and so deservedly popular as that of Dr. Goldsmith. Whether this be owing to its attractive and perfectly intelligible style, or to the vivid impression which his simple and clear narrative of the facts never fails to leave, it is not now important to enquire. The fact of its established classical character, is sufficient to justify the publisher in selecting the most approved edition of this work, to be revised and adapted to the use of schools in our own country.

The mass of illustrative matter, consisting of notes, tables, engravings, &c., which the reader will find in the present edition, may be regarded as adding greatly to its value; and the complete and careful series of questions appended to each section will claim the especial notice of teachers.

CONTENTS.

CHAP.		PAGE
I.	—The Ancient Britons	7
II.	—The Saxons	15
III.	—The Invasion of the Danes	21
IV.	—William the Conqueror	41
V.	—William Rufus	45
VI.	—Henry I	49
VII.	—Stephen	53
VIII.	—Henry II	57
IX.	—Richard I	68
X.	—John	73
XI.	—Henry III	79
XII.	—Edward I	85
XIII.	—Edward II	94
XIV.	—Edward III	99
XV.	—Richard II	109
XVI.	—Henry IV	116
XVII.	—Henry V	120
XVIII.	—Henry VI	124
XIX.	—Edward IV	134
XX.	—Edward V	135
XXI.	—Richard III	138
XXII.	—Henry VII	141
XXIII.	—Henry VIII	149
XXIV.	—Edward VI	168
XXV.	—Mary	173
XXVI.	—Elizabeth	180
XXVII.	—James I	200
XXVIII.	—Charles I	210
XXIX.	—Oliver Cromwell	235
XXX.	—Charles II	251
XXXI.	—James II	269
XXXII.	—William III	271
XXXIII.	—Anne	288
XXXIV.	—George I	308
XXXV.	—George II	317
XXXVI.	—George III	364
XXXVII.	—George IV	423
XXXVIII.	—William IV	437
XXXIX.	—Victoria	458
XL.	—Sketch of the Progress of Literature, Science, and the Arts, during the Present Century	491
XLI.	—The British Constitution	501
	Appendix	509

INTRODUCTORY CHAPTER.

Brief Sketch of the Saxon Idols from which the Days of the Week received their names.

THE idols which our Saxon ancestors worshipped were various; but those which are delineated in the Frontispiece, and from which the days of the week derive their names, were the principal objects of their adoration.

The Idol of the SUN.

This idol, which represented the glorious luminary of the day, was the chief object of their adoration. It is described like the bust of a man, set upon a pillar; holding, with outstretched arms, a burning wheel before his breast. The first day of the week was especially dedicated to its adoration, which they termed the *Sun's daeg;* hence is derived the word SUNDAY.

The Idol of the MOON.

The next was the Idol of the MOON, which they worshipped on the second day of the week, called by them *Moon's daeg;* and since by us, MONDAY.

The form of this Idol is intended to represent a woman, habited in a short coat and a hood, with two long ears. The moon which she holds in her hand designates the quality.

The Idol of TUISCO.

TUISCO was at first deified as the father and ruler of the Teutonic race, but in course of time he was worshipped as the son of the earth. From him came the Saxon words *Tuisco's daeg,* which we call TUESDAY.

He is represented standing on a pedestal, as an old venerable sage, clothed with the skin of an animal, and holding a sceptre in the right hand.

The Idol WODEN, or ODIN.

WODEN, or ODIN, was the supreme divinity of the Northern nations. This hero is supposed to have emigrated from the East, but from what country, or at what time, is not known. His exploits form the greatest part of the mythological creed of the Northern nations, and his achievements are magnified beyond all credibility. The name of the fourth day of the week, called by the Saxons *Woden's daeg,* and by us WEDNESDAY, is derived from this personage.

Woden is represented in a bold and martial attitude, clad in armour, with a broad sword uplifted in his right hand.

The Idol THOR.

Thor, the eldest and bravest of the sons of *Woden* and *Friga*, was, after his parents, considered as the greatest god among the Saxons and

Danes. To him the fifth day of the week, called by them *Thor's daeg*, and by us THURSDAY, was consecrated.

Thor is represented as sitting on a throne, with a crown of gold on his head, adorned with a circle in front, wherein were set twelve bright-burnished gold stars, and with a regal sceptre in his right hand.

The Idol FRIGA, or FREA.

FRIGA, or FREA, was the wife of Woden or Odin; and, next to him, the most revered divinity among the heathen Saxons, Danes, and other Northern nations. In the most ancient times, Friga, or Frea, was the same with the goddess *Hertha* or *Earth*. To her the sixth day of the week was consecrated, which by the Saxons was written *Friya's daeg*, corresponding with our FRIDAY.

Friga is represented with a drawn sword in her right hand, and a bow in her left.

The Idol SEATER.

The Idol SEATER is represented on a pedestal, whereon is placed a *perch*, on the sharp-prickled back of which he stood. His head was uncovered and his visage lean. In his left hand he held up a wheel, and in his right was a pail of water, wherein were flowers and fruits; and his dress consisted of a long coat, girded with linen.

The appellation given to the day of his celebration is still retained. The Saxons named it *Seater's daeg*, which we call SATURDAY.

It will be seen in our explanation of the Mythological plate, that the names of the *days of the week* owe their origin to the names given by the Saxons to their chief idols. We shall here observe, that the names which they gave to the *months* were singularly descriptive of the seasons, and, therefore, we subjoin them: remarking, by the way, that the names of the months adopted by the French during the Revolution, though more elegant, were not more appropriate than those of the Saxons, whose ideas they appear to have borrowed.—Their first month was styled

Midwinter Monath .... DECEMBER.
Aefter Yula ...... (or after Christmas) .... JANUARY.
Sol Monath ...... (From the returning sun) .... FEBRUARY.
Rethe Monath .... (Rugged Month) .... MARCH.
Easter Monath ... {(From a Saxon goddess, whose name we still preserve).} APRIL.
Trimilchi .... (From cows being milked thrice a day)... MAY.
Sere Monath ...... (Dry Month) .... JUNE.
Mæd Monath ..... (The meads being then in bloom) .... JULY.
Weod Monath .... (From the luxuriance of weeds) .... AUGUST.
Hæfast Monath .. (Harvest Month) .... SEPTEMBER
Winter Fyllish ... {(From winter approaching with the full moon of that month).} OCTOBER.
Blot Monath ...... {(From the blood of cattle slain that month and stored for winter provision)} NOVEMBER.

THE
HISTORY OF ENGLAND

CHAPTER I.

THE ANCIENT BRITONS.

OF BRITAIN,* FROM THE INVASION OF JULIUS CÆSAR,† B. C. 54,
TO THE ABDICATION OF THE ROMANS.‡

SECTION I.

*Theirs was the science of a martial race,
To shape the lance or decorate the shield;
E'en the fair virgin stain'd her native grace
To give new horrors to the tented field.*

1. BRITAIN was but very little known to the rest of the world before the time of the Romans. The coasts opposite Gaul § were frequented by merchants, who traded thither for such commodities as the natives were able to produce, and who, it is thought, after a time, possessed themselves of all the maritime places where they had at first been permitted to reside. 2. Finding the country fertile, and commodiously situated for trade, they settled upon the seaside, and introduced the practice of agriculture; but it was very different with the inland inhabitants of the country, who considered themselves as the lawful possessors of the soil, and avoided all correspondence with the new-comers, whom they viewed as intruders upon their property,‖ and therefore harassed by repeated wars.

---

* Britain, the name given to England, Scotland, and Wales, united.
† Julius Cæsar was a most eloquent writer and successful warrior; he assumed the title of emperor, which roused the jealousy of many of the principal Roman citizens, by whom he was assassinated in the senate-house, in the 56th year of his age.
‡ The ancient inhabitants of Rome in Italy.
§ Gaul was the ancient name of France.
‖ Geoffrey of Monmouth, an ancient English historian, says, that the British isles were first peopled 1100 years before Christ, and asserts that Brutus, the great grandson of Æneas, colonized them with the descendants of those Trojans, who, after the destruction of Troy, settled in Greece or Italy. This account is, however, unsupported by any genuine historical documents, and is, therefore, now treated as purely fabulous, though in less enlightened ages a story so romantic easily passed current.

3. The inland inhabitants are represented as extremely numerous, living in cottages thatched with straw, and feeding large herds of cattle. They lived mostly upon milk, or flesh produced by the chase.* What clothes they wore to cover any part of their bodies, were usually the skins of beasts; but the arms, legs, and thighs were left naked, and were usually painted blue. 4. Their hair, which was long, flowed down upon their backs and shoulders; while their beards were kept close shaven, except upon the upper lip, where they were suffered to grow. The dress of savage nations is everywhere pretty much the same, being calculated rather to inspire terror than to excite love or respect.

5. As to the government, it consisted of several small principalities, each under its respective leader; and this seems to be the earliest mode of dominion with which mankind are acquainted, and is deduced from the natural privileges of paternal authority. Upon great and imminent dangers, a commander-in-chief was chosen by common consent, in a general assembly; and to him was committed the conduct of the general interest, the power of making peace or leading to war, and the administration of justice.

6. Their forces consisted chiefly of foot, and yet they could bring a considerable number of horse into the field upon great occasions. They likewise used chariots in battle, which, with short scythes fastened to the ends of the axletrees, inflicted terrible wounds, spreading horror and devastation wheresoever they drove.† 7. Nor while the chariots were thus destroying, were the warriors who conducted them unemployed: they darted their javelins against the enemy, ran along the beam, leaped upon the ground, resumed their seat, stopped or turned their horses at full speed, and sometimes cunningly retreated to draw the enemy into confusion.

8. The religion of the Britons was one of the most considerable parts of their government; and the Druids,‡

---

* The ancient Britons were so habitually regular and temperate, that they only began to grow old at a hundred and twenty years.—PLUTARCH, De Placitis Philosophæ.

† Cæsar gives a most animated description of the dexterity of the Britons in managing their war-chariots, which he ascribes to constant use and incessant exercise; thereby intimating that the Britons were continually engaged in intestine wars.—Cæsar's Com., lib. iv.

‡ The Druids were divided into three different classes; the Bards, who were the heroic historians and genealogical poets; the Vates who were the sacred musicians the religious poets and the pretended prophets; the third

An Ancient Briton.

who were the guardians of it, possessed great authority among them. No species of superstition was ever more terrible than theirs: besides the severe penalties which they were permitted to inflict in this world, they inculcated the eternal transmigration of souls, and thus extended their authority as far as the fears of their votaries.* 9. They

class, which was by far the most numerous, and who performed all the other offices of religion, were called by the general name of Druids, which appellation was commonly given to the whole fraternity. Their supreme chief was styled the Arch-druid. To the priesthood were also attached a number of females called Druidesses, who were likewise divided into three classes. Those of the first vowed perpetual virginity, and lived together sequestered from the rest of the world: these were great pretenders to divination, prophecy, and miracles, and were highly venerated by the people. The second class consisted of certain devotees, who, though married, spent the greater part of their time with the Druids in assisting in the offices of religion, occasionally returning to their husbands. The third and lowest class waited on the Druids, and performed the most servile offices about the temples, &c. The priesthood, in the most ancient times, was hereditary in all countries, and was particularly so in the Celtic nations; where the order of Druids did not only descend to their posterity, but the office of priest was likewise hereditary in families.

* Among a people so credulous as the ancient Britons, it is no wonder that those who possessed such high authority among them as the Druids, practiced the greatest impositions: accordingly we read, that the Druids were in the habit of borrowing large sums of the people, which they promised to repay in the other world.—Druidæ pecuniam mutuo accipiebant in posteriore vita reddituri.—*Particius.*

sacrificed human victims, which they burnt in large wicker-idols, made so capacious as to contain a multitude of persons at once, who were thus consumed together. To these rites, tending to impress ignorance with awe, they added the austerity of their manners and the simplicity of their lives. They lived in woods, caves, and in hollow trees; their food was acorns and berries, and their drink water. These acts caused the people, not only to respect, but almost to adore them. The most remarkable Druidical monument in England is the circle of stones on Salisbury plains, called Stonehenge. It appears to have been a great national temple.

10. It may be easily supposed that the manners of the people took a tincture from the discipline of their teachers. Their lives were simple, but they were marked with cruelty and fierceness; their courage was great, but neither dignified by mercy nor perseverance.

Cæsar invading Britain.

11. The Britons had long remained in this rude but independent state, when Cæsar, having overrun Gaul with his victories, and willing still further to extend his fame, determined upon the conquest of a country that seemed to promise an easy triumph; accordingly when the troops designed for the expedition were embarked, he set sail for Britain about midnight, and the next morning arrived on the coast near Dover, where he saw the rocks and cliffs covered with armed men to oppose his landing.

12. The Britons had chosen Cassivelau'nus* for their commander-in-chief; but the petty princes under his command, either desiring his station, or suspecting his fidelity, threw off their allegiance. 13. Some of them fled with their forces into the internal parts of the kingdom, others submitted to Cæsar, till at length Cassivelau'nus himself, weakened by so many desertions, resolved upon making what terms he was able while he yet had power to keep the field. 14. The conditions offered by Cæsar, and accepted by him, were, that he should send to the continent double the number of hostages first demanded, and that he should acknowledge subjection to the Romans. Cæsar, however, was obliged to return once more to compel the Britons to complete their stipulated treaties.

Questions for Examination.

1. Was Britain well known before the time of its invasion by the Romans? By whom were, at that time, the coasts opposite Gaul frequented?
2. Who introduced the practice of agriculture?
3, 4. Describe the inland inhabitants.
5. Of what did the Government of the ancient Britons consist?
6, 7. What was their chief force?
8. Who were the ministers of their religion?
9. Did they ever sacrifice human victims?
10. What were the manners of the people?
11. Who first determined on the conquest of Britain?
12, 13. Whom did the Britons choose for their leader?
14. What conditions were offered by Cæsar, and accepted by Cassivelaunus?

SECTION II.

Great Boadicea———
Thy very fall perpetuates thy fame,
And Suetonius' laurels droop with shame.—*Dibdin.*

1. Upon the accession of Augus'tus,† that emperor had formed a design of visiting Britain, but was diverted from it by the unexpected revolt of the Panno'nians.‡

Tiberius,§ wisely judging the empire already too extensive, made no attempt upon Britain. From that time the natives began to improve in all the arts which contribute to the advancement of human nature.

2. The wild extravagances of Calig'ula, ‖ by which he

---

* Sometimes written Cassibelau'nus, or Cassibe'lan.
† Augustus was the son of Julius Cæsar's niece adopted by Cæsar. He was the second emperor of Rome.
‡ The people of Hungary, which country was formerly called Pannonia.
§ The third emperor of Rome.
‖ A Roman emperor, the successor of Tiberius.

threatened Britain with an invasion, served rather to expose him to ridicule than the island to danger. At length, the Romans, in the reign of Clau'dius,* began to think seriously of reducing them under their dominion. The expedition for this purpose was conducted in the beginning by Plau'tius and other commanders, with that success which usually attended the Roman arms.

3. Carac'tacus was the first who seemed willing, by a vigorous effort, to rescue his country, and repel its insulting and rapacious conquerors. This rude soldier, though with inferior forces, continued, for above nine years, to oppose and harass the Romans; till at length he was totally routed and taken prisoner by Osto'rius Scap'ula, who sent him in triumph to Rome. 4. While Carac tacus was being led through Rome, he appeared no way dejected at the amazing concourse of spectators that were gathered upon this occasion; but casting his eyes on the splendours that surrounded him, " Alas!" cried he, " how is it possible that a people possessed of such magnificence at home, could envy me a humble cottage in Britain!" The emperor was affected by the British hero's misfortunes, and won by his address. He ordered him to be unchained on the spot, and set at liberty with the rest of the captives.

5. The cruel treatment of Boadi'cea, queen of the Ice'ni, drove the Britons once more into open rebellion. Prasat'agus, king of the Ice'ni, at his death had bequeathed one half his dominions to the Romans, and the other to his daughters, thus hoping, by the sacrifice of a part, to secure the rest to his family. But it had a different effect; for the Roman procurator immediately took possession of the whole: and when Boadi'cea, the widow of the deceased, attempted to remonstrate, he ordered her to be scourged like a slave, and made slaves of her daughters. 6. These outrages were sufficient to produce a revolt throughout the island. The Ice'ni, as being the most deeply interested in the quarrel, were the first to take arms; all the other states soon followed the example; and Boadi'cea, a woman of great beauty and masculine spirit, was appointed to head the common forces, which amounted to two hundred and thirty thousand fighting men. 7. These, exasperated by their wrongs, attacked several of the Roman settlements and colonies with success: Suetoni'us, who commanded the Roman forces, hastened to relieve London, which was al-

* The son of Drusus, and successor of Caligula.

ready a flourishing colony; but found on his arrival, that it would be requisite for the general safety to abandon that place to the merciless fury of the enemy. 8. London was soon, therefore, reduced to ashes; such of the inhabitants as remained in it were massacred, and the Romans, with all other strangers, to the number of seventy thousand, were cruelly put to the sword. Flushed with these successes, the Britons no longer sought to avoid the enemy, but boldly came to the place where Suetoni'us awaited their arrival, posted in a very advantageous manner with a body of ten thousand men. 9. The battle was obstinate and bloody. Boadi'cea herself appeared in a chariot with her two daughters, and harangued her army with masculine intrepidity; but the irregular and undisciplined bravery of her troops was unable to resist the cool intrepidity of the Romans. They were routed with great slaughter; eighty thousand perished in the field, and an infinite number were made prisoners; while Boadi'cea herself, fearing to fall into the hands of the enraged victor, put an end to her life by poison.

10. The general who firmly established the dominion of the Romans in this island was Ju'lius Agric'ola,* who governed it during the reigns of Vespa'sian,† Ti'tus,‡ and Domi'tian,§ and distinguished himself as well by his courage as humanity.

For several years after the time of Agric'ola, a profound peace seems to have prevailed in Britain, and little mention is made of the affairs of the island by any historian.

11. At length, however, Rome, that had for ages given laws to nations, and diffused slavery and oppression over the known world, began to sink under her own magnificence. Mankind, as if by a general consent, rose up to vindicate their natural freedom; almost every nation asserting that independence of which they had been so long unjustly deprived.

12. During these struggles the British youth were frequently drawn away into Gaul, to give ineffectual succour

* Julius Agricola was the father-in-law of Tacitus, the celebrated historian.
† Vespasian was the tenth Roman emperor, he was valiant, but very avaricious.
‡ Titus was the eleventh Roman emperor, the son of Vespasian; he was so good a man that he was called " the delight of mankind."
§ Domitian was the twelfth Roman emperor, and brother to Titus: he was a great persecutor of the Christians, and of a most cruel disposition.

to the various contenders for the empire, who, failing in every attempt, only left the name of tyrants behind them.* In the mean time, as the Roman forces decreased in Britain, the Picts and Scots† continued still more boldly to infest the northern parts; and crossing the friths, which the Romans could not guard, in little wicker-boats covered with leather, filled the country, wherever they came, with slaughter and consternation.

13. The Romans therefore finding it impossible to stand their ground in Britain, in the reign of the emperor Valentin'ian took their last leave of the island, after being masters of it for nearly four hundred years, and now left the natives to the choice of their own government and kings. They gave them the best instructions the calamitous times would permit, for exercising their arms, and repairing their ramparts; and helped them to erect a new wall of stone across the island, for they had not at that time artisans skiful enough among themselves to repair that which had been built by the emperor Sev'erus. The ruins of this wall, and the fortresses by which the Roman colonies were defended, are among the most interesting relics of antiquity in England.

Questions for Examination.

1. What prevented Augustus from visiting Britain ?
  Did Tiberius make an attempt upon Britain ?
2. What exposed Caligula to ridicule ?
3. Who was the first person that was willing to repel the invaders ?
  How long did Caractacus harass the Romans?
4. What remarks did Caractacus make on witnessing the splendour of Rome?
5. What caused the Britons to rebel?
  Who commanded Boadicea to be ill-treated?
6. What were the consequences?
7. Who commanded the Roman forces at that time?
8. What was the fate of London and its inhabitants?
9. Describe Boadicea's conduct, and the result of this battle.
10. At what time did peace prevail in Great Britain?
11. What was the situation of Rome at this time?
12. What were the nations that infested the northern parts?
13. When did the Romans take their leave of Britain? And how long had they been masters of it?

---

* According to the "*Notitia Imperii*," no less than twelve British corps of infantry and cavalry were constantly dispersed in the distant provinces of the empire; while foreign soldiers were, according to the invariable policy of the Romans, stationed in Britain.

† The names by which the inhabitants of Scotland were at that time distinguished. "The Picts (so called from *Pictish*, a plunderer, and not from *Picti*, painted), and the Scots, from *Scuite*, a wanderer, in the Celtic tongue, were only different tribes of Caledonians."—*Dr. Henry.*

CHAPTER II.

THE SAXONS.

SECTION I.

*But hark! what foreign drum on Thanet's isle
Proclaims assistance? 'Tis the Saxon band
By Hengist led and Horsa; see they smile,
And greet their hosts with false insiduous hand.—Dibdin.*

1. (A. D. 447.) THE Britons, being now left to themselves, considered their new liberties as their greatest calamity. The Picts and Scots, uniting together, began to look upon Britain as their own, and attacked the northern wall, which the Romans had built to keep off their incursions, with success. Having thus opened to themselves a passage, they ravaged the whole country with impunity, while the Britons sought precarious shelter in the woods and mountains.*

2. It was in this deplorable and enfeebled state that the Britons had recourse to the Saxons, a brave people; who for their strength and valour, were formidable to all the German nations around them, and supposed to be more than a match for the gods themselves. They were a people restless and bold, who considered war as their trade; and were, in consequence, taught to consider victory as a doubtful advantage, but courage as a certain good. 3. A nation however entirely addicted to war, has seldom wanted the imputation of cruelty; as those terrors which are opposed without fear are often inflicted without regret. The Saxons are represented as a very cruel nation: but we must remember that their enemies have drawn the picture.

4. It was no disagreeable circumstance to these ambitious people to be invited into a country upon which they had for ages been forming designs. In consequence, therefore, of the solemn invitation of Vor'tigern, who was then king of Britain, they arrived with fifteen hundred men, under the command of Hen'gist and Hor'sa, who were brothers, and

---

* In this extremity, they made application for succour to Ætius, prefect of Gaul, in the following remarkable words:—"The groans of the wretched Britons, to the thrice-appointed Consul Ætius,—The barbarians drive us into the sea, and the sea forces us back on the swords of the barbarians, so that we have nothing left us but the wretched choice of being either drowned or murdered." Ætius was, however, too closely engaged in opposing Attila, the renowned king of the Huns (who, from the havoc he made wherever his sword was drawn, was denominated "*The scourge of God,*") to bestow any attention on the Britons.

landed on the Isle of Than'et.* 5. There they did not long remain inactive; but being joined by the British forces, they boldly marched against the Picts and Scots, who had advanced as far as Lincolnshire, and soon gained a complete victory over them. (A. D. 450.)

The Saxons, however, being sensible of the fertility of the country to which they came, and the barrenness of that which they had left behind, invited over great numbers of their countrymen to become sharers in their new expedition. 6. Accordingly they received a fresh supply of five thousand men, who passed over in seventeen vessels, and soon made a permanent establishment in the island.

The British historians, in order to account for the easy conquest of their country by the Saxons, assign their treachery, not less than their valour, as a principal cause.

7. They allege, that Vor'tigern was artfully inveigled into a passion for Rowe'na, the daughter of Hen'gist; and, in order to marry her, was induced to settle the fertile province of Kent upon her father, whence the Saxons could never after be removed.† It is alleged, also, that upon the death of Vor'timer, which happened shortly after the victory he gained at Eg'glesford, Vor'tigern, his father, was reinstated upon the throne. 8. It is added that this weak monarch, accepting of a festival from Hen'gist, three hundred of his nobility were treacherously slaughtered, and himself detained captive.

After the death of Hen'gist, several other German tribes, allured by the success of their countrymen, went over in great numbers. 9. A body of Saxons, under the conduct of Ella and his three sons, had some time before laid the foundation of the kingdom of the South Saxons, though not without great opposition and bloodshed. This new kingdom included Surrey, Sussex, and the New Forest; and extended to the frontier of Kent.

10. Another tribe of the Saxons, under the command of Cerdic, and his son Kenrick, landed in the west, and from thence took the name of West Saxons. These met with

* Thanet is an island of Kent. Margate and Ramsgate are its principal towns.

† Our old English historians say, that when the beautiful Rowena was first introduced to Vortigern, "she presented him on her knee with a cup of wine, saying 'Wacs heal, hlaford cyning,' or 'Be of health, Lord king!' to which Vortigern, being instructed in the custom, answered, 'Drinc heal,' or, 'I drink your health.'"—It is proper here to observe, however, that some able historians have declared, that no authentic documents exist concerning these stories of Vortigern and Rowena, or of the slaughter of the British nobles; and that they are inclined to believe the whole a fiction, or at least very much exaggerated.

a very vigorous opposition from the natives, but, being reinforced from Germany,* and assisted by their countrymen on the island, they routed the Britons, and although retarded in their progress by the celebrated king Arthur,† they had strength enough to keep possession of the conquest they had already made. Cerdic, therefore, with his son Kenrick, established the third Saxon kingdom in the island, namely, that of the West Saxons, including the counties of Hants, Dorset, Wilts, Berks, and the Isle of Wight.

11. It was in opposing this Saxon invader that the celebrated prince Arthur acquired his fame. However unsuccessful all his valour might have been in the end, yet his name made so great a figure in the fabulous annals of the times, that some notice must be taken of him. 12. This prince is of such obscure origin, that some authors suppose him to be the son of King Ambro'sius,‡ and others only his nephew; others again affirm that he was a Cornish prince, and son of Gurlois, king of that province. However this may be, it is certain he was a commander of great valour; and, could courage alone have repaired the miserable state of the Britons, his might have been effectual. 13. According to the most authentic historians, he worsted the Saxons in twelve successive battles. In one of these, namely, that fought at Caerbadon, in Berks, it is asserted that he killed no less than four hundred and forty of the enemy with his own hand. But the Saxons were too numerous and powerful to be extirpated by the desultory efforts of single valour; so that a peace, and not a conquest, was the immediate fruit of his victories. 14. The enemy, therefore, still gained ground; and this prince, in the decline of life, had the mortification, from some domestic troubles of his own, to be a patient spectator of their encroachments. His first wife had been carried off by Menlas, king of Somersetshire, who detained her a whole year at Glastonbury,§ until Arthur, discovering the place of her retreat, advanced with an army against the seducer, and obliged him to give her back. 15. In his second wife, perhaps, he may have been more fortunate, as we have no mention made of her; but it was otherwise with his third consort, who was car-

* A large country of Europe, comprising many kingdoms and states.
† A British prince, who established Christianity at York, in the room of paganism or worshipping of idols.
‡ King of the Britons.
§ Glastonbury is a town in Somersetshire, noted for a famous abbey.

ried off by his own nephew, Mordred. This produced a rebellion, in which the king and his traitorous kinsman, meeting in battle, slew each other.

Questions for Examination.

1. Who ravaged England with impunity?
2. To whom did the Britons have recourse for assistance in their distress?
3. What character is given of the Saxons*
4. Where did the Saxons land?
5. Whom did the Saxons defeat?
6. By what means can the easy conquest of Britain be accounted for?
7. How did the Saxons obtain possession of the province of Kent?
8. Were not many of the British nobility treacherously slaughtered?
9. Who laid the foundations of the South Saxon kingdom?
10. Who gave rise to the name of the West Saxons?
11, 12. What celebrated British prince opposed the Saxons with success?
13. What extraordinary feat of valour is related of him?
14. What domestic troubles afflicted Arthur in the decline of life?

SECTION II

While undecided yet which part should fall,
Which nation rise, the glorious Lord of all.—Creech.

1. (A.D. 575.) In the meantime, while the Saxons were thus gaining ground in the west, their countrymen were not less active in the other parts of the island. Adventurers still continuing to pour over from Germany, one body of them, under the command of Uffa, seized upon the Counties of Cambridge, Suffolk, and Norfolk, and gave their commander the title of king of the East Angles,* which was the fourth Saxon kingdom founded in Britain.

2. Another body of these adventurers formed a kingdom under the title of East Saxony, or Essex, comprehending Essex, Middlesex, and part of Hertfordshire. This kingdom, which was dismembered from that of Kent, formed the fifth Saxon principality founded in Britain.

3. The kingdom of Mercia was the sixth which was established by these fierce invaders, comprehending all the middle counties, from the banks of the Severn to the frontiers of the two last-named kingdoms.

The seventh and last kingdom which they obtained was that of Northumberland,† one of the most powerful and extensive of them all. This was formed from the union of

---

* Comprehending Norfolk, Suffolk, Cambridge, and the Isle of Ely.
† Northumberland, that is the land north of the river Humber, contained six counties in England, and extended as far as the Frith of Edinburgh, in Scotland.

two smaller Saxon kingdoms, the one called Berni'cia, containing the present county of Northumberland and the bishoprick of Durham; the subjects of the other, called Dei'ri, extending themselves over Lancashire and Yorkshire. 4. These kingdoms were united in the person of Ethelred, king of Northumberland, by the expulsion of Edwin, his brother-in-law, from the kingdom of the Dei'ri and the seizure of his dominions. In this manner, the natives being overpowered or entirely expelled, seven kingdoms were established in Britain, which have since been well known by the name of the Saxon heptarchy.

5. The Saxons, being thus well established in all the desirable parts of the island, and having no longer the Britons to contend with, began to quarrel among themselves. A country divided into a number of petty independent principalities, must ever be subject to contention, as jealousy and ambition have more frequent incentives to operate. 6. After a series, therefore, of battles, treasons, and stratagems, all their petty principalities fell under the power of Egbert, king of Wessex, whose merits deserved dominion, and whose prudence secured his conquests. By him all the kingdoms of the heptarchy were united under one common jurisdiction; but to give splendour to his authority, a general council of the clergy and laity was summoned at Winchester, where he was solemnly crowned king of England, by which name the united kingdom was thenceforward called.

7. Thus about four hundred years after the first arrival of the Saxons in Britain, all the petty settlements were united into one great state, and nothing offered but prospects of peace, security, and increasing refinement.

It was about this period that St. Gregory undertook to send missionaries among the Saxons, to convert them to Christianity. 8. It is said, that before his elevation to the papal chair he chanced one day to pass through the slave-market at Rome, and perceiving some children of great beauty, who were set up for sale, he enquired about their country, and finding they were English pagans, he is said to have cried out in the Latin language, Non Angli sed Angeli, forent, si essent Christiani,—"They would not be English, but angels, had they been Christians."* 9. From

* Inquiring further the name of their province, he was answered Deiri (a district of Northumberland). "Deiri," replied St. Gregory, "that is good; they are called to the mercy of God from his anger, that is, DE IRA. But

that time he was struck with an ardent desire to convert that unenlightened nation, and ordered a monk named Augustine, and others of the same fraternity, to undertake the mission into Britain

This pious monk, upon his first landing upon the Isle of Thanet, sent one of his interpreters to Eth'elbert the Kentish king, declaring he was come from Rome with offers of eternal salvation. 10. The king immediately ordered them to be furnished with all necessaries, and even visited them, though without declaring himself as yet in their favour. Augustine, however, encouraged by this favourable reception, and now seeing a prospect of success, proceeded with redoubled zeal to preach the gospel. 11. The king openly espoused the Christian religion, while his example wrought so successfully on his subjects that numbers of them came voluntarily to be baptized, the missionaries loudly declaring against any coercive means towards their conversion. In this manner the other kingdoms, one after the other, embraced the faith: and England was soon as famous for its superstition, as it had once been for its averseness to Christianity.

The Saxon ecclesiastics were in general men of great piety and learning. The most celebrated among them was the venerable Bede, born A. D. 673, died A. D. 735, whose history of the Anglo-Saxon Church was so highly valued by King Alfred, that he translated it from the Latin language, in which it was written, into the Saxon.

Questions for Examination.

1. Whence did adventurers continue to come?
   What counties formed the fourth kingdom of the Saxons?
2. What counties did the fifth Saxon kingdom comprehend?
3. What was the sixth kingdom called?
   What was the seventh kingdom? and how was it formed.
4. What was the general name given to the seven Saxon kingdoms?
5. What happened to the Saxons after the Britons were subdued?
6. Under whose power did all the petty principalities fall?
7. At about what period were missionaries sent among the Saxons to convert them to Christianity?
8, 9. What was the circumstance which occasioned the sending missionaries into Britain?
10. How were the missionaries received by the Saxon monarch?
11. What effect was produced by the king's example?

---

what is the king of that province named?" He was told ÆLLA, or ALLA. 'Alleluiah!" cried he, "we must endeavour that the praises of God be sung in that country."—*Hume.*

CHAPTER III.

THE INVASION OF THE DANES.

FROM THE END OF THE HEPTARCHY TO THE REIGN OF WILLIAM THE CONQUEROR.

SECTION I.

> The Danes! the Danes!" the young and aged cry,
> And mothers press their infants as they fly."—*Dibdin.*

1. (A. D. 832.) Peace and unanimity had been scarcely established in England, when a mighty swarm of those nations called Danes* and Northmen, subsequently corrupted into Normen or Normans, who had possessed the country bordering on the Baltic,† began to level their fury against England. A small body of them at first landed on the coasts, with a view to learn the state of the country; and having committed some depredations, fled to their ships for safety.

2. About seven years after this first attempt they made a descent upon the kingdom of Northumberland, where they pillaged a monastery; but, their fleet being shattered by a storm, they were defeated by the inhabitants and put to the sword. It was not till about five years after the accession of Egbert ‡ that their invasions became truly formidable. From that time they continued with unceasing ferocity, until the whole kingdom was reduced to a state of the most distressing bondage.§

3. Though often repulsed, they always obtained their end of spoiling the country and carrying the plunder away. It was their method to avoid coming, if possible, to a general engagement; but, scattering themselves over the face of the country, they carried away indiscriminately, as well the inhabitants themselves as all their movable possessions.

4. At length, however, they resolved upon making a settle-

---

* The Danes were inhabitants of Denmark, a kingdom in the north of Europe.
† The Baltic is an inland sea in the north of Europe.
‡ Egbert was the first sole monarch in England.
§ Nothing could be more dreadful than the manner in which these fierce barbarians carried on their excursions; they spared neither age nor sex, and each commander urged the soldiers to inhumanity. One of their celebrated chieftains, named Oliver, gained from his dislike to the favorite amusement of his soldiers (that of tossing children on the point of their spears), the contemptuous surname of Bumakal, or "The Preserver of Children."

ment in the country; and landing on the Isle of Thanet, stationed themselves there. In this place they kept their ground, notwithstanding a bloody victory gained over them by Eth'elwolf. The reign of Eth'elbald, his successor, was of no long continuance; however, in a short space, he crowded together a number of vices sufficient to render his name odious to posterity.

5. This prince was succeeded by his brother Eth'elred, a brave commander, but whose valour was insufficient to repress the Danish incursions. In these exploits he was always assisted by his younger brother, Alfred, afterwards surnamed the Great, who sacrificed all private resentment to the public good, having been deprived by the king of a large patrimony. 6. It was during Eth'elred's reign that the Danes, penetrating into Mercia, took up their winter-quarters at Nottingham; whence the king, attempting to dislodge them, received a wound in the battle, of which he died, leaving his brother Alfred the inheritance of a kingdom that was now reduced to the brink of ruin.

7. The Danes had already subdued Northumberland and East Anglia, and had penetrated into the very heart of Wessex. The Mercians were united against Alfred; the dependence upon the other provinces of the empire was but precarious: the lands lay uncultivated, through fear of continual incursions; and all the churches and monasteries were burnt to the ground. In this terrible situation of affairs, nothing appeared but objects of terror, and every hope was lost in despair. 8. The wisdom and virtues of one man alone were found sufficient to bring back happiness, security, and order; and all the calamities of the time found redress from Alfred.

9. This prince seemed born, not only to defend his bleeding country, but even to adorn humanity. He had given very early instances of those great virtues which afterwards gave splendour to his reign; and was anointed by Pope Leo as future king, when he was sent by his father, for his education, to Rome. On his return thence, he became every day more the object of his father's fond affections; and that perhaps was the reason why his education was at first neglected. He had attained the age of twenty before he was made acquainted with the lowest elements of literature; but hearing some Saxon poems read, which recounted the praise of heroes, his whole mind was roused, not only to obtain a similitude of glory, but also to be able to transmit

that glory to posterity. 10. Encouraged by the queen his mother, and assisted by a penetrating genius, he soon learned to read these compositions, and proceed thence to a knowledge of Latin authors, who directed his taste and rectified his ambition.

He was scarcely come to the throne when he was obliged to oppose the Danes, who had seized Wilton,* and were exercising their usual ravages on the country around. 11. He marched against them with the few troops he could assemble on a sudden, and a desperate battle was fought, to the disadvantage of the English. But it was not in the power of misfortune to abate the king's diligence, though it repressed his power to do good. He was in a little time enabled to hazard another engagement; so that the enemy, dreading his courage and activity, proposed terms of peace, which he did not think proper to refuse. 12. They, by this treaty, agreed to relinquish the kingdom; but instead of complying with their engagements, they only removed from one place to another, burning and destroying wherever they came.

CONTEMPORARY SOVEREIGNS.

Popes.	A.D.		A.D.	Kings of Scotland.	A.D.
Gregory IV	823	Theophilus I	829		
Sergius II	844	Michael III	842	Congallus III	824
Leo IV	847	*Emperors of the West,*		Dongallus	829
Benedict III	855	*and Kings of France.*		Alpinus	834
Nicholas I	858			Kennethus II	849
		Lewis I	814	Donaldus V	859
Emperors of the East.		Lotharius	840	Constantius II	865
Michael II	821	Lewis II	855		

EMINENT PERSONS.

In the reign of Egbert: Earls Osmond and Dudda. Bishops Wigfurth and Herefurth.—*In the reigns of Ethelbald and Ethelbert:* Swithun, bishop of Winchester. Orsyck, earl of Hampton. Lambert and Ethelbard, archbishops of Canterbury.—*In the reign of Ethelred:* Osbricht and Ella, Northumbrian princes, who were killed while bravely opposing the Danes.

Questions for Examination.

1. What enemies disturbed the tranquillity which England enjoyed after the union of the seven Saxon kingdoms?
   What mode of warfare was practised by the Danes?
2. What loss did the Danes suffer by sea?
3. What did the Danes carry away?
4. Where did they at length establish themselves?
5. Who succeeded Ethelbald?
   By whom was Ethelred assisted?

---

* Wilton is the county town of Wiltshire, though Salisbury is now its principal place.

6. What was the cause of Ethelred's death? and to whom did he leave the kingdom?
7, 8. What was the cause of the lands remaining uncultivated?
9, 10. What is related of Alfred's youth and early disposition?
11. What was the success of this prince against the Danes?
12. In what manner did the Danes observe their treaty with Alfred?

SECTION II.

Replete with soul, the monarch stood alone,
And built on freedom's basis, England's throne:
A legislator, parent, warrior, sage,
He died, the light of a benighted age.—*Dibdin*.

1. (A. D. 877.) ALFRED, thus opposed to an enemy whom no stationary force could resist, and no treaty could bind, found himself unable to repel the efforts of those ravagers who from all quarters invaded him. New swarms of the enemy arrived every year upon the coast, and fresh invasions were still projected. Some of his subjects, therefore, left their country, and retired into Wales,* or fled to the continent. Others submitted to the conqueror, and purchased their lives by their freedom. 2. In this universal defection, Alfred vainly attempted to remind them of the duty they owed their country and their king; but, finding his remonstrances ineffectual, he was obliged to give way to the wretched necessity of the times. Accordingly, relinquishing the ensigns of his dignity, and dismissing his servants, he dressed himself in the habit of a peasant, and lived for some time in the house of a herdsman, who had been intrusted with the care of his cattle. 3. In this manner, though abandoned by the world, and fearing an enemy in every quarter, still he resolved to continue in his country, to catch the slightest occasion for bringing it relief. In his solitary retreat, which was in the county of Somerset, at the confluence of the rivers Parret and Thone, he amused himself with music, and supported his humble lot with the hopes of better fortune. 4. It is said, that one day, being commanded by the herdsman's wife, who was ignorant of his quality, to take care of some cakes which were baking by the fire, he happened to let them burn, on which she severely upbraided him for neglect.

Previous to his retirement, Alfred had concerted measures for assembling a few trusty friends, whenever an opportunity should offer of annoying the enemy, who were in possession of the whole country. 5. This chosen band, still faithful

---

* Wales consists of twelve counties on the west of England, annexed to it by Edward the First.

to their monarch, took shelter in the forest and marshes of Somerset, and thence made occasional irruptions upon straggling parties of the enemy. Their success in this rapacious and dreary method of living, encouraged many more to join their society, till at length, sufficiently augmented, they repaired to their monarch, who had by that time been reduced by famine to the last extremity.*

6. Meanwhile Ubba, the chief of the Danish commanders, carried terror over the whole land, and now ravaged the country of Wales without opposition. The only place where he found resistance was in his return from the castle of Kenwith, into which the Earl of Devonshire had retired with a small body of troops. 7. This gallant soldier, finding himself unable to sustain the siege, and knowing the danger of surrendering to a perfidious enemy, was resolved, by one desperate effort, to sally out and force his way through the besiegers, sword in hand. The proposal was embraced by all his followers: while the Danes, secure in their numbers, and in their contempt of the enemy, were not only routed with great slaughter, but Ubba, their general, was slain.

8. This victory once more restored courage to the dispirited Saxons; and Alfred, taking advantage of their favour-

---

* The life of Alfred is full of the most interesting events. Among numerous anecdotes related of him by the old English historians, the following we think worthy of a place in this work, as it affords a striking illustration of his benevolence, and is a proof of the privations, in common with his trusty adherents, underwent during their seclusion in Somersetshire:—"It happened one day during the winter, which proved uncommonly severe, that he had sent all his attendants out to endeavour to procure fish, or some kind of provisions; so difficult was the enterprise esteemed, that the king and queen only were excused from the employment. When they were gone, the king, as was his custom, whenever he had an opportunity, took a book, and began reading, whilst Elswitha was employed in her domestic concerns; they had not long continued thus engaged, before a poor pilgrim, accidentally passing that way, knocked at the gate, and begged they would give him something to eat. The humane king called Elswitha, and desired her to give the poor man part of what provision there was in the fort; the queen, finding only one loaf, brought it to Alfred to show how slender their store was, at the same time representing the distress the family would labour under, should they return from their foraging unsuccessful. The king, not deterred by this scanty view from his charitable purpose, but rather internally rejoicing at this trial of his humanity, cheerfully gave the poor Christian one half of the loaf; consoling the queen with this religious reflection: 'That he who could feed five thousand with five loaves and two fishes, could make (if it so pleased him) that half of the loaf suffice for more than their necessities.' When the traveller departed, the king returned to his reading, and felt that satisfaction which most surely results from a beneficent action. Nor was it long unrewarded, for his companions returned with so great a quantity of provisions, that they were not exposed to any similar inconveniences during their seclusion."

ble disposition, prepared to animate them to a vigorous exertion of their superiority. He soon, therefore, apprized them of the place of his retreat, and instructed them to be ready with all their strength at a minute's warning. 9. But still none was found who would undertake to give intelligence of the forces and posture of the enemy. Not knowing, therefore, a person in whom he could confide, he undertook this dangerous task himself. In the simple dress of a shepherd, with his harp in his hand, he entered the Danish camp, tried all his musical arts to please, and was so much admired, that he was brought even into the presence of Guthrum, the Danish prince, with whom he remained some days. 10. He there remarked the supine security of the Danes, their contempt of the English, their negligence in foraging and plundering, and their dissolute wasting of such ill-gotten booty. Having made his observations, he returned to his retreat; and, detaching proper emissaries among his subjects, appointed them to meet him in the forest of Selwood, a summons which they gladly obeyed.

11. It was against the most unguarded quarter of the enemy that Alfred made his most violent attack; while the Danes, surprised to behold an army of English, whom they considered as totally subdued, made but a faint resistance. Notwithstanding the superiority of their numbers, they were routed with great slaughter; and though such as escaped fled for refuge into a fortified camp in the neighbourhood, yet, being unprovided for a siege, in less than a fortnight they were compelled to surrender at discretion, 12. By the conqueror's permission, those who did not choose to embrace Christianity embarked for Flanders,* under the command of one of their generals, called Hastings. Guthrum, their prince, became a convert, with thirty of his nobles, and the king himself answered for him at the font.

13. Alfred had now attained the meridian of glory; he possessed a greater extent of territory than had ever been enjoyed by any of his predecessors; the kings of Wales did him homage for their possessions, the Northumbrians† received a king of his appointing, and no enemy appeared to give him the least apprehensions, or excite an alarm. 14. In this state of prosperity and profound tranquillity, which lasted for twelve years, Alfred was diligently employed in cultivating the arts of peace, and in repairing the damages which the kingdom had sustained by war.

*Now a part of the Netherlands. † The inhabitants of Northumberland.

15. His care was to polish the country by arts, as he had protected it by arms; and he is said to have drawn up a body of laws.* His care for the encouragement of learning did not a little tend to improve the morals and restrain the barbarous habits of the people. When he came to the throne, he found the English sunk into the grossest ignorance and barbarism, proceeding from the continual disorders of the government, and from the ravages of the Danes. He himself complains, that on his accession, he knew not one person south of the Thames who could so much as interpret the Latin service.† 16. To remedy this deficiency, he invited over the most celebrated scholars from all parts of Europe; he founded, or at least re-established, the University of Oxford, and endowed it with many privileges; and he gave, in his own example, the strongest incentives to study. 17. He usually divided his time into three equal portions: one was given to sleep, and to the refection of his body by diet and exercise; another to the despatch of business; and the third to study and devotion.‡ He made considerable progress in the different studies of grammar, rhetoric, philosophy, architecture, and geometry. He was an excellent historian; he understood music; he was acknowledged to be the best Saxon poet of the age, and left many works behind him, some of which remain to this day. 18. To give a character of this prince would

---

* Alfred established a regular militia throughout England, and raised a considerable naval force, by which means he was enabled to repel the future incursions of the Danes. He afterwards established a regular police, dividing the kingdom into counties, and the counties into hundreds and tithings. So well regulated was the police which he established, that it is said he had golden bracelets hung up near the highways, which no robber dared to touch. Yet he never deviated from the nicest regard to the liberty of his people; and there is a remarkable sentiment preserved in his will, namely, that "*It is just the English should for ever remain as free as their own thoughts.*"

† So little, indeed, was learning attended to by the great, that Asser, the biographer of Alfred, mentions with astonishment, that the king taught his youngest son, Ethelward, to read, before he made him acquainted with hunting.

‡ The piety of Alfred was as conspicuous as his prowess; and, in those days of ignorance, he enlightened, by his pen no less than by his example, the people over whom he swayed the sceptre. One of his literary labours was the rendering the Holy Gospels into the Saxon tongue, from which we extract the Lord's Prayer, and insert it here as a specimen of the language spoken by the English at that period:

"Fæder ure thu the earth on heafenum, si thin mama gehagog, to be cume thin rice, Gevurthe hin willa on earthen swa swa on heafenum, urne go dægwanlican hlaf syle us to dæg; and forgyf us ure gyltas, swa swa we forgivath urum gyltendum, and ne geldde thu us on consenung ac alyse us of yfle." (Si it 3wa.)—*Medullæ Historiæ Anglicanæ.*

be to sum up those qualities which constitute perfection. Even virtues seemingly opposite were happily blended in his disposition; persevering, yet flexible; moderate, yet enterprising; just, yet merciful; stern in command, yet gentle in conversation. Nature also, as if desirous that such admirable qualities of mind should be set off to the greatest advantage, had bestowed upon him all bodily accomplishments, vigour, dignity, and an engaging, open countenance. 19. He died at Oxford on the 25th of October, 900 and was buried at Winchester.

CONTEMPORARY SOVEREIGNS.

Popes.	A.D.		A.D.		A.D
John VIII	872	Leo VI	886	Lewis III	899
Martin II	882				
Adrian III	884	*Emperors of the West,*		*Kings of Scotland.*	
Stephen VI	885	*and Kings of France.*		Constantine II	863
Formosus	891	Lewis II	855	Ethus	878
		Charles I	873	Gregory	880
Emperors of the East.		Charles II	880	Donaldus VI	898
Basilus I	867	Arnold	888		

EMINENT PERSONS.

Oldune, earl of Devon, who killed Hubba the Dane, and took the famous Reafern, or enchanted standard. Ulfredus, Trelotegaldus, Celnorth, Ethelred, and Plerumbus, were successively archbishops of Canterbury in this reign.

Questions for Examination.

1. What effect had the continual ravages of the Danes upon the English?
2, 3. How did Alfred act in this emergency?
4. What anecdote is related of Alfred during his concealment?
5. How did those who still remained faithful to Alfred conduct themselves?
6. What benevolent act is related of this monarch? (*See the Note.*)
7. What desperate effort did the Earl of Devonshire resolve on? And what was the consequence?
8. What was the advantage gained by Alfred's courage?
9. By what stratagem did Alfred get intelligence of the enemy's situation?
10, 11. What observations did he make during his stay in the Danish camp?
12. What became of the Danes after their defeat?
13. What kings paid homage to Alfred?
14, 15, 16. How was Alfred employed during the peace?
17. For what purpose did Alfred divide his time into three equal portions? And what were his accomplishments?
18. What is the general character given of Alfred?
19. Where did Alfred die, and at what place was he buried?

SECTION III.

*Priest-ridden by a man
Of an unbounded stomach, ever ranking
Himself with princes.—Shakespeare.*

1. (A.D. 901.) His second son, Edward,* succeeded him on the throne. To him succeeded Athelstan, his natural son, the illegitimacy of his birth not being then deemed a sufficient obstacle to his inheriting the crown. He died at Gloucester, after a reign of sixteen years, and was succeeded by his brother Edmund, who, like the rest of his predecessors, met with disturbance from the Northumbrians on his accession to the throne; but his activity soon defeated their attempts. 2. The resentment this monarch bore to men of an abandoned way of living was the cause of his death. He was killed by Leolff, a robber, at a feast, where this villain had the insolence to intrude into the king's presence. His brother, Edred, was appointed to succeed him; and like his predecessors this monarch found himself at the head of a rebellious and refractory people. 3. Edred implicitly submitted to the directions of Dunstan the monk, both in church and state; and the kingdom was in a fair way of being turned into a papal province by this zealous ecclesiastic; but he was checked in the midst of his career, by the death of the king, who died of a quinsy, in the tenth year of his reign.—A.D. 955.

4. Edwy, his nephew, who ascended the throne, his own sons being yet unfit to govern, was a prince of great personal accomplishments, and of martial disposition. But he was now come to the government of a kingdom in which he had an enemy to contend with against whom all military virtues could be of little service. 5. Dunstan, who had governed during the former reign, was resolved to remit nothing of his authority in this; and Edwy, immediately upon his accession, found himself involved in a quarrel with the monks; whose rage neither his accomplishments nor his virtues could mitigate.

6. Among other instances of their cruelty, the following is recorded:—There was a lady of the royal blood named Elgiva, whose beauty had made a strong impression upon

---

* Surnamed Edward *the Elder*, from being the first of that name who sat on the throne of England. He obtained many victories over the Northumbrian rebels, built several castles, and fortified different cities. He also founded the University of Cambridge, in 915. He is said to have been nearly equal to his father in military courage, but greatly inferior to him in mental accomplishments. He reigned 24 years.

Dunstan separating Edwy and Elgiva.

the young monarch's heart. He had even ventured to marry her contrary to the advice of his councillors, as she was within the degrees of affinity prohibited by the canon law. 6. On the day of his coronation, while his nobility were giving loose to the more noisy pleasures of wine and festivity in the great hall, Edwy retired to his wife's apartments, where, in company with her mother, he enjoyed the more pleasing satisfaction of her conversation. Dunstan no sooner perceived his absence, than, conjecturing the reason, he rushed furiously into the apartment, and, upbraiding him with all the bitterness of ecclesiastical rancour, dragged him forth in the most outrageous manner.

8. Dunstan, it seems, was not without his enemies, for the king was advised to punish this insult by bringing him to account for the money with which he had been intrusted during the last reign. This account the haughty monk refused to give in; wherefore he was deprived of all the ecclesiastical and civil emoluments of which he had been in possession, and banished the kingdom. 9. His exile only served to increase the reputation of his sanctity with the people. Among the rest, Odo, archbishop of Canterbury,* was so far transported with the spirit of party, that he pronounced a divorce between Edwy and Elgiva. The king was unable to resist the indignation of the church, and consented to surrender his beautiful wife to its fury. Accord-

* An ancient city of Kent, of which county it is the capital.

ingly, Odo sent into the palace a party of soldiers, who seized the queen, and, by his orders, branded her on the face with a hot iron. 10. Not contented with this cruel vengeance, they carried her by force into Ireland, and there commanded her to remain in perpetual exile. This injunction, however, was too distressing for that faithful woman to comply with; for being cured of her wound, and having obliterated the marks which had been made to deface her beauty, she once more ventured to return to the king, whom she still regarded as her husband. But misfortune continued to pursue her. 11. She was taken prisoner by a party whom the archbishop had appointed to observe her conduct, and was put to death in a most cruel manner. The sinews of her limbs being cut, and her body mangled, she was thus left to expire in the most cruel agony. In the mean time a secret revolt against Edwy became almost general; and Dunstan put himself at the head of the party. 12. The malcontents at last proceeded to open rebellion; and having placed Edgar, the king's youngest brother, a boy of about thirteen years of age, at their head, they soon put him in possession of all the northern parts of the kingdom. Edwy's power, and the number of his adherents, every day declining, he was at last obliged to consent to a partition of the kingdom; but his death, which happened soon after, freed his enemies from all further inquietude, and gave Edgar peaceable possession of the government.

13. Edgar being placed on the throne by the influence of the monks, affected to be entirely guided by their directions in all his succeeding transactions.

Little worthy of notice is mentioned of this monarch, except his amour with Elfrida, which is of too singular a nature to be omitted. 14. Edgar had long heard of the beauty of a young lady, whose name was Elfrida, daughter to the Earl of Devonshire; but unwilling to credit common fame in this particular, he sent Ethelwald, his favourite friend, to see and inform him if Elfrida was, indeed, that incomparable woman report had described her. 15. Ethelwald, arriving at the earl's, had no sooner set his eyes upon that nobleman's daughter than he became desperately enamoured of her himself. Such was the violence of his passion, that, forgetting his master's intention, he solicited only his own interest, and demanded for himself the beautiful Elfrida from her father in marriage. The favourite of a king was not likely to find a refusal; the earl gave his consent, and the nuptials were performed in private. 16. Upon his return to court, which was shortly after, he assured the king that riches alone, and her high quality, had been the cause of her high fame, and he appeared amazed how the world could talk so much and so unjustly of her charms. The king was satisfied, and no longer felt any curiosity, while Ethelwald secretly triumphed in his address. 17. When he had, by this deceit, weaned the king from his purpose, he took an opportunity, after some time, of turning the conversation on Elfrida, representing that, though the fortune of the earl of Devonshire's daughter would be a trifle to a king, yet it would be an immense acquisition to a needy subject. He therefore humbly entreated permission to pay his addresses to her, as she was the richest heiress in the kingdom. 18. A request so seemingly reasonable was readily complied with; Ethelwald returned to his wife, and their nuptials were solemnized in public.

His greatest care however, was employed in keeping her from court; and he took every precaution to prevent her from appearing before a king so susceptible of love, while she was so capable of inspiring that passion. But it was impossible to keep his treachery long concealed. 19. Edgar was soon informed of the whole transaction; but dissembling his resentment, he took occasion to visit that part of the country where this miracle of beauty was detained, accompanied by Ethelwald, who reluctantly attended him thither. Upon coming near the lady's habitation, he told him that he had a desire to see his wife, of whom he had formerly heard so much, and desired to be introduced as his acquaintance. 20. Ethelwald, thunderstruck at the proposal, did all in his power, but in vain, to dissuade him. All he could obtain was permission to go before, on pretence of preparing for the king's reception. On his arrival, he fell at his wife's feet confessing what he had done to be possessed of her charms, and conjuring her to conceal as much as possible her beauty from the king, who was too susceptible of its power. 21. Elfrida, little obliged to him for a passion that had deprived her of a crown, promised compliance; but, prompted either by vanity or revenge, adorned her person with the most exquisite art, and called up all her beauty on the occasion. The event answered her expectations; the king no sooner saw than he loved her, and was instantly resolved to obtain her. 22. The better to effect his intentions, he concealed his passion from the husband, and took leave with a seeming indifference; but his revenge was not the less certain and faithful. Ethelwald was sometime after sent into Northumberland, upon pretence of urgent affairs, and was found murdered in the wood by the way. 23. Some say he was stabbed by the king's own hands; some that he only commanded the assassination. However this be, Elfrida was invited soon after to court by the king's own order, and their nuptials were performed with the usual solemnity.

This monarch died, after a reign of sixteen years, in the thirty-third year of his age, being succeeded by his son Edward, whom he had by his first marriage with the daughter of the earl of Ordmer.*

CONTEMPORARY SOVEREIGNS.

Popes.	A.D.		A.D.		A.D.
Benedict IV	900	Benedict VI	972	Otho I	936
Leo V	904	Donius II	972	Otho II	973
Sergius III	905				
Anastasius III	910	*Emperors of the East.*		*Kings of France.*	
Lado	912	Leo VI	886	Charles III	899
John X	913	Constantine Porphy-		Lewis IV	936
Leo VII	928	rogenitus	910	Lothaire I	954
Stephen VIII	929	Romanus the young-			
John XI	931	er	959	*Kings of Scotland.*	
Leo VI	936	Nicephorus	963	Constantine III	909
Stephen IX	939	Zenrises	970	Malcolm I	943
Martin III	943			Indulphus	958
Agapetus	950	*Emperors of the West.*		Duffus	967
John XII	956	Lewis III	899	Culenus	972
Benedict V	964	Conrad I	912		
John XIII	965	Henry I	919		

EMINENT PERSONS.

In the reign of Edward: Ethelfrida, sister of Edward the Elder, a great warrior. and very instrumental in assisting to gain her brother's victories. Atholme, archbishop of Canterbury. — *In the reign of Athelstan:* Guy, earl of Warwick, who is said to have killed the Danish giant Colbrand in single combat at Winchester, and performed many other extraordinary actions. Terketyl, a successful warrior, an abbot of Croyland, and chancellor of England. Wolston, archbishop of Canterbury.—*In the reign of Edred:* Dunstan, abbot of Glastonbury. Odo, archbishop of Canterbury.—*In the reign of Edgar:* Dunstan and Elsius, archbishops of Canterbury.

---

* Until the reign of Edgar, England was much infested with wolves. The king, however, was indefatigable in hunting and destroying them; but finding that those which escaped took shelter in the mountains and forest of Wales, he changed the tribute of money imposed on that country into an annual tribute of 300 wolves' heads; this produced such diligence in hunting them, that their extirpation was soon effected.

Questions for Examination.

2. What was the cause of Edward's death? and who succeeded him?
3. To whose directions did Edred submit?
4. Who succeeded Edred?
6. Whom did Edwy marry?
7. What happened on the day of his coronation?
8. On what account was Dunstan banished the kingdom?
9. By whose orders was the queen seized?
14. Who was Elfrida, and whom did Edgar send to her?
15. How did Ethelwald perform his mission?
16, 17, 18. Relate what followed?
19. How did the king act on hearing the whole transaction?
20. What did Ethelwald request of his wife?
21. What was the result of her non-compliance?
22. How did Ethelwald die?
23. How long did Edgar reign? and by whom was he succeeded?

SECTION IV.

> Cut off in all the blossom of my sin,
> Unhousel'd, unanointed, unanneal'd,
> No reck'ning made, but sent to my account
> With all my imperfections on my head.—*Shakspeare.*

1. (A. D. 975.) EDWARD, surnamed the Martyr, was made king by the interest of the monks, and lived but four years after his accession. In this reign there is nothing remarkable if we except his tragical and memorable end.

2. Hunting one day near Corfe Castle, where Elfrida, his mother-in-law resided, he thought it his duty to pay her a visit, although he was not attended by any of his retinue. There desiring some liquor to be brought him, as he was thirsty, while he was yet holding the cup to his head, one of Elfrida's domestics, instructed for that purpose, stabbed him in the back. The king, finding himself wounded, put spurs to his horse; but fainting with the loss of blood, he fell from the saddle, and his foot sticking in the stirrup, he was dragged along by his horse till he died.

3. Ethelred the Second, surnamed the Unready, the son of Edgar and Elfrida, succeeded; a weak and irresolute monarch, incapable of governing the kingdom, or providing for its safety. During his reign the bold and terrible enemies, the Danes, who seemed not to be loaded with the same accumulation of vice and folly as the English, were daily gaining ground. 4. The weakness and inexperience of Ethelred appeared to give a favourable opportunity for renewing their depredations; and, accordingly, they landed on several parts of the coast, spreading their usual terror and devastation. A.D. 981.

As they lived indiscriminately among the English, a resolution was taken for a general massacre; and Ethelred, by a policy incident to weak princes, embraced the cruel resolution of putting them all to the sword. 5. This plot was carried on with such secrecy, that it was executed in one day, and all the Danes in England were destroyed without mercy. But this massacre, so perfidious in the contriving, and so cruel in the execution, instead of ending the long miseries of the people, only prepared the way for greater calamities.

While the English were yet congratulating each other upon their late deliverance from an inveterate enemy, Sweyn, king of Denmark, who had been informed of their treacherous cruelties, appeared off the western coast with a large fleet, meditating slaughter and furious with revenge. Ethelred was obliged to fly into Normandy, and the whole country thus came under the power of Sweyn, his victorious rival.

7. Canute, afterwards surnamed the Great, succeeded Sweyn as king of Denmark, and also as general of the Danish forces in England. The contest between him and Edmund Ironside, successor to Ethelred, was managed with great obstinacy and perseverance; the first battle that was fought appeared indecisive; a second followed, in which the Danes were victorious; but Edmund still having interest enough to bring a third army into the field, the Danish and English nobility, equally harassed by these convulsions, obliged their kings to come to a compromise and to divide the kingdom between them by treaty.* Canute reserved to himself the northern parts of the kingdom; the southern parts were left to Edmund; but this prince being murdered about a month after the treaty, by his two chamberlains, at Oxford, Canute was left in peaceable possession of the whole kingdom. A. D. 1017,

Canute † is represented, by some historians, as one of the first characters in those barbarous ages. The piety of the

* In the battle which was fought at Athelmey, Edmund, perceiving Canute at the head of his forces, rode off from his own, and Canute advancing, a furious combat ensued, in which, according to the author of the *Medullæ Historiæ Anglicanæ*, Canute was wounded, and first proposed forbearance; and this, it is said, led to the division of the kingdom. By Canute's accession to the throne, a termination was put to a war with the Danes, which had almost, without intermission, raged for 200 years.

† In the latter part of his life, to atone for his many acts of violence, he built churches, endowed monasteries, imported relics, and made a pilgrimage to Rome.

latter part of his life, and the resolute valour of the former, were topics that filled the mouths of his courtiers with flattery and praise. 9. They even affected to think his power uncontrollable, and that all things would be obedient to his command. Canute, sensible of their adulation, is said to have taken the following method to reprove them. He ordered his chair to be set on the sea-shore while the tide was coming in, and commanded the sea to retire. 10. "Thou art under my dominion," cried he, "the land upon which I sit is mine; I charge thee, therefore, to approach no farther, nor dare to wet the feet of thy sovereign." He feigned to sit some time in expectation of submission, till the waves began to surround him, then turning to his courtiers, he observed, That the titles of Lord and master belonged only to Him whom both earth and seas were ready to obey. 11. Thus feared and respected, he lived many years, honoured with the surname of Great for his power, but deserving it still more for his virtues. He died at Shaftesbury,* in the nineteenth year of his reign, leaving behind him three sons, Sweyn, Harold, and Hardicanute. Sweyn was crowned king of Norway, Hardicanute was put in possession of Denmark, and Harold succeeded his father on the English throne. A. D. 1036.

12. To Harold succeeded his brother, Hardicanute, whose title was readily acknowleged both by the Danes and the English; and upon his arrival from the continent, he was received with the most extravagant demonstrations of joy. This king's violent and unjust government was of but short duration. He died two years after his accession in consequence of excess at the marriage of a Danish lord which was celebrated at Lambeth.

13. The disorders of the Danish monarchs once more induced the English to place a monarch of the Saxon line upon the throne, and accordingly Edward, surnamed the Confessor, was by the general consent crowned king A. D. 1041.

The English, who had long groaned under a foreign yoke, now set no bounds to their joy, at finding the line of their ancient monarchs restored.

14. As he had been bred in the Norman court, he showed, in every instance, a predilection for the customs, laws, and even the natives of that country; and among the rest of his faults, though he married Editha, the daughter of God-

* A market town in Dorchester.

win, yet, either from mistaken piety or fixed aversion, during his whole reign he abstained from her society.*

15. Thus having no legitimate issue, and being wholly engrossed, during the continuance of a long reign, with the visions of superstition, he was at last surprised by sickness, which brought him to his end, on 5th of January, in the sixty-fifth year of his age and twenty-fifth of his reign.

16. Harold, the son of a popular nobleman, whose name was Godwin, and whose virtues seemed to give a right to his pretensions, ascended the throne without any opposition. But neither his valour, his justice, nor his popularity were able to secure him from the misfortunes attendant upon an ill-grounded title. His pretensions were opposed by William duke of Normandy, who insisted that the crown belonged of right to him, it being bequeathed to him by Edward the Confessor.†

Questions for Examination.

1. By whose interest was Edward the Martyr crowned king?
2. Relate the circumstances attending the king's death?
3. Who succeeded Edward?
4. What was the conduct of the Danes during Ethelred's reign?
5. What method did Ethelred take to destroy the Danes?
6. What was the consequence of Ethelred's perfidy?
7. By whom was Sweyn succeeded?
9. Did Canute reprove his courtiers for their flattery?
10. Repeat the words Canute made use of on this occasion?
11. Where did Canute die? and what issue did he leave?
13. Whom did the English place on the throne upon the death of Hardicanute?
14. Where had Edward the Confessor been bred? and what predilections had he in consequence?
15. How long did Edward reign?
16. What were the pretensions of William duke Normandy to the English throne?

SECTION. V.

Ah! who can tell the horrors of that day
When Harold fell on the ensanguined field,
Where rank 'gainst rank rushed on in dread array,
With jav'lin, arrow, battle-axe, and shield.—*Brown.*

1. (A. D. 1066.) WILLIAM, who was afterwards called the Conqueror, was natural son of Robert duke of Normandy. His mother's name was Arlette, a beautiful maid of Falaise, whom Robert fell in love with as she stood gazing at the door while he passed through the town. William, who was

---
* This contributed to gain him the title of Saint and Confessor.
† Edward the Confessor converted a small monastery into the beautiful cathedral called Westminster Abbey, where he built his own sepulchre, and which, until very lately, has been the usual burial place of the English monarchs.

the offspring of this amour, owed a part of his greatness to his birth, but still more to his own personal merit. 2. His body was vigorous, his mind capacious and noble, and his courage not to be repressed by apparent danger. Upon coming to his dukedom of Normandy, though yet very young, he on all sides opposed his rebellious subjects, and repressed foreign invaders, while his valour and conduct prevailed in every action. 3. The tranquillity which he had thus established in his dominions induced him to extend his views; and some overtures made by Edward the Confessor, in the latter part of his reign, who was wavering in the choice of a successor, inflamed his ambition with a desire of succeeding to the English throne. 4. The pope himself was not behind the rest in favouring his pretensions; and, either influenced by the apparent justice of his claims, or by the hopes of extending the authority of the church, he immediately pronounced Harold a usurper. With such favourable incentives, William soon found himself at the head of a chosen army of sixty thousand men, all equipped in the most warlike and splendid manner. 5. It was in the beginning of summer that he embarked this powerful body on board a fleet of three hundred sail; and after some small opposition from the weather, landed at Pevensey,* on the coast of Sussex, with resolute tranquillity.

6. Harold, who seemed resolved to defend his right to the crown and retain that sovereignty which he had received from the people, who only had a right to bestow it, was now returning, flushed with conquest, from defeating the Norwegians who had invaded the kindgdom, with all the forces he had employed in that expedition, and all he could invite or collect in the country through which he passed. His army was composed of active and valiant troops, in high spirits, strongly attached to their king, and eager to engage.

7. On the other hand, the army of William consisted of the flower of the continent, and had long been inured to danger. The men of Brittany, Boulogne, Flanders, Poictou, Maine, Orleans, France, and Normandy, were all voluntarily united under his command. England never before, nor ever since, saw two such armies drawn up to dispute its crown. 8. The day before the battle, William sent an offer to Harold to decide the quarrel between them by single combat, and thus to spare the blood of thousands: but Harold refused, and said he would leave it to the God of armies to determine. Both armies, therefore, that night pitched in

*A small town in Sussex.

sight of each other, expecting the dawning of the day with impatience. The English passed the night in songs and feasting, the Normans in devotion and prayer.

(Oct. 13, 1066.) 9. The next morning, at seven, as soon as day appeared, both armies were drawn up in array against each other. Harold appeared in the centre of his forces, leading on his army on foot, that his men might be more encouraged by seeing their king exposed to an equality of danger. William fought on horseback, leading on his army, that moved at once, singing the songs of Roland, one of the famous chiefs of their country. 10. The Normans began to fight with their cross-bows, which, at first, galled and surprised the English; and as their ranks were close, their arrows did great execution. But soon they came to closer fight, and the English with their bills hewed down their adversaries with great slaughter. Confusion was spreading among the ranks, when William, who found himself on the brink of destruction, hastened with a select band to the relief of his forces. 11. His presence restored the suspense of battle; he was seen in every place, endeavouring to pierce the ranks of the enemy, and had three horses slain under him. At length, perceiving that the English continued impenetrable, he pretended to give ground, which, as he expected, drew the enemy from their ranks, and he was instantly ready to take advantage of their disorder. 12. Upon a signal given, the Normans immediately returned to the charge with greater fury than before, broke the English troops and pursued them to a rising ground. It was in this extremity that Harold was seen flying from rank to rank rallying and inspiring his troops with vigour; and though he had toiled all day, till near nightfall, in front of his Kentish men, yet he still seemed unabated in force or courage, keeping his men to the post of honour.

13. Once more, therefore, victory seemed to turn against the Normans, and they fell in great numbers, so that the fierceness and obstinacy of this memorable battle was often renewed by the courage of the leaders, whenever that of the soldiers began to slacken. Fortune at length determined a victory that valour was unable to decide.

14. Harold, making a furious onset at the head of his troops against the Norman heavy-armed infantry, was shot into the brains by an arrow; and his two valiant brothers, fighting by his side, shared the same fate. He fell with his sword in his hand, admidst heaps of slain; and after the bat-

tle, the royal corpse could hardly be distinguished among the dead.*

This was the end of the Saxon monarchy in England, which had continued for more than six hundred years.

CONTEMPORARY SOVEREIGNS.

Popes.	A.D.	Emperors of the East.	A.D.	Kings of France.	A.D.
Benedict VII	975				
John XIV	984	Basilius II	975	Lothaire I	954
John XV	985	Constantine X	1025	Louis V	986
Gregory V	996	Romanus III	1028	Hugh Capet	987
Silvester II	999	Michael IV	1034	Robert II	997
John XVI	1003	Michael V	1041	Henry I	1031
John XVII	1004	Constantine XI	1042	Philip I	1060
Sergius IV	1009	Theodore (emp)	1054		
Benedict VIII	1012	Michael VI	1056		
John XVIII	1024	Isaac Comnenus	1059	Kings of Scotland.	
Benedict IX	1033	Constantine XII	1059		
Gregory VI	1044			Culenus	972
Clement II	1046	Emperors of the West.		Kenneth III	977
Damascus II	1048	Otho II	973	Constantine IV	1002
Leo IX	1049	Otho III	983	Grimus	1005
Victor II	1055	Henry II	1002	Malcolm II	1054
Stephen X	1057	Conrad II	1024	Duncan I	1031
Nicholas II	1059	Henry III	1039	Macbeth	1040
Alexander II	1061	Henry IV	1056	Malcolm III	1057

EMINENT PERSONS.

In the reigns of Edward the Martyr, Ethelred II., and Edmund: the duke of Mercia, who took part with Elfrida and the clergy, against the king. Dunstan, Ethelgar, Elfric, Siricus, Alphage, and Livingus, archbishops of Canterbury.—*In the reigns of Canute, Harold, Hardicanute, and Edward the Confessor:* Elnothus, Edsine, and Robert, archbishops of Canterbury. Goodwin, earl of Kent, whose estates, being afterwards swallowed by inundations of the sea, are now denominated the Goodwin Sands.—*In the reign of Harold II:* Leofwin and Gurf, brothers to the king. Stigand, archbishop of Canterbury. Tosti, earl of Northumberland.

Questions for Examination.

1. Who was William the Conqueror?
2. When and where did William land?
6, 7. Of what were the armies of Harold and William composed?
8. How did the two armies pass the night previous to the battle?
9. In what way did Harold and William lead their respective armies to battle?
11, 12, 13. Describe the conduct of William and Harold?
14. How did Harold fall?
How long did the Saxon monarchy continue in England?

---

*The English in this battle neither used the long-bow nor cross-bow, but both were used by the Normans. The English forces were nearly all infantry, while by far the greater part of the Norman army was composed of cavalry. It is therefore probable, that to the want of cavalry, and the not using any missive weapons, may be in a great measure attributed the defeat of Harold's army. Certain it is, that the victory remained undecided from nine in the morning till the close of the day, when the death of the king, who had slain many Normans with his own hand, finally turned the scale.

CHAPTER IV

WILLIAM THE CONQUEROR.

Born 1024. Died Sept. 9, 1087. Began to reign Dec. 25th, 1066. Reigned 21 years.

William the Conqueror receiving the crown of England.

> A furious victor's partial will prevailed,
> All prostrate lay; and in the secret shade,
> Deep stung but fearful indignation gnashed
> His teeth. *Thomson.*

1. (A. D. 1066). As soon as William passed the Thames at Wallingford, Stigand, the primate, made submission to him in the name of the clergy: and before he came within sight of the city, all the chief nobility came into his camp, and declared their intention of yielding to his authority. William was glad of being peaceably put in possession of a throne which several of his predecessors had not gained without repeated victories.

2. But, in order to give his invasion all the sanction possible, he was crowned at Westminster by the archbishop of York, and took the oath usual in the times of the Saxon and Danish kings: which was to protect and defend the church, to observe the laws of the realm, and to govern the people with impartiality. Having thus secured the government, and, by a mixture of rigour and lenity, brought the English to an entire submission, he resolved to return to the continent, there to enjoy the triumph and congratulations of his ancient subjects.

3. In the meantime the absence of the Conqueror in England produced the most fatal effects. His officers, being no longer controlled by his justice, thought this a fit opportunity for extortion; while the English, no longer awed by his presence, thought it the happiest occasion for vindicating their freedom.

4. The English had entered into a conspiracy to cut off their invaders, and fixed the day for their intended massacre, which was to be on Ash-Wednesday, during the time of divine service, when all the Normans would be unarmed as penitents, according to the discipline of the times. But William's return quickly disconcerted all their schemes: and from that time forward he began to lose all confidence in his English subjects, and to regard them as inveterate and irreconcilable enemies. 5. He had already raised such a number of fortresses in the kingdom, that he no longer dreaded the tumultuous or transient efforts of a discontented multitude; he therefore determined to treat them as a conquered nation;* to indulge his own avarice, and that of his followers, by numerous confiscations; and to secure his power by humbling all who were able to make any resistance. 6. He proceeded to confiscate all the estates of the English gentry, and to grant them liberally to his Norman followers. Thus all the ancient and honourable families were reduced to beggary, and the English found themselves entirely excluded from every road that led either to honour or preferment.

7. To keep the clergy as much as possible in his interests, he appointed none but his own countrymen to the most considerable church dignities, and even displaced Stigand, archbishop of Canterbury, upon some frivolous pretence.

William having crushed several conspiracies, and, by punishing the malcontents, thus secured the peace of his dominions, now expected rest from his labours; and, find-

---

* So mercilessly did the treat the people whom he had coquered, and so determined was he to incapacitate them from future resistance to his power, that on the Northumbrians having revolted in 1070, he gave orders to lay waste the fine fertile lands between the rivers Humber and Tees, for the extent of sixty miles. Many flourishing towns, fine villages, and noble country seats were accordingly burnt down; the implements of husbandry destroyed and the cattle driven away. The great Lord Lyttleton, speaking of these cruel devastations, and those occasioned by the "Forest laws," observes that Attila did no more deserve the name of the "Scourge of God" than this merciless tyrant, nor did he, nor any other destroyer of nations make more havoc in an enmy's country than William did in his own.

ing none either willing or powerful enough to oppose him, he hoped that the end of his reign would be marked with prosperity and peace. 8. But such is the blindness of human hope, that he found enemies where he least expected them; and such, too, as served to imbitter all the latter part of his life. His last troubles were excited by his own children, from the opposing of whom he could expect to reap neither glory nor gain. He had three sons, Robert, William, and Henry, besides several daughters. 9. Robert, his eldest son, surnamed Curthose from the shortness of his legs, was a prince who inherited all the bravery of his family and nation, but was rather bold than prudent; and was often heard to express his jealousy of his two brothers, William and Henry. These, by greater assiduity, had wrought upon the credulity and affections of the king, and consequently were the more obnoxious to Robert. 10. A mind, therefore, so well prepared for resentment soon found or made cause for an open rupture. The princes were one day in sport together, and in the idle petulance of play, took it in their heads to throw water over their elder brother as he passed through the court, on leaving their apartment. Robert, all alive to suspicion, quickly turned this frolic into studied indignity; and having these jealousies further inflamed by one of his favourites, he drew his sword, and ran up stairs, with intent to take revenge. 11. The whole castle was quickly filled with tumult, and it was not without some difficulty that the king himself was able to appease it. But he could not allay the animosity which, from that moment, ever after prevailed in his family. Robert, attended by several of his confederates, withdrew to Rouen that very night, hoping to surprise the castle, but his design was defeated by the governor.

12. The flame being thus kindled, the popular character of the prince, and a sympathy of manners, engaged all the young nobility of Normandy and Maine, as well as Anjou and Brittany, to espouse his quarrel; even his mother it is said supported him by secret remittances, and aided him in this obstinate resistance by private encouragement. This unnatural contest continued for several years to inflame the Norman state, and William was at last obliged to have recourse to England, for supporting his authority against his son. 13. Accordingly, drawing an army of Englishmen together, he led them over to Normandy, where he soon compelled Robert and his adherents to quit the field, and he was quickly reinstated in all his dominions.*

* In one of the battles between the forces of William and his son Robert,

William had scarcely put an end to this transaction, when he felt a very severe blow in the death of Matilda his queen; and in addition to this domestic calamity, he received information of a general insurrection in the Norman government.

14. Upon his arrival on the continent, he found that the insurgents had been secretly assisted and excited by the king of France, whose policy consisted in thus lessening the Norman power, by creating dissensions among the nobles of its different provinces. William's displeasure was not a little increased by the account he received of some railleries which that monarch had thrown out against him. This so provoked the English monarch, that he sent him word, that he should soon set the kingdom of France in a flame.

15. In order to perform this promise, he levied a strong army, and, entering the isle of France, destroyed and burned all the villages and houses without opposition, and took the town of Mantua, which he reduced to ashes. But the progress of these hostilities was stopped by an accident, which shortly after put an end to William's life.

His horse chancing to place his fore-foot on some hot ashes, plunged so violently, that the rider was thrown forward, and bruised upon the pommel of the saddle to such a degree, that he suffered a relapse, of which he died, shortly after, at a little village near Rouen. Sept. 9, 1087.*

CONTEMPORARY SOVEREIGNS.

Popes.		King of France.
A.D.	A.D.	A.D.
Alexander II..... 1061	Romanus IV..... 1063	Philip I.......... 1060
Gregory VII..... 1073	Michael VII...... 1071	
Victor III........ 1086	Nicephorus I..... 1078	Kings of Scotland.
	Alexis I.......... 1081	Malcolm III...... 1059
Emperors of the East.	Emperor of the West.	Donald VIII..... 1068
Constantine XII.. 1059	Henry IV........ 1056	

the latter happened to engage the king, whose face was concealed by his helmet, and both of them being valiant, a fierce combat ensued till the young prince wounded his father in the arm, and unhorsed him. On his calling out for assistance, his voice discovered him to be his son, who, struck with remorse, threw himself at his father's feet and craved pardon for his offence, but William, who was highly exasperated, gave him his malediction. He was, however, afterwards reconciled to him, and on his return to England, Robert was successfully employed in retaliating an invasion of Malcolm, king of Scotland.

* In this reign justices of the peace were first appointed in England. The Tower of London was built. A general survey of all the lands of the kingdom made, their value, proprietors, quality of the soil, &c., and entered in a register, called Doomsday-book, which is still preserved in the exchequer, and is considered the most valuable monument of antiquity, possessed by any nation. The curfew (or cover fire) bell established, at which signal all fires and candles were arbitrarily extinguished at eight o'clock in the evening.

EMINENT PERSONS.

Prince Edgar Atheling, Stigand and Lanfranc, archbishops of Canterbury. Edwin and Mocar, earls of Northumberland and Mercia.

Questions for Examination.

1. In what manner was William received by the nobility and clergy?
2. Where and by whom was he crowned?
4. What conspiracy did the English enter into?
5. In what way did William determine to treat his English subjects?
6, 7. What measures did he adopt to degrade the English?
9. What were the troubles which afflicted William?
10, 11. What frolic was it that led to the serious consequences that followed?
12. Who espoused Robert's cause?
13. What happened in one of the engagements between the forces of the king and his son? (*See the Note.*)
14. What inducement had the king of France to assist the insurgents?
15. What caused William's death?
What valuable ancient record is preserved in the exchequer, and what was its use? (*See the Note,*)

CHAPTER V.

WILLIAM RUFUS.

Born 1060. Died August 2nd, 1100. Began to reign Sept. 9th, 1087. Reigned 12¾ years.

> And that Red King, who, while of old
> Through Boldrewood the chase he led,
> By his loved huntsman's arrow bled.—*Walter Scott.*

1. (A. D. 1087.) WILLIAM, surnamed Rufus, from the colour of his hair, was appointed, by the king's will, his successor, while the elder son, Robert, was left in possession of Normandy. Nevertheless, the Norman barons were from the beginning displeased at the division of the empire by the late king: they eagerly desired a union as before, and looked upon Robert as the proper owner of the whole. A powerful conspiracy was therfore carried on against William; and Odo, the late king's brother, undertook to conduct it to maturity.

2. William, sensible of the danger that threatened him, endeavoured to gain the affections of the native English, whom he prevailed upon by promises of future good treat-

ment, and preference in the distribution of his favours, to espouse his interests. 3. He was soon, therefore, in the field; and at the head of a numerous army, showed himself in readiness to oppose all who should dispute his pretensions. In the mean time Robert, instead of employing himself in levies, to support his friends in England, squandered his resources away in idle expenses and unmerited benefits, so that he procrastinated his departure till the opportunity was lost; while William exerted himself with incredible activity to dissipate the confederacy before his brother could arrive. 4. Nor was this difficult to effect. The conspirators had, in consequence of Robert's assurances, taken possession of some fortresses; but the appearance of the king soon reduced them to implore his mercy. He granted them their lives; but confiscated all their estates and banished them the kingdom.

5. A new breach was made some time after between the brothers, on which Rufus found means to encroach still farther upon Robert's possessions. Every conspiracy thus detected served to enrich the king, who took care to apply to his own use those treasures which had been amassed for the purpose of dethroning him.

6. (A. D. 1097.) But the memory of these transient broils and unsuccessful treasons, was now totally eclipsed by one of the most noted enterprises that ever adorned the annals of nations, or excited the attention of mankind: I mean the crusades, which were now first projected. Peter the Hermit, a native of Amiens, in Picardy, was a man of great zeal, courage, and piety. 7. He had made a pilgrimage to the holy sepulchre at Jerusalem, and beheld with indignation the cruel manner in which the Christians were treated by the infidels, who were in possession of that place.

He preached the crusade over Europe, by the pope's permission, and men of all ranks flew to arms with the utmost alacrity to rescue the Holy Land from the infidels, and each bore the sign of the cross upon his right shoulder, as a mark of their devotion to the cause. 8. In the midst of the universal ardour that was diffused over Europe, men were not entirely forgetful of their temporal interests; for some, hoping for a more magnificent settlement in the soft regions of Asia, sold their European property for whatever they could obtain, contented with receiving anything for what they were predetermined to relinquish. 9. Among the princes who felt and acknowledged this general spirit of enterprise, was Robert duke of Normandy. The crusade was entirely adapted to his inclinations and his circumstances; he was brave, zealous, covetous of glory, poor, harassed by insurrections, and, what was more than all, naturally fond of change. In order therefore to supply money to defray the necessary charges of so expensive an undertaking, he offered to mortgage his dukedom in Normandy to his brother Rufus for a stipulated sum of money. 10. This sum, which was no greater than ten thousand marks, was readily promised by Rufus, whose ambition was upon the watch to seize every advantage.

But though the cession of Maine and Normandy greatly increased the king's territories, they added but little to his real power, and his new subjects were composed of men of independent spirits, more ready to dispute than to obey his commands. Many were the revolts and insurrections which he was obliged to quell in person; and no sooner was one conspiracy suppressed than another rose to give him disquietude.

However, Rufus proceeded careless of approbation or censure; and continued to extend his dominions, either by purchase or conquest. 12. The earl of Poictiers and Guienne, inflamed with a desire of going upon the crusade, had gathered an immense multitude for that expedition, but wanted money to forward his preparations. He had recourse, therefore, to Rufus, and offered to mortgage all his dominions, without much considering what would become of his unhappy subjects that he thus disposed of.

13. The king accepted this offer with his usual avidity, and had prepared a fleet and an army in order to take possession of the rich provinces thus consigned to his trust. But an accident put an end to all his ambitious projects: he was shot by an arrow that Sir Walter Tyrrel* discharged at a deer in the New Forest, which, glancing from a tree, † struck the king to the heart. 14. He dropped dead instantaneously; while the innocent author of his death, terrified

* A French gentleman, remarkable for his skill in archery.
† It is a no less interesting historical fact, than a botanical curiosity abundantly proving the longevity of the oak, that this celebrated tree is now standing, though in the last stage of decay, near Malwood Castle, in the centre of the New Forest. It was first paled round by an order of Charles II.
  The rampart which surrounds the Tower of London and Westminster Hall, are the principal monuments which remain of Rufus' reign. At the time of his death he was forty-two years of age, and had reigned thirteen.

at the accident, put spurs to his horse, hastened to the sea-shore, embarked for France, and joined the crusade that was then setting out for Jerusalem.

CONTEMPORARY SOVEREIGNS.

Popes.	Emperors of the East.	King of France.
A.D.	A.D.	A.D.
Victor III........ 1086	Alexis I.......... 1081	Philip I.......... 1060
Urban II........ 1088		
Pascal II........ 1099	Emperor of the West.	King of Scotland.
	Henry IV....... 1056	Donald VIII.... 1060

EMINENT PERSONS.

Lanfranc and Anselm, archbishops of Canterbury. Odo, bishop of Bayeux. Flambard, bishop of Durham.

Questions for Examination.

1. Who succeeded William the Conqueror?
2. By what means did Rufus induce the English to support his interest?
3. How did Robert employ his money?
5. What was the conduct of the king on the detection of conspiracies against him?
7. Relate the origin of the crusades.
9. What is the character of the duke of Normandy!
12. Who offered to mortgage his dominions to Rufus?
13. What caused the death of Rufus?

CHAPTER VI.

HENRY I.

Born 1068. Died December 2d, 1135. Began to reign August 5th, 1100. Reigned 35 years.

> But who shall teach my harp to gain
> A sound of that romantic strain;
> Whose Anglo-Norman tones whilere
> Could win the royal Henry's ear? —*Dibdin.*

1. (A. D. 1100.) HENRY, surnamed Beauclerc,* the late king's younger brother, who had been hunting in the New Forest when Rufus was slain, took the earliest advantage of the occasion, and, hastening to Winchester, resolved to secure the royal treasures, which he knew to be the best assistant in seconding his aims. The barons, as well as the people, acquiesced in a claim which they were unprovided to resist, and yielded obedience, from the fear of immediate danger.

2. Henry, to ingratiate himself with the people, expelled from court all the ministers of his brother's debauchery and arbitrary power. One thing only remained to confirm his claims without danger of a rival. The English remembered the Saxon monarchs with gratitude, and beheld them excluded the throne with regret. 3. There still remained some of the descendants of that favourite line; and amonst others, Matilda the niece of Edgar Atheling; which lady, having declined all pretension to royalty, was bred in a convent, and had actually taken the veil. 4. Upon her Henry first fixed his eyes as a proper consort, by whose means the long breach between the Saxon and Norman interest would be finally united. It only remained to get over the scruple of her being a nun; but this a council devoted to his interests readily admitted, and Matilda being pronounced free to marry, the nuptials were celebrated with great pomp and solemnity.†

5. It was at this unfavourable juncture that Robert returned from abroad; and, after taking possession of his

---

* "Henry was called 'Beauclerc' from his attention to learning; he had heard his father say, that 'Illiterate kings were little better than crowned asses,' and determined not to come under that description." —*Camden.*

† Queen Matilda was the delight of the English, both on account of her descent and goodness of heart. To her we owe the first stone arched bridges England ever possessed; she built two at Stratford, in Essex, (thence called De Arcubus, or Le Bow), where she had nearly been drowned for want of such a convenience.

native dominions, laid his claim to the crown of England. But proposals for an accommodation being made, it was stipulated that Robert, upon the payment of a certain sum, should resign his pretensions to England; and that, if either of the princes died without issue, the other should succeed to his dominions. This treaty being ratified, the armies on each side were disbanded: and Robert, having lived two months in the utmost harmony with his brother, returned in peace to his own dominions.

6. But Robert's indiscretion soon rendered him unfit to govern any state; he was totally averse to business, and only studious of the more splendid amusements or enjoyments of life. His servants pillaged him without compunction; and he is described as lying whole days in bed for want of clothes of which they had robbed him. 7. His subjects were treated still more deplorably; for, being under the command of petty and rapacious tyrants, who plundered them without mercy, the whole country was become a scene of violence and depredation. It was in this miserable exigence that the Normans at length had recourse to Henry, from whose wise administration of his own dominions, they expected a similitude of prosperity, should he take the reins of theirs. Henry very readily promised to redress their grievances, as he knew it would be the direct method to second his own ambition. The year ensuing, therefore, he landed in Normandy, with a strong army, took possession of the principal towns; and a battle ensuing, Robert's forces were totally overthrown, and he himself taken prisoner, with nearly ten thousand of his men, and all the considerable barons who had adhered to his misfortunes. This victory was followed by the final reduction of Normandy, while Henry returned in triumph to England, leading with him his captive brother, who, after a life of bravery, generosity, and truth, now found himself deprived, not only of his patrimony and friends, but also his freedom. Henry, unmindful of his brother's former magnanimity with regard to him, detained him a prisoner during the remainder of his life, which was no less than twenty-eight years; and he died in the castle of Cardiff, Glamorganshire. 10. It is even said by some that he was deprived of his sight by a red-hot copper basin applied to his eyes; while his brother attempted to stifle the reproaches of his conscience, by founding the abbey of Reading, which was then considered a sufficient atonement for every degree of barbarity.

HENRY I.

11. Fortune now seemed to smile upon Henry, and promise a long succession of felicity. He was in peaceable possession of two powerful states, and had a son, who was acknowledged his undisputed heir, arrived at his eighteenth year, whom he loved most tenderly. His daughter Matilda was also married to the emperor Henry V. of Germany, and she had been sent to that court, while yet but eight years old, for her education. 12. All his prospects, however, were at once clouded by unforeseen misfortunes, and accidents, which tinctured his remaining years with misery. The king, from the facility with which he usurped the crown, dreading that his family might be subverted with the same ease, took care to have his son recognized as his successor by the states of England, and carried him over to Normandy, to receive the homage of the barons of that duchy. 13. After performing this requisite ceremony, Henry, returning triumphantly to England, brought with him a numerous retinue of the chief nobility, who seemed to share in his success. In one of the vessels of the fleet, his son and several young noblemen, the companions of his pleasures, went together, to render the passage more agreeable. The king set sail from Harfleur,* and was soon carried by a fair wind out of sight of land. 14. The prince was detained by some accident; and his sailors, as well as their captain, Fitz-Stephen, having spent the interval in drinking, became so disordered, that they ran the ship upon a rock, and immediately it was dashed to pieces. The prince was put into the boat and might have escaped, had he not been called back by the cries of Maud, his natural sister. He was at first conveyed out of danger himself, but could not leave a person so dear to perish without an effort to save her. He therefore prevailed upon the sailors to row back and take her in. 15. The approach of the boat giving several others, who had been left upon the wreck, the hopes of saving their lives, numbers leaped in, and the whole went to the bottom. About a hundred and forty young noblemen of the principal families of England and Normandy, were lost on this occasion. A butcher of Rouen was the only person on board who escaped; he clung to the mast and was taken up the next morning by some fishermen. 16. Fitz-Stephen, the captain, while the butcher was thus buffeting the waves for his life, swam up to him and enquired if the prince was yet living; when being told

* A town of Normandy in France.

that he had perished, "then I will not outlive him," said the captain, and immediately sunk to the bottom. The shrieks of these unfortunate people were heard from the shore, and the noise even reached the king's ship, but the cause was then unknown. 17. Henry entertained hopes, for three days, that his son had put into some distant port in England; but when certain intelligence of the calamity was brought to him he fainted away, and was never seen to smile from that moment till the day of his death, which followed some time after at St. Denis, a little town in Normandy, from eating too plentifully of lampreys, a dish he was particularly fond of. He died, in the sixty-seventh year of his age, and the thirty-fifth of his reign, leaving by will his daughter Matilda heiress of all his dominions.

Questions for Examination.

1. On the death of Rufus, what was the conduct of Henry?
2. What method did Henry take to ingratiate himself in his subjects, favour?
4. To whom was Henry married?
5. Was there any other claimant to the crown of England?
6, 7. What was the conduct of Robert, at this time, and to what disasters did it lead?
9. In what way was the captive Robert treated by his brother?
11. What was the situation of Henry at this time?
12. For what purpose did Henry carry his son to Normandy?
15. Relate the fatal accident that befel many of the nobility?
17. What was the cause of the king's death?

CONTEMPORARY SOVEREIGNS.

Popes.	A.D.		A.D.		A.D.
Pascal II.	1099	John Comnenus..	1118	Louis IV.	1108
Gelastius II.	1118				
Calixtus II.	1119	*Emperors of the West.*		*Kings of Scotland.*	
Honorius II.	1124	Henry IV.	1056		
Innocent II.	1130	Henry V.	1106	Donald VIII.	1068
		Lotharius.	1125	Edgar.	1108
Emperors of the East.				Alexander.	1117
		Kings of France.		David.	1124
Alexis I.	1081	Philip I.	1060		

EMINENT PERSONS.

Anselm and Radulph, archbishops of Canterbury. William Crito, son of duke Robert of Normandy. Robert earl of Shrewsbury. The Empress Matilda.*

---

* She was the only daughter and surviving legitimate child of Henry; she was married to Henry V. emperor of Germany, but having become a widow in the year 1126, she returned to her father's court and continued to receive the honorary title of empress. In the following year Henry, while

CHAPTER VII.

STEPHEN.

Born 1104. Died Oct. 25th, 1154. Began to reign Dec. 26, 1135. Reigned 18¾ years.

> Contending armies now for empire fight,
> And civil war distracts Britannia's isle;
> Matilda now asserts her regal right,—
> Now dauntless Stephen's cause is seen to smile.
> Thus mad ambition prompts to desperate deeds,
> And, for a phantom, thus a nation bleeds.—*Macdonald*

1. (A. D. 1135.) No sooner was the king known to be dead, than Stephen, son of Adela, the king's sister, and the count of Blois,* conscious of his own power and influence, resolved to secure himself the possession of what he so long desired. He speedily hastened from Normandy, and, arriving at London, was immediately saluted king by all the lower ranks of people. 2. Being thus secure of the people, his next step was to gain over the clergy; and, for that purpose, his brother, the bishop of Winchester, exerted all his influence among them with great success.† Thus was Stephen made king by one of those speedy revolutions which ever mark the barbarity of a state in which they are customary.

3. The first acts of a usurper are always popular. Stephen, in order to secure his tottering throne, passed a charter granting several privileges to the different orders of the state:—To the nobility a permission to hunt in their own forests; to the clergy, a speedy filling of all vacant benefices; and to the people, a restoration of the laws of Edward the Confessor. To fix himself still more securely, he took possession of the royal treasures at Winchester, and had his title ratified by the pope with a part of the money.

4. It was not long, however, that Matilda delayed asserting her claim to the crown. She landed upon the coast of in Normandy, became attached to Geoffry Martel, the young count of Anjou, who had changed his name to Plantagenet, from his custom of wearing in his helmet a bunch of flowering broom (*plante-de-genêt*,) instead of a plume; not content with becoming his godfather in chilvary, the king resolved that Matilda should receive the young count of Anjou as her second husband. This marriage was contracted without the consent of the estates of the realms of England and Normandy; being therefore deemed illegal, it afforded Stephen a pretext for usurping the throne.—*William of Malmesbury.*

* A city of France.

† "Stephen was a man of great facetiousness, and much of his success is to be imputed to the familiar pleasantry of his conversation.— *William of Malmesbury.*

Sussex, assisted by Robert, earl of Gloucester, natural son of the late king. The whole of Matilda's retinue upon this occasion amounted to no more than one hundred and forty knights, who immediately took possession of Arundel castle; but the nature of her claim soon increased the number of her partisans, and her forces every day seemed to gain ground upon those of her antagonist. 5. Meantime Stephen being assured of her arrival, flew to besiege Arundel, where she had taken refuge, and where she was protected by the queen dowager, who secretly favoured her pretensions. This fortress was too feeble to promise a long defence; and would have soon been taken had it not been represented to the king, that as it was a castle belonging to the queen dowager, it would be an infringement on the respect due to her to attempt taking it by force.

6. There was a spirit of generosity mixed with the rudeness of the times that unaccountably prevailed in many transactions. Stephen permitted Matilda to come forth in safety, and had her conveyed with security to Bristol, another fortress equally strong with that from which he permitted her to retire. 7. It would be tedious to relate the various skirmishes on either side, in pursuance of their respective pretensions; it will suffice to say that Matilda's forces increased every day, while her antagonist seemed every hour to become weaker; and a victory gained by the queen threw Stephen from the throne into a prison, and exalted Matilda in his room. Matilda was crowned at Winchester with all imaginable solemnity.

8. Matilda, however, was unfit for government. She affected to treat the nobility with a degree of disdain to which they had long been unaccustomed; so that the fickle nation once more began to pity their deposed king, and repent the steps they had taken in her favour. The bishop of Winchester was not remiss in fomenting these discontents; and when he found the people ripe for a tumult, detached a party of his friends and vassals to block up the city of London, where the queen then resided. At the same time measures were taken to instigate the Londoners to a revolt, and to seize her person. Matilda, having timely notice of this conspiracy, fled to Winchester, whither the bishop, still her secret enemy, followed her, watching an opportunity to ruin her cause. His party was soon sufficiently strong to bid the queen open defiance, and to besiege her in the very place where she first received his

Imprisonment of King Stephen.

benediction. 10. There she continued for some time; but the town being pressed by a famine, she was obliged to escape; while her brother, the earl of Gloucester, endeavouring to follow, was taken prisoner, and exchanged for Stephen, who still continued a captive. Thus a sudden revolution once more took place; Matilda was deposed, and obliged to seek for safety in Oxford. Stephen was again recognised as the king, and taken from his dungeon to be replaced on the throne.

11. But he was now to enter the lists with a new opposer, who was every day coming to maturity, and growing more formidable. This was Henry, the son of Matilda, who had now reached his sixteenth year; and gave the greatest hopes of being one day a valiant leader and a consummate politician.

12. With the wishes of the people in his favour young Henry was resolved to claim his hereditary kingdom, and to dispute once more Stephen's usurped pretensions; he accordingly made an invasion on England, where he was immediately joined by almost all the barons of the kingdom.

13. In the meantime, Stephen, alarmed at the power and popularity of his young rival, tried every method to anticipate the purpose of an invasion; but finding it impossible to turn the torrent, he was obliged to have recourse to treaty. It was, therefore, agreed, by all parties, that Stephen should reign during his life; and that justice should

be administered in his name; that Henry should, on Stephen's death, succeed to the kingdom; and William, Stephen's son, should inherit Boulogne and his patrimonial estate. 14. After all the barons had sworn to this treaty, which filled the whole kingdom with joy, Henry evacuated England; and Stephen returned to the peaceful enjoyment of his throne. His reign, however, was soon after terminated by his death, which happened about a year after the treaty at Canterbury, where he was interred.

Questions for Examination.

1. Who succeeded Henry the first?
2. What measures were taken to secure the throne?
3. What were the first acts of Stephen?
4. Was there no opposition to Stephen?
6. What was Stephen's conduct towards Matilda?
7. Did Matilda succeed in recovering the throne?
8. Had Matilda's conduct any serious consequences?
10. Whither did Matilda flee for safety?
  In what manner did she escape?
11. Had Stephen any new opposer?
12. Who joined Henry when he invaded England?
13. Of what nature was the treaty between the two parties?

CONTEMPORARY SOVEREIGNS.

Popes.	A.D.		A.D.	*Kings of France.*	A.D.
Celestine II.	1143	Man. Comnenus.	1143		
Lucius II.	1144			Louis VI.	1108
Eugenius III.	1145	*Emperors of the West.*		Louis VII.	1137
Anastasius IV.	1153				
Adrian IV.	1154	Lothaire II.	1125	*King of Scotland.*	
		Conrad III.	1138		
Emperors of the East.		Frederic I.	1152	David I.	1124
John Comnenus.	1118				

EMINENT PERSONS.

John of Salisbury, Henry of Huntingdon, Roger de Hoveden, Geoffry of Monmouth (historians); Curboil and Theobald, archbishops of Canterbury; Thurston, archbishop of York, and lieutenant to the king who appointed Ralph, bishop of Durham, his general against the Scots; Robert, earl of Gloucester; Ranulph, earl of Chester.

CHAPTER VIII.

HENRY II.

Born 1132. Died July 6th, 1189. Began to reign Dec. 8th, 1154.* Reigned 34¾ years.

SECTION I.

*Plantagenet, from civil broils
The land awhile respired, and all was peace;
Then Becket rose, and, impotent of mind,
Bid murd'rous priests the sov'reign frown contemn,
And with unhallowed crozier, bruised the crown.—Shenstone.*

1. (A. D. 1155.) The first act of Henry's government gave the people a happy omen of his future wise administration. Conscious of his power, he began to correct those abuses, and to resume those privileges, which had been extorted from the weakness or the credulity of his predecessors. He immediately dismissed those mercenary soldiers who committed infinite disorders in the nation.
2. He resumed many of those benefactions which had been made to churches and monasteries in the former reigns. He gave charters to several towns, by which the citizens claimed their freedom and privileges, independent of any superior but himself. These charters were the groundwork of English liberty. The struggles which had before this time been, whether the king, or the barons, or the clergy, should be despotic over the people, now began to assume a new aspect; and a fourth order, namely, that of the more opulent of the people, began to claim a share in administration. Thus was the feudal government first impaired; and liberty began to be more equally diffused throughout the nation.
4. Henry being thus become the most powerful prince of his age, the undisputed monarch of England, possessed of more than a third of France, and having humbled the barons that would circumscribe his power, he might naturally be expected to reign with very little opposition for the future. But it happened otherwise. He found the severest mortifications from a quarter where he least expected resistance.
5. The famous Thomas a Becket, the first man of English extraction who had, since the Norman conquest, risen to any share of power, was the son of a citizen of London.

* He was on the continent at the time of Stephen's death, and the commencement of his reign is dated from the day of his landing in England.

Having received his early education in the schools of that metropolis, he resided sometime at Paris; and, on his return, became clerk in the Sheriff's office. From that humble station he rose, through the gradations of office, until at last he was made archbishop of Canterbury—a dignity second only to that of the king.*

5. No sooner was he fixed in this high station, which rendered him for life the second person in the kingdom, than he endeavoured to retrieve the character of sanctity which his former levities might have appeared to oppose. He was in his person the most mortified man that could be seen. He wore sackcloth next to his skin. He changed it so seldom, that it was filled with dirt and vermin. His usual diet was bread; his drink water, which he rendered farther unpalatable by the mixture of unsavory herbs.

7. His back was mangled with frequent discipline. He every day washed on his knees the feet of thirteen beggars. Thus pretending to sanctity, he set up for being a defender of the privileges of the clergy, which had for a long time been enormous, and which it was Henry's aim to abridge.

8. An opportunity soon offered, and gave him a popular pretext for beginning his intended reformation. A man in holy orders had debauched the daughter of a gentleman in Worcestershire; and then murdered the father to prevent

---

* The parentage of this extraordinary man was truly romantic. His father, Gilbert Beck, or Becket, while serving as a private soldier in Palestine, was taken prisoner by a Saracen chief. He had the good fortune to engage the affections of his master's daughter, and by her aid made his escape. She soon after took the desperate resolution of quitting her home and country in search of the object of her love, and though the only two words of any western language which she knew were *London* and *Gilbert* set out for Europe. By the aid of the former word she secured a passage on board an English vessel: and when she was landed on the banks of the Thames, she ran from street to street, calling out the latter name until chance brought her into the presence of Gilbert himself. The strangeness of the event excited universal attention, and the young Saracen, after being baptized by the Christian name of Matilda, became the wife of Gilbert Becket. Thomas was their eldest son, and was educated in all the learning and accomplishments of the age. He was in early life taken under the patronage of Thibaut or Theobald, archbishop of Canterbury, and by the favour of that prelate was permitted to enjoy indulgences which the Norman conquerors had prohibited to all of Saxon descent. During the reign of Stephen, Becket and his patron were warm supporters of Henry's claim to the English Crown, and in consequence he was rewarded at the commencement of the new reign with the high office of chancellor of England. In this situation he was distinguished by his zeal in defence of the royal prerogative, and by the extravagant pomp and luxury of his establishment. Henry, believing that the companion of his games, his wars, and even his debaucheries, would be subservient to his desires of limiting the power of the church, elevated Becket to the see of Canterbury, but found, too late, that he had only given to the holy see a zealous champion, and to himself a dangerous antagonist.

the effects of his resentment. The atrociousness of the crime produced a spirit of indignation among the people; and the king insisted that the assassin should be tried by the civil magistrate. This Becket opposed, alleging the privileges of the church.

9. In order to determine this matter, the king summoned a general council of the nobility and prelates at Clarendon, to whom he submitted this great and important affair, and desired their concurrence. These councils seem at that time convened rather to give authenticity to the king's decrees, than to enact laws that were to bind their posterity. A number of regulations were then drawn up which were afterwards well known under the title of the Constitutions of Clarendon, and were then voted without opposition. 10. By these regulations it was enacted, that clergymen accused of any crime should be tried in the civil courts; that laymen should not be tried in the spiritual courts, except by legal and reputable witnesses. These, with some others of less consequence, or implied in the above, to the number of sixteen, were readily subscribed to by all the bishops present: Becket himself, who at first showed some reluctance, added his name to the number. But Alexander who was then pope, condemned them in the strongest terms; abrogated, annulled, and rejected them.

11. This produced a contest between the king and Becket, who, having attained the highest honours the monarch could bestow, took part with his holiness. In the midst of this dispute, Becket, with an intrepidity peculiar to himself, arraying himself in his episcopal vestments, and with the cross in his hand, went forward to the king's palace, and, entering the royal apartments, sat down, holding up his cross as his banner of protection. 12. There he put himself, in the most solemn manner, under the protection of the supreme pontiff; and, upon receiving a refusal of permission to leave the kingdom, he secretly withdrew in disguise, and at last found means to cross over to the continent.

The intrepidity of Becket, joined to his apparent sanctity, gained him a favorable reception upon the continent, both from the people and the governors.

13. The pope and he were not remiss to retort their fulminations, and to shake the very foundation of the king's authority. Becket compared himself to Christ, who had been condemned by a lay tribunal, and who was crucified

anew in the present oppressions, under which the church labored. But he did not rest in complaints only. 14. He issued out a censure, excommunicating the king's chief ministers by name, all that were concerned in sequestering the revenues of his see, and all who obeyed or favoured the constitutions of Clarendon.

Frequent attempts indeed were made towards an accommodation; but the mutual jealousies which each bore the other, and their anxiety not to lose the least advantage in the negociation, often protracted this desirable treaty.

Questions for Examination.

1. What were the first acts of Henry's power?
2. What was the ground-work of English liberty?
4. Describe the possessions of Henry at this time?
5. Who was Thomas à Becket?
   How did he rise to be archbishop of Canterbury?
6. What was the character and manner of life of Becket?
9. What proceeding took place at the council of Clarendon?
10. What were these regulations?
11. 12. Describe Becket's conduct in the king's palace.
13. To whom did Becket compare himself? and why?
14. How did Becket act?

SECTION II.

Still must that tongue some wounding message bring,
And still thy priestly pride provoke thy king.—Pope.

1. (A. D.) 1170. At length, however, the mutual aim of both made a reconciliation necessary; but nothing could exceed the insolence with which Becket conducted himself upon his first landing in England. Instead of retiring quietly to his diocese, with that modesty which became a man just pardoned by his king, he made a progress through Kent, in all the splendour and magnificence of a sovereign pontiff. 2. As he approached Southwark, the clergy, the laity, men of all ranks and ages, came forth to meet him, and celebrated his triumphal entry with hymns of joy. Thus confident of the voice and hearts of the people, he began to launch forth his thunders against those who had been his former opposers. The archbishop of York, who had crowned Henry's eldest son in his absence, was the first against whom he denounced sentence of suspension. 2. The bishops of London and Salisbury he actually excommunicated. One man he excommunicated for having spoken against him; and another for having cut off the tail of one of his horses.

Death of Thomas à Becket.

Henry was then in Normandy, while the primate was thus triumphantly parading through the kingdom; and it was not without the utmost indignation that he received information of his turbulent insolence. 4. When the suspended and excommunicated prelates arrived with their complaints, his anger knew no bounds. He broke forth into the most acrimonious expressions against that arrogant churchman, whom he had raised from the lowest station to be the plague of his life, and the continual disturber of his government. The archbishop of York remarked to him, that so long as Becket lived, he could never expect to enjoy peace or tranquillity: and the king himself burst out into an exclamation, that he had no friends about him, or he would not so long have been exposed to the insults of that ungrateful hypocrite.* 5. These words excited the attention of the whole court, and armed four of his resolute attendants to gratify their monarch's secret inclination. The conspirators being joined by some assistants at the place of their meeting, proceeded to Canterbury with all that haste their bloody intentions required. 6. Advancing

* The words made use of by the king on this occasion are said to be as follow:—" 'Is there not one of the crew of lazy, cowardly knights, whom I maintain, that will rid me of this turbulent priest, who came to court but t'other day on a lame horse, with nothing but his wallet behind him?' This speech unfortunately animated to action Reginald Fitzurse, William de Tracy, Hugh de Morvil, and Richard Brito."— *Berington's Life of Thomas à Becket.*

directly to Becket's house, and entering his apartment, they reproached him very fiercely for the rashness and insolence of his conduct. During the altercation, the time approached for Becket to assist at vespers, whither he went unguarded, the conspirators following, and preparing for their attempt.
7. As soon as he reached the altar, where it is just to think he aspired to the glory of martyrdom, they all fell upon him; and having cloven his head with repeated blows he dropped down dead before the altar of St. Benedict,* which was besmeared with his blood and brains.

8. Nothing could exceed the king's consternation upon receiving the first news of this prelate's catastrophe. He was instantly sensible that the murder would be ultimately imputed to him: and, at length, in order to divert the minds of the people to a different object, he undertook an expedition to Ireland. A. D. 1172.

9. Ireland was at that time in pretty much the same situation that England had been after the first invasion of the Saxons. They had been early converted to Christianity; and for three or four centuries after possessed a very large proportion of the learning of the times. Being undisturbed by foreign invasions, and perhaps too poor to invite the rapacity of conquerors, they enjoyed a peaceful life, which they gave up to piety, and such learning as was then thought necessary to promote it. 10. Of their learning, their arts, their piety, and even their polished manners, too many monuments remain to this day for us to make the least doubt concerning them; but it is equally true, that in time they fell from these advantages: their degenerate posterity, at the period we are now speaking of, were wrapped in the darkest barbarity.

11. At the time when Henry first planned the invasion of the island, it was divided into five principalities; namely, Leinster, Meath, Munster, Ulster, and Connaught; each governed by its respective monarch. As it has been usual for one or other of those to take the lead in the wars, he was denominated sole monarch of the kingdom, and possessed of power resembling that of the early Saxon monarchs in England. Roderic O'Connor, king of Connaught, was then advanced to this dignity, and Dermot M'Morrough, was king of Leinster. 12. This last-named prince, a weak, licentious tyrant, had carried off the daughter of the king of

---

* St. Benedict, the founder of the religious order which bears his name, was born in Italy about the year 480, and early embraced a solitary life

Meath, who, being strengthened by the alliance of the king of Connaught, invaded Dermot's dominions, and expelled him from his kingdom. The prince, thus justly punished, had recourse to Henry, who was at that time in Guienne; and offered to hold his kingdom of the English crown, in case he recovered it by the king's assistance. 13. Henry readily accepted the offer; but being at that time embarrassed by more near interests, he only gave to Dermot letters patent, by which he empowered all his subjects to aid the Irish prince in the recovery of his dominions. Dermot, relying on this authority, returned to Bristol, where, after some difficulty, he formed a treaty with Richard, surnamed Strongbow, earl of Pembroke, who agreed to reinstate him in his dominions, upon condition of his being married to his daughter Eva, and declared heir of all his territory. 14. Being thus assured of assistance, he returned privately to Ireland, and concealed himself during the winter in the monastery of Ferns, which he had founded. Robert Fitzstephens was the first knight who was able, in the ensuing spring, to fulfil his engagements, by landing with a hundred and thirty knights, sixty esquires, and three hundred archers. 15. They were soon after joined by Maurice Pendergast, who, about the same time, brought over ten knights and sixty archers; and with this small body of forces they resolved on besieging Wexford, which was to be theirs by treaty. The town was quickly reduced; and the adventurers being reinforced by another body of men to the amount of a hundred and fifty, under the command of Maurice Fitzgerald, composed an army that struck the barbarous natives with awe. 16. Roderic, the chief monarch of the island, ventured to oppose them, but he was defeated; and soon after the prince of Ossory was obliged to submit, and give hostages for his future conduct.

17. Dermot being thus reinstated in his hereditary dominions, soon began to conceive hopes of extending the limits of his power, and making himself master of Ireland. With these views he endeavoured to expedite Strongbow, who, being personally prohibited by the king, was not yet come over. Dermot tried to inflame his ambition by the glory of the conquest, and his avarice by the advantages it would procure. He expatiated on the cowardice of the natives, and the certainty of his success. 18. Strongbow first sent over Raymond, one of his retinue, with ten knights and seventy archers; and receiving permission shortly after for

himself, he landed with two hundred horse and a hundred archers. All these English forces now joining together, became irresistible; and though the whole number did not amount to a thousand, yet such was the barbarous state of the natives, that they were every where put to the rout. The city of Waterford quickly surrendered; Dublin was taken by assault; and Strongbow soon after marrying Eva, according to treaty, became master of the kingdom of Leinster upon Dermot's decease.

19. The island being thus in a manner wholly subdued, for nothing was capable of opposing the further progress of the English arms, Henry became willing to share in person these honours which the adventurers had already secured. 20. He, therefore, shortly after landed in Ireland, at the head of five hundred knights and some soldiers; not so much to conquer a disputed territory, as to take possession of a kingdom. Thus after a trifling effort, in which very little money was expended, and little blood shed, that beautiful island became, as it still continues to be, an appendage to the British crown.

Questions for Examination.

2. 3. How did Becket conduct himself on his return to England?
4. In what manner did Henry receive the complaints of Becket's insolence?
5. 6. What was the consequence of Henry's resentment?
7. By what means did Henry divert the minds of the people?
9. 10. What was the situation of Ireland at this time?
11. By whom was it governed?
12. What occasioned the interference of Henry?
13. What followed this interference?
15. What further means were taken to subdue Ireland?
18. What was the success of the English on their invading Ireland?
20. For what purpose did Henry go to Ireland?

SECTION III.

A maid unmatch'd in manners as in face.
Skill'd in each art, and crown'd with every grace.—*Pope.*

1. (A. D. 1173.) The joy which this conquest diffused was very great; but troubles of a domestic nature served to render the remainder of Henry's life a scene of turbulence and disquietude.

Young Harry, the king's eldest son, was taught to believe himself injured, when, upon being crowned as partner in the kingdom, he was not admitted into a share of the administration. 2. His discontents were shared by his brothers Geoffrey and Richard, whom the queen persuaded to assert

Henry II. on his pilgrimage to Canterbury.

their titles to the territories assigned them. Queen Eleanor herself was meditating an escape to the court of France whither her sons had retired, and had put on man's apparel for that purpose, when she was seized by the king's order and put in confinement. 3. Thus Henry saw all his long perspective of future happiness totally clouded; his sons scarcely yet arrived at manhood, eager to share the spoils of their father's possessions; his queen warmly encouraging these undutiful princes in their rebellion; and many potentates of Europe not ashamed to lend them assistance to support these pretensions.

4. It was not long before the young princes had sufficient influence upon the continent to raise a powerful confederacy in their favour. Henry, therefore, knowing the influence of superstition over the minds of the people, and perhaps apprehensive that a part of his troubles arose from the displeasure of heaven, resolved to do penance at the shrine of St. Thomas, at Canterbury, for that was the name given to Becket upon his canonization. As soon as he came within sight of the church of Canterbury, alighting from his horse, he walked barefoot towards the town, and prostrated himself before the shrine* of the saint. Next day he received absolution; and, departing for London, was acquainted with the

* Here he was scourged by the monks, and passed the whole day and night fasting on the bare stones.

agreeable news of a victory over the Scots, obtained on the very day of his absolution.

5. From that time Henry's affairs began to wear a better aspect: the barons, who had revolted, or were preparing for a revolt, made instant submission; they delivered up their castles to the victor; and England, in a few weeks, was restored to perfect tranquillity. 6. Young Henry, who was ready to embark with a large army, to second the efforts of the English insurgents, finding all disturbances quieted at home, abandoned all thoughts of the expedition. This prince died soon after, in the twenty-sixth year of his age, of a fever, at Martel, not without the deepest remorse for his undutiful conduct towards his father.

7. As this prince left no posterity, Richard was become heir in his room; and he soon discovered the same ardent ambition that had misled his elder brother. A crusade having been once more projected, Richard, who had long wished to have all the glory of such an expedition to himself, and who could not bear to have even his father a partner in his victories, entered into a confederacy with the king of France, who promised to confirm him in those wishes at which he so ardently aspired. 8. By this, Henry found himself obliged to give up all hopes of taking the cross, and compelled to enter upon a war with France and his eldest son, who were unnaturally leagued against him.

9. At last, however, a treaty was concluded, in which he was obliged to submit to many mortifying concessions: but still more so, when, upon demanding a list of the barons that it was stipulated he should pardon, he found his son John, his favourite child, among the number. He had long borne an infirm state of body with calm resignation. He had seen his children rebel without much emotion; but when he saw that child, whose interest always lay next to his heart, among the number of those who were in rebellion against him, he could no longer contain his indignation. He broke out into expressions of the utmost despair; cursed the day on which he had received his miserable being; and bestowed on his ungrateful children a malediction, which he never after could be prevailed upon to retract. 10. The more his heart was disposed to friendship and affection, the more he resented this barbarous return; and now not having one corner in his heart where he could look for comfort or fly for refuge from his conflicting passions, he lost all his former vivacity. A lingering fever, caused by a broken

heart, soon after terminated his life and his miseries. He died at the castle of the Chinon, near Saumur, in the fifty-eighth year of his age, and in the thirty-fifth of his reign, in the course of which he displayed all the abilities of a politician, all the sagacity of a legislator, and all the magnanimity of a hero; sullied, however, by many instances of cruelty and perfidy, which were too commonly the characteristics of all the Plantagenets.

Questions for Examination.

2. By what means did Eleanor endeavour to escape?
3. In what way were Henry's prospects of future happiness clouded?
4. What was the penance performed by Henry?
5. At what time did the affairs of Henry wear a better aspect?
6. Who endeavoured to assist the insurgents?
7. Did another of Henry's sons enter into a conspiracy? and what was the consequence?
8. What were the misfortunes which led Henry to curse the day of his birth, and to bestow a malediction on his children?
10. What caused the death of Henry?
    What was his character?

CONTEMPORARY SOVEREIGNS.

Popes.	A.D.		A.D.		A.D.
Adrian IV*......	1154	Isaac Angelus....	1185	Sancho I.........	1185
Alexander III ...	1159				
Lucius III.......	1181	*Emperor of the West.*		*King of Denmark.*	
Urban III........	1185	Frederick I....	1152	Waldemar I.†....	1157
Gregory VIII....	1187				
Clement III......	1188	*Kings of France.*		*Kings of Scotland.*	
		Louis VII........	1137	David I..........	1124
Emperors of the East.		Philip Augustus..	1180	Malcolm IV......	1153
Man. Comnenus..	1143			William..........	1165
Alexis II.........	1180	*Kings of Portugal.*			
Andronicus I.....	1183	Alphonso........	1102		

EMINENT PERSONS.

Theobold, Becket, Richard, and Baldwin, archbishops of Canterbury; Strongbow, earl of Pembroke; William Longsword, earl of Salisbury; Geoffrey, archbishop of York; and Morgan, bishop of Durham—natural sons of the king—the two former by fair Rosamond, the latter by a daughter of Sir Ralph Blewet. Hugh Lacy, and Ralph de Glanville, justiciaries of Ireland and England. Bertrand de Boru.‡

---

* Pope Adrian was an Englishman, by name Nicholas Breakspear; he was choked by a fly in the fifth year of his popedom.—*Med. Hist. August.*
† The regular succession and history of Denmark do not properly commence till the accession of Waldemar I. (called the Great), who considerably enlarged and civilized the country.
‡ Though not properly a subject of the British crown, this extraordinary man exercised no little influence on the fortunes of Henry. He was lord of a small territory lying between the continental possessions of Henry and France: he saw that his only hope of retaining independence rested on the continued hostility of these great powers, and used all his efforts

CHAPTER IX.

RICHARD I.

Born 1157. Died April 6th, 1199. Began to reign August 13, 1189. Reigned 9¾ years.

> Against whose fury and unmatched force
> The aweless lion could not wage the fight,
> Nor keep his princely heart from Richard's hand.—*Shakspeare.*

1. (A. D. 1189.) RICHARD, surnamed *Cœur de Lion*, upon his ascending the throne, was still inflamed with the desire of going upon the crusade: and at length the king having got a sufficient supply for his undertaking, having even sold his superiority over the kingdom of Scotland, which had been acquired in the last reign, for a moderate sum, he set out for the Holy Land, whither he was impelled by repeated messages from king Philip II. of France, who was ready to embark in the same enterprise.

2. The first place of rendezvous for the two armies of England and France, was the plain of Vevelay, on the borders of Burgundy; where, when Richard and Philip arrived, they found their armies amounting to a hundred thousand fighting men. Here the French prince and the English entered into the most solemn engagements of mutual support, and determined to conduct the armies to the Holy Land by Sea; they were obliged, however, by stress of weather, to take shelter at Messina,* the capital of Sicily, where they were detained during the whole winter. 3. Richard took up his quarters in the suburbs, and possessed himself of a small fort, which commanded the harbour. Philip quartered his troops in the town, and lived upon good terms with the Sicilian king.

---

to keep them constantly at war. Being both a politician and a poet, he exaggerated the causes of quarrel which constantly arise between adjoining states, and in bitter satires alternately reproached each government with cowardly submission to its rival. He stimulated the sons of Henry to make war against their father, and young Henry especially was chiefly urged into the field by the satirical verses of Boru. After the death of the young prince, Henry besieged Bertrand's castle and made him prisoner. When brought into the monarch's presence, the king sarcastically said to his captive, "I think, Bertrand, thy wit has failed thee." "Yes, my lord," replied Bertraud, "it failed me on the day that the valiant young king, your son, expired: on that day I lost sense, wit, and knowledge." Struck at the unexpected mention of his son's name, the king fainted, and on his recovery granted Bertrand a full pardon.—*History of the Troubadours.*

* This place suffered much by an earthquake in 1783. It is famous for its wines, and is the finest harbour in the Mediterranean.

Many were the mistrusts and the mutual conciliations between these two monarchs, which were very probably inflamed by the Sicilian king's endeavours. At length, however, having settled all controversies, they set sail for the Holy Land, where the French arrived long before the English.

4. Upon the arrival of the English army in Palestine, however, fortune was seen to declare more openly in favour of the common cause. The French and English princes seemed to forget their secret jealousies, and to act in concert. But shortly after, Philip, from the bad state of his health, returned to France, leaving Richard ten thousand of his troops, under the command of the duke of Burgundy. 5. Richard, now left conductor of the war, went on from victory to victory. The Christian adventurers, under his command, determined to besiege the renowned city of Ascalon, in order to prepare the way for attacking Jerusalem with greater advantage. Saladin, the most heroic of the Saracen monarchs, was resolved to dispute their march, and placed himself upon the road with an army of three hundred thousand men. This was a day equal to Richard's wishes; this an enemy worthy his highest ambition. 6. The English crusaders were victorious. Richard, when the wings of his army were defeated, led on the main body in person, and restored the battle. The Saracens fled in the utmost confusion, and no less than forty thousand of their number perished on the field of battle.* Ascalon soon surrendered after this victory; other cities of less note followed the example; Richard was at last able to advance within sight of Jerusalem, the object of his long and ardent expectations.

7. But just at this glorious juncture, his ambition was to suffer a total overthrow; upon reviewing his forces, and considering his abilities to prosecute the siege, he found that his army was so wasted with famine, fatigue, and even victory, that they were neither able nor willing to second the

* So celebrated was the courage of the English king, even in the enemy's army, and so dreaded was his name, that the Saracens would say to their restive horses, "What do you start at? do you think you see king Richard?" Nor was his zealous industry less remarkable than his courage. To encourage the soldiers in repairing the ruined walls of Acre, Cœur de Lion not only laboured in person, but appointed hours for other leaders to work at the head of their men. All cheerfully obeyed, except the duke of Austria, who sent word that his father having been neither bricklayer nor mason, he had not learned either business. The English king hearing this insolent speech repeated to his face by the haughty duke, kicked him out of his tent, and ordered his banner to be disgraced.—*Brompton.*

views of their commander. 8. It appeared, therefore, absolutely necessary to come to an accommodation with Saladin, and a truce for three years was accordingly concluded; in which it was agreed, that the sea-port towns of Palestine should remain in the hands of the Christians; and that all of that religion should be permitted to make their pilgrimage to Jerusalem in perfect security.*

9. Richard having thus concluded his expedition with more glory than advantage, began to think of returning home; but being obliged to return through Germany, in the habit of a pilgrim, he was arrested by Leopold, duke of Austria, who commanded him to be imprisoned, and loaded with shackles, to the disgrace of honour and humanity. The emperor soon after required the prisoner to be delivered up to him, and stipulated a large sum of money to the duke as a reward of his services. 10. Thus, the king of England, who had long filled the world with his fame, was basely thrown into a dungeon, and loaded with irons, by those who expected to reap a sordid advantage from his misfortunes. It was a long time before his subjects in England knew what was become of their beloved monarch. 11. So little intercourse was there between different nations at that time, that this discovery is said by some to have been made by a poor French minstrel, who, playing upon his harp, near the fortress in which Richard was confined, a tune which he knew that unhappy monarch was fond of, he was answered by the king from within, who, with his harp, played the same tune, and thus discovered the place of his confinement.

12. However, the English at length prevailed upon this barbarous monarch, who now saw that he could no longer detain his prisoner, to listen to terms of accommodation. A ransom was agreed upon, which amounted to a hundred and fifty thousand marks, or one hundred thousand pounds of our money, upon the payment of which, Richard was once more restored to his expecting subjects.

13. Nothing could exceed the joy of the English upon seeing their monarch return, after all his achievements and sufferings.

---

* There was a magnanimity and generosity in Saladin rarely seen. It is recorded, that once during this campaign, Richard was dangerously sick, and his disorder requiring fresh fruit, and snow to render it cool, the generous Saracen sent both in profusion, and thus saved the life of the only foe he dreaded.—(*Vita Saladina.*)

He made his entry into London in triumph; and such was the profusion of wealth shown by the citizens, that the German lords who attended him were heard to say, that if the emperor had known of their affluence he would not so easily have parted with their king, He soon after ordered himself to be crowned anew at Winchester. He convoked a general council at Nottingham, at which he confiscated all his brother John's possessions, who had basely endeavoured to prolong his captivity and gone over to the king of France with that intent. However he pardoned him soon after, with this generous remark: "I wish I could as easily forget my brother's offence as he will my pardon."

14. Richard's death was occasioned by a singular accident. A vassal of the crown had taken possession of a treasure, which was found by one of the peasants in digging a field in France; and to secure the remainder, he sent part of it to the king. Richard, as superior lord, sensible that he had a right to the whole, insisted on its being sent to him; and upon refusal, attacked the castle of Chalus, where he understood this treasure had been deposited. 15. On the fourth day of the siege, as he was riding round the place to observe where the assault might be given with the fairest probability of success, he was aimed at by Bertrand de Gourdon, an archer from the castle, and pierced in the shoulder with an arrow. The wound was not in itself dangerous; but an unskilful surgeon, endeavouring to disengage the arrow from the flesh, so rankled the wound, that it mortified, and brought on fatal symptoms. 16. Richard, when he found his end approaching, made a will, in which he bequeathed the kingdom, with all his treasure, to his brother John, except a fourth part, which he distributed among his servants. He ordered also that the archer who had shot him should be brought into his presence, and demanded what injury he had done him, that he should take away his life? The prisoner answered with deliberate intrepidity: 17. "You killed, with your own hand, my father and my two brothers, and you intended to have hanged me. I am now in your power, and my torments may give you revenge; but I will endure them with pleasure, since it is my consolation that I have rid the world of a tyrant." Richard, struck with this answer, ordered the soldier to be presented with one hundred shillings, and set at liberty; but Marcade, the general under him, like a true ruffian, ordered him to be flayed alive, and them hanged. Richard died in

the tenth year of his reign and the forty-second of his age, leaving only one (natural) son, named Philip, behind him.

Questions for Examination.

1. With whom did Richard embark for the crusades?
2. Of what numbers did the armies consist?
4. On Philip's return to France, who was left to conduct the war?
5. Who opposed Richard on his march to besiege Jerusalem?
6. Can you repeat the particulars of the battle?
8. What circumstance induced Richard to come to an accommodation with Saladin?
9. In returning home, what happened to Richard?
11. How was it discovered that Richard was a prisoner?
12. By what means did Richard recover his liberty?
13. Who endeavoured to prolong Richard's captivity? and what was his remark on this occasion?
15. Can you relate the singular accident which caused the death of Richard?
17. What was the answer of the person who shot the king?

CONTEMPORARY SOVEREIGNS.

Popes	A.D.		A.D.	*Kings of*	A.D.
Clement III.	1188	Alexis III.	1195		
Celestine III.	1191			*France*. Phillip II.	1180
Innocent III.	1198	*Emperors of the West.*		*Portugal*. San. I.	1180
		Frederic I.	1152	*Denmark*. Can. V.	1182
Emperors of the East.		Henry VI.	1190	*Scotland.* William	1165
Isaac II.	1186	Philip I.	1197		

EMINENT PERSONS.

Hubert, archbishop of Canterbury; Henry Fitzalwyn, first lord mayor of London; William Longchamps, bishop of Ely, regent in Richard's absence; Robin Hood and Little John, the celebrated outlaws.

CHAPTER X.

JOHN.

Born 1165. Died October 7th, 1216. Began to reign April 6th, 1199. Reigned 17½ years.

SECTION I.

> When faithless John usurped the sullied crown,
> What ample tyranny! Six tedious years
> Our helpless fathers in despair obey'd
> The Papal interdict: and who obey'd
> The Sovereign plundered?—*Shenstone.*

1. (A. D. 1199.) John,* who was readily put in possession of the English throne, lost no time to second his interest on the continent; and his first care was to recover the revolted provinces from young Arthur, his nephew. But from the pride and cruelty of his temper, he soon became hateful to his subjects; and his putting his nephew, who had a right to the crown, to death, with his own hand in prison, served to render him completely hateful.

2. Hitherto John was rather hateful to his subjects than contemptible; they rather dreaded than despised him. But he soon shewed that he might be offended, if not without resentment, at least with impunity. It was the fate of this vicious prince to make those the enemies of himself whom he wanted abilities to make the enemies of each other. The clergy had for some time acted as a community independent of the crown, and had their elections of each other generally confirmed by the pope, to whom alone they owed subjection. 3. However, the election of archbishops had for some time been a continual subject of dispute between the suffragan bishops and the Augustine monks, and both had precedents to confirm their pretensions. John sided with the bishops, and sent two knights of his train, who were fit instruments for such a prince, to expel the monks from their convent, and to take possession of their revenues. 4. The pope was not displeased with these divisions; and instead of electing either of the persons appointed by the contending parties, he nominated Stephen Langton as archbishop of Canterbury. John, however, refusing to admit the man of the pope's choosing, the kingdom was put under an interdict. This instrument of terror, in the hands of the see of Rome, was calculated to strike the senses in the highest degree, and to operate upon the

---

* Surnamed *Sans Terre,* or *Lackland.*

superstitious minds of the people. 5. By it a stop was immediately put to divine service, and to the administration of all the sacraments but baptism. The church-doors were shut; the statues of the saints were laid on the ground; the dead were refused Christian burial, and were thrown into ditches on the highways, without the usual rites or any funeral solemnity.

6. No situation could be more deplorable than that of John upon this occasion—furious at his indignities, jealous of his subjects, and apprehending an enemy in every face. It is said that, fearing a conspiracy against his life, he shut himself up a whole night in the castle of Nottingham, and suffered none to approach his person. But what was his consternation when he found that the pope had actually given away his kingdom to the monarch of France, and that the prince of that country was actually preparing an army to take possession of his crown!

7. John, who, unsettled and apprehensive, scarcely knew where to turn, was still able to make an expiring effort to receive the enemy. All hated as he was, the natural enmity between the French and the English, the name of king, which he still retained, and some remaining power, put him at the head of sixty thousand men—a sufficient number indeed, but not to be relied on—and with these he advanced to Dover. 8. Europe now regarded the important preparations on both sides with impatience; and the decisive blow was soon expected, in which the church was to triumph or to be overthrown. But neither Philip nor John had ability equal to the pontiff by whom they were actuated; who appeared on this occasion too refined a politician for either. He only intended to make use of Philip's power to intimidate his refractory son, not to destroy him. 9. He intimated, therefore, to John, by his legate, that there was but one way to secure himself from impending danger; which was to put himself under the pope's protection, who was a merciful father, and still willing to receive a repentant sinner to his bosom. John was too much intimidated by the manifest danger of his situation not to embrace every means offered for his safety. He assented to the truth of the legate's remonstrances, and took an oath to perform whatever stipulation the pope should impose. 10. John having thus sworn to the performance of an unknown command, the artful Italian so well managed the barons, and so effectually intimidated the king, that he

persuaded him to take the most extraordinary oath in all the records of history, before all the people, kneeling upon his knees, and with his hands held up between those of the legate.

11. "I, John, by the grace of God, king of England and lord of Ireland, in order to expiate my sins, from my own free will, and the advice of my barons, give to the church of Rome, to pope Innocent, and his successors, the kingdom of England, and all other prerogatives of my crown. I will hereafter hold them as the pope's vassal. I will be faithful to God, to the church of Rome, to the pope my master, and his successors legitimately elected. I promise to pay him a tribute of a thousand marks yearly; to wit, seven hundred for the kingdom of England, and three hundred for the kingdom of Ireland." 12. Having thus done homage to the legate, and agreed to reinstate Langton in the primacy, he received the crown, which he had been supposed to have forfeited, while the legate trampled under his feet the tribute which John had consented to pay. Thus, by this most scandalous concession, John once more averted the threatened blow.

In this manner, by repeated acts of cruelty, by expeditions without effect, and humiliations without reserve, John was become the detestation of all mankind.

Questions for Examination.

1. What was the conduct of John on succeeding to the throne?
2. 3. Of what nature was the disagreement between the king and the clergy which produced such serious consequences to the nation?
4. Why was the kingdom put under an interdict?
5. What were the consequences of it?
6. To what distress was John reduced?
9. To what humiliating concessions did John submit?
11. What oath did the king take?
12. What degrading ceremony followed?

SECTION II.

This is the place
Where England's ancient barons, clad in arms,
And stern with conquest, from their tyrant king
(Then rendered tame) did challenge and secure
The charter of thy freedom.—*Akenside.*

1. (A.D. 1215.) THE barons had long been forming a confederacy against him; but their union was broken, or their aims disappointed, by various and unforeseen accidents. At length, however, they assembled a large body of men at Stamford, and thence, elated by their power, they marched to Brackley, about fifteen miles from Oxford, the

place where the court then resided. 2. John, hearing of their approach, sent the archbishop of Canterbury, the earl of Pembroke and others of the council, to know the particulars of their request, and what those liberties were which they so earnestly importuned him to grant. The barons delivered a schedule, containing the chief articles of their demands, and of which the former charters of Henry and Edward the Confessor formed the ground-work. No sooner were those shown to the king, than he burst into a furious passion, and asked why the barons did not also demand his kingdom? swearing that the would never comply with such exorbitant demands! But the confederacy was now too strong to fear much from the consequences of his resentment. 3. They chose Robert Fitzwalter for their general, whom they dignified with the title of "mareschal of the army of God, and of the holy church," and proceeded, without further ceremony, to make war upon the king. They besieged Northampton; they took Bedford; they were joyfully received in London. They wrote circular letters to all the nobility and gentlemen who had not yet declared in their favour, and menaced their estates with devastation in case of refusal or delay.

4. John, struck with terror, first offered to refer all differences to the pope alone, or eight barons; four to be chosen by himself and four by the confederates. This the barons scornfully rejected. He then assured them that he would submit at discretion; and that it was his supreme pleasure to grant all their demands; a conference was accordingly appointed and all things adjusted for this most important treaty.

5. The ground where the king's commissioners met the barons was between Staines and Windsor,* at a place called Runimede, still held in reverence by posterity as the spot where the standard of freedom was first erected in England. There the barons appeared with a vast number of knights and warriors, on the fifteenth day of June, while those on the king's part came a day or two after. Both sides encamped apart like open enemies. The debates between power and precedent are generally but of short continuance. 6. The barons, having arms in their hands, would admit but few abatements; and the king's agents being for the most part in their interests, few debates

---

* Here is the strongest castle in England; it was the general residence of his late majesty, and was originally built by William the Conqueror.

King John compelled to ratify Magna Charta.

ensued. After some days the king, with a facility that was somewhat suspicious, signed and sealed the charter required of him; a charter which continues in force to this day, and is the famous bulwark of English liberty, which now goes by the name of MAGNA CHARTA. 7. This famous deed either granted or secured freedom to those orders of the kingdom that were already possessed of freedom; namely, to the clergy, the barons, and the gentlemen: as for the inferior and the greater part of the people, they were as yet held as slaves, and it was long before they could come to a participation of legal protection.

8. John, however, could not long brook these concessions that were extorted from his fears; he therefore took the first opportunity of denying to be the least governed by them.

9. This produced a second civil war, in which the barons were obliged to have recourse to the king of France for assistance. Thus England saw nothing but a prospect of being every way undone. If John succeeded, a tyrannical and implacable monarch was to be their tormentor; if the French king was to prevail, the country was ever after to submit to a more powerful monarchy, and was to become a province of France. What neither human prudence could foresee nor policy suggest, was brought about by a happy and unexpected accident.

10. John had assembled a considerable army, with a view to make one great effort for the crown; and at the head of a large body of troops, resolved to penetrate into the heart of the kingdom. With these resolutions he departed from Lynn, which, for its fidelity, he had distinguished with many marks of favour, and directed his route towards Lincolnshire. His road lay along the shore, which was overflowed at high-water; but not being apprised of this, or being ignorant of the tide of the place, he lost all his carriages, treasure, and baggage, by its influx. 11. He himself escaped with the greatest difficulty, and arrived at the abbey of Swinstead, where his grief for the loss he had sustained, and the distracted state of affairs, threw him into a fever which soon appeared to be fatal. Next day, being unable to ride on horseback, he was carried in a litter to the castle of Seaford, and thence removed to Newark, where, after having made his will, he died, in the fifty-first year of his age and the eighteenth of his detested reign.*

12. Seldom has any throne been disgraced by a monarch so depraved as John; before his accession he had rebelled against a fond father, and treacherously attempted the life of a generous brother: to secure himself on the throne he murdered his nephew, prince Arthur, and detained his niece, the princess Eleanora, in perpetual imprisonment. He repudiated one wife and imprisoned another, and violated his faith to both with the most abandoned profligacy. He showed his contempt for religion by habitually swearing, and wantonly violating the most solemn oaths. If he was a bad man, he was a worse king; he subjected himself to the ignominious yoke of Rome; he suffered France to take possession of the Norman provinces, almost without a struggle; and at home he acted the part of a lustful and bloody tyrant, sporting with the honours, the fortunes, and the lives of his unhappy subjects. Yet, by the blessing of Providence, his tyranny became the source of the greatest benefits to posterity, since his intolerable oppression drove the barons into rebellion, and procured them the great charter, which was the first foundation of British freedom.

* King John once demanded 10,500 marks from a Jew of Bristol; and, on his refusal, ordered one of his teeth to be drawn every day till he should comply. The Jew lost seven teeth, and then paid the sum required of him.

Questions for Examination.

1. Did the barons assemble an army in opposition to the king?
2. What were their demands? and what answer did the king return?
3, 4. What consequences followed?
5, 6. Can you mention the circumstances which attended the signing of Magna Charta?
8. What produced a second civil war?
9. What great effort did John resolve to make?
10, 11. What was the accident which befell John, and accelerated his death?
12. What was the character of John?

CONTEMPORARY SOVEREIGNS.

Popes.				Kings of	
	A.D.	Alexis V.	1204 A.D.		A.D.
Innocent III.	1198	Theodore I.	1205	*France.* Philip II.	1189
Honorius III.	1215			*Portug.* Sancho I.	1185
		Emperors of the West.		Adolphus II.	1212
Emperors of the East.		Philip.	1187	*Den.* Waldemar II.	1202
Alexis III.	1195	Otho IV.	1208	*Scotland.* William.	1165
Alexis IV.	1203	Frederick II.	1211	Alexander II.	1214

EMINENT PERSONS.

Stephen Langton, archbishop of Canterbury; he divided our Bible into chapters and verses. Robert Fitzwalter, general of the barons' army. John de Courcy, earl of Ulster, famous for his strength and prowess. Prince Arthur, nephew to the king, by whom he is supposed to have been murdered.

CHAPTER XI.

HENRY III.

Born 1207. Died Nov. 16th, 1272. Began to reign October the 17th, 1216. Reigned 56 years.

SECTION I.

Humane, indulgent, kind ev'n to a fault;
Yet wanting energy when cares assault.
His reign, though turbulent, an instance brings
Of " Mercy thronèd in the heart of Kings."—Dibdin.

1. (A. D. 1216.) A CLAIM was made, upon the death of John, in favour of young Henry, the son of the late king, who was now but nine years of age. The earl of Pembroke, a nobleman of great worth and valour who had

faithfully adhered to John in all the fluctuations of his fortune, determined to support his declining interests, and had him solemnly crowned by the bishops of Winchester, Bath, and Gloucester.

2. The young king was of a character the very opposite to his father; as he grew up to man's estate, he was found to be gentle, merciful, and humane; he appeared easy and good-natured to his dependents, but no way formidable to his enemies. Without activity or vigour, he was unfit to govern in war; without distrust or suspicion, he was imposed upon in times of peace.

3. As weak princes are never without governing favourites he first placed his affections on Hubert de Burgh, and he becoming obnoxious to the people, the place was soon supplied by Peter Des Roches, bishop of Winchester, a Poictevin by birth, a man remarkable for his arbitrary conduct, for his courage, and his abilities. Henry, in pursuance of this prelate's advice, invited over a great number of Poictevins; and other foreigners, who, having neither principles nor fortunes at home were willing to adopt whatever schemes their employers should propose. 4. Every office and command was bestowed on these unprincipled strangers, whose avarice and rapacity were exceeded only by their pride and insolence. So unjust a partiality to strangers very naturally excited the jealousy of the barons; and they even ventured to assure the king, that, if he did not dismiss all foreigners from court, they would drive both him and them out of the kingdom; but their anger was scarcely kept within bounds when they saw a new swarm of these intruders come over from Gascony, with Isabella, the king's mother, who had some time before been married to the Count de la Marche. 5. To these just causes of complaint were added the king's unsuccessful expedition to the continent, his total want of economy, and his oppressive exactions, which were but the result of the former. The kingdom therefore waited with gloomy resolution, determined to take vengeance when the general discontent arrived at maturity.

6. This imprudent preference, joined to a thousand other illegal evasions of justice, at last impelled Simon Montford, earl of Leicester, to attempt an innovation in the government, and to wrest the sceptre from the feeble hand that held it. This nobleman was the son of the famous general who commanded against the Albigenses, a sect of enthusiasts that had been destroyed some time before in the kingdom of Sa-

voy. He was married to the king's sister; and by his power and address was possessed of a strong interest in the nation; having gained equally the affections of the great and the little.

7. The place where the formidable confederacy which he had formed first discovered itself was in the parliament house, where the barons appeared in complete armour. The king, upon his entry, asked them what was their intention; to which they submissively replied, to make him their sovereign by confirming his power, and to have their grievances redressed. 8. Henry, who was ready enough to promise whatever was demanded, instantly assured them of his intention to give all possible satisfaction; and, for that purpose, summoned a parliament at Oxford, to digest a new plan of government, and to elect proper persons who were to be intrusted with the chief authority. This parliament, afterwards called the "mad parliament," went expeditiously to work upon the business of reformation. 9. Twenty-four barons were appointed, with supreme authority, to reform the abuses of the state, and Leicester was placed at their head. The whole state in their hands underwent a complete alteration; all its former officers were displaced; and creatures of the twenty-four barons were put into their room. They not only abridged the authority of the king, but the efficacy of parliament, giving up to twelve persons all parliamentary power between each session. Thus, these insolent nobles after having trampled upon the crown, threw prostrate the rights of the people, and a vile oligarchy was on the point of being established for ever.

10. The first opposition that was made to these usurpations was from a power which but lately began to take a place in the constitution. The knights of the shire, who for some time had begun to be regularly assembled in a separate house, now first perceived these grievances, and complained against them. They represented that their own interests and power seemed the only aim of all their decrees; and they even called upon the king's eldest son, prince Edward, to interpose his authority, and save the sinking nation.

Questions for Examination.

1. By whom was the interest of the young king secured
2. What is the character given of him?
3. Who were his favourites?

4. By what means did he excite the jealousy of the barons?
6. Who attempted an innovation in the government?
7. What are the particulars of the conspiracy formed by the barons?
9. In whom was the supreme authority vested?
10. By whom were these usurpations opposed, and of what did they complain?

SECTION II.

*The fate of war, capricious, now ordains
That Edward, Henry's son, shall break his chains.—Dyrlin.*

1. (A. D. 1264.) PRINCE EDWARD was at this time about twenty-two years of age. The hopes, which were conceived of his abilities and his integrity rendered him an important personage in the transactions of the times, and in some measure atoned for the father's imbecility. He had, at a very early age, given the strongest proofs of courage, of wisdom, and of constancy. At first, indeed, when applied to, appearing sensible of what his father had suffered by levity and breach of promise, he refused some time to listen to the people's earnest application; but, being at last persuaded to concur, a parliament was called, in which the king assumed his former authority.

2. This being considered as a breach of the late convention, a civil war ensued, in which, in a pitched battle, the earl of Leicester became victorious, and the king was taken prisoner, but soon after exchanged for Prince Edward, who was to remain as a hostage to ensure the punctual observance of the former agreement.

With all these advantages, however, Leicester was not so entirely secure but that he still feared the combination of the foreign states against him, as well as the internal machinations of the royal party. In order, therefore, to secure his ill-acquired power, he was obliged to have recourse to an aid till now entirely unknown in England, namely, that of the body of the people. 4. He called a parliament, where, besides the barons of his own party, and several ecclesiastics, who were not immediate tenants of the crown, he ordered returns to be made of two knights from every shire; and also deputies from the boroughs, which had been hitherto considered as too inconsiderable to have a voice in legislation. This is the first confused outline of an English house of commons. The people had been gaining some consideration since the gradual diminution of the force of the feudal system.

5. This parliament, however, was found not so very com

plying as he expected. Many of the barons who had hitherto steadfastly adhered to his party, appeared disgusted at his immoderate ambition; and many of the people, who found that a change of masters was not a change for happiness, began to wish for the re-establishment of the royal family. 6. In this exigence, Leicester, finding himself unable to oppose the concurring wishes of the nation, was resolved to make a merit of what he could not prevent; and he accordingly released prince Edward from confinement, and had him introduced at Westminster-hall, where his freedom was confirmed by the unanimous voice of the barons. But though Leicester had all the popularity of restoring the prince, yet he was politic enough to keep him still guarded by his emissaries, who watched all his motions and frustrated all his aims.

7. The prince, therefore, upon hearing that the Duke of Gloucester was up in arms in his cause, took an opportunity to escape from his guards, and put himself at the head of his party. A battle soon after ensued; but the earl's army having been exhausted by famine on the mountains of Wales, were but ill able to sustain the impetuosity of young Edward's attack, who bore down upon them with incredible fury. During this terrible day, Leicester behaved with astonishing intrepidity; and kept up the spirit of the action from two o'clock in the morning till nine at night. 8. At last his horse being killed under him, he was compelled to fight on foot; and though he demanded quarter, yet the adverse party refused it, with a barbarity common enough in the times we are describing. The old king, who was placed in front of the battle, was soon wounded in the shoulder; and, not being known by his friends, he was on the point of being killed by a soldier; but crying out, "I am Henry of Winchester, the king!" he was saved by a knight of the royal army. 9. Prince Edward, hearing the voice of his father, instantly ran to the the spot where he lay, and had him conducted to a place of safety. The body of Leicester being found among the dead, was barbarously mangled by one Roger Mortimer; and then, with an accumulation of inhumanity, sent to the wretched widow as a testimony of the royal party's success.

10. This victory proved decisive; and the prince, having thus restored peace to the kingdom, found his affairs so firmly established, that he resolved upon taking the cross, which was at that time the highest object of human ambition.

In pursuance of this resolution, Edward sailed from England with a large army, and arrived at the camp of Lewis, king of France, which lay before Tunis, where he had the misfortune to hear of that good monarch's death before his arrival. The prince, however, no way discouraged by this event, continued his voyage, and arrived at the Holy Land in safety.

11. He was scarcely departed upon this pious expedition when the health of the old king began to decline; and he found not only his own constitution, but also that of the state, in such a dangerous situation, that he wrote letters to his son, pressing him to return with all dispatch. 12. At last, being overcome with the cares of government, and the infirmities of age, he ordered himself to be removed by easy journeys, from St. Edmunds to Westminster, and that same night expired, in the sixty-fourth year of his age, and in the fifty-seventh of his reign, the longest to be met with in the annals of England, until that of George the Third.*

Questions for Examination.

1. What were the circumstances which warranted the hopes conceived by prince Henry?
2. What was the result of the battle between the king and Leicester?
3, 4. By what means did Leicester endeavour to secure his power?
5. Did the Parliament comply with his wishes?
6. Why did Leicester resolve to release prince Edward?
7, 8, 9. Can you relate the circumstance which took place in the action between prince Edward and Leicester?
10. What were Edward's determination and conduct after this victory?
11. During Edward's absence, what was the situation of the king and the nation?
12. At what age did Henry die? and how long did he reign?

---

* The interest paid in this reign for money in the East Indies, amounted, it is said, to twenty-five, and even sometimes to thirty-six per cent. But instances occurred in England of fifty per cent. being paid for money. No wonder, therefore, that the Jews, who were the only money-lenders, should be tempted to stay in the kingdom, notwithstanding the grievous extortions that were practiced on them.

Henry granted a charter to the town of Newcastle, in which he gave the inhabitants a license to dig coal.

The houses of the city of London were, till this period, mostly thatched with *straw*, for it appears that an order was issued, that all houses therein should be covered with tiles or slate, instead of straw; more especially such as stood in the best streets, which were then but few in comparison with the present, for where Cheapside now stands (which is the heart of the city), was at that time a field, the principal part of the city lying more eastward. From Temple Bar to the city (then the *village*,) of Westminster, where the Strand now stands, was no more than a mere highway or country road, having, however, many noblemen's houses and gardens adjoining to it, which have since given names to streets there erected. This indeed was the case in several subsequent reigns.

CONTEMPORARY SOVEREIGNS.

Popes.	A.D.		A.D.		A.D.
Honorious III	1216	Michael VIII	1259	Alphonsus IV	1247
Gregory IX	1227			*Kings of Denmark.*	
Celestine IV	1241	*Emperor of the West.*		Waldemar	1202
Innocent IV	1243	Frederick II.	1211	Eric VI	1240
Alexander IV	1254			Abel I	1250
Urbain IV	1261	*Kings of France.*		Christopher I	1252
Clement IV	1265	Philip II	1280	Eric VIII	1259
Gregory X	1271	Louis VIII	1223		
		St. Louis IX	1226	*King of Sweden.*	
Emperors of the East.		Philip III	1270	Waldemar	1250
Theodore I	1204				
John III	1222	*Kings of Portugal.*		*Kings of Scotland.*	
Theodore II	1225	Alphonso III	1202	Alexander II	1214
John IV	1259	Sancho II	1233	Alexander III	1249

EMINENT PERSONS.

Richard Magnus, Edmund of Abingdon, Boniface, and Robert Kilwarby, archbishops of Canterbury. Les Roches, bishop of Winchester, and Lord Chancellor.* Earl of Pembroke, protector. Montford, Earl of Leicester, general of the barons.

CHAPTER XII.

EDWARD I.

Born 1236. Died July 7th, 1307. Began to reign Nov. 16th, 1272. Reigned 34 years.

> The red cross flies in holy land,
> The Saracen his crescent waves,
> And English Edward's gallant band
> Seek proud renown or glorious graves.—*Dibdin.*

1. (A. D. 1272.) WHILE the unfortunate Henry was thus vainly struggling with the ungovernable spirit of his subjects, his son and successor, Edward,† was employed in the holy wars, where he revived the glory of the English name, and made the enemies of Christianity tremble. He was stabbed, however, by one of those Mahometan enthusiasists, called Assassins, as he was one day sitting in his tent, and was cured, not without great difficulty. 2. Some say that he

---

* In the reigns of the earlier Norman kings the Lord Chancellor was usually a clergyman, and was frequently styled the keeper of the king's conscience The Court of Chancery did not exist under the Saxon Dynasty.
† From the great length and slenderness of his legs, he was surnamed *Longshanks.*

owed his safety to the piety of Eleanora, his wife, who sucked the poison from the wound, to save his life at the hazard of her own.

Though the death of the late king happened while the successor was so far from home, yet measures had been so well taken, that the crown was transferred with the greatest tranquillity.

3. As Edward was now come to an undisputed throne, the opposite interests were proportionably feeble. The barons were exhausted by long and mutual dissensions; the clergy were divided in their interests, and agreed only in one point, to hate the pope, who had for some time drained them with impunity: the people, by some insurrections against the convents, appeared to hate the clergy with equal animosity. But these disagreeing orders concurred in one point, that of esteeming and reverencing the king, who therefore thought this the most favourable conjuncture for uniting England with Wales. 4. The Welsh had for many ages enjoyed their own laws, language, customs, and opinions. They were the remains of the ancient Britons, who had escaped Roman and Saxon invasions, and still preserved their freedom and their country uncontaminated by the admission of foreign conquerors. 5. But as they were, from their number, incapable of withstanding their more powerful neighbours on the plain, their chief defence lay in the inaccsesible mountains, those natural bulwarks of the country. Whenever England was distressed by faction at home, or its forces called off by wars abroad, the Welch made it a constant practice to pour in their irregular troops, and lay the open country waste wherever they came. 6. Nothing could be more pernicious to a country than several neighbouring independent principalities, under different commanders, and pursuing different interests; the mutual jealousies of such were sure to harass the people; and whenever victory was purchased, it was always at the expense of the general welfare. 7. Sensible of this, Edward had long wished to reduce that incursive people, and had ordered Llewelyn to do homage for his territories: which summons the Welsh prince refused to obey, unless the king's own son should be delivered as a hostage for his safe return. The king was not displeased at this refusal, as it served to give him a pretext for his intended invasion. He therefore levied an army against Llewelyn, and marched into his country with certain assurance of success,

8. Upon the approach of Edward, the Welsh prince took refuge among the inaccessible mountains of Snowdon,* and there resolved to maintain his ground, without trusting to the chance of a battle. These were the steep retreats that had for many ages defended his ancestors against all the attempts of the Roman and Saxon conquerors. But Edward, equally vigorous and cautious, having explored every part of his way, pierced into the very centre of Llewelyn's territories, and approached the Welsh army in its vast retreats. 9. Here, after extorting submission from the Welsh prince, the king retired. But an idle prophecy, in which it was foretold by Merlin that Llewelyn was to be the restorer of Bruton's empire in Britain, was an inducement sufficiently strong to persuade this prince to revolt once more, and hazard a decisive battle against the English. 10. With this view he marched into Radnorshire, and, passing the river Wye, his troops were surprised and defeated by Edward Mortimer, while he himself was absent from his army upon a conference with some of the barons of that country. Upon his return, seeing the dreadful situation of his affairs, he ran desperately into the midst of the enemy, and quickly found that death he so ardently sought for. David, the brother of this unfortunate prince, soon after fell in the same cause; and with him expired the independence of the Welsh nation, A. D. 1282. 11. It was soon after united to the kingdom of England, and made a principality, and given to the eldest son of the king. Foreign conquest might add to their glory, but this added to the felicity of the kingdom. The Welsh are now blended with the conquerors, and in the revolution of a few ages, all national animosity was entirely forgotten.

12. Soon after, the death of Margaret, queen of Scotland, gave him hopes of adding Scotland also to his dominions. The death of this princess produced a most ardent dispute about the succession to the Scottish throne, it being claimed by no less than twelve competitors. The claims, however, of all the other candidates were reduced to three, who were the descendants of the Earl of Huntingdon by three daughters: John Hastings, who claimed in right of his mother, as one of the co-heiresses of the crown; John Baliol, who alleged his right, as being descended from the eldest daughter, who was his grandmother; and Robert Bruce, who was

---

* From the summit of which may be seen part of Ireland, Scotland, England, and all North Wales.

Baliol surrendering his crown to Edward I.

the actual son of the second daughter. This dispute being referred to Edward's decision, with a strong degree of assurance he claimed the crown for himself, and appointed Baliol his deputy.

13. Baliol being thus placed on the Scottish throne, less a king than a vassal, Edward's first step was sufficient to convince that people of his intentions to stretch the prerogative to the utmost. Upon the most frivolous pretence, he sent six different summonses for Baliol to appear in London, at different times in one year; so that the poor Scottish king soon perceived that he was possessed of the name only, but not the authority of a sovereign. Willing, therefore, to shake off the yoke of so troublesome a master, Baliol revolted, and procured the pope's absolution from his former oath of homage.

14. But no power the Scots could bring into the field was able to withstand the victorious army of Edward. He overthrew their forces in many engagements; and thus becoming undisputed master of the kingdom, he took every precaution to secure his title, and to abolish those distinctions which might be apt to keep the nation in its former independence. Baliol was carried a prisoner to London and compelled to surrender his crown; and Edward carefully destroyed all records and monuments of antiquity that inspired the Scots with a spirit of national pride.

EDWARD I.

Questions for Examination.

1. What disaster befell Edward in the Holy Land?
2. To whose care is it said he owed his life?
3. What was the situation of the kingdom at Edward's accession?
4. What was the state of the Welsh at this time?
5. What was the constant practice of the Welsh towards England?
7. What method did Edward pursue to reduce Wales?
8. What was its success?
9. What induced Llewelyn again to revolt?
10. What followed this defeat?
11. To whom was the principality of Wales given after its union with England?
12. What happened, at this time, that gave Edward hopes of adding Scotland to his dominions?
How many competitors claimed the Scottish throne? and what were the names of the three principal?
13. What method did Baliol take to shake off the yoke of Edward?
15. What was the result of this struggle for independence?

SECTION II.

Still are the Scots determined to oppose
And treat intruding Edward's friends as foes;
Till the revengeful king, in proud array,
Swears to make Scotland bend beneath his sway.—*Macdonald.*

1. (A. D. 1296.) These expeditions, however, terminated rather in glory than advantage; the expenses which were requisite for carrying on the war were not only burdensome to the king, but even, in the event, threatened to shake him on his throne. In order at first to set the great machine in motion, he raised considerable supplies by means of his parliaments, and that august body was then first modelled by him into the form in which it continues to this day. 2. As a great part of the property of the kingdom was, by the introduction of commerce and the improvement of agriculture, transferred from the barons to the lower classes of the people, so their consent was now thought necessary for the raising any considerable supplies. For this reason he issued writs to the sheriffs, enjoining them to send to parliament along with two knights of the shire (as in the former reign) two deputies from each borough within their county; and these provided with sufficient power from their constituents to grant such demands as they should think reasonable for the safety of the state. 3. One of the first efforts, therefore, was to oblige the king's council to sign the Magna Charta, and to add a clause to secure the nation forever against all impositions and taxes without the consent of parliament. This the king's council (for Edward was at that time in Flanders) readily agreed to sign; and the king himself, when

it was sent over to him, after some hesitation thought proper to do the same. These concessions he again continued after his return; and though it is probable he was averse to granting them, yet he was at last brought to give a plenary consent to all the articles which were demanded of him. Thus, after the contest of an age, the Magna Charta was finally established; nor was it the least circumstance in its favour, that its confirmation was procured from one of the greatest and boldest princes that ever swayed the English sceptre.

5. In the mean time William Wallace,* so celebrated in Scottish story, attempted to rescue Scotland from the English yoke. He was a younger son of a gentleman who lived in the western part of the kingdom. He was a man of a gigantic stature, incredible strength, and amazing intrepidity; eagerly desirous of independence, and possessed with the most disinterested spirit of patriotism. To this man had resorted all those who were obnoxious to the English government; the proud, the bold, the criminal, and the ambitious.

6. These, bred among dangers and hardships themselves, could not forbear admiring in their leader a degree of patience under fatigue and famine, which they supposed beyond the power of human nature to endure; he soon, therefore, became the principal object of their affection and their esteem. His first exploits were confined to petty ravages, and occasional attacks upon the English; but he soon overthrew the English armies and slew their generals.

7. Edward, who had been over in Flanders while these misfortunes happened in England, hastened back with impatience to restore his authority, and secure his former conquest. He quickly levied the whole force of his dominions, and at the head of a hundred thousand men directed his course to the north, fully resolved to take vengeance upon the Scots for their late defection.

A battle was fought at Falkirk, in which Edward gained a complete victory, leaving twelve thousand of the Scots, or, as some will have it, fifty thousand, dead upon the field, while the English had not a hundred slain. A blow so dreadful had not as yet entirely crushed the spirit of the Scottish nation; and after a short interval they began to breathe from their calamities. 9. Wallace, who had gained

* He was of an ancient family, and was chosen regent of Scotland during the captivity of Baliol.

all their regards by his valour, shewed that he still merited them more by his declining the rewards of ambition. Perceiving how much he was envied by the nobility, and knowing how prejudicial that envy would prove to the interests of his country, he resigned the regency of the kingdom, and humbled himself to a private station. 10. He proposed Cummin as the most proper person to supply his room; and that nobleman endeavoured to show himself worthy of this pre-eminence. He soon began to annoy the enemy; and not content with a defensive war, made incursions into the southern counties of the kingdom, which Edward had imagined wholly subdued. They attacked an army of English lying at Roslin, near Edinburgh, and gained a complete victory.

11. But it was not easy for any circumstances of bad fortune to repress the enterprising spirit of the king. He assembled a great fleet and army; and entering the frontiers of Scotland, appeared with a force which the enemy could not think of resisting in the open field. Assured of success, he marched along, and traversed the kingdom from one end to the other, ravaging the open country, taking all the castles, and receiving the submissions of all the nobles. 12. There seemed to remain only one obstacle to the final destruction of the Scottish monarchy, and that was William Wallace, who still continued refractory; and wandering with a few forces from mountain to mountain, preserved his native independence, and usual good fortune. But even their feeble hopes from him were soon disappointed; he was betrayed into the king's hands by Sir John Monteith, his friend, whom he had made acquainted with the place of his concealment, being surprised by him as he lay asleep in the neighbourhood of Glasgow. 13. The king, willing to strike the Scots with an example of severity, ordered him to be conducted in chains to London, where he was hanged, drawn, and quartered, with the most brutal ferocity.

Robert Bruce, who had been one of the competitors for the crown, but was long kept prisoner in London, at length escaping from his guards, resolved to strike for his country's freedom. 14. Having murdered one of the king's servants, he left himself no resource but to confirm by desperate valour what he had begun in cruelty, and he soon expelled such of the English forces as had fixed themselves in the kingdom. Soon after, he was solemnly crowned king, by the bishop of St. Andrew's, in the abbey of Scone; and numbers flocked to his standard, resolved to confirm his pretensions. 15. Thus, after twice conquering the kingdom, and as often pardoning the delinquents; after having spread his victories in every quarter of the country, and receiving the most humble submissions; the old king saw that his whole work was to begin afresh, and that nothing but the final destruction of the inhabitants, could give him assurance of tranquillity. But no difficulties could repress the ardent spirit of this monarch, who, though now verging towards his decline, yet resolved to strike a parting blow and to make the Scots once more tremble at his appearance. 16. He vowed revenge against the whole nation; and averred that nothing but reducing them to the completest bondage could satisfy his resentment. He summoned his prelates, nobility, and all who held by knight's service, to meet him at Carlisle, which was appointed as the general rendezvous: and in the mean time he detached a body of forces before him to Scotland, under the command of Aymer de Valence, who began the threatened infliction by a complete victory over Bruce, near Methven, in Perthshire. 17. Immediately after this dreadful blow, the resentful king appeared in person, entering Scotland with his army divided into two parts, and expecting to find, in the opposition of the people, a pretext for punishing them. But this brave prince, who was never cruel but from motives of policy, could not strike the poor submitting natives, who made no resistance. His anger was disappointed in their humiliation; and he was ashamed to extirpate those who only opposed patience to his indignation. 18. His death put an end to the apprehensions of the Scots, and effectually rescued their country from total subjection. He sickened and died at Carlisle, of a dysentery: enjoining his son with his last breath, to prosecute the enterprise, and never to desist till he had finally subdued the kingdom. He expired July 7, 1307, in the sixty-ninth year of his age, and the thirty-fifth of his reign; after having added more to the solid interests of the kingdom than any of those who went before or succeeded him.

Questions for Examination.

1. What circumstances led to the modelling the parliament into its present form?
2. What was the manner observed in framing the parliament?
3. What was one of their first efforts?

4. Was the king at first favourable to the measure?
5. By whom was an attempt made to rescue Scotland from the English yoke?
6. Who were the first adherents of Wallace?
7. With what number of troops did Edward march towards the north?
8. Did any engagement take place between the forces of Edward and Wallace?
What was the issue of this engagement?
9. What was the conduct of Wallace afterwards?
12. In what manner was Wallace afterwards surprised?
13. What was the manner of his death?
14. What took place after Bruce's escape from London?
15. What was the conduct of the king on this occasion?
18. Where did the king die? and what enterprise did he enjoin his son to prosecute?

CONTEMPORARY SOVEREIGNS.

Popes.	A.D.
Gregory X	1271
Innocent V	1276
Adrian V	1276
John XXI	1276
Nicholas III	1277
Martin IV	1281
Honorius IV	1285
Nicholas IV	1288
Celestine V	1294
Boniface VIII	1294
Benedict IX	1303
Clement V	1305

Emperors of the East.	A.D.
Michael VIII	1259

	A.D.
Andronicus II	1283
Emperors of the West.	
Frederick II*	1212
Rodolphus I	1273
Adolphus of Nassau	1291
Albert	1298
Kings of France.	
Philip III	1270
Philip IV	1285
Kings of Portugal.	
Adolphus III	1247
Dennis	1275

Kings of Denmark.	A.D.
Eric VII	1259
Eric VIII	1286
Kings of Sweden.	
Magnus II	1279
Birger II	1209
Kings of Scotland.	
Alexander III	1246
John Baliol	1293
Robert Bruce	1306

EMINENT PERSONAGES.

John Peckham, Robert Winchelsea, Walter Reynolds, and John Stratford, archbishops of Canterbury. Richard, earl of Cornwall. Rodger Bigod, earl of Norfolk. Humphrey Bohun, earl of Hereford. John Plantagenet, earl of Warwick. Roger Bacon. Wickliffe.†

---

* After the death of Frederick II. there was an interregnum in the Western empire until Rodolphus, during which the following princes either reigned or were elected: Conrad III.; William, earl of Holland; Richard, earl of Cornwall; Edward IV.; and Alphonso, king of Castile. —*Lochman.*

† Wickliffe was the first preacher of the reformed doctrines in England; he was the author of a valuable translation of the New Testament, and of several able tracts on the usurpations of the Romish Church.

CHAPTER XIII.
EDWARD II.

Born 1284. Died Sep. 21, 1327. Began to reign July 7, 1307. Reigned 20 years.

SECTION I.

Immersed in soft effeminacy's down,
The feeble prince his subjects' good neglects
For minions, who monopolize the crown,
And stain the sceptre which their vice protects.—Dibdin.

1. (A.D. 1307.) EDWARD, surnamed Caernarvon,* was in the twenty-third year of his age when he succeeded his father; of an agreeable figure, of a mild, harmless disposition, and apparently addicted to few vices. But he soon gave symptoms of his unfitness to succeed so great a monarch as his father; he was rather fond of the enjoyment of his power, than of securing it, and, lulled by the flattery of his courtiers, he thought he had done enough for glory when he accepted the crown. 2. Instead, therefore, of prosecuting the war against Scotland, according to the injunctions he had received from his dying father, he took no steps to check the progress of Bruce: his march into that country being rather a procession of pageantry than a warlike expedition.

3. Weak monarchs are ever governed by favourites; and the first that Edward placed his affections upon was Piers Gavestone, the son of a Gascon knight, who had been employed in the service of the late king. The young man was adorned with every accomplishment of person and mind that was capable of creating affection; but he was utterly destitute of those qualities of heart and understanding that serve to procure esteem. He was handsome, witty, brave and active; but then he was vicious, effeminate, debauched, and trifling. These were qualities entirely adapted to the taste of the young monarch, and he seemed to think no rewards equal to his deserts. 4. Gavestone, on the other hand, intoxicated with his power, became haughty and overbearing, and treated the English nobility, from whom it is probable he received marks of contempt, with scorn and derision. A conspiracy, therefore, was soon formed against him, at the head of which queen Isabel and the earl of Lancaster, a nobleman of great power, were associated.

5. It was easy to perceive that a combination of the nobles, while the queen secretly assisted their designs,

* From the place of his birth, Caernarvon Castle, in Wales.

would be too powerful against the efforts of a weak king and a vain favourite. The king, timid and wavering, banished him (A. D. 1312) at their solicitation, and recalled him soon after. This was sufficient to spread an alarm over the whole kingdom: all the great barons flew to arms, and the earl of Lancaster put himself at the head of this irresistible confederacy. The unhappy Edward, instead of attempting to make resistance, sought only for safety. Ever happy in the company of his favourite, he embarked at Teignmouth, and sailed with him to Scarborough, where he left Gavestone as in a place of safety, and then went back to York himself, either to raise an army to oppose his enemies or by his presence to allay their animosity. 6. In the meantime, Gavestone was besieged in Scarborough by the earl of Pembroke; and had the garrison been sufficiently supplied with provisions, the place would have been impregnable. But Gavestone, sensible of the bad condition of the garrison, took the earliest opportunity to offer terms of capitulation. He stipulated that he should remain in Pembroke's hands as a prisoner for two months; and that endeavours should be used in the meantime for a general accommodation. 7. But Pembroke had no intention that he should escape so easily; he ordered him to be conducted to the castle of Deddington, near Banbury, where, on pretence of other business, he left him with a feeble guard, of which the earl of Warwick having received information, attacked the castle in which the unfortunate Gavestone was confined, and quickly made himself master of his person. The earls of Lancaster, Hereford, and Arundel were soon apprised of Warwick's success, and informed that their common enemy was now in custody in Warwick castle. 8. Thither therefore they hastened with the utmost expedition to hold a consultation upon the fate of their prisoner. This was of no long continuance, they unanimously resolved to put him to death, as an enemy to the kingdom, and gave him no time to prepare for his execution. They instantly had him conveyed to a place called Blacklow-hill, where a Welsh executioner, provided for that purpose, severed his head from his body.

9. To add to Edward's misfortunes, he soon after suffered a most signal defeat from the Scots' army under Bruce, near Bannockburn;* and this drove him once more to seek

---

* Near Stirling. Edward was so sure of conquest that he brought with him Baston, a Carmeitte, and a famous poet, to celebrate his victory.

for relief in some favourite's company. 10. The name of his new favourite was Hugh de Spenser, a young man of a noble English family, of some merit, and very engaging accomplishments. His father was a person of a much more estimable character than the son; he was venerable for his years, and respected through life for his wisdom, his valour, and his integrity. 11. But these excellent qualities were all diminished and vilified from the moment he and his son began to share the king's favour, who even dispossessed some lords unjustly of their estates, in order to accumulate them upon his favourite. This was a pretext the king's enemies had been long seeking for; the earls of Lancaster and Hereford flew to arms; sentence was procured from parliament of perpetual exile against the two Spensers, and a forfeiture of their fortunes and estates. 12. The king, however, at last rousing from his lethargy, took the field in defence of his beloved Spenser, and at the head of thirty thousand men pressed the earl of Lancaster so closely, that he had not time to collect his forces together, and, flying from one place to another, he was at last stopped in his way towards Scotland by Sir Andrew Harcla, and made prisoner. 13. As he had formerly shown little mercy to Gavestone, there was very little extended to him upon this occasion. He was condemned by a court-martial: and led, mounted on a lean horse, to an eminence near Pomfret, in circumstances of the greatest indignity, where he was beheaded by a Londoner.

14. A rebellion, thus crushed, served only to increase the pride and rapacity of young Spenser; most of the forfeitures were seized for his use—and in his promptitude to seize the delinqnents, he was guilty of many acts of rapine and injustice.*

Questions for Examination.

1. What was the disposition of Edward II?
2. What was his conduct in regard to Scotland?
3. What was the character of Gavestone, the king's first favourite?
4. Who formed a conspiracy against the king?
5. What was the conduct of the king on this occasion?

*In the year 1315, the perpetual rains and cold weather having not only destroyed the harvest but produced a mortality among the cattle, the parliament endeavoured to moderate the prices of provisions. The rates established were, of our present money, as follows: for the best ox, not corn fed, 2*l* 8*s*., corn fed, 3*l* 12*s*.; a fat hog, two years old, 10*s*.; a fat wether, unshorn, 5*s*., shorn, 3*s*. 6*d*.; a fat goose sevenpence halfpenny; a fat capon, 6*d*.; a fat hen 3*d*; two chickens, 3*d*.; four pigeons, 3*d*.; and twenty-four eggs, 3*d*.

6. Where was Gavestone besieged? and on what conditions did he surrender himself?
7, 8. Were these conditions observed? and what was the conduct of the nobles towards him?
9. What misfortune did Edward experience in Scotland?
10. Who were the Spensers?
11. On what pretext did the king's enemies fly to arms?
12. How did the king act on this emergency?
13. What was the manner of executing the earl of Lancaster?

SECTION II.

Mark what convulsions heave his martyr'd breast.—*Lewis.*

1. (A.D. 1325.) But he was now to oppose a more formidable enemy in Queen Isabella, a cruel, haughty woman, who fled over to France, and refused to appear in England till Spenser was removed from the royal presence, and banished the kingdom. By this reply she gained two very considerable advantages: she became popular in England, where Spenser was universally disliked; and she had the pleasure of enjoying the company of a young nobleman, whose name was Mortimer, upon whom she had lately placed her affections, and whom she indulged with all the familiarities that her criminal passion could confer. 2. The queen's court now, therefore, became a sanctuary for all the malcontents who were banished their own country, or who chose to come over. Accordingly, soon after, accompanied by three thousand men-at-arms, she set out from Dort* harbour, and landed safely, without opposition, on the coast of Suffolk. She had no sooner appeared than there seemed a general revolt in her favour: and the unfortunate king found the spirit of disloyalty was not confined to the capital alone, but diffused over the whole kingdom. 3. He had placed some dependence upon the garrison which was stationed in the castle of Bristol, under the command of the elder Spenser; but they mutinied against their governor, and that unfortunate favourite was delivered up, and condemned by the tumultuous barons to the most ignominious death. He was hanged on a gibbet, in his armour: his body was cut in pieces and thrown to the dogs; and his head was sent to Winchester, where it was set upon a pole, and exposed to the populace.

* Dort, or Dordrecht, is a city of Holland, situated on an island of the Meuse. By an irruption of the river Meuse, seventy-two villages and one hundred thousand persons were lost. It is said to have been occasioned by the malice of a man, who wished to inundate his neighbour's ground by destroying the dyke near his house.

4. Young Spenser, the unhappy son, did not long survive his father; he was taken, with some others who had followed the fortunes of the wretched king, in an obscure convent in Wales, and the merciless victors resolved to glut their revenge in adding insult to cruelty. The queen had not patience to wait the formality of a trial, but ordered him immediately to be led forth before the insulting populace, and seemed to take a savage pleasure in feasting her eyes with his distresses. 5. The gibbet erected for his execution was fifty feet high; his head was sent to London, where the citizens received it in brutal triumph, and fixed it on the bridge Several other lords also shared his fate; all deserving pity in deed, had they not themselves formerly justified the present inhumanity by setting a cruel example.

6. In the meantime, the king, who hoped to find refuge in Wales, was quickly discovered, and delivered up to his adversaries, who expressed their satisfaction in the grossness of their treatment. He was conducted to the capital, amidst the insults and reproaches of the people, and confined in the Tower. A charge was soon after exhibited against him, in which no other crimes but his incapacity to govern, his indolence, his love of pleasure, and his being swayed by evil counsellors, were objected against him. His deposition was quickly voted by parliament; he was assigned a pension for his support; his son Edward, a youth of fourteen, was fixed upon to succeed him, and the queen was appointed regent during the minority. 7. The deposed monarch but a short time survived his misfortunes; he was sent from prison to prison, a wretched outcast, and the sport of his inhuman keepers. He had been at first consigned to the custody of the Earl of Lancaster, but this nobleman showing some marks of respect and pity, he was taken out of his hands, and delivered over to Lords Berkeley, Montravers and Gournay, who were intrusted with the charge of guarding him a month about. 8. Whatever his treatment from Lord Berkeley might have been, the other two seemed resolved that he should enjoy none of the comforts of life while in their custody. They practiced every kind of indignity upon him, as if their design had been to accelerate his death by the bitterness of his sufferings. (A.D. 1328.) But when his persecutors saw that his death might not arrive, even under every cruelty, till a revolution had been made in his favour, they resolved to rid themselves of their fears by destroying him at once. 9. Accordingly his two keepers, Gournay and Montravers,

came to Berkeley castle, where Edward was then confined, and murdered him by a most cruel and torturing process, which left no marks of external violence.

Question for examination.

1. What other enemy had Edward now to oppose?
2. Was there any revolt in the queen's favour? and by whom was she accompanied?
3. What happened to the elder Spenser?
5. In what manner was the younger Spenser executed?
6. What were the proceedings against the king?
7. Did the king long survive his misfortunes?
8. Can you relate the indignities practiced upon him?
9. What was the manner of the king's murder? and by whom was it committed?

CONTEMPORARY SOVEREIGNS.

Popes.		*Kings of Denmark.*
A.D.	A.D.	A D.
Clement V....... 1305	Lewis IV........ 1314	Eric VIII........ 1286
John XII........ 1316	*Kings of France.*	Christopher II... 1319
	Philip IV........ 1284	
Emperors of the East.	Lewis X......... 1314	*Kings of Sweden.*
Andronicus II... 1283	Philip V......... 1316	Berger II......... 1290
Andronicus III.. 1320	Charles IV...... 1322	Magnus III...... 1320
Emperors of the West.	*Kings of Portugal.*	*King of Scotland.*
Albert I.......... 1298	Dennis.......... 1272	Robert Bruce.... 1306
Henry VIII...... 1304	Alphonsus IV.... 1325	

EMINENT PERSONS.

John Offord, archbishop of Canterbury. Thomas Plantagenet, earl of Lancaster. Roger, lord Mortimer; Piers Gavestone and the two Spensers, favourites of the king.

CHAPTER XIV

EDWARD III.

Born 1312. Died June 21, 1377. Began to reign Sept. 22, 1327. Reigned nearly 50 years.

SECTION I.

With form and aspect to command respect,
With mind, desert, and talent to protect,
Edward presents a model to admire;
His subjects' hearts before their sovereign bend,
The widow's guardian and the orphan's sire:
Foe to the vicious, to the good a friend.—*Dibdin.*

1. (A.D. 1327.) THE Parliament by which young Edward was raised to the throne, during the life of his father, appointed twelve persons as his privy council, to direct the operations of the government. Mortimer the queen's favourite,

who might naturally be set down as one of the members, artfully excluded himself, under a pretended show of moderation; but at the same time he secretly influenced all the measures that came under their deliberation. 2. He caused the greater part of the royal revenues to be settled on the queen-dowager, and he seldom took the trouble to consult the ministers of government in any public undertaking. The king himself was even so besieged by the favourite's creatures, that no access could be procured to him, and the whole sovereign authority was shared between Mortimer and the queen, who took no care to conceal her criminal attachment.

3. At length, however, Edward was resolved to shake off an authority that was odious to the nation, and particularly restrictive upon him. But such was the power of the favourite, that it required as much precaution to overturn the usurper as to establish the throne. The queen and Mortimer had for some time chosen the castle of Nottingham for the place of their residence; it was strictly guarded, the gates locked every evening, and the keys carried to the queen. 4. It was therefore agreed between the king and some of the barons, who secretly entered into his designs, to seize upon them in the fortress; and for that purpose Sir William Bland, the governor, was induced to admit them by a secret subterraneous passage, which had been formerly contrived for an outlet, but was now hidden with rubbish, and known only to one or two. It was by this, therefore, the noblemen in the king's interest entered in the night; and Mortimer, without having it in his power to make any resistance, was seized in apartments adjoining those of the queen. 5. It was in vain that she endeavoured to protect him; in vain she entreated them to spare her "gentle Mortimer"; the barons, deaf to her entreaties, denied her that pity which she had so often refused to others. Her paramour was condemned by the parliament, which was then sitting, without being permitted to make his defence, or even examining a witness against him. He was hanged on a gibbet, at a place called Elms, about a mile from London, where his body was left hanging for two days after. 6. The queen, who certainly was the most culpable, was shielded by the dignity of her station; she was only disgraced from all share of power, and confined for life in the castle of Risings, with a pension of three thousand pounds a year. From this confinement she was never after set free; and though

the king annually paid her a visit of decent ceremony, yet she found herself abandoned to universal contempt and detestation; and continued, for about twenty-five years after, a miserable monument of blighted ambition.

7. In order still more to secure the people's affections, Edward made a successful irruption into Scotland, in which, in one battle, fought at Halidon hill, about thirty thousand of the Scots were slain. Soon after he turned his arms against France, which was at that time particularly unfortunate. Three sons of Philip the Fair, in full parliament, accused their wives of adultery; and in consequence of this accusation they were condemned and imprisoned for life.

8. Lewis Hutin, successor to the crown of France, caused his wife to be strangled, and her lovers to be flayed alive. After his death, as he left only a daughter, his next brother, Philip the Tall, assumed the crown in prejudice of the daughter, and vindicated his title by the Salic law, which laid it down that no female should succeed to the crown. Edward, however, urged his pretensions, as being, by his mother Isabella, who was daughter to Philip the Fair, and sister to the three last kings of France, rightful heir to the crown. But first he, in a formal manner, consulted his parliament on the propriety of the undertaking, obtained their approbation, received a proper supply of wool, which he intended to barter with the Flemings; and being attended with a body of English forces, and several of his nobility, he sailed into Flanders, big with his intended conquests.

9. The first great advantage gained by the English was in a naval engagement on the coast of Flanders, in which the French lost two hundred and thirty ships, and had thirty thousand of their seamen and two of their admirals slain.

10. The intelligence of Edward's landing and the devastation caused by his troops, who dispersed themselves over the whole face of the country, soon spread universal consternation through the French court. Caen was taken and plundered by the English without mercy; the villages and towns, even up to Paris, shared the same fate; and the French had no other resource, but by breaking down their bridges to attempt putting a stop to the invader's career.

11. Philip, then king of France, was not idle in making preparations to repress the enemy. He had stationed one of his generals, Godemar de Faye, with an army on the opposite side of the river Somme, over which Edward was to

pass; while he himself, at the head of one hundred thousand fighting men, advanced to give the English battle.

12. As both armies had for some time been in sight of each other, nothing was so eagerly expected on each side as a battle; and although the forces were extremely disproportionate, the English amounting only to thirty thousand, the French to a hundred and twenty thousand, yet Edward resolved to indulge the impetuosity of his troops, and to put all to the hazard of a battle. He accordingly chose his ground with advantage, near the village of Crecy,* and there determined to wait with tranquillity the shock of the enemy. He drew up his men on a gentle ascent, and divided them into three lines. The first was commanded by the young prince of Wales; the second was conducted by the earls of Northampton and Arundel; and the third, kept as a body of reserve, was headed by the king in person.

13. On the other side, Philip, impelled by resentment, and confident of his numbers, was more solicitous in bringing the enemy to an engagement than prudent in taking measures for its success. He led on his army in three bodies opposite to those of the English. The first line consisted of fifteen thousand Genoese cross-bow men, the second body was led by the king of France's brother, and he himself was at the head of the third.

Question for Examination.

2. By whom, and in what manner, were the operations of the government conducted?
4. What was the conduct of the king at this time?
5. What was the fate of Mortimer?
   What was the queen's punishment?
7. In what undertaking did Edward succeed?
8. What is the Salic law?
9. What was the first advantage gained by the English?
10. What did the English in France?
11. What preparations did the king of France make to oppose Edward?
12. Where did Edward choose his ground?
    How did he draw up his army? and who conducted it?
13. How did Philip lead on his army?

* Here the King of Bohemia was slain, and the motto, "*Ich dien,*" *I serve*, was found under the ostrich feathers which he wore on his helmet Edward the Black Prince, adopted this motto, and it has ever since continued to be the motto of the prince of Wales. At this battle cannon were first made use of.

SECTION II.

*In frequent showers their shafs the archers hail'd
In headlong charge successive hosts assail'd;
But motionless as his own island's rocks,
Undaunted, Edward met their furious shocks.—Cooke.*

1. (A. D. 1346.) ABOUT three in the afternoon, the famous battle of Crecy began, by the French king's ordering the Genoese archers to charge, but they were so fatigued with their march that they cried out for a little rest before they should engage. The count Alençon, being informed of their petition, rode up, and reviled them as cowards, commanding them to begin their onset without delay. Their reluctance to begin was still more increased by a heavy shower, which fell at that instant, and relaxed their bow-strings: so that the discharge they made produced but very little effect. 2. On the other hand the Enlish archers, who had kept their bows in cases, and were favoured by a sudden gleam of sunshine, that rather dazzled the enemy, let fly their arrows so thick, and with such good aim, that nothing was to be seen among the Genoese but hurry, terror, and dismay. The young prince of Wales had presence of mind to take advantage of their confusion and to lead on his line to the charge. The French cavalry, however, commanded by the Count Alençon, wheeling round, sustained the combat and began to hem the English in. 3. The earls of Arundel and Northampton now came to assist the prince, who appeared foremost in the very shock; and wherever he appeared, turned the fortune of the day. The thickest of the battle was now gathered round him, and the valour of a boy filled even veterans with astonishment; but their surprise at his courage could not but give way to their fears for his safety. Being apprehensive that some mischance might happen to him at the end, an officer was despatched to the king, desiring that succours might be sent to the prince's relief. 4. Edward, who had all this time, with great tranquillity, viewed the engagement from a windmill, demanded, with seeming deliberation, if his son were dead; but being answered that he still lived and was giving astonishing instances of his valour, "Then tell my generals," cried the king, "that he shall have no assistance from me; the honour of the day shall be his; let him show himself worthy of the profession of arms, and let him be indebted to his own merit alone for victory." 5. This speech being reported to the prince and his attendants, inspired them with new courage; they made a fresh attack upon the French cavalry, and Count Alençon, their bravest

King Edward III. and the Burgesses of Calais.

commander, was slain. This was the beginning of their total overthrow; the French, being now without a competent leader, were thrown into confusion; the whole army took to flight, and were put to the sword by the pursuers without mercy, till night stopped the carnage. 6. Never was a victory more seasonable, or less bloody to the English, than this. Notwithstanding the great slaughter of the enemy, the conquerors lost but one squire, three knights, and a few of inferior rank.

But this victory was attended with still more substantial advantages; for Edward, as moderate in conquest as prudent in his methods to obtain it, resolved to secure an easy entrance into France for the future. 7. With this view he laid siege to Calais, at that time defended by John de Vienne, an experienced commander, and supplied with everything necessary for defence. These operations, though slow, were at length successful. It was in vain that the governor made a noble defence, that he excluded all the useless mouths from the city, which Edward generously permitted to pass. 8. Edward resolved to reduce it by famine; and it was at length taken, after a twelvemonths' siege, the defendants having been reduced to the last extremity. He resolved to punish the obstinacy of the townsmen by the death of six of the most considerable citizens, who offered themselves, with ropes round their necks, to satiate his indignation; but he spared their lives at the intercession of the queen.

9. While Edward was reaping victories upon the continent, the Scots, ever willing to embrace a favourable opportunity of rapine and revenge, invaded the frontiers with a numerous army, headed by David Bruce. their king. This unexpected invasion, at such a juncture, alarmed the English, but was not capable of intimidating them. 10. Lionel, Edward's son, who was left guardian of England during his father's absence, was yet too young to take upon him the command of an army; but the victories on the continent seemed to inpire even women with valour. Philippa, Edward's queen, took upon her the conduct of the field, and prepared to repulse the enemy in person: accordingly, having made Lord Percy general under her, she met the Scots at a place called Nevil's Cross, near Durham, and offered them battle. 11. The Scots king was no less impatient to engage; he imagined that he might obtain an easy victory against undisciplined troops, and headed by a woman. But he was miserably deceived. His army was quickly routed and driven from the field. Fifteen thousand of his men were cut to pieces; and he himself, with many of his nobles and knights, were taken prisoners, and carried in triumph to London, A. D. 1346.

12. A victory gained by the Black prince,* near Poictiers, followed not long after, in which John, king of France, was taken prisoner, and led in triumph through London, amidst an amazing concourse of spectators. Two kings, prisoners in the same court, and at the same time, were considered as glorious achievements; but all that England gained by them was only glory. Whatever was won in France, with all the dangers of war, and the expense of preparation, was successively and in a manner silently lost, without the mortification of a defeat.

13. The English, by their frequent supplies, had been quite exhausted, and were unable to continue an army in the field. Charles, who had succeeded his father John, who died a prisoner in the Savoy, on the other hand, cautiously forebore to come to any decisive engagement; but was content to let his enemies waste their strength in attempts to plunder a fortified country. When they were tired, he then was sure to sally forth, and possess himself of such places as they were not strong enough to defend. 14. He first fell

---

* Edward, the Prince of Wales. He was called the Black Prince from the color of his armour.

upon Ponthieu; the citizens of Abbeville opened their gates to him; those of St. Valois, Rue, and Crotoy imitated the example, and the whole country was, in a little time, reduced to total submission. The southern provinces were, in the same manner, invaded by his generals with equal success; while the Black Prince, destitute of supplies from England, and wasted by a cruel and consumptive disorder, was obliged to return to his native country, leaving the affairs of the south of France in a most desperate condition. 15. But what of all other things served to cast a gloom over the latter part of this splendid reign was the approaching death of the Black Prince, whose constitution showed, but too manifestly, the symptoms of a speedy dissolution. This valiant and accomplished prince died in the forty-sixth year of his age, leaving behind him a character without a single blemish; and a degree of sorrow among the people that time could scarcely alleviate.

16. The king was most sensibly affected with the loss of his son, and tried every art to allay his uneasiness. He removed himself entirely from the duties and burdens of the state, and left his kingdom to be plundered by a set of rapacious ministers. He did not survive the consequences of his bad conduct, but died about a year after the prince, at Sheene, in Surrey, deserted by all his courtiers, even by those who had grown rich by his bounty. He expired in the sixty-fifth year of his age, and fifty-first of his reign, 1377; a prince more admired than beloved by his subjects and more an object of their applause than their sorrow.

17. It was in this reign that the order of the Garter was instituted; the number was to consist of twenty-four persons besides the king. A story prevails, but unsupported by any ancient authority, that the Countess of Salisbury, at a ball, happening to drop her garter, the king took it up and presented it to her, with these words, "*Honi soi qui mal y pense;*"—"Evil be to him that evil thinks." This accident, it is said, gave rise to the order and the motto,* A. D. 1349.

Edward left many children by his queen, Philippa of

---

* "Some do affirm, that this order beganne fyrst by King Richard Cœur de Lion, at the siege of the citie of Acres, where in his greate necessytie there was but twenty-five knights that firmlye and sureiye abode by him where he caused all of them to wear thonges of blue leythere aboute their legges, and afterwards they were called knights."—*Rastell's Chronicle.*

Hainault. His eldest son, the Black Prince, died before him; but he left a son named Richard, who succeeded to the throne.*

Questions for Examination.

1. Describe the situation and conduct of the Genoese archers.
2. What circumstances operated in favour of the English archers? What advantage did the Prince of Wales take of it?
3. What astonishing bravery did the prince display?
4. What answer did the king make, when he was requested to send relief to the prince?
6. How many did the English lose in the battle?
8. How long did Edward besiege Calais?
9. What did the Scots in the meantime?
10. What female prepared to repulse the enemy?
11. What was the fate of the Scots?
12. What did England gain by its royal prisoners?
14. What obliged the Black Prince to return to England?
15. What character is given of the prince?
17. When was the order of the Garter instituted? What accident is said to have given rise to the institution of this order?

CONTEMPORARY SOVEREIGNS.

Popes.	A.D.	A.D.
A.D.	Charles IV........1347	Waldemar III.....1340
John XII..........1316		Olaus III..........1375
Benedict XI.......1334	*Kings of France.*	
Clement VI........1342	Charles IV.....1322	*Kings of Sweden.*
Innocent VI.......1352	Philip VI.........1328	Magnus III........1320
Urban V...........1362	John I............1353	Albert............1363
Gregory XI........1370	Charles V.........1364	
		Kings of Scotland.
Emperors of the East.	*Kings of Portugal.*	Robert Bruce......1306
Andronicus III....1320	Alphonsus IV.....1325	David II..........1330
John V............1341	Pedro I...........1357	Edward Baliol ... 1332
John VI...........1355	Ferdinand I......1367	David II. (restor.)1342
		Robert (Stuart) II. 1370
Emperors of the West.	*Kings of Denmark.*	
Louis IV..........1314	Christopher II.....1319	

EMINENT PERSONS.

Thomas Bradwardin, Simon Islip, Simon Langham, William Whittlesey, and Simon Sudbury, archbishops of Canterbury. Edward, the Black Prince, John Lord Chandos. Latimer, the lord chamberlain, &c.

---

* In this reign the statute of high-treason was first enacted. St. Stephens chapel (now the house of commons) was built, and Windsor castle changed from a fortress to a palace.

CHAPTER XV.

RICHARD II.

Born 1367. Deposed Sept. 30, 1399. Died Jan. 10, 1400. Began to reign June 21, 1377. Reigned 22¼ years.

SECTION I.

*Sprung from a sire and grandsire of renown,
Yet he was scarce deserving of a crown.—Egerton.*

1. (A. D. 1377.) RICHARD the Second was but eleven years old when he came to the throne of his grandfather, and found the people discontented and poor, the nobles proud and rebellious. As he was a minor, the government was vested in the hands of his three uncles, the Dukes of Lancaster, York, and Gloucester; and as the late king had left the kingdom involved in many dangerous and expensive wars, which demanded large and constant supplies, the murmurs of the people increased in proportion. 2. The expenses of armaments to face the enemy on every side and the want of economy in the administration, entirely exhausted the treasury; and a new tax of three groats on every person above fifteen was granted by parliament as a supply. The indignation of the people had been for some time increasing; but a tax so unequitable, in which the rich paid no more than the poor, kindled the resentment of the latter into a flame. 3. It began in Essex, where a report was industriously spread that the peasants were to be destroyed, their houses burned, and their farms plundered. A blacksmith, well known by the name of Wat Tyler, was the first that incited them to arms. The tax-gatherers coming to the man's house while he was at work, demanded payment for his daughter, which he refused, alleging she was under the age mentioned in the act. 4. One of the brutal collectors insisted on her being a full-grown woman, and behaved in the most indecent manner. This provoked the father to such a degree, that he instantly struck him dead with a blow of his hammer. The standers-by applauded his spirit, and one and all resolved to defend his conduct. He was considered as a champion in the cause and appointed the leader and spokesman of the people. 5. It is easy to imagine the disorders committed by this tumultuous rabble; the whole neighbourhood rose in arms; they burned

and plundered wherever they came, and revenged upon their former masters all those insults which they had long sustained with impunity. As the discontent was general, the insurgents increased in proportion as they approached the capital. The flame soon propagated itself into Kent, Herefordshire, Surrey, Suffolk, Norfolk, Cambridge, and Lincoln.

6. They were found to amount to above a hundred thousand men by the time they arrived at Blackheath. At the head of one party of these was Wat Tyler, who led his men into Smithfield, where he was met by the king, who invited him to a conference, under a pretence of hearing and redressing his grievances. Tyler, ordering his companions to retire till he should give them a signal, boldly ventured to meet the king in the midst of his retinue, and accordingly began the conference. 7. The demands of this demagogue are censured by all the historians of the time as insolent and extravagant; and yet nothing can be more just than those they have delivered for him. He required that all slaves should be set free, and all commonages should be open to the poor as well as the rich; and that a general pardon should be passed for the late outrages. 8. Whilst he made these demands, he now and then lifted up his sword in a menacing manner; which insolence so raised the indignation of William Walworth, then mayor of London, attending on the king, that, without considering the danger to which he exposed his majesty, he stunned Tyler with a blow of his mace, while one of the king's knights, riding up, despatched him with his sword. 9. The mutineers, seeing their leader fall, prepared themselves to take revenge; and their bows were now bent for execution, when Richard, though not yet quite sixteen years of age, rode up to the rebels, and with admirable presence of mind, cried out, "What, my people, will you then kill your king? Be not concerned for the loss of your leader; I myself will now be your general; follow me now into the field, and you shall have whatever you desire." The awed multitude immediately desisted: they followed the king, as if mechanically, into the field, and there he granted them the same charter that he had before given to their companions, but which he soon afterwards revoked in parliament.*

* Gower, the poet, wrote some Latin verses on this rebellion, part of which are here inserted, as a specimen of the literature of this reign; nor will they be less acceptable, we trust, from the ludicrous effect produced by putting English nick-names into a Latin dress.

10. Hitherto the king had acted under the control of the regency, who did all they could devise to abridge his power. However, in an extraordinary council of the nobility, assembled after Easter, he, to the astonishment of all present, desired to know his age; and being told that he was turned of two-and-twenty, he alleged that it was time then for him to govern without help; and that there was no reason that he should be deprived of those rights which the meanest of his subjects enjoyed.

11. Being thus set at liberty to conduct the business of government at discretion, it quickly appeared that he wanted those arts that are usually found to procure a lasting respect; he was fond of luxurious pleasure and idle ostentation; he admitted the meanest ranks to his familiarity; and his conversation was not adapted to impress them with a reverence for his morals or abilities. 12. The cruelty shown to the Duke of Gloucester, who, upon slight suspicions, was sent to confinement in Calais, and there murdered in prison, with some other acts equally arbitrary, did not fail to increase those animosities which had already taken deep root in the kingdom. The aggrandizement of some new favourites contributed still more to make the king odious; but though he seemed resolved, by all his actions, to set his subjects against him, it was accident that gave occasion for his overthrow. 13. The Duke of Hereford appeared in parliament, and accused the Duke of Norfolk of having spoken seditious words against his majesty in a private conversation. Norfolk denied the charge, gave Hereford the lie, and offered to prove his innocence by single combat.

"WATTE vocat cui THOMA venit, neque SYMME retardat,
   BATQUE, GIBBE simul, HYKKE venire subent.
COLLE furit quem BOBBE juvat, nocumenta parantes,
   Cum quibus ad damnum WILLE coire volat.
GRIGGE rapit, dum DAVIE strepit, comes est quibus HOBBE
   LARKIN et in medio non minor esse putat.
HUDDE ferit, quem JUDDE terit, dum TIBBE juvatur,
   JACKE domosque viros vellit, et ense necat," &c.

Which are thus humorously translated by ANDREWS.

"WAT cries, TOM flies, nor SYMKIN stays aside;
   And BATT, and GIBB, and HYKE, they summon loud;
COLLIN and Hob combustibles provide,
   While WILL the mischief forwards in the crowd;
GREG hawls, BOB bawls, and DAVY joins the cry,
   With LARY, not the least among the throng;
HODGE drubs, JUDE scrubs, while TIB stands grinning by,
   And JACK with sword and fire-brand madly strides along."

As proofs were wanting for legal trial, the lords readily acquiesced in that mode of determination; the time and place were appointed, and the whole nation waited with anxious suspense for the event. 14. At length the day arrived, on which the duel was to be fought; and the champions having just begun their career, the king stopped the combat, and ordered both the combatants to leave the kingdom. The Duke of Norfolk he banished for life, but the Duke of Hereford only for ten years. Thus the one was condemned to exile without being charged with any offence, and the other without being convicted of any crime. The Duke of Norfolk was overwhelmed with grief and despondence at the judgment awarded against him: he retired to Venice, where in a little time after, he died of a broken heart. 15. Hereford's behaviour on this occasion was resigned and submissive, which so pleased the king, that he consented to shorten the date of his banishment four years; and he also granted him letters patent, ensuring him the enjoyment of any inheritance which should fall to him during his absence; but upon the death of his father, the Duke of Lancaster, which happened shortly after, Richard revoked those letters, and retained the possession of the Lancaster estate to himself A.D. 1388.

Questions for Examination.

1. At what age and under what circumstances did Richard come to the throne?
2. In whose hands was the government vested?
3. Who was the first person that excited the people to arms?
5, 6. What disorders were committed by the rebels? and who was their leader?
7. What conditions were requested from the king by Wat Tyler?
8. By whom was Wat Tyler slain?
9. What was the conduct of the king on this occasion?
10. Did the subsequent conduct of the king serve to make him respected by his subjects?
13. What gave occasion to his overthrow?
14. With what severity did the king treat Norfolk and Hereford?

SECTION. II.

Oh! let us then intestine discord shun:
We ne'er can be but by ourselves undone.—*Savage.*

1. (A. D. 1398.) SUCH complicated injuries served to inflame the resentment of Hereford against the king: and although he had hitherto concealed it, he now set no bounds to his indignation, but even conceived a desire of dethroning

a person who had shown himself so unworthy of power. Indeed, no man could be better qualified for an enterprise of this nature than the Earl of Hereford: he was cool, cautious, discerning, and resolute. 2. He had served with distinction against the infidels of Lithuania; and he had thus joined to his other merits those of piety and valour. He was stimulated by private injuries, and had alliance and fortune sufficient to give weight to his measures. He only waited the absence of the king from England to put his schemes into execution; and Richard's going over into Ireland to quell an insurrection there, was the opportunity he had long looked for.

3. Accordingly he instantly embarked at Nantz, with a retinue of sixty persons, in three small vessels, and landed at Ravenspur, in Yorkshire. The Earl of Northumberland, who had long been a malcontent, together with Henry Percy, his son, who, from his ardent valour, was surnamed Hotspur, immediately joined them with their forces. After this junction the concourse of people coming to enlist under his banner was so great, that in a few days his army amounted to sixty thousand men.

4. While these things were transacting in England, Richard continued in Ireland in perfect security. Contrary winds, for three weeks together, prevented his receiving any news of the rebellion which had begun in his native dominions; wherefore, upon landing at Milford Haven with a body of twenty thousand men, he saw himself in a dreadful situation, in the midst of an enraged people, without any friend on whom to rely; and forsaken by those who, in the sunshine of his power, had only contributed to fan his follies. 5. His little army gradually began to desert him, till at last he found that he had not above six thousand men who followed his standard. Thus not knowing whom to trust, or where to turn, he saw no other hopes of safety but to throw himself upon the generosity of the enemy, and to gain from pity what he could not obtain by arms. He therefore sent Hereford word that he was ready to submit to whatever terms he thought proper to prescribe, and that he earnestly desired a conference. 6. For this purpose the earl appointed him to meet at a castle within about ten miles of Chester, where he came next day with his army. Richard, who the day before had been brought thither by the Duke of Northumberland, descrying his rival's approach from the walls, went down to receive him;

while Hereford, after some ceremony, entered the castle in complete armour, only his head was bare, in compliment to the fallen king. 7. Richard received him with that open air for which he had been remarkable, and kindly bade him welcome. "My lord king," returned the earl, with a cool respectful bow, "I am come sooner than you appointed, because your people say, that for one-and-twenty years you have governed with rigour and indiscretion. They are very ill satisfied with your conduct; but if it please God, I will help you to govern them better for the time to come." To this declaration the king made no other answer but " Fair cousin, since it pleases you it pleases us likewise."

8. But Hereford's haughty answer was not the only mortification the unfortunate Richard was to endure. After a short conversation with some of the king's attendants, Hereford ordered the king's horses to be brought out of the stable; and the wretched animals being produced, Richard was placed upon one, and his favourite, the earl of Salisbury, on the other. 9. In this mean equipage they rode to Chester; and were conveyed to the castle with a great noise of trumpets, and through a vast concourse of people, who were no way moved at the sight. In this manner he was led triumphantly along from town to town, amidst multitudes who scoffed at him, and extolled his rivals. "Long live the good Duke of Lancaster, our deliverer!" was the general cry; but as for the king, to use the pathetic words of the poet, "None cried God bless him!" 10. Thus, after repeated indignities, he was confined a close prisoner in the Tower, there, if possible, to undergo a still greater variety of studied insolence and flagrant contempt. The wretched monarch, humbled in this manner, began to lose the pride of a king with the splendors of royalty, and his spirit sunk to his circumstances. There was no great difficulty, therefore, in inducing him to sign a deed, by which he renounced his crown, as being unqualified for governing the kingdom. 11. Upon this resignation Hereford founded his principal claim: but, willing to fortify his pretensions with every appearance of justice, he called a parliament, which was readily brought to approve and confirm his claim. A frivolous charge, of thirty-three articles, was drawn up, and found valid against the king; upon which he was solemnly deposed, and the Earl of Hereford elected in his stead, by the title of Henry the Fourth. 12. Thus

H

Richard II. surrendering his crown.

began the contest between the houses of York and Lancaster, which, for several years after, deluged the kingdom with blood; and yet, in the end, contributed to settle and confirm the constitution.

13. When Richard was deposed, the Earl of Northumberland made a motion in the house of peers, demanding the advice of parliament with regard to the future treatment of the deposed king. To this they replied, that he should be imprisoned in some secure place, where his friends and partizans should not be able to find him. This was accordingly put in practice; but while he still continued alive, the usurper could not remain in safety. Indeed, some conspiracies and commotions which followed soon after, induced Henry to wish for Richard's death; in consequence of which, one of those assassins that are found in every court, ready to commit the most horrid crimes for reward, went down to the place of this unfortunate monarch's confinement in the castle of Pomfret, and, with eight of his followers, rushed into his apartments. 12. The king, concluding their design was to take away his life, resolved not to fall unrevenged, but to sell it as dearly as he could; wherefore, wresting a pole-axe from one of the murderers, he soon laid four of their number dead at his feet. But he was at

length overpowered, and struck dead by the blow of a pole-axe; although some assert that he was starved in prison. 15. Thus died the unfortunate Richard, in the thirty-fourth year of his age, and the twenty-third of his reign. Though his conduct was blameable, yet the punishment he suffered was greater than his offences; and in the end his sufferings made more converts to his family and cause than ever his most meritorious actions could have procured them. He left no posterity, either legitimate or otherwise.

Questions for Examination.

1. By whom was the king opposed ?
3. By whom was Hereford joined on his arrival in England ?
4. In what manner did the king conduct himself ?
6. Can you mention the indignities the king afterwards suffered ?
7. How did Richard receive the Earl of Hereford ? and what passed at the interview between them ?
8, 9. To what other mortifications was the king obliged to submit ?
10. What circumstances preceded his resignation of the crown ?
11. By whom was he succeeded ?
12. What dreadful contest now commenced ?
13. After Richard was deposed, in what manner was he treated ?
14. Relate the circumstances which attended the murder of Richard.
15. Describe his character.

CONTEMPORARY SOVEREIGNS.

Popes.	A.D.	Kings of France.	A.D.		A.D.
Gregory XI	1370			Margaret	1385
Urbain VI	1378	Charles V	1364		
Boniface IX	1389	Charles VI	1380	*Queen of Sweden.*	
				Margaret held Sweden with	
Emperors of the East.		*Kings of Portugal.*		Denmark	1397
John VI	1355	Ferdinand	1367		
Emanuel II	1391	John I	1385		
				Kings of Scotland.	
Emperors of the West		King and Queen of *Denmark.*		Robert II	1370
Charles IV	1347			Robert III	1390
Winceslaus	1378	Glaus III	1375		

EMINENT PERSONS.

William Courtney, and Thomas Arundel, archbishops of Canterbury. William Walworth, lord mayor of London. Roger Mortimer, earl of March, grandson to Clarence, heir apparent. Henry of Bolingbroke. Vere, duke of Ireland. William of Wykeham, bishop of Winchester, founder of Winchester College, and of Merton College, Oxford.

CHAPTER XVI.

HENRY IV.

Born 1367. Died March 20, 1413. Began to reign October 1, 1399. Reigned 13 years.

> Heaven knows what bye-paths and crooked ways
> I met this crown ; and I myself know well
> How troublsome it sat upon my brow.—*Shakespeare.*

1. (A. D. 1399.) Henry soon found that the throne of a usurper is but a bed of thorns. Such violent animosities broke out among the barons in the first session of this parliament, that forty challenges were given and received, and forty gauntlets were thrown down as pledges of the sincerity of their resentment. But though these commotions were seemingly suppressed by his moderation for that time, yet one conspiracy broke out after another, and were detected in the formation, or actually punished in the field.

2. That formed against him by the Earl of Northumberland was the most formidable. It was in a skirmish between the Scots and English that Archibald, Earl of Douglas, with many of the Scots nobility, were taken prisoners by the Earl of Northumberland, and carried to Alnwick castle. When Henry received intelligence of this victory, he sent the earl orders not to ransom his prisoners, as he intended to detain them, in order to increase his demands in making peace with Scotland. 3. This message was highly resented by the Earl of Northumberland, who, by the laws of war that prevailed in that age, had a right to the ransom of all such as he had taken in battle. The command was still more irksome, as he considered the king his debtor, both for his security and his crown. Accordingly, stung with this supposed injury, he resolved to overturn a throne which he had the chief hand in establishing.

4. A scheme was laid in which the Scots and Welsh were to unite their forces, and to assist Northumberland in elevating Mortimer, as the true heir to the crown of England. When all things were prepared for the intended insurrection, the earl had the mortification to find himself unable to lead on the troops, being seized with a sudden illness at Berwick. But the want of his presence was well supplied by his son, Henry Percy, surnamed Hotspur, who took the command of the troops, and marched them towards Shrewsbury, in order to join his forces with those of Glen-

dower, a Welsh chieftain, who for some time before had been exchanged from prison, and had now advanced with his forces as far as Shropshire. 5. Upon the junction of these two armies they published a manifesto, which aggravated their real grievances, and invented more. In the meantime, Henry, who had received no intelligence of their designs, was at first greatly surprised at the news of this rebellion. But fortune seemed to befriend him on this occasion; he had a small army in readiness, which he had levied for an intended war against the Scots, and knowing the importance of despatch against such active enemies, he instantly hurried down to Shrewsbury, that he might give the rebels battle.

6. Upon the approach of the two armies, both sides seemed willing to give a colour to their cause by shewing a desire of reconciliation; but when they came to open their mutual demands, the treaty was turned into abuse and recrimination. On one side was objected rebellion and ingratitude; on the other, tyranny and usurpation. 7. The two armies were pretty nearly equal, each consisting of about twelve thousand men; the animosity on both sides was inflamed to the highest pitch; and no prudence nor military skill could determine on which side the victory might incline; accordingly a very bloody engagement ensued, in which the generals on both sides exerted themselves with great bravery. Henry was seen everywhere in the thickest of the fight; while his valiant son, who was afterwards the renowned conqueror of France, fought by his side; and, though wounded in the face by an arrow, still kept the field, and performed astonishing acts of valour. 8. On the other side, the daring Hotspur supported that renown which he had arquired in so many bloody engagements, and everywhere sought out the king as a noble object of indignation. At last, however, his death from an unknown hand decided the victory; and the fortune of Henry once more prevailed. On that bloody day, it is said that no less than two thousand three hundred gentlemen were slain, and about six thousand private men, of whom two-thirds were of Hotspur's army.

9. While this furious transaction was going forward, Northumberland, who was lately recovered from his indisposition, was advancing with a body of troops to reinforce the army of malcontents, and take upon him the command; but hearing by the way of his son's and brother's misfortune he dismissed his troops, not daring to keep the field with so small a force, before an army superior in number, and

flushed with recent victory. 10. The earl, therefore, for a while, attempted to find safety by flight; but at last, being pressed by his pursuers, and finding himself totally without resource, he chose rather to throw himself upon the king's mercy than lead a precarious and indigent life in exile. Upon his appearing before Henry at York, he pretended that his sole intention in arming was to mediate between the two parties; and this, though but a very weak apology, seemed to satisfy the king. Northumberland, therefore, received a pardon; Henry probably thinking that he was sufficiently punished by the loss of his army and the death of his favourite son.

11. By these means Henry seemed to surmount all his troubles; and the calm which was thus produced was employed by him in endeavours to acquire popularity, which he had lost by the severities exercised during the preceding part of his reign. For that reason, he often permitted the house of commons to assume powers which had not been usually exercised by their predecessors. (A.D. 1407.) 12. In the sixth year of his reign, when they voted him the supplies, they appointed treasurers of their own, to see the money disbursed for the purpose intended; and required them to deliver in their accounts to the house. They proposed thirty very important articles for the government of the king's household; and, on the whole, preserved their privileges and freedom more entire during his reign than in that of any of his predecessors. 13. But while the king thus laboured, not without success, to retrieve the reputation he had lost, his son Henry, the prince of Wales, seemed equally bent on incurring the public aversion. He became notorious for all kinds of debauchery, and ever chose to be surrounded by a set of wretches, who took pride in committing the most illegal acts, with the prince at their head. 14. The king was not a little mortified at this degeneracy in his eldest son, who seemed entirely forgetful of his station; although he had already exhibited repeated proofs of his valorous conduct and generosity. Such were the excesses into which he ran, that one of his dissolute companions having been brought to trial before Sir William Gascoigne, chief justice of the king's bench, for some misdemeanor, the prince was so exasperated at the issue of the trial, that he struck the judge in open court. 15. The venerable magistrate, who knew the reverence that was due to his station, behaved with a dignity that became his office,

and immediately ordered the prince to be committed to prison. When this transaction was reported to the king, who was an excellent judge of mankind, he could not help exclaiming in a transport—" Happy is the king that has a magistrate endowed with courage to execute the laws upon such an offender; still more happy in having a son willing to submit to such a chastisement!" This, in fact, is one of the first great instances we read in the English history of a magistrate doing justice in opposition to power; since, upon many former occasions, we find the judges only ministers of royal caprice.

16. Henry, whose health had for some time been declining, did not long outlive this transaction. He was subject to fits, which bereaved him for the time of his senses; and which at last brought on his death at Westminster, in the forty-sixth year of his age, and the fourteenth of his reign.

Questions for Examination.

1. In what situation did Henry find himself on ascending the throne?
2. Who was the most formidable opponent of Henry?
4. For what purpose were the Scots and Welsh to unite their forces?
7. Relate the valorous conduct of the king and of the prince.
8. What was the fate of Hotspur?
10. What became of the earl of Northumberland?
12. What at this time were the powers assumed by the house of commons?
13. What was the conduct of the prince of Wales?
15. For what offence did the chief justice imprison him?
What did the king exclaim when he heard of the prince's committal?
16. What caused the death of the king?

CONTEMPORARY SOVEREIGNS.

Popes.	Emperors of the West.	King and Queen of Denmark and Sweden.
A.D.	A.D.	A.D.
Boniface IX.......1389	Winceslaus........1378	
Innocent VII.....1404	Robert le Pet.....1400	Margaret...........1335
Gregory XII......1406	Sigismund 1410	Eric XIII.........1411
Alexander V......1409	*King of France.*	
John XXIII......1410	Charles VI...........1380	*King of Scotland.*
		Robert III........1390
Emperor of the East.	*King of Portugal.*	
Emanuel II.......1391	John I..............1385	

EMINENT PERSONS.

Thomas Arundel, archbishop of Canterbury; Edward Mortimer; Henry Percy, surnamed Hotspur; Chief Justice Gascoigne; Sir Robert Knowles; Sir Richard Whittington, lord mayor of London; John Gower, and Geoffrey Chaucer.

CHAPTER XVII.

HENRY V.

Born 1388. Died Aug. 31, 1422. Began to reign March 20, 1413. Reigned 9½ years.

Now terror seemed to make the field its own.—Egerton.

1. (A.D. 1413.) THE first steps taken by the young king confirmed all those prepossessions entertained in his favour. He called together his former abandoned companions: acquainted them with his intended reformation; exhorted them to follow his example; and thus dismissed them from his presence, allowing them a competency to subsist upon till he saw them worthy of further promotion. 2. The faithful ministers of his father at first began to tremble for their former justice in the administration of their duty; but he soon eased them of their fears by taking them into his friendship and confidence. Sir William Gascoigne, who thought himself the most obnoxious, met with praise instead of reproaches, and was exhorted to persevere in the same rigorous and impartial execution of justice.

3. About this time the heresy of Wickliffe,[*] or Lollardism, as it was called, began to spread every day more and more, while it received a new lustre from the protection and preaching of Sir John Oldcastle, baron of Cobham, who had been one of the king's domestics, and stood high in his favour. The primate, however, indicted this nobleman, and, with the assistance of his suffragans, condemned him, as a heretic, to be burnt alive. 4. Cobham, however, escaping from the Tower, in which he was confined, the day before his execution, privately went up to London to take a signal revenge on his enemies. But the king, apprised of his intentions, ordered that the city gates should be shut; and coming by night with his guards into St. Giles's-fields seized such of the conspirators as appeared, and afterwards laid hold of several parties that were hastening to the ap-

---

[*] John Wickliffe, a celebrated English divine, was the father of the reformation of the English Church from popery. He first opposed the authority of the pope, and, being cited to appear before the bishop of London, it caused great tumult. His tenets were solemnly condemned in an assembly held at Oxford; he, however, escaped the malice of his enemies, and died peaceably at Lutterworth, in 1384.

pointed place. 5. Some of these were executed, but the greater number pardoned. Cobham himself found means of escaping for that time, but he was taken about four years after; and never did the cruelty of man invent, or crimes draw down, such torment as he was made to endure. He was hung up with a chain by the middle, and thus, at a slow fire, burned, or rather roasted, alive.

6. Henry, to turn the minds of the people from such hideous scenes, resolved to take advantage of the troubles in which France at that time was engaged; and assembling a great fleet and army at Southampton, landed at Harfleur, at the head of an army of six thousand men-at-arms, and twenty-four thousand foot, mostly archers. But although the enemy made but a feeble resistance, yet the climate seemed to fight against the English, a contagious dysentery carrying off three parts of Henry's army. 7. The English monarch, when it was too late, began to repent of his rash inroad into a country where disease and a powerful army everywhere threatened destruction; he, therefore, began to think of retiring into Calais.

The enemy, however, resolved to intercept his retreat; and after he had passed the small river of Tertois, at Blangi, he was surprised to observe, from the heights, the whole French army drawn up in the plains of Agincourt,* and so posted, that it was impossible for him to proceed on his march without coming to an engagement. 8. No situation could be more unfavourable than that in which he found himself. His army was wasted with disease; the soldiers' spirits worn down with fatigue, destitute of provisions, and discouraged by their retreat. Their whole body amounted to but nine thousand men, and these were to sustain the shock of an enemy nearly ten times their number, headed by expert generals, and plentifully supplied with provisions. 9. As the enemy were so much superior, he drew up his army on a narrow ground between two woods, which guarded each flank; and he patiently expected, in that position, the attack of the enemy. The constable of France was at the head of one army, and Henry himself, with Edward, Duke of York, commanded the other. 10. For a time both armies, as if afraid to begin, kept silently gazing at each other, neither willing to

---

*Agincourt is a village in the province of Artois, formerly part of the French Netherlands

break their ranks by making the onset; which, Henry perceiving, with a cheerful countenance cried out, "My friends, since they will not begin, it is ours to set the example; come on, and the blessed Trinity be our protection!" Upon this the whole army set forward with a shout, while the French still waited their approach with intrepidity. 11. The English archers, who had long been famous for their great skill, first let fly a shower of arrows three feet long, which did great execution. The French cavalry advancing to repel these two hundred bowmen, who lay till then concealed, rising on a sudden let fly among them, and produced such a confusion, that the archers threw by their arrows, and, rushing in, fell upon them sword in hand. The French at first repulsed the assailants, who were enfeebled by disease; but they soon made up the defect by their valour; and, resolving to conquer or die, burst in upon the enemy with such impetuosity, that the French were soon obliged to give way.

12. They were overthrown in every part of the field; their numbers being crowded into a very narrow space, were incapable of either flying or making any resistance, so that they covered the ground with heaps of slain. After all appearance of opposition was over, there was heard an alarm from behind, which proceeded from a number of peasants who had fallen on the English baggage, and were putting those who guarded it to the sword. 13. Henry, now seeing the enemy on all sides of him, began to entertain apprehensions from his prisoners, the number of whom exceeded even that of his army. He thought it necessary, therefore, to issue general orders for putting them to death; but on a discovery of a certainty of his victory, he stopped the slaughter, and was still able to save a great number. 14. This severity tarnished the glory which his victory would otherwise have acquired; but all the heroism of that age is tinctured with barbarity. In this battle the French lost ten thousand men and fourteen thousand prisoners: the English only forty men in all.*

15. France was at that time (A.D. 1417) in a wretched situation; the whole kingdom appeared as one vast theatre

---

*The duke of York and the earl of Suffolk were among the few who fell in this battle on the side of the English. Also three valiant Welshmen, named Davy Gam, Roger Vaughan, Walker, Lloyd, who had rescued the king, and were afterwards knighted by him as they lay bleeding to death.—*Monstrelet.*

of crimes, murders, injustice, and devastation. The duke of Orleans was assassinated by the duke of Burgundy; and the duke of Burgundy, in his turn, fell by the treachery of the dauphin.

16. A state of imbecility into which Charles had fallen made him passive in every transaction; and Henry, at last, by conquests and negociation, caused himself to be elected heir to the crown. The principal articles of this treaty were, that Henry should espouse the princess Catharine, daughter of the king of France; that king Charles should enjoy the title and dignity for life, but that Henry should be declared heir to the crown, and should be intrusted with the present administration of the Government; that France and England should for ever be united under one king, but should still retain their respective laws and privileges.

17. In consequence of this, while Henry was everywhere victorious he fixed his residence in Paris; and while Charles had but a small court, he was attended with a very magnificent one. (A.D. 1421.) On Whit-Sunday, the two kings and their two queens, with crowns on their heads, dined together in public; Charles receiving apparent homage, but Henry commanding with absolute authority.*

18. Henry, at that time, when his glory had nearly reached its summit, and both crowns were just devolved upon him, was seized with a fistula, a disorder which, from the unskilfulness of the physicians of the time, soon became mortal. He expired with the same intrepidity with which he had lived, in the thirty-fourth year of his age and the tenth of his reign.

Questions for Examination.

1. What were the first steps taken by the young king?
3. What remarkable circumstance did the heresy of Wickliffe produce?
5. What was the melancholy fate of Sir John Oldcastle, baron of Cobham?

---

* The revenues of government, and the grants of parliament, were so inadequate to Henry's expensive armies and expeditions that he was forced to pawn his crown to his uncle, Cardinal Beaufort, for a large sum; and certain jewels to the lord mayor of London, for ten thousand marks. He was also obliged to pledge two gold cased basons, weighing together 28lb. 8oz. to two canons of St. Paul's for six hundred marks: and two golden shells to the dean of Lincoln for one hundred more. The cost of his army was great; each knight received 20s per diem, a squire 10s. and each archer 6s. Besides which, he had a costly band of music, among which were the ten clarions, wh.ch played an hour night and morning, before his tent.—*Bertrand de Moleville.*

6. What caused Henry to assemble an army in France? What was the amount of his army?
7. Where did the enemy attempt to intercept his retreat?
8. In what condition was the English army?
9. Who commanded the respective armies?
10. Relate the particulars of the battle of Agincourt?
14. What tarnished the glory of this victory? What was the situation of France?
15. What were the principal articles of treaty between England and France?
18. What was the age of Henry at his death, and how long did he reign?

CONTEMPORARY SOVEREIGNS.

Popes.	Emperor of the West.	King of Denmark and Sweden.
A.D.	A.D.	
John XXIII......1410	Sigismund........1410	
Martin V.........1417		A.D.
	King of France.	Eric XIII.........1411
Emperor of the East.	Charles IV........1380	
Emanuel II.......1394		King of Scotland.
	King of Portugal.	Robert III........1390
	John I............1385	

EMINENT PERSONS.

Henry Chicheley, archbishop of Canterbury; Cardinal Beaufort, bishop of Winchester, younger son of John of Gaunt, and preceptor to Henry the Fifth and Sixth. Talbot, earl of Shrewsbury.

CHAPTER XVIII.

HENRY VI.

Born 1421. Deposed March 5, 1461. Died April 21, 1471. Began to reign August 31, 1422. Reigned 38½ years.

SECTION I.

From fields obscure darts forth a village maid.—Dibdin.

1. (A. D. 1422.) THE duke of Bedford, one of the most accomplished princes of the age, and equally experienced both in the cabinet and the field, was appointed by parliament protector of England, defender of the church, and first counsellor to the king during his minority; as he was not yet a year old: and as France was the great object that engrossed all consideration, he attempted to exert the efforts of the nation upon the continent with all his vigor.

2. A new revolution was produced in that kingdom, by

means apparently the most unlikely to be attended with success. In the village of Domreni, near Vaucoleurs, on the borders of Lorraine, there lived a country girl, about twenty-seven years of age, called Joan of Arc. This girl had been a servant at a small inn, and in that humble station had submitted to those hardy employments which fit the body for the fatigues of war. She was of an irreproachable life, and had hitherto testified none of those enterprising qualities which displayed themselves soon after. 3. Her mind, however, brooding with melancholy steadfastness upon the miserable situation of her country, began to feel several impulses, which she was willing to mistake for the inspirations of Heaven. Convinced of the reality of her own admonitions she had recourse to one Baudricourt, governor of Vaucoleurs, and informed him of her destination by Heaven to free her native country from its fierce invaders. Baudricourt treated her at first with some neglect: but her importunities at length prevailed, and willing to make trial of her pretensions, he gave her some attendants, who conducted her to the French court, which at that time resided at Chinon.

4. The French court were probably sensible of the weakness of her pretensions; but they were willing to make use of every artifice to support their declining fortunes. It was therefore, given out that Joan was actually inspired; that she was able to discover the king among the number of his courtiers, although he had laid aside all the distinctions of his authority; that she had told him some secrets which were only known to himself; and that she had demanded and minutely described a sword in the church of St. Catherine de Firebois, which she had never seen. 5. In this manner the minds of the vulgar being prepared for her appearance, she was armed cap-à-pie, and shown in that martial dress to the people. She was then brought before the doctors of the university, and they, tinctured with the credulity of the times, or willing to second the imposture, declared that she had actually received her commission from above.

5. When the preparations for her mission were completely blazoned, their next aim was to send her against the enemy. The English were at that time besieging the city of Orleans, the last resource of Charles, and everything promised them a speedy surrender. Joan undertook to raise the siege; and to render herself still more remarkable girded herself with the miraculous sword, of which she had before such extra-

ordinary notices. Thus equipped, she ordered all the soldiers to confess themselves before they set out; she displayed in her hand a consecrated banner, and assured the troops of certain success. 7. Such confidence on her side soon raised the spirits of the French army; and even the English who pretended to despise her efforts, felt themselves secretly influenced with the terrors of her mission; and relaxing in their endeavours, the siege was raised with great precipitation. From being attacked, the French now in turn became the aggressors. One victory followed another; and at length the French king was solemnly crowned at Rheims, which Joan had promised should come to pass.

8. A tide of success followed the performance of this solemnity; but Joan having thrown herself into the city of Compeign, with a body of troops, that was then besieged by the Duke of Burgundy, she was taken prisoner in a sally which she headed against the enemy, the governor shutting the gates behind. The Duke of Bedford was no sooner informed of her being taken, than he purchased her of the count Vendome, who had made her prisoner, and ordered her to be committed to close confinement. 9. The credulity of both nations was at the time so great, that nothing was too absurd to gain belief that coincided with their passions. As Joan, but a little before, from her successes, was regarded as a saint, she was now, upon her captivity, considered as a sorceress, forsaken by the demon who had granted her a fallacious and temporary assistance; and accordingly, being tried at Rouen, she was found guilty of heresy and witchcraft, and sentenced to be burnt alive, which was executed with the most ignorant malignity.

10. From this period the English affairs became totally irretrievable. The city of Paris returned once more to a sense of its duty. Thus ground was continually, though slowly, gained by the French; and in the lapse of a few years, Calais alone remained of all the conquests that had been made in France; and this was but a small compensation for the blood and treasure which had been lavished in that country, and which only served to gratify ambition with transient applause.* (A.D. 1443.)

* The duke of Bedford died about this time; and when the dauphin of France was advised to demolish the monument of black marble which had been erected to his memory, he generously replied, "Let him repose in peace; and let us be thankful that he does repose. Were he to awake, he wou'd make the stoutest of us tremble."

11. But the incapacity of Henry began to appear in a fuller light; and a foreign war being now extinguished, the people began to prepare for the horrors of intestine strife. In this period of calamity a new interest was revived, which had lain dormant in the times of prosperity and triumph. Richard, Duke of York, was descended, by the mother's side, from Lionel, one of the sons of Edward the Third; whereas the reigning king was descended from John of Gaunt, a younger son of the same monarch: Richard, therefore, stood plainly in succession before Henry; and he began to think the weakness and unpopularity of the present reign a favourable moment for ambition. The ensign of Richard was a white rose, that of Henry a red: and this gave name to the two factions, whose animosity was now about to drench the kingdom with slaughter.

12. Among the number of complaints which the unpopularity of the government gave rise to, there were some which even excited insurrection; particularly that headed by John Cade, which was of the most dangerous nature. This man was a native of Ireland, who had been obliged to fly over to France for his crimes; but seeing the people upon his return, prepared for violent measures, he assumed the name of Mortimer; and at the head of twenty thousand Kentish men, advanced towards the capital, and encamped at Blackheath. The king, being informed of this commotion, sent a message to demand the cause of their assembling in arms, and Cade, in the name of the community, answered that their only aim was to punish evil ministers, and to procure a redress of grievances for the people. 13. But committing some abuses and engaging with the citizens, he was abandoned by most of his followers; and retreating to Rochester, was obliged to fly alone into the woods of Kent, where, a price being set upon his head by proclamation, he was discovered and slain.*

14. In the meantime the duke of York secretly fomented these disturbances, and, pretending to espouse the cause of the people, still secretly aspired to the crown; and though he wished nothing so ardently, yet he was for some time prevented by his own scruples from seizing it. What his in-

---

*The inscription on Cade's standard consisted of the following doggerel, sufficiently indicative of the levelling doctrines of him and his rebel companions:—

"When Adam delv'd and Eve span,
Who was then a gentleman?"

trigues failed to bring about, accidents produced according to his desires. 15. The king falling into a distemper, which so far increased his natural imbecility that it even rendered him incapable of maintaining the appearance of royalty, York was appointed lieutenant and protector of the kingdom, with powers to hold and open parliaments at pleasure.

Question for Examination.

1. What happened on the death of the king?
2, 3. Relate the history of Joan of Arc.
4. By what artifices did the French court support their declining fortunes?
6. What enterprise did Joan undertake?
7. Were the French successful?
8. In what manner was Joan of Arc made prisoner?
9. What was the fate of this extraordinary woman?
10. In what state were the English affairs at this time?
11. What new interest was now revived against Henry? and to what consequences did it lead?
12. Mention the particulars of an insurrection which took place, and the cause which occasioned it?
13. What was the fate of the principal conspirators?
14. Who secretly fomented these disturbances?
15. Who was appointed protector of the kingdom, and on what occasion?

SECTION II.

> While second Richard's blood for vengeance calls,
> Doom'd for his grandsire's guilt, poor Henry falls.—*Savage.*

1. (A.D. 1452.) BEING thus invested with a plenitude of power, he continued in the enjoyment of it for some time; but at length the unhappy king recovered from his lethargic complaint; and, as if waking from a dream, perceived with surprise that he was stripped of all his authority. Henry was married to Margaret of Anjou,* a woman of a masculine understanding, who obliged him to take the field, and in a manner dragged him to it, where both sides came to an engagement, in which the Yorkists gained a complete victory.†
2. The king himself being wounded, and having taken shelter in a cottage near the field of battle, was taken prisoner, and treated by the victor with great respect and tenderness.

Henry was now merely a prisoner, treated with the splendid forms of royalty; yet, indolent and sickly, he seemed

---

* Daughter of René, titular king of Sicily, an ambitious, enterprising and courageous woman. She supported the rights of her husband with great fortitude and activity, till the fatal defeat at Tewkesbury, which put an end to all her enterprises.
† This battle was the first of St. Alban's.

pleased with his situation, and did not regret that power which was not to be exercised without fatigue. But Margaret once more induced him to assert his prerogative. 3. The contending parties met at Bloreheath, on the borders of Staffordshire, Sept. 23, 1459, and the Yorkists gained some advantages; but Sir Andrew Trollop deserted with all his men to the king; and this so intimidated the whole army of the Yorkists, that they separated the next day without striking a single blow. Several other engagements followed, with various success; Margaret being at one time victorious, at another in exile: the victory upon Wakefield green,* in which the duke of York was slain, seemed to fix her good fortune.

4. But the earl of Warwick, who now put himself at the head of the Yorkists, was one of the most celebrated generals of the age, formed for times of trouble, extremely artful, and incontestably brave, equally skilful in council and the field; and inspired with a degree of hatred against the queen that nothing could suppress. He commanded an army, in which he led about the captive king, to give a sanction of his attempts. 5. Upon the approach of the Lancastrians, he conducted his forces, strengthened by a body of Londoners, who were very affectionate to his cause, and gave battle to the queen at St. Alban's. In this, however, he was defeated. About two thousand of the Yorkists perished in the battle, and the person of the king again fell into the hands of his own party, to be treated with apparent respect, but real contempt.

6. In the mean time young Edward, the eldest son of the late duke of York, began to repair the losses his party had lately sustained, and to give spirit to the Yorkists. This prince, in the bloom of youth, remarkable for the beauty of his person, his bravery, and popular deportment, advanced towards London with the remainder of Warwick's army; and, obliging Margaret to retire, entered the city amidst the acclamations of the people. Perceiving his own popularity, he supposed that now was the time to lay his claim to the crown; and his friend Warwick, assembling the citizens to St. John's Fields, pronounced a harangue, setting forth the title of Edward, and inveighing against the tyranny and usurpation of the house of Lancaster. (A.D. 1461.) 7. Both sides at length met near Towton, in the county of York, to

---

* In the West Riding of Yorkshire.

decide the fate of the empire, and never was England depopulated by so terrible an engagement. It was a dreadful sight to behold a hundred thousand men of the same country engaged against each other; and all to satisfy the ambition of the weakest or the worst of mankind. While the army of Edward was advancing to the charge, there happened a great fall of snow, which, driving full in the face of the enemy, blinded them; and this advantage, seconded by an impetuous onset, decided the victory in his favour. Edward issued orders to give no quarter; and a bloody slaughter ensued, in which nearly forty thousand of the Lancastrians were slain.

8. The weak and unfortunate Henry, always imprudent and always unsuccessful, was taken prisoner, carried to London with great ignominy, and conducted to the Tower. Margaret was rather more fortunate: she contrived to escape out of the kingdom, and took refuge with her father in Flanders.*

9. Edward being now, by means of the earl of Warwick, fixed upon the throne, reigned in peace and security, while his title was recognised by parliament, and universally submitted to by the people. (A.D. 1464.) He began, therefore, to give loose to his favourite passions, and a spirit of gallantry, mixed with cruelty, was seen to prevail in his court. The very same palace which one day exhibited a spectacle of horror, was to be seen the day following with a mask or a pageant; and the king would at once gallant a mistress and inspect an execution. 10. In order to turn him from these pursuits, which were calculated to render him unpopular, the earl of Warwick advised him to marry; and with his consent went over to France, to procure Bona of Savoy, as queen, and the match was accordingly concluded. But whilst the earl was hastening the negociation in France, the

*Margaret, flying with her son into a forest, was attacked during the night by robbers, who despoiled her of her rings and jewels, and treated her with the utmost indignity. The partition of this great booty having raised a violent quarrel among them, she took an opportunity of flying with her son into the thickest part of the forest, where she wandered till she was overcome with hunger and fatigue. While in this wretched condition, she saw a robber approaching her with his naked sword; she suddenly embraced the resolution of trusting entirely to his faith and generosity, and, presenting to him the young prince, "Here, my friend," said she, "I commit to your care the safety of the king's son." The man struck with the singularity of the event, and recalled to virtue by the flattering confidence reposed in him, vowed not only to abstain from all injury against the princess, but to devote himself entirely to her service. By his means she reached the sea-coast and embarked for Flanders.—*DeMolevillle*, &c.

king himself rendered it abortive at home, by marrying Elizabeth Grey,* with whom he had fallen in love, and whom he had vainly endeavoured to debauch. 11. Having thus given Warwick real cause of offence, he was resolved to widen the breach by driving him from the council. Warwick, whose prudence was equal to his bravery, soon made use of both to assist his revenge; and formed such a combination against Edward, that he was in his turn obliged to fly the kingdom. Thus, once more, the poor, passive king Henry was released from prison to be placed upon a dangerous throne. A parliament was called, which confirmed Henry's title with great solemnity; and Warwick was himself received among the people under the title of king maker.

12. But Edward's party, though repressed, was not destroyed. Though an exile in Holland, he had many partisans at home; and, after an absence of nine months, being seconded by a small body of troops, granted to him by the duke of Burgundy, he made a descent at Ravenspur, in Yorkshire. Though, at first, he was coolly received by the English, yet his army increased upon his march, while his moderation and feigned humility still added to the number of his partisans. London, at that time ever ready to admit the most powerful, opened her gates to him; and the wretched Henry was once more plucked from a throne to be sent back to his former mansion.

13. Nothing now, therefore, remained to Warwick, but to cut short an anxious suspense, by hazarding a battle. Edward's fortune prevailed. They met at St. Albans, and the Lancastrians were defeated; while Warwick himself, leading a chosen body of troops into the thickest of the slaughter, fell, in the midst of his enemies, covered with wounds.

Margaret, receiving the fatal news of the death of the brave Warwick, and the total destruction of her party, gave way to her grief, for the first time, in a torrent of tears; and yielding to her unhappy fate, took sanctuary in the abbey of Beaulieu, in Hampshire.

14. She had not been long in this melancholy abode

---

* Elizabeth Grey was the daughter of sir Richard Woodville. The king first saw her at court, whether she had repaired to present a petition for the recovery of the confiscated lands of her late husband, sir John Grey, who was slain in arms on the side of Henry. She told Edward when he first addressed her on the subject of his love, that though too humble to be his wife, she was too high to become his concubine.

before she found some few friends still waiting to assist her fallen fortunes. She had now fought battles in almost every province in England; Tewkesbury park was the last scene that terminated her attempts. 15. The duke of Somerset headed her army; a man who had shared her dangers, and had ever been steady in her cause. When Edward first attacked him in his intrenchments, he repulsed him with such vigour, that the enemy retired with precipitation; upon which the duke, supposing them routed, pursued, and ordered lord Wenlock to support his charge. But, unfortunately, this lord disobeyed his orders; and Somerset's forces were soon overpowered by numbers. 16. In this dreadful exigence, the duke finding that all was over, became ungovernable in his rage; and beholding Wenlock inactive, and remaining in the very place where he had first drawn up his men, giving way to his fury, with his heavy battle-axe in both hands he ran upon the coward, and with one blow dashed out his brains.

17. The queen and the prince were taken prisoners after the battle, and brought in the presence of Edward. The young prince appeared before the conqueror with undaunted majesty; and being asked, in an insulting manner, how he dared to invade England without leave, more mindful of his high birth than of his ruined fortunes, he boldly replied, "I have entered the dominions of my father, to revenge his injuries and to redress my own." 18. The barbarous Edward, enraged at his intrepidity, struck him on the mouth with his gauntlet; and this served as a signal for further brutality: the dukes of Gloucester, Clarence, and others, like wild beasts, rushing on the unarmed youth at once, stabbed him to the heart with their daggers. To complete the tragedy, Henry himself was soon after murdered in cold blood. Of all those that were taken, none were suffered to survive but Margaret herself. 19. It was perhaps expected that she would be ransomed by the king of France; and in this they were not deceived, as that monarch paid the king of England fifty thousand crowns for her freedom. This extraordinary woman, after having sustained the cause of her husband in twelve battles, after having survived her friends, fortunes, and children, died a few years after in privacy in France, very miserable indeed; but with few other claims to our pity except her courage and her distresses.*

* During this and several previous reigns, a most absurd fashion was followed by the people. It was customary to wear the beaks or points of

HENRY VI.

Questions for Examination.

1. What was the issue of the first battle between the houses of York and Lancaster?
2. What was the fortune of Henry?
3. Where did the contending parties next meet? What circumstances gave the advantage to Henry's party?
4. Who was the commander of the Yorkists?
5. What was his success?
6. Who now laid claim to the crown?
7. What were the particulars of the action at Towton?
8. What happened to Margaret and the young prince after the battle?
9. How did Edward conduct himself after his accession?
11. For what reason did Warwick combine against Edward? By what title was Warwick received among the people?
13. What was the fortune of the next battle?
14. What followed this engagement?
17. What was the answer of the young prince to Edward?
18. What was his treatment? What was the fate of Henry?
19. What of Margaret?

CONTEMPORARY SOVEREIGNS.

Popes.	A.D.		A.D.		A.D.
Martin V.	1417	took Constantino-		Edward	1433
Eugenius VI.	1431	ple by storm, May		Alphonsus	1438
Nicholas V.	1447	29.	1453		
Calixtus III.	1455			*Kings of Denmark and*	
Pius II.	1458	*Emperors of the West.*		*Sweden.*	
		Sigismund	1410	Eric IX.	1411
Emperors of the East.		Albert II.	1438	Christopher III.	1439
Emanuel II.	1391	Frederick III.	1440	Christian I.	1448
John VII.	1429				
Constantine III.,		*Kings of France.*		*Kings of Scotland.*	
and last Christian		Charles VII.	1452	Robert III.	1390
emperor. Suc-		Louis XI.	1461	James I.	1424
ceeded by his				James II.	1437
conqueror, Ma-		*Kings of Portugal.*		James III.	1460
homet II., who		John 1.	1385		

EMINENT PERSONS.

John Stratford and John Kemp, archbishops of Canterbury. De la Pole, duke of Suffolk. The dukes of Bedford, Gloucester, Exeter, and bishop of Winchester, regents and guardians to the king. Richard, duke of York.

---

their shoes so long that it was necessary to tie them up to their knees with laces or chains to enable them to walk without stumbling; gentlemen used for this purpose chains made of silver, or silver gilt, and others used laces. This ridiculous custom was now (A.D. 1467,) prohibited on the forfeiture of twenty shillings, and the pain of cursing by the clergy. Whatever absurdities in dress may have been rendered fashionable in modern times, certainly none have exceeded this folly of our ancestors.

CHAPTER XIX.

EDWARD IV.

Born 1411. Died April 9th, 1482. Began to reign March 5th, 1461.
Reigned 22 years.

Edward, to each voluptuous vice a slave.
Cruel, intemp'rate, vain, suspicious, brave.—*Egerton.*

1. (A.D. 1478.) EDWARD, being now free from great enemies, turned to the punishment of those of lesser note; so that the gibbets were hung with his adversaries, and their estates confiscated to his use.

Whilst he was rendering himself terrible on the one hand, he was immersed in abandoned pleasures on the other. Nature, it seems, was not unfavourable to him in personal charms; as he was universally allowed to be the handsomest man of his time. 2. His courtiers also seemed willing to encourage those debaucheries in which they had a share; and the clergy, as they themselves practised every kind of lewdness with impunity, were ever ready to lend absolution to all his failings. The truth is, enormous vices had been of late too common.

Among his other cruelties, that to his brother, the duke of Clarence, is the most remarkable. The king, hunting one day in the park of Thomas Burdet, a creature of the duke's, killed a white buck, which was a great favourite of the owner. Burdet, vexed at the loss, broke into a passion, and wished the horns of the deer in the belly of the person who had advised the king to that insult. For this trifling exclamation, Burdet was tried for his life, and publicly executed at Tyburn. 4. The duke of Clarence, upon the death of his friend, vented his grief in renewed reproaches against his brother, and exclaimed against the iniquity of the sentence. The king, highly offended with this liberty, or using that as a pretext against him had him arraigned before the house of peers, and appeared in person as his accuser. 5. In those times of confusion, every crime alleged by the prevailing party was fatal; the duke was found guilty; and, being granted a choice of the manner in which he would die, was privately drowned in a butt of malmsey in the Tower; a whimsical choice, and implying that he had an extraordinary passion for that liquor.

6. However, if this monarch's reign was tyrannical, it was but short; while he was employed in making preparation for a war with France, he was seized with a distemper, of which he expired in the forty-second year of his age, and, counting from the deposition of the late king, in the twenty-third of his reign.

Questions for Examination.

1. What was now the conduct of Edward?
2. For what was Burdet tried and executed?
4. Relate the cruelty of Edward towards his brother?
5. What kind of death did the duke of Clarence prefer?
6. How long did Edward the Fourth reign?

CONTEMPORARY SOVEREIGNS.

Popes.	A.D.		A.D.	*Kings of Denmark and Sweden.*	
Pius II	1458	Bajazet II	1481		
Paul II	1464				A.D.
Sextus IV	1471	*King of France.*		Christian I	1448
		Louis IX	1461	John I	1481
Emperor of Germany.					
Frederic II	1440	*Kings of Portugal.*		*King of Scotland.*	
		Alphonsus V	1438	James III	1469
Emperors of the Turks.		John II	1481		
Mahomet II	1453				

EMINENT PERSONS.

Thomas Borlieur, archbishop of Canterbury: Nevil, earl of Warwick, called the king-maker; Beaufort, duke of Somerset; Richard, duke of Gloucester; Tiptoft, earl of Worcester; William Caxton, mercer of London, the first printer (practiced his art in Westminister abbey, 1471). Jane Shore.

CHAPTER XX.
EDWARD V.

Born 1470. Died June, 1483. Began to reign April 9, 1483. Reigned 8 months.

What's this
That rises like the issue of a king,
And bears upon his baby brow the round
And top of sov'reignty? *Shakespeare.*

1. (A.D. 1483.) THE duke of Gloucester, who had been made protector of the realm, upon a pretence of guarding the persons of the late king's children from danger, conveyed them both to the Tower.

Having thus secured them, his next step was to spread a report of their illegitimacy; and by pretended obstacles, to put off the day appointed for young Edward's coronation. His next aim was to dispatch Lord Hastings, whom he knew to be warmly in the young king's interest.

7. Having summoned Lord Hastings to a council in the Tower, he entered the room knitting his brows, biting his lips, and showing, by a frequent change of countenance, the signs of some inward perturbation. A silence ensued for some time; and the lords of the council looked upon each other, not without reason, expecting some horrid catastrophe. 3. Laying bare his arm, all shrivelled and decayed, he accused Jane Shore and her accomplices of having produced this deformity by their sorceries; upon which Hastings cried, "If they have committed such a crime, they deserve punishment."—"If!" cried the protector, with a loud voice; "dost thou answer me with ifs? I tell thee they have conspired my death; and that thou, traitor, art an accomplice in the crime." 4. He struck the table twice with his hand, and the room was instantly filled with armed men. "I arrest thee," continued he, turning to Hastings, "for high treason;" and at the same time gave him in charge to the soldiers. Hastings was obliged to make a short confession to the next priest that was at hand; the protector crying out, by St. Paul, that he would not dine till he had seen his head taken off. He was accordingly hurried out to the little green before Tower chapel, and there beheaded on a log of wood that accidentally lay in the way.

5. Jane Shore, the late king's favourite, was the next that felt his indignation. This unfortunate woman was an enemy too humble to excite his jealousy: yet, as he had accused her of witchcraft, of which all the world saw she was innocent, he thought proper to make her an example for those faults of which she was really guilty. 6. She had been formerly deluded from her husband, who was a goldsmith in Lombard-street, and continued to live with Edward, the most guiltless favourite in his abandoned court. It was very probable that the people were not displeased at seeing one again reduced to her former meanness who had for a while been raised above them and enjoyed the smiles of a court. 7. The charge against her was too notorious to be denied; she pleaded guilty, and was accordingly condemned to walk barefooted through the city, and to do penance in St Paul's church in a white sheet, with a wax

EDWARD V.

taper in her hand before thousands of spectators. She lived above forty years after this sentence, and was reduced to the most extreme indigence.

8. The Protector now began to throw off the mask, and to deny his pretended regard for the sons of the late king, thinking it high time to aspire to the crown more openly. He had previously gained over the duke of Buckingham, a man of talents and power, by bribes and promises of future favour. This nobleman, therefore, used all his arts to cajole the populace and citizens at St. Paul's cross; and, construing their silence into consent, his followers cried "Long live king Richard!" Soon after, the mayor and aldermen waiting upon Richard with an offer of the crown, he accepted it with seeming reluctance.

Questions for Examination.

1. What was the conduct of the duke of Gloucester towards the young princes?
2. 3. By what vile arts did he get rid of lord Hastings?
5. Who next felt his indignation?
6. Who was Jane Shore?
7. What punishment did she suffer?
8. In what manner did Richard contrive to procure an offer of the crown?

CONTEMPORARY SOVEREIGNS.

Pope. A.D.	*King of France.*	*King of Denmark and Sweden..*
Sextus IV.........1471	A.D.	A.D.
	Charles VIII......1483	John.............1481
Emperor of Germany.		
Frederick III.....1440	*King of Portugal.*	
	John II............1481	*King of Scotland.*
Emperor the Turks.		James III.........1460
Bajazet II.........1481		

EMINENT PERSONS.

Richard, duke of Gloucester, protector. Edward, earl of Warwick; Margaret, countess of Salisbury (children of George, duke of Clarence). Earl Grey. Marquis of Dorset. William Lord Hastings.

CHAPTER XXI.

RICHARD III.

Born 1450. Died Aug. 23, 1485. Began to reign June 27, 1483. Reigned 2 years.

> Tetchy and wayward was his infancy;
> His school-days frightful, desperate, wild, and furious;
> His prime of manhood, daring, bold, and venturous;
> His age confirm'd, proud, subtle, sly, and bloody.—*Shakespeare.*

1.* (A.D. 1483.) ONE crime ever draws on another; justice will revolt against fraud, and usurpation requires security. As soon, therefore, as Richard was seated upon the throne, he sent the governor of the Tower orders to put the two young princes to death; but this brave man, whose name was Brackenbury, refused to be made the instrument of a tyrant's will; but submissively answered, that he knew not how to imbrue his hand in innocent blood. A fit instrument, however, was not long wanting; Sir James Tyrrel readily undertook the office, and Brackenbury was ordered to resign to him the keys for one night. Tyrrel, choosing three associates, Slater, Deighton, and Forest, came in the night-time to the door of the chamber where the princes were lodged, and, sending in the assassins, he bid them execute their commission, while he himself stayed without. They found the young princes in bed, and fallen into a sound sleep: after suffocating them with a bolster and pillows, they showed their naked bodies to Tyrrel, who ordered them to be buried at the stair's foot, deep in the ground under a heap of stones.

3. But while the usurper thus endeavoured to establish his power, he found it threatened in a quarter where he least expected an attack. The duke of Buckingham, who had been instrumental in placing him on the throne, now took disgust, being refused some confiscated lands for which he solicited. He therefore levied a body of men in Wales, and advanced with hasty marches towards Gloucester, where he designed to cross the Severn. 4. Just at that time the river was swollen to such a degree, that the country on both sides was deluged, and even the tops of some hills were covered with water. The inundation continued for ten days; during which Buckingham's army, composed of

---

* See the note at the end of the reign of Henry VII.

Welshmen, could neither pass the river nor find subsistence on their own side; they were therefore obliged to disperse, and return home, notwithstanding all the dukes's efforts to prolong their stay. 5. In this helpless situation, the duke, after a short deliberation, took refuge at the house of one Bannister, who had been his servant, and who had received repeated obligations from his family; but the wicked seldom find, as they seldom exert, friendship. Bannister, unable to resist the temptation of a large reward that was set upon the duke's head, went and betrayed him to the sheriff of Shropshire; who, surrounding the house with armed men, seized the duke, in the habit of a peasant, and conducted him to Salisbury; where he was instantly tried, condemned, and executed, according to the summary method practised in those days.

6. Amidst the perplexity caused by many disagreeable occurrences, the king received information that the earl of Richmond was making preparations to land in England, and assert his claims to the crown. Richard, who knew not in what quarter he might expect the invader, had taken post at Nottingham, in the centre of the kingdom; and had given commission to several of his creatures to oppose the enemy wherever he should land.

7. Some time after, however, the earl of Richmond, who was a descendant from John of Gaunt, by the female line, resolved to strike for the crown. He had been obliged to quit the kingdom; but he now, knowing how odious the king was, set out from Harfleur, in Normandy, with a retinue of about two thousand persons, and, after a voyage of six days, arrived at Milford-Haven in Wales, where he landed without opposition.

8. Upon news of this descent, Richard, who was possessed of courage and military conduct, his only virtues, instantly resolved to meet his antagonist and decide their mutual pretensions by a battle. Richmond, on the other hand, being reinforced by Sir Thomas Bouchier, Sir Walter Hungerford, and others, to the number of about six thousand, boldly advanced with the same intention; and in a few days both armies drew near Bosworth-field,* where the contest that had now for more than forty years filled the kingdom with civil commotions and deluged its plains with blood, was determined by the death of Richard, who was

---

* In Leicestershire. The battle fought at this place was the last of thirteen between the houses of York and Lancaster.

slain in battle: while Richmond was saluted king, by the title of Henry the Seventh.*

Questions for Examination.

1. What was the first act of Richard?
2. In what manner were his orders executed?
3. From what quarter and on what occasion was Richard first threatened?
4. What obliged Buckingham's army to disperse?
5. What was the fate of the duke of Buckingham?
6. With what new opposer did Richard now contend?
7. Where did Richmond land?
8. By whom was he joined?
   Where did the armies meet?
   What was the result of the battle?

CONTEMPORARY SOVEREIGNS.

Popes.	A.D.	King of France.	A.D.	King of Denmark and Sweden.	A.D.
Sextus IV	1471	Charles VIII	1483	John	1481
Innocent VIII	1484				
Emperor of Germany.		*King of Portugal,*		*King of Scotland.*	
Frederick II	1440	John II	1481	James III	1460
Emperor of the Turks.					
Bajazet II	1481				

EMINENT PERSONS.

Henry Tudor, earl of Richmond. Stafford, duke of Buckingham. Vere, earl of Oxford. Thomas, Lord Stanley. Howard, duke of Norfolk. Francis, viscount Lovel. Sir Richard Ratcliffe. Sir William Catesby.

---

* Richard's body, after being exposed, was buried in the church of the Grey Friars, at Leicester. Henry VII. bestowed a monument on it, which was demolished at the dissolution of abbeys under Henry VIII.; and the monarch's stone coffin actually served for a horse trough, at the White Horse Inn. "Sic transit gloria mundi!"

CHAPTER XXII.
HENRY VII.

Born 1456. Died April 22, 1509. Began to reign Aug. 23, 1485. Reigned 23½ years.

SECTION I.

> But oh ! how altered was the mournful tone?
> When Harry Richmond, armed with title true,
> His baldrick 'cross his shoulder flung,
> And with enliv'ning trumpet blew
> A call to arms that through the island rung !
> His claim announcing to the English throne.—*Dibdin.*

1. (A.D. 1485.) HENRY's first care, upon coming to the throne, was to marry the princess Elizabeth, daughter of Edward the Fourth; and thus he blended the interest of the houses of York and Lancaster, so that ever after they were incapable of distinction.

2. A great part of the miseries of his predecessors proceeded from their poverty, which was mostly occasioned by riot and dissipation. Henry saw that money alone could turn the scale of power in his favour; and, therefore, hoarded up all the confiscations of his enemies with the utmost frugality.

Immediately after his marriage with Elizabeth, he issued a general pardon to all such as chose to accept it; but people were become so turbulent and factious, by a long course of civil war, that no governor could rule them, nor any king please; so that one rebellion seemed extinguished only to give rise to another.

3. There lived in Oxford one Richard Simon, a priest, who, possessing some subtlety, and more rashness, trained up Lambert Simnel, a baker's son, to counterfeit the person of the earl of Warwick, the son of the duke of Clarence, who was smothered in a butt of malmsey. But, as the impostor was not calculated to bear a close inspection, it was thought proper to show him first at a distance; and Ireland was judged the fittest theatre for him to support his assumed character.

4. In this manner Simnel, being joined by Lord Lovel, and one or two lords more of the discontented party, resolved to pass over into England; and accordingly landed in Lancashire, whence he marched to York, expecting the country would rise and join him as he marched along. But in this he was deceived; the people, averse to join a body of German and Irish troops, by whom he was sup-

ported, and kept in awe by the king's reputation, remained in tranquillity, or gave all their assistance to the royal cause.

5. The opposite armies met at Stoke, in the county of Nottingham, and fought a battle, which was more bloody, and more obstinately disputed than could have been expected from the inequality of their forces. 6. But a victory at length declared in favour of the king, and it proved decisive. Lord Lincoln perished in the field of battle; Lord Lovel was never more heard of, and it is supposed he shared the same fate. Simnel, with his tutor Simon, were taken prisoners; and four thousand of the common men fell in the battle. Simon, being a priest, could not be tried by the civil power, and was only committed to close confinement. 7. Simnel was too contemptible to excite the king's fear or resentment: he was pardoned, and made a scullion in the king's kitchen, whence he was afterwards advanced to the rank of falconer, in which mean employment he died.

8. A fresh insurrection began in Yorkshire. The people resisting the commissioners who were appointed to levy the taxes, the earl of Northumberland attempted to enforce the king's command; but the populace, being by this taught to believe that he was the adviser of their oppressions, flew to arms, attacked his house, and put him to death. The mutineers did not stop there; but, by the advice of one John Archamber, a seditious fellow of mean appearance, they chose sir John Egremont for their leader, and prepared themselves for a vigorous resistance. 9. The king, upon hearing of this rash proceeding, immediately levied a force which he put under the earl of Surrey; and this nobleman, encountering the rebels, dissipated the tumult, and took their leader, Archamber, prisoner. Archamber was shortly after executed, but sir John Egremont fled to the court of the duchess of Burgundy, the usual retreat of all who were obnoxious to government in England.

10. One would have imagined, that from the ill success of Simnel's imposture, few would be willing to embark in another of a similar kind; however, the old duchess of Burgundy, rather irritated than discouraged by the failure of her past enterprises, was determined to disturb that government which she could not subvert, A. D. 1492. She first procured a report to be spread that the young duke of York, said to have been murdered in the Tower, was still living; and finding the rumour greedily received, she soon

produced a young man who assumed his name and character. 11. The person chosen to sustain this part was one Osbeck, or Warbeck, the son of a converted Jew, who had been over in England during the reign of Edward IV., where he had this son named Peter, but corrupted, after the Flemish manner, into Peterkin, or Perkin. 12. The duchess of Burgundy found this youth entirely suited to her purposes; and her lessons, instructing him to personate the duke of York, were easily learned and strongly retained by a youth of very quick apprehension. In short, his graceful air, his courtly address, his easy manner, and elegant conversation, were capable of imposing upon all but such as were conscious of the imposture.

The English, ever ready to revolt, gave credit to all these absurdities; while the young man's prudence, conversation, and deportment served to confirm what their disaffection and credulity had begun.

13. Among those who secretly abetted the cause of Perkin were lord Fitzwalter, sir Simon Mountford, sir Thomas Thwaits, and sir Robert Clifford. But the person of the greatest weight, and the most dangerous opposition, was sir William Stanley, the lord chamberlain, and brother to the famous lord Stanley, who had contributed to place Henry on the throne. This personage, either moved by a blind credulity, or more probably by a restless ambition, entered into a regular conspiracy against the king; and a correspondence was settled between the malcontents in England and those in Flanders.

14. While this plot was thus carrying on in all quarters, Henry was not inattentive to the designs of his enemies. He spared neither labour nor expense to detect the falsehood of the pretender to his crown; and was equally assiduous in finding out who were his secret abettors. For this purpose he dispersed his spies through all Flanders, and brought over, by large bribes, some of those whom he knew to be in the enemy's interest. 15. Among these, sir Robert Clifford was the most remarkable, both for his consequence, and the confidence with which he was trusted. From this person Henry learnt the whole of Perkin's birth and adventures, together with the names of all those who had secretly combined to assist him. The king was pleased with the discovery; but the more trust he gave to his spies, the higher resentment did he feign against them.

16. At first he was struck with indignation at the ingra-

titude of many of those about him; but concealing his resentment for a proper opportunity, he almost at the same instant arrested Fitzwalter, Mountford, and Thwaits, together with William Danbury, Robert Ratcliff, Thomas Cressenor and Thomas Astwood. All these were arraigned, convicted, and condemned for high treason. Mountford, Ratcliff, and Danbury were immediately executed; the rest received a pardon.

Questions for Examination.

1. What was Henry's first care?
2. What prudent measures did he take to secure his power?
3. Who counterfeited the person of the Earl of Warwick?
4. By whom was Simnel joined?
5, 6. What were the consequences of this rebellion?
7. What became of Simnel?
8. What caused a fresh insurrection? and what was the conduct of the mutineers?
10. What other imposture was now undertaken?
11. Who was chosen to personate the duke of York?
12. Who instructed Perkin to personate him?
13. Who were his abettors?
14, 15. What was Henry's conduct on this occasion?
16. What was the fate of those who opposed the king?

SECTION II.

James backed the cause of that weak prince,
Warbeck that Flemish counterfeit,
Who on the gibbet paid the cheat.—*Scott*.

1. (A. D. 1494.) THE young adventurer, thus finding his hopes frustrated in England, went next to try his fortune in Scotland. In that country his luck seemed greater than in England—James IV., the king of that country, receiving him with great cordiality. He was seduced to believe the story of his birth and adventures; and he carried his confidence so far, as to give him in marriage lady Catherine Gordon, daughter of the earl of Huntley, and a near kinswoman of his own—a young lady eminent for virtue as well as beauty. 2. But not content with these instances of favour, he was resolved to attempt setting him on the throne of England. It was naturally expected that, upon Perkin's first appearance in that kingdom, all the friends of the house of York would rise in his favour. Upon this ground, therefore, the king of Scotland entered England with a numerous army, and proclaimed the young adventurer wherever he went. But Perkin's pretensions, attended

by repeated disappointments, were now become stale, even in the eyes of the populace; so that, contrary to expectation, none were found to second his views.

3. In this manner the restless Perkin, being dismissed Scotland, and meeting with a very cold reception from the Flemings, who now desired to be at peace with the English, resolved to continue his scheme of opposition, and took refuge among the wilds and fastnesses of Ireland. A.D. 1497. Impatient of an inactive life, he held a consultation with his followers, Herne, Skelton, and Astley, three broken tradesmen; and by their advice he resolved to try the affections of the Cornishmen; and he no sooner made his appearance among them at Bodmid, in Cornwall, than the populace, to the number of three thousand, flocked to his standard. 4. Elated with this appearance of success, he took on him, for the first time, the title of Richard the Fourth, king of England; and, not to suffer the spirits of his adherents to languish, he led them to the gates of Exeter. Finding the inhabitants obstinate in refusing to admit him, and being unprovided with artillery to force an entrance, he broke up the siege of Exeter, and retired to Taunton. 5. His followers, by this time, amounted to seven thousand men, and appeared ready to defend his cause; but his heart failed him upon being informed that the king was coming down to oppose him; and instead of bringing his men into the field, he privately deserted them, and took sanctuary in the monastery of Leauheu, in the New Forest. His wretched adherents, left to the king's mercy, found him still willing to pardon; and, except a few of the ringleaders, none were treated with capital severity.

6. At the same time some other persons were employed to treat with Perkin, and to persuade him, under promise of a pardon, to deliver himself up to justice, and to confess and explain all the circumstances of his imposture. His affairs being altogether desperate, he embraced the king's offer without hesitation, and quitted the sanctuary. Henry being desirous of seeing him, he was brought to court, and conducted through the streets of London in a kind of mock triumph, amidst the derision and insults of the populace, which he bore with the most dignified resignation. 7. He was then compelled to sign a confession of his former life and conduct, which was printed and dispersed throughout the nation; but it was so defective and contradictory, that instead of explaining his pretended imposture, it left it still

K

more doubtful than before; and this youth's real pretensions are to this very day an object of dispute among the learned. After attempting once or twice to escape from custody, he was hanged at Tyburn; and several of his adherents suffered the same ignominious death.

8. There had been hitherto nothing in this reign but plots, treasons, insurrections, impostures, and executions; and it is probable that Henry's severity proceeded from the continual alarm in which they held him. It is certain that no prince ever loved peace more than he; and much of the ill-will of his subjects arose from his attempts to repress their inclinations for war. The usual preface to all his treaties was, "That, when Christ came into the world peace was sung; and when he went out of the world, peace was bequeathed."

9. He had all along two points in view; one to depress the nobility and clergy, and the other to exalt and humanise the populace. With this view he procured an act, by which the nobility were granted a power of disposing of their estates; a law infinitely pleasing to the commons, and not disagreeable even to the nobles, since they had thus an immediate resource for supplying their taste for prodigality, and answering the demands of their creditors. The blow reached them in their posterity alone; but they were too ignorant to be affected by such distant distresses.

10. He was not remiss also in abridging the pope's power, while at the same time he professed the utmost submission to his commands, and the greatest respect for the clergy. But while he thus employed his power in lowering the influence of the nobles and clergy, he was using every art to extend the privileges of the people. In fact, his greatest efforts were directed to promote trade and commerce, because they naturally introduced a spirit of liberty, and disengaged them from all dependence, except upon the laws and the king. 11. Before this great era, all our towns owed their origin to some strong castle in the neighbourhood, where some powerful lord generally resided. These were at once fortresses for protection, and prisons for all sorts of criminals. In this castle there was usually a garrison armed and provided, depending entirely on the nobleman's support and assistance. 12. To these seats of protection, artificers, victuallers, and shopkeepers naturally resorted, and settled on some adjacent spot, to furnish the lord and his attendants with all the necessaries they might

require. The farmers, also, and the husbandmen, in the neighbourhood, built their houses there, to be protected against the numerous gangs of robbers, called Robertsmen, that hid themselves in the woods by day, and infested the open country by night. 13. Henry endeavoured to bring the towns from such a neighbourhood, by inviting the inhabitants to a more commercial situation. He attempted to teach them frugality, and a just payment of debts, by his own example; and never once omitted the rights of the merchant, in all his treaties with foreign princes.

14. Henry having seen England, in a great measure, civilized by his endeavours, his people pay their taxes without constraint, the nobles confessing subordination, the laws alone inflicting punishment, the towns beginning to live independent of the powerful, commerce every day increasing, the spirit of faction extinguished, and foreigners either fearing England or seeking its alliance, he began to see the approaches of his end, and died of the gout in his stomach, (A. D. 1509,) having lived fifty-two years, and reigned twenty-three.

The reign of Henry VII. produced so many beneficial changes in the condition of England, and the manners of its people, that many historians have attributed to the monarch a larger share of wisdom and virtue than is justly his due. He was a faithless friend, a bitter enemy, a cruel husband to an amiable consort, an undutiful son to his venerable mother, a careless father, and an ungenerous master. He maintained peace because his avarice disinclined him to the expenses of war; he increased the power of the people through jealousy of the nobles; and he checked the papal encroachments because they interfered with his taxes. Inordinate love of money and unrelenting hatred of the house of York* were his ruling passions, and the chief sources of all his vices and his troubles.

---

* The pretensions of Perkin Warbeck, the last who claimed the crown in right of the house of York, will naturally occur to the reader's mind, and some anxiety will be felt to learn whether he was really an unfortunate prince or a crafty impostor. The latter opinion seems to have prevailed principally on the authority of Shakespeare and Lord Bacon, certainly the two greatest names in our literature, but as certainly witnesses wholly unworthy of credit in the present instance. They wrote to please queen Elizabeth, who was naturally anxious to raise the character of her grandfather Henry VII and depreciate that of his rival Richard III.

The first point to be ascertained is the fact of the murder of the two young princes, and this, which would at once have decided the pretensions of Warbeck, was so far from being proved, that the inquisition taken and published by Henry's command is so full of contradictions and

Questions for Examination.

1. Where next did the young adventurer try his fortune? and what was his success?
3. After his disappointment in Scotland, what was Perkin's future scheme of opposition?
4. What title did Perkin assume?
5. What was his conduct afterwards?
6. In what manner did Henry treat him?
7. Of what nature was his confession, and what his fate?
8. From what cause proceeded Henry's severity? What was his usual preface to his treaties?
9. What were the two points which Henry had always in view, and what plan did he pursue to attain them?
10. How did he abridge the power of the pope?
11, 12 Before this era, what was the state of the towns in England?
13, 14. By what means did Henry civilize his country? When did the king die and what was his character?

CONTEMPORARY SOVEREIGNS.

Popes.	A.D.	Kings of France.	A.D.		A.D.
Innocent VIII.	1484			Emanuel	1495
Alexander VI.	1492	Charles VIII.	1493		
Pius III.	1503	Louis XII.	1498	*King of Denmark and*	
Julius III.	1503			*Sweden.*	
		King & Queen of Spain		John	1481
Emperors of Germany.		Ferdinand * the			
Frederick II.	1440	Catholic, and		*Kings of Scotland,*	
Maximilian I.	1493	Isabella	1475	James III	1460
				James IV	1489
Emperor of the Turks.		*Kings of Portugal.*			
Bajazet II.	1481	John	1481		

palpable absurdities, that Henry himself never made use of it in any of his later declarations. Besides, the persons who were said to have confessed the murder were never brought to trial for the crime.

The next evidence brought forward on the side of Henry is the confession extorted from Warbeck after he was made prisoner. Like the former, it bears internal evidence of its own falsehood, though the unfortunate young man is said to have repeated it at the time of his death.

On the other side we have the evidence of the duchess of Burgundy, who could have had no possible motive for joining in such a foul conspiracy against the husband of her own neice; and to say nothing of a host of friends of the house of York, we have the negative evidence of the dowager-queen, whom Henry kept in close confinement from the moment of Warbeck's appearance. To have brought him into her presence would at once have set the question at rest, for surely the mother would have known whether it was her son or not that stood before her. But Henry took especial care to prevent such an interview; and the inference is, that he had just reason to dread that its consequences would be a confirmation of Warbeck's pretensions.—T.

* Till this period, Spain had been divided into three different governments, viz. Leon, Castile and Arragon, under distinct sovereigns; but by the marriage of Ferdinand and Isabella, heiress of Castile and Arragon, the whole was united in one kingdom.

EMINENT PERSONS.

John Morton, Henry Chicheley, Thomas Langton, archbishop of Canterbury. Margaret, countess of Richmond, mother of the king. Cardinal Morton, lord chancellor. Fox, bishop of Winchester. Sebastian Cabot, a great navigator. Epson and Dudley, extortionate ministers of the king.

CHAPTER XXIII.

HENRY VIII.

Born 1491. Died January 28, 1547. Began to reign April 22, 1509, reigned 37½ years.

SECTION I.

*Now Henry reigns, to learning much inclin'd,
But of strong passions and a savage mind.—Egerton.*

1. (A.D. 1509.) No prince ever came to the throne with a conjuncture of circumstances more in his favour than Henry the Eighth, who now, in the eighteenth year of his age, undertook the Government of the kingdom. As he was at the head of a formidable army, fifty thousand strong, and as a war with France was the most pleasing to the people, he determined to head his forces for the conquest of that kingdom. 2. But France was not threatened by him alone; the Swiss, in another quarter, with twenty-five thousand men were preparing to invade it; while Ferdinand of Arragon, whom no treaties could bind, was only waiting for a convenient opportunity of attack on his side to advantage. Never was the French monarchy in so distressed a situation; but the errors of its assailants procured its safety. 3. After an ostentatious but ineffectual campaign, a truce was concluded between the two kingdoms; and Henry continued to dissipate, in more peaceful follies, those immense sums which had been amassed by his predecessor for very different purposes.

4. In this manner, while his pleasures on the one hand engrossed Henry's time, the preparations for repeated expeditions exhausted his treasures on the other. As it was natural to suppose the old ministers, who were appointed by his father, to direct him, would not willingly concur in these idle projects, Henry had, for some time, discontinued asking their advice, and chiefly confided in the counsels of

Thomas, afterwards Cardinal Wolsey, who seemed to second him in his favourite pursuits. 5. Wolsey was a minister who complied with all his master's inclinations, and flattered him in every scheme to which his sanguine and impetuous temper was inclined. He was the son of a private gentleman at Ipswich. He was sent to Oxford so early, that he was a bachelor at fourteen, and at that time was called the boy bachelor. He rose by degrees, upon quitting college, from one preferment to another, till he was made rector of Lymington by the marquis of Dorset, whose children he had instructed. 6. He was soon recommended as chaplain to Henry the Seventh; and being employed by that monarch in a secret negociation respecting his intended marriage with Margaret of Savoy, he acquitted himself to the king's satisfaction, and obtained the praise both of diligence and dexterity. 7. That prince, having given him a commission to Maximilian, who at that time resided at Brussels, was surprised in less than three days to see Wolsey present himself before him; and supposing he had been delinquent, began to reprove this delay. Wolsey, however, surprised him with an assurance that he had just returned from Brussels, and had successfully fulfilled all his majesty's commands. 8. His despatch on that occasion procured him the deanery of Lincoln; and in this situation it was that he was introduced by Fox, bishop of Winchester, to the young king's notice, in hopes that he would have talents to supplant the earl of Surrey, who was the favourite at that time; and in this Fox was not out in his conjectures. Presently after being introduced at court, he was made a privy councillor; and as such had frequent opportunities of ingratiating himself with the young king, as he appeared at once complying, submissive, and entreprising. 9. Wolsey used every art to suit himself to the royal temper; he sung, laughed, and danced with every libertine of the court; neither his own years, which were nearly forty, nor his character as a clergyman, were any restraint upon him, or tended to check by ill-timed severities the gayety of his companions. To such a weak and vicious monarch as Henry, qualities of this nature were highly pleasing; and Wolsey was soon acknowledged as the chief favourite, and to him was intrusted the chief administration of affairs.

10. The people began to see with indignation the new favourite's mean condescensions to the king, and his arrogance to themselves. They had long regarded the vicious

haughtiness and the unbecoming splendour of the clergy with envy and detestation; and Wolsey's greatness served to bring a new odium upon that body, already too much the object of the people's dislike. His character, being now placed in a more conspicuous point of light, daily began to manifest itself the more. 11. Insatiable in his acquisitions, but still more magnificent in his expense; of extensive capacity, but still more unbounded in enterprise; ambitious of power, but still more desirous of glory; insinuating, engaging, persuasive, and at other times lofty, elevated, and commanding; haughty to his equals, but affable to his dependents; oppressive to the people, but liberal to his friends; more generous than grateful; formed to take the ascendant in every intercourse, but vain enough not to cover his real superiority.

12. In order to divert the envy of the public from his inordinate exaltation, he soon entered into a correspondence with Francis the First of France, who had taken many methods to work upon his vanity, and at last succeeded. In consequence of that monarch's wishes, Henry was persuaded by the cardinal to an interview with that prince. This expensive congress was held between Guines and Andres, near Calais, within the English pale, in compliment to Henry for crossing the sea.

Question for Examination.

1. What combination of circumstances favoured Henry the Eighth on coming to the throne?
3. What was the conduct of Henry after the truce with France?
4. In what counsels did Henry chiefly confide?
5. Whose son was Cardinal Wolsey?
6. What disgraceful circumstance happened to Wolsey?
7. 8. What circumstance led to Wolsey's advancement?
9. What were the arts used by Wolsey to please the king?
10. What were the consequences?
11. In what manner did Wolsey's character now manifest itself?
12. With whom did he enter into a correspondence?

SECTION II.

At Guines, where France and England met
In dazzling panoply of gold.—*Dibdin.*

1. (A. D. 1520.) SOME months before, a defiance had been sent by the two kings to each other's court, and through all the chief cities of Europe, importing that Henry and

Francis, with fourteen aids, would be ready in the plains of Picardy to answer all comers, that were gentlemen, at tilt and tournay.* Accordingly, the monarchs, now all gorgeously apparelled, entered the lists on horseback, Francis surrounded with Henry's guards, and Henry with those of Francis. 2. They were both at that time the most comely personages of their age, and prided themselves on their expertness in military exercises. The ladies were the judges in these feats of chivalry, and they put an end to the encounter whenever they thought proper. In these martial exercises, the crafty French monarch gratified Henry's vanity by allowing him to enjoy a petty pre eminence in these pastimes.

3. By this time all the immense treasures of the late king were quite exhausted on empty pageants, guilty pleasures, or vain treaties, or expeditions. But the king relied on Wolsey alone for replenishing his coffers; and no person could be fitter for the purpose. 4. His first care was to get a large sum of money from the people, under the title of a benevolence; which, added to its being extorted, had the mortification of being considered as a free gift. Henry little minded the manner of its being raised, provided he had the enjoyment of it; however, his minister met with some opposition in his attempts to levy these extorted contributions. In the first place, having exacted a considerable sum from the clergy, he next addressed himself to the house of commons: but they only granted him half the supplies he demanded. 5. Wolsey was at first highly offended at their parsimony, and desired to be heard in the house; but as this would have destroyed the very form and constitution of that august body, they replied, that none could be permitted to sit and argue there but such as had been elected members. This was the first attempt made in this reign to render the king master of the debates in parliament. Wolsey first paved the way, and, unfortunately for the kingdom, Henry too well improved upon his plans soon after.

6. Hitherto the administration of all affairs was carried on by Wolsey; for the king was contented to lose, in the embraces of his mistresses, all the complaints of his subjects; and the cardinal undertook to keep him ignorant in order to continue his uncontrolled authority. But now a period was approaching that was to put an end to this

* This game was instituted by Henry I. of Germany, A.D. 919, and abolished in 1560.

minister's exorbitant power. One of the most extraordinary and important revolutions that ever employed the attention of man was now ripe for execution. This was no less a change than the Reformation. 7. The vices and impositions of the church of Rome were now almost come to a head; and the increase of arts and learning among the laity, propagated by means of printing, which had been lately invented, began to make them resist that power, which was originally founded on deceit. (A. D. 1519.) Leo the Tenth was at that time pope, and eagerly employed in building the church of St. Peter, at Rome. In order to procure money for carrying on that expensive undertaking, he gave a commission for selling indulgences, a practice that had often been tried before. 8. These were to free the purchaser from the pains of purgatory; and they would serve even for one's friends, if purchased with that intention. The Augustine friars* had usually been employed in Saxony, to preach the indulgences, and from this trust had derived both profit and consideration; but the pope's minister, supposing that they had found out illicit methods of secreting the money, transferred this lucrative employment from them to the Dominicans.† 9. Martin Luther, professor in the university of Wirtemberg, was an Augustine monk, and one of those who resented this transfer of the sale of indulgences from one order to another. He began to shew his indignation by preaching against their efficacy; and being naturally of a fiery temper, and provoked by opposition, he inveighed against the authority of the pope himself. Being driven hard by his adversaries, still as he enlarged his reading, in order to support his tenets, he discovered some new abuse or error in the church of Rome. 10. In this dispute, it was the fate of Henry to be champion on both sides. His father, who had given him the education of a scholar, permitted him to be instructed in school divinity, which then was the principal object of learned inquiry. Henry, therefore, willing to convince the world of his abilities in that science, obtained the pope's permission to read the works of Luther, which

---

* They observed the rule of St. Augustine, prescribed them by pope Alexander IV. in 1256. This rule was, to have all things in common; the rich, who entered among them, were compelled to sell their possessions and give them to the poor.

† In some places called jacobins, and in others predicants, or preaching friars; they were obliged to take a vow of absolute poverty, and to abandon entirely their revenues and possessions.

had been forbidden under pain of excommunization. 11. In consequence of this, the king defended the seven sacraments, out of St. Thomas Aquinas; and shewed some dexterity in this science, though it is thought that Wolsey had the chief hand in directing him. A book being thus finished in haste, it was sent to Rome for the pope's approbation, which it was natural to suppose would not be withheld. The pontiff, ravished with its eloquence and depth, compared it to the labours of St. Jerome, or St. Augustine, and rewarded the author of it with the title of DEFENDER OF THE FAITH; little imagining that Henry was soon to be one of the most terrible enemies that ever the church of Rome had to contend with.

Questions for Examination.

1, 2. Relate the particulars of the congress that took place in the plains of Picardy.
3. In what manner were the late king's treasures exhausted?
4. How were the king's coffers replenished?
5. What was the first attempt made to render the king master of the debates in parliament?
6. Why did Wolsey endeavour to keep the king ignorant of the complaints of his subjects?
7. What practices led to the Reformation?
9. In what manner did Luther oppose the transfer of the sale of indulgences?
10, 11. What was the king's conduct on this occasion, and what was his reward?

SECTION III.

When thunderstruck, that eagle Wolsey fell.—*Young*.

1. (A. D. 1527.) Henry had now been eighteen years married to Catharine of Arragon, who had been brought over from Spain, and married to his eldest brother, who died a few months after. But, notwithstanding the submissive deference paid for the indulgence of the church, Henry's marriage with this princess did not pass without scruple and hesitation, both on his own side and on that of the people. 2. However, his scruples were carried forward, though perhaps not at first excited by a motive much more powerful than the tacit suggestion of his conscience. It happened that among the maids of honour then attending the queen, there was one Anna Bullen, the daughter of sir Thomas Bullen, a gentleman of distinction, and related to most of the nobility. He had been employed by the king

in several embassies, and was married to a daughter of the duke of Norfolk. 3. The beauty of Anna surpassed whatever had hitherto appeared at this voluptuous court; and her education, which she had received at Paris, set off her personal charms. Henry, who had never learned the art of restraining any passion that he desired to gratify, saw and loved her; but, of course, could not marry her without previously divorcing his wife, queen Catharine of Arragon. 4. This obstacle, therefore, he hardly undertook to remove; and as his own queen was now become hateful to him, in order to procure a divorce, he alleged that his conscience rebuked him for having so long been married to the wife of his brother. In this pretended perplexity, therefore, he applied to Clement the Seventh, who owed him many obligations, desiring him to dissolve the bull of the former pope, which had given him permission to marry Catherine; and to declare that it was not in the power even of the holy see, to dispense with the law so strictly enjoined in Scripture. 5. The unfortunate pope, unwilling to grant, yet afraid to refuse, continued to promise, recant, dispute, and temporize; hoping that the king's passion would never hold out during the tedious course of an ecclesiastical controversy. In this he was entirely mistaken. Henry had been long taught to dispute as well as he, and quickly found or wrested many texts in Scripture to favour his opinions, or his passions. 6. During the course of a long perplexing negotiation, on the issue of which Henry's happiness seemed to depend, he had at first expected to find in his favourite Wolsey a warm defender and a steady adherent: but in this he found himself mistaken. Wolsey seemed to be in pretty much the same dilemma with the pope. On the one hand, he was to please his master the king, from whom he had received a thousand marks of favour; and on the other hand, he feared to disoblige the pope, whose servant he more immediately was, and who, besides, had power to punish his disobedience. 7. He therefore, resolved to continue neuter in the controversy; and, though of all men the most haughty, he gave way on this occasion to Campeggio the pope's nuncio, in all things, pretending a deference to his skill in canon law. Wolsey's scheme of temporizing was highly displeasing to the king; but for a while he endeavoured to stifle his resentment, until he could act with more fatal certainty. He for some time looked out for a man of equal abilities and less art; and it was not long before accident threw in his way one Thomas Cranmer, of greater talents, and probably of more integrity.

8. Thus finding himself provided with a person who could supply Wolsey's place, he appeared less reserved in his resentments against that prelate. The attorney-general was ordered to prepare a bill of indictment against him; and he was soon after commanded to resign the great seal. Crimes are easily found out against a favourite in disgrace, and the courtiers did not fail to increase the catalogue of his errors. He was ordered to depart from York place palace; and all his furniture and plate were converted to the king's use. 9. The inventory of his goods being taken, they were found to exceed even the most extravagant surmises. He was soon after arrested by the earl of Northumberland, at the king's command, for high treason, and preparations were made for conducting him from York, where he then resided, to London, in order to take his trial. 10. He at first refused to comply with the requisition, as being a cardinal; but finding the earl bent on performing his commission, he complied, and set out by easy journeys to London, to appear as a criminal, where he had acted as a king. In his way he stayed a fortnight at the earl of Shrewsbury's; where one day, at dinner, he was taken ill, not without violent suspicions of having poisoned himself. Being brought forward from thence, he with much difficulty reached Leicester abbey; where the monks coming out to meet him, he said, "Father Abbot, I am come to lay my bones among you:" and immediately ordered his bed to be prepared. 11. As his disorder increased, an officer being placed near him, at once to guard and attend him, he spoke to him a little before he expired to this effect: "Had I but served God as diligently as I have served the king, he would not have given me over in my gray hairs. But this is the just reward I must receive for my indulgent pains and study; not regarding my service to God, but only to my prince." He died soon after, in all the pangs of remorse, and left a life which had all along been rendered turbid by ambition, and wretched by mean assiduities.

12. The tie that held Henry to the church being thus broken, he resolved to keep no farther measures with the pontiff. He, therefore, privately married Anna Bullen, whom he had created marchioness of Pembroke; the duke of Norfolk, uncle to the new queen, her father, and Dr.

Death of Queen Catharine of Arragon.

Cranmer, being present at the ceremony. Soon after, circumstances compelled him publicly to own his marriage; and, to cover his disobedience to the pope with an appearance of triumph, he passed with his beautiful bride through London with a magnificence greater than had ever been known before. But though Henry had thus seceded from the church, yet he had not addicted himself to the system of the reformers.

13. As the monks had all along shown him the greatest resistance, he resolved at once to deprive them of future power to injure him. He accordingly empowered Thomas Cromwell, who was now made secretary of state, to send commissioners into the several counties of England to inspect the monasteries, and to report with rigorous exactness the conduct and deportment of such as were resident there. This employment was readily undertaken by some creatures of the court, namely, Layton, London, Price, Gage, Peter, and Bellasis, who are said to have discovered monstrous disorders in many of the religious houses. The accusations, whether true or false, were urged with great clamour against these communities, and a general horror was excited in the nation against them.

14. Queen Catharine of Arragon, Henry's first wife lived in retirement after her divorce until her decease. She was one of the brightest characters of English history. Her character and death are admirably depicted by Shakspeare.

Questions for Examination.

1. Who was Henry's first wife?
2. Whom did he afterwards wish to obtain?
3. What description is given of Anna Bullen?
4. What pretence did Henry allege to procure a divorce?
5. What was the conduct of the pope?
6. What were the circumstances which put an end to Wolsey's power?
8. In what manner did the king act towards him?
9. What account is given of the inventory of his goods?
10. What circumstances preceded the death of Wolsey?
11. Relate Wolsey's expression immediately before his death.
12. What followed Wolsey's death?
13. What commission did the king give to Cromwell?
14. What is said of queen Catharine?

SECTION IV.

*Tyrannic cruelty, voluptuous pride,
Insatiable licentiousness and guilt,
So share this monarch, we can ne'er decide
On what one vice his ruling wish was built.*—*Dibdin.*

1. (A.D. 1536.) A NEW visitation of the religious houses was soon after appointed, and fresh crimes were also produced; so that his severities were conducted with such seeming justice and success, that in less than two years he became possessed of all monastic revenues. These, on the whole, amounted to six hundred and forty-five, of which twenty-eight had abbots who enjoyed a seat in parliament. Ninety colleges were demolished in several counties; two thousand three hundred and seventy-four chantries and free chapels, and a hundred and ten hospitals. 2. The whole revenue of these establishments amounted to one hundred and sixty-one thousand pounds, which was about the twentieth part of the national income. But as great murmurs were excited by some on this occasion, Henry took care that all those who could be useful to him, or even dangerous in case of opposition, should be sharers in the spoil. He either made a gift of the revenues of the convents to his principal courtiers, or sold them at low prices, or exchanged them for other lands on very disadvantageous terms.

3. Henry's opinions were at length delivered in a law, which, from its horrid consequences, was afterwards termed the Bloody Statute; by which it was ordained, that whoever, by word or writing, denied transubstantiation, whoever maintained that the communion in both kinds was necessary, whoever asserted that it was lawful for priests to marry, whoever alleged that vows of chastity might be broken, whoever maintained that private masses were unprofitable, or that auricular confession was unnecessary, should be found

guilty of heresy and burned or hanged as the court should determine. 4. As the people were at that time chiefly composed of those who followed the opinions of Luther, and such as still adhered to the pope, this statute, with Henry's former decrees, in some measure included both, and opened a field for persecution, which soon after produced its dreadful harvests. Bainham and Bilney were burned for their opposition to popery. Sir Thomas More and bishop Fisher were beheaded for denying the king's supremacy.

5. These severities, however, were preceded by one of a different nature, arising neither from religious nor political causes, but merely from a tyrannical caprice. Anna Bullen, his queen, had always been favourable to the Reformation, and consequently had many enemies on that account, who only waited some fit occasion to destroy her credit with the king, and that occasion presented itself but too soon. 6. The king's passion was by this time abated, and he became as desirous to divorce the queen as he had formerly been to marry her. He was now fallen in love, if we may so prostitute the expression, with another, and was desirous to marry Jane Seymour, who had for some time been maid of honor to the queen.

7. In the meantime her enemies were not remiss in raising an accusation against her. The duke of Norfolk, from his attachment to the old religion, took care to produce several witnesses, accusing her of impropriety with some of the meaner servants of the court. Four persons were particularly pointed out as her favourites; Henry Norris, groom of the stole; Weston and Breton, gentlemen of the king's bed chamber; together with Mark Smeaton, a musician. 8. Accordingly, soon after, Norris, Weston, Breton, and Smeaton were tried in Westminster-hall; when Smeaton was prevailed upon, by the promise of a pardon, to confess a criminal correspondence with the queen; but he was never confronted with her he accused; and his execution with the rest, shortly after, served to acquit her of the charge. 9. Norris, who had been much in the king's favour, had an offer of his life if he would confess his crime, and accuse his mistress; but he rejected the proposal with contempt, and died professing her innocence and his own. The queen and her brother were tried by a jury of peers; but upon what proof or pretence the crime was urged against them is unknown: the cheif evidence, it is said, amounted to no more than that Rochford had been seen to lean on her

bed before some company. 10. Part of the charge against her was, that she had declared to her attendants that the king never had her heart: which was considered as a slander upon the throne, and strained into a breach of law by statute, by which it was declared criminal to throw any slander upon the king, queen, or their issue. The unhappy queen, though unassisted by council, defended herself with great judgment and presence of mind: and the spectators could not forbear declaring her entirely innocent. 11. She answered distinctly to all the charges brought against her: but the king's authority was not to be controlled; she was declared guilty and her sentence ran that she should be burned or beheaded at the king's pleasure. On the morning of her execution, her sentence being mitigated into beheading, she sent for Kingstone, the keeper of the Tower, to whom, upon entering the prison, she said, "Mr. Kingstone, I hear I am not to die till noon, and I am sorry for it; for I thought to be dead before this time, and free from a life of pain." 12. The keeper attempting to comfort her by assuring her the pain would be very little, she replied, "I have heard the executioner is very expert; and (clasping her neck with her hands, laughing) I have but a little neck." When brought to the scaffold, from a consideration of her child Elizabeth's welfare, she would not inflame the minds of the spectators against her persecutors, but contented herself with saying that "she was come to die as she was sentenced by the law." 13. She would accuse none, nor say anything of the ground upon which she was judged; she prayed heartily for the king, and called him a most merciful and gentle prince; that he had always been to her a good and gracious sovereign; and if that any one should think proper to canvass her cause, she desired him to judge the best." She was beheaded by the executioner of Calais, who was brought over, as much more expert than any in England. 14. The very next day after her execution he married the lady Jane Seymour, his cruel heart being no way softened by the wretched fate of one that had been so lately the object of his warmest affections. He also ordered his parliament to give him a divorce between her sentence and execution, and thus endeavoured to render Elizabeth, the only child he had by her, illegitimate, as he had in the same manner, formerly, Mary, his only child by queen Catherine.

HENRY VIII.

Questions for Examination.

1. What monastic revenues now came into the king's possession?
2. What was the amount of these revenues?
3. What were the opinions of Henry?
4. What were the horrid consequences?
5. What tyrannical act preceded these severities?
7. Relate the charges alleged against Anna Bullen.
9. What is said to have been the chief evidence against her?
10. What strange charge was brought against her?
11. What was her behaviour at the trial?
12, 13. What at her execution?
14. In what manner did the king act after her execution?

SECTION V.

*Superior Cranmer, in a crowd alone,
Dares friendship with the virtuous fallen own.—Dibdin.*

1. (A.D. 1537.) In the midst of these commotions the fires of Smithfield were seen to blaze with unusual fierceness. Those who adhered to the pope, or those who followed the doctrines of Luther, were equally the objects of royal vengeance and ecclesiastical persecution. From the multiplied alterations which were made in the national systems of belief, mostly drawn up by Henry himself, few knew what to think, or what to profess. 2. They were ready enough to follow his doctrines, how inconsistent or contradictory soever; but, as he was continually changing them himself, they could hardly pursue so fast as he advanced before them. Thomas Cromwell, raised by the king's caprice from being a blacksmith's son to be a royal favourite (for tyrants ever raise their favourites from the lowest of the people), together with Cranmer, now become archbishop of Canterbury, were both seen to favour the Reformation with all their endeavours. 3. On the other hand, Gardiner, bishop of Winchester, together with the duke of Norfolk, were for leading the king back to his original faith. In fact, Henry submitted to neither; his pride had long been so inflamed by flattery, that he thought himself entitled to regulate, by his own single opinion, the religious faith of the whole nation.

4. Soon after, no less than five hundred persons were imprisoned for contradicting the opinions delivered in the Bloody Statute, and received protection only from the lenity of Cromwell. Lambert, a schoolmaster, and doctor Barnes, who had been instrumental in Lambert's execution, felt the

L

severity of the persecuting spirit; and, by a bill in parliament, without any trial, were condemned to the flames, discussing theological questions at the very stake. With Barnes were executed one Gerrard, and Jerome, for the same opinions. Three Catholics also, whose names were Abel, Featherstone, and Powel, were dragged upon the same hurdles to execution; and who declared that the most grievous part of their punishment was the being coupled with such heretical miscreants as were united in the same calamity.

5. During these horrid transactions, Henry was resolved to take another queen, Jane Seymour having died; and after some negotiations upon the continent, he contracted marriage with Anne of Cleves, his aim being, by her means, to fortify his alliance with the princes of Germany. 6. His aversion, however, to the queen secretly increased every day; and he at length resolved to get rid of her and his prime minister together. He had a strong cause of dislike to him for his late unpropitious alliance; and a new motive was soon added for increasing his displeasure. Henry had fixed his affection on Catharine Howard, niece to the duke of Norfolk; and the only method of gratifying this new passion was, as in the former cases, discarding the present queen to make room for a new one. The duke of Norfolk had long been Cromwell's mortal enemy, and eagerly embraced this opportunity to destroy a man he considered as his rival. 7. He therefore made use of all his niece's arts to ruin the favourite; and when this project was ripe for execution, he obtained a commission from the king to arrest Cromwell for high-treason. His disgrace was no sooner known, than all his friends forsoook him, except Cranmer, who wrote such a letter to Henry in his behalf, as no other man in the kingdom would have presumed to offer. However, he was accused in parliament of heresy and treason; and without even being heard in his own defence, condemned to suffer the pains of death, as the king should think proper to direct. 8. When he was brought to the scaffold his regard for his son hindered him from expatiating upon his own innocence. He thanked God for bringing him to death for his transgressions; confessed he had often been seduced, but that he now died in the Catholic faith.

But the measure of Henry's severities was not yet filled up. He had thought himself very happy in his new marriage. He was so captivated with the queen's accomplishments, that he gave public thanks for his felicity, and desired his confessor to join with him in the same thanksgiving. 9. This joy, however, was of very short duration. While the king was at York, upon an intended conference with the king of Scotland, a man of the name of Lassels waited upon Cranmer at London; and, from the information of his sister, who had been servant to the duchess-dowager of Norfolk, he gave a very surprising account of the queen's criminality. When the queen was first examined relative to her crime, she denied the charge; but afterwards, finding that her accomplices were her accusers, she confessed her crime in part, but denied some of the circumstances. 10. Three maids of honour, who were admitted to her secrets, still further alleged her guilt; and some of them made such confessions as tended to augment the nature of her crime. The servile parliament, upon being informed of the queen's crime and confession, quickly found her guilty, and petitioned the king that she might be punished with death; that the same penalty might be inflicted on the lady Rochford, her friend and confidant; and that her grandmother, the duchess-dowager of Norfolk, together with her father, mother, and nine others, men and women, as having been privy to the queen's irregularities, should participate in her punishment. With this petition the king was most graciously pleased to agree; they were condemned to death by an act of attainder, which at the same time, made it capital for all persons to conceal their knowledge of the criminality of any future queen. 11. The queen was beheaded on Tower-hill, together with the lady Rochford, who found no great degree of compassion, as she had herself before tampered in blood.

Questions for Examination.

1. What cruel persecution followed the multiplied alterations in the national belief?
2. Who favoured the Reformation;
3. Who endeavoured to lead the king back to popery?
5. Upon whom did Henry fix his affections?
6. What caused Henry's dislike to Cromwell? and what was the consequence?

9. In what manner was the king informed of the criminality of his queen?
10. Who were the witnesses that alleged her guilt?
11. What was the fate of the queen?

SECTION VI.

*I would not have such a heart in my bosom
For the dignity of the whole body.*—*Shakspeare.*

1. (A. D. 1543.) In about a year after the death of the last queen, Henry once more changed his condition, by marrying his sixth and last wife, Catharine Parr, who was a widow. She was the widow of the late lord Latimer; and was considered as a woman of discretion and virtue. She had already passed the meridian of life, and managed this capricious tyrant's temper with prudence and success.

2. Still, however, the king's severity to his subjects continued as fierce as ever. For some time he had been incommoded by an ulcer in his leg; the pain of which, added to his corpulence and other infirmities, increased his natural irascibility to such a degree, that scarcely any of his domestics approached him without terror. It was not to be expected, therefore, that any who differed from him in opinion should, at this time particularly, hope for pardon.

3. Though his health was declining apace, yet his implacable cruelties were not the less frequent. His resentment was diffused indiscriminately to all; at one time a protestant, and at another a catholic, were the objects of his severity. The duke of Norfolk, and his son, the earl of Surrey, were the last that felt the injustice of the tyrant's groundless suspicions. 4. The duke was a nobleman who had served the king with talent and fidelity; his son was a young man of the most promising hopes, who excelled in every accomplishment that became a scholar, a courtier, and a soldier. He excelled in all the military exercises which were then in request; he encouraged the fine arts by his practice and example; and it is remarkable that he was the first who brought our language, in his poetical pieces, to any degree of refinement. 5. He celebrated the fair Geraldine in all his sonnets, and maintained her superior beauty in all places of public contention. These

qualifications, however, were no safeguard to him against Henry's suspicions; he had dropped some expressions of resentment against the king's ministers, upon being displaced from the government of Bologne; and the whole family was become obnoxious from the late conduct of Catharine Howard the queen, who was executed. 6. From these motives, therefore, private orders were given to arrest father and son; and accordingly they were arrested both on the same day and confined in the Tower. Surrey being a commoner, his trial was the more expeditious; and as to proofs, there were many informers base enough to betray the intimacies of private confidence, and all the connections of blood. The duchess-dowager of Richmond, Surrey's own sister, enlisted herself among the number of his accusers; and sir Richard Southwell, also, his most intimate friend, charged him with infidelity to the king. 7. It would seem that at this dreary period, there was neither faith nor honour to be found in all the nation. Surrey denied the charge, and challenged his accuser to single combat. This favour was refused him; and it was alleged that he had quartered the arms of Edward the Confessor on his escutcheon, which alone was sufficient to convict him of aspiring to the crown. To this he could make no reply; and indeed any answer would have been needless; for neither parliaments nor juries, during this reign, seemed to be guided by any other proofs but the will of the crown. 8. This young nobleman was, therefore, condemned for high treason, notwithstanding his eloquent and spirited defence; and the sentence was soon after executed upon him on Tower-hill. In the meantime the duke endeavoured to mollify the king by letters of submission; but the monster's hard heart was rarely subject to tender impressions. 9. The parliament meeting on the fourteenth day of January (A.D. 1546), a bill of attainder was found against the duke of Norfolk; as it was thought he could not so easily have been convicted on a fair hearing by his peers. The death-warrant was made out, and immediately sent to the lieutenant of the Tower. The duke prepared for death; the following morning was to be his last; but an event of greater consequence to the kingdom intervened, and prevented his execution.

10. The king had been for some time approaching fast towards his end; and for several days all those about his person plainly saw that his speedy death was inevitable,

The disorder in his leg was now grown extremely painful; and this, added to his monstrous corpulency, which rendered him unable to stir, made him more furious than a chained lion. He had been very stern and severe; he was now outrageous. In this state he had continued for nearly four years before his death, the terror of all, and the tormentor of himself; his courtiers having no inclination to make an enemy of him, as they were more ardently employed in conspiring the death of each other.* 11. In this manner, therefore, he was suffered to struggle, without any of his domestics having the courage to warn him of his approaching end; as more than once, during this reign, persons had been put to death for foretelling the death of the king. At last, sir Anthony Denny had the courage to disclose to him this dreadful secret; and, contrary to his usual custom, he received the tidings with an expression of resignation. 12. His anguish and remorse were at this time greater than can be expressed; he desired that Cranmer might be sent for; but before that prelate could arrive he was speechless. Cranmer desired him to give some sign of his dying in the faith of Christ; he squeezed his hand and immediately expired, after a reign of thirty-seven years and nine months, in the fifty-sixth year of his age.

13. Some kings have been tyrants from contradiction and revolt; some from being misled by favourites; and some from a spirit of party; but Henry was cruel from a

*The irritability of the king was so ungovernable, that many fell victims to it; and his queen, who constantly attended him with the most tender and dutiful care, had also, as will be seen by the following account, nearly fallen a sacrifice. Henry's favourite topic of conversation was theology, and Catharine had unwarily ventured to raise objections against his arguments. Henry, highly provoked that she should presume to differ from his opinion, complained of her obstinacy to Gardiner, bishop of Winchester, the chancellor, who inflamed his anger by representing the queen as a dangerous heretic. Hurried by their insinuations, he went so far as to direct the chancellor to draw up aricles of impeachment, which he besigned. This paper fortunately fell into the hands of one of the queen's friends, who immediately carried the intelligence to her. Next morning she paid her usual visit to the king, and finding him disposed to challenge her to an argument on divinity, she modestly declined the conversation, saying, that it did not become a weak woman to dispute with one, who, by his superior learning, was entitled to dictate, not only to her, but to the whole world; and that if ever she had ventured to object to anything he advanced, it was only for the sake of her own instruction, and to engage him upon topics which diverted his pains. This seasonable piece of flattery suddenly revived his affections, and the chancellor coming soon after, with a numerous escort, to seize the queen and carry her to the Tower, the king treated him very roughly, calling him knave, fool, and beast, and commanded him to be gone.—*De Moleville's Great Britain.*

depraved disposition alone; cruel in government, cruel in religion, and cruel in his family. Our divines have taken some pains to vindicate the character of this brutal prince, as if his conduct and our Reformation had any connexion with each other. There is nothing so absurd as to defend the one by the other; the most noble designs are brought about by the most vicious instruments: for we see even that cruelty and injustice were thought necessary to be employed in our holy redemption.

Questions for Examination.

1. To whom was the king now married?
2. What at this time increased the king's irascibility?
3. Who were the last who felt this severity?
4. 5. What character is given of the earl of Surrey?
6. Who appeared among the number of Surrey's accusers?
7. What was the chief charge alleged against this nobleman?
8. Where was he executed?
9. What was the fate of his father, duke of Norfolk?
10. What description is given of the king during his illness?

CONTEMPERARY SOVEREIGNS.

Popes.	*Kings of France.*	
A.D.	A.D.	A.D.
Julius II..........1503	Louis XII.........1498	Christian II.......1513
Leo X............1513	Francis I..........1515	*Kings of Denmark alone.*
Adrian VI........1522		
Clement VII......1523	*Kings and Qu. of Spain*	Frederick I.......1524
Paul III..........1534	Philip I...........1504	Christian III......1533
	Joan..............1506	
Emperors of Germany,	Charles I..........1516	*King of Sweden alone.*
Maximilian I......1493		Gustavus Vasa*...1522
Charles V.........1519	*Kings of Portugal.*	
	Emanuel..........1495	*Kings and Queen of Scotland.*
Emperors of the Turks.	John III..........1512	
Bajazet II.........1481	*Kings of Denmark and Sweden.*	James IV.........1498
Selim I............1512		James V..........1514
Soliman II........1520	John.............1481	Mary.............1542

EMINENT PERSONS.

Thomas Cranmer, archbishop of Canterbury; cardinal Wolsey and sir Thomas More, lord Chancellors; Thomas, lord Cromwell; Gardiner, bishop of Winchester; Henry Howard, earl of Surrey; Nicholas, lord Vaux; John Bourchier, lord Berners; George Boleyn, Viscount Rochford; John, lord Lumley; Edward, lord Sheffield; dean Collet.

---

*GUSTAVUS VASA delivered Sweden from the Danish yoke, and for his recompense was elected its independent sovereign.

CHAPTER XXIV.

EDWARD VI.

Born 1537. Died July 6, 1553. Began to reign Jan. 29, 1547. Reigned 6½ years.

> Men perish in advance, as if the sun
> Should set ere noon.   *Young.*

1. (A.D. 1547.) Henry the Eighth was succeeded on the throne by his only son, Edward the Sixth, now in the ninth year of his age. The late king, in his will, which he expected would be implicitly obeyed, fixed the majority of the prince at the completion of his eighteenth year; and in the mean time appointed sixteen executors of his will, to whom, during the minority, he intrusted the government of the king and kingdom; the duke of Somerset, as protector, being placed at their head.

2. The protector, in his schemes for advancing the Reformation, had always recourse to the counsels of Cranmer; who, being a man of moderation and prudence, was averse to violent changes, and determined to bring over the people by insensible innovations to his own peculiar system.

3. A committee of bishops and divines had been appointed by the council to frame a liturgy for the service of the church; and this work was executed with great moderation, precision, and accuracy. A law was also enacted, permitting priests to marry; the ceremony of auricular confession, though not abolished, was left at the discretion of the people, who were not displeased at being freed from the spiritual tyranny of their instructors; the doctrine of the real presence was the last tenet of popery that was wholly abandoned by the people, as both the clergy and laity were loth to renounce so miraculous a benefit as it was asserted to be.

4. However, at last, not only this, but all the principal opinions and practices of the catholic religion, contrary to what the scripture authorizes, were abolished; and the Reformation, such as we have it, was almost entirely completed in England. With all these innovations the people and clergy in general acquiesced; and Gardiner and Bonner were the only persons whose opposition was thought of any weight; they were, therefore, sent to the Tower, and threatened with the king's further displeasure in case of disobedience. (A.D. 1548.)

5. For all these the protector gained great applause and popularity; but he was raised to an enviable degree of eminence, and his enemies were numerous in proportion to his exaltation. Of all the ministers at that time in council, Dudley, earl of Warwick, was the most artful, ambitious, and unprincipled. Resolved, at any rate, to possess the principal place under the king, he cared not what means were to be used in acquiring it. However, unwilling to throw off the mask, he covered the most exorbitant views under the fairest appearances. Having associated himself with the earl of Southampton, he formed a strong party in the council, who were determined to free themselves from the control the protector assumed over them. That nobleman was, in fact, now grown obnoxious to a very prevailing party in the kingdom. 7. He was hated by the nobles for his superior magnificence and power; he was hated by the catholic party for his regard to the Reformation; he was disliked by many for his severity to his brother; besides, the great estate he had raised at the expense of the church and the crown rendered him obnoxious to all. The palace* which he was then building in the Strand served also, by its munificence, and still more so by the unjust methods that were taking to raise it, to expose him to the censures of the public. The parish church of St. Mary, with three bishops' houses, were pulled down to furnish ground and materials for the structure.

8. He was soon afterwards sent to the Tower; and the chief article of which he was accused was the usurpation of the government, and taking all the power into his own hands; but his great riches were the real cause. Several others of a slighter tint were added to invigorate this accusation, but none of them could be said to amount to high-treason. 9. In consequence of these, a bill of attainder was preferred against him in the house of lords; but Somerset contrived for this time to elude the rigour of their sentence, by having previously, on his knees, confessed the charge before the members of the council. 10. In consequence of this confession, he was deprived of all his offices and goods, together with a great part of his landed estates, which were forfeited to the use of the crown. This fine on his estate was soon after remitted by the king; and Somerset, once more, contrary to the expectation of all, recovered his lib-

* Still called Somerset House.

erty. He was even readmitted into the council. Happy for him if his ambition had not revived with his security!

11. In fact, he could not help now and then bursting out into invectives against the king and government, which were quickly carried to his secret enemy, the earl of Warwick, who was now become the duke of Northumberland. As he was surrounded with that nobleman's creatures, they took care to reveal all the designs which they had themselves first suggested, and Somerset soon found the fatal effects of his rival's resentment. 12. He was, by Northumberland's command, arrested, with many more accused of being his partisans; and was, with his wife, the duchess, also thrown into prison. He was now accused of having formed a design to raise an insurrection in the North; of attacking the train-bands on a muster day; of plotting to secure the Tower, and to excite a rebellion in London.

13. These charges he strenuously denied; but he confessed one of as heinous nature, which was, that he had laid a project for murdering Northumberland, Northampton, and Pembroke at a banquet, which was to be given them by lord Paget. He was soon after brought to trial before the Marquis of Winchester, who sat as high-steward on the occasion, with twenty-seven peers more, including Northumberland, Pembroke, and Northampton, who were at once his judges and accusers; and being found guilty, was brought to the scaffold on Tower-hill, where he appeared without the least emotion, in the midst of a vast concourse of the populace, by whom he was beloved. 14. He spoke to them with great composure, protesting that he had always promoted the service of his king, and the interest of true religion, to the best of his power. The people attested their belief of what he said by crying out, "It is most true." An universal tumult was beginning to take place; but Somerset desiring them to be still, and not interrupt his last meditations, but to join with him in prayer, he laid down his head, and submitted to the stroke of the executioner.

15. In the meantime, Northumberland had long aimed at the first authority; and the infirm state of the king's health opened alluring prospects to his ambition. He represented to that young prince that his sisters, Mary and Elizabeth, who were appointed by Henry's will to succeed in failure of direct heirs to the crown, had been declared illegitimate by parliament; that the queen of Scots, his aunt, stood excluded by the king's will, and, being an alien also,

lost all right of succeeding. 16. And, as the three princesses were thus legally excluded, the succession naturally devolved to the marchioness of Dorset whose next heir was the lady Jane Grey, a lady every way accomplished for government, as well as by the charms of her person as the virtues and acquirements of her mind. The king, who had long submitted to all the politic views of this designing minister, agreed to have the succession submitted to council, where Northumberland had influence soon after to procure an easy concurrence.

17. In the meantime, as the king's health declined, the minister laboured to strengthen his own interests and connexions. His first aim was to secure the interests of the marquis of Dorset, father of lady Jane Grey, by procuring for him the title of duke of Suffolk, which was lately become extinct. Having thus obliged this nobleman, he then proposed a match between his fourth son, lord Guildford Dudley, and the lady Jane Grey. 18. Still bent on spreading his interests as widely as possible, he married his own daughter to Lord Hastings, and had these marriages solemnized with all possible pomp and festivity. Meanwhile, Edward continued to languish, and several fatal symptoms of consumption began to appear. It was hoped, however, that youth and temperance might get the better of his disorders; and, from their love, the people were unwilling to think him in danger. 19. It had been remarked, indeed, by some, that his health was visibly seen to decline from the moment that the Dudleys were brought about his person. The character of Northumberland might have justly given some colour to suspicion; and his removing all, except his own emissaries, from about the king, still farther increased the distrusts of the people. Northumberland, however, was no way uneasy at their murmurs; he was assiduous in his attendance upon the king, and professed the most anxious concern for his safety; but still drove forward his darling scheme of transferring the succession to his own daughter-in-law.

20. The young king was put into the hands of an ignorant woman, who very confidently undertook his cure. After the use of medicines, all the bad symptoms increased to a most violent degree; he felt a difficulty of speech and breathing; his pulse failed; his legs swelled; his colour became livid, and many other symptoms appeared of his approaching end. He expired at Greenwich, in the six-

King Edward VI. refusing to place his foot on the Bible.

teenth year of his age, and the seventh of his reign, greatly regretted by all, and his early virtues gave a prospect of the continuance of a happy reign, July 6, 1553.

An anecdote is related of this king to illustrate his piety and reverence for the Scriptures. When in his library, one day, being desirous to reach a book on a high shelf, he was offered a large Bible as a footstool. But he refused the offer, with strong expressions of disapprobation towards the attendant who had made it.

Questions for Examination.

1. Who succeeded Henry the Eighth?
   Who was appointed protector during the king's minority?
2, 3. By what methods was the Reformation begun and completed?
4. Who were sent to the tower for their aversion to the Reformation?
5. By whom was the protector opposed?
7. For what reasons was he universally disliked?
8. What was the chief article of accusation against him?
9. By what means did he elude the rigour of his sentence?
10. Did the protector regain his authority?
11. In what manner did he then conduct himself?
12. By whose command was he afterwards arrested?
   Of what was he accused?
13. What confession did he make?
14. What was his behaviour when brought to the scaffold?
15. Who next aspired to the chief authority?
16, 17. What means did he take to secure it?
18, 19. What circumstances preceded the king's death?
20. Where and at what age did Edward the Sixth die?

CONTEMPORARY SOVEREIGNS.

Popes. A.D.	Emperor of the Turks. A.D.	King of Denmark. A.D.
Paul III.............1534	Soliman II..........1520	Charles II..........1534
Julius III..........1550	King of France.	King of Sweden.
Emperor of Germany and King of Spain.	Henry II...........1547	Gustavus Vasa....1522
Charles V..........1547	King of Portugal.	Queen of Scotland.
	John III...........1541	Mary..............1542

EMINENT PERSONS.

Cranmer, archbishop of Canterbury. Heath and Day, bishops of Worcester and Chichester. Lord Seymour. Dukes of Somerset and Northumberland. Guildford, lord Dudley. Lady Jane Grey.

CHAPTER XXV.

MARY.

Born 1516. Died December 1, 1558. Began to reign July 16, 1553. Reigned 5 years.

*When persecuting zeal made royal sport
With royal innocence in Mary's court,
Then Bonner, blythe as shepherd at a wake,
Enjoy'd the show, and danced about the stake.—Cowper.*

1. (A.D. 1553.) Upon the death of Edward, two candidates put in their pretensions to the crown;—Mary, Henry's daughter by Catharine of Arragon, relying on the justice of her cause; and lady Jane Grey, being nominated in the late young king's will, and upon the support of the duke of Northumberland, her father-in-law. Mary was strongly bigoted to the popish superstitions, having been bred up among churchmen, and having been even taught to prefer martyrdom to a denial of her belief. 2. As she had lived in continual restraint, she was reserved and gloomy; she had, even during the life of her father, the resolution to maintain her sentiments, and refused to comply with his new institutions. Her zeal had rendered her furious; and she was not only blindly attached to her religious opinions, but even to the popish clergy who maintained them. 3. On the other hand, Jane Grey was strongly attached to the Reformers; and though yet but sixteen, her judgment had attained to such a degree of maturity as few have been found to possess. All historians agree that the solidity of her understanding, improved by continual application, rendered her the wonder of her age. Jane, who was in a great measure ignorant of

all the transactions in her favour, was struck with equal grief and surprise when she received intelligence of them. She shed a flood of tears, appeared inconsolable, and it was not without the utmost difficulty that she yielded to the entreaties of Northumberland, and the duke her father. 4. Orders were given also for proclaiming her throughout the kingdom; but these were but very remissly obeyed. When she was proclaimed in the city, the people heard her accession made public without any signs of pleasure; no applause ensued, and some even expressed their scorn and contempt.

5. In the meantime, Mary, who had retired, upon the news of the king's death, to Kenning Hall, in Norfolk, sent circular letters to all the great towns and nobility in the kingdom, reminding them of her right, and commanding them to proclaim her without delay. Her claims soon became irresistible; in a little time she found herself at the head of forty thousand men; while the few who attended Northumberland continued irresolute, and he even feared to lead them to the encounter.

6. Lady Jane, thus finding that all was lost, resigned her royalty, which she had held but ten days, with marks of real satisfaction, and retired with her mother to their own habitation. Northumberland, also, who found his affairs desperate, and that it was impossible to stem the tide of popular opposition, attempted to quit the kingdom; but he was prevented by the band of pensioner-guards, who informed him that he must stay to justify their conduct in being led out against their lawful sovereign. Thus circumvented on all sides, he delivered himself up to Mary, and was soon afterwards executed in a summary way. Sentence was also pronounced against lady Jane and lord Guildford, but without any intention for the present of putting it into execution.

7. Mary now entered London, and with very little effusion of blood saw herself joyfully proclaimed, and peaceably settled on the throne. This was a flattering prospect; but soon the pleasing phantom was dissolved. Mary was morose, and a bigot; she was resolved to give back their former power to the clergy; and thus once more to involve the kingdom in all the horrors from which it had just emerged. Gardiner, Tunstal, Day, Heath, and Vesey, who had been confined or suffered losses, for their catholic opinions during the late reign, were taken from prison, reinstated in their sees, and their former sentences repealed.

8. A parliament, which the queen called soon after, seemed willing to concur in all her measures: they at one blow repealed all the statutes, with regard to religion, which had passed during the reign of her predecessors; so that the national religion was again placed on the same footing on which it stood in the early part of the reign of Henry the Eighth.
9. While religion was thus returning to its primitive abuses, the queen's ministers, who were willing to strengthen her power, by a catholic alliance, had been for some time looking out for a proper consort; and they at length chose Philip, prince of Spain, son to the celebrated Charles the Fifth. In order to avoid any disagreeable remonstrance from the people, the articles of marriage were drawn as favourable as possible to the interest and honour of England. and this in some measure stilled the clamours that had already been begun against it.
10. The discontents of the people rose to such a pitch, that an insurrection, headed by sir Thomas Wyat, succeeded; but Wyat, being made prisoner, was condemned and executed, with some of his adherents. But what excited the compassion of the people most of all, was the execution of lady Jane Grey and her husband, lord Guildford Dudley, who were involved in the punishment, though not in the guilt of this insurrection. 11. Two days after Wyat was apprehended, lady Jane and her husband were ordered to prepare for death. Lady Jane, who had long before seen the threatening blow, was no way surprised at the message, but bore it with heroic resolution; and being informed that she had three days to prepare, she seemed displeased at so long a delay. 12. On the day of her execution her husband desired permission to see her; but this she refused, as she knew the parting would be too tender for her fortitude to withstand. The place at first designed for their execution was without the Tower; but their youth, beauty, and innocence being likely to raise an insurrection among the people, orders were given that they should be executed within the verge of the Tower. 13. Lord Dudley was the first that suffered; and while the lady Jane was being conducted to the place of execution, the officers of the Tower met her, bearing along the headless body of her husband streaming with blood, in order to be interred in the Tower chapel. She looked on the corpse for some time without any emotion: and then, with a sigh, desired them

Death of Lady Jane Grey.

to proceed. 14. On the scaffold she made a speech, in which she alleged that her offence was not the having laid her hand upon the crown, but the not rejecting it with sufficient constancy; that she had less erred through ambition than filial obedience; and she willingly accepted death as the only atonement she could make to the injured state; and was ready by her punishment to show, that innocence is no plea in excuse for deeds that tend to injure the community. After speaking to this effect, she caused herself to be disrobed by her women, and, with a steady, serene countenance, submitted to the executioner.

15. At the head of those who drove these violent measures forward were Gardiner, bishop of Winchester, and cardinal Pole, who was now returned from Italy. Pole, who was nearly allied by birth to the royal family, had always conscientiously adhered to the catholic religion, and had incurred Henry's displeasure, not only by refusing to assent to his measures, but by writing against him. 16. It was for this adherence that he was cherished by the pope, and now sent over to England as legate from the holy see. Gardiner was a man of a very different character; his chief aim was to please the reigning prince, and he had shown already many instances of his prudent conformity.

Questions for Examination.

1. What were the pretensions of the two candidates for the crown?
2. What was the character of Mary?
3. What is said of lady Jane Grey?
4. In what manner was her proclamation received?
5. How did Mary act, and what was her success?
6. What was the fate of the duke of Northumberland?
7. What was Mary's conduct after her accession?
8. Did the parliament concur in her religious views?
9. What plan was resolved on to strengthen the Catholic power?
11. What was the fate of lady Jane Grey and her husband?
12, 14. Mention the circumstances that attended their execution.
15, 16. Who were the instigators of those violent measures?

SECTION II.

*Curst superstition, which deludes the mind,
And makes it to the tender feelings blind.—Anon.*

1. (A. D. 1554.) A PERSECUTION, therefore, began by the martyrdom of Hooper, bishop of Gloucester, and Rogers, prebendary of Saint Paul's. They were examined by commissioners appointed by the queen, with the chancellor at the head of them. Saunders and Taylor, two other clergymen, whose zeal had been distinguished in carrying on the Reformation, were the next that suffered.

2. Bonner, bishop of London, bloated at once with rage and luxury, let loose his vengeance without restraint, and seemed to take a pleasure in the pains of the unhappy sufferers; while the queen, by her letters, exhorted him to pursue the pious work without pity or interruption. Soon after, in obedience to her commands, Ridley, bishop of London, and the venerable Latimer, bishop of Worcester, were condemned together. 3. Ridley had been one of the ablest champions for the Reformation; his piety, learning, and solidity of judgment were admired by his friends and dreaded by his enemies. The night before his execution, he invited the mayor of Oxford and his wife to see him; and when he beheld him it melted him to tears; he himself appeared quite unmoved, inwardly supported and comforted in that hour of agony. When he was brought to the stake to be burnt, he found his old friend, Latimer, there before him. 4. Of all the prelates of that age, Latimer was the most remarkable for his unaffected piety, and the simplicity of his manners. He had never learnt to flatter in courts; and his open rebuke was dreaded by all the great, who at that time too much deserved it. 5. His sermons, which

remain to this day, show that he had much learning and much wit; and there is an air of sincerity running through them, not to be found elsewhere. When Ridley began to comfort his ancient friend, Latimer was as ready on his part to return the kind office. "Be of good cheer, brother," cried he; "we shall this day kindle such a torch in England, as, I trust in God, shall never be extinguished." 6. A furious bigot ascended to preach to them and the people, while the fire was preparing; and Ridley gave a most serious attention to his discourse. No way distracted by the preparations about him, he heard him to the last, and then told him he was ready to answer all he had preached upon, if he were permitted a short indulgence; but this was refused him. At length fire was set to the pile; Latimer was soon out of pain: but Ridley continued to suffer much longer, his legs being consumed before the fire reached his vitals.

7. Cranmer's death followed soon after, and struck the whole nation with horror. His love of life had formerly prevailed. In an unguarded moment he was induced to sign a paper condemning the Reformation; and now his enemies, as we are told of the devil, after having rendered him completely wretched, resolved to destroy him.

8. Being led to the stake, and the fire beginning to be kindled around him, he stretched forth his right hand, and held it in the flames till it was consumed, while he frequently cried out, in the midst of his sufferings, "That unworthy hand!" at the same time exhibiting no appearance of pain or disorder. When the fire attacked his body, he seemed to be quite insensible to his tortures: his mind was wholly occupied upon the hopes of a future reward. After his body was destroyed, his heart was found entire; an emblem of the constancy with which he suffered.

9. It was computed that, during this persecution, two hundred and seventy-seven persons suffered by fire, besides those punished by imprisonment, fines and confiscations. Among those who suffered by fire, were five bishops, twenty-one clergymen, eight lay gentlemen, eighty-four tradesmen, one hundred husbandmen, fifty-five women, and four children. All this was terrible; and yet the temporal affairs of the kingdom did not seem to be more successful.

10. (A. D. 1557.) Calais, that had now for above two hundred years been in possession of the English, was attacked, and by a sudden and unexpected assault, being

blockaded on every side, was obliged to capitulate; so that in less than eight days, the duke of Guise recovered the city that had been in possession of the English since the time of Edward the Third, who had spent eleven months in besieging it. This loss filled the whole kingdom with murmurs, and the queen with despair; she was heard to say, that, when dead, the name of Calais would be found engraven upon her heart.

11. These complicated evils, a murmuring people, an increasing heresy, a disdainful husband, and an unsuccessful war, made dreadful depredations on Mary's constitution. She began to appear consumptive, and this rendered her mind still more morose and bigoted. The people now, therefore, began to turn their thoughts to her successor; and the princess Elizabeth came into a greater degree of consideration than before. 12. Mary had been long in a very declining state of health; and having mistaken the nature of her disease, she made use of an improper regimen, which had increased her disorder. Every reflection now tormented her. The consciousness of being hated by her subjects, and the prospect of Elizabeth's succession, whom she hated, preyed upon her mind, and threw her into a lingering fever, of which she died, after a short and unfortunate reign of five years, four months, and eleven days, in the forty-third year of her age.

Questions for Examination.

1. Who were the first in this reign who suffered martyrdom for their religion?
2. Who were the principal actors in this persecution?
3, 4. Describe the behaviour and character of Ridley and Latimer?
6. What words did Latimer make use of at the stake to his friend and fellow-sufferer?
8. What is said of the character and death of Cranmer?
9. How many persons are said to have been burnt on account of their religious tenets?
10. By what means was Calais obliged to capitulate?
11. What hastened Mary's death?
12. How long did she reign?

CONTEMPORARY SOVEREIGNS.

Popes.	A.D.	King of France. A.D.	King of Denmark. A.D.
Julius III.	1550	Henry 1547	Frederic II. 1549
Marcellus II.	1555		
Paul IV.	1555		
		King of Spain,	King of Sweden.
Emperor of Germany.		Philip II 1555	Gustavus Vasa....1522
Charles V.	1519		
		King of Portugal.	Queen of Scotland.
Emperor of the Turks.		John III .... .1521	Mary............1542
Soliman II.	1520		

EMINENT PERSONS.

Archbishop Cranmer; bishops Ridley, Hooper, Latimer, Feries, Rogers, Saunders, Taylor, and many others of the clergy who suffered for their religion. Cardinal Pole, bishops Gardiner, Bonner, Thirlby, &c., who were fiery supporters of the papal powers.* Lord Stafford.

CHAPTER XXVI.

ELIZABETH.

Born 1533. Died March 24, 1603. Began to reign November 7, 1558. Reigned 44½ years.

SECTION I.

1. (A. D. 1558.) NOTHING could exceed the joy that was diffused among the people upon the accession of Elizabeth, who now came to the throne without any opposition.

This favourite of the people, from the beginning, resolved upon reforming the church, even while she was held in the constraints of a prison; and now, upon coming to the crown, she immediately set about it. A parliament soon after completed what the prerogative had begun; act after act was passed in favour of the Reformation; and in a single session the form of religion was established as we at present have the happiness to enjoy it.

2. A state of permanent felicity is not to be expected here; and Mary Stuart, commonly called Mary queen of Scots, was the first person that excited the fears or the resentment of Elizabeth. Henry the Seventh had married his eldest daughter, Margaret, to James, king of Scotland, who dying, left no issue that came to maturity except Mary

---

* "The common net at that time for catching protestants was the real presence, and this net was used to catch the princess Elizabeth ; for being asked one time what she thought of the words of God, this is my body, whether she thought it the true body of Christ that was in the sacrament, it is said, that, after some pausing, she thus answered :—
        Christ was the word that spake it,
        He took the bread and brake it,
        And what the word did make it,
        That I believe and take it.
Which, though it may seem but a slight expression, yet had it more solidness than at first sight appears ; at least it served her turn at that time to escape the net, which by direct answer she could not have done."

afterwards surnamed Mary queen of Scots. 3. At a very early age, this princess, being possessed of every accomplishment of person and mind, was married to Francis, the dauphin of France, who dying, left her a widow at the age of nineteen. Upon the death of Francis, Mary, the widow, still seemed disposed to keep up the title; but finding herself exposed to the persecutions of the dowager-queen, who now began to take the lead in France, she returned home to Scotland, where she found the people strongly impressed with the gloomy enthusiasm of the times. 4. A difference of religion between the sovereign and the people is ever productive of bad effects; since it is apt to produce contempt on the one side, and jealousy on the other. Mary could not avoid regarding the sour manners of the reforming clergy, who now bore sway among the Scots, with a mixture of ridicule and hatred; while they, on the other hand, could not look tamely on gayeties and levities which she introduced among them, without abhorrence and resentment. The jealousy thus excited began every day to grow stronger; the clergy only waited for some indiscretion in the queen to fly out into open opposition; and her imprudence but too soon gave them sufficient opportunity.

5. Mary, upon her return, had married the earl of Darnley; but having been dazzled by the pleasing exterior of her new lover, she had entirely forgotten to look to the accomplishments of his mind. Darnley was but a weak and ignorant man; violent, yet variable in his enterprises; insolent, yet credulous, and easily governed by flatterers. She soon, therefore, began to convert her admiration into disgust; and Darnley, enraged at her increasing coldness, pointed his vengeance against every person he supposed the cause of this change in her sentiments and behaviour.

6. There was then in the court one David Rizzio, the son of a musician at Turin, himself a musician, whom Mary took into her confidence. She consulted him on all occasions; no favours could be obtained but by his intercession; and all suitors were first obliged to gain Rizzio to their interests by presents or by flattery. 7. It was easy to persuade a man of Darnley's jealous and uxorious temper that Rizzio was the person who had estranged the queen's affections from him; and a surmise once conceived became to him a certainty. He soon, therefore, consulted with some lords of his party; who, acompanying him into the queen's apartments, where Rizzio then was, they dragged

him into the antechamber, where he was despatched with fifty-six wounds; the unhappy princess continuing her lamentations while they were perpetrating their horrid crime.
8. Being informed, however, of his fate, Mary at once dried her tears, and said she would weep no more, for she would now think of revenge. She, therefore, concealed her resentment, and so far imposed upon Darnley her husband, that he put himself under her protection, and soon after attended her to Edinburgh, where he was told the place would be favourable to his health.
9. Mary lived in the palace of Holyrood-house; but as the situation of that place was low, and the concourse of people about the court necessarily attended with noise, which might disturb him in his present infirm state, she fitted up an apartment for him in a solitary house at some distance, called the Kirk of Field. Mary there gave him marks of kindness and attachment; she conversed cordially with him; and she lay some nights in a room under his.
10. It was on the ninth of February that she told him she would pass that night in the palace, because the marriage of one of her servants was to be there celebrated in her presence. But dreadful consequences ensued. About two o'clock in the morning, the whole city was much alarmed at hearing a great noise; the house in which Darnley lay was blown up with gunpowder. His dead body was found at some distance in a neighbouring field, but without any marks of violence or contusion. No doubt could be entertained that Darnley was murdered; and the general suspicion fell upon Bothwell, a person lately taken into Mary's favour, as the perpetrator.
11. One crime led on to another; Bothwell, though accused of being stained with the husband's blood, though universally odious to the people, had the confidence, while Mary was on her way to Stirling, on a visit to her son, to seize her at the head of a body of eight hundred horse, and to carry her to Dunbar, where he forced her to yield to his purposes. It was then thought by the people that the measure of his crimes was complete; and that he who was supposed to kill the queen's husband, and to have possessed himself of her person, could expect no mercy; but they were astonished upon finding, instead of disgrace, that Bothwell was taken into more than former favour; and to crown all, that he was married to Mary, having divorced his own wife to procure his union.

13. This was a fatal alliance to Mary; and the people were now wound up, by the complication of her guilt, to pay very little deference to her authority. An association was formed that took Mary prisoner, and sent her into confinement to the castle of Lochlevin, situated on a lake of that name, where she suffered all the severities of an unkind keeper, an upbraiding conscience, with a feeling heart.

14. The calamities of the great, even though justly deserved, seldom fail of creating pity, and procuring friends. Mary, by her charms and promises, had engaged a young gentleman, whose name was George Douglas, to assist her in escaping from the place where she was confined; and this he effected by conveying her in disguise in a small boat, rowed by himself, ashore. It was now that the news of her enlargement being spread abroad, all the loyalty of the people seemed to revive once more, and in a few days she saw herself at the head of six thousand men.

Questions for Examination.

1. What were the first acts of Elizabeth in favour of?
2. Who was the first person that excited her resentment? From whom was Mary queen of Scots descended?
3. To whom was she first married?
4. Why is the difference in religion between the sovereign and the people apt to produce bad effects?
5. Describe the character of the earl of Darnley?
6. Who was David Rizzio?
7. What was the fate of Rizzio?
8. On what did Mary determine in consequence?
9. How did she affect to treat her husband?
10. Relate the circumstances of the earl of Darnley's death.
13. Where was Mary confined?
14. By what means did she escape?

SECTION II.

But malice, envy, cruelty and spleen,
To death doom'd Scotia's dear devoted queen.—*Macdonald.*

1. (A. D. 1568.) A BATTLE was fought at Langside, near Glasgow, which was entirely decisive against the queen of Scots; and now, being totally ruined, she fled southward from the field of battle with great precipitation, and came with a few attendants to the borders of England, where she hoped for protection from Elizabeth; who, instead of protecting, ordered her to be put in confinement, yet treated her with all proper marks of respect. 2. She was accord-

ingly sent to Tutbury castle, in the county of Stafford, and put into the custody of the earl of Shrewsbury; where she had hopes given her of one day coming into favour; and that, unless her own obstinacy prevented, an accommodation might at last take place.

3. The duke of Norfolk was the only peer who enjoyed the highest title of nobility in England; and the qualities of his mind were correspondent to his high station. Beneficent, affable, and generous, he had acquired the affections of the people; and yet, from his moderation, he had never alarmed the jealousy of the sovereign. He was at this time a widower; and being of a suitable age to espouse the queen of Scots, her own attractions, as well as his interest, made him desirous of the match. Elizabeth, however, dreaded such a union, and the duke was soon after made prisoner, and sent to the Tower. Upon his releasement from thence, new projects were set on foot by the enemies of the queen and the reformed religion, secretly fomented by Rodolphi, an instrument of the court of Rome, and the bishop of Ross, Mary's minister in England. 5. It was concerted by them that Norfolk should renew his designs upon Mary, and raise her to the throne, to which it is probable he was prompted by passion as well as by interest; and this nobleman entering into their scheme, he, from being at first only ambitious, now became criminal. His servants were brought to make full confession of their master's guilt; and the bishop of Ross, soon after finding the whole discovered, did not scruple to confirm their testimony. 6. The duke was instantly committed to the Tower, and ordered to prepare for his trial. A jury of twenty-five peers unanimously passed sentence upon him; and the queen, four months after, reluctantly signed the warrant for his execution. He died with great calmness and constancy; and, though he cleared himself of any disloyal intentions against the queen's authority, he acknowledged the justice of the sentence by which he suffered.

7. These conspiracies served to prepare the way for Mary's ruin, whose greatest misfortunes proceeded rather from the violence of her friends than the malignity of her enemies. Elizabeth's ministers had long been waiting for some signal instance of the captive queen's enmity, which they could easily convert into treason; and this was not long wanting. 8. About this time (A. D. 1586), one John Ballard, a popish priest, who had been bred in the English

seminary at Rheims, resolved to compass the death of the queen, whom he considered as the enemy of his religion; and with that gloomy resolution came over to England in the disguise of a soldier, with the assumed name of captain Fortescue. He bent his endeavours to bring about at once the project of an assassination, an insurrection, and an invasion. 9. The first person he addressed himself to was Anthony Babington, of Dethic, in the county of Derby, a young gentleman of good family, and possessed of a very plentiful fortune. This person had been long remarkable for his zeal in the catholic cause, and in particular for his attachment to the captive queen. He, therefore, came readily into the plot, and procured the concurrence and assistance of some other associates in this dangerous undertaking. 10. The next step was to apprise Mary of the conspiracy formed in her favour; and this they effected by conveying their letters to her, by the means of a brewer that supplied the family with ale, through a chink in the wall of her apartment. In these, Babington informed her of a design laid for a foreign invasion, the plan of an insurrection at home, the scheme for her delivery, and the conspiracy for assassinating the usurper, by six noble gentlemen, as he termed them, all of them his private friends, who, from the zeal which they bore the catholic cause, and her majesty's service, would undertake the tragical execution. 11. To these Mary replied, that she approved highly of the design; that the gentlemen might expect all the rewards which it should ever be in her power to confer; and that the death of Elizabeth was a necessary circumstance, previous to any further attempts, either for her delivery or the intended insurrection.

12. The plot being thus ripe for execution, and the evidence against the conspirators incontestable, Walsingham, who was privately informed of all, resolved to suspend their punishment no longer. A warrant was accordingly issued out for the apprehension of Babington and the rest of the conspirators, who covered themselves with various disguises, and endeavoured to keep themselves concealed. But they were soon discovered, thrown into prison, and brought to trial. In their examination they contradicted each other, and the leaders were obliged to make a full confession of the truth. Fourteen were condemned and executed; seven of whom died acknowledging their crime.

13. The execution of these wretched men only prepared the way for one of still greater importance, in which a captive queen was to submit to the unjust decision of those who had no right but that of power to condemn her. Accordingly a commission was issued to forty peers, with five judges, or the major part of them, to try and pass sentence upon Mary, daughter and heir of James the Fifth, king of Scotland, commonly called queen of Scots, and dowager of France. 14. Thirty-six of these commissioners arriving at the castle of Fotheringay on the 11th of November, 1586, presented her with a letter from Elizabeth, commanding her to submit to a trial for a late conspiracy. The principal charge against her was urged by sergeant Gaudy, who accused her with knowing, approving, and consenting to Babington's conspiracy. This charge was supported by Babington's confession, and by the copies which were taken of their correspondence, in which her approbation of the queen's murder was expressly declared.

15. Whatever might have been this queen's offences, it is certain that her treatment was very severe. She desired to be put in possession of such notes as she had taken preparatory to her trial; but this was refused her. She demanded a copy of her protest; but her request was not complied with. She even required an advocate to plead her cause against so many learned lawyers as had undertaken to urge her accusations; but all her demands were rejected, and, after an adjournment of some days, sentence of death was pronounced against her in the Star Chamber, in Westminster, all the commissioners except two being present.

Independent of the affairs of Mary queen of Scots, the contents of this section are barren of information. It must not, however, be supposed, that a period of eighteen years of the reign of Elizabeth afforded no matter worthy of the notice of the historian; and we shall therefore endeavour to supply the deficiency by the following brief chronological memoranda:—On St. Bartholomew's day, 1572, a dreadful massacre of the protestants took place in France; a circumstance which proved very detrimental to the Scottish queen, as many of her adherents, who were protestants, dreaded her attachment to a religion that allowed its votaries to employ such abominable measures. In 1573, Elizabeth found means, by economy, without imposing any additional burdens on her subjects, to discharge with interest, not only all the debts she had incurred in her reign, but those of Edward VI. her brother, and of her sister Mary. In 1574, so great a dearth prevailed in England, that wheat sold for six shillings a bushel. In 1577, pocket-watches were first brought into England from Germany. In 1579, a proclamation was issued, prohibiting the enlarging of the city of London; to effect which, it was ordered that no new houses should be built within three miles of the gates of the city. In the same year the Turkey Company was established. In 1580, the use of coaches was first introduced into England by the earl of Arundel. Before that time the queen, on public occasions, rode on horseback behind her chamberlain.

In the year 1580, also, Francis Drake, the first Englishman who circumnavigated the globe, returned from his voyage. He brought home with him immense treasures, which he had taken from the Spaniards; and many of the English courtiers, dreading the Spanish power, advised Elizabeth to discountenance the gallant adventurer. But the queen, who admired valor, and was allured by the prospects of sharing the booty, conferred on him the honour of knighthood, and accepted a banquet from him at Deptford, on board the ship which had achieved so memorable a voyage.

Questions for Examination.

1. Where did Mary fly after her defeat at Langside?
2. Where was she confined?
3. Describe the character of the duke of Norfolk?
4. Of what was he desirous?
5. What were the designs of the duke of Norfolk?
6. What were the consequences?
8. What conspiracy was now formed in Mary's favour?
10. By what means was Mary informed of it?
12. what was the fate of the conspirators?
14. What was the principal charge alleged against Mary?
15. What favours were refused her previous to her sentence?

SECTION III.

*Dejected pity by her side,
Her soul-subduing voice applied.—Collins.*

1. (A.D. 1586.) WHETHER Elizabeth was really sincere in her apparent reluctance to execute Mary, is a question which, though usually given against her, I will not take upon me to determine. Certainly there were great arts used by her courtiers to incline her to the side of severity; as they had everything to fear from the resentment of Mary in case she ever succeeded to the throne. 2. Accordingly the kingdom was now filled with rumors of plots, treasons, and insurrections; and the queen continually kept in alarm by fictitious dangers. She, therefore, appeared to be in great terror and perplexity; she was observed to sit much alone, and mutter to herself half sentences, importing the difficulty and distress to which she was reduced. 3. In this situation she one day called her secretary, Davison, whom she ordered to draw out secretly the warrant for Mary's execution, informing him that she intended keeping it by her, in case any attempt should be made for the delivery of that princess. She signed the warrant, and then commanded it to be carried to the chancellor, to have the seal affixed to it. 4. Next morning, however, she sent two gentlemen successively to desire that Davison would not go to the chancellor until she should see him; but Davison telling her that the warrant had been already sealed, she seemed displeased at his precipitation. Davison, who probably wished himself to see the sentence executed, laid the affair before the council, who unanimously resolved that the warrant should be immediately put in execution; and promised to justify Davison to the queen. 5. Accordingly, the fatal instrument was delivered to Beale, who summoned the noblemen to whom it was directed, namely, the earls of Shrewsbury, Derby, Kent, and Cumberland; and these together set out for Fotheringay-castle, accompanied by two executioners to dispatch their bloody commission.

6. Mary heard of the arrival of her executioners, who ordered her to prepare for death at eight o'clock the next morning. Early on the fatal morning she dressed herself in a rich habit of silk and velvet, the only one which she had reserved for this solemn occasion. Thomas Andrews, the under-sheriff of the county, then entering the room, he informed her that the hour was come, and that he must

attend her to the place of execution. 7. She replied that she was ready, and, bidding her servants farewell, she proceeded, supported by two of her guards, and followed the sheriff with a serene, composed aspect, with a long veil of linen on her head, and in her hand, a crucifix of ivory.

8. She then passed into another hall, the noblemen and the sheriff going before, and Melvil, her master of the household, bearing up her train, where was a scaffold erected, and covered with black. As soon as she was seated, Beale began to read the warrant for her execution. Then Fletcher, dean of Peterborough, standing without the rails, repeated a long exhortation, which she desired him to forbear, as she was firmly resolved to die in the catholic religion. The room was crowded with spectators, who beheld her with pity and distress; while her beauty, though dimmed by age and affliction, gleamed through her sufferings and was still remarkable in this fatal moment. 9. The two executioners kneeling, and asking her pardon, she said she forgave them, and all the authors of her death, as freely as she hoped for forgiveness from her Maker; and then once more made a solemn protestation of her innocence. Her eyes were then covered with a linen handkerchief; and she laid herself down without any fear or trepidation. Then reciting a psalm, and repeating a pious ejaculation her head was severed from her body, at two strokes by the executioners.

10. Thus perished Mary, in the forty-fifth year of her age, and the nineteenth of her captivity in England. She was a woman of great accomplishments; and the beauty of her person, the graces of her air, and charms of her conversation, combined to make her one of the most amiable of women, and to produce a deep impression on all who had intercourse with her. She was ambitious and active in her temper, yet inclined to cheerfulness and society. She partook sufficiently of manlike virtues to give her vigour in the prosecution of her purposes, without relinquishing those soft graces which compose the proper ornament of her sex. Such indeed were, on the one hand, her natural advantages and her acquirements, and on the other her faults, that an enumeration of her qualities might seem to be a panegyric; while an account of her conduct must, in some parts, wear the aspect of severe satire and invective.

Her numerous misfortunes, the solitude of her long captivity, and the persecution to which she had been exposed on account of her religion, had produced in her a degree of bigotry in her later years: and such were the prevalent spirit and principles of the age, that we need not wonder if her zeal, her resentment, and her interest uniting, induced her to give consent to a design which conspirators, actuated by the first of these motives only, had formed against the life of Elizabeth.

In contemplating the contentions of mankind, we find almost ever both sides culpable; Mary, who was stained with crimes that deserved punishment, was put to death by a princess who had no just pretensions to inflict punishment on her equal.

11. In the meantime, Philip, King of Spain, who had long meditated the destruction of England, and whose extensive power gave him grounds to hope for success, now began to put his projects into execution. The point on which he rested his glory and the perpetual object of his schemes, was to support the catholic religion and exterminate the Reformation. The revolt of his subjects in the Netherlands still more inflamed his resentment against the English, as they had encouraged that insurrection, and assisted the revolters. He had, therefore, for some time been making preparations to attack England by a powerful invasion; and now every part of his vast empire resounded with the noise of armaments, and every art was used to levy supplies for that great design.

12. The marquis of Santa Cruz, a sea-officer of great reputation and experience, was destined to command the fleet, which consisted of a hundred and thirty vessels, of a greater size than any that had hitherto been seen in Europe. The duke of Parma was to conduct the land forces, twenty thousand of whom were on board the fleet, and thirty-four thousand more were assembled in the Netherlands, ready to be transported into England. No doubt was entertained of this fleet's success; and it was ostentatiously styled the Invincible Armada.

13. Nothing could exceed the terror and consternation which all ranks of people felt in England upon the news of this terrible armada being under sail to invade them. A fleet of not above thirty ships of war, and those very small in comparison, was all that was to oppose it at sea; and as for resisting it by land, that was supposed to be impossible, as the Spanish army was composed of men well-disciplined, and long inured to danger.

14. Although the English fleet was much inferior in number and size of shipping to that of the enemy, yet it was much more manageable; the dexterity and courage of the mariners being greatly superior. Lord Howard of Effingham, a man of great courage and capacity, as lord admiral, took upon him the command of the navy.

15. Drake, Hawkins, and Frobisher, the most renowned seamen in Europe, served under him; while a small squadron, consisting of forty vessels, English and Flemish, commanded by lord Seymour, lay off Dunkirk, in order to intercept the duke of Parma. This was the preparation made by the English; while all the Protestant powers in Europe regarded the enterprise as the critical event which was to decide for ever the fate of their religion.

Questions for Examination.

2. With what rumours was the kingdom filled?
3. What orders did Elizabeth give to her Secretary?
5. To whom was the warrant of Mary's death delivered?
6. 7. 8. Relate the particulars of her execution,
9. What was her behaviour at the fatal hour?
11. Who now meditated the destruction of England?
    What was the chief object of his schemes?
12. Who were his principal officers?
    What was the amount of the Spanish forces?
13. What was the number of the English ships?
14. Who commanded them?
15. What other preparations were made by the English?

SECTION IV.

*Destruction follows where her flag is seen,
And haughty Spaniards stoop to Britain's queen.—Anon.*

1. (A. D. 1588.) IN the mean time, while the Spanish armada was preparing to sail, the admiral Santa Cruz died, as likewise the vice-admiral Palino; and the command of the expedition was given to the duke de Medina Sidonia, a person utterly inexperienced in sea affairs; and this, in some measure, served to frustrate the design. But some other accidents also contributed to its failure. 2. Upon leaving the port of Lisbon, the armada the next day met with a violent tempest, which sunk several of the smallest of their shipping, and obliged the fleet to put back into harbour. After some time spent in refitting, they again put to sea; where they took a fisherman, who gave them intelligence that the English fleet, hearing of the dispersion of the armada in a storm, had retired back into Plymouth harbour, and most of the mariners were discharged. 3. From this false intelligence, the Spanish admiral, instead of going directly to the coast of Flanders, to take in the troops stationed there as he had been instructed, resolved to sail for Plymouth, and destroy the shipping laid up in that harbour. But Effingham, the English admiral, was very well prepared to receive them; he had just got out of port when he saw the Spanish armada coming full sail towards him, disposed in the form of a half moon, and stretching seven miles from one extremity to the other. 4. However, the English admiral, seconded by Drake, Hawkins, and Frobisher, attacked the armada at a distance, pouring in their broadsides with admirable dexterity. They did not choose to engage the enemy more closely, because they were greatly inferior in the number of ships, guns, and weight of metal; nor could they pretend to board such lofty ships without manifest disadvantage. However, two Spanish galleons were disabled and taken. 5. As the armada advanced up the channel, the English still followed, and infested their rear; and their fleet continually increasing from different ports, they soon found themselves in a capacity to attack the Spanish fleet more nearly, and accordingly fell upon them while they were as yet taking shelter in the port of Calais. 6. To increase their confusion, Howard took eight of his smaller ships, and filling them with combustible materials, sent them, as if they had been fire-ships, one

after the other, into the midst of the enemy. The Spaniards taking them for what they seemed to be, immediately took flight, in great disorder; while the English, profiting by their panic, took or destroyed about twelve of the enemy.

7. This was a fatal blow to Spain; the duke de Medina Sidonia, being thus driven to the coast of Zealand, held a council of war, in which it was resolved, that, as their ammunition began to fail, as their ships had received great damage, and the duke of Parma had refused to venture his army under their protection, they should return to Spain by sailing round the Orkneys, as the winds were contrary to his passage directly back. 8. Accordingly they proceeded northward, and were followed by the English fleet as far as Flamborough-head, where they were terribly shattered by a storm. Seventeen of the ships, having five thousand men on board, were afterwards cast away on the Western isles, and the coast of Ireland. Of the whole armada, three-and-fifty ships only returned to Spain, in a miserable condition; and the seamen, as well as soldiers, who remained, only served by their accounts to intimidate their countrymen from attempting to renew so dangerous an expedition.

9. From being invaded, the English, in their turn, attacked the Spaniards. Of those who made the most signal figure in the depredations upon Spain, was the young earl of Essex, a nobleman of great bravery, generosity, and genius; and fitted not only for the foremost ranks in war by his valour, but to conduct the intrigues of court by his eloquence and address. 10. In all the masques which were then performed, the earl and Elizabeth were generally coupled as partners; and although she was almost sixty, and he not half so old, yet her vanity overlooked the disparity; the world told her she was young, and she herself was willing to think so. This young earl's interest in the queen's affections, as may naturally be supposed, promoted his interests in the state; and he conducted all things at his discretion. 11. But young and inexperienced as he was, he at length began to fancy that the popularity he possessed, and the flatteries he received, were given to his merits, and not to his favour. In a debate before the queen, between him and Burleigh, about the choice of a governor for Ireland, he was so heated in the argument, that he entirely forgot both the rules and duties of civility. 12. He turned his back on the queen in a contemptuous manner, which so provoked her resentment,

that she instantly gave him a box on the ear. Instead of recollecting himself, and making the submission due to her sex and station, he clapped his hand to his sword, and swore he would not bear such usage even from her father. This offence, though very great, was overlooked by the queen: her partiality was so prevalent, that she reinstated him in her former favour, and her kindness seemed to have acquired new force from that short interruption of anger and resentment. 13. The death also of his rival, Lord Burleigh, which happened shortly after, seemed to confirm his power. At that time the earl of Tyrone headed the rebellious natives of Ireland; who, not yet thoroughly brought into subjection by the English, took every opportunity to make incursions upon the more civilized inhabitants, and slew all they were able to overpower. 14. To subdue these was an employment that Essex thought worthy of his ambition; nor were his enemies displeased at thus removing him from court, where he obstructed all their private aims of preferment. But it ended in his ruin. Instead of attacking the enemy in their grand retreat in Ulster, he led his forces into the province of Munster, where he only exhausted his strength, and lost his opportunity against a people that submitted at his approach, but took up arms when he retired. 15. This issue of an enterprise, from which much was expected, did not fail to provoke the queen most sensibly; and her anger was still more heightened by the peevish and impatient letters which he daily wrote to her and the council. But her resentment against him was still more justly let loose, when she found that, leaving the place of his appointment and without any permission demanded or obtained, he returned from Ireland, to make his complaints to herself in person.

16. Though Elizabeth was justly offended, yet he soon won upon her temper to pardon him. He was now ordered to continue a prisoner in his own house till the queen's further pleasure should be known, and it is probable that the discretion of a few months might have reinstated him in all his former employments; but the impetuosity of his character would not suffer him to wait for a slow redress of what he considered as wrongs: and the queen's refusing his request to continue him in possesion of a lucrative monopoly of sweet wines, which he had long enjoyed, spurred him on to the most violent and guilty measures. (A. D. 1600.) 17. Having long built with fond credulity on his

great popularity, he began to hope, from the assistance of the giddy multitude, that revenge upon his enemies in council, which he supposed was denied him from the throne. His greatest dependence was upon the professions of the citizens of London, whose schemes of religion and government he appeared entirely to approve; and while he gratified the puritans, by railing at the government of the church, he pleased the envious, by exposing the faults of those in power. 18. Among other criminal projects, the result of blind rage and despair, it was resolved that Sir Christopher Blount, one of his creatures, should, with a choice detachment, possess himself of the palace gates; that Sir John Davis should seize the hall; sir Charles Danvers, the guard chamber; while Essex himself should rush in from the Mews, attended by a body of his partisans, into the queen's presence, and entreat her to remove his and her enemies, to assemble a new parliament, and to correct the defects of the present administration.

Questions for Examination.

1. 2. What were the circumstances that contributed to retard the armada?
4. Describe the gallant conduct of the English?
7. 8. What were the consequences?
9. What was the character of the earl of Essex?
12 How did he behave to the queen?
13. What expedition did he undertake?
14. What was his success?
15, 16. In what manner did he increase the queen's resentment?
17. From whom did Essex expect assistance?
18. On what project did he afterwards resolve?

SECTION V.

Raleigh, with hopes of new discoveries fired,
And all the depths of human wit inspired,
Moved o'er the western world in search of fame,
Adding fresh glory to Eliza's name.—*Dr. King.*

1. (A. D. 1601.) WHILE Essex was deliberating upon the manner in which he should proceed, he received a private note, by which he was warned to provide for his own safety. He now, therefore, consulted with his friends, touching the emergency of their situation; they were destitute of arms and ammunition, while the guards at the palace were doubled, so that any attack there would be fruitless. 2. While he and his confidants were in consultation, a person, probably employed by his enemies, came in, as a messenger from the citizens, with tenders of friendship and

assistance against all his adversaries. Wild as the project was of raising the city in the present terrible conjuncture, it was resolved on; but the execution of it was delayed till the day following.

8. Early in the morning of the next day he was attended by his friends, the earls of Rutland and Southampton, the lords Sandes, Parker, and Monteagle, with three hundred persons of distinction. The doors of Essex-house were immediately locked, to prevent all strangers from entering; and the earl now discovered his scheme for raising the city more fully to all the conspirators. In the mean time, sir Walter Raleigh sending a message to Ferdinando Georges, this officer had a conference with him in a boat on the Thames, and there discovered all their proceedings. 4. The earl of Essex, who now saw that all was to be hazarded, resolved to leave his house, and to sally forth to make an insurrection in the city. But he had made a very wrong estimate in expecting that popularity alone would aid him in time of danger; he issued out with about two hundred followers, armed only with swords; and in his passage to the city was joined by the earl of Bedford and lord Cromwell. 5. As he passed through the streets, he cried aloud, "For the queen! for the queen! a plot is laid for my life;" hoping to engage the populace to rise; but they had received orders from the mayor to keep within their houses, so that he was not joined by a single person. 6. In this manner, attended by a few of his followers, the rest having privately retired, he made towards the river; and, taking a boat, arrived once more at Essex-house, where he began to make preparations for his defence. But his case was too desperate for any remedy from valour; wherefore, after demanding in vain for hostages and conditions from his besiegers, he surrendered at discretion, requesting only civil treatment and a fair and impartial hearing.

7. Essex and Southampton were immediately carried to the archbishop's palace at Lambeth, whence they were the next day conveyed to the tower, and tried by the peers on the nineteenth of February following. Little could be urged in their defence; their guilt was too flagrant; and though it deserved pity, it could not meet an acquittal. Essex, after condemnation, was visited by that religious horror which seemed to attend him in all his disgraces. He was terrified almost to despair by the ghostly remonstrances of his own chaplain; he was reconciled to his

Queen Elizabeth signing the death warrant of Essex.

enemies, and made a full confession of his conspiracy. 8. It is alleged upon this occasion, that he had strong hopes of pardon from the irresolution which the queen seemed to discover before she signed the warrant for his execution. She had given him formerly a ring, which she desired him to send her in any emergency of this nature, and that it should procure his safety and protection. This ring was actually sent by the countess of Nottingham, who, being a concealed enemy to the unfortunate earl, never delivered it; while Elizabeth was secretly fired at his obstinacy in making no application for mercy or forgiveness. 9. The fact is, she appeared herself as much an object of pity as the unfortunate nobleman she was induced to condemn. She signed the warrant for his execution; she countermanded it; she again resolved on his death, and again felt a new return of tenderness. At last she gave her consent to his execution, and was never seen to enjoy one happy day more.

10. With the death of her favourite Essex, all Elizabeth's pleasures seemed to expire; she afterwards went through the business of the state merely from habit, but her satisfactions were no more. His distress was more than sufficient to destroy the remains of her constitution; and her end was now visibly seen to approach. Her voice soon after left her; she fell into a lethargic slumber, which continued some

hours; and she expired gently, without a groan, in the seventieth year of her age, and the forty-fifth of her reign.

11. Her character differed with her circumstances: in the beginning she was moderate and humble; towards the end of her reign haughty and severe. Though she was possessed of excellent sense, yet she never had the discernment to discover that she wanted beauty; and to flatter her charms at the age of sixty-five was the surest road to her favour and esteem.

12. But whatever were her personal defects, as a queen she is ever to be remembered by the English with gratitude. It is true, indeed, that she carried her prerogative in parliament to its highest pitch, so that it was tacitly allowed in that assembly that she was above all laws, and could make and unmake them at pleasure; yet still she was so wise and good as seldom to exert that power which she claimed, and to enforce few acts of her prerogative which were not for the benefit of her people. 13. It is true, in like manner, that the English, during her reign, were put in possession of no new or splendid acquisitions; but commerce was daily growing up among them, and the people began to find that the theatre of their truest conquests was to be on the bosom of the ocean. A nation, which had hitherto been the object of every invasion, and a prey to every plunderer, now asserted its strength in turn, and became terrible to its invaders. 14. The successful voyages of the Spaniards and Portuguese began to excite their emulation, and they planned several expeditions for discovering a shorter passage to the East Indies. The famous Sir Walter Raleigh, without any assistance from government, colonized New England; while internal commerce was making equal improvements; and many Flemings, persecuted in their native country, found, together with their arts and industry, an easy asylum in England. 15. Thus the whole island seemed as if roused from her long habits of barbarity; arts, commerce, and legislation began to acquire new strength every day; and such was the state of learning at that time, that some fix that period as the Augustan age of England. Sir Walter Raleigh and Hooker are considered as among the first improvers of our language. 16. Spenser and Shakspeare are too well known as poets to be praised here; but, of all mankind, Francis Bacon, lord Verulam, who flourished in this reign, deserves, as a philosopher, the highest applause; his style is copious and correct, and his wit is only surpassed

by his learning and penetration. 17. If we look through history, and consider the rise of kingdoms, we shall scarcely find an instance of a people becoming, in so short a time, wise, powerful, and happy. Liberty, it is true, still continued to fluctuate; Elizabeth knew her own power, and stretched it to the very verge of despotism; but, now that commerce was introduced, liberty soon after followed; for there never was a nation that was perfectly commercial that submitted long to slavery.

Questions for Examination.
1. What project did Essex resolve on for rising the city?
3, 4, 5. How did he proceed to effect this?
6, 7. What was the fate of Essex and Southampton?
8. What induced Essex to have hopes of pardon?
9. What was Elizabeth's conduct on this occasion?
10. Did Elizabeth long survive the death of her favourite?
11. What was her character?
13. What was the political condition of England at the death of Elizabeth?
14. Did any important events take place during her reign?
15. What was the state of learning, and what eminent men flourished at this time?

CONTEMPORARY SOVEREIGNS.

Popes.	A.D.		A.D.	Union of Spain and Portugal.	
Paul IV.	1555	Selim II.	1566		A.D.
Pius IV.	1559	Amurath III.	1574	Philip II.	1580
Pius V.	1565	Mahomet III.	1595	Philip III.	1597
Gregory XIII.	1572	*Kings of France.*		*Kings of Denmark.*	
Sextus V.	1585	Henry II.	1547	Christian IV.	1558
Urban VII.	1590	Francis II.	1559	Frederick II.	1559
Gregory XIV.	1590	Charles IX.	1560	*Kings of Sweden.*	
Innocent IX.	1591	Henry III.	1574	Eric X.	1556
Clement VIII.	1592	Henry IV.	1589	John III.	1569
Emperors of Germany.		*King of Spain.*		Sigismund.	1592
Ferdinand I.	1558	Philip II.	1555	*Queen and King of Scotland.*	
Maximilian II.	1564	*Kings of Portugal.*			
Rodolphus II.	1576	Sebastian.	1557	Mary.	1542
Emperors of the Turks.		Henry.	1579	James VI.	1567
Soliman II.	1520				

EMINENT PERSONS.

Shakspeare. Spenser. Bacon. Sir Philip Sidney. Sir Walter Raleigh.* Sir Francis Drake. Lord Howard of Effingham. Cecil. Lord Burleigh. Robert Dudley, earl of Leicester. Sir Martin Frobisher. Sir John Hawkins, &c. &c.

* Sir Walter Raleigh is said to have attracted Elizabeth's notice by a delicate act of gallantry. When the queen, in one of her customary walks, hesitated about passing a miry spot, Raleigh, then a young adventurer, threw his cloak before her as a carpet. He was immediately invited to court, and the most brilliant prospects began to open before him.

CHAPTER XXVII.

JAMES I.

Born 1556. Died March 27, 1625. Began to reign March 24, 1603. Reigned 22 years over Great Britain, 58 years (nearly) over Scotland.

> Now, on the great and glorious queen's demise,
> The Scottish James her vacant place supplies;
> Uniting into one, both crowns he claims,
> And then, conjunctively, Great Britain names.—*Egerton*.

1. (A.D. 1603.) JAMES the Sixth of Scotland, and the First of England, the son of Mary, came to the throne with the universal approbation of all orders of the state, as in his person were united every claim that either descent, bequest, or parliamentary sanction could confer. However, in the very beginning of his reign, a conspiracy was set on foot, the particulars of which are but obscurely related. 2. It is said to have been begun by lord Grey, lord Cobham, and sir Walter Raleigh, who were all condemned to die, but had their sentence mitigated by the king. Cobham and Grey were pardoned after they had laid their heads on the block. Raleigh was reprieved, but remained in confinement many years afterwards, and at last suffered for his offence, which was never proved.

3. Mild as this monarch was in toleration, there was a project contrived in the very beginning of his reign for the re-establishment of popery, which, were it not a fact known to all the world, could scarcely be credited by posterity. This was the gunpowder plot, than which a more horrid or terrible scheme never entered into the human heart to conceive.

4. The Roman Catholics had expected great favour and indulgence on the accession of James, both as a descendant of Mary, a rigid Catholic, and also as having shown some partiality to that religion in his youth; but they soon discovered their mistake, and were at once surprised and enraged to find James, on all occasions, express his resolution of strictly exercising the laws enacted against them, and of persevering in the conduct of his predecessor. This declaration determined them upon more desperate measures; and they at length formed a resolution of destroying the king and both houses of parliament at a blow. The scheme was first broached by Robert Catesby, a gentleman of good parts and ancient family; who conceived that a train of gunpowder

might be so placed under the parliament-house as to blow up the king and all the members at once.

6. How horrid soever the contrivance might appear, yet every member seemed faithful and secret in the league, and about two months before the sitting of parliament they hired a house, in the name of Percy, adjoining to that in which the parliament was to assemble. 7. Their first intention was to bore a way under the parliament-house from that which they occupied, and they set themselves labouring at the task; but when they had pierced the wall, which was three yards in thickness, on approaching the other side they were surprised to find that the house was vaulted underneath, and that a magazine of coals was usually deposited there. 8. From their disappointment on this account they were soon relieved, by information that the coals were then selling off, and that the vaults would then be let to the highest bidder. They therefore seized the opportunity of hiring the place, and bought the remaining quantity of coals with which it was then stored, as if for their own use. 9. The next thing done was to convey thither thirty-six barrels of gunpowder, which had been purchased in Holland; and the whole was covered with coals and fagots, bought for that purpose. Then the doors of the cellar were boldly thrown open, and every body admitted as if it contained nothing dangerous.

10. Confident of success, they now began to plan the remaining part of their project. The king, queen, prince Henry, the king's eldest son, were all expected to be present at the opening of parliament. The king's second son, by reason of his tender age, would be absent, and it was resolved that Percy should seize or assassinate him. The princess Elizabeth, a child likewise, was kept at lord Harrington's house in Warwickshire; and sir Everard Digby was to seize her, and immediately proclaim her queen.

11. The day for the sitting of parliament now approached. Never was treason more secret or ruin more apparently inevitable: the hour was expected with impatience, and the conspirators gloried in their meditated guilt. The dreadful secret, though communicated to above twenty persons, had been inviolably kept during the space of a year and a half. When all the motives of pity, justice, and safety were too weak, a remorse of private friendship saved the kingdom.

12. Sir Henry Percy, one of the conspirators, conceived a design of saving the life of lord Monteagle, his intimate

friend and companion, who also was of the same persuasio[n] with himself. About ten days before the meeting of parli[a]ment, this nobleman, upon his return to town, received [a] letter from a person unknown, and delivered by one wh[o] fled as soon as he had discharged his message. 13. Th[e] letter was to this effect: "My lord, stay away from th[e] parliament; for God and man have concurred to punish th[e] wickedness of the times. And think not slightly of th[e] advertisement, but retire yourself into your county, whe[re] you may expect the event in safety. For though there b[e] no appearance of any stir, yet I say they will receive a te[r]rible blow this parliament; and yet they shall not see wh[o] hurts them. This counsel is not to be condemned, becau[se] it may do you good, and can do you no harm. For th[e] danger is passed as soon as you have burned the letter."

14. The contents of this mysterious letter surprised an[d] puzzled the nobleman to whom it was addressed; an[d] though inclined to think it a foolish attempt to affright an[d] ridicule him, yet he judged it safest to carry it to lord Sali[s]bury, secretary of state. 15. Lord Salisbury, too, was i[n]clined to give little attention to it, yet thought proper to la[y] it before the king in council, who came to town a few day[s] after. None of the council were able to make any thing [of] it, although it appeared serious and alarming. In the un[i]versal agitation between doubt and apprehension, the kin[g] was the first who penetrated the meaning of this dark epistle[.] 16. He concluded that some sudden danger was preparin[g] by gunpowder; and it was thought advisable to inspect al[l] the vaults below the houses of parliament. This care be[longed to the earl of Suffolk, lord chamberlain, who pur[posely delayed the search till the day before the meeting o[f] parliament, November 5, 1605. He remarked those grea[t] piles of fagots which lay in the vault under the house o[f] peers, and seized a man preparing for a terrible enterprise[,] dressed in a cloak and boots, with a dark lantern in hi[s] hand. 17. This was no other than Guy Fawkes who ha[d] just deposited every part of the train for its taking fire th[e] next morning, the matches and other combustibles bein[g] found in his pockets. The whole design was now discov[ered; but the atrociousness of his guilt, and the despair o[f] pardon inspiring him with resolution, he told the officers o[f] justice, with an undaunted air, that, had he blown them an[d] himself up together, he had been happy. Before the coun[cil he displayed the same intrepid firmness, mixed even wit[h]

Seizure of Guy Fawkes.

scorn and disdain, refusing to discover his associates, and showing no concern but for the failure of his enterprise. But his bold spirit was at length subdued; being confined in the Tower for two or three days, and the rack just shewn him, his courage, fatigued with so long an effort, at last failed him, and he made a full discovery of all his accomplices.

Questions for Examination.

1. Who succeeded Elizabeth?
2. What conspiracy was set on foot at the commencement of this reign?
3. What project was contrived for the re-establishment of popery?
5. By whom was it first broached?
6–9. In what manner was the project endeavoured to be carried into effect?
10. Who were expected to be present at the opening of parliament?
11. To how many persons had the plot been revealed?
12. What circumstance saved the kingdom?
13. What were the contents of Percy's letter?
15. Who was the first to discover the meaning of the letter?
16. Can you relate the measures taken to prevent the apprehended danger?
17. What was the name of the person engaged in this enterprise, and what was his conduct on being discovered?

SECTION II.

Yet Raleigh left a deathless name,
To learning dear, and dear to fame.—Dibdin.

1. (A. D. 1695.) CATESBY, Percy, and the conspirators who were in London, hearing that Fawkes was arrested, fled with all speed to Warwickshire, where sir Everard

Digby, relying on the success of the plot, was already in arms. But the country soon began to take the alarm, and wherever they turned, they found a superior force ready to oppose them. 2. In this exigence, beset on all sides, they resolved, to the number of about eighty persons, to fly no further, but to make a stand at a house in Warwickshire, to defend it to the last, and sell their lives as dearly as possible. But even this miserable consolation was denied them; a spark of fire happening to fall among some gunpowder that was laid to dry, it blew up, and so maimed the principal conspirators, that the survivors resolved to open the gate, and sally out against the multitude that surrounded the house. 3. Some were instantly cut to pieces; Catesby, Percy, and Winter, standing back to back, fought long and desperately, till in the end the two first fell covered with wounds, and Winter was taken alive. Those that survived the slaughter were tried and convicted; several fell by the hands of the executioner, and others experienced the king's mercy. The jesuits, Garnet and Oldcorn, who were privy to the plot, suffered with the rest; and, notwithstanding the atrociousness of their treason, Garnet was considered by his party as a martyr, and miracles were said to have been wrought by his blood.

4. The sagacity with which the king first discovered the plot raised the opinion of his wisdom among the people, but the folly with which he gave himself up to his favourites quickly undeceived the nation. (A.D. 1612.) In the first rank of these stood Robert Carr, a youth of a good family in Scotland, who, after having passed some time in his travels, arrived in London, at about twenty years of age. All his natural accomplishments consisted in a pleasing visage; and all his acquired abilities in an easy and graceful demeanour.

5. This youth was considered as a most rising man at court; he was knighted, created viscount Rochester, honoured with the order of the garter, made a privy councillor, and, to raise him to the highest pitch of honour, he was at last created earl of Somerset.

6. This was an advancement which some regarded with envy; but the wiser part of mankind looked upon it with contempt and ridicule, sensible that ungrounded attachments are seldom of long continuance. Some time after, being accused and convicted, from private motives, of poisoning Sir Thomas Overbury in the tower, he fell under the king's

displeasure; and, being driven from court, spent the remainder of his life in contempt and self-conviction.

7. But the king had not been so improvident as to part with one favourite until he had provided himself with another. This was George Villiers, a youth of one and twenty, the younger brother of a good family, who was returned about that time from his travels, and whom the enemies of Somerset had taken occasion to throw in the king's way, certain that his beauty and fashionable manners would do the rest. 8. Accordingly he had been placed at a comedy full in the king's view and immediately caught the monarch's affections. In the course of a few years, he was created viscount Villiers, earl, marquis, and duke of Buckingham, knight of the garter, master of the horse, chief justice in eyre, warden of the cinque ports, master of the king's bench office, steward of Westminster, constable of Windsor, and lord high admiral of England.

9. The universal murmur which these foolish attachments produced was soon after heightened by an act of severity, which still continues as the blackest stain upon this monarch's memory. The brave and learned Raleigh had been confined in the Tower almost from the very beginning of James' accession, for a conspiracy which had never been proved against him; and in that abode of wretchedness he wrote several valuable performances which are still in the highest esteem. 10. His long sufferings, and his ingenious writings, had now turned the tide of popular opinion in his favour; and they who once detested the enemy of Essex, could not now help pitying the captivity of this philosophical soldier. He himself still struggled for freedom; and perhaps it was with this desire that he spread the report of his having discovered a gold mine in Guiana, which was sufficient to enrich not only the adventurers who should seize it, but afford immense treasures to the nation. 11. The king, either believing his assertions, or willing to subject him to further disgrace, granted him a commission to try his fortune in quest of these golden schemes; but still reserved his former sentence as a check upon his future behaviour.

12. Raleigh was not long in making preparations for this adventure, which, from the sanguine manner in which he carried it on, many thought he believed to be as promising as he described it. He bent his course to Guiana, and remaining himself at the mouth of the river Orinoko with five of the largest ships, he sent the rest up the stream, under

the command of his son and captain Kemmis, a person tirely devoted to his interest. 13. But, instead of a coun abounding in gold, as the adventurers were taught to expe they found the Spaniards had been warned of their approa and were prepared in arms to receive them. Young leigh, to encourage his men, called out "That was the t mine," meaning the town of St. Thomas which he v approaching; and "that none but fools looked for any othei but just as he was speaking he received a shot, of which immediately expired. This was followed by another a appointment; for when the English took possession of town they found nothing in it of any value.

14. Raleigh in this forlorn situation, found now that his hopes were over; and saw his misfortunes still furtl aggravated by the reproaches of those whom he had und taken to command. Nothing could be more deplorable th his situation, particularly when he was told that he must carried back to England, to answer for his conduct to t king. 15. It is pretended that he employed many artific first to engage them to attack the Spanish settlements at time of peace, and, failing of that, to make his escape in France. But all of those proving unsuccessful, he was livered into the king's hands and strictly examined, as w as his fellow-adventurers, before the privy council. Cou Gondemar, the Spanish ambassalor, made heavy complai against the expedition; and the king declared that Ralei had express orders to avoid all disputes and hostilit against the Spaniards. 16. Wherefore to give the court Spain a particular instance of his attachment, he signed t warrant for his execution; not for the present offence, for his former conspiracy. This great man died with same fortitude he had testified through life; he observe as he felt the edge of the axe, that it was a sharp but a su remedy for all evils; his harangue to the people was ca and eloquent; and he laid his head down on the block w the utmost indifference.

Questions for Examination.

1. What measures were taken by the principal conspirators?
3. What was their fate?
4. Who was king James' first favourite?
6. How did Somerset fall under the king's displeasure?
7. Who was the king's next favourite?
8. What honours did he confer on him?
   For what was sir Walter Raleigh confined in the Tower?

10. What report did Raleigh spread?
12—15. Mention the particulars relating to this expedition?
16. What was the fate of this great man?
What was his behaviour at his execution?

SECTION II.

*Though scorned abroad, bewilder'd in a maze
Of fruitless treaties, while at home enslaved,
He lost his people's confidence and love.—Thomson.*

1. (A.D. 1618.) BUT there soon appeared very apparent reasons for James' partiality to the court of Spain. This monarch had entertained an opinion which was peculiar to himself, that in marrying his son Charles, the prince of Wales, any alliance below that of royalty would be unworthy of him; he, therefore, was obliged to seek, either in the court of France or Spain, a suitable match, and he was taught to think of the latter. 2. Gondemar, who was an ambassador from the court, perceiving this weak monarch's partiality to a crowned head, made an offer of the second daughter of Spain to prince Charles; and that he might render the temptation irresistible, he gave hopes of an immense fortune which should attend the princess. However, this was a negotiation which was not likely soon to be ended; and from the time the idea was first started, James saw five years elapse without bringing the treaty to any kind of conclusion.

3. A delay of this kind was very displeasing to the king, who had all along an eye on the great fortune of the princess; nor was it less disagreeable to prince Charles, who, bred up with the ideas of romantic passion, was in love without ever seeing the object of his affections. In this general tedium of delay, a project entered the head of Villiers, who had for some years ruled the king with absolute authority, that was fitter to be conceived by the knight of a romance than by a minister and a statesman. 4. It was projected that the prince should himself travel in disguise into Spain, and visit the princess of that country in person. Buckingham, who wanted to ingratiate himself with the prince, offered to be his companion; and the king, whose business it was to check so wild a scheme, gave his consent to this hopeful proposal. 5. Their adventures on this strange project would fill novels; and have actually been made the subject of many. Charles was the knight-errant, and Buckingham was the squire. The match, however,

broke off, for what reasons historians do not assign; but, if we may credit the novelists of that time, the prince had already fixed his affections upon the daughter of Henry IV. of France, whom he married shortly after.

6. It may be easily supposed that these mismanagements were seen and felt by the people. The house of commons was become by this time quite unmanageable; the prodigality of James to his favourites had made his necessities so many, that he was contented to sell the different branches of his prerogative to the commons, one after the other, to procure supplies. In proportion as they perceived his wants, they found out new grievances; and every grant of money was sure to come with a petition for redress. The struggles between him and the parliament had been growing more and more violent every session; and the very last advanced their pretensions to such a degree, that he began to take the alarm: but these evils, which the weakness of this monarch had contributed to give birth to, fell upon his successor.

7. These domestic troubles were attended by others still more important in Germany, and which produced in the end most dangerous effects. The king's eldest daughter had been married to Frederic, the elector palatine of Germany; and this prince, revolting against the emperor Ferdinand the Second, was defeated in a decisive battle, and obliged to take refuge in Holland. 8. His affinity to the English crown, his misfortunes, but particularly the Protestant religion, for which he had contended, were strong motives to the people of England to wish well to his cause; and frequent addresses were sent from the commons to induce James to take a part in the German contest, and to replace the exiled prince upon the throne of his ancestors. 9. James at first attempted to ward off the misfortunes of his son-in-law by negotiation, A. D. 1620; but this proving utterly ineffectual it was at last resolved to rescue the palatinate from the emperor by force of arms. Accordingly, war was declared against Spain and the emperor; six thousand men were sent over into Holland, to assist prince Maurice in his schemes against those powers; the people were everywhere elated at the courage of their king, and were satisfied with any war which was to exterminate the papists. 10. This army was followed by another, consisting of twelve thousand men, commanded by count Mansfeldt; and the court of France promised its assistance. But the English were disappointed in all their views; the troops being em-

barked at Dover, upon sailing to Calais they found no orders for their admission. After waiting in vain for some time, they were obliged to sail towards Zealand, where no proper measures were yet concerted for their disembarkation. 11. Meanwhile a pestilential disease crept in among the forces, so long cooped up in narrow vessels; half the army died while on board; and the other half, weakened by sickness, appeared too small a body to march into the palatinate; and thus ended this ill-concerted and fruitless expedition.

12. Whether this misfortune had any effect upon James' constitution is uncertain; but he was soon after seized with a tertian ague, which, when his courtiers assured him from the proverb that it was health for a king, he replied, that the proverb was made for a young king. (A. D. 1625.) After some fits he found himself extremely weakened, and sent for the prince, whom he exhorted to persevere in the Protestant religion; then, preparing with decency and courage to meet his end, he expired, after a reign over England of twenty-two years, and in the fifty-ninth year of his age.

Questions for Examination.
1. What were the reasons for James' partiality to Spain?
2. What offer was made by the Spanish ambassador?
4. What project was formed by Villiers, and by whom was it undertaken?
5. What was its success?
6. How did the house of commons act towards James?
7—11. Relate the circumstances that occurred in Germany.
12. In what manner did the king conduct himself previously to his death? How long did he reign?

CONTEMPORARY SOVEREIGNS.

Popes		*Emperors of the Turks.*		*Kings of Spain and Portugal.*	
	A.D.		A.D.		A.D.
Clement VIII	1592	Achmet I	1603	Philip III	1597
Leo XI	1605	Mustapha I	1617	Philip IV	1621
Paul III	1605	Osman I	1618	*King of Denmark.*	
Gregory XV	1621	Mustapha I. re-			
Urban VIII	1623	stored	1622	Christian IV	1588
		Amurath IV	1623		
Emperors of Germany.		*Kings of France.*		*Kings of Sweden.*	
Rodolphus II	1576			Sigismund	1592
Matthias I	1612	Henry IV	1589	Charles IX	1606
Ferdinand II	1619	Louis XIII	1610	Gustavus II	1611

EMINENT PERONS.

Henry, prince of Wales. Carr, earl of Somerset. Villiers, duke of Buckingham. Lord chancellor Bacon. WILLIAM SHAKSPEARE. Sir Walter Raleigh. Sir Hugh Middleton. Lord chancellor Maitland. W. A., earl of Stirling. Sir M. Kerr, earl of Ancram. J. Hamilton, earl of Haddington. James, duke of Hamilton. Henry Carey, lord Falkland.

G. Calvert, lord Baltimore. Robert Carey, earl of Monmouth. Sir M. Cecil, earl of Salisbury. Henry Howard, earl of Northampton. Lord chancellor Ellesmere. Sir Faulke Greville, lord Brooke. G. Carew, earl of Totness. W. Herbert, earl of Pembroke. Sir Dudley Carleton, viscount Dorchester. E. Cecil, viscount Wimbledon, &c., &c.

CHAPTER XXVIII.

CHARLES I.

Born 1600. Died January 30, 1649. Began to reign March 27, 1625. Reigned 23¾ years.

SECTION I.

*The monarch's deeds shall large allowance claim,
With whom too often, to a nation's shame,
Success is virtue and misfortune blame.—Dibdin.*

1. (A. D. 1625.) FEW princes ever ascended the throne with more apparent advantages than Charles; and none ever encountered more real difficulties. Indeed, he undertook the reigns of government with a fixed persuasion that his popularity was sufficient to carry every measure. 2. He had been loaded with a treaty for defending the prince palatine, his brother-in-law, in the last reign; and the war declared for that purpose was to be carried on with vigour in this. But war was more easily declared than supplies granted. After some reluctance, the commons voted him two subsidies; a sum far from being sufficient to support him in his intended equipment.

3. To supply the want of parliamentary aid, Charles had recourse to some of the ancient methods of extortion, practiced by sovereigns when in necessitous circumstances. That kind of tax called a benevolence was ordered to be exacted, and privy seals were issued accordingly. With this the people were obliged, though reluctantly, to comply; it was in fact authorised by many precedents; but no precedent whatsoever could give a sanction to injustice.

4. After an ineffectual expedition to Cadiz, another attempt was made to obtain supplies in a more regular and constitutional manner than before. Another parliament was accordingly called; and though some steps were taken to exclude the more popular leaders of the last house of commons, by nominating them sheriffs of counties, yet the present parliament seemed more refractory than the former.

5. When the king laid before the house his necessities, and asked for a supply, they voted him only three subsidies, which amounted to about sixty thousand pounds, a sum no way adequate to the importance of the war, or the necessities of the state. In order, therefore, to gain a sufficient supply, a commission was openly granted to compound with the catholics, and agree for a dispensation of the penal laws against them. He borrowed a sum of money from the nobility, whose contributions came in but slowly. 6. But the greatest stretch of his power was in the levying of ship-money. In order to equip a fleet (at least this was the pretence made), each of the maritime towns was required, with the assistance of the adjacent counties, to arm as many vessels as were appointed them. The city of London was rated at twenty ships. This was the commencement of a tax, which, afterwards, being carried to such violent lengths, created such discontents in the nation.

7. War being soon after declared against France, a fleet was sent out, under the command of Buckingham, to relieve Rochelle, a maritime town in that kingdom, that had long enjoyed its privileges, independent of the French king; but that had for some time embraced the reformed religion, and now was besieged with a formidable army. This expedition was as unfortunate as that to the coast of Spain. 8. The duke's measures were so ill concerted, that the inhabitants of the city shut their gates, and refused to admit allies, of whose coming they were not previously informed. Instead of attacking the island of Olderon, which was fertile and defenceless, he bent his course to the isle of Rhé, which was garrisoned and well fortified. He attempted there to starve out the garrison of St. Martin's castle, which was plentifully supplied with provisions by sea. 9. By that time the French had landed their forces privately at another part of the island; so that Buckingham was at last obliged to retreat, but with such precipitation, that two-thirds of his army were cut to pieces before he could re-embark, though he was the last man of the whole army that quitted the shore. 10. This proof of his personal courage, however, was but a small subject of consolation for the disgrace which his country had sustained, for his own person would have been the last they would have regretted.

11. The contest between the king and the commons every day grew warmer. The officers of the custom-house were summoned before the commons, to give an account by what

authority they seized the goods of the merchants who had refused to pay the duty of tonnage and poundage, which they alleged was levied without the sanction of law. The barons of the exchequer were examined concerning their decrees on that head; and the sheriff of London committed to the Tower for his activity in supporting the custom-house officers. 12. These were bold measures; but the commons went still further, by a resolution to examine into religious grievances, and a new spirit of intolerance began to appear. A. D. 1629. The king, therefore, resolved to dissolve a parliament which he found himself unable to manage; and sir John Finch, the speaker, just as the question concerning tonnage and poundage was going to be put, rose up, and informed the house that he had a command from the king to adjourn.

13. The house upon this was in an uproar; the speaker was pushed back into his chair, and forcibly held in it by Hollis and Valentine, till a short remonstrance was framed, and passed by acclamation rather than vote. In this hasty production, papists and Arminians were declared capital enemies to the state; tonnage and poundage were condemned as contrary to the law; and not only those who raised that duty, but those who paid it, were considered as guilty of capital crimes.

14. In consequence of this violent procedure, sir Miles Hobart, sir Peter Haymen, Selden, Coriton, Long, and Strode, were, by the king's order, committed to prison under pretence of sedition. But the same temerity that impelled Charles to imprison them, induced him to grant them a release. 15. Sir John Elliot, Hollis, and Valentine were summoned before the king's bench; but they, refusing to appear before an inferior tribunal for faults committed in a superior, were condemned to be imprisoned during the king's pleasure; the two former to pay a fine of a thousand pounds each, and the latter five hundred, and to find sureties for their good behaviour. The members triumphed in their sufferings, while they had the whole kingdom as spectators and applauders of their fortitude.

16. In the meantime, while the king was thus distressed by the obstinacy of the commons, he felt a much severer blow by the death of his favourite, the duke of Buckingham, who fell a sacrifice to his unpopularity. 17. It had been resolved once more to undertake the raising of the siege of Rochelle; and the earl of Denbigh, brother-in-law to Buck-

ingham, was sent thither, but returned without effecting any thing. In order to repair this disgrace, the duke of Buckingham went in person to Portsmouth to hurry on another expedition, and punish such as had endeavoured to defraud the crown of the legal assessments. 18. In the general discontent that prevailed against that nobleman, it was daily expected that some severe measures would be resolved on; and he was stigmatized as the tyrant and betrayer of his country. There was one Felton who caught the general contagion,—an Irishman of good family, who had served under the duke as lieutenant, but had resigned, on being refused his rank on the death of his captain, who had been killed at the isle of Rhé. 19. This man was naturally melancholy, courageous, and enthusiastic; he felt for the country, as if labouring under a calamity which he thought it in the power of his single arm to remove. He therefore, resolved to kill the duke, and thus revenge his own private injuries, while he did service also to God and man. 20. Animated in this manner with gloomy zeal and mistaken patriotism, he travelled down to Portsmouth alone, and entered the town while the duke was surrounded by his levee and giving out the necessary orders for embarkation. While he was speaking to one of his colonels, Felton struck him over an officer's shoulder in the breast with his knife. 21. The duke had only time to say, "The villain has killed me," when he fell at the colonel's feet, and instantly expired. No one had seen the blow, nor the person who gave it; but a hat being picked up, on the inside of which was sewed a paper containing four or five lines of the remonstrance of the commons against the duke, it was concluded that this hat must belong to the assassin; and while they were employed in conjectures whose it should be, a man without a hat was seen walking very composedly before the door, and was heard to cry out, "I am he!" 22. He disdained denying a murder in which he gloried; and averred that he looked upon the duke as an enemy to his country, and, as such, deserving to suffer. When asked at whose instigation he had perpetrated that horrid deed, he answered that they need not trouble themselves in that inquiry; that his conscience was his only prompter, and that no man on earth could dispose him to act against its dictates. He suffered with the same degree of constancy to the last; nor were there many wanting who admired, not only his fortitude, but the action for which he suffered.

Questions for Examination.

1. Who succeeded James ?
3—6. What methods were taken to procure supplies ?
7—10. What success attended Buckingham's expedition to France ?
11. What followed the contest between the king and the commons ?
13. What uproar was excited by the king's command to adjourn ?
14, 15. Under what pretence did the king send many of the members to prison ?
17—21. Relate the circumstances which attended the assassination of the duke of Buckingham.
What was the conduct of the assassin ?

SECTION I.

When civil dudgeon first grew high,
And men fell out, they knew not why.—*Butler*.

1. (A. D. 1627.) THE king's first measure, now being left without a minister and a parliament, was a prudent one. He made a peace with the two crowns against whom he had hitherto waged war, which had been entered upon without necessity and conducted without glory. 2. Being freed from these embarrassments, he bent his whole attention to the management of the internal policy of the kingdom, and took two men as his associates in this task, who still acted an under part to himself. These were, sir Thomas Wentworth, afterwards created earl of Strafford; and Laud, afterwards archbishop of Canterbury.

3. While Laud, therefore, during this long interval, ruled the church, the king and Strafford undertook to manage the temporal interests of the nation. A declaration was dispersed, implying that during this reign no more parliaments would be summoned; and every measure of the king but too well served to confirm the suspicion.

4. Tonnage and poundage were continued to be levied by royal authority alone; custom-house officers received orders from the council to enter any house whatever, in search of suspected goods; compositions were openly made with papists, and their religion was become a regular part of the revenue. 5. The high commission court and the court of the star-chamber exercised their power, independent of any law, upon several bold innovators in liberty, who only gloried in their sufferings, and contributed to render government odious and contemptible. Prynne, a barrister at Lincolns'-Inn; Burton, a divine; and Bastwick, a physician, were tried before this tribunal for schismatical libels, in which they attacked, with great severity and intemperate

zeal, the ceremonies of the church of England. They were condemned to be pilloried, to lose their ears, and to pay five thousand pounds to the king.

6. Every year, every month, every day, gave fresh instances, during this long intermission of parliaments, of the resolution of the court to throw them off for ever; but the levying of ship money, as it was called, being a general burden, was universally complained of as a national grievance. This was a tax which had, in former reigns, been levied without the consent of parliament, but then the exigency of the state demanded such a supply. 7. John Hampden a gentleman of fortune in Buckinghamshire, refused to comply with the tax, and resolved to bring it to a legal determination. He had been rated at twenty shillings for his estate, which he refused to pay; and the case was argued twelve days in the exchequer chamber, before all the judges of England. 8. The nation regarded, with the utmost anxiety, the result of a trial that was to fix the limits of the king's power. All the judges, four only excepted, gave sentence in favour of the crown; while Hampden, who lost his cause, was more than sufficiently recompensed by the applause of the people.

9. The discontent and opposition which the king met with, in maintaining episcopacy among his English subjects might, one would think, hinder him from attempting to introduce it among those of Scotland, where it was generally hateful. Having published an order for reading the liturgy in the principal church in Edinburgh, the people received it with clamours and imprecations. 10. The seditious disposition in that kingdom, which had hitherto been kept within bounds, was now too furious for restraint, and the insurrection became general over all the country, and the Scots flew to arms with great animosity.

11. Yet still the king could not think of desisting from his design; and so prepossessed was he in favour of royal right, that he thought the very name of king, when forcibly urged, would induce them to return to their duty. Instead, therefore, of fighting with his opponents, he entered upon a treaty with them; so that a suspension of arms was soon agreed upon, and a treaty of peace concluded, which neither side intended to observe; and then both parties agreed to disband their forces. After much altercation, and many treaties signed and broken, both parties had recourse

once more to arms, and nothing but blood could satiate the contenders.

12. War being thus resolved on, the king took every method as before for raising money to support it. Ship-money was levied as usual; some other arbitrary taxes were exacted from the reluctant people with great severity, but these were far from being sufficient; and there now remained only one method more, the long-neglected method of a parliamentary supply.

13. The new house of commons, however, could not be induced to treat the Scots, who were of the same principles with themselves and contending against the same ceremonies, as enemies of the state. They regarded them as friends and brothers, who first rose to teach them a duty it was incumbent on all virtuous minds to imitate. The king, therefore, could reap no other fruits from this assembly than murmurings and complaints. 14. Every method he had taken to supply himself with money was declared an abuse, and breach of the constitution. The king, therefore, finding no hopes of a compliance with his requests, but recrimination instead of redress, once more dissolved the parliament, to try the most feasible methods of removing his necessities.

15. His necessities, however, continuing, the parliament was called, which did not cease sitting till they overturned the constitution. Without any interval they entered upon business, and, by unanimous consent, they struck a blow that might be regarded as decisive. Instead of granting the demand of subsidies, they impeached the earl of Strafford, the king's first minister, and had him arraigned before the house of peers for high-treason. 16. After a long and eloquent speech, delivered without premeditation, in which he confuted all the accusations of his enemies, he was found guilty by both houses of parliament; and nothing remained but for the king to give his consent to the bill of attainder. Charles, who loved Strafford tenderly, hesitated, and seemed reluctant, trying every expedient to put off so dreadful a duty as that of signing the warrant for his execution. 17. While he continued in this agitation of mind, not knowing how to act, his doubts were at last silenced by an act of heroic bravery in the condemned lord. He received a letter from that unfortunate nobleman, desiring that his life might be made the sacrifice of mutual reconciliation between the

king and the people; adding, that he was prepared to die, and to a willing mind there could be no injury. 18. This instance of noble generosity was but ill repaid by his master, who complied with his request. He consented to sign the fatal bill by commission. Strafford was beheaded on Tower-hill, behaving with all that composed dignity of resolution that was expected from his character.

19. In this universal rage for punishment, the parliament fell with great justice on two courts, which had been erected under arbitrary kings, and had seldom been employed but in cases of necessity. These were, the high commission court, and the court of star-chamber. A bill unanimously passed the houses to abolish both; and in them to annihilate the principal and most dangerous articles in the king's prerogative.

20. In the midst of these troubles an insurrection in the northern counties of Ireland, accompanied by several acts of atrocious cruelty, excited great alarm throughout the empire. The insurgents might have been easily subdued; but the king's deputies in Ireland, eager to make their fortunes by trading in confiscations, averred, that all the catholics in the kingdom were involved in the guilt of this rebellion, and by wicked arts changed the local disturbance into a general civil war. Many wanton murders were committed on both sides; religious zeal added bitterness to political animosity; the hatred of heresy by one party, and of popery by the other, led men to perpetrate and palliate crimes shocking to human nature. The war lasted several years; four hostile parties had armies in Ireland, the native Irish, the descendants of the early settlers, usually called "the lords of the pale," the royalists, and the puritans, who supported the supremacy of the English parliament. The last party, though infinitely the weakest, finally triumphed by taking advantage of the dissensions and errors of the other three.

21. The king, aware that he was already suspected of a secret attachment to popery, and that the northern Irish pretended to have his authority for taking up arms, used every means in his power to put down the rebellion. But he was no longer able to effect this desirable object; the native Irish and the lords of the pale, frequently deceived before, would not trust the royal promises; Parsons and Borlase, the lords justice of Ireland, refused to obey the king's commands: and the English parliament gladly used

the Irish war as a pretext for levying soldiers; for every one now clearly foresaw that the disputes between the king and the parliament must finally be decided by the sword. Many insinuations were thrown out that he had himself fomented this rebellion, and no money could be spared for the extinction of distant dangers, when they pretended that the kingdom was threatened with greater at home.

It was now that the republican spirit began to appear without any disguise in the present parliament; and that party, instead of attacking the faults of the king, resolved to destroy monarchy.

Questions for Examination.

1. What was the king's first measure after Buckingham's death?
2, 3. By whom was the king assisted in his government?
4. In what manner did the custom-house officers exact taxes?
5. What is said respecting the court of star-chamber?
6. What tax was the most generally complained of?
7, 8. By whom was the tax of ship-money opposed, and what were the consequences?
9—12. What produced an insurrection in Scotland, and afterwards war?
13. How were the Scotch regarded by the new parliament?
15. What was the conduct of the next parliament?
16—18. Describe the particulars of the trial and death of the earl of Strafford?
19. What were the next proceedings of parliament?
20. What insurrection took place in Ireland?
21. How was the king treated by his parliament on this occasion? What spirit now openly manifested itself?

SECTION III.

*The son and father loose mild nature's ties,
And by a brother's hand a brother dies.—Egerton.*

1. (A. D. 1641.) THE leaders of opposition began their operations by a resolution to attack episcopacy, which was one of the strongest bulwarks of the royal power. They accused thirteen bishops of high-treason, for enacting canons without the consent of parliament; and endeavoured to to prevail upon the house of peers to exclude all the prelates from their seats and votes in that august assembly. The bishops saw the storm that was gathering against them; and, probably to avert its effects, they resolved to attend their duty in the house of lords no longer.

2. This was a fatal blow to the royal interest; but it soon felt a much greater from the king's own imprudence. Charles had long suppressed his resentment, and only

strove to satisfy the commons by the greatness of his concessions; but, finding that all his compliances had but increased their demands, he could no longer restrain it. 3. He gave orders to Herbert, his attorney general, to enter an accusation of high treason in the house of peers against lord Kimbolton, one of the most popular men of his party, gether with five commoners; sir Arthur Haslerig, Hollis, Hampden, Pym, and Strode. 4. The articles were, that they had traitorously endeavoured to subvert the fundamental laws and government of the kingdom; to deprive the king of his regal power, and to impose on his subjects an arbitrary and tyrannical authority. Men had scarcely leisure to wonder at the precipitancy and imprudence of his impeachment when they were astonished by another measure still more rash and unsupported. 5. The next day the king himself was seen to enter the house of commons alone, advancing through the hall, while all the members stood up to receive him. The speaker withrew from the chair, and the king took possession of it. Having seated himself, and having looking around for some time, he told the house that he was sorry for the occasion that had forced him thither; that he was come in person to seize the members whom he had accused of high-treason, seeing they would not deliver them up to his sergeant-at-arms. He then sat down for some time, to see if the accused were present, but they had escaped a few minutes before his entry.

6. Thus disappointed, perplexed, and not knowing on whom to rely, he next proceeded,—amidst the clamours of the populace, who continued to cry out, "Privilege! privilege!"—to the common council of the city, and made his complaints to them. The common council only answered his complaints with a contemptuous silence; and, on his return, one of the populace, more insolent than the rest, cried out, "To your tents, O Israel!" a watch-word among the Jews when they intended to abandon their princes.

7. Being returned to Windsor, he began to reflect on the rashness of his former proceedings, and now, too late, resolved to make some atonement. He therefore, wrote to the parliament, informing them that he desisted from his former proceedings against the accused members; and assured them that upon all occasions he would be as careful of their privileges as of his life or his crown. Thus his former violence had rendered him hateful to his com.

mons, and his present submission now rendered him contemptible.

8. The power of appointing generals and levying armies was still a remaining prerogative of the crown. The commons having, therefore, first magnified their terrors of popery, which perhaps they actually dreaded, they proceeded to petition that the Tower might be put into their hands, and that Hull, Portsmouth, and the fleet should be intrusted to persons of their choosing. These were requests, the complying with which levelled all that remained of the ancient constitution; however, such was the necessity of the times, that they were first contested, and then granted. 9. At last, every compliance only increased the avidity of making fresh demands; the commons desired to have a militia, raised and governed by such officers and commanders as they should nominate, under pretext of securing them from the Irish papists, of whom they professed to be in great apprehension.

10. It was here that Charles first ventured to put a stop to these concessions, and being urged to give up the command of the army for an appointed time, he was so exasperated that he exclaimed "No, not for an hour." This peremptory refusal broke off all further treaty; and both sides were resolved to have recourse to arms.

11. No period since England began could show so many instances of courage, abilities, and virtue, as the present fatal opposition called forth into exertion, A.D. 1642. Now was the time when talents of all kinds, unchecked by authority, were called from the lower ranks of life, to dispute for power and pre-eminence.

12. Manifestos on the one side and on the other were now dispersed throughout the whole kingdom; and the people were universally divided between two factions, distinguished by the names of cavaliers and roundheads. The king's forces appeared in a very low condition; besides the trained bands of the country, raised by sir John Digby, the sheriff, he had not got together three hundred infantry. 13. His cavalry, which composed his chief strength, exceeded not eight hundred, and were very ill provided with arms. However, he was soon gradually reinforced from all quarters, but not being then in a condition to face his enemies, he thought it prudent to retire by slow marches to Derby, and thence to Shrewsbury, in order to countenance the levies which his friends were making in those quarters.

14. In the meantime the parliament was not remiss in preparations on their side. They had a magazine of arms at Hull, and sir John Hotham was appointed governor of that place by government. The forces also, which had been everywhere raised on pretence of the service of Ireland, were now more openly enlisted by the parliament for their own purposes, and the command given to the earl of Essex, a bold man, who rather desired to see monarchy abridged than totally destroyed; and in London no less than four thousand men were enlisted in one day.

15. Edge-hill was the first place where the two armies were put in array against each other, and the country drenched in civil slaughter. It was a dreadful sight to see above thirty thousand of the bravest men in the world, instead of employing their courage abroad, turning it against each other, while the dearest friends and nearest kinsmen embraced opposite sides, and prepared to bury their private regards in factious hatred. After an engagement of some hours, animosity seemed to be wearied out, and both sides separated with equal loss. Five thousand men are said to have been found dead on the field of battle.

Questions for Examination.

1. What was the first act of the leaders of the opposition?
By what means did the bishops avert the impending storm?
2, 3. What was the king's conduct on this occasion?
4. What were the articles of impeachment?
5. How did the king conduct himself when he went to the house of commons?
6. How did the common-council afterwards receive him?
7. What were the consequences of his rashness?
8, 9. What were the next demands of the commons?
10. On what occasion did the king stop all further concessions?
What was the result?
12. By what means were the contending parties distinguished?
13. In what situation were the king's forces?
14. What preparations did the parliament make?
15. Where did the armies first meet?
What was the issue of the battle?

SECTION IV.

To live with Freedom or to die with Fame.—*Day.*

1. (A. D. 1643.) IT would be tedious, and no way instructive, to enter into the marchings and counter-marchings of these undisciplined and ill-conducted armies; war was

a new trade to the English, as they had not seen a hostile engagement in the island for nearly a century before. The queen came to reinforce the royal party; she had brought soldiers and ammunition from Holland, and immediately departed to furnish more. 2. But the parliament, who knew its own consequence and strength, was no way discouraged. Their demands seemed to increase in proportion to their losses; and as they were repressed in the field, they grew more haughty in the cabinet. Such governors as gave up their fortresses to the king were attainted of high-treason. 3. It was in vain for the king to send proposals after any success; this only raised their pride and their animosity. But though this desire in the king to make peace with his subjects was the highest encomium on his humanity, yet his long negotiations, one of which was carried on at Oxford, were faulty as a warrior. He wasted that time in altercation and treaty which he should have employed in vigorous exertions in the field.

4. However, his first campaign, upon the whole, wore a favourable aspect. One victory followed after another; Cornwall was reduced to peace and obedience under the king; a victory was gained over the parliamentarians at Stratton-Hill, in Cornwall; another at Roundway Down, about two miles from Devizes; and a third at Chalgrave Field. Bristol was besieged and taken, and Gloucester was invested; the battle of Newbury was favourable to the royal cause; and great hopes of success were formed from an army in the north, raised by the marquis of Newcastle.

5. In this first campaign, the two bravest and greatest men of their respective parties were killed; as if it was intended, by the kindness of Providence, that they should be exempted from seeing the miseries and the slaughter which were shortly to ensue; these were John Hampden, and Lucius Cary, lord Falkland,—the first in a skirmish against prince Rupert; the other in the battle of Newbury, which followed shortly after.

6. Hampden, whom we have seen, in the beginning of these troubles, refusing to pay the ship-money, gained, by his inflexible integrity, the esteem even of his enemies. To these he added affability in conversation, temper, art, eloquence in debate, and penetration in council.

7. Falkland was still a greater loss, and greater character. He added to Hampden's severe principles a politeness and elegance but then beginning to be known in England. He

had boldly withstood the king's pretensions while he saw him making a bad use of his power; but, when he perceived the design of parliament to overturn the religion and the constitution of the country, he changed his side, and steadfastly attached himself to the crown. 8. From the beginning of the civil war, his natural cheerfulness and vivacity forsook him; he became melancholy, sad, pale, and negligent of his person, and seemed to wish for death. His usual cry among his friends, after a deep silence and frequent sighs, was "Peace! peace!" He now said, upon the morning of the engagement, that he was weary of the times, and should leave them before night. He was shot by a musket-ball in the chest; and his body was next morning found among a heap of slain. His writings, his elegance, his justice, and his courage deserved each a death of glory; and they found it.

9. The king, that he might make preparations during the winter for the ensuing campaign, and to oppose the designs of the Westminster parliament, called one at Oxford; and this was the first time that England saw two parliaments sitting at the same time. His house of peers was pretty full; his house of commons consisted of about one hundred and forty, which amounted to not above half of the other house of commons. From this shadow of a parliament he received some supplies, after which it was prorogued, and never after assembled.

10. In the meantime, the parliament were equally active on their side. They passed an ordinance commanding all the inhabitants of London and its neighbourhood to retrench a meal a week, and to pay the value of it for the support of the public cause. 11. But, what was more effectual, the Scots, who considered their claims as similar, led a strong body to their assistance. They levied an army of fourteen thousand men in the east under the earl of Manchester; they had an army of ten thousand men under Essex; another, of nearly the same force, under sir William Waller. These were superior to any force the king could bring into the field; and were well appointed with ammunition, provisions and pay.

12. Hostilities, which even during the winter season had never been wholly discontinued, were renewed in spring with their usual fury, and served to desolate the kingdom, without deciding victory. (A.D. 1644.) Each county joined that side to which it was addicted, from motives of conviction, interest, or fear, though some observed a perfect neu-

trality. Several frequently petitioned for peace; and all the wise and good were earnest in the cry. 13. What particularly deserves remark was an attempt of the women of London, who, to the number of two or three thousand, went in a body to the house of commons, earnestly demanding a peace—"Give us those traitors," said they, "that are against a peace: give them, that we may tear them to pieces." The guards found some difficulty in quelling this insurrection, and one or two women lost their lives in the affray.

14. The battle of Marston Moor was the beginning of the king's misfortunes and disgrace. The Scots and parliamentarian army had joined, and were besieging York, when prince Rupert, joined by the marquis of Newcastle, determined to raise the siege. Both armies drew up on Marston Moor, to the number of fifty thousand, and the victory seemed long undecided between them. 15. Rupert, who commanded the right wing of the royalists, was opposed by Oliver Cromwell, who now first came into notice, at the head of a body of troops which he had taken care to levy and discipline. Cromwell was victorious; he pushed his opponents off the field, followed the vanquished, returned to a second engagement, and a second victory; the prince's whole train of artillery was taken, and the royalists never after recovered the blow.

16. William Laud, archbishop of Canterbury, was sent to the Tower in the beginning of the civil war. He was now brought to his trial, condemned, and executed. And it was a melancholy consideration, that in those times of trouble, the best men on either side were those who chiefly suffered.

17. The death of Laud was followed by a total alteration of the ceremonies of the church. The liturgy was, by a public act, abolished the day he died, as if he had been the only obstacle to its former removal. The church of England was, in all respects, brought to a conformity to the puritanical establishment; while the citizens of London and the Scots' army gave public thanks for so happy an alteration.

Questions for Examination.

1. Who reinforced the royal party?
2. What courage did the parliament display?
4, 5. In the first campaign, where were the principal battles fought?
6. Describe the character of Hampden.
7. Describe the character of Falkland.

8. How was his death occasioned?
9. Where did the king summon a parliament, and what were their proceedings?
10. What ordinance was now passed?
11. What other measures were taken in opposition to the king?
12. What was the situation of the kingdom?
13. What earnest desire for peace did the women of London discover?
14, 15. Describe the particulars of the battle of Marston Moor.
16. What was the fate of archbishop Laud?
17. What followed his execution?

SECTION V.

*Guile, violence, and murder seized on man,
And, for milky streams, with blood the rivers ran.—Thomson.*

1. (A.D. 1645.) THE well-disputed battle, which decided the fate of Charles, was fought at Naseby, a village in Northamptonshire. The main body of the royal army was commanded by lord Astley; prince Rupert led the right wing, sir Marmaduke Langdale the left; and the king himself headed the body of reserve. 2. On the opposite side, Fairfax and Skippon commanded the main body. Cromwell led on the right wing, and Ireton, his son-in-law, the left. Prince Rupert attacked the left wing with his usual impetuosity and success; they were broken, and pursued as far as the village; but he lost time in attempting to make himself master of their artillery. 3. Cromwell, in the meantime, was equally successful on his side, and broke through the enemy's horse, after a very obstinate resistance. While these were thus engaged, the infantry on both sides maintained the conflict with equal ardour; but, in spite of the efforts of Fairfax and Skippon, their battalions began to give way. At this critical period Cromwell returned with his victorious forces, and charged the king's infantry in flank with such vigour, that a total rout began to ensue. 4. By this time prince Rupert had rejoined the king, and the small body of reserve: but his troops, though victorious, could not be brought to a second charge. The king, perceiving the battle wholly lost, was obliged to abandon the field to his enemies, who took all his cannon, baggage, and about fifty thousand prisoners.

5. The battle of Naseby put the parliamentarians in possession of almost all the strong cities of the kingdom, Bristol, Bridgewater, Chester, Sherborn, and Bath. Exeter was besieged; and all the king's troops in the western counties being entirely dispersed, Fairfax pressed the place,

and it surrendered at discretion. The king, thus surrounded, harassed on every side, retreated to Oxford, that, in all conditions of his fortune, had held steady to his cause; and there he resolved to offer new terms to his incensed pursuers.

6. In the meantime Fairfax was approaching with a powerful and victorious army, and was taking the proper measures for laying siege to Oxford, which promised an easy surrender. To be taken captive, and led in triumph by his insolent subjects, was what Charles justly abhorred: and every insult and violence was to be dreaded from the soldiery, who had felt the effects of his opposition.

7. In this desperate extremity he embraced a measure, which, in any other situation, might justly lie under the imputation of imprudence and indiscretion. He took the fatal resolution of giving himself up to the Scots army, who had never testified such implacable animosity against him; but he soon found that, instead of treating him as a king, they insulted him as a captive.

8. The English parliament, being informed of the king's captivity, immediately entered into a treaty with the Scots about delivering up their prisoner. This was soon adjusted. They agreed, that upon payment of four hundred thousand pounds, they would deliver up the king to his enemies, and this was cheerfully complied with. An action so atrocious may be palliated, but can never be defended; they returned home laden with plunder, and the reproaches of all good men.

9. The civil war was now over; the king had absolved his followers from their allegiance; and the parliament had now no enemy to fear, except those very troops by which they had extended their overgrown authority. But, in proportion as the terror of the king's power diminished, the divisions between the members which composed the parliament became more apparent. 10. The majority in the house were of the Presbyterian sect, who were for having clergy; but the majority of the army were staunch independents, who admitted of no clergy; but thought that every man had a right to instruct his fellows. At the head of this sect was Cromwell, who secretly directed their operations, and invigorated all their measures.

11. Oliver Cromwell, whose talents now began to appear in full lustre, was the son of a private gentleman of Huntington; but, being the son of a second brother, he inherited

a very small paternal fortune. From accident or intrigue he was chosen a member for the town of Cambridge in the long parliament; but he seemed at first to possess no oratorical talents; his person being ungraceful, his dress slovenly, his elocution homely, tedious, obscure, and embarrassed. 12. He made up, however, by zeal and perseverance what he wanted in natural powers; and, being endowed with unshaken intrepidity, much dissimulation, and a thorough conviction of the rectitude of his cause, he rose, through the gradations of preferment, to the post of lieutenant-general under Fairfax; but, in reality, possessing the supreme command over the whole army.

13. The army now began to consider themselves as a body distinct from the commonwealth; and complained that they had secured the general tranquillity, while they were at the same time deprived of the priviliges of Euglishmen. In opposition, therefore, to the parliament of Westminster, a military parliament was formed, composed of the officers and common soldiers of each regiment. 14. The principal officers formed a council to represent the body of peers; the soldiers elected two men out of each company, to represent the house of commons, and these were called the agitators of the army. Cromwell took care to be one of the number, and thus contrived an easy method of secretly conducting and promoting the sedition of the army.

15. The unhappy king, in the meantime, continued a prisoner at Holmby Castle; and as his countenance might add some authority to that side which should obtain it, Cromwell, who secretly conducted all the measures of the army, while he apparently exclaimed against their violence, resolved to seize the king's person. 16. Accordingly, a party of five hundred horse appearing at Holmby Castle, under the command of one Joyce, conducted the king to the army near Cambridge. The next day Cromwell arrived among them, where he was received with acclamations of joy, and was instantly invested with the supreme command.

Questions for Examination.

1. Where was the battle fought that decided the fate of Charles? Who were the leaders of the king's army?
2. By whom was the parliamentary army conducted?
4. What was the issue of the battle?
5. What towns surrendered to the parliamentarians after this engagement?
6. Where did the king fly for refuge?

7. On what measures did he now resolve?
8. What atrocious act was committed towards the king?
10. What were the parties which composed the parliament?
11. Who was Oliver Cromwell?
12. To what post in the army did he rise?
14. In what manner was a council formed from the army?
15. Where was the place of the king's confinement?
16. By whose command was he taken and conducted to the army?

SECTION VI.

*Though always by prosperity undone,
Yet in adversity this monarch shone.—Egerton.*

1. (A.D. 1647.) THE house of commons was now divided into parties, as usual; one part opposing, but the majority, with the two speakers at their head, encouraging the army. In such a universal confusion, it is not to be expected that anything less than a separation of the parties could take place; and accordingly the two speakers, with sixty-two members, secretly retired from the house, and threw themselves under the protection of the army, which was then at Hounslow-heath. 2. They were received with shouts and acclamations; their integrity was extolled; and the whole body of the soldiery, a formidable force of twenty thousand men, now moved forward, to reinstate them in their former seats and stations.

3. In the meantime, that part of the house which was left behind resolved to act with vigour, and resist the encroachments of the army. They chose new speakers, they gave orders for enlisting troops, they ordered the trainbands to man the lines; and the whole city boldly resolved to resist the invasion. But this resolution only held while the enemy was thought at a distance: for when the formidable force of Cromwell appeared, all was obedience and submission; the gates were opened to the general, who attended the speakers, and the rest of the members, peaceably to their habitations. 4. The eleven impeached members, being accused as causers of the tumult, were expelled, and most of them retired to the continent. The mayor, sheriff, and three aldermen were sent to the Tower; several citizens and officers of the militia were committed to prison, and the lines about the city were levelled to the ground. The command of the Tower was given to Fairfax, the general; and the parliament offered him their hearty thanks for having disobeyed their commands.

4. It now only remained to dispose of the king, who had

been sent by the army a prisoner to Hampton Court; from whence he attempted to escape, but was once more made prisoner in the Isle of Wight and confined in Carrisbrook Castle.

6. While the king continued in this forlorn situation, the parliament, new modelled as it was by the army, was every day growing more feeble and factious. He still, therefore, continued to negociate with the parliament for settling the unspeakable calamities of the kingdom. The parliament saw no other method of destroying the military power than to depress it by the kingly; and frequent proposals for an accommodation passed between the captive king and the commons.

7. But it was now too late; their power was soon totally to expire; for the rebellious army, crowned with success, was returned from the destruction of their enemies; and, sensible of their own power, with furious remonstrances began to demand vengeance on their king. At the same time they advanced to Windsor; and sending an officer to seize the king's person, where he was lately sent under confinement, they conveyed him to Hurst Castle, in Hampshire, opposite the Isle of Wight. 8. The commons, however, though destitute of all hopes of prevailing, had still courage to resist; and attempted, in the face of the whole army, to close their treaty with the king. But the next day colonel Pride, at the head of two regiments, blockaded the house, seized in the passage forty-one members of the Presbyterian party, and sent them to a low room belonging to the house, that passed by the denomination of hell. 9. Above a hundred, and sixty members more were excluded; and none were allowed to enter but the most furious and determined of the Independents, in all not exceeding sixty. This atrocious invasion of the parliamentary rights commonly passed by the name of Pride's Purge, and the remaining members were called the Rump. These soon voted that the transactions of the house a few days before were entirely illegal, and that their general's conduct was just and necessary.

10. A committee was appointed to bring in a charge against the king; and a vote passed, declaring it treason in a king to levy war against his parliament. A high court of justice was accordingly appointed, to try his majesty for this new-invented treason.

11. Colonel Harrison, the son of a butcher was com-

manded to conduct the king from Hurst Castle to Winsdor, and from thence to London. His afflicted subjects, who ran to have a sight of their sovereign, were greatly affected at the change that appeared in his face and person. He had allowed his beard to grow; his hair was become venerably gray, rather by the pressure of anxiety than the hand of time; while his apparel bore the marks of misfortune and decay. 12. Thus he stood a solitary figure of majesty in distress, which even his adversaries could not behold without reverence and compassion. He had been long attended only by an old decrepit servant, whose name was sir Phillip Warwick, who could only deplore his master's fate, without being able to revenge his cause. 13. All the exterior symbols of sovereignty were now withdrawn; and his new attendants had orders to serve him without ceremony. The duke of Hamilton, who was reserved for the same punishment with his master, having leave to take a last farewell as he departed from Windsor, threw himself at the king's feet, crying out, "My dear master!" 14. The unhappy monarch raised him up, and, embracing him tenderly replied, while tears ran down his cheeks, "I have indeed been a dear master to you." These were severe distresses; however he could not be persuaded that his adversaries would bring him to a formal trial; but he every moment expected to be despatched by private assassination.

15. From the sixth to the twentieth of January was spent in making preparations for this extraordinary trial. The court of justice consisted of a hundred and thirty-three persons, named by the commons; but of these never above seventy sat upon the trial. The members were chiefly composed of the principal officers of the army, most of them of very mean birth, together with some of the lower house, and a few citizens of London. Bradshaw, a lawyer, was chosen president; Coke was appointed solicitor for the people of England; Dorislaus, Steele, and Aske were named assistants. The court sat in Westminster-hall.

16. The king now was conducted from Windsor to St. James's, and the next day was brought before the high court to take his trial. When he was brought forward, he was conducted by the mace-bearer to a chair placed within the bar. Though long detained a prisoner, and now produced as a criminal, he still sustained the dignity of a king; he surveyed the members of the court with a stern and haughty air; and, without moving his hat, sat down

while the members also were covered. 17. His charge was then read by the solicitor, accusing him of having been the cause of all the bloodshed which followed since the commencement of the war; at that part of the charge he could not suppress a smile of contempt and indignation. After his charge was finished, Bradshaw directed his discourse to the king, and told him that the court expected his answer.

Questions for Examination.

1. What measures were pursued by the majority of the house of commons?
2. How were they received by the army?
3. What was the conduct of the remaining members?
4. To whom was the command of the Tower given?
5. Did not the king escape from the place of his confinement? Where was he taken?
6. Did he continue to negotiate with the parliament?
7—9. Describe the conduct of the army on this occasion.
11, 12. What was now the appearance of the king?
13. What passed between him and the duke of Hamilton?
15. How many persons sat on the king's trial?
16. Who were the chief?
17. What was his behaviour on his trial? What was the charge alleged against him?

SECTION VII.

*Nor agonies, nor livid death, disgrace
The sacred features of the monarch's face;
In the cold visage, mournfully serene,
The same indignant majesty is seen.—Rowe's Lucan.*

1. (A.D. 1648.) THE king, with great temper, entered upon his defence, by denying the authority of the court. He represented, that having been engaged in a treaty with his two houses of parliament, and having finished almost every article, he expected a different treatment from that which he now received. He perceived, he said, no appearance of an upper house, which was necessary to constitute a just tribunal. 2. That he was himself the king and the fountain of law, and, consequently, could not be tried by laws to which he had never given his assent; that having been intrusted with the liberties of the people, he would not now betray them, by recognising a power founded in usurpation; that he was willing, before a proper tribunal, to enter into the particulars of his defence; but that before them he must decline any apology or plea of innocence, lest he should be considered as the betrayer of, and not a martyr for, the constitution.

3. Bradshaw, in order to support the authority of the

court, insisted that they had received their power from the people, the source of all right. He pressed the prisoner not to decline the authority of the court, which was delegated by the commons of England; and he interrupted and overruled the king in his attempts to reply.

4. In this manner the king was three times produced before the court, and as often he persisted in declining its jurisdiction. The fourth and last time he was brought before the self-created tribunal; as he was proceeding thither, he was insulted by the soldiers and the mob, who exclaimed, "Justice! justice! execution! execution!" but he continued undaunted. His judges, having now examined some witnesses, by whom it was proved that the king had appeared in arms against the forces commissioned by parliament, pronounced sentence against him.

5. The conduct of the king, under all these instances of low-bred malice, was great, firm, and equal; in going through the hall, the soldiers and the rabble were again instigated to cry out, "Justice and execution!" They reviled him with the most bitter reproaches. Among other insults, one miscreant presumed to spit in the face of his sovereign. He patiently bore their insolence. "Poor souls," cried he, "they would treat their generals in the same manner for sixpence." 6. Those of the populace who still retained the feelings of humanity, expressed their sorrow in sighs and tears. A soldier, more compassionate than the rest, could not help imploring a blessing upon his royal head. An officer, overhearing him, struck the honest sentinel to the ground before the king, who could not help saying that the punishment exceeded the offence.

7. After returning from this solemn mockery of justice, the unhappy monarch petitioned the house for permission to see his children, and desired the attendance of Dr. Juxon, bishop of London, to assist in his private devotions. Both requests were immediately granted, and three days were allowed to prepare for the execution of the sentence. This interval was spent by Charles in the exercises of devotion, and in administering consolation to his unhappy family. 8. During the progress of the trial, the French and Dutch ambassadors vainly interceded in his behalf; and the Scots, who had set the first example of resistance to his authority, now remonstrated against the violence offered to his person and dignity. 9. After his condemnation, the queen and the prince of Wales wrote the most pathetic letters to the par

Execution of King Charles I., 1649.

liament, but nothing could divert the stern regicides from their atrocious design.

10. The king was confined in the palace of St. James's, but the place selected for erecting the scaffold was the street before the palace of Whitehall. 11. On the morning of the execution he rose early, and, having spent some time in private devotion, received the sacrament from the hands of bishop Juxon; he was then conducted on foot through the park to Whitehall, and partook of some slight refreshment; after a brief delay, he advanced to the place of execution, attended still by his friend and servant, Dr. Juxon, who used every exertion to soothe the last moments of his unfortunate master. 12. The scaffold, which was covered with black, was guarded by a regiment of soldiers, under the command of colonel Tomlinson, and under it were to be seen a block, the axe, and two executioners in masks. The people, in immense crowds, stood at a great distance, in dreadful expectation of the event. The king surveyed all these solemn preparations with calm composure; and as he could not expect to be heard by the people at a distance, he addressed himself to the few persons who stood around him.

13. He there justified his own innocence in the late fatal war; and observed, that he had not taken arms till after the parliament had shewn him the example. That he had no other object in his warlike preparations than to preserve that

authority entire, which had been transmitted to him by his ancestors; but though innocent towards his people, he acknowledged the equity of his execution in the eyes of his Maker. 14. He owned that he was justly punished for having consented to the execution of an unjust sentence upon the earl of Strafford. He forgave all his enemies; exhorted the people to return to their obedience, and acknowledged his son as his successor; and signed his attachment to the Protestant religion, as professed in the church of England. So strong was the impression his dying words made upon the few who could hear him, that colonel Tomlinson himself, to whose care he had been committed, acknowledged himself a convert.

15. While he was preparing himself for the block, bishop Juxon called out to him, "There is, sir, but one stage more, which, though turbulent and troublesome, is yet a very short one. It will soon carry you a great way. It will carry you from earth to heaven; and there you shall find, to your great joy, the prize to which you hasten, a crown of glory." 16. "I go," replied the king, "from a corruptible to an incorruptible crown, where no disturbance can have place." —" You exchange," replied the bishop, a temporal for an eternal crown; a good exchange!" Charles, having taken off his cloak, delivered his George to the prelate, pronouncing the word "Remember!" Then he laid his neck on the block, and, stretching out his hands as a signal, one of the executioners severed his head from his body at a blow; while the other, holding it up, exclaimed, "This is the head of a traitor!" 17. The spectators testified their horror of the sad spectacle in sighs, tears, and lamentations; the tide of their duty and affection began to return; and each blamed himself either with active disloyalty to his king, or a passive compliance with his destroyers.

18. Charles was executed in the forty-ninth year of his age, and the twenty-fourth of his reign. He was of a middle stature, robust, and well-proportioned. His visage was pleasing but melancholy; and it is probable that the continued troubles in which he was involved might have made that impression on his countenance. As for his character, the reader will deduce it, with more precision and satisfaction to himself, from the detail of his conduct, than from any summary given of it by the historian.

Questions for Examination.

1, 2. What did the king urge in his defence?
3. What was the answer of Bradshaw?
4. What treatment did he receive from the soldiers?
5. With what patience did he bear their reproaches, and what was his remark?
7, 8. What followed the king's condemnation?
9, 10. What spot was chosen as the place of the king's execution?
12. What preparations were made for his trial?
13, 14. What did he say in his address to the people?
15, 16. What conversation passed between the king and bishop Juxon?
17. What effect had his execution on the minds of the people?
18. How long did Charles reign?

CONTEMPORARY SOVEREIGNS.

Popes. A.D.	Emperors of the Turks. A.D.	King of Spain and Portugal. A.D.
Urbain VIII......1623	Amurath IV.. ..1623	Philip IV.........1621
Innocent X.......1644	Ibrahim...........1649	
	Mahomet IV......1643	Portugal alone.*
Emperors of Germany.	Kings of France.	
Ferdinand II.....1619	Louis XIII,.......1620	John IV..........1640
Ferdinand III....1637	Louis XIV........1643	

EMINENT PERSONAGES.

Archbishop Laud. Earl of Strafford. John Hampden. Lucius Cary, lord Falkland. Harry Cary, Lord Falkland. H. Montague, earl of Manchester. R. Greville, lord Brooke. Lord-keeper Littleton. Arthur, lord Capel. Lord Edward Herbert, of Cherbury. G. Stanley, earl of Derby. J. Digby, earl of Bristol. Ulicke de Burgh, marquis of Clanricarde, and earl of St. Albans. Henry Carey, earl of Monmouth. Mildmay Fane, earl of Westmoreland. E. Somerset, marquis of Worcester.

CHAPTER XXIX.

OLIVER CROMWELL.

Born 1599. Died September 3, 1658. Became lord protector December 16, 1653. Ruled 4½ years.

THE COMMONWEALTH.

SECTION I.

Though cunning, bold; and though intrepid, sage.—Egerton.

1. (A. D. 1649.) CROMWELL, who had secretly solicited and contrived the king's death, now began to feel wishes to which he had been hitherto a stranger. His prospects widening as he rose, his first principles of liberty were

---

* The Portuguese shook off the Spanish yoke, and elected John, duke of Braganza, their king.

all lost in the unbounded stretch of power that lay before him.

2. Having been appointed to command the army in Ireland, he prosecuted the war in that kingdom with his usual success. He had to combat against the royalists, commanded by the duke of Ormond, and the native Irish, led on by O'Neil. But such ill-connected and barbarous troops could give very little opposition to Cromwell's more numerous forces, conducted by such a general, and emboldened by long success. He soon overran the whole country; and, after some time, all the towns revolted in his favour, and opened their gates at his approach. 3. But, in these conquests, as in all the rest of his actions, there appeared a brutal ferocity, that would tarnish the most heroic valour. In order to intimidate the natives from defending their towns, he, with a barbarous policy, put every garrison that made any resistance to the sword.

4. After his return to England, upon taking his seat, he received the thanks of the house, by the mouth of the speaker, for the services he had done the commonwealth in Ireland. They then proceeded to deliberate upon choosing a general for conducting the war in Scotland, where they had espoused the royal cause, and placed young Charles, the son of their late monarch, on the throne. Fairfax refusing this command upon principle, as he had all along declined opposing the Presbyterians, the command necessarily devolved upon Cromwell, who boldly set forward for Scotland, at the head of an army of sixteen thousand men.

5. The Scots in the mean time, who had invited over their wretched king to be a prisoner, not a ruler among them, prepared to meet the invasion. (A. D. 1650.) A battle soon ensued, in which they, though double the number of the English, were soon put to flight, and pursued with great slaughter, while Cromwell did not lose above forty men in all.

6. In this terrible exigence young Charles embraced a resolution worthy a prince who was willing to hazard all for empire. Observing that the way was open to England, he resolved immediately to march into that country, where he expected to be reinforced by all the royalists in that part of the kingdom.

7. But he soon found himself disappointed in the expectation of increasing his army. The Scots, terrified at the prospect of so hazardous an enterprise, fell from him in great

numbers. The English, affrighted at the name of his opponent, dreaded to join him; but his mortifications were still more increased as he arrived at Worcester, when, informed that Cromwell was marching with hasty strides from Scotland, with an army increased to forty thousand men.

8. The news had scarcely arrived, when that active general himself appeared; and falling upon the town on all sides, broke in upon the disordered royalists. The streets were strewed with slaughter; the whole Scots' army were either killed or taken prisoners; and the king himself, having given many proofs of personal valour, was obliged to fly.

9. Imagination can scarcely conceive adventures more romantic or distress more severe, than those which attended the young king's flight from the scene of slaughter. After various escapes, and one-and-forty days' concealment, he landed safely at Feschamp in Normandy; no less than forty men and women having, at different times, been privy to his escape.

10. The particulars of Charles' escape, after the battle of Worcester are truly interesting. He left the fatal scene of action accompanied by the duke of Buckingham, the earls of Derby and Lauderdale, the lords Talbot, Wilmot, and fifty horse; and, without halting, arrived at Whiteladies, twenty-five miles from Worcester, at five o'clock in the morning. There he thought it best for his safety to separate from his companions; and, without intrusting them with his intentions, he went to Boscobel, a lone house in Staffordshire, inhabited by one Penderell, a farmer, whose fidelity remained unshaken, though death was denounced against all who concealed the king, and a great reward promised to any one who should betray him. Penderell, and his four brothers, having clothed the king in a garb like their own, led him into the neighbouring wood, put a bill into his hand, and employed themselves in cutting faggots with him. For better concealment he mounted upon an oak where he sheltered himself among the branches and leaves for twenty-four hours. There he saw several soldiers passing in search of him. This tree was afterwards called the royal oak, and for many years was regarded by the neighbourhood with great veneration. Thence he passed with imminent danger from one cottage to another, feeling all the varieties of famine, fatigue, and pain, till he reached the house of Mr. Lane, a gentleman of good reputation and fortune in Staffordshire. In this station the king remained many days in quiet and security,

Thence he went to one of Mr. Lane's relations, within five miles of Bristol, where he intended to embark; but finding that no ship was to sail for a month from that place, he was obliged to go elsewhere for a passage, and escaped from being discovered and arrested at Lyme, only by a few minutes. Charles passed through many other adventures, assumed different disguises, in every step was exposed to imminent dangers, and received daily proofs of uncorrupted fidelity. A little bark was at last found at Brighthelmstone, (at that time a small fishing-town in Sussex, but now a place of considerable magnitude and opulence,) where his majesty embarked, and arrived safely at Feschamp, in Normandy, October 22.

11. In the meantime, Cromwell, crowned with success, returned in triumph to London, where he was met by the speaker of the house, accompanied by the mayor of London, and the magistrates, in all their formalities. His first care was to take advantage of his late success, by depressing the Scots, who had so lately withstood the work of the gospel, as he called it. 12. An act was passed for abolishing royalty in Scotland, and annexing that kingdom, as a conquered province, to the English commonwealth. It was empowered, however, to send some members to the English parliament. Judges were appointed to distribute justice; and the people of that country, now freed from the tyranny of the ecclesiastics, were not much dissatisfied with their present government. The prudent conduct of Monk, who was left by Cromwell to complete their subjection, served much to reconcile the minds of the people, harassed with dissensions, of which they never well understood the cause.

13. In this manner, the English parliament, by the means of Cromwell, spread their uncontested authority over all the British dominions. Ireland was totally subdued by Ireton and Ludlow. All the settlements in America, that had declared for the royal cause, were obliged to submit; Jersey, Guernsey, Scilly, and the Isle of Man, were brought easily under subjection. Thus mankind saw, with astonishment, a parliament composed of sixty or seventy obscure and illiterate members governing a great empire with unanimity and success 14. Without any acknowledged subordination except a council of state, consisting of thirty-eight, to whom all addresses were made, they levied armies, maintained fleets, and gave laws to the neighbouring powers of Europe. 15. The finances were managed with economy and exact-

ness. Few private persons became rich by the plunder of the public; the revenues of the crown, the lands of the bishops, and a tax of a hundred and twenty thousand pounds each month, supplied the wants of the government, and gave vigour to all their proceedings.

Questions for Examination.

1. What was the nature of Cromwell's ambition?
2. What success attended him in Ireland?
3. What cruelty tarnished his victories?
4. Whom did the parliament appoint to the command of the army against Scotland?
5. What was Cromwell's success?
6. What resolution did prince Charles embrace?
7. What news did the prince receive at Worcester?
8. What was the result of his undertaking?
9. What were his sufferings, and how did he escape?
10. Mention more particularly the incidents of this escape?
11. What was Cromwell's first care after his return?
12. What act was now passed respecting Scotland?
13—15. What was the state of the British empire at this time?

SECTION II.

An evil soul, producing holy writ,
Is like a villain with a smiling cheek;
A goodly apple rotten at the core.—Shakspeare.

1. (A. D. 1652.) THE parliament, having thus reduced their native dominions to perfect obedience, next resolved to chastise the Dutch, who had given but very slight cause of complaint. It happened that one doctor Dorislaus, who was of the number of the late king's judges, being sent by the parliament as their envoy to Holland, was assassinated by one of the royal party, who had taken refuge there. 2. Some time after, also, Mr. St. John, appointed their ambassador to that court, was insulted by the friends of the prince of Orange. These were thought motives sufficient to induce the commonwealth of England to declare war against them. The parliament's chief dependence lay in the activity and courage of Blake, their admiral; who though he had not embarked in naval command till late in life, yet surpassed all that went before him in courage and dexterity. 3. On the other side, the Dutch opposed to him

their famous admiral Von Tromp, to whom they have never since produced an equal. Many were the engagements between these celebrated admirals, and various was their success. Sea fights, in general, seldom prove decisive; and the vanquished are soon seen to make head against the victor. Several dreadful encounters, therefore, rather served to shew the excellence of the admirals than to determine their superiority. 4. The Dutch, however, who felt many great disadvantages by the loss of their trade, and by the total suspension of their fisheries, were willing to treat for a peace; but the parliament gave them a very unfavourable answer. It was the policy of that body to keep their navy on foot as long as they could; rightly judging, that, while the force of the nation was exerting by sea, it would diminish the power of general Cromwell by land, which was become very formidable to them.

5. This great aspirer, however, quickly perceived their designs; and, from the first, saw that they dreaded his growing power, and wished its diminution. All his measures were conducted with a bold intrepidity that marked his character, and he now saw that it was not necessary to wear the mask of subordination any longer. Secure, therefore, in the attachment of the army, he resolved to make another daring effort; and persuaded the officers to present a petition for payment of arrears and redress of grievances, which he knew would be rejected by the commons with disdain. 6. The petition was soon drawn up and presented, in which the officers, after demanding their arrears, desired the parliament to consider how many years they had sat; and what professions they had formerly made of their intentions to new-model the house, and establish freedom on the broadest basis.

7. The house was highly offended at the presumption of the army, although they had seen, but too lately, that their own power was wholly founded on that very presumption. They appointed a committee to prepare an act ordaining that all persons who presented such petitions for the future should be deemed guilty of high-treason. To this the officers made a very warm remonstrance, and the parliament as angry a reply; while the breach between them every moment grew wider. 8. This was what Cromwell had long wished, and had long foreseen. He was sitting in the council with his officers, when informed of the subject on which the house was deliberating; upon which he rose up

Cromwell dismissing the parliament.

in the most seeming fury, and, turning to major Vernon, he cried out that he was compelled to do a thing that made the very hairs of his head stand on end. 9. Then hastening to the house with three hundred soldiers, and, with the marks of violent indignation on his countenance, he entered. Stamping with his foot, which was the signal for the soldiers to enter, the place was immediately filled with armed men. Then addressing himself to the members: "For shame," said he, "get you gone. Give place to honester men; to those who will more faithfully discharge their trust. 10. You are no longer a parliament: I tell you you are no longer a parliament: the Lord has done with you." Sir Harry Vane exclaiming against this conduct: "Sir Harry," cried Cromwell, with a loud voice, " O! sir Harry Vane, the Lord deliver me from sir Harry Vane." He then, in the coarsest and most violent manner, reproached many of the members, by name, with their vices. "It is you," continued he, "that have forced me upon this. 11. I have sought the Lord night and day, that he would rather slay me than put me upon this work." Then pointing to the mace, "Take away," cried he, "that bauble." After which, turning out all the members, and clearing the hall, he ordered the doors to be locked, and, putting the key in his pocket, returned to Whitehall.

12. The persons selected for his next parliament were the lowest, meanest, and the most ignorant among the citizens, and the very dregs of the fanatics. He was well apprised, that, during the administration of such a group of characters, he alone must govern, or that they must soon throw up the reins of government, which they were unqualified to guide. Accordingly, their practice justified his sagacity. One of them particularly, who was called Praise God Barebone, a canting leather seller, gave his name to this odd assembly, and it was called Barebone's Parliament.

13. The very vulgar now began to exclaim against so foolish a legislature; and they themselves seemed not insensible of the ridicule which every day was thrown out against them. Accordingly, by concert, they met earlier than the rest of their fraternity, and observing to each other that this parliament had sat long enough, they hastened to Cromwell, with Rouse their speaker at their head, and into his hands they resigned the authority with which he had invested them.

Questions for Examination.

1. What circumstances produced a war with the Dutch?
2. On what admiral did the English place their chief dependence?
3. To whom was Blake opposed?
4. What was the result of the war?
5. What petition did Cromwell persuade the officers to present?
7. In what manner did the parliament receive the petition?
8—11. Relate the particulars of this dispute, and its result.
12. Of whom was the next parliament composed, and what was it called?
13. To whom did they resign their authority?

SECTION III.

Established violence and lawless might,
Avowed and hallowed by the name of right.—*Rowe's Lucan.*

1. (A. D. 1653.) CROMWELL accepted their resignation with pleasure; but being told that some of the members were refractory, he sent colonel White to clear the house of such as ventured to remain there. They had placed one Moyer in the chair by the time the colonel arrived, and, being asked by the colonel what they did there, Moyer replied, very gravely, that they were seeking the Lord. "Then may you go elsewhere," cried White, "for, to my certain knowledge, the Lord has not been here these many years."

2. This shadow of a parliament being dissolved, the officers, by their own authority, declared Cromwell protector

of the commonwealth of England. He was to be addressed by the title of highness; and his power was proclaimed in London, and other parts of the kingdom. Thus an obscure and vulgar man, at the age of fifty-three, rose to unbounded power; first by following small events in his favour, and at length by directing great ones.

3. Cromwell chose his council from among his officers, who had been the companions of his dangers and his victories, to each of whom he assigned a pension of one thousand pounds a year. He took care to have his troops, upon whose fidelity he depended for support, paid a month in advance; the magazines were also well provided, and the public treasure managed with frugality and care; while his activity, vigilance, and resolution were such, that he discovered every conspiracy against his person, and every plot for an insurrection, before they took effect.

4. His management of foreign affairs, though his schemes were by no means political, yet well corresponded with his character, and for a while were attended with success. The Dutch, having been humbled by repeated defeats, and totally abridged of their commercial concerns, were obliged at last to sue for peace, which he gave them upon terms rather too favourable. 5. He insisted upon their paying deference to the British flag; he compelled them to abandon the interest of the king, and to pay eighty-five thousand pounds, as an indemnification for former expenses; and to restore the English East India Company a part of those dominions of which they had been dispossessed by the Dutch, during the former reign, in that distant part of the world.

6. He was not less successful in his negotiation with the court of France. Cardinal Mazarin, by whom the affairs of that kingdom were conducted, deemed it necessary to pay deference to the protector; and desirous rather to prevail by dexterity than violence, submitted to Cromwell's imperious character, and thus procured ends equally beneficial to both.

7. The court of Spain was not less assiduous in its endeavours to gain his friendship, but was not so successful. This vast monarchy, which, but a few years before, had threatened the liberties of Europe, was now reduced so low as to be scarcely able to defend itself. Cromwell, however, who knew nothing of foreign politics, still continued to regard its power with an eye of jealousy, and came into an association with France to depress it still more. 8. He lent that court a body of six thousand men to attack the Spanish

dominions in the Netherlands; and, upon obtaining a signal victory by his assistance at Dunes, the French put Dunkirk, which they had just taken from the Spaniards, into his hands, as a reward for his attachment.

9. But it was by sea that he humbled the power of Spain with still more effectual success. Blake, who had long made himself formidable to the Dutch, and whose fame was spread over Europe, now became still more dreadful to the Spanish monarchy. He sailed with a fleet into the Mediterranean, whether, since the time of the crusades, no English fleet had ever ventured to advance. He there conquered all that dared to oppose him. 10. Casting anchor before Leghorn, he demanded and obtained satisfaction for some injuries which the English commerce had suffered from the duke of Tuscany. He next sailed to Algiers, and compelled the Dey to make peace, and to restrain his piratical subjects from further injuring the English. 11. (A. D. 1655.) He then went to Tunis, and, having made the same demands, was desired by the Dey of that place to look at the two castles, Porto Forino and Goletta, and do his utmost. Blake shewed him that he was not slow in accepting the challange; entered that harbour, burned the shipping there, and then sailed out triumphantly to pursue his voyage. At Cadiz he took two galleons, valued at nearly two millions of dollars. 12. At the Canaries he burned a Spanish fleet of sixteen ships; and returning home to England, to enjoy the fame of his noble actions, as he came within sight of his native country he expired. This gallant man, though he fought for an usurper, was yet adverse to his cause; he was a zealous republican in principle, and his aim was to serve his country, not to establish a tyrant. "It is still our duty," he would say to the seamen, "to fight for our country into whatever hands the government may fall."

13. At the same time that Blake's expeditions were going forward, there was another carried on under the command of admirals Penn and Venables, with about four thousand land forces, to attack the island of Hispaniola. Failing, however, in this, and being driven off the place by the Spaniards, they steered to Jamaica, which was surrendered to them without a blow. So little was thought of the importance of this conquest, that, upon the return of the expedition, Penn and Venables were sent to the Tower, for their failure in the principal object of their expedition.

14. But it must not be supposed that Cromwell's situation

was at that time enviable. Perhaps no situation, however mean or loaded with contempt, could be more truly distressing than his at the time the nation were loading him with congratulations and addresses. He had by this time rendered himself hateful to every party; and he owed his safety to their mutual hatred and diffidence of each other. 15. His arts of dissimulation had been long exhausted; none could now be deceived by them; those of his own party and principles disdained the use to which he had converted his zeal and professions. The truth seems to be, if we may use the phrase taken from common life, he had begun with being a dupe to his own enthusiasm, and ended with being a sharper.

16. The whole nation silently detested his adminstration, but he had not still been reduced to the extreme of wretchedness, if he could have found domestic consolation. Fleetwood, his son-in-law, actuated with the wildest zeal, detested that character which could use religious professions for the purposes of temporal advancement. 17. His eldest daughter, married to Fleetwood, had adopted republican principles so vehemently, that she could not behold even her own father intrusted with uncontrollable power. His other daughters were no less sanguine in favour of the royal cause; but, above all, Mrs. Claypole, his favourite daughter, upon her death-bed, upbraided him with all those crimes that had led him to trample on the throne.

18. Every hour added some new disquietude. Lord Fairfax, sir William Waller, and many of the heads of the Presbyterians, had secretly entered into an engagement to destroy him. His administration, so expensive both at home and abroad, had exhausted his revenue, and he was left considerably in debt. 19. One conspiracy was no sooner detected, than another rose from its ruins; and, to increase the calamity, he was now taught, upon reasoning principles, that his death was not only desirable, but his assassination would be meritorious. A book was published by colonel Titus, a man who had formerly been attached to his cause, entitled, "Killing no Murder." 20. Of all the pamphlets that came forth at that time, or perhaps of those that have since appeared, this was the most eloquent and masterly. "Shall we," said this popular declaimer, "who would not suffer the lion to invade us, tamely stand to be devoured by the wolf?" Cromwell read this spirited treatise and was never seen to smile more.

Questions for Examination.

1. Mention what followed the resignation of this parliament?
2. What important events succeeded?
3—5. What were the first acts of Cromwell?
6, 7. In what manner did he act towards France and Spain?
9—12. Relate the bold and successful enterprises of admiral Blake?
13. What other admirals did Cromwell employ, and with what success?
14, 15. What was Cromwell's situation at this time?
16, 17. What were his domestic troubles?
18. Who entered into an engagement to destroy him?
19. What effect had the pamphlet written by colonel Titus on him?

SECTION IV

> He left a name at which the world grew pale,
> To point a moral or adorn a tale.—*Johnson.*

1. (A. D. 1658.) ALL peace was now forever banished from his mind; and he found that the grandeur to which he had sacrificed his former peace was only an inlet to fresh inquietudes. The fears of assassination haunted him in all his walks, and were perpetually present in his imagination. He wore armour under his clothes, and always kept pistols in his pockets. 2. His aspect was clouded by a settled gloom, and he regarded every stranger with a glance of timid suspicion. He always travelled with hurry, and was ever attended by a numerous guard. He never returned from any place by the road he went; and seldom slept above three nights together in the same chamber. Society terrified him, as there he might meet an enemy; solitude was terrible, as he was there unguarded by every friend.

3. A tertian ague came kindly at last to deliver him from this life of horror and anxiety. For the space of a week no dangerous symtoms appeared; and in the intervals of the fits he was able to walk abroad. At length the fever increased, and he became delirious. He was just able to answer yes to the demand, whether his son Richard should be appointed to succeed him. He died on the third day of September, the very day which he had always considered as the most fortunate of his life; he was then fifty-nine years old, and had usurped the government nine years.

4. Whatever might have been the difference of interests after the death of the usurper, the influence of his name was still sufficient to get Richard, his son, proclaimed protector in his room. But the army, discontented with such a leader, established a meeting at general Fleetwood's, which, as he dwelt at Wallingford-house, was called the cabal of Wal-

lingford. The result of their deliberation was a remonstrance, that the command of the army should be intrusted to some person in whom they might all confide; and it was plainly given to understand that the young protector was not that person.

5. Richard wanted resolution to defend the title that had been conferred upon him; he soon signed his own abdication in form, and retired to live, several years after his resignation, at first on the continent, and afterwards upon his paternal fortune at home. He was thought by the ignorant to be unworthy the happiness of his exaltation; but he knew, by his tranquillity in private, that he had made the most fortunate exchange.

While Richard Cromwell was on his travels, under an assumed name, he was introduced to the prince of Conti, who, talking of England, broke out into admiration of Cromwell's courage and capacity: " But as for that poor pitiful fellow, Richard," said he, " what has become of him? How could he be such a blockhead as to reap no greater benefit from all his father's crimes and successes?" We have, however, abundant proof that Richard was fonder of the social virtues than of noisy fame, and justly appreciated the calm enjoyments of retirement. When, on assuming the protectorship, one of his adherents pressed him to exert more vigour against the royalists, he said "I positively forbid shedding the blood of a single man in my cause. I would rather relinquish the post I hold, than proceed to such unwarrantable extremities. I wish to retain my situation no longer than shall be consistent with the public good, and the wishes of those I govern." His peaceful and quiet life extended to the age of 86; and he died in the year 1712, at the latter end of queen Anne's reign.

6. The officers, being once more left to themselves, determined to replace the remnant of the old parliament which had beheaded the king, and which Cromwell had so disgracefully turned out of the house.

7. The rump parliament, for that was the name it went by, being now reinstated, was yet very vigorous in its attempts to lessen the power by which it was replaced. The officers of the army, therefore, came to a resolution, usual enough in those times, to dissolve that assembly by which they were so vehemently opposed. 8. Accordingly, Lambert, one of the generals, drew up a chosen body of troops, and, placing them in the streets which led to Westminster

hall, when the speaker, Lenthall, proceeded in his carriage to the house, he ordered the horses to be turned, and very civilly conducted him home. The other members were likewise intercepted, and the army returned to their quarters to observe a solemn feast, which generally either preceded or attended their outrages.

9. During these transactions, general Monk was at the head of eight thousand veterans in Scotland, and beheld the distractions of his native country with but slender hopes of relieving it.

10. Whatever might have been his designs, it was impossible to cover them with greater secrecy than he did. As soon as he put his army in motion, to inquire into the cause of the disturbances in the capital, his countenance was eagerly sought by all the contending parties. He still, however, continued to march his army towards the capital; the whole country equally in doubt as to his motives, and astonished at his reserve. But Monk continued his inflexible taciturnity, and at last came to St. Albans, within a few miles of London.

11. He there sent the rump parliament, who had resumed their seat, a message, desiring them to remove such forces as remained in London to country quarters. In the meantime, the house of commons having passed votes for the composure of the kingdom, dissolved themselves, and gave orders for the immediate assembling of a new parliament.

12. As yet the new parliament was not assembled, and no person had hitherto dived into the designs of the general. (A. D. 1660.) He still persevered in his reserve; and although the calling of a new parliament was but, in other words, to restore the king, yet his expressions never once betrayed the secret of his bosom. Nothing but a security of confidence at last extorted the confession from him. 13. He had been intimate with one Morrice, a gentleman of Devonshire, of a sedentary studious disposition, and with him alone did he deliberate upon the great and dangerous enterprise of the restoration. Sir John Granville, who had a commission from the king, applied for access to the general; he was desired to communicate his business to Morrice. 14. Granville refused, though twice urged, to deliver his message to any but the general himself; so that Monk, finding he could depend upon this minister's secrecy, opened to him his whole intentions; but, with his usual caution, still scrupled to commit anything to paper. In consequence of

this, the king left the Spanish territories, where he very narrowly escaped being detained at Breda by the governor, under the pretence of treating him with proper respect and formality. Thence he retired into Holland, where he resolved to wait for further advice.

15. At length the long-expected day for the sitting of a free parliament arrived. The affections of all were turned towards the king; yet such were their fears, and such dangers attended a freedom of speech, that no one dared for some days to make any mention of his name. All this time Monk, with his usual reserve, tried their temper, and examined the ardour of their wishes; at length he gave directions to Annesly, president of the council, to inform them that sir John Granville, a servant of the king, had been sent over by his majesty, and was now at the door with a letter to the commons.

16. Nothing could exceed the joy and transport with which this message was received. The members, for a moment, forgot the dignity of their situations, and indulged in a loud acclamation of applause. Granville was called in, and the letter eagerly read. A moment's pause was scarcely allowed: all at once the house burst into a universal assent to the king's proposals; and to diffuse the joy more widely, it was voted that the letter and indemnity should immediately be published.

17. Charles II. entered London on the twenty-ninth of May, which was his birth-day. An innumerable concourse of people lined the way wherever he passed, and rent the air with their acclamations. They had been so long distracted by unrelenting factions, oppressed and alarmed by a succession of tyrannies, that they could no longer suppress these emotions of delight, to behold their constitution restored, or rather, like a phœnix, appearing more beautiful and vigourous from the ruins of its former conflagration.

18. Fanaticism, with its long train of gloomy terrors, fled at the approach of freedom; the arts of society and peace began to return; and it had been happy for the people if the arts of luxury had not entered in their train.*

---

* A great number of religious sects sprung up in England during the civil wars. That of the Quakers was the most remarkable. The founder was George Fox, born at Drayton, in Lancashire, in 1624,

Questions for Examination.

1, 2. What was the state of Cromwell's mind, and what was his conduct previous to his death?
3. When did he die? at what age? and how long did he reign?
5. What mode of life did Richard Cromwell prefer?
6. What measures were now determined upon?
7, 8. What consequences followed?
9—12. What was now the conduct of general Monk?
13. In whom did general Monk confide?
16. Relate the particulars which preceded the king's restoration?
17. At what time did Charles II. enter London, and what was his reception?

CONTEMPORARY SOVEREIGNS.

Popes.	King of France.	King of Denmark.
A.D.	A.D.	A.D.
Innocent X......1644	Louis XIV......1649	
Alexander VII....1655		Frederick III.....1648
Emperors of Germany.	*King of Spain.*	
Ferdinand III....1637	Philip IV.........1621	*King and Queen of Sweden.*
Leopold..........1658	*Kings of Portugal.*	
Emperor of the Turks.	John IV.........1640	Christiana........1633
Mahomet IV......1649	Alphonso........1656	Charles X.........1653

EMINENT PERSONS.

JOHN MILTON;* Waller; Davenant; Cowley; sir John Denham; Harrington; Harvey; Clarendon; Selden; Hobbs. Admirals Blake Montague, &c.; Generals Bradshaw, Ireton, Fairfax, Monk, Lambert, Fleetwood; the earl of Essex; sir Henry Vane; Bulstrode Whiterock, lord keeper.

---

* Milton was the greatest epic poet that England, perhaps that the world has ever produced. He held the situation of Latin Secretary under Oliver Cromwell, and was permitted to retain the emoluments of his office after he had become blind. After the Restoration he was deprived of his office; and it was amid all the distress arising from blindness, age, and poverty, that Paradise Lost, the most sublime poem which adorns any language, was written.

CHAPTER XXX.

CHARLES II.

Born 1630. Died February 6, 1685. Began to reign May 29, 1660. Reigned 24¾ years.

SECTION I.

*Already quench'd sedition's brand,
And zeal, which burnt it, only warms the land.*—*Dryden.*

1. (A. D. 1661.) WHEN Charles came to the throne he was thirty years of age, possessed of an agreeable person, an elegant address, and an engaging manner. His whole demeanour and behaviour was well calculated to support and increase popularity. Accustomed, during his exile, to live cheerfully among his courtiers, he carried the same endearing familiarities to the throne; and, from the levity of his temper, no injuries were dreaded from his former resentments. 2. But it was soon found that all these advantages were merely superficial. His indolence and love of pleasure made him averse to all kinds of business; his familiarities were prostituted to the worst as well as to the best of his subjects; and he took no care to reward his former friends, as he had taken few steps to be avenged of his former enemies.

3. Though an act of indemnity was passed, those, who had an immediate hand in the king's death were excepted. —Cromwell, Ireton, and Bradshaw, though dead, were considered as proper objects of resentment; their bodies were dug from their graves, dragged to the place of execution, and, after hanging some time, buried under the gallows. 4. Of the rest who sat in judgment in the late monarch's trial, some were dead, and some thought worthy of pardon. Ten only, out of fourscore, were devoted to destruction. These were enthusiasts, who had all along acted from principle, and who, in the general spirit of rage excited against them, shewed a fortitude that might do honour to a better cause.

5. This was the time for the king to have made himself independent of all parliaments; and it is said that Southampton, one of his ministers, had thought of procuring his master, from the commons, the grant of a revenue of two millions a year, which would have effectually rendered him

absolute; but in this his views were obstructed by the great Clarendon, who, though attached to the king, was still more the friend of liberty and the laws. 6. Charles, however, was no way interested in these opposite views of his ministers; he only desired money in order to prosecute his pleasures; and, provided he had that, he little regarded the manner in which it was obtained.

7. His continual exigencies drove him constantly to measures no way suited to his inclination. Among others was his marriage, celebrated at this time, with Catharine, infanta of Portugal, who, though a virtuous princess, possessed, as it would seem, but few personal attractions. It was the portion of this princess that the needy monarch was enamoured of, which amounted to three hundred thousand pounds, together with the fortresses of Tangier in Africa, and of Bombay in the East Indies. 8. The chancellor Clarendon, the duke of Ormond, and Southampton, urged many reasons against this match, and opposed it with all their influence; but the king disregarded their advice, and the inauspicious marriage was celebrated accordingly.

9. It was probably with a view of recruiting the supply for his pleasure that he was induced to declare war against the Dutch, as the money appointed for that purpose would go through his hands. In this naval war, which continued to rage for some years with great fierceness, much blood was spilt and great treasure exhausted, until at last a treaty was concluded at Breda, by which the colony of New York was ceded by the Dutch to the English, and considered as a most valuable acquisition.

10. This treaty was considered as inglorious to the English, as they failed in gaining any redress upon the complaints which gave rise to it. Lord Clarendon particularly gained a share of blame, both for having advised an unnecessary war, and then for concluding a disgraceful peace. He had been long declining in the king's favour, and he was no less displeasing to the majority of the people.

11. This seemed the signal for the earl's enemies to step in, and effect his entire overthrow. A charge was opened against him in the house of commons, by Mr. Seymour, consisting of seventeen articles. These, which were only a catalogue of the popular rumours before mentioned, appeared, at first sight, false and frivolous. However, Clarendon, finding the popular torrent, united to the violence of power, running with impetuosity against him, thought proper to withdraw to France.

12. Having thus got rid of his virtuous minister, the king soon after resigned himself to the direction of a set of men who afterwards went by the appellation of the Cabal, from the initials of the names of which it was composed.

13. The first of them, sir Thomas Clifford, was a man of a daring and impetuous spirit, rendered more dangerous by eloquence and intrigue. Lord Ashley, soon after known by the name of Lord Shaftesbury, was turbulent, ambitious, subtle, and enterprising. The duke of Buckingham was gay, capricious, with some wit, and great vivacity. Arlington was a man of very moderate capacity; his intentions were good, but he wanted courage to persevere in them. Lastly, the duke of Lauderdale, who was not defective in natural, and still less in acquired talents; but neither was his address graceful, nor his understanding just: he was ambitious, obstinate, insolent, and sullen. 14. These were the men to whom Charles gave up the conduct of his affairs, and who plunged the remaining part of his reign in difficulties, which produced the most dangerous symptoms.

15. From this inauspicious combination the people had entertained violent jealousies against the court. The fears and discontents of the nation were vented without restraint; the apprehensions of a popish successor, an abandoned court, and a parliament, which, though sometimes assertors of liberty, yet which had now continued for seventeen years without change, naturally rendered the minds of mankind timid and suspicious, and they only wanted objects on which to wreak their ill-humours.

The gloom which hung over the public mind was still further increased by two fearful calamities. In the year 1665 the plague broke out in London, and raged so dreadfully that 68,596 persons died within the bills of mortality. The following year was as fearfully distinguished by the great fire of London, in which eighty-nine churches and 13,200 houses were consumed. The ruins of the city extended over 436 acres, from the Tower along the river to the Temple, and from the north-east gate along the city wall to Holborn-bridge. Prompted by blind rage, some ascribed the guilt of this accidental conflagration to the republicans, others to the catholics; though it is not easy to conceive how the burning of London could serve the purposes of either party. As the papists were the chief objects of public detestation, the rumour, which threw the guilt on them was favourably received by the people. No proof,

Dreadful fire in London, 1666.

however, or even presumption, after the strictest inquiry by a committee of parliament, ever appeared to authorize such a calumny; yet in order to give countenance to the popular prejudice, the inscription engraved by authority on the monument ascribed the calamity to this hated sect. This clause was erased by James II. after his ascension, but was again restored after the revolution. So credulous, as well as obstinate, are the people in believing every thing which flatters their prevailing passions!

Questions for Examination.

1. What engaging qualities did Charles possess?
2. Were these advantages of outward behaviour solid?
3, 4. What proceedings were taken against those who were concerned in the king's death?
5. What proposition did Southampton make in favour of Charles and who opposed it?
7. Whom did the king marry, and what was his inducement?
9. What is supposed to have induced the king to declare war against the Dutch?
10. In what way did Lord Clarendon incur blame?
11. To what country did Clarendon withdraw?
12. What appellation was given to the new ministers?
13. Who were they?
15. What consequences followed their appointment?

SECTION II.

*Some genuine plots on their authors were fix'd
With plots to invent plots, most curiously mix'd;
For Dangerfield, Bedloe, and Oates found a Tongue
To affirm half the natives deserved to be hung.—Dibdin.*

1. (A. D. 1670.) WHEN the spirit of the English is once roused, they either find objects of suspicion, or make them. On the 13th of August, one Kirby, a chemist, accosted the king, as he was walking in the park. "Sir," said he "keep within the company; your enemies have a design upon your life, and you may be shot in this very walk." 2. Being questioned in consequence of this strange intimation, he offered to produce one doctor Tongue, a weak, credulous clergyman, who told him that two persons, named Grove and Pickering, were engaged to murder the king; and that Sir George Wakeman, the queen's physician, had undertaken the same task by poison. 3. Tongue was introduced to the king with a bundle of papers relating to this pretended conspiracy, and was referred to the lord-treasurer Danby. He there declared that the papers were thrust under his door; and he afterwards asserted that he knew the author of them, who desired that his name might be concealed, as he dreaded the resentment of the jesuits.

4. This information appeared so vague and unsatisfactory that the King concluded the whole was a fiction. However, Tongue was not to be repressed in the ardour of his loyalty; he went again to the lord-treasurer, and told him that a packet of letters, written by jesuits concerned in the plot, was that night put into the post-house at Windsor, directed to one Bedingfield, a jesuit, who was confessor to the duke of York, and who resided there. These letters had actually been received a few hours before by the duke; but he had shown them to the king as a forgery, of which he knew neither the drift nor the meaning.

5. Titus Oates, who was the fountain of all this dreadful intelligence was produced soon after, who, with seeming reluctance, came to give his evidence. This Titus Oates was an abandoned miscreant, obscure, illiterate, vulgar, and indigent. He had been once indicted for perjury, was afterwards chaplain on board a man-of-war, and dismissed for criminal practices. 6. He then professed himself a Roman catholic, and crossed the sea to St. Omer's, where he was for some time maintained in the English seminary of that city. At a time that he was supposed to have been intrusted with a secret involving the fate of kings, he was allowed to

remain in such necessity, that Kirby was obliged to supply him with daily bread.

7. He had two methods to proceed; either to ingratiate himself by this information with the ministry, or to alarm the people, and thus turn their fears to his advantage. He chose the latter method. 8. He went, therefore, with his companions, to Sir Edmondsbury Godfrey, a noted and active justice of the peace, and before him deposed to a narrative dressed up in terrors fit to make an impression on the vulgar. The pope, he said, considered himself as entitled to the possession of England and Ireland, on account of the heresy of the prince and people, and had accordingly assumed the soverignty of these kingdoms. 9. The king, who was ridiculed by the jesuits, was solemnly tried by them, and condemned as a heretic. Grove and Pickering, to make sure work, were employed to shoot the king, and that too with silver bullets. The duke of York was to be offered the crown in consequence of the success of these probable schemes on condition of extirpating the protestant religion. Upon his refusal, "To pot James must go!" as the Jesuits were said to express it.

10. In consequence of this dreadful information, sufficiently marked with absurdity, vulgarity and contradictions, Titus Oates became the favourite of the people, notwithstanding, during his examination before the council, he so betrayed the grossness of his impostures, that he contradicted himself in every step of his narration.

11. A great number of the jesuits mentioned by Oates were immediately taken into custody. Coleman, secretary to the duke of York, who was said to have acted so strenuous a part in the conspiracy, at first retired, and next day surrendered himself to the secretery of state; and some of his papers, by Oates' directions, were secured.

12. In this fluctuation of passions an accident served to confirm the prejudices of the people, and to put it beyond a doubt that Oates' narrative was nothing but the truth. Sir Edmondsbury Godfrey, who had been so active in unravelling the whole mystery of the popish machinations, after having been missing some days, was found dead in a ditch by Primrose-hill, on the way to Hampstead. 13. The cause of his death remains, and must still continue, a secret; but the people, already enraged against the papists, did not hesitate a moment to ascribe it to them. The body of Godfrey was carried through the streets, in procession, preceded

by seventy clergymen; and every one who saw it made no doubt that his death could be only caused by the papists. 14. Even the better sort of people were infected with the vulgar prejudice; and such was the general conviction of popish guilt, that no person, with any regard to personal safety, could express the least doubt concerning the information of Oates, or the murder of Godfrey.

15. In order to continue and propagate the alarm, the parliament affected to believe it true. An address was voted for a solemn fast. It was requested that all papers tending to throw light upon so horrible a conspiracy might be laid before the house; that all papists should remove from London; that access should be denied at court to all unknown and suspicious persons; and that the train-bands in London and Westminster should be in readiness to march. 16. Oates was recommended to parliament by the king. He was lodged in Whitehall, and encouraged by a pension of twelve hundred pounds a year to proceed in forging new informations.

The encouragement given to Oates did not fail to bring in others also, who hoped to profit by the delusion of the times. 17. William Bedloe, a man, if possible, more infamous than Oates, appeared next upon the stage. He was, like the former, of very low birth, and had been noted for several cheats and thefts. This man, at his own desire, was arrested at Bristol, and conveyed to London, where he declared before the council that he had seen the body of Sir Edmondsbury Godfrey at Somerset-house where the queen lived. 18. He said that a servant of Lord Bellasis offered to give him four thousand pounds if he would carry it off; and, finding all his information greedily received, he confirmed and heightened Oates' plot with aggravated horrors.

19. Thus encouraged by the general voice in their favour, the witnesses, who had all along enlarged their narratives in proportion as they were eagerly received, went a step further and ventured to accuse the queen. The commons, in an address to the king, gave countenance to this scandalous accusation; the lords rejected it with becoming disdain.

Questions for Examination.

1. In what manner did Kirby address the king?
2—4. Relate the circumstances of a pretended conspiracy.
5. What was the character of the principal actor in this business?
7—11. By what means did he proceed?
12—14. What accident served to confirm the prejudices of the people?

15. What means were taken to continue the alarm?
16. How was Oates treated by the government?
17. What other delusion followed?
19. Whom did they afterwards venture to accuse?

SECTION III.

> O think what anxious moments pass between
> The birth of plots, and their last fatal periods
> O 'tis a dreadful interval of time,
> Made up of horror all, and big with death.—*Addison.*

1. (A. D. 1675.) EDWARD COLEMAN, secretary to the duke of York, was the first who was brought to trial, as being most obnoxious to those who pretended to fear the introduction of popery. Bedloe swore that he received a commission, signed by the superior of the Jesuits, appointing him papal secretary of state, and that he had consented to the king's assassination. 2. After this unfortunate man's sentence, thus procured by these vipers, many members of both houses offered to interpose in his behalf, if he would make ample confession; but as he was, in reality, possessed of no treasonable secrets, he would not procure life by falsehood and imposture. He suffered with calmness and constancy; and, to the last, persisted in the strongest protestations of his innocence.

The trial of Coleman was succeeded by those of Ireland, Pickering and Grove. They protested their innocence, but were found guilty. The unhappy men went to execution protesting their innocence, a circumstance, which made no impression on the spectators; but their being jesuits banished even pity for their sufferings.

4. Hill, Green, and Berry, were tried upon the evidence of one Miles Prance, for the murder of Godfrey; but though Bedloe's narrative, and Prance's information were totally irreconcilable, and though their testimony was invalidated by contrary evidence, all was in vain; the prisoners were condemned and executed. They all denied their guilt at execution; and, as Berry died a protestant, this circumstance was regarded as very considerable.

5. Whitebread, provincial of the jesuits, Fenwick, Gaven, Turner, and Harcourt, all of them of the same order, were brought to their trial; and Langhorne soon after. Besides Oates and Bedloe, Dugdale, a new witness, appeared against the prisoners. This man spread the alarm still further, and even asserted that two hundred thousand papists in England were ready to take up arms. 6. The prisoners proved, by

sixteen witnesses from St. Omer's that Oates was in that seminary at the time he swore he was in London. But, as they were papists, their testimony could gain no manner of credit. All pleas availed them nothing; but the jesuits and Langhorne were condemned and executed; with their last breath denying the crime for which they died.

7. The informers had less success on the trial of sir George Wakeman, the queen's physician, who, though they swore with their usual animosity, was acquitted. His condemnation would have involved the queen in his guilt; and it is probable the judge and the jury were afraid of venturing so far.

8. The earl of Stafford, nearly two years after, was the last man that fell a sacrifice to these bloody wretches: the witnesses produced against him were Oates, Dugdale, and Tuberville. Oates swore that he saw Fenwick, the jesuit, deliver Stafford a commission from the general of the jesuits, constituting him paymaster of the papal army. 9. The clamour and outrage of the populace against the prisoner was very great; he was found guilty, and condemned to be hanged and quartered; but the king changed his sentence into that of beheading. He was executed on Tower-hill, where even his persecutors could not forbear shedding tears at that serene fortitude which shone in every feature, motion and accent of this aged nobleman.

10. This parliament had continued to sit for seventeen years without interruption, wherefore a new one was called; in which was passed the celebrated statute called the Habeas Corpus Act, which confirms the subject in an absolute security from oppressive power. By this act it was prohibited to send any one to prison beyond the sea; no judge, under severe penalties, was to refuse to any prisoner his writ of habeas corpus; by which the jailer was to produce in court the body of the prisoner, whence the writ had its name, and to certify the cause of its detainer and imprisonment.

11. If the jail lie within twenty miles of the judge, the writ must be conveyed in three days, and so proportionably for greater distances. Every prisoner must be indicted the first term of his commitment, and brought to trial the subsequent term; and no man, after being enlarged by court can be recommitted for the same offence.

12. The Meal-tub Plot, as it was called, soon followed the former. One Dangerfield, more infamous, if possible than Oates and Bedloe, a wretch who had been set in the

pillory, scourged, branded, and transported for felony and coining, hatched a plot, in conjunction with a person whose name was Cellier, a Roman catholic of abandoned character. Dangerfield began by declaring that there was a design on foot to set up a new form of government, and remove the king and the royal family. 13. He communicated this intelligence to the king and the duke of York, who supplied him with money, and countenanced his discovery. He hid some seditious papers in the lodgings of one colonel Mansel; and then brought the custom-house officers to his apartment, to search for smuggled merchandise. The papers were found: and the council, having examined the affair, concluded they were forged by Dangerfield. 14. They ordered all the places he frequented to be searched; and in the house of Cellier the whole scheme of the conspiracy was discovered upon paper, concealed in a meal-tub, whence the plot had its name. Dangerfield, being committed to Newgate, made an ample confession of the forgery, which, though probably entirely of his own contrivance, he ascribed to the earl of Castlemain, the countess of Powis, and the five lords in the Tower. 15. He said that the design was to suborn witnesses to prove a charge of perjury upon Oates, to assassinate the earl of Shaftesbury, to accuse the dukes of Monmouth and Buckingham, the earls of Essex, Halifax, and others, of having been concerned in the conspiracy against the king and his brother. Upon this information the earl of Castlemain and the countess of Powis were sent to the Tower, and the king himself was suspected of encouraging this imposture.

16. The chief point which the present house of commons laboured to obtain was the exclusion bill, which, though the former house had voted, was never passed into a law. Shaftesbury, and many considerable men of the party, had rendered themselves so obnoxious to the duke of York, that they could find safety in no measure but in his ruin. Monmouth's friends hoped that the exclusion of James would make room for their own patron. 17. The duke of York's professed bigotry to the catholic superstition influenced numbers, and his tyrannies, which were practised without control while he continued in Scotland, rendered his name odious to thousands. In a week, therefore, after the commencement of the session, a motion was made for bringing in a bill for excluding him from the succession to the throne,

and a committee was appointed for that purpose. The debates were carried on with great violence on both sides. The king was present during the whole debate; and had the pleasure of seeing the bill thrown out by a very great majority.

Questions for Examination.

1. Who was first brought to trial?
2. What was his behaviour at his execution?
3, 4. Who were the next that suffered?
5. What others were tried for their lives?
6. By what means did they prove their innocence?
7. Which of the accused was acquitted?
8. Who was the last that fell a victim to these wretches? What was the evidence against him?
9. What sentence was passed upon the earl of Stafford? What effect had his fortitude on the beholders of his death?
10, 11. What were the particulars of the Habeas Corpus Act?
12. What plot was now laid, and who was the principal actor in it?
13. How and when was it discovered?
16, 17. What now engaged the attention of the Commons?

SECTION IV.

Yet sometimes nations will decline so low
From Virtue, which is reason, that no wrong,
But justice, and some fatal course annex'd,
Deprives them of their outward liberty,
Their inward lost.—Milton.

1. (A. D. 1683.) EACH party had for some time reviled and ridiculed the other in pamphlets and libels; and this practice at last was attended with an accident that deserves notice. One Fitzharris, an Irish papist, dependent on the duchess of Portsmouth, one of the king's favourites, used to supply her with these occasional publications. 2. But he was resolved to add to their number by his own endeavours; and he employed one Everhard, a Scotchman, to write a libel against the king and the duke of York. The Scot was actually a spy for the opposite party; and supposing this a trick to entrap him, he discovered the whole to sir William Waller, an eminent justice of the peace; and to convince him of the truth of his information, posted him and two other persons, privately, where they heard the whole conference between Fitzharris and himself. 3. The libel composed between them was replete with utmost rancour and scurrility. Waller carried the intelligence to the king, and obtained a warrant for committing Fitzharris, who happened at that very time to have a copy of the libel in his pocket. Seeing himself in the hands of a party from which he expected no mercy, he

resolved to side with them, and throw the odium of the libel on the court, who, he said, were willing to draw out a libel which should be imputed to the exclusioners, and thus render them hateful to the people. 4. He enhanced his services with the country party by a new popish plot, still more tremendous than any of the foregoing. He brought in the duke of York, as a principal accomplice in the plot, and as a contriver in the murder of sir Edmondsbury Godfrey.

5. The king imprisoned Fitzharris; the commons avowed his cause. They voted that he should be impeached by themselves, to secure him from the ordinary forms of justice; the lords rejected the impeachment; the commons asserted their right; a commotion was likely to ensue; and the king, to break off the contest, went to the house, and dissolved the parliament, with a fixed resolution never to call another.

6. This vigorous measure was a blow that the parliament had never expected; and nothing but the necessity of the times could have justified the king's manner of proceeding. From that moment, which ended the parliamentary commotions, Charles seemed to rule with despotic power; and he was resolved to leave the succession to his brother, but clogged with all the faults and misfortunes of his own administration. 7. His temper, which had always been easy and merciful, now became arbitrary, and even cruel; he entertained spies and informers round the throne, and imprisoned all such as he thought most daring in their designs.

8. He resolved to humble the Presbyterians; these were divested of their employments and their places; and their offices given to such as held with the court, and approved the doctrine of non-resistance. The clergy began to testify their zeal and their principles by their writings and their sermons; but though among these the partisans of the king were the most numerous, those of the opposite faction were the most enterprising. 9. The king openly espoused the cause of the former; and thus placing himself at the head of a faction, he deprived the city of London, which had long headed the popular party, of their charter. It was not till after an abject submission that he returned it to them, having previously subjected the election of their magistrates to his immediate authority.

10. Terrors also were not wanting to confirm this new

species of monarchy. Fitzharris was brought to trial before a jury, and condemned and executed. The whole gang of spies, witnesses, informers, and suborners, which had long been encouraged and supported by the leading patriots, finding now that the king was entirely master, turned short upon their ancient drivers, and offered their evidence against those who had first put them in motion. The king's ministers, with a horrid satisfaction, gave them countenance and encouragement; so that soon the same cruelties, and the same injustice, were practised against presbyterian schemes, that had been employed against catholic treasons.

11. The first person that fell under the displeasure of the ministry was one Stephen College, a London joiner, who had become so noted for his zeal against popery, that he went by the name of the protestant joiner. He had attended the city members to Oxford armed with sword and pistol; he had been sometimes heard to speak irreverently of the king, and was now presented by the grand jury of London as guilty of sedition. 12. A jury, at Oxford, after half an hour's deliberation, brought him in guilty; and the spectators testified their inhuman pleasure with a shout of applause. He bore his fate with unshaken fortitude; and at the place of execution denied the crime for which he had been condemned.

13. The power of the crown became at this time irresistible (A. D. 1683), the city of London having been deprived of their charter, which was restored only upon terms of submission; and the giving up the nomination of their own magistrates was so mortifying a circumstance, that all the other Corporations in England soon began to fear the same treatment, and were successively induced to surrender their charters into the hands of the king. Considerable sums were exacted for restoring these charters; and all the offices of power and profit were left at the disposal of the crown. 14. Resistance now, however justifiable, could not be safe; and all prudent men saw no other expedient, but peaceably submitting to the present grievances. But there was a party in England that still cherished their former ideas of freedom, and were resolved to hazard every danger in its defence.

15. The duke of Monmouth, the king's natural son, engaged the earl of Macclesfield, lord Brandon, sir Gilbert Gerrard, and other gentlemen in Cheshire, in this cause. Lord Russel fixed a correspondance with Sir William Courtney, sir

Francis Rowles, and sir Francis Drake, who promised to raise the west. Shaftesbury, with one Ferguson, an independent clergymen, and a restless plotter, managed the city, upon which the confederates chiefly relied. It was now that this turbulent man found his schemes most likely to take effect.

16. After the disappointment and destruction of a hundred plots, he at last began to be sure of this. But this scheme, like all the former, was disappointed. The caution of lord Russel, who induced the duke of Monmouth to put off the enterprise, saved the kingdom from the horrors of a civil war; while Shaftesbury was so struck with the sense of his impending danger, that he left his house, and, lurking about the city, attempted, but in vain, to drive the Londoners into open insurrection. 17. At last, enraged at the numberless cautions and delays which clogged and defeated his projects he threatened to begin with his friends alone. However, after a long struggle between fear and rage, he abandoned all hopes of success, and fled out of the kingdom to Amsterdam, where he ended his turbulent life soon after, without being pitied by his friends or feared by his enemies.

Questions for Examination.

1, 2. What incident next deserves notice?
3, 4. How did the commons act on this occasion, and what was the consequence?
5. How did the dispute end between the king and parliament?
7. What was now the temper of the king?
8. How did the clergy act?
9. Of what did the king deprive the city of London?
10. What was now the conduct of the spies?
11, 12. Who first fell under the ministry's displeasure, and on what occasion?
13, 14. What resulted from the great power of the crown?
15. By whom was resistance made?
16, 17. What was the issue of it?

SECTION V.

> But let the bold conspirator beware,
> For heav'n makes princes its peculiar care.—*Dryden.*

1. (A. D. 1684.) THE loss of Shaftesbury, though it retarded the views of the conspirators, did not suppress them. A council of six was elected, consisting of Monmouth, Rus-

sel, Essex, Howard, Algernon Sidney, and John Hampden, grandson to the great man of that name.

2. Such, together with the duke of Argyle, were the leaders of this conspiracy. But there was also a set of subordinate conspirators who frequently met together and carried on projects quite unknown to Monmouth and his council. Among these men were colonel Rumsey, an old republican officer, together with lieutenant-colonel Walcot, of the same stamp; Goodenough, under-sheriff of London, a zealous and noted party-man; Ferguson, an independent minister; and several attorneys, merchants, and tradesmen of London. 3. But colonel Rumsey and Ferguson were the only persons that had access to the great leaders of the conspiracy. These men in their meetings embraced the most desperate resolutions. They proposed to assassinate the king on his way to Newmarket; Rumble, one of the party, possessed a farm upon that road called the Rye-house, and thence the conspiracy was denominated the Rye-house plot. 4. They deliberated upon a scheme of stopping the king's coach by overturning a cart on the highway at this place, and shooting him through the hedges. The house in which the king lived at Newmarket took fire accidentally, and he was obliged to leave Newmarket eight days sooner than was expected, to which circumstance his safety was ascribed.

5. Among the conspirators was one Keiling, who, finding himself in danger of a prosecution for arresting the lord-mayor of London, resolved to earn his pardon by discovering this plot to the ministry. Colonel Rumsey, and West, a lawyer, no sooner understood that this man had informed against them, than they agreed to save themselves by turning king's evidence, and they surrendered themselves accordingly. 6. Monmouth absconded; Russel was sent to the Tower; Grey escaped; Howard was taken, concealed in a chimney; Essex, Sidney, and Hampden were soon after arrested, and had the mortification to find lord Howard an evidence against them.

7. Walcot was first brought to trial and condemned, together with Hone and Rouse, two associates in the conspiracy, upon the evidence of Rumsey, West, and Sheppard. They died penitent, acknowledging the justice of the sentence by which they were executed. A much greater sacrifice was shortly after to follow. This was the Lord Russel, son of the earl of Bedford, a nobleman of num-

berless good qualities, and led into this conspiracy from a conviction of the duke of York's intention to restore popery. 8. He was liberal, popular, humane, and brave. All his virtues were so many crimes in the present suspicious disposition of the court. The chief evidence against him was lord Howard, a man of very bad character, one of the conspirators who was now contented to take life upon such terms, and to accept of infamous safety. 9. This witness swore that Russel was engaged in the design of an insurrection; but he acquitted him; as he did also Rumsey and West, of being privy to the assassination. The jury, who were zealous royalists, after a short deliberation, brought the prisoner in guilty, and he was condemned to suffer beheading. The scaffold for his execution was erected in Lincoln's-inn-fields; he laid his head on the block without the least change of countenance, and at two strokes it was severed from his body.

10. The celebrated Algernon Sidney, son to the earl of Leicester, was next brought to his trial. He had been formerly engaged in the parliamentary army against the late king, and was even named on the high court of justice that tried him, but he had not taken his seat among the judges. 11. He had ever opposed Cromwell's usurpation, and went into voluntary banishment on the restoration. His affairs, however, requiring his return, he applied to the king for a pardon, and obtained his request. But all his hopes and all his reasoning were founded upon republican principles. For his adored republic he had written and fought and went into banishment and ventured to return. 12. It may easily be conceived how obnoxious a man of such principles was to a court that now was not even content to be without limitations to its power. They went so far as to take illegal methods to procure his condemnation. The only witness that deposed against Sidney was lord Howard, and the law required two. 13. In order therefore, to make out a second witness, they had recourse to a very extraordinary expedient. In ransacking his closet, some discourses on government were found in his own handwriting, containing principles favourable to liberty, and in themselves no way subversive of a limited government. By overstraining, some of these were construed into treason. 14. It was in vain he alleged that papers were no evidence; that it could not be proved they were written by him; that if proved, the papers themselves contained nothing criminal. His defence

was overruled; the violent and inhuman Jefferies, who was now chief-justice, easily prevailed on a partial jury to bring him in guilty, and his execution followed soon after. 15. One can scarce contemplate the transactions of this reign without horror. Such a picture of factious guilt on each side; a court at once immersed in sensuality and blood, a people armed against each other with the most deadly animosity, and no single party to be found with sense enough to stem the general torrent of rancour and factious suspicion.

Hampden was tried soon after, and as there was nothing to affect his life, he was fined forty thousand pounds. Holloway, a merchant of Bristol, who had fled to the West Indies, was brought over, condemned, and executed. Sir Thomas Armstrong also, who had fled to Holland, was brought over, and shared the same fate. 17. Lord Essex, who had been imprisoned in the Tower, was found in an apartment with his throat cut; but whether he was guilty of suicide, or whether the bigotry of the times might not have induced some assassin to commit the crime, cannot now be known.

This was the last blood that was shed for an imputation of plots or conspiracies, which continued during the greatest part of this reign.

18. At this period the goverment of Charles was as absolute as that of any monarch in Europe; but happily, for mankind, his tyranny was but of short duration. The king was seized with a sudden fit, which resembled an apoplexy; and although he was recovered by bleeding, yet he languished only for a few days, and then expired, in the fifty-fifth year of his age, and twenty-fifth of his reign. During his illness some clergymen of the church of England attended him, to whom he discovered a total indifference. Catholic priests were brought to his bedside, and from their hands he received the rites of their communion.

In this reign was begun the celebrated naval hospital at Greenwich. The design was by Inigo Jones, and it was intended as a royal palace. It remained unfinished till the reign of William III., when it was converted to its present use. It was enlarged by the addition of three wings, enriched by donations, and by a tax of 6d. a month from every seaman; and it now supports 3000 boarders, and pays pensions to 5400 in different parts of the kingdom.

The reign of Charles II., which some preposterously represent as our Augustan age, retarded the progress of polite literature; and the immeasurable licentiousness indulged,

Greenwich Hospital.

or rather applauded at court, was more destructive to the fine arts, than even the court nonsense and enthusiasm of the preceding period.—HUME.

Bishop Burnet, in his History of his own Times, says, there were apparent suspicions that Charles had been poisoned. He also observes that the king's body was indecently neglected; his funeral was very mean; he did not lie in state; no mourning was given, and the expense of it was not equal to what an ordinary nobleman's funeral will amount to.

Questions for Examination.

1. What new conspiracy was formed?
2. Who were the subordinate conspirators?
3, 4. What were their desperate resolutions?
5. In what manner was this plot discovered?
6. What was the fate of the conspirators?
7. What eminent noblemen was concerned in this conspiracy?
8. Describe the character of Russel. Who was principal evidence against him?
9. Where did lord Russel suffer? 10. Who was the next brought to trial?
11. Describe the character and conduct of Algernon Sidney.
12, 13. What methods were taken to procure his condemnation?
14. Was his defence attended to, and by whom was he tried?
15. What dreadful picture did the kingdom now present?
16, 17. What other persons suffered?
18. Describe the manner of the death of the king.

CONTEMPORARY SOVEREIGNS.

Popes.	A.D.	*Emperor of the Turks.*		*Kings of Portugal.*	
Alexander VII	1655		A.D.		A.D.
Clement IX	1667	Mahomet IV	1649	Alphonso VI	1656
Innocent XI	1676			Pedro II	1688
Clement X	1679	*King of France.*		*Kings of Denmark.*	
		Louis XIV	1643	Frederick III	1648
Emperor of Germany.		*Kings of Spain.*		Christian V	1576
		Philip IV	1621	*King of Sweden.*	
Leopold	1658	Charles II	1665	Charles XI	1660

EMINENT PERSONS.

Hyde, earl of Clarendon; Villiers, duke of Buckingham;* Butler, duke of Ormond; Cooper, earl of Shaftesbury; sir William Temple; Algernon Sidney; Wentworth Dillon, earl of Roscommon; R. Boyle, earl of Orrery; G. Mackenzie, earl of Cromarty; G. Monk, duke of Albemarle; C. Stanley, earl of Derby; Montague, earl of Sandwich; J. Powlet, marquis of Winchester; W. Cavendish, duke of Newcastle; G. Digby, carl of Bristol; Denzil, lord Hollis; Dudley, lord North; J. Touchet, earl of Castlehaven and baron Audley; H. Pierpont, marquis of Dorchester; J. Wilmot, carl of Rochester*; Anthony Ashley; Heneage Finch, earl of Nottingham; Francis North; lord-keeper Guildford; J. Roberts, carl of Radnor; Arthur Annesly, earl of Anglesea; marquis of Argyle; H. Finch, earl of Winchelsea; A. Carry, lord Falkland; Anne, countess of Dorset, Pembroke, and Montgomery; Margaret, duchess of Newcastle.

CHAPTER XXXI.

JAMES II.

Born 1633. Began to reign February 6, 1685. Abdicated the throne, January 22, 1688. Reigned 2½ years.

SECTION I.

*Near Bridgewater, the fatal place
Of Monmouth's downfall and disgrace,
The hopeless duke, half starved, half drowned,
In covert of a ditch was found.*—Dibdin.

1. (A. D. 1685.) THE duke of York, who succeeded his brother by the title of king James the Second, had been bred

---

*The strange character of this highly-gifted but profligate nobleman, is thus graphically described by Dryden:

"A man so various that he seemed to be
Not one, but all mankind's epitome:
Stiff in opinion—always in the wrong—
Was everything by starts, but nothing long;
Who in the course of one revolving moon
Was chemist, fiddler, statesman, and buffoon."

He died in wretchedness. Pope thus describes the miserable end of his career:

"In the worst inn's worst room, with mat half hung,
The George and Garter dangling from that bed,
Where tawdry yellow strove with dirty red,
Great Villiers lies—alas! how changed from him
That life of pleasure, and that soul of whim?
There, victor of his health, of fortune, friends,.
And fame, the lord of useless thousands ends."

† Rochester was equally celebrated for his wit and profligacy. His mock epitaph on Charles II. contains a severe but just character of that monarch:

"Here lies our mutton-eating king,
Whose word no man relies on:
He never said a foolish thing,
And never did a wise one."

a papist by his mother, and was strongly bigoted to his principles. He went openly to mass with all the ensigns of his dignity, and even sent one Caryl as his agent to Rome, to make submission to the pope, and to pave the way for the readmission of England into the bosom of the catholic church.

2. A conspiracy, set on foot by the duke of Monmouth, was the first disturbance in this reign. He had, since his last conspiracy, been pardoned, but was ordered to depart the kingdom, and had retired to Holland. Being dismissed from thence by the prince of Orange, upon James's accession he went to Brussels, where finding himself still pursued by the king's severity, he resolved to retaliate, and make an attempt upon the kingdom. 3. He had ever been the darling of the people; and some averred that Charles had married his mother, and owned Monmouth's legitimacy at his death. The duke of Argyle seconded his views in Scotland, and they formed the scheme of a double insurrection; so that, while Monmouth should attempt to make a rising in the west, Argyle was also to try his endeavours in the north.

4. Argyle was the first who landed in Scotland, where he published his manifestoes, put himself at the head of two thousand five hundred men, and strove to influence the people in his cause. But a formidable body of the king's forces coming against him, his army fell away, and he himself, after being wounded in attempting to escape, was taken prisoner by a peasant, who found him standing up to his neck in a pool of water. He was thence carried to Edinburgh, where, after enduring many indignities with a gallant spirit, he was publicly executed.

5. Meanwhile Monmouth was by this time landed in Dorsetshire, with scarcely a hundred followers. However, his name was so popular, so great was the hatred of the people both for the person and religion of James, that in four days he had assembled a body of above two thousand men.

6. Being advanced to Taunton, his numbers had increased to six thousand men; and he was obliged every day, for want of arms, to dismiss numbers who crowded to his standard. He entered Bridgewater, Wells, and Frome, and was proclaimed in all those places; but he lost the hour of action in receiving and claiming these empty honours.

7. The king was not a little alarmed at his invasion; but still more so at the success of an undertaking that at first appeared desperate. Six regiments of British troops were recalled from Holland, and a body of regulars, to the num-

ber of three thousand men, were sent, under the command of the earls of Feversham and Churchill, to check the progress of the rebels. 8. They took post at Sedgemore, a village in the neighbourhood of Bridgewater, and were joined by the militia of the country in considerable numbers. It was there that Monmouth resolved, by desperate effort, to lose his life or gain the kingdom. The negligent disposition made by Feversham invited him to the attack; and his faithful followers showed what courage and principle could do against discipline and numbers. 9. They drove the royal infantry from their ground, and were upon the point of gaining the victory, when the misconduct of Monmouth, and the cowardice of lord Grey, who commanded the horse, brought all to ruin. This noblemen fled at the first onset; and the rebels being charged in flank by the victorious army, gave way, after three hours' contest. 10. About three hundred were killed in the engagement, and a thousand in the pursuit; and thus ended an enterprise rashly begun, and more feebly conducted.

Monmouth fled from the field of battle about twenty miles, till his horse sunk under him. He then alighted, and, changing his clothes with a shepherd, fled on foot, attended by a German count, who had accompanied him from Holland. 11. Being quite exhausted with hunger and fatigue, they both lay down in a field, and covered themselves with fern. The shepherd being found in Monmouth's clothes by the pursuers, increased the diligence of the search; and by the means of blood-hounds he was detected in this miserable situation, with raw peas in his pocket, which he had gathered in the fields to sustain life. 12. He wrote the most submissive letters to the king; and that monarch, willing to feast his eyes with the miseries of a fallen enemy, gave him an audience. At this interview the duke fell upon his knees, and begged his life in the most abject terms. He even signed a paper, offered him by the king, declaring his own illegitimacy; and then the stern tyrant assured him that his crime was of such a nature as could not be pardoned. 13. The duke, perceiving that he had nothing to hope from the clemency of his uncle, re-collected his spirits, rose up, and retired with an air of disdain. He was followed to the scaffold with great compassion from the populace. He warned the executioner not to fall into the same error which he had committed in beheading Russel, where it had been neccessary to redouble the blow. 14. But this only increased the severity of the punishment; the man was seized with a universal trepidation, and he struck a feeble blow, upon which the duke raised his head from the block, as if to reproach him; he gently laid down his head a second time, and the executioner struck him again and again to no purpose. He at last threw the axe down; but the sheriff compelled him to resume the attempt, and at two more blows the head was severed from the body. 15. Such was the end of James, duke of Monmouth, the darling of the English people. He was brave, sincere, and good-natured, open to flattery, and by that seduced into an enterprise which exceeded his capacity.

16. But it were well for the insurgents, and fortunate for the king, if the blood that was now shed had been thought a sufficient expiation for the late offence. The victorious army behaved with the most savage cruelty to the prisoners taken after the battle. Feversham, immediately after the victory, hanged up above twenty prisoners.

17. The military severities of the commanders were still inferior to the legal slaughters committed by judge Jefferies, who was sent down to try the delinquents. The natural brutality of this man's temper was inflamed by continual intoxication. He told the prisoners, that if they would save him the trouble of trying them, they might expect some favour, otherwise he would execute the law upon them with the utmost severity. 18. Many poor wretches were thus allured into a confession, and found that it only hastened their destruction. No less than eighty were executed at Dorchester; and, on the whole, at Exeter, Taunton, and Wells, two hundred and fifty-one are computed to have fallen by the hands of the executioner.

Questions for Examination.

1. In what manner did James act on succeeding to the throne?
2, 3. What was the first disturbance in this reign, and who were the principals concerned in it?
4. What success attended Argyle's attempt?
5—10. Relate the particulars of Monmouth's invasion?
11. In what situation was he found?
12. What was his conduct after he was taken?
13, 14. Relate what happened at his execution?
15. What was his character?
16. How were the prisoners treated?
17. What was the conduct of judge Jefferies?
18. How many rebels are said to have been executed?

SECTION II.

> With persecution arm'd, the sacred code
> Of law he dashes thoughtless to the ground.—*Valpy.*

1. (A. D. 1686.) In ecclesiastical matters, James proceeded with still greater injustice. Among those who distinguished themselves against popery was one Dr. Sharpe, a clergyman of London, who declaimed with just severity against those who changed their religion by such arguments as the popish missionaries were able to produce. 2. This being supposed to reflect upon the king, gave great offence at court; and positive orders were given to the bishop of London to suspend Sharpe, till his majesty's pleasure should be further known. The bishop refused to comply; and the king resolved to punish the bishop himself for disobedience.

3. To effect his design, an ecclesiastical commission was issued out, by which seven commissioners were invested with a full and unlimited authority over the whole church of England. Before this tribunal the bishop was summoned, and not only he, but Sharpe, the preacher, suspended.

4. The next step was to allow the liberty of conscience to all sectaries; and he was taught to believe, that the truth of the catholic religion would then, upon a fair trial, gain the victory. He, therefore, issued a declaration of general indulgence, and asserted that non-conformity to the established religion was no longer penal.

5. To complete his work, he publicly sent the earl of Castlemain ambassador extraordinary to Rome, in order to express his obedience to the pope, and to reconcile his kingdom to the catholic communion. Never was there so much contempt thrown upon an embassy that was so boldly undertaken. The court of Rome expected but little success from measures so blindly conducted. They were sensible that the king was openly striking at those laws and opinions, which it was his business to undermine in silence and security.

6. The jesuits soon after were permitted to erect colleges in different parts of the kingdom; they exercised the catholic worship in the most public manner; and four catholic bishops, consecrated in the king's chapel, were sent through the kindom to exercise their episcopal functions, under the title of apostolic vicars.

7. Father Francis, a benedictine monk, was recommended by the king to the university of Cambridge, for a degree of master of arts. But his religion was a stumbling-block which the university could not get over; and they presented a petition, beseeching the king to recall his mandate. 8. Their petition was disregarded and their deputies denied a hearing: the vice-chancellor himself was summoned to appear before the high commission court, and deprived of his office; yet the university persisted, and Father Francis was refused.

9. The place of president of Magdalen college, one of the richest foundations in Europe, being vacant, the king sent a mandate in favour of one Farmer, a new convert to popery, and a man of bad character in other respects. The fellows of the college made very submissive applications to the king for recalling his mandate; they refused admitting the candidate; and James, finding them resolute in the defence of their privileges, ejected them all except two.

10. A second declaration for liberty of conscience was published about the same time with the former; but with this peculiar injuction, that all divines should read it after service in their churches. (A. D. 1688.) The clergy were known universally to disapprove of these measures, and they were now resolved to disobey an order dictated by the most bigoted motives. They were determined to trust their cause to the favour of the people, and that universal jealousy which prevailed against the encroachment of the crown. 11. The first champions of this service of danger were Loyde, bishop of St. Asaph; Ken, of Bath and Wells; Turner, of Ely; Lake, of Chichester; White, of Peterborough; and Trelawney, of Bristol. These, together with Sancroft, the primate, concerted the address, in the form of a petition to the king, which, with the warmest expressions of zeal and submission, remonstrated that they could not read his declaration consistent with their consciences, or the respect they owed the protestant religion.

12. The king, in a fury, summoned the bishops before the council, and there questioned them whether they would acknowledge their petition. They for sometime declined giving an answer; but being urged by the chancellor, they at last owned it. On their refusal to give bail, an order was immediately drawn for their commitment to the tower, and the crown lawyers received directions to prosecute them for a seditious libel.

Questions for Examination.

1. In what way did Dr. Sharpe give offence to the king?
2. What was the conduct of James on that occasion?
3. By what means did he effect his design?
4. What was his next step?
5. Whom did he send ambassador extraordinary to Rome, and how was the embassy received?
6. Relate the further proceedings of James?
7. What took place at Magdalen college?
8. What were the consequences of another declaration?
9. Who were the first that disobeyed the king's mandate?
10. In what manner did James act on this occasion?

SECTION III.

> Forsaken thus, he other thoughts revolves.
> To quit the realm, and many a scheme resolves:
> But let him go, nor heed, though thus you make
> The gentle duke his lonely journey take.—*Hoole.*

1. (A. D. 1688.) THE twenty-ninth day of June was fixed for their trial; and their return was more splendidly attended than their imprisonment. The cause was looked upon as involving the fate of the nation; and future freedom, or future slavery, awaited the decision. The dispute was learnedly managed by the lawyers on both sides. 2. Holloway and Powel, two of the judges, declared themselves in favour of the bishops. The jury withdrew into a chamber, where they passed the whole night; but next morning they returned into court, and pronounced the bishops not guilty. 3. Westminster-hall instantly rang with loud acclamations, which were communicated to the whole extent of the city. They even reached the camp at Hounslow, where the king was at dinner, in lord Feversham's tent. His majesty demanded the cause of these rejoicings, and being informed that it was nothing but the soldiers shouting at the delivery of the bishops, "Call you that nothing," cried he, "but so much the worse for them!"

4. It was in this posture of affairs that all people turned their eyes upon William, prince of Orange, who had married Mary, the eldest daughter of king James.

William was a prince who had, from his earliest entrance into business, been immersed in dangers, calamities, and politics. The ambition of France, and the jealousies of Holland, had served to sharpen his talents, and to give him a propensity for intrigue.

5. This politic prince now plainly saw that James had incurred the most violent hatred of his subjects. (A. D.

1688.) He was minutely informed of their discontents; and by seeming to discourage, still farther increased them, hoping to gain the kingdom for himself in the sequel.

6. The time when the prince entered upon this enterprise was just when the people were in a flame about the recent insult offered to their Bishops. He had before this made considerable augmentations to the Dutch fleet, and the ships were then lying ready in the harbour. Some additional troops were also levied, and sums of money raised for other purposes were converted to the advancement of this expedition.

7. So well concerted were his measures, that, in three days, above four hundred transports were hired; the army fell down the rivers and canals from Nimeguen, with all necessary stores; and the prince set sail from Helvoetsluys, with a fleet of nearly five hundred vessels, and an army of above fourteen thousand men.

It was given out that this invasion was intended for the coast of France; and many of the English, who saw the fleet pass along their coasts, little expected to see it land on their own shores. Thus, after a voyage of two days, the prince landed his army at the village of Broxholme, at Torbay, on the fifth of November, which was the anniversary of the gunpowder treason.

8. But though the invitation from the English was very general, the prince had for some time the mortification to find himself joined by very few. He marched first to Exeter, where the country people had been so much terrified at the executions which had ensued on Monmouth's rebellion, that they continued to observe a strict neutrality. 9. He remained for ten days in expectation of being joined by the malcontents, and at last began to despair of success. But just when he began to deliberate about re-embarking his forces, he was joined by several persons of consequence, and the whole country soon after came flocking to his standard. The nobility, clergy, officers, and even the king's own servants and creatures, were unanimous in deserting James. 10. Lord Churchill had been raised from the rank of a page, and had been invested with a high command in the army; had been created a peer, and owed his whole fortune to the king's bounty; even he deserted among the rest, and carried with him the duke of Grafton, the natural son of the late king, colonel Berkeley, and some others.

11. The prince of Denmark, and Anne, his favourite

daughter, perceiving the desperation of his circumstances, resolved to leave him, and take part with the prevailing side. When he was told that the prince and princess had followed the rest of his favourites, he was stung with most bitter anguish. "God help me," cried he, in the extremity of his agony, "my own children have forsaken me!"

12. The king, alarmed every day more and more with the prospect of a general disaffection, was resolved to hearken to those who advised his quitting the kingdom. To prepare for this he first sent away the queen, who arrived safely at Calais, under the conduct of Count Lauzun, an old favourite of the French king. He himself soon after disappeared in the night time, attended only by sir Edward Hale, a new convert; but was discovered and brought back by the mob.

But shortly after, being confined at Rochester, and observing that he was entirely neglected by his own subjects, he resolved to seek safety from the king of France, the only friend he had still remaining. 14. He accordingly fled to the sea-side, attended by his natural son, the duke of Berwick, where he embarked for the continent, and arrived in safety at Ambleteuse in Picardy, from whence he hastened to the court of France, where he still enjoyed the empty title of a king, and the appellation of a saint, which flattered him more.

15. The king having thus abdicated the throne, the next consideration was the appointing a successor. (A. D. 1688.) Some declared for a regent; others, that the princess of Orange should be invested with regal power, and the young prince considered as supposititious. After a long debate in both houses, a new sovereign was preferred to a regent, by a majority of two voices. It was agreed that the prince and princess of Orange should reign jointly as king and queen of England, while the administration of government should be placed in the hands of the prince only.

Questions for Examination.

1—3. Relate the circumstances which attended the bishops' trial?
4. To whom did the people look for deliverance?
5. What was the situation of the people when William entered upon this enterprise?
7. What measures did William concert to effect the invasion of England?
Where did he land?
10. By whom was the king deserted?
11. What exclamation did the king make when he was told that the prince and princess had forsaken him?

12. What resolution did the king adopt?
14. To what court did James repair?
15. What followed the king's abdication?

CONTEMPORARY SOVEREIGNS.

Pope.		King of Portugal.
A.D.	A.D.	A.D.
Innocent XI......1676	Solyman I........1687	Pedro II..........1683

Emperor of Germany.	King of France.	King of Denmark.
Leopold............1658	Louis XIV........1643	Christian V.......1678

Emperors of the Turks.	King of Spain.	King of Sweden.
Mahomet IV......1649	Charles II........1665	Charles XI........1660

EMINENT PERSONS.

The duke of Monmouth; Spencer, earl of Sunderland; Prince James, otherwise called the Pretender; Judge Jefferies; Colonel Kirk; G Saville, marquis of Halifax; George, earl of Berkely; Thomas Osburn, duke of Leeds; H. Booth, lord Delamore, and earl of Warrington; C. Sackville, earl Dorset; H. Cavendish, duke of Devonshire; J. Thomson, lord Haversham; Colin Lindsay, earl of Balcarras; James Dalrymple, viscount Stair; R. Graham, viscount Preston; Roger Palmer, earl of Castlemain.

CHAPTER XXXII.
WILLIAM III.

Born 1650. Died March 8, 1702. Landed in England, November 5, 1688. Began to reign January 22, 1689. Reigned 13 years.

SECTION I.

———By turns they tell,
And listen, each with emulous glory fired,
How William conquer'd, and how France retired,
How Providence o'er William's temples held,
On Boyne's propitious banks the heav'nly shield.—*Prior.*

1. (A. D. 1687.) WILLIAM was no sooner elected to the throne, than he began to experience the difficulty of governing a people, who were more ready to examine the commands of their superiors than to obey them.

2. His reign commenced with an attempt similar to that which had been the principal cause of all the disturbances in the preceding reign, and which had excluded the monarch from the throne. William was a Calvinist, and consequently averse to persecution; he therefore began by attempting those laws which enjoined uniformity of worship; and, though he could not entirely succeed in his design, a toleration was granted to such dissenters as should take the oaths of allegiance, and hold no private conventicle.

3. In the meantime, James, whose authority was still

acknowleged in Ireland, embarked at Brest for that kingdom, and on May 22d arrived at Kinsale. He soon after made his public entry into Dublin, amidst the acclamations of the inhabitants. He found the appearance of things in that country equal to his most sanguine expectations. Tyrconnel, the lord-lieutenant, was devoted to his interests; his old army was steady, and a new one raised, amounting together to nearly forty thousand men.

4. As soon as the season would permit, he went to lay siege to Londonderry, a town of small importance in itself, but rendered famous by the stand it made on this occasion.

5. The besieged endured the most poignant sufferings from fatigue and famine, until at last relieved by a storeship, that happily broke the boom laid across the river to prevent a supply. The joy of the inhabitants at this unexpected relief was only equalled by the rage and disappointment of the besiegers. The army of James was so dispirited by the success of this enterprise, that they abandoned the siege in the night; and retired with precipitation, after having lost about nine thousand men before the place.

6. It was upon the opposite sides of the river Boyne that both armies came in sight of each other, inflamed with all the animosities arising from a difference of religion, hatred, and revenge. (A. D. 1690.) The river Boyne at this place was not so deep but that men might wade over on foot; however, the banks were rugged, and rendered dangerous by old houses and ditches, which served to defend the latent enemy. 7. William, who now headed the protestant army, had no sooner arrived, than he rode along the side of the river in sight of both armies, to make proper observations upon the plan of battle; but in the meantime, being, perceived by the enemy, a cannon was privately brought out, and planted against him where he was sitting. The shot killed several of his followers, and he himself was wounded in the shoulder.

8. Early the next morning, at six o'clock, king William gave orders to force a passage over the river This the army undertook in three different places; and after a furious cannonading, the battle began with unusual vigour. The Irish troops, though reckoned the best in Europe abroad, have always fought indifferently at home. 9. After an obstinate resistance, they fled with precipitation, leaving the French and Swiss regiments, who came to their assistance, to make the best retreat they could. William led on his

Battle of Aughrim, and Death of General St. Ruth.

horse in person; and contributed by his activity and vigilance to secure the victory. James was not in the battle, but stood aloof during the action, on the hill of Dunmore, surrounded with some squadrons of horse: and at intervals was heard to exclaim, when he saw his own troops repulsing those of the enemy, "O spare my English subjects!"

10. The Irish lost about fifteen hundred men, and the protestants about one-third of that number. The victory was splendid, and almost decisive; but the death of the duke of Schomberg, who was shot as he was crossing the water, seemed to outweigh the whole loss sustained by the enemy.

11. The last battle fought in favour of James was at Aughrim. (A. D. 1691.) The enemy fought with surprising fury, and the horse were several times repulsed; but the English wading through the middle of a bog up to the waist in mud and rallying with some difficulty on the firm ground on the other side, renewed the combat with great fury. 12. St. Ruth, the Irish general, being killed, his fate so discouraged his troops, that they gave way on all sides, and retreated to Limerick, where they resolved to make a final stand, after having lost above five thousand of the flower of their army. 13. Limerick, the last retreat of the Irish forces, made a brave defence; but soon seeing the enemy advanced within ten paces of the bridge foot, and perceiving themselves surrounded on all sides, they determined to capitulate; a negociation was immediately

begun, and hostilities ceased on both sides. 14. The Roman catholics, by this capitulation, were restored to the enjoyment of those liberties in the exercise of their religion which they had possessed in the reign of king Charles the Second. All persons were indulged with free leave to remove with their families and effects to any other country except England and Scotland. In consequence of this, above fourteen thousand of those who had fought for king James went over into France, having transports provided by government for conveying them thither.

Questions for Examination.

1, 2. What were the first acts of William ?
3. In what manner was James received in Ireland ?
4. What was the state of affairs in that country ?
5. Relate the particulars of the seige of Londonderry ?
6. Where did the armies first meet ?
7. By what means was William wounded ?
8, 9. What was the issue of this battle ?
Describe the conduct of the rival kings during his engagement.
10. What loss did each side sustain ?
11. Where was the next battle fought ?
12. How many of the Irish fell in this engagement ?
13. What was the last place of their retreat ?
14. What were the articles of their capitulation ?

SECTION II.

Yet Fame shall stay and bend to William's praise.
Of him her thousand ears shall hear triumphant lays ;
Of him her tongue shall talk, on him her eyes shall gaze.—*Congreve.*

1. (A. D. 1692.) JAMES was now reduced to the lowest state of despondence : his designs upon England were quite frustrated, so that nothing was left his friends but the hopes of assassinating the monarch on the throne. These base attempts, as barbarous as they were useless, were not entirely disagreeable to the temper of James. 2. It is said he encouraged and proposed them ; but they all proved unserviceable to his cause, and only ended in the destruction of the undertakers. From that time till he died, which was about seven years, he continued to reside at St. Germains, a pensioner on the bounty of Louis, and assisted by occasional liberalities from his daughter and friends in England. He died on the sixteenth day of September, in the year 1700, after having laboured under a tedious sickness; and many miracles, as the people thought, were wrought at his tomb. 3. Indeed, the latter part of his life was calculated to inspire the superstitious with reverance for his piety. He subjected himself to acts of uncommon penance and

mortification. He frequently visited the poor monks of La Trappe, who were edified by his humble and pious deportment. 4. His pride and arbitrary temper seemed to have vanished with his greatness; he became affable, kind, and easy to all his dependents; and at his last illness conjured his son to prefer religion to every worldly advantage,—a counsel which that prince strictly obeyed. He died with great marks of devotion, and was interred, at his own request, in the church of the English benedictines at Paris, without any funeral solemnity.

5. William, upon accepting of the crown, was resolved to preserve, as much as he was able, that share of prerogative which still was left him. But at length he became fatigued with opposing the laws which parliament every day were laying round his authority, and gave up the contest. 6. He admitted every restraint upon the prerogative in England, upon the condition of being properly supplied with the means of humbling the power of France. War and the balance of power in Europe, were all he knew, or indeed desired to understand. Provided the parliament furnished him with supplies for these purposes, he permitted them to rule the internal polity at their pleasure. 7. For the prosecution of the war with France, the sums of money granted to him were incredible. The nation, not content with furnishing him with such sums of money as they were capable of raising by the taxes of the year, mortgaged these taxes and involved themselves in debts which they have never since been able to discharge. 8. For all that profusion of wealth granted to maintain the imaginary balance of Europe, England received in return the empty reward of military glory in Flanders, and the consciousness of having given their allies, particularly the Dutch, frequent opportunities of being ungrateful.

The war with France continued during the greatest part of this king's reign; but at length the treaty of Ryswick, A. D. 1697, put an end to those contentions, in which England had engaged without policy and came off without advantage.

9. In the general pacification, her interest seemed entirely deserted; and for all the treasures she had sent to the continent, and all the blood which she had shed there, the only equivalent she received was an acknowledgment of king William's title from the king of France.

10. William was naturally of a very feeble constitution; and it was by this time almost exhausted by a series of con-

tinual disquietude and action. He had endeavoured to repair his constitution, or at least to conceal its decay, by exercise and riding. On the twenty-first day of February, in riding to Hampton-Court from Kensington, his horse fell under him, and he was thrown with such violence, that his collar-bone was fractured. His attendants conveyed him to the palace at Hampton-court, where the fracture was reduced, and in the evening he returned to Kensington in his coach. 11. The jolting of the carriage disunited the fracture once more, and the bones were again replaced, under Bidloo, his physician. This in a robust constitution would have been a trifling misfortune; but in him it was fatal. For sometime he appeared in a fair way of recovery; but, falling asleep on his couch, he was seized with a shivering, which terminated in a fever and diarrhœa, which soon became dangerous and desperate. 12. Perceiving his end approaching, the objects of his former care still lay next his heart; and the fate of Europe seemed to remove the sensations he might be supposed to feel for his own. The earl of Albermarle arriving from Holland, he conferred with him in private on the posture of affairs abroad. Two days after, having received the sacrament from archbishop Tenison, he expired in the fifty-second year of his age, after having reigned thirteen years.

Questions for Examination.

1. To what situation was James reduced, and what were the designs of his friends?
2. When and where did James die?
3. How did the exiled monarch spend the latter part of his life?
4. What counsel did he give to his son in his last illness?
5. What was William's resolution on accepting the crown?
6. Did his actions correspond with that resolution?
7. In what manner did William act?
8, 9. What consequences resulted from the war with France?
10, 11. What accident happened to William, and what were the consequences?
12. What object lay nearest his heart?
How long did William reign, and what was his age?

CONTEMPORARY SOVEREIGNS.

Popes.	A. D.		A. D.	King of Portugal.	A. D.
Alexander VIII.	1689	Achmet II.	1691	Pedro II.	1683
Innocent XII.	1691	Mustapha II.	1695		
Clement XI.	1700	*King of France.*		*King of Denmark.*	
Emperor of Germany.		Louis XIV.	1643	Christian V.	1670
Leopold.	1658	*Kings of Spain.*		*Kings of Sweden.*	
Emperors of the Turks.		Charles II.	1665	Charles XI.	1660
Soliman III.	1687	Phillip V.	1700	Charles XII.	1690

EMINENT PERSONS.

SIR ISAAC NEWTON ; JOHN LOCKE ; Archbishop Tillotson ; Bishop Burnet; duke Schomberg ; General Schomberg, son of the duke ; Montague, earl of Halifax; Russel, earl of Oxford ; John, lord Somers ; Anthony Ashley Cooper, earl of Shaftesbury (grandson to the nobleman mentioned in a former reign) ; Sheffield, duke of Buckingham ; John, lord Cutts ; admiral Russel, lord Berkely, &c.

CHAPTER XXXIII.

ANNE.

Born 1664. Died August, 1714. Began to reign March 8, 1702. Reigned 12½ years.

SECTION I.

> Ye active streams, where'er your waters flow,
> Let distant climes and farthest nations know
> What ye from Thames and Danube have been taught,
> How Anne commanded, and how Marlboro' fought.—*Prior.*

1. (A. D. 1702.) ANNE, married to prince George of Denmark, ascended the throne in the thirty-eight year of her age, to the general satisfaction of all parties. She was the second daughter of King James, by his first wife, the daughter of chancellor Hyde, afterwards earl of Clarendon. Upon coming to the crown, she resolved to declare war against France, and communicated her intentions to the house of commons, by whom it was approved, and war was proclaimed accordingly.

2. This declaration of war on the part of the English, was seconded by similar declarations by the Dutch and Germans on the same day. The French monarch could not suppress his anger at such a combination, but his chief resentment fell upon the Dutch. He declared with great emotion, that, as for these gentlemen pedlars, the Dutch, they should one day repent their insolence and presumption in declaring war against one whose power they had formerly felt and dreaded. 3. However, the affairs of the allies were no way influenced by his threats. The duke of Marlborough had his views gratified, in being appointed general of the English forces; and he was still farther flattered by the Dutch, who, though the earl of Athlone had a right to share the command, appointed Marlborough generalissimo of the allied army. 4. And it must be confessed, that few men shone more, either in debate or action, than he; serene in the midst of danger, and indefatigable in the cabinet; so

Marlborough.

that he became the most formidable enemy to France that England ever produced, since the conquering times of Cressy and Agincourt.

5. A great part of the history of this reign consists in battles fought upon the continent, which, though of very little advantage to the interest of the nation, were very great additions to its honour. These triumphs, it is true, are passed away, and nothing remains of them but the names of Blenheim, Ramilies, Oudenarde, and Malplaquet, where the allied army gained great, but (with respect to England) useless victories.

6. A conquest of much greater national importance was gained with less expense of blood and treasure in Spain. The ministry of England, understanding that the French were employed in equipping a strong squadron in Brest, sent out Sir Cloudesly Shovel and sir John Rooke to watch their motions. Sir George, however, had further orders to convoy a body of forces in transport-ships to Barcelona, upon which a fruitless attack was made by the prince of Hesse.

7. Finding no hopes, therefore, from this expedition, in two days after the troops were re-embarked, Sir George Rooke, joined by sir Cloudesly, called a council of war on board the fleet, as they lay off the coast of Africa. In this they resolved to make an attempt upon Gibraltar, a city then belonging to the Spaniards, at that time ill provided with a garrison, as neither expecting nor fearing such an attempt.

8. The town of Gibraltar stands upon a tongue of land, as the mariners called it, and defended by a rock inaccessible on every side but one. The prince of Hesse landed his troops, to the number of eight hundred, on the continent adjoining, and summoned the town to surrender, but without effect. 9. Next day the admiral gave orders for cannonading the town; and perceiving that the enemy were driven from their fortifications at a place called the South Mole Head, ordered captain Whitaker to arm all the boats, and assault that quarter. Those officers who happened to be nearest the Mole immediately manned their boats without orders, and entered the fortifications sword in hand. 10. But they were premature; for the Spaniards sprung a mine, by which two lieutenants and about one hundred men were killed or wounded. Nevertheless, the two captains, Hicks and Jumper, took possession of a platform, and kept their ground until they were sustained by captain Whitaker, and the rest of the seamen, who took a redoubt between the Mole and the town by storm. Then the governor capitulated, and the prince of Hesse entered the place, amazed at the success of the attempt, considering the strength of the fortifications.

11. When the news of this conquest was brought to England, it was for some time in debate whether it was a capture worth thanking the admiral for. It was at last considered, as unworthy of public gratitude; and, while the Duke of Marlborough was extolled for useless services, sir George Rooke was left to neglect, and soon displaced from his command for having so essentially served his country. A striking instance, that, even in the most enlightened age, popular applause is most usually misplaced. 12. Gibraltar has ever since remained in the possession of the English, and continues of the utmost use in refitting that part of the navy destined to annoy an enemy, or protect our trade in the Mediterranean. Here the English have a repository capable of containing all things necessary for the repairing of fleets or the equipment of armies.

13. While the English were thus victorious by land and sea, a new scene of contention was opened on the side of Spain, where the ambition of the European princes exerted itself with the same fury that had filled the rest of the continent. Philip the Fourth, grandson of Louis the Fourteenth, had been placed upon the throne of that kingdom, and had been received with the joyful concurrence of the greatest part of his subjects. 14. He had also been nominated successor

to the crown by the late king of Spain's will. But, in a former treaty among the powers of Europe, Charles, son of the Emperor of Germany, was appointed heir to that crown; and this treaty had been guaranteed by France herself, though she now resolved to reverse that consent in favour of a descendant of the house of Bourbon. 15. Charles was still farther led on to put in for the crown of Spain by the invitations of the Catalonians, who declared in his favour, and by the assistance of the English and the Portuguese, who promised to arm in his cause. He was furnished with two hundred transports, thirty ships of war, and nine thousand men, for the conquest of that extensive empire. But the earl of Peterborough, a man of romantic bravery, offered to conduct them; and his single service was thought equivalent to armies.

16. The earl of Peterborough was one of the most singular and extraordinary men of the age in which he lived. When yet but fifteen, he fought against the Moors in Africa; at twenty he assisted in compassing the revolution; and he now carried on the war in Spain almost at his own expense: his friendship for the duke Charles being one of his chief motives to this great undertaking. He was deformed in his person; but of a mind the most generous, honourable, and active. His first attempt upon landing in Spain was the taking of Barcelona, a strong city, with a garrison of five thousand men, while the whole army amounted to little more than nine thousand. The prince of Hesse was killed in this action.

17. These successes, however, were but of short continuance; Peterborough being recalled, and the army under Charles being commanded by the Lord Galway. This nobleman, having received intelligence that the enemy, under the command of the duke of Berwick, was posted near the town of Almanza, he advanced thither to give him battle. 18. The conflict began about two in the afternoon, and the whole front of each army was fully engaged. The centre, consisting chiefly of battalions from Great Britain and Holland, seemed at first victorious; but the Portuguese horse, by whom they were supported, betaking themselves to flight in the first charge, the English troops were flanked and surrounded on every side. 19. In this dreadful emergency they formed themselves into a square, and retired to an eminence, where, being ignorant of the country and destitute of all supplies, they were obliged to surrender prisoners of

Death of the prince of Hesse at Barcelona.

war, to the number of ten thousand men. This victory was complete and decisive; and all Spain, except the Province of Catalonia, returned to their duty to Philip their sovereign.

Questions for Examination.

1. Who succeeded William?
Against whom did Anne declare war?
2. How did the French monarch express his anger?
3. Who was appointed generalissimo?
4. What is his character?
5. Where did the nation gain great victories?
6, 7. What important conquest was next obtained?
8, 10 Relate the patriculars?
11. What opinion did the nation entertain of it?
12. Was not this opinion unfounded?
13—15. What new scenes of contention arose?
16. What were the character and conduct of the earl of Peterborough?
18, 19. Relate the particulars of the battle of Almanza.

SECTION II.

Henceforth, she said, in each returning year,
One stem the thistle and the rose shall bear;
The thistle's lasting grace—thou, O my rose, shall be;
The warlike thistle's arm a sure defence to thee.—*Rowe.*

1. (A. D. 1707.) THE councils of the queen had hitherto been governed by a whig ministry; for, though the duke of Marlborough had first started in the tory interest, he soon joined the opposite faction, as he found them most sincere

in their desires to humble the power of France. The whigs, therefore, still pursued the schemes of the late king; and, impressed with a republican spirit of liberty, strove to humble despotism in every part of Europe. 2. In a government, where the reasoning of individuals, retired from power, generally leads those who command, the designs of the ministry must alter as the people happen to change. The people, in fact, were beginning to change. But previous to the disgrace of the whig ministry, whose fall was now hastening, a measure of the greatest importance took place in parliament; a measure that had been wished by many, but thought too difficult for execution. 3. What I mean is, the union between the two kingdoms of England and Scotland: which, though they were governed by one sovereign since the accession of James the First, yet were still ruled by their respective parliaments, and often professed to pursue opposite interests and different designs.

4. The attempt for a union was begun at the commencement of this reign; but some disputes arising relative to the trade of the East, the conference was broken up, and it was thought that an adjustment would be impossible. 5. It was revived by an act in either parliament, granting power to commissioners, named on the part of both nations, to treat on the preliminary articles of a union, which should afterwards undergo a more thorough discussion by the legislative body of both kingdoms. The choice of these commissioners was left to the queen, and she took care that none should be employed but such as heartily wished to promote so desirable a measure.

6. Accordingly, the queen having appointed commissioners on both sides, they met in the council-chamber of the Cockpit, near Whitehall, which was the place appointed for the conferences. As the queen frequently exhorted the commissioners to despatch, the articles of this famous Union were soon agreed to and signed by the commissioners; and it only remained to lay them before the parliaments of both nations.

7. In this famous treaty it was stipulated that the succession to the United Kingdom should be vested in the house of Hanover; that the united kingdoms should be represented by one and the same parliament; that all the subjects of Great Britain should enjoy a communion of privileges and advantages. 8. That they should have the same allowance

and privileges with respect to commerce and customs; that the laws concerning public right, civil government, and policy, should be the same through the two united kingdoms; but that no alteration should be made in the laws which concerned private rights, except for the evident benefit of the subjects of Scotland. 9. That the courts of session, and all other courts of judicature in Scotland, should remain as then constituted by the laws of that kingdom, with the same authority and privileges as before the union; and that Scotland should be represented in the parliament of Great Britain by sixteen peers and forty-five commoners, to be elected in such a manner as should be settled by the present parliament of Scotland. 10. That all peers of Scotland should be considered as peers of Great Britain, and rank immediately after the English peers of the like degree at the time of the union, and before such as should be created after it; that they should enjoy all privileges of English peers, except that of sitting or voting in parliament, or sitting upon the trial of peers; and that all the insignia of royalty and government should remain as they were. 11. That all laws or statutes in either kingdom, as far as they may be inconsistent with the terms of these articles, should cease, and be declared void by the respective parliaments of the two kingdoms. These were the principal articles of the union; and it only remained to obtain the sanction of the legislature of both kingdoms to give them authority.

12. The arguments of these different assemblies were suited to the audience. To induce the Scots parliament to come into the measure, it was alleged, by the ministry and their supporters, that an entire and perfect union would be the solid foundation of a lasting peace. It would secure their religion, liberty, and property; remove the animosities that prevailed amongst themselves, and the jealousies that subsisted between the two nations. 13. It would increase their strength, riches, and commerce; the whole island would be joined in affection, and freed from all apprehensions of different interests; it would be enabled to resist all its enemies, support the Protestant interests, and maintain the liberties of Europe. It was observed, that the less the wheels of government were clogged by a multiplicity of councils, the more vigorous would be their exertions. 14. They were shown that the taxes, which, in consequence of this union, they were to pay, were by no means so pro-

portionally great as their share in the legislature; that their taxes did not amount to a seventeenth part of those supplied by the English; and yet their share in the legislature was not a tenth part less. Such were the arguments in favour of the union addressed to the Scots' parliament. 15. In the English houses it was observed, that a powerful and dangerous nation would thus for ever be prevented from giving them any disturbance. That, in case of any future rupture, England had everything to lose, and nothing to gain, against a nation that was courageous and poor.

16. On the other hand, the Scots were fired with indignation at the thought of losing their ancient and independent government. The nobility found themselves degraded in point of dignity and influence, by being excluded from their seats in parliament. The trading part of the nation beheld their commerce loaded with heavy duties, and considered their new privileges of trading to the English plantations in the West Indies as a very uncertain advantage. 17. In the English houses it was also observed, that the union of a rich with a poor nation would always be beneficial to the latter, and that the former could only hope for a participation of their necessities. It was said that the Scots reluctantly yielded to this coalition, and it might be likened to a marriage with a woman against her consent. 18. It was supposed to be a union made up of so many unmatched pieces and such incongruous ingredients, that it could never take effect. It was complained that the proportion of the land-tax paid by the Scots was small, and unequal to their share in the legislature.

19. At length, notwithstanding all opposition made by the tories, every article in the union was approved by a great majority in both parliaments. Thus all were obliged to acquiesce in a union of which they at first had not the sagacity to distinguish the advantage.

Questions for Examination.

1. By whom had the queen's counsels hitherto been governed?
2, 3. What important measure took place in parliament?
4-6. By what means was the union effected?
7-11. Relate the stipulations contained in this famous treaty.
12-14. What arguments were used to induce the Scots to come into the measure?
15. What arguments were made use of to the English?
16. In what manner did the Scots receive this message?
17. How was it received by the English?
18. What opinion was held concerning it?
19. Did the measure succeed?

SECTION III.

*Of Church and State, who dearest deems
Should carefully avoid extremes.—Dibdin.*

1. (A.D. 1708.) In the meantime the whig ministry was every day declining. Among the number of those whom the duchess of Marlborough had introduced to the queen to contribute to her private amusement, was one Mrs. Masham, her own kinswoman, whom she had raised from indigence and obscurity. The duchess, having gained the ascendant over the queen, became petulant and insolent, and relaxed in those arts by which she had risen. 2. Mrs. Masham, who had her fortune to make, was more humble and assiduous; she flattered the foibles of the queen, and assented to her prepossessions. She soon saw the queen's inclination to the tory set of opinions, their divine right and passive obedience; and instead of attempting to thwart her, as the duchess had done, she joined in with her partiality, and even outdid her in her own way.

3. This lady was, in fact, the tool of Mr. Harley, secretary of state, who also some time before had insinuated himself into the queen's good graces, and who had determined to sap the credit of the whig ministers. His aim was to unite the tory interest under his own shelter, and to expel the whigs from the advantages which they had long enjoyed under government.

4. In this career of his ambition he chose for his coadjutor, Henry St. John, afterwards the famous lord Bolingbroke; a man of great eloquence and a greater ambition; enterprising, restless, active, and haughty, with some wit and little principle. To this juncto was added Sir Simon Harcourt, a lawyer, who was a man of great abilities.

5. It was now perceived that the people themselves began to be weary of a whig ministry, whom they formerly caressed. To them they imputed the burdens under which they groaned,—burdens which they had been hitherto animated to bear by the pomp of triumph, but the load of which they felt in a pause of success.

6. Harley, afterwards known by the title of lord Oxford, was at the bottom of all these complaints; and though they did not produce an immediate effect, yet they did not fail of a growing and steady operation.

7. At length the whig party of the ministry opened their eyes to the intrigues of the tories. But it was now too late:

they had entirely lost the confidence of the queen. Harley soon threw off the mask of friendship, and took more vigorous measures for the prosecution of his designs. In him the queen reposed all her trust, though he had now no visible concern in the administration. 8. The first triumph of the tories, in which the queen discovered a public partiality in their favour, was seen in a transaction of no great importance in itself but from the consequence it produced. The parties of the nation were eager to engage, and they wanted but the watchword to begin. This was given by a man neither of abilities, property, nor power; but whom accident brought forward on this occasion.

9. Henry Sacheverel was a clergyman bred at Oxford, of narrow intellects and an overheated imagination. He had acquired some popularity among those who had distinguished themselves by the name of high churchmen, and had taken all occasions to vent his animosity against the dissenters. At the summer assizes at Derby, he held forth in that strain before the judges. On the fifth of November, in St. Paul's church, he, in a violent declamation, defended the doctrine of non-resistance, inveighed against the toleration of dissenters, declared the church was dangerously attacked by its enemies, and slightly defended by its false friends. 10. He sounded the trumpet for the zealous, and exhorted the people to put on the whole armour of God. Sir Samuel Gerrard, lord mayor, countenanced this harangue, which, though very weak both in matter and style, was published under his protection, and extolled by the tories as a masterpiece of writing. These sermons owed all their celebrity to the complexion of the times, and they are now deservedly neglected.

11. Mr. Dolbon, son of the archbishop of York, laid a complaint before the house of commons against these rhapsodies, and thus gave force to what would soon have been forgotten. The most violent paragraphs were read, and the sermons were voted scandalous and seditious libels. Sacheverel was brought to the bar of the house; and he, far from disowning the writing of them, gloried in what he had done and mentioned the encouragement he had received to publish them from the lord mayor, who was then present.

12. Being ordered to withdraw, it was resolved to impeach him of high crimes and misdemeanours at the bar of the house of lords; Mr. Dolbon was fixed upon to conduct the prosecution, in the name of the commons of England. A

committee was appointed to draw up articles of impeachment; Sacheverel was taken into custody, and a day was appointed for his trial before the lords in Westminster-hall.

13. The eyes of the whole kingdom were turned upon this very extraordinary trial, which lasted three weeks, and excluded all other public business for the time. The queen herself was every day present as a private spectator, whilst vast multitudes attended the culprit each day as he went to the hall, shouting as he passed, or silently praying for his success. The managers for the commons, were sir Joseph Jekyl, Mr. Eyre, solicitor-general, sir Peter King, recorder-general Stanhope, sir Thomas Parker, and Mr. Walpole. 14. The doctor was defended by sir Simon Harcourt and Mr. Philips, and assisted by doctor Atterbury, doctor Smallridge, and doctor Friend. While the trial continued, nothing could exceed the violence and outrage of the populace. They surrounded the queen's sedan, exclaiming, "God bless your majesty and the church! We hope your majesty is for doctor Sacheverel." 15. They destroyed several meeting-houses, plundered the dwellings of many eminent dissenters, and even proposed to attack the bank. The queen, in compliance with the request of the commons, published a proclamation for suppressing the tumults; and several persons were apprehended and tried for high-treason. Two were convicted, and sentenced to die; but neither suffered.

16. When the commons had gone through their charge, the managers for Sacheverel undertook his defence with great art and eloquence. He afterwards recited a speech himself, which, from the difference found between it and his sermons, seemed evidently the work of another. 17. In it he solemnly justified his intentions towards the queen and her government. He spoke in the most respectful terms of the Revolution and of the Protestant succession. He maintained the doctrine of non-resistance as the tenet of the church in which he was brought up; and in a pathetic conclusion endeavoured to excite the pity of his audience.

Questions for Examination.

1. What circumstances led to the fall of the whig ministers?
4. Who were the principal persons opposed to them?
5. What made the people dissatisfied?
6. Who was the cause of their discontent?
7. In whom did the queen repose her trust?
8. In what accident originated the contention between the two parties?
9. What was the subject of Sacheverel's writings?

10. Who countenanced and extolled them?
11. What notice did parliament take of these writings?
12. What followed?
13. Who were the managers for the commons?
14. By whom was he defended?
What was the conduct of the populace?
15. What outrages did they commit?
16, 17. What was the purport of Sacheverel's defence?

SECTION IV.

*Next to the thunderer let Anne stand,
In piety supremo as in command;
Fam'd for victorious arms and generous aid,
Young Austria's refuge and fierce Bourbon's dread.--Lansdowne.*

1. (A.D. 1709.) AT length after much obstinate dispute and virulent altercation Sacheverel was found guilty by a majority of seventeen voices; but no less than four-and thirty peers entered a protest against this decision. He was prohibited from preaching for three years; and his two sermons were ordered to be burnt by the hand of the common hangman, in presence of the lord mayor and the two sheriffs. The lenity of this sentence, which was in a great measure owing to the dread of popular resentment, was considered by the tories as a triumph.

2. Such was the complexion of the times, when the queen thought proper to summon a new parliament; and being a friend to the tories herself, she gave the people an opportunity of indulging themselves in choosing representatives to her mind. In fact, very few were returned but such as had distinguished themselves by their zeal against the whig administration.

3. In the meantime the campaign in Flanders was conducted with the most brilliant success. The duke of Marlborough had every motive to continue the war, as it gratified not only his ambition, but his avarice,—a passion that obscured his shining abilities.

4. The king of France appeared extremely desirous of a peace, and resolved to solicit a conference. He employed one Perkum, resident of the duke of Holstein at the Hague, to negotiate upon this subject, and he ventured also to solicit the duke himself in private. A conference was at length begun at Gertruydenburg, under the influence of Marlborough, Eugene, and Zinzendorf, who were all three, from private motives, entirely averse to the treaty. 5. Upon this occasion the French ministers were subjected to every spe-

cies of mortification. Spies were placed upon all their conduct. Their master was insulted, and their letters were opened; till at last Louis resolved to hazard another campaign. 6. It was only by insensible degrees that the queen seemed to acquire courage enough to second her inclinations, and depose a ministry that had long been disagreeable to her. Harley, however, who still shared her confidence, did not fail to inculcate the popularity, the justice, and the security of such a measure; and, in consequence of his advice, she began the changes, by transferring the post of lord chamberlain from the duke of Kent to the duke of Shrewsbury, who had lately voted with the tories and maintained an intimate correspondence with Mr. Harley. 7. Soon after, the earl of Sunderland, secretary of state, and son-in-law to the duke of Marlborough, was displaced, and the earl of Dartmouth put in his room. Finding that she was rather applauded than condemned for this resolute proceeding, she resolved to become entirely free.

8. Soon after, the earl of Godolphin was divested of his office, and the treasury put in commission, subjected to the direction of Mr. Harley, who was appointed chancellor of the exchequer, and under-treasurer. 9. The earl of Rochester was declared president of the council, in the room of lord Somers. The staff of the lord steward, being taken from the duke of Devonshire, was given to the duke of Buckingham; and Mr. Boyle was removed from the secretary's office to make way for Mr. Henry St. John. The lord chancellor having resigned the great seal, it was first put in commission, and then given to sir Simon Harcourt. 10. The earl of Wharton surrendered his commission of lord-lieutenant of Ireland, and that employment was conferred upon the duke of Ormond. Mr. George Greenville was appointed secretary of war, in the room of Mr. Robert Walpole. And, in a word, there was not one whig left in any office of the state, except the duke of Marlborough. He was still continued the reluctant general of the army; but he justly considered himself as a ruin entirely undermined, and just ready to fall.

11. But the triumph was not yet complete until the parliament was brought to confirm and approve the queen's choice. The queen, in her speech, recommended the prosecution of the war with vigour. The Parliament were ardent in their expressions of zeal and unanimity. They exhorted her to discountenance all such principles and

measures as had lately threatened her royal crown and dignity. This was but an opening to what soon after followed.

12. The duke of Marlborough, who but a few months before had been so highly extolled and caressed by the representatives of the people, was now become the object of their hatred and reproach. His avarice was justly upbraided; his protracting the war was said to arise from that motive. Instances were everywhere given of his fraud and extortion. These might be true; but party had no moderation, and even his courage and conduct were called in question.

13. To mortify the duke still more, the thanks of the house of commons were voted to the earl of Peterborough for his services in Spain, when they were refused to the duke for those in Flanders; and the lord-keeper, who delivered them to Peterborough, took occasion to drop some reflection against the mercenary disposition of his rival.

14. Nothing now, therefore, remained of the whig system, upon which this reign was begun, but the war, which continued to rage as fiercely as ever, and which increased in expense every year as it went on. It was the resolution of the present ministry to put an end to it at any rate, as it had involved the nation in debt almost to bankruptcy; and as it promised, instead of humbling the enemy, only to become habitual to the constitution.

15. It only remained to remove the duke of Marlborough from his post, as he would endeavour to traverse all their negotiations. But here again a difficulty started: this step could not be taken without giving offence to the Dutch, who placed entire confidence in him; they were obliged, therefore, to wait for some convenient occasion. Upon his return from the campaign, he was accused of having taken a bribe of six thousand pounds a year from a Jew who contracted to supply the army with bread; and the queen thought proper to dismiss him from all his employments. 16. This was the pretext made use of, though his fall had been predetermined; and though his receiving such a bribe was not the real cause of his removal, yet candour must confess that it ought to have been so.

In the meantime, Prior, much more famous as a poet than as a statesman, was sent over with proposals to France; and Menager, a man of no great station, returned with Prior to London, with full powers to treat upon the preliminaries.

17. The ministry having got thus far, the great difficulty

still lay before them of making the terms of peace agreeable to all the confederates. The earl of Strafford, who had been lately recalled from the Hague, where he resided as ambassador, was now sent back to Holland, with orders to communicate to the pensionary Heinsius the preliminary proposals, to signify the queen's approbation of them, and to propose a place where the plenipotentiaries should assemble. 18. The Dutch were very averse to begin the conference, upon the inspection of the preliminaries. They sent over an envoy to attempt to turn the queen from her resolution; but, finding their efforts vain, they fixed upon Utrecht as a place of general conference, and they granted passports to the French ministers accordingly.

19. The conference began at Utrecht, under the conduct of Robinson, bishop of Bristol, lord privy-seal, and the earl of Strafford, on the side of the English; of Buys and Vanderdusson, on the part of the Dutch; and of the marshal d'Exelles, the cardinal Polignac, and Mr. Menager, on behalf of France. The ministers of the emperor and of the duke of Savoy assisted, and the other allies sent also plenipotentiaries, though with the utmost reluctance. 20. As England and France were the only two powers that were seriously inclined to peace, it may be supposed that all the other deputies served rather to retard than advance its progress. They met rather to start new difficulties and widen the breach, than to quiet the dissensions of Europe.

Questions for Examination.

1. Was Sacheverel found guilty?
   What was his sentence?
2. Which party prevailed in the new parliament?
3-5. What took place in Flanders?
6-10. What change in the ministry took place?
11. In what manner did the parliament act?
12, 13. What conduct was observed towards the duke of Marlborough?
14. What was the resolution of the present ministry?
15. With what crime was Marlborough charged?
16, 17. What proceedings were now adopted?
18. Were the Dutch averse to the measure?
19. Where did the conference begin? By whom was it conducted?
20. What retarded its progress?

SECTION V.

*No reign than Anne's in war more justly crown'd,
No reign for learning justly more renow'd,
Elizabeth a Shakespeare own'd;
Charles could a Milton boast;
But Anne saw Newton high enthron'd
Amid the heavenly host.—Dibdin.*

1. (A.D. 1712.) The English ministers, therefore, finding multiplied obstructions from the deliberations of their allies, set on foot a private negociation with France. They stipulated certain advantages for the subjects of Great Britain in a concerted plan of peace. They resolved to enter into such mutual confidence with the French as would anticipate all clandestine transactions to the prejudice of the coalition.

2. In the beginning of August, secretary St. John, who had been created lord viscount Bolingbroke, was sent to the court of Versailles to remove all obstructions to the separate treaty. He was accompanied by Mr. Prior and the abbe Gualtier, and treated with the most distinguished marks of respect. He was caressed by the French king and the marquis de Torcy, with whom he adjusted the principal interests of the duke of Savoy and the elector of Bavaria.

3. At length, the treaties of peace and commerce between England and France being agreed on by the plenipotentiaries on either side, and ratified by the queen, she acquainted the parliament of the steps she had taken.

4. The articles of this famous treaty were longer canvassed, and more warmly debated, than those of any other treaty read of in history. The number of different interests concerned, and the great enmity and jealousy subsisting between all, made it impossible that all could be satisfied; and indeed there seemed no other method of obtaining peace but that which was taken,—for the two principal powers concerned to make their own articles, and to leave the rest for a subject of future discussion.

5. The first stipulation was, that Philip, now acknowledged king of Spain, should renounce all right to the crown of France; the union of two such powerful kingdoms being thought dangerous to the liberties of Europe. It was agreed that the duke of Berri, Philip's brother, and after him in succession, should also renounce his right to the crown of Spain, in case he became king of France. 6. It was stipulated that the duke Savoy should possess the island of Sicily, with the title of king, together with Fenistrelles, and other places on the continent; which increase

of dominion was in some measure made out of the spoils of the French monarchy. The Dutch had that barrier granted them which they so long sought after; and if the crown of France was deprived of some dominions to enrich the duke of Savoy, on the other hand the house of Austria was taxed to supply the wants of the Hollanders, who were put in possession of the strongest towns in Flanders. 7. With regard to England, its glory and its interests were secured. The fortifications of Dunkirk, a harbour that might be dangerous to their trade in time of war, were ordered to be demolished, and its port destroyed. Spain gave up all right to Gibraltar and the Island of Minorca. France resigned her pretensions to Hudson's Bay, Nova Scotia, and Newfoundland; but they were left in possession of Cape Breton, and the liberty of drying their fish upon the shore. 8. Among these articles, glorious to the English nation, their setting free the French Protestants confined in the prisons and galleys for their religion, was not the least meritorious. For the emperor, it was stipulated, that he should possess the kingdom of Naples, the duchy of Milan, and the Netherlands. The king of Prussia was to have Upper Guelder; and a time was fixed for the emperor's acceding to these articles, as he had for some time obstinately refused to assist at the negociation. 9. Thus Europe seemed to be formed into one great republic, the different members of which were cantoned out to different governors, and the ambition of any one state amenable to the tribunal of all. Thus it appears that the English ministry did justice to all the world; but their country denied that justice to them.

10. But while the whigs were attacking the tory ministers from without, these were in much greater danger from their own internal dissensions. Lord Oxford and Lord Bolingbroke, though they had started with the same principles and designs, yet, having vanquished other opposers, now began to turn their strength against each other. Both began to form separate interests, and to adopt different principles. Oxford's plan was the more moderate; Bolingbroke's the more vigorous, but the more secure. 11. Oxford, it was thought, was entirely for the Hanoverian succession; Bolingbroke had some hopes of bringing in the pretender. But though they hated each other most sincerely, yet they were for a while kept together for the good offices of their friends and adherents, who had the melancholy prospect of

seeing the citadel of their hopes, while openly besieged from without, secretly undermined within.

12. This was a mortifying prospect for the tories; but it was more particularly displeasing to the queen, who daily saw her favourite minister declining, while her own health kept pace with their contentions. Her constitution was now quite broken. One fit of sickness succeeded another; and what completed the ruin of her health was the anxiety of her mind. These dissensions had such an effect upon her spirits and constitution, that she declared she could not outlive it, and immediately sank into a state of lethargic insensibility. Notwithstanding all the medicines which the physicians could prescribe, the distemper gained ground so fast, that the day afterwards they despaired of her life, and the privy council was assembled on the occasion.

All the members, without distinction, being summoned from the different parts of the kingdom, began to provide for the security of the constitution. 14. They sent a letter to the elector of Hanover, informing him of the queen's desperate situation, and desiring him to repair to Holland, where he would be attended by a British squadron to convey him to England. At the same time they despatched instructions to the earl of Strafford, at the Hague, to desire the states-general to be ready to perform the guarantee of thr Protestant succession. 15. Precautions were taken to secure the seaports; and the command of the fleet was bestowed upon the earl of Berkeley, a professed whig. These measures, which were all dictated by that party, answered a double end. It argued their own alacrity in the cause of their new sovereign, and seemed to imply a danger to the state from the disaffection of the opposite interest.

16. On the thirtieth of July, the queen seeming somewhat relieved by medicines, rose from her bed about eight o'clock and walked a little. After some time, casting her eyes on a clock that stood in her chamber, she continued to gaze on it for some minutes. One of the ladies in waiting asked her what she saw there more than usual, to which the queen only answered by turning her eyes upon her with a dying look. 17. She was soon after seized with a fit of apoplexy. She continued all night in a state of stupefaction, and expired the next morning, in the forty-ninth year of her age. She reigned more than twelve years over a people that was now risen to the highest pitch of refinement, and had attained by their wisdom all the advantages

of opulence, and, by their valour, all the happiness of security and conquest.*

Questions for Examination.

1, 2. What circumstances preceded the treaty with France?
3, 4. After its conclusion, in what manner was it received?
5. What was the first stipulation?
6. What the next?
7. How did the treaty regard England?
8. Which article of the treaty was meritorious to the English nation? What were the stipulations regarding the emperor and the king of Prussia?
9. What appearance did Europe now exhibit?
10. What dissensions took place between Oxford and Bollingbroke?
11. What was thought to be their different views?
12. What effect had this discussion on the queen?
13-15. When the queen's life was despaired of, what measures were taken?
16. What immediately preceded the queen's death?
17. How long did she reign?
What was the situation of England at her death?

CONTEMPORARY SOVEREIGNS.

Popes		A.D.		A.D.
		Achmet III......1703	John V.........	1707
	A.D.			
Clement XI......1700		King of France.		King of Denmark.
Emperors of Germany.		Louis XIV......1643		Frederick IV...1669
Leopold.........1658		King of Spain.		King of Sweden.
Joseph I........1705				
Charles VI......1711		Philip V.......1700		Charles XII......1697
Emperors of the Turks.		Kings of Portugal.		King of Prussia.
Mustapha II....1695		Pedro II.......1683		Frederick I......1701

* It has been a subject of general remark, that England flourished more under the reigns of Elizabeth and Anne than under those of its most distinguished kings. Though the actions and principles of these princesses were widely different, yet their reigns were equally remembered with gratitude by their subjects, and both of them have acquired the endearing epithets of "good queens." With a pleasing countenance and melodious voice, were united in the person of queen Anne those amiable virtues, which add so great a lustre to the charms of beauty, and place the female character in so admirable a light. Good-natured, affable, and kind, she was an affectionate wife, a tender mother, a warm friend, a generous patroness, and a benevolent and merciful sovereign. Though she was deficient in the shining qualities of Queen Elizabeth, yet she surpassed that princess in her fondness for her subjects; and as Elizabeth acquired the good-will of the English by the greatness of her actions, so Anne was beloved by her people because she evinced a maternal affection for them. Nor should the fact pass unnoticed, that, notwithstanding the prevalence of factions and the dissensions of parties, during this reign the blood of no subject was shed for treason.

GEORGE I.

EMINENT PERSONS.

Churchill, duke of Marlborough; lord Bolingbroke, sir William Temple; Boyle, earl of Orrery; Swift; Sydney, earl of Godolphin; Harley, earl of Oxford; Mordount, earl of Peterborough; Howard, earl of Suffolk; D. Finch, earl of Nottingham; G. Grenville, lord Landsdowne; Philip, duke of Wharton; R. lord Raymond; lord-chancellor King; T. lord Paget; Sarah, duchess of Marlborough.

CHAPTER XXXIV.

GEORGE I.

Born 1660, Died June 11, 1727. Began to reign August 1, 1714. Reigned 12¾ years.

SECTION I.

*The common weal should be the first pursuit
Of the crown'd warrior; for the royal brows
The people first enwreath'd.—Seward.*

1. (A.D. 1714.) PURSUANT to the act of succession, George the First, son of Ernest Augustus, first elector of Brunswick, and the princess Sophia, grand-daughter to

*John Churchill, duke of Marlborough, was the son of sir Winston Churchill, and was born at Ashe, in Devonshire, in 1650. At the age of 12 he became page to the duke of York. About 1666 he was made an ensign in the guards, and served for some time at Tangier; and this seems to have decided him in the choice of a profession. He was a great favourite at court, and the duchess of Cleveland presented him £5,000, with which he purchased a life annuity. In 1772 he accompanied the duke of Monmouth to the continent as a captain of grenadiers, and there fought under the great Turenne, with whom he was known by the name of the handsome Englishman. At the siege of Maestritcht he distinguished himself so highly as to receive the public thanks of the king of France. Returning to England, he advanced from one post to another. On the accession of James II, he was created baron Churchill of Sundridge; and, on that of William and Mary, earl of Marlborough. When Anne took the throne in 1702, he was made captain-general of all the forces at home and abroad, and sent plenipotentiary to the Hague, where he was also made captain-general by the states. This was followed by a series of the most splendid campaigns ever made by the armies of England. But in 1711 he was removed from his command by a ministry that was opposed to him. At the accession of George I he was reinstated. After assisting in the defeat of the rebellion in 1715, he withdrew from public employments, and died in 1722, in the 73d year of his age.

The duchess, his widow, a lady of great ambition and avarice, became very celebrated, and died in 1744, after amassing great wealth.

The palace which was built for him by the nation at Woodstock, near Oxford, after his celebrated victory at Blenhiem, is one of the finest structures in the kingdom.

The architect, sir John Vanburgh, has been censured as having built it in too heavy a style; and this caused the mock epitaph on him to be received with much favour:

<blockquote>Lie heavy on him, earth; for he
Laid many a heavy load on thee.</blockquote>

But many consider the criticism unjust.

James the First, ascended the British throne. His mature age, he being now fifty-four years old, his sagacity and experience, his numerous alliances, and the general tranquility of Europe, all contributed to establish his interests, and to promise him a peaceable and happy reign. 2. His abilities, though not shining, were solid; he was of a very different disposition from the Stuart family, whom he succeeded. These were known, to a proverb, for leaving their friends in extremity. George, on the contrary, soon after his arrival in England was heard to say, "My maxim is, never to abandon my friends, to do justice to all the world, and to fear no man."

3. To these qualifications of resolution and perseverance, he joined great application to business. However, one fault with respect to England remained behind,—he studied the interests of those subjects he had left, more than the interests of those he came to govern.

4. The queen had no sooner resigned her breath, than the privy-council met; and three instruments were produced, by which the elector appointed several of his known adherents to be added as lord-justices to seven great officers of the kingdom. Orders were immediately issued out for proclaiming George king of England, Scotland, and Ireland. The regency appointed the earl of Dorset to carry him the intimation of his accession to the crown, and to attend him on his journey to England. They sent the general officers, in whom they could confide, to their posts; they reinforced the garrison at Portsmouth, and appointed the celebrated Mr. Addison secretary of state. 5. To mortify the late ministry the more, lord Bolingbroke was obliged to wait every morning in the passage among the servants with his bag of papers, where there were persons purposely placed to insult and deride him. No tumult appeared, no commotion arose, against the accession of the new king; and this gave a strong proof that no rational measures were even taken to obstruct his exaltation.

6. When he first landed at Greenwich, he was received by the duke of Northumberland, captain of the life-guard, and the lords of the regency. When he retired to his bedchamber, he sent for such of the nobility as had distinguished themselves by their zeal for his succession. But the duke of Ormond, the lord-chancellor, and the lord-treasurer, found themselves excluded.

7. The king of a faction is but the sovereign of half his

subjects. Of this, however, the new elected monarch did not seem to be sensible. It was his misfortune, and consequently that of the nation, that he was hemmed round by men who soured him with their own interests. None now but the leaders of a party were admitted into employment. The whigs, while they pretended to secure the crown for their king, were, with all possible arts, confirming their own interests, extending their connexions, and giving laws to the sovereign. 8. An instantaneous and total change was made in all the offices of trust, honour and advantage. The whigs governed the senate and the court, whom they would have oppressed; bound the lower orders of people with severe laws, and kept them at a distance by vile distinctions; and taught them to call this—liberty!

9. These partialities soon raised discontents among the people, and the king's attachment considerably increased the discontents throughout the kingdom. The clamour of the church's being in danger was revived. Birmingham, Bristol, Norwich, and Reading, still remembered the spirit with which they had declared for Sacheverel; and now the cry was, "Down with the whigs, and Sacheverel for ever!"

10. Upon the first meeting of the new parliament, in which the whigs, with the king at their head, were predominant, nothing was expected but the most violent measures against the late ministry, nor were the expectations of mankind disappointed. (A.D. 1714).

11. The lords professed their hopes that the king would be able to recover the reputation of the kingdom on the continent, the loss of which they affected to deplore. The commons went much further: they declared their resolution to trace out those measures by which the country was depressed; they resolved to seek after those abettors on whom the pretender seemed to ground his hopes; and they determined to bring such to condign punishment.

12. It was the artifice, during this and the succeeding reign, to stigmatize all those who testified their discontent against government, as papists and jacobites. All who attempted to speak against the violence of their measures, were reproached as designing to bring in the pretender; and most people were consequently afraid to murmur, since discontent was so near akin to treason. The people, therefore, beheld the violence of their conduct in silent fright, internally disapproving, yet not daring to avow their detestation.

13. A committee was appointed, consisting of twenty persons, to inspect all the papers relative to the late negotiation for peace, and to pick out such of them as might serve as subjects of accusation against the late ministry. After some time spent in this disquisition, Mr. Walpole, as chairman of the committee, declared to the house that a report was drawn up; and in the mean time moved that a warrant might be issued for apprehending Mr. Mathew Prior and Mr. Thomas Harley, who, being in the house, were immediately taken into custody. 14. He then impeached lord Bolingbroke of high treason. This struck some of the members with amazement; but they were still more astonished when lord Coningsby, rising up, was heard to say, "The worthy chairman has impeached the hand, but I impeach the head; he has impeached the scholar, and I the master; I impeach Robert earl of Oxford and the earl of Mortimer of high-treason and of other crimes and misdemeanours."

Questions for Examination.

1. Under what circumstances did George I. ascend the throne?
2. What were his abilities and disposition? What was his maxim?
3. What fault was atributed to him?
4. What was the first act of the privy council?
5. In what manner was Bolingbroke treated?
6. By whom was the king received on his landing?
7. By whom was the king advised, and what was the result?
8. 9. What did these partialities produce?
10. 11. In what manner did the new parliament act?
12. What did their proceedings produce?
13] 14. For what purpose was a committee appointed?

SECTION II.

Where Scotland's cloud-capp'd hills appear,
See Mar the rebel standard rear:
The rash Pretender's hopes are vain.
His followers dispersed or slain.—*Davies.*

1. (A.D. 1714.) WHEN lord Oxford appeared in the house of lords the day following, he was avoided by the peers as infectious; and he had now an opportunity of discovering the baseness of mankind. When the articles were read against him in the house of commons, a warm debate arose upon that in which he was charged with having advised the French king of the manner of gaining Tournay from the Dutch. 2. Mr. Walpole alleged that it was treason. Sir Joseph Jekyl, a known whig, said that he could never be of opinion that it amounted to treason. It was his principle,

he said, to do justice to all men, from the highest to the lowest. He hoped he might pretend to some knowledge of the law, and would not scruple to declare, upon this part of the question, in favour of the criminal. 3. To this, Walpole answered, with great warmth, that there were several persons, both in and out of the committee, who did not in the least yield to that member in point of honesty, and exceeded him in the knowledge of the laws, and yet were satisfied that the charge in that article amounted to high treason. 4. This point being decided against the earl, and the other articles proved by the house, the lord Coningsby, attended by the whig members, impeached him soon after at the bar of the house of lords; demanding, at the same time, that he might lose his seat, and be committed to custody. When this point came to be debated in the house of lords a violent altercation ensued. Those who still adhered to the deposed minister, maintained the injustice and danger of such proceedings. 5. At last the earl himself rose up, and, with great tranquillity, observed, that, for his own part, he always acted by the immediate directions and command of the queen, his mistress; he had never offended against any known law, and was unconcerned for the life of an insignificant old man. Next day he was brought to the bar, where he received a copy of his indictment, and was allowed a month to prepare his answer. Though Dr. Mead declared, that if the earl should be sent to the Tower, his life would be in danger, it was carried in the house that he should be committed.

6. At the same time the duke of Ormond and lord Bolingbroke, having omitted to surrender themselves (for they had actually fled to the continent) within a limited time, it was ordered that the earl-marshall should raze out their names and arms from among the list of peers; and inventories were taken of their estates and possessions, which were declared forfeited to the crown.

7. Lord Oxford, being confined in the Tower, continued there for two years, during which time the nation was in a continual ferment, from an actual rebellion that was carried on unsuccessfully. After the execution of some lords who were taken in arms, the nation seemed glutted with blood, and that was the time that lord Oxford petitioned to be brought to trial. 8. He knew that the fury of the nation was spent on objects that were really culpable, and expected that his case would look like innocence itself compared to

theirs. A day, therefore, at his own request, was assigned him, and the commons were ordered to prepare for their charge. At the appointed time the peers repaired to the court in Westminster-hall, where lord Cowper presided as lord high steward. 9. But a dispute arising between the lords and commons concerning the mode of his trial, the lords voted that the prisoner should be set at liberty. To this dispute he probably owed the security of his title and fortune; for as to the articles importing him guilty of high treason, they were at once malignant and frivolous, so that his life was in no manner of danger.

10. In the mean time these vindictive proceedings excited the indignation of the people, who perceived that the avenues to royal favour were closed against all but a faction. The flames of rebellion were actually kindled in Scotland. The earl of Mar, assembling three hundred of his own vassals in the Highlands, proclaimed the pretender at Castledown, and set up his standard at a place called Braemar, assuming the title of lieutenant-general of his majesty's forces. 11. To second these attempts, two vessels arrived in Scotland from France, with arms, ammunition, and a number of officers, together with assurances to the earl, that the Pretender himself would shortly come over to head his own forces. The earl, in consequence of this promise, soon found himself at the head of ten thousand men, well armed and provided. 12. The duke of Argyle, apprized of his intentions, and at any rate willing to prove his attachment to the present government, resolved to give him battle in the neighbourhood of Dumblane, though his forces did not amount to half the number of the enemy. After an engagement which continued several hours, in the evening both sides drew off, and both sides claimed the victory. 13. Though the possession of the field was kept by neither, yet certainly all the honour and all the advantages of the day belonged to the duke of Argyle. It was sufficient for him to have interrupted the progress of the enemy; for, in their circumstances, delay was defeat. The earl of Mar soon found his disappointment and losses increase. The castle of Inverness, of which he was in possession, was delivered up to the king by lord Lovat, who had hitherto professed to act in the interest of the Pretender. 14. The marquis of Tullibardine forsook the earl, in order to defend his own part of the country; and many of the clans, seeing no likelihood of coming soon to a second engagement, returned quietly home; for

an irregular army is much easier led to battle, than induced to bear the fatigues of a campaign.

15. In the mean time the rebellion was much more unsuccessfully prosecuted in England. From the time the Pretender had undertaken this wild project at Paris, in which the duke of Ormond and lord Bolingbroke were engaged, lord Stair, the English ambassador there, had penetrated all his designs, and sent faithful accounts of all his measures, and of all his adherents, to the ministry at home. Upon the first rumour, therefore, of an insurrection, they imprisoned several lords and gentlemen, of whom they had a suspicion.

16. The earls of Home, Wintown, Kinnoul, and others, were committed to the castle of Edinburgh. The king obtained leave from the lower house to seize sir William Wyndham, sir John Packington, Harvey Combe, and others. The lords Lansdowne and Duplin were taken into custody. Sir William Wyndham's father-in-law, the duke of Somerset, offered to become bound for his appearance, but this surety was refused.

Questions for Examination.

1. What was the conduct of the peers towards lord Oxford?
2. In what way was he defended by sir John Jekyl?
3. What was the answer of Walpole?
4. Who impeached the earl of Oxford before the lords?
5. What answer did his lordship make to the charge?
6. What proceedings were taken against Ormond and Bolingbroke?
7. In what state was the nation at this time?
8. Under what circumstances did Oxford request his trial?
9. What occasioned his being set at liberty?
10. What excited the indignation of the people?
11-14. Relate the particulars of the rebellion of Scotland.
15. Who, penetrating into the wild project of the pretender, sent accounts of all his measures?
16. Who were imprisoned in consequence?

SECTION III.

Swift to the north his troops he leads,
O'er rapid floods and hills of snow;
No toil the glorious march impedes
That bears the Briton to the foe.—*Anon.*

1. (A.D. 1715.) ALL these precautions were not able to stop the insurrection in the western counties, where it was already begun. However, all their preparations were weak and ill-conducted; every measure was betrayed to government as soon as projected, and many revolts suppressed in the very outset. 2. The university of Oxford was treated with great severity on this occasion. Major-general Pepper, with

a strong detachment of dragoons, took possession of the city at daybreak, declaring that he would instantly shoot any of the students who should presume to appear without the limits of their respective colleges. The insurrections in the northern counties came to greater maturity. 3. In the month of October, 1715, the earl of Derwentwater and Mr. Foster took the field with a large body of horse, and being joined by some gentlemen from the borders of Scotland, proclaimed the Pretender. Their first attempt was to seize upon Newcastle, in which they had many friends; but they found the gates shut against them and were obliged to retire to Hexham. 4. To oppose these, general Carpenter was detached by government with a body of nine hundred men, and an engagement was hourly expected. The rebels had proceeded by way of Kendal and Lancaster to Preston, of which place they took possession without any resistance. But this was the last stage of their ill-advised incursion; for general Wills, at the head of seven thousand men, came up to the town to attack them, and from his activity there was no escaping. They now, therefore, began to raise barricades, and to place the town in a posture of defence, repulsing the first attack of the royal army with success. Next day, however, Wills was reinforced by Carpenter, and the town was invested on all sides. In this deplorable situation, to which they were reduced by their own rashness, Foster hoped to capitulate with the general, and accordingly sent colonel Oxburgh, who had been taken prisoner, with a trumpeter, to propose a capitulation. 6. This, however, Wills refused, alleging that he would not treat with rebels, and the only favour they had to expect was to be spared from immediate slaughter. These were hard terms, yet no better could be obtained. They accordingly laid down their arms, and were put under a strong guard; all the noblemen and leaders were secured, and a few of the officers tried for deserting from the royal army, and shot by order of a court-martial. The common men were imprisoned at Chester and Liverpool; the noblemen and considerable officers were sent to London, and led through the streets, pinioned and bound together, to intimidate their party.

7. The Pretender might, by this time, have been convinced of the vanity of his expectations, in supposing that the whole country would rise up in his cause. His affairs were actually desperate; yet, with his usual infatuation, he resolved to hazard his person among his friends in Scotland

at a time when such a measure was too late for success. 8. Passing, therefore, through France in disguise, and embarking in a small vessel at Dunkirk, he arrived, after a passage of a few days, on the coast of Scotland, with only six gentlemen in his train. He passed unknown through Aberdeen to Feterosse, where he was met by the earl of Mar, and about thirty noblemen and gentlemen of the first quality. 9. There he was solemnly proclaimed. His declaration, dated at Commercy, was printed and dispersed. He went from thence to Dundee, where he made a public entry, and in two days more he arrived at Scoon, where he intended to have the ceremony of the coronation performed. He ordered thanksgivings to be made for his safe arrival; he enjoined the ministers to pray for him in their churches; and without the smallest share of power, went through the ceremonies of royalty, which threw an air of ridicule on all his conduct. 10. Having thus spent some time in unimportant parade, he resolved to abandon the enterprise with the same levity with which it was undertaken. Having made a speech to his grand council, he informed them of his want of money, arms, and ammuunition, for undertaking a campaign, and therefore deplored that he was compelled to leave them. He once more embarked on board a small French ship that lay in the harbour of Montrose, accompanied by severals lords, his adherents, and in five days arrived at Gravelin.

11. In this manner ended a rebellion, which nothing but imbecility could project, and nothing but rashness could support. But though the enemy was no more, the fury of the victors did not seem in the least to abate with success. The law was now put in force with all its terrors; and the prisons of London were crowded with those deluded wretches, whom the ministry seemed resolved not to pardon.

12. The commons, in their address to the crown, declared they would prosecute in the most rigorous manner the authors of the late rebellion. In consequence of which the earls of Derwentwater, Nithisdale, Carnwath, and Wintown, the lords Widrington, Kenmuir, and Nairne, were impeached, and, upon pleading guilty, all but lord Wintown received sentence of death. No entreaties could soften the minstry to spare these unhappy men. The countess of Derwentwater, with her sister, and several other ladies of the first distinction, being introduced into the presence of the king, besought his clemency for her husband, but without effect.

13. Orders were dispatched for executing the lords Der-

Countess of Derwenwater interceding for her husband.

wentwater, Nithisdale, and Kenmuir immediately; the rest were respited to a farther time. Nithisdale, however, had the good fortune to escape in women's clothes, which were brought to him by his mother, the night before he was to have been executed. Derwentwater and Kenmuir were brought to the scaffold on Tower-hill at the time appointed. Both underwent their sentence with calm intrepidity, pitied by all, and seemingly less moved themselves than those who beheld them.

14. In the beginning of April, commissioners for trying the rebels met in the court of common pleas, when bills were found against Mr. Forster, Mr. Mackintosh, and twenty of their confederates.

15. Forster escaped from Newgate, and reached the continent in safety; the rest pleaded not guilty. Pitts, the keeper of Newgate, being suspected of having connived at Forster's escape, was tried for his life, but acquitted. Yet, notwithstanding this, Mackintosh and several other prisoners broke from Newgate, after having mastered the keeper and tnrnkey, and disarmed the sentinel. 16. The court proceeded to the trial of those that remained; four or five were hanged, drawn, and quartered at Tyburn; two-and-twenty were executed at Preston and Manchester; and about a thousand prisoners experienced the king's mercy, if such it might be called, by being transported to North America.

17. A rupture with Spain, which ensued some time after, served once more to raise the declining expectations of the pretender and his adherents. It was hoped that, by the assistance of cardinal Alberoni, the Spanish minister, a new insurrection might be carried on in England. The duke of Ormond was the person fixed upon to conduct this expedition; and he obtained from the Spanish court a fleet of ten ships of war and transports, having on board six thousand regular troops, with arms for twelve thousand more. 18. But fortune was still as unfavourable as ever. Having set sail, and proceeded as far as Cape Finisterre, he was encountered by a violent storm, which disabled his fleet and frustrated the expedition. This misfortune, together with the bad success of the Spanish arms in Sicily, and in other parts of Europe, induced Philip to wish for peace; and he at last consented to sign the quadruple alliance. This was at that time thought an immense acquisition; but England, though she procured the ratification, had no share in the advantage of the treaty.

Questions for Examination.

1. Of what nature was the insurrection in the western counties?
2. In what manner was the university of Oxford treated?
3. By whom was the pretender first proclaimed?
4. Relate the manner in which they were opposed.
5. 6. What was the result of the siege of Preston?
8. 9. What was the next proceeding of the Pretender?
10. What was his conduct on abandoning this enterprise?
11. What was the conduct of the victors?
12. What was the declaration of the commons? and what was the consequence?
13. What orders were now despatched?
14–16. Relate the particulars which regarded the other rebels.
17. What rupture raised the declining hopes of tho Pretender?
18. What was the result?

SECTION IV.

The South Sea bubble now appears,
Which caused some smiles, some countless tears,
And set half Europe by the ears.—*Dibdin.*

1. (A.D. 1721) IT was about this time that one John Law, a Scotchman, had cheated France by erecting a company under the name of the Mississippi, which promised that deluded people great wealth, but which ended in involving the French nation in great distress. It was now that the people of England were deceived by a project entirely similar, which is remembered by the name of the South

Sea Scheme, and which was felt long after by thousands. 2. To explain this as concisely as possible, it is to be observed, that ever since the revolution under king William, the government, not having had sufficient supplies granted by parliament, or what was granted requiring time to be collected, they were obliged to borrow money from several different companies of merchants, and, among the rest, from that company which traded to the South Sea. The South Sea company having made up their debt to the government ten millions, instead of six hundred thousand pounds, which they usually received as interest, were satisfied with five hundred thousand pounds.

3. It was in this situation of things that one Blount, who had been bred a scrivener, and was possessed of all the cunning and plausibility requisite for such an undertaking, proposed to the ministry, in the name of the South Sea company, to buy up all the debts of the different companies of merchants, and thus to become the sole creditor of the state. 4. The terms he offered to government were extremely advantageous. The South Sea company was to redeem the debts of the nation out of the hands of the private proprietors, who were creditors to the government, upon whatever terms they could agree on; and for the interest of this money, which they had thus redeemed, and taken into their own hands, they would be contented to be allowed by government, for six years, five per cent.; then the interest should be reduced to four per cent.; and should at any time be redeemable by parliament. 5. But now came the part of the scheme big with fraud and ruin. As the directors of the South Sea company could not of themselves be supposed to possess money sufficient to buy up the debts of the nation, they were empowered to raise it by opening a subscription to a scheme for trading to the South Seas, from which commerce immense ideal advantages were promised by the cunning directors, and still greater expected by the rapacious credulity of the people. All persons therefore, who were creditors to the government, were invited to come in, and exchange their stocks for that of the South Sea company.

6. The directors' books were no sooner opened for the first subscription, than crowds came to make the exchange of their stock for South Sea stock. The delusion was artfully continued, and spread. Subscriptions in a very few days sold for double the price they had been bought at.

The scheme succeeded even beyond the proprietor's hopes, and the whole nation was infected with a spirit of avaricious enterprise. The infatuation prevailed; the stock increased to a surprising degree, and to nearly ten times the value of what it was subscribed for.

7. After a few months, however, the people awoke from their dreams of riches, and found that all the advantages they expected were merely imaginary, while thousands of families were involved in one common ruin.

8. The principal delinquents were punished by parliament with a forfeiture of all such possessions and estates as they had acquired during the continuance of this popular phrensy, and some care also was taken to redress the sufferers. The discontents occasioned by these public calamities once more gave the disaffected party hopes of succeeding. But in all their councils they were weak, divided, and wavering.

9. The first person that was seized upon suspicion was Francis Atterbury, bishop of Rochester, a prelate long obnoxious to the present government, and possessed of abilities to render him formidable to any ministry he opposed. His papers were seized, and he himself confined to the Tower. Soon after, the duke of Norfolk, the Earl of Orrery, the lords North and Grey, and some others of inferior rank, were arrested and imprisoned. Of all these, however, only the bishop, who was banished, and one Mr. Layer, who was hanged at Tyburn, felt the severity of government, the proofs against the rest amounting to no convictive evidence.

10. The commons about this time, finding many abuses had crept into the court of Chancery, which either impeded justice or rendered it venal, resolved to impeach the chancellor Thomas, earl of Macclesfield, at the bar of the house of lords, for high crimes and misdemeanours. 11. This was one of the most laborious and best-contested trials in the annals of England. The trial lasted twenty days. The earl proved that the sums he had received for the sale of places in chancery had been usually received by former lord chancellors; but reason told that such receipts were contrary to strict justice. Equity, therefore, prevailed above precedent; the earl was convicted of fraudulent practices, and condemned to a fine of thirty thousand pounds. with imprisonment till the sum should be paid, which was accordingly discharged about six weeks after.

12. In this manner, the corruption, venality, and avarice

of the times had increased with the riches and luxury of the nation. Commerce introduced fraud, and wealth introduced prodigality.

It must be owned that the parliament made some new efforts to check the progress of vice and immorality, which now began to be diffused through every rank of life. But they were supported neither by the co-operation of the ministry, nor the voice of the people.

13. It was now two years since the king had visited his electoral dominions of Hanover. He therefore, soon after the breaking up of the parliament, prepared for a journey thither. A. D. 1727.) Having appointed a regency in his absence, he embarked for Holland, and lay, upon his landing, at a little town called Voet. Next day he proceeded on his journey, and, in two days more, between ten and eleven at night, arrived at Delden, to all appearance in perfect health. 14. He supped there very heartily, and continued his progress early the next morning, but between eight and nine ordered his coach to stop. It being perceived that one of of his hands lay motionless, Monsieur Fabrice who had formerly been servant to the king of Sweden, and who now attended king George, attempted to quicken the circulation, by chafing it between his hands. 15. As this had no effect, the surgeon, who followed on horseback, was called, and he also rubbed it with spirits. Soon after, the king's tongue began to swell, and he had just strength enough to bid them hasten to Osnaburgh; then, falling insensibly into Fabrice's arms, he never recovered, but expired about eleven o'clock the next morning, in the sixty-eighth year of his age and the thirteenth of his reign.

Questions for Examination.

1. What was the project of the South Sea scheme?
2. Explain the nature of it?
3. What proposition was made to the ministry?
4. What were the terms?
5. What part of the scheme was full of fraud and ruin?
6. What success attended it?
7. How were the principal delinquents punished?
8.
9. What persons were now seized as obnoxious to government?
10. On what charge was the earl of Macclesfield impeached?
11. Relate the particulars of his trial.
12. What was now the state of the nation?
13. About what time did the king prepare to visit his electoral dominions?
14. What happened on his progress thither?
15. In what manner did the king die? and what was his age?

CONTEMPORARY SOVEREIGNS.

Popes.	A.D.	Empress of Russia.		King of Denmark.	
Clement XI	1700		A.D.		A.D.
Innocent XIII	1721	Catherine I	1725	Frederick IV	1699
Benedict XIII	1724				

Emperor of Germany.		Kings of France.		King and Queen of Sweden.	
Charles VI	1711	Louis XIV	1643		
		Louis XV	1715	Charles XII	1697
Emperor of the Turks.				Utricia Leonora	1718
Achmet III	1708	King of Spain,			
		Philip V	1700	King of Prussia.	
Emperor of Russia.				Frederick II	1713
Peter the Great, first		King of Portugal.			
emperor	1722	John V	1707		

EMINENT PERSONS.

Sir William Wyndham; Sir Robert Walpole; William Pulteney; Francis, bishop Atterbury; John, lord Harvey: John Perceval, earl of Egmont, &c, &c.

CHAPTER XXXV.

GEORGE II.

Born 1688. Died October 25, 1760. Began to reign June 11, 1727. Reigned 33¼ years.

SECTION I.

The royal sire to realms of bliss removed,
(Like the famed phœnix) from his pyre shall spring
Successive Georges, gracious and beloved,
And good and glorious as the parent king.—Cunningham.

1. (A.D. 1727.) UPON the death of George the First, his son George the Second came to the crown; a man of inferior abilities to the late king, and strongly biased with a partiality to his dominions on the continent. The chief person, and he who shortly after engrossed the greatest share of power under him, was sir Robert Walpole, who had risen from low beginnings, through two successive reigns, into great estimation. 2. He was considered as a martyr to his cause in the reign of queen Anne; and when the tory party could no longer oppress him, he still preserved the hatred against them with which he set out. To defend the declining prerogative of the crown might, perhaps, have been the first object of his attention; but soon after, those very measures by which he pretended to secure it, proved the most effectual means to lessen it. By corrupting the house of commons, he increased their riches

and power; and they were not averse to voting away those millions which he permitted them so liberally to share.

3. As such a tendency in him naturally produced opposition, he was possessed of a most phlegmatic insensibility to reproach, and a calm dispassionate manner of reasoning upon such topics as he desired should be believed. His discourse was fluent, but without dignity, and his manner convincing from its apparent want of art.

4. The Spaniards were the first nation who showed the futility of the treaties of the former reign to bind, when any advantage was to be produced by infraction. The people of our West India Islands had long carried on an illicit trade with the subjects of Spain upon the continent, but, whenever detected, were rigorously punished, and their cargoes confiscated to the crown. In this temerity of adventure, on the one hand, and in the vigilance of pursuit and punishment on the other, it must often have happened that the innocent must suffer with the guilty; and many complaints were made, perhaps founded in justice, that the English merchants were plundered by the Spanish king's vessels upon the southern coast of America, as if they were pirates.

6. The English ministry, unwilling to credit every report which was inflamed by resentment or urged by avarice, expected to remedy the evils complained of by their favourite system of treaty, and in the meantime promised the nation redress. At length, however, the complaints became more general, and the merchants remonstrated by petition to the house of commons, who entered into a deliberation on the subject. 7. They examined the evidence of several who had been unjustly seized, and treated with great cruelty. One man, the master of a trading vessel, had been used by the Spaniards in a most shocking manner; he gave in his evidence with great precision, informed the house of the manner they had plundered and stripped him, of their cutting off his ears, and of their preparing to put him to death. "I then looked up," said he, "to my God for pardon, and to my country for revenge."

8. These accounts raised a flame among the people, which it was neither the minister's interest nor perhaps that of the nation to indulge; new negotiations were set on foot, and new mediators offered their interposition. A treaty was signed at Vienna, between the emperor, the king of Great Britain, and the king of Spain, which settled the

peace of Europe upon its former footing, and put off the threatening war for a time. 9. By this treaty the king of England conceived hopes that all war would be at an end. Don Carlos, upon the death of the Duke of Parma, was, by the assistance of an English fleet, put in peaceable possession of Parma and Placentia, while six thousand Spaniards were quietly admitted and quartered in the duchy of Tuscany, to secure for him the reversion of that dukedom.

10. An interval of peace succeeded, in which nothing remarkable happened, and scarcely any contest ensued, except in the British parliament, where the disputes between the court and country party were carried on with unceasing animosity.

11. (A.D. 1731.) A society of men, in this interested age of seeming benevolence, had united themselves into a company, by the name of the Charitable Corporation; and their professed intention was to lend money at legal interest to the poor, upon small pledges, and to persons of higher rank upon proper security. Their capital was at first limited to thirty thousand pounds, but they afterwards increased it to six hundred thousand. 12. This money was supplied by subscription, and the care of conducting the capital was intrusted in a proper number of directors. This company having continued for more than twenty years, the cashier, George Robinson, member for Marlow, and the warehouse-keeper, John Thompson, disappeared in one day. Five hundred thousand pounds of capital was found to be sunk and embezzled by means which the proprietors could not discover. 13. They, therefore, in a petition, represented to the house the manner in which they had been defrauded, and the distress to which many of the petitioners were reduced. A secret committee being appointed to examine into this grievance, a most iniquitous scene of fraud was discovered, which had been carried on by Robinson and Thompson, in concert with some of the directors, for embezzling the capital and cheating the proprietors. Many persons of rank and quality were concerned in this infamous conspiracy; and even some of the first characters in the nation did not escape censure. 14. A spirit of avarice and rapacity infected every rank of life about this time: no less than six members of parliament were expelled for the most sordid acts of knavery,—Sir Robert Sutton, sir Archibald Grant, and George Robinson, for their frauds in the management of the Charitable Corporation scheme; Denis Bond

and sergeant Birch, for a fraudulent sale of the unfortunate earl of Derwentwater's large estate; and, lastly, John Ward, of Hackney, for forgery. 15. Luxury had given birth to prodigality, and that was the parent of the meanest arts of peculation. It was asserted in the house of lords, at that time, that not one shilling of the forfeited estates was ever applied to the service of the public, but became the reward of fraud and venality.

Questions for Examination.

1. By whom was George the First succeeded?
   Who engrossed the greatest share of power under him?
2. 3. What measures did Walpole pursue? what was his character?
4. 5. Under what circumstances did the dispute with Spain originate?
6. What was the conduct of the English ministry?
7. Relate the evidence of one who had been treated with great cruelty by the Spaniards.
8. What for a time prevented the threatening war?
10. In the interval of peace did any thing remarkable happen?
11. What was the origin of the Charitable Corporation?
12. By whom was its capital embezzled?
13. What followed the detection of this fraud?
14. What members of parliament were expelled for the most sordid acts of knavery?
15. What remarkable assertion was made in the house of lords at this time?

SECTION II.

Of Spain dissatisfied once more we tell;
On England's triumphs, too, the muse might dwell,
And sing how Vernon fought and Porto Bello fell.—Dibdin.

1. (A.D. 1732.) A SCHEME, set on foot by sir Robert Walpole, soon after engrossed the attention of the public, which was to fix a general excise. The minister introduced it into the house, by going into detail of the frauds practised by the factors in London, who were employed by the American planters in selling their tobacco. 2. To prevent these frauds, he proposed, that, instead of having the custom levied in the usual manner upon tobacco, all hereafter to be imported should be lodged in warehouses appointed for that purpose by the officers of the crown; that it should from thence be sold, upon paying the duty of fourpence a pound, when the proprietor found a purchaser. 3. This proposal raised a violent ferment, not less within doors than without. It was asserted that it would expose the factors to such hardships that they would not be able to continue their trade, and that

such a scheme would not even prevent the frauds complained of. It was added, that a number of additional excisemen and warehouse-keepers would thus be employed, which would at once render the ministry formidable, and the people dependent. 4. Such were the arguments made use of to stir up the citizens to oppose this law; arguments rather specious than solid, since, with all its disadvantages, the tax upon tobacco would thus be more safely and expeditiously collected, and the avenues to numberless frauds would be shut up. The people, however, were raised into such a ferment, that the parliament-house was surrounded with multitudes, who intimidated the ministry, and compelled them to drop the design. The miscarriage of the bill was celebrated with public rejoicings in London and Westminister, and the minister was burned in effigy by the populace of London.

5. Ever since the treaty of Utrecht, the Spaniards in America had insulted and distressed the commerce of Great Britain, and the British merchants had attempted to carry on an illicit trade in their dominions. A right which the English merchants claimed by treaty, of cutting logwood in the bay of Campeachy, gave them frequent opportunities of pushing in contraband commodities upon the continent; so that, to suppress the evil, the Spaniards were resolved to annihilate the claim. 6. This liberty of cutting logwood had often been acknowledged, but never clearly ascertained; in all former treaties it was considered as an object of too little importance to make a separate article in any negotiation. The Spanish vessels appointed for protecting the coast, continued their severities upon the English; many of the subjects of Britain were sent to dig in the mines of Potosi, and deprived of all means of conveying their complaints to those who might send them redress. 7. One remonstrance followed another to the court of Madrid of this violation of treaty; but the only answers given were promises of inquiry which produced no reformation. Our merchants complained loudly of these outrages, but the ministers vainly expected from negotiations that redress which was only to be obtained by arms.

8. The fears discovered by the court of Great Britain only served to increase the insolence of the enemy; and their guard-ships continued to seize, not only all the guilty, but the innocent, whom they found sailing along the Spanish Main. At last, however, the complaints of the English

merchants were loud enough to interest the house of commons; their letters and memorials were produced, and their grievances enforced by council at the bar of the house. 9. It was soon found that the money which Spain had agreed to pay to the court of Great Britain was withheld, and no reason assigned for the delay. The minister, therefore, to gratify the general ardour, and to atone for his former deficiencies, assured the house that he would put the nation in a condition for war. Soon after, letters of reprisal were granted against the Spaniards; and this being on both sides considered as an actual commencement of hostilities, both diligently set forward their armaments by sea and land. 10. In this threatening situation, the French minister at the Hague declared that his master was obliged by treaty to assist the king of Spain; so that the alliances, which but twenty years before had taken place, were now quite reversed. At that time, France and England were combined against Spain: at present France and Spain were united against England: such little hopes can statesmen place upon the firmest treaties, where there is no superior power to compel the observance.

11. (A.D. 1739.) A rupture between England and Spain being now become unavoidable, the people, who had long clamoured for war, began to feel uncommon alacrity at its approach; and the ministry, finding it inevitable, began to be as earnest in preparation. Orders were issued for augmenting the land forces, and for raising a body of marines. War was declared with proper solemnity, and soon after, two rich Spanish prizes were taken in the Mediterranean. 12. Admiral Vernon, a man of more courage than experience, of more confidence than skill, was sent as commander of a fleet into the West Indies, to distress the enemy in that part of the globe. He had asserted in the house of commons, that Porto Bello, a fort and harbour in South America, could be easily destroyed, and that he himself would undertake to reduce it with six ships only. 13. A project which appeared so wild and impossible was ridiculed by the ministry; but as he still insisted upon the proposal, they complied with his request, hoping that his want of success might repress the confidence of his party. In this, however, they were disappointed; for with six ships only he attacked and demolished all the fortifications of the place, and came away victorious with scarcely the loss of a man. This victory was magnified at home in all the strains of

panegyric, and the triumph was far superior to the value of the conquest.

14. While vigorous preparations were making in other departments, a squadron of ships was equipped for distressing the enemy in the South Seas, the command of which was given to commodore Anson. This fleet was destined to sail through the Straits of Magellan, and, steering northward along the coast of Chili and Peru, to co-operate occasionally with admiral Vernon across the isthmus of Darien. The delays and mistakes of the ministry frustrated that part of the scheme, which was originally well laid. 15. When it was too late in the season, the commodore set out with five ships of the line, a frigate and two smaller ships, with about fourteen hundred men. Having reached the coast of Brazil, he refreshed his men for some time on the island of St. Catherine, a spot that enjoys all the fruitfulness and verdure of the luxurious tropical climate. From thence he steered downward into the cold and tempestuous regions of the South; and, about five months after, meeting a terrible tempest, he doubled Cape Horn. 16. By this time his fleet was dispersed, and his crew deplorably disabled with the scurvy; so that with much difficulty he gained the delightful island of Juan Fernandez. There he was joined by one ship, and a vessel of seven guns. From thence advancing northward, he landed on the coast of Chili, and attacked the city of Paita by night. 17. In this bold attempt he made no use of his shipping, nor even disembarked all his men : a few soldiers, favoured by darkness, sufficed to fill the whole town with terror and confusion. The governor of the garrison, and the inhabitants, fled on all sides: accustomed to be severe, they expected severity. In the mean time a small body of the English kept possession of the town for three days, stripping it of treasures and merchandise to a considerable amount, and then setting it on fire.

Questions for Examination.

1. What scheme now engrossed the public attention?
2. How did the minister propose to effect it?
3. What were the arguments used in opposition to this measure?
4. What was their success?
5. From what cause originated the dispute?
6. What was the conduct of the Spaniards?
7. What measures were taken by the English merchants?
8. What continued to be the conduct of the enemy?
9. What induced the minister to gratify the general ardour of the nation? In what manner did the war commence?

10. Under what pretence did France assist Spain?
11. What was the feeling of the people at the approach of the war?
12. What did admiral Vernon assert in the house of commons?
13. Relate the success of his expedition.
14-17. Describe the proceedings of the squadron under commodore Anson from its sailing to the taking of Paita.

SECTION III.

But what are wreaths in battle won!
And what the tribute of amaze
Which man too oft mistaken pays
To the vain idol shrine of false renown!—Anon.

1. (A.D.1740.) Soon after, this small squadron advanced as far as Panama, situated on the isthmus of Darien, on the western side of the great American continent. The commodore now placed all his hopes in taking one of those valuable Spanish ships which trade from the Philippine islands to Mexico. Not above one or two at the most of these immensely rich ships went from one continent to the other in a year; they were therefore, very large, in order to carry a sufficiency of treasure, and proportionably strong to defend it. 2. In hopes of meeting with one of these, the commodore, with his little fleet, traversed the Pacific Ocean; but the scurvy once more visiting his crew, several of his men died and nearly all were disabled. In this exigence, having brought all his men into one vessel, and set fire to another, he steered for the island of Tinian, which lies about half way between the new world and the old. 3. In this charming abode he continued for some time, till his men recovered their health, and his ship was refitted for sailing.

Thus refitted, he set forward for China, where he laid in proper stores for once more traversing back that immense ocean, in which he had before suffered such incredible difficulties. 4. Having accordingly taken some Dutch and Indian sailors on board, he again steered towards America, and at length, after various toils, discovered the Spanish galleon he had so long and ardently expected. This vessel was built as well for the purpose of war as for merchandise. It mounted sixty guns and five hundred men, while the crew of the commodore did not amount to half that number. 5. However, the victory was on the side of the English, and they returned home with their prize, which was estimated at three hundred and thirteen thousand pounds sterling, while the different captures that had been made before amounted to as much more. Thus, after a voyage of three years, conducted with astonishing perseverance and intrepidity, the public sustained the loss of a noble fleet but a few individuals became possessed of immense riches.

6. In the mean time the English conducted other operations against the enemy with amazing activity. When Anson set out, it was with a design of acting a subordinate part to a formidable armament designed for the coast of New Spain, consisting of twenty-nine ships of the line, and almost an equal number of frigates, furnished with all kinds of warlike stores, nearly fifteen thousand seamen, and as many land-forces. Never was a fleet more completely equipped, nor never had the nation more sanguine hopes of success. Lord Cathcart was appointed to command the land-forces; but he dying on the passage the command devolved upon general Wentworth, whose abilities were supposed to be unequal to the trust reposed in him.

7. When the forces were landed at Carthagena, they erected a battery, with which they made a breach in the principal fort, while Vernon, who commanded the fleet, sent a number of ships into the harbour to divide the fire of the enemy, and to co-operate with the army on shore. 8. The breach being deemed practicable, a body of troops were commanded to storm; but the Spaniards deserted the forts, which if possessed of courage, they might have defended with success. The troops, upon gaining this advantage, were advanced a good deal nearer the city; but there they met a much greater opposition than they had expected. 9. It was found, or at least asserted, that the fleet could not lie near enough to batter the town, and that nothing remained but to attempt one of the forts by scaling. The leaders of the fleet and the army began mutually to accuse each other, each asserting the probability of what the other denied. At length, Wentworth, stimulated by the admiral's reproach, resolved to try the dangerous experiment, and ordered that fort St. Lazare should be attempted by escalade. 10. Nothing could be more unfortunate than this undertaking. The forces marching up to the attack, the guides were slain, and they mistook their way. Instead of attempting the weakest part of the fort, they advanced to where it was the strongest, and where they were exposed to the fire of the town. Colonel Grant, who commanded the grenadiers, was killed in the beginning. 11. Soon after, it was found that their scaling-ladders were too short; the officers were perplexed for want of orders, and the troops stood ex-

posed to the whole fire of the enemy, without knowing how to proceed. After bearing a dreadful fire for some hours with great intrepidity, they at length retreated, leaving six hundred men dead on the spot. 12. The terrors of the climate soon began to be more dreaded than those of war; the rainy season came on with such violence that it was impossible for the troops to continue encamped; and the mortality of the season now began to attack them in all its frightful varieties. To these calamities, sufficient to quell any enterprise, was added the dissension between the land and sea commanders, who blamed each other for every failure, and became frantic with mutual recrimination. They only, therefore, at last, could be brought to agree in one mortifying measure, which was to re-embark the troops, and withdraw them as quickly as possible from this scene of slaughter and contagion.

13. This fatal miscarriage, which tarnished the British glory, was no sooner known in England, than the kingdom was filled with murmurs and discontent. The loudest burst of indignation was directed at the minister; and they who once praised him for success that he did not merit, condemned him now for a failure of which he was guiltless.

14. (A.D. 1741.) The minister, finding the indignation of the house of commons turned against him, tried every art to break that confederacy, which he knew he had not strength to oppose. The resentment of the people had been raised against him to an extravagant height; and their leaders taught them to expect very signal justice on their supposed oppressor. At length, finding his post untenable, he declared he would never sit more in that house; the next day the king adjourned both houses of parliament for a few days, and in the interim sir Robert Walpole was created earl of Oxford, and resigned all his employments.

15. But the pleasure of his defeat was but of short duration: it soon appeared that those who declared most loudly for the liberty of the people, had adopted new measures with their new employments. The new converts were branded as betrayers of the interests of their country; but particularly the resentment of the people fell upon Pulteney, earl of Bath, who had long declaimed against that very conduct he now seemed earnest to pursue. 16. He had been the idol of the people, and considered as one of the most illustrious champions that ever defended the cause of freedom; but allured, perhaps, with the hope of go-

verning in Walpole's place, he was contented to give up his popularity for ambition. The king, however, treated him with that neglect which he merited; he was laid aside for life, and continued a wretched survivor of all his former importance.

Questions for Examination.

1-4. Relate briefly the further proceedings of the squadron under commodore Anson till the capture of the rich Spanish galleon.
5. What was the result of this enterprise?
6. What other operations were undertaken?
7-9. Describe the particulars of the siege of Carthagena.
10. 11. What causes rendered it unsuccessful?
12. What was then the situation of the English troops?
13. What was the consequence of this miscarriage?
14. What was the ministers' conduct?
15. Did the conduct of his successors render them favourites of the people? On whom particularly did the public resentment fall?
16. In what light had Pulteney formerly been considered by the people?

SECTION IV.

By turns each army gains the vantage-ground,
The cannons roar, and carnage spreads around.—*Duncan.*

1. (A. D. 1740.) THE emperor dying in the year 1740, the French began to think this a favourable opportunity for exerting their ambition once more. Regardless of treaties, particularly that called the Pragmatic sanction, by which the reversion of all the late emperor's dominions was settled upon his daughter, they caused the elector of Bavaria to be crowned emperor. Thus the queen of Hungary, daughter to Charles the Sixth, descended from an illustrious line of emperors, saw herself stripped of her inheritance, and left for a whole year deserted by all Europe, and without any hopes of succour. 2. She had scarcely closed her father's eyes, when she lost Silesia, by an irruption of the young king of Prussia, who seized the opportunity of her defenceless state to renew his ancient pretensions to that province, of which it must be owned his ancestors had been unjustly deprived. France, Saxony, and Bavaria attacked the rest of her dominions. England was the only ally that seemed willing to espouse her helpless condition. Sardinia and Holland soon after came to her assistance, and last of all Russia acceded to a union in her favour.

3. It may now be demanded what cause Britain had to intermeddle in those continental schemes. It can only be answered, that the interests of Hanover, and the security

of that electorate, depended upon nicely balancing the different interests of the empire; and the English ministry were willing to gratify the king.

4. Accordingly the king sent a body of English forces into the Netherlands, which he had augmented by sixteen thousand Hanoverians, to make a diversion upon the dominions of France, in the queen of Hungary's favour; and by the assistance of these the queen of Hungary soon began to turn the scale of victory on her side. 5. The French were driven out of Bohemia. Her general, prince Charles, at the head of a large army, invaded the dominions of Bavaria. Her rival, the nominal emperor, was obliged to fly before her, and, being abandoned by his allies and stripped of even his hereditary dominions, retired to Frankfort, where he lived in obscurity.

6. (A.D. 1743.) The French, in order to prevent the junction of the Austrian and the British forces, assembled an army of sixty thousand men on the river Mayne, under the command of marshall Noailles, who posted his troops upon the east side of that river. The British forces, to the number of forty thousand, pushed forward on the other side into a country were they found themselves entirely destitute of provisions, the French having cut off all means of their being supplied. 7. The king of England arrived at the camp while his army was in this deplorable situation; wherefore he resolved to penetrate forward to join twelve thousand Hanoverians and Hessians, who had reached Hanau. With this view he decamped; but before his army had reached three leagues, he found that the enemy had enclosed him on every side, near a village called Dettingen.

8. Nothing now presented themselves but the most mortifying prospects. If he fought the enemy, it must be at the greatest disadvantage; if he continued inactive, there was a certainty of being starved; and a retreat for all was impossible. The impetuosity of the French troops saved his whole army. They passed a defile, which they should have been contented to guard; and, under the command of the duke of Grammont, their horse charged the English foot with great fury. They were received with intrepidity and resolution; so that they were obliged to give way, and repassed the Mayne with precipitation, with the loss of five thousand men.

9. Meanwhile the French went on with vigour on every side. They projected an invasion of England; and Charles,

the son of the old pretender, departed from Rome, in the disguise of a Spanish courier, for Paris, where he had an audience of the French king.

10. The family had long been the dupes of France; but it was thought that at present there were serious resolutions formed in their favour. The troops destined for the expedition amounted to fifteen thousand men; preparations were made for embarking them at Dunkirk and at other of the ports nearest to England, under the eye of the young Pretender. 11. The duke de Roquefeuille, with twenty ships of the line was to see them safely landed in England; and the famous count Saxe was to command them when put on shore. But the whole project was disconcerted by the appearance of sir John Norris, who, with a superior fleet, made up to attack them. The French fleet was thus obliged to put back; a very hard gale of wind damaged their transports beyond redress: and the French, now frustrated in their scheme of a sudden descent, thought fit openly to declare war.

12. The French, therefore, entered upon the war with great alacrity. They besieged Fribourg, and in the beginning of the succeeding campaign invested the strong city of Tournay. Although the allies were inferior in number, and although commanded by the duke of Cumberland, yet they resolved, if possible, to save the city by hazarding a battle. They accordingly marched against the enemy, and took post in sight of the French, who were encamped on an eminence, the village of St. Antoine on the right, a wood on the left, and the town of Fontenoy before them. 13. This advantageous situation did not repress the ardour of the English, who began to attack at two o'clock in the morning, and, pressing forward, bore down all opposition. They were for nearly an hour victorious, and confident of success, while Saxe, a soldier of fortune, who commanded the French army, was at that time sick of the same disorder of which he afterwards died. However, he was carried about to all the posts in a litter, and assured his attendants, that, notwithstanding all unfavourable appearances, the day was his own. 14. A column of the English, without any command, but by mere mechanical courage had advanced upon the enemy's lines, which, opening, formed an avenue on each side to receive them. It was then that the French artillery on the three sides began to play on this forlorn body, which, though they continued for a long time unshaken, were obliged at last to retreat.

15. This was one of the most bloody battles that had been fought in this age; the allies left on the field nearly twelve thousand men, and the French bought their victory with nearly an equal number of slain.

This blow, by which Tournay was taken by the French, gave them such a manifest superiority all the rest of the campaign, that they kept the fruits of the victory during the whole continuance of the war.

Questions for Examination.

1. On the death of the emperor of Austria, what was the conduct of the French?
2. Describe the situation of the emperor's daughter.
3. What cause had Britain to intermeddle in continental schemes?
4. 5. With what success was Britain's interference attended?
6–8. Relate the circumstances which preceded and attended the battle of Dettingen.
9. What other project did the French endeavour to effect?
10. 11. What success attended their measures?
12. What preceded the battle of Fontenoy?
13. 14. Relate the particulars of this battle.
15. What loss did each side experience?

SECTION V.

But still to darken the dread gloom of war,
Misguided Stuart drew rebellion's sword:
E'en Derby saw his vaunting banners wave,
And Scottish chieftains hail'd him as their lord.—*Valpy.*

1. (A. D. 1745.) BUT though bad success attended the British arms by land and sea, yet, these being distant evils, the English seemed only to complain from honourable motives, and murmured at distresses of which they had but a very remote prospect. A civil war was now going to be kindled in their own dominions, which mixed terrors with their complaints; and which, while it increased their perplexities, only cemented their union.

2. It was at this period that the son of the old Pretender resolved to make an effort for gaining the British crown. Charles Edward, the adventurer in question, had been bred in a luxurious court without partaking of its effeminacy. He was enterprising and ambitious; but either from inexperience or natural inability, utterly unequal to the bold undertaking. He was long flattered by the rash, the susperstitious, and the needy: he was taught to believe that the kingdom was ripe for a revolt, and that it could no longer bear the immense load of taxes with which it was burdened.

3. Being now, therefore, furnished with some money, and

with still larger promises from France, who fanned his ambition, he embarked for Scotland on board a small frigate, accompanied by the marquis of Tullibardine, sir Thomas Sheridan, and a few other desperate adventurers. Thus, for the conquest of the whole British empire, he only brought with him seven officers, and arms for two thousand men.

4. The boldness of this enterprise astonished all Europe. It awakened the fears of the pusillanimous, the ardour of the brave, and the pity of the wise. But by this time the young adventurer was arrived at Perth, where the unnecessary ceremony was performed of proclaiming his father king of Great Britain. 5. From thence, descending with his forces from the mountains, they seemed to gather as they went forward; and, advancing to Edinburgh, they entered that city without opposition. There again the pageantry of proclamation was performed; and there he promised to dissolve the union, which was considered as one of the grievances of the country. However, the castle of that city still held out, and he was unprovided with cannon to besiege it.

6. In the mean time, sir John Cope, who had pursued the rebels through the Highlands, but had declined meeting them in [their descent, being now reinforced by two regiments of dragoons, resolved to march towards Edinburgh and give the enemy battle. The young adventurer, whose forces were rather superior though undisciplined, attacked him near Preston-pans, about twelve miles from the capital, and in a few minutes put him and his troops to flight. 7. This victory, by which the king lost five hundred men, gave the rebels great influence; and had the Pretender taken advantage of the general consternation and marched directly for England, the consequences might have been fatal to freedom. But he was amused by the promise of succours which never came; and thus induced to remain at Edinburgh, to enjoy the triumphs of an unimportant victory, and to be treated as a monarch.

8. While the young Pretender was thus trifling away his time at Edinburgh (for, in dangerous enterprises, delay is but defeat,) the ministry of Great Britain took every precaution to oppose him with success. Six thousand Dutch troops, that had come over to the assistance of the crown, were despatched northward, under the command of general Wade. The duke of Cumberland soon after arrived from Flanders, and was followed by another detachment of dragoons and infantry, well disciplined and inured to action. Besides

these, volunteers offered in every part of the kingdom, and every county exerted a vigorous spirit of indignation both against the ambition, the religion, and the allies of the young Pretender.

9. However, he had been bred in a school that taught him maxims very different from those that then prevailed in England. Though he might have brought civil war, and all the calamities attending it, with him into the kingdom, he had been taught that the assertion of his right was a duty incumbent upon him, and the altering the constitution, and perhaps the religion, of his country, an object of laudable ambition. 10. Thus animated, he went forward with vigour; and having, upon frequent consultations with his officers, come to a resolution of making an irruption into England, he entered the country by the western border, and invested Carlisle, which surrendered in less than three days. He there found a considerable quantity of arms, and there too he caused his father to be proclaimed king.

11. General Wade, being apprized of his progress, advanced across the country from the opposite shore; but receiving intelligence that the enemy was two days' march before him, he retired to his former station. The young Pretender, thus unopposed, resolved to penetrate farther into the kingdom, having received assurances from France that a considerable body of troops would be landed on the southern coasts, to make a diversion in his favour. 12. He was flattered also with the hopes of being joined by a considerable number of malecontents as he passed forward, and that his army would increase on his march. Accordingly, leaving a small garrison in Carlisle, which he should rather have left defenceless, he advanced to Penrith marching on foot in a Highland dress, and continued his irruption till he came to Manchester, where he established his head-quarters.

13. He was there joined by about two hundred English, who were formed into a regiment, under the command of colonel Townley. From thence he pursued his march to Derby, intending to go by the way of Chester into Wales, where he hoped to be joined by a great number of followers; but the factions among his own chiefs prevented his proceeding to that part of the kingdom.

14. He was by this time advanced within a hundred miles of the capital, which was filled with perplexity and consternation, Had he proceeded in his career with that expedition which he had hitherto used, he might have made

himself master of the metropolis, where he would certainly have been joined by a considerable number of his well-wishers, who waited impatiently for his approach.

Questions for Examination.
1. What was the situation of England at this time?
2. By whom was an effort made to gain the English crown?
3. Under what circumstances was it undertaken?
5. What were the first proceedings of the Pretender?
6. With what success did he attack sir John Cope?
7. What were the consequences of this victory?
8. What precautions were taken by the English ministry?
What was the conduct of the Pretender?
11. By whom was an attempt made to oppose him? and what was its result?
12. To what place did he next proceed?
13. By whom was he joined? and whither did he next march?
14. What might have been the results had he proceeded with expedition?

SECTION VI.

Ill-fated youth; Culloden's bloody field
Sunk the vain fabrics of ambition low.
Press'd with fatigue and hunger, long he roam'd,
'Mid scenes of danger and 'mid sights of woe.—*Valpy.*

1. (A. D. 1745.) IN the mean time the king resolved to take the field in person. But he found safety from the discontents which now began to prevail in the Pretender's army. In fact, he was but the nominal leader of his forces; as his generals, the chiefs of the highland clans, were, from their education, ignorant, and averse to subordination. They had, from the beginning, began to embrace opposite systems of operation, and to contend with each other for pre-eminnence; but they seemed now unanimous in returning to their own country once more.

2. The rebels accordingly effected their retreat to Carlisle without any loss, and from thence crossed the rivers Eden and Solway, into Scotland. In these marches, however, they preserved all the rules of war; they abstained in a great measure from plunder; they levied contributions on the towns as they passed along; and with unaccountable caution left a garrison at Carlisle, which shortly after was obliged to surrender to the duke of Cumberland at discretion, to the number of four hundred men.

3. The Pretender, being returned to Scotland, proceeded to Glasgow, from which city he exacted severe contributions. He advanced from thence to Stirling, where he was joined by lord Lewis Gordon, at the head of some forces

which had been assembled in his absence. Other clans, to the number of two thousand, came in likewise ; and from some supplies of money which he received from Spain, and from some skirmishes, in which he was successful against the royalists, his affairs began to wear a most promising aspect. 4. Being joined by lord Drummond, he invested the castle of Stirling, commanded by general Blakeney ; but the rebel forces, being unused to sieges, consumed much time to no purpose. It was during this attempt that general Hawley, who commanded a considerable body of forces near Edinburgh, undertook to raise the siege, and advanced towards the rebel army as far as Falkirk. After two days spent in mutually examining each other's strength, the rebels, being ardent to engage, were led on in full spirits to attack the king's army. 5. The Pretender, who was in the front line, gave the signal to engage, and the first fire put Hawley's forces into confusion. The horse retreated with precipitation and fell upon their own infantry ; while the rebels following up the blow, the greatest part of the royal army fled with the utmost precipitation. They retired in confusion to Edinburgh, leaving the conquerors in possession of their tents, their artillery, and the field of battle.

6. Thus far the affairs of the rebel army seemed not unprosperous ; but here was an end of all their triumphs. The duke of Cumberland, at that time the favourite of the English army, had been recalled from Flanders, and put himself at the head of the troops, at Edinburgh, which consisted of about fourteen thousand men. 7. With these he advanced to Aberdeen, where he was joined by several of the Scotch nobility attached to the house of Hanover ; and having revived the drooping spirits of his army, he resolved to find out the enemy, who retreated at his approach. After having refreshed his troops at Aberdeen for some time, he renewed his march, and in twelve days he came up to the banks of the deep and rapid river Spey. This was the place where the rebels might have disputed his passage, but they lost every advantage in disputing with each other. 8. They seemed now totally void of all counsel and subordination, without conduct and without unanimity. After a variety of contests among each other, they resolved to wait their pursuers upon the plains of Culloden, a place about nine miles distant from Inverness, embosomed in hills, except on that side which was open to the sea. There they drew up in order of battle, to the number of eight thousand men, in

three divisions, supplied with some pieces of artillery, ill manned and served.

9. The battle began about one o'clock in the afternoon; the cannon of the king's army did dreadful execution among the rebels, while theirs was totally unserviceable. One of the great errors in all the Pretender's warlike measures, was his subjecting wild and undisciplined troops to the forms of artful war, and thus repressing their native ardour, from which alone he could hope for success. 10. After they had kept in their ranks and withstood the English fire for some time, they at length became impatient for closer engagement; and about five hundred of them made an irruption upon the left wing of the enemy with their accustomed ferocity. The first line being disordered by this onset, two battalions advanced to support it and galled the enemy with a terrible close discharge. 11. At the same time the dragoons under Hawley, and the Argyleshire militia pulling down a parkwall feebly defended, fell among them sword in hand, with great slaughter. In less than thirty minutes they were totally routed, and the field covered with their wounded and slain to the number of three thousand men. The French troops on the left did not fire a shot, but stood inactive during the engagement, and afterwards surrendered themselves prisoners of war. 12. An entire body of the clans marched off the field in order, while the rest were routed with great slaughter, and their leaders obliged with reluctance to retire. Civil war is in itself terrible, but much more so when heightened by unnecessary cruelty. How guilty soever an enemy may be, it is the duty of a brave soldier to remember that he is only to fight an opposer, and not a suppliant. 13. The victory was in every respect decisive, and humanity to the conquered would have rendered it glorious. But little mercy was shown here; the conquerors were seen to refuse quarter to the wounded, the unarmed, the defenceless; some were slain who were only excited by curiosity to become spectators of the combat, and soldiers were seen to anticipate the base employment of the executioner. 14. The duke, immediately after the action, ordered six-and-thirty deserters to be executed. The conquerors spread terror wherever they came: and, after a short space, the whole country round was one dreadful scene of plunder, slaughter, and desolation; justice was forgotten, and vengeance assumed the name.

Questions for Examination.

1. What was the situation of the Pretender's army?
2. To what place did the rebels retreat?
3. By whom were they joined?
4. What success attended them in besieging Stirling castle? Who attempted to raise the siege?
5. With what success did the rebels attack the royal army?
6. What ended their triumphs?
7. What was the conduct of the duke of Cumberland?
8. What was the determination of the rebel army? What was the amount of their forces?
9–12. Relate the particulars and result of the battle of Culloden.
13. 14. What was the conduct of the conquerors?

SECTION VII.

The quality of mercy is not strain'd,—
It droppeth as a gentle rain from heaven
Upon the place beneath; it is twice bless'd,—
It blesseth him that gives and him that takes.—*Shakspeare.*

1. (A.D. 1746.) IN this manner were blasted all the hopes and all the ambition of the young adventurer. One short hour deprived him of imaginary thrones and sceptres, and reduced him from a nominal king to a distressed, forlorn outcast, shunned by all mankind except those who sought his destruction. To the good and the brave, subsequent distress often atones for former guilt; and while reason would speak for punishment, our hearts plead for mercy.

2. Immediately after the engagement, he fled away with a captain of Fitz-James's cavalry; and when their horses were fatigued, they both alighted, and separately sought for safety. He for some days wandered in this country, naturally wild, but now rendered more formidable by war, a wretched spectator of all those horrors which were the result of his ill-grounded ambition.

3. There is a striking similitude between his adventures and those of Charles the Second upon his escape from Worcester. He sometimes found refuge in caves and in cottages, without attendants, and dependent on the wretched natives who could pity but not relieve him. Sometimes he lay in forests, with one or two companions of his distress, continually pursued by the troops of the conqueror, as there was a reward of thirty thousand pounds offered for taking him, dead or alive. 4. Sheridan, an Irish adventurer, was the person who kept most faithfully by him, and inspired him with courage to support such incredible hardships. He had occasion, in the course of his concealments, to trust his life to the fidelity of above fifty individuals,

whose veneration for his family prevailed above their avarice.

5. One day, having walked from morning till night, he ventured to enter a house, the owner of which he well knew was attached to the opposite party. As he entered, he addressed the master of the house in the following manner: "The son of your king comes to beg a little bread, and a few clothes. I know your present attachment to my adversaries, but I believe you have sufficient honour not to abuse my confidence or to take advantage of my distressed situation. Take these rags, that have for some time been my only covering: you may probably restore them to me one day when I shall be seated on the throne of Great Britain." 6. The master of the house was touched with pity at his distress; he assisted him as far as he was able, and never divulged the secret. There were few of those who even wished his destruction, that would choose to be the immediate actors in it, as it would have subjected them to the resentment of a numerous party.

7. In this manner he continued to wander among the frightful wilds of Glengarry for near six months, often hemmed round by his pursuers, but still rescued by some lucky accident from the impending danger. At length a privateer of St. Maloes, hired by his adherents, arrived in Lochnanach, in which he embarked in the most wretched attire. He was clad in a short coat of black frieze, threadbare, over which was a common Highland plaid, girt round by a belt from which were suspended a pistol and a dagger. He had not been shifted for many weeks; his eyes were hollow, his visage wan, and his constitution greatly impaired by famine and fatigue. 8. He was accompanied by Sullivan and Sheridan, two Irish adherents, who had shared all his calamities, together with Cameron of Lochiel, and his brother, and a few other exiles. They set sail for France; and after having been chased by two English men-of-war, they arrived in safety at a place called Roseau, near Morlaix, in Bretagne. Perhaps he would have found it more difficult to escape, had not the vigilance of his pursuers been relaxed by a report that he was already slain.

9. In the meantime, while the Pretender was thus pursued, the scaffold and the gibbets were preparing for his adherents. Seventeen officers of the rebel army were hanged, drawn, and quartered, at Kennington-common, in the neighbourhood of London. Their constancy in death

gained more proselytes to their cause than even perhaps their victories would have obtained. Nine were executed in the same manner at Carlisle, and eleven at York. A few obtained pardon, and a considerable number of common men were transported to the plantations in North America.

10. The earls of Kilmarnock and Cromartie, and the lord Balmerino, were tried by their peers, and found guilty. Cromartie was pardoned, and the rest were beheaded on Tower-hill.

In this manner, victory, defeat, negotiation, treachery, and rebellion, succeeded each other rapidly for some years, till all sides began to think themselves growing more feeble, and gaining no solid advantage.

11. A negotiation was, therefore, resolved upon; and the contending powers agreed to come to a congress at Aix-la-Chapelle, where the earl of Sanford and sir Thomas Robinson assisted as plenipotentiaries from the king of Great Britain. This treaty was begun upon the preliminary condition of restoring all conquests made during the war. 12. From thence great hopes were expected of conditions both favourable and honourable to the English; but the treaty still remains a lasting mark of precipitate counsels and English disgrace. By this it was agreed, that all prisoners on each side should be mutually restored and all conquests given up. That the Duchies of Parma, Placentia, and Guastalla, should be ceded to don Philip, heir-apparent to the Spanish throne, and to his heirs; but in case of his succeeding to the crown of Spain, then these dominions should revert to the house of Austria. 13. It was confirmed that the fortifications of Dunkirk to the sea should be demolished; that the English ships annually sent with slaves to the coast of New Spain should have this privilege continued for four years; that the king of Prussia should be confirmed in the possession of Silesia, which he had lately conquered; and that the queen of Hungary should be secured in her patrimonial dominions. 14. But one article of this peace was more displeasing and afflictive to the English than all the rest. It was stipulated that the king of Great Britain should, immediately after the ratification of this treaty, send two persons of rank and distinction to France, as hostages, until restitution should be made of Cape Breton, and all other conquests which England had made during the war. 15. This was a mortifying clause; but, to add to the general error of the negotiation, no men

tion was made of the searching the vessels of England in the American seas, upon which the war was originally begun. The limits of their respective possessions in North America were not ascertained; nor did they receive any equivalent for those forts which they restored to the enemy.

16. The treaty of Utrecht had long been the object of reproach to those by whom it was made; but with all its faults, the treaty now concluded was by far more despicable and erroneous. Yet such was the spirit of the times, that the treaty of Utrecht was branded with universal contempt, and the treaty of Aix-la Chapelle was extolled with the highest strains of praise.

17. This treaty, which some asserted would serve for a bond of permanent amity, was, properly speaking, but a temporary truce; a cessation from hostilities, which both sides were unable to continue. Though the war between England and France was actually hushed up in Europe, yet in the East and the West Indies it still went forward with undiminished vehemence; both sides still willing to offend still offending, and yet both complaining of the infraction.

Questions for Examination.

1, 2. In what situation was the Pretender after the battle of Culloden?
3. Whose adventures did his resemble?
4. Who was his most faithful attendant?
5. In what manner did he address one of his opponents?
7. By what means did he escape? and what was his appearance?
8. By whom was he accompanied?
9. In what manner were his adherents punished?
10. What noblemen were beheaded?
11. What led to a negotiation between Great Britain and Spain?
12. What hopes were expected from this treaty? What was the result?
13. What were its conditions?
14. Which article of peace was very displeasing to the English?
15. What was another error in the negotiation?
16. What opinion was held of this treaty?

SECTION VIII.

In distant climes we wage unequal war,
And transatlantic broils our comfort mar.—*Jones.*

1. (A.D. 1750.) A NEW colony having been formed in North America, in the province of Nova Scotia, it was thought that thither the waste of an exuberant nation might well be drained off; and those bold spirits kept in employment at a distance, who might be dangerous if suffered to continue in idleness at home. Nova Scotia was a place

where men might be imprisoned, but not maintained; it was cold, barren, and incapable of successful cultivation. 2. The new colony, therefore, was maintained there with some expense to the government in the beginning; and such as were permitted, soon went southward to the milder climates, where they were invited by an untenanted and fertile soil. Thus did the nation ungratefully send off her hardy veterans to perish on inhospitable shores, and this they were taught to believe would extend their dominions.

3. However, it was for this barren spot that the English and French revived the war, which soon after spread with such terrible devastation over every part of the globe. The native Indians bordering upon the deserts of Nova Scotia, a fierce and savage people, looked from the first with jealousy upon these new settlers; and they considered the vicinity of the English as an encroachment upon their native possessions. 4. The French, who were neighbours in like manner, and who were still impressed with natural animosity, fomented these suspicions in the natives, and represented the English (and with regard to this colony this representation might be true) as enterprising and severe. Commissaries were, therefore, appointed, to meet at Paris, to compromise these disputes; but these conferences were rendered abortive by the cavillings of men who could not be supposed to understand the subject in debate.

5. As this seemed to be the first place where the dissensions took their rise for a new war, it may be necessary to be a little more minute. The French had been the first cultivators of Nova Scotia, and, by great industry and long perseverance, had rendered the soil, naturally barren, somewhat fertile, and capable of sustaining nature, with some assistance from Europe. This country, however, had frequently changed masters, and at length the English were settled in the possession, and acknowledged as the rightful owners, by the treaty of Utrecht. 6. The possession of this country was reckoned necessary to defend the English colonies to the north, and to preserve their superiority in the fisheries in that part of the world. The French, however, who had been long settled in the back part of the country, resolved to use every method to dispossess the new-comers, and spirited up the Indians to more open hostilities, which were represented to the English ministry for some time without redress.

7. Soon after this, another source of dispute began to be

seen in the same part of the world, and promised as much uneasiness as the former. The French, pretending to have first discovered the mouth of the river Mississippi, claimed the whole adjacent country towards New Mexico on the east, and quite to the Appalachian mountains on the west. 8. In order to assert their claims, they found several English, who had settled beyond these mountains from motives of commerce, and who had also been invited by the natural beauties of the country; they dispossessed them of their new settlements, and built such forts as would command the whole country round about.

9. Not in America alone, but also in Asia, the seeds of a new war were preparing to be expended. On the coasts of Malabar, the English and French had, in fact, never ceased from hostilities.

(A.D. 1756.) The ministry, however, in England now began a very vigorous exertion in defence of their colonies, who refused to defend themselves. Four operations were undertaken in America at the same time. Of these, one was commanded by colonel Monckton, who had orders to drive the French from the encroachments upon the province of Nova Scotia. 10. The second, more to the south, was directed against Crown Point, under the command of general Johnson. The third, under the conduct of general Shirley, was destined to Niagara, to secure the forts on that river. And the fourth was farther southward still, against Fort du Quesne, under general Braddock.

11. In these expeditions, Monckton was successful; Johnson also was victorious, though he failed in taking the fort against which he was sent; Shirley was thought to have lost the season for operation by delay; Braddock was vigorous and active, but suffered a defeat. This bold commander, who had been recommended to this service by the duke of Cumberland, set forward upon this expedition in June, and left the cultivated parts of the country on the 10th, at the head of two thousand two hundred men, directing his march to that part of the country whence major Washington had retreated the year before. 12. Being at length within ten miles of the French fort he was appointed to besiege, and marching forward through the forest with full confidence of success, on a sudden his whole army was astonished by a general discharge of arms both in front and flank, from an enemy that still remained unseen. It was now too late to think of retreating; the troops had passed into the defile,

which the enemy had artfully permitted them to do before they offered to fire. 13. The vanguard of the English now, therefore, fell back in consternation upon the main body, and the panic soon became general. The officers alone disdained to fly, while Braddock himself still continued to command his brave associates, discovering at once the greatest intrepidity and the greatest imprudence. 14. An enthusiast to the discipline of war, he disdained to fly from the field, or to permit his men to quit their ranks, when their only method of treating the Indian army was by precipitate attack, or an immediate desertion of the field of battle. At length Braddock, having received a musket-shot through the lungs, dropped, and a total confusion ensued. All the artillery, ammunition, and baggage of the army was left to the enemy, and the loss sustained by the English army might amount to seven hundred men. The remnant of the army in this emergency was saved by the courage and ability of Washington.

15. The murmurs, fears, and dissensions which this defeat gave rise to, gave the French an opportunity of carrying on their designs in another quarter. The Island of Minorca, which we had taken from the Spaniards in the reign of queen Anne, was secured to England by repeated treaties. But the ministry at this time, being blinded by domestic terrors, had neglected to take sufficient precaution for its defence, so that the garrison was weak, and no way fitted to stand a vigorous siege. 16. The French, therefore, landed near the fortification of St. Philip, which was reckoned one of the strongest in Europe, and commanded by general Blakeney, who was brave indeed, but rather superannuated. The siege was carried on with vigour, and for some time as obstinately defended on the side of the English; but the place was at length obliged to capitulate.

Questions for Examination.

1. 2. From what motive was the new colony in Nova Scotia furnished with inhabitants?
3. What was the cause of the renewing of the war?
4. Where were the commissaries appointed to meet to settle these disputes?
  What rendered these conferences abortive?
5. Who had been the first cultivators of Nova Scotia?
  Who had been acknowledged rightful owners of this country?
6. What method did the French use to dispossess the English?
8. What other conduct of the French contributed to hasten the war?
9, 10. What operations were undertaken by the English?
11. What success attended them?

12, 13. Relate the particulars of General Braddock's expedition.
14. What was the result of it?
15, 16. What other enterprise did the French undertake? and with what success.

SECTION IX.

*How many traitors to their God and king
Escape the death which was reserv'd for Byng!*—*Anon.*

1. (A. D. 1757.) The ministry, being apprised of this unexpected attack, resolved to raise the siege if possible, and sent out admiral Byng, with ten ships of war, with orders to relieve Minorca at any rate. Byng accordingly sailed from Gibraltar, where he was refused any assistance of men from the governor of that garrison, under a pretence that his own fortifications were in danger. 2. Upon his approaching the island, he saw the French banners displayed upon the shore, and the English colours still flying on the castle of St. Philip. He had been ordered to throw a body of troops into the garrison, but this he thought too hazardous an undertaking, nor did even make an attempt. While he was thus deliberating between his fears and his duty, his attention was quickly called off by the appearance of a French fleet, that seemed of nearly equal force to his own. 3. Confounded by a variety of measures, he seemed resolved to pursue none, and, therefore, gave orders to form the line of battle, and act upon the defensive. Byng had been long praised for his skill in naval tactics; and perhaps, valuing most those talents for which he was most praised he sacrificed all claims to courage to the applause for naval discipline. The French fleet advanced, a part of the English fleet engaged; the admiral still kept aloof, and gave very plausible reasons for not coming into action. The French fleet, therefore, slowly sailed away, and no other opportunity ever offered of coming to a closer engagement.

4. Nothing could exceed the resentment of the nation upon being informed of Byng's conduct. The ministry were not averse to throwing from themselves the blame of those measures which were attended with such indifferent success, and they secretly fanned the flame. 5. The news which soon after arrived of the surrender of the garrison to the French, drove the general ferment almost to frenzy. In the meantime Byng continued at Gibraltar, quite satisfied with his own conduct, and little expecting the dreadful storm that was gathering against him at home. Orders,

however, were soon sent out for putting him under an arrest, and for carrying him to England. 6. Upon his arrival, he was committed to close custody in Greenwich hospital, and some arts used to inflame the populace against him, who want no incentives to injure and condemn their superiors. Several addresses were sent up from different counties demanding justice on the delinquent, which the ministry were willing to second. 7. He was soon after tried by a court-martial in the harbour of Portsmouth, where, after a trial which continued several days, his judges were agreed that he had not done his utmost during the engagement to destroy the enemy, and therefore they adjudged him to suffer death by the twelfth article of war. At the same time, however, they recommended him as an object of mercy, as they considered his conduct rather as the effect of error than of cowardice. By this sentence they expected to satisfy at once the resentment of the nation, and yet screen themselves from conscious severity. 8. The government was resolved upon shewing him no mercy; the parliament was applied to in his favour, but they found no circumstance in his conduct that could invalidate the former sentence. Being thus abandoned to his fate, he maintained to the last a degree of fortitude and serenity that no way betrayed any timidity or cowardice. On the day fixed for his execution, which was on board a man-of-war, in the harbour of Portsmouth, he advanced, from the cabin where he had been imprisoned, upon deck, the place appointed for him to suffer. 9. After delivering a paper, containing the strongest assertions of his innocence, he came forward to the place where he was to kneel down, and for some time persisted in not covering his face; but his friends representing that his looks would possibly intimidate the soldiers who were to shoot him, and prevent their taking a proper aim, he had his eyes bound with a handkerchief; and then giving the signal for the soldiers to fire, he was killed instantaneously. There appears some severity in Byng's punishment; but it certainly produced soon after very beneficial effects to the nation.

10. In the progress of the war the forces of the contending powers of Europe were now drawn out in the following manner. England opposed France in America, Asia, and on the ocean. France attacked Hanover on the continent of Europe. This country the king of Prussia undertook to protect; while England promised him troops

Death of Admiral Byng.

and money to assist in the operations. Then, again, Austria had her aims at the dominions of Prussia, and drew the elector of Saxony into the same designs. In these views she was seconded by France and Sweden, and by Russia, who had hopes of acquiring a settlement in the west of Europe.

11. The east was the quarter in which success first began to dawn upon the British arms. The affairs of the English seemed to gain the ascendency by the conduct of Mr. Clive. This gentleman had at first entered the company's service in a civil capacity; but finding his talents more adapted to war, he gave up his clerkship, and joined among the troops as a volunteer. His courage, which is all that subordinate officers can at first shew, soon became remarkable; but his conduct, expedition, and military skill soon after became so conspicuous as to raise him to the first rank in the army.

12. The first advantage that was obtained from his activity and courage was the clearing of the province of Arcot. Soon after, the French general was taken prisoner; and the nabob, whom the English supported, was reinstated in the government of which he had formerly been deprived.

13. The prince of the greatest power in that country declared war against the English from motives of personal resentment; and, levying a numerous army, laid siege to

Calcutta, one of the principal British forts in that part of the world; but which was not in a state of strength to defend itself against the attack even of barbarians. The fort was taken, having been deserted by the commander; and the garrison, to the number of a hundred and forty-six persons, were made prisoners.

14. They expected the usual treatment of prisoners of war, and were therefore the less vigorous in their defence; but they soon found what mercy was to be expected from a savage conqueror. They were all crowded together into a narrow prison, called the Black Hole, of about eighteen feet square, and received air only by two small windows to the west, which by no means afforded a sufficient circulation. 15. It is terrible to reflect on the situation of these unfortunate men, shut up in this narrow place, in the burning climate of the east, and suffocating each other. Their first efforts, upon perceiving the effects of their horrid confinement, were to break open the door of the prison; but as it opened inwards, they soon found that impossible. They next endeavoured to excite the compassion or the avarice of the guard, by offering him a large sum of money for his assistance in removing them into separate prisons; but with this he was not able to comply, as the viceroy was asleep and no person dared to disturb him. 16. They were now, therefore, left to die without hopes of relief; and the whole prison was filled with groans, shrieks, contest, and despair. This turbulence, however, soon after sunk into a calm still more hideous! their efforts of strength and courage were over, and an expiring languor succeeded. In the morning, when the keepers came to visit the prison, all was horror, silence, and desolation. Of a hundred and forty-six who had entered alive, twenty-three only survived, and of these the greatest part died of putrid fevers upon being set free.

17. The destruction of this important fortress served to interrupt the prosperous success of the English company; but the fortune of Mr. Clive, backed by the activity of an English fleet under admiral Watson, still turned the scale in their favour. Among the number of those who felt the power of the English in that part of the world was the famous Tullagee Angria, a piratical prince, who had long infested the Indian ocean, and made the princes on the coast his tributaries. He maintained a large number of galleys, and with these he attacked the largest ships, and almost ever with success. 18. As the company had been

greatly harrassed by his depredations, they resolved to subdue such a dangerous enemy, and attack him in his own fortress. In pursuance of this resolution, admiral Watson and colonel Clive sailed into his harbour of Geriah; and though they sustained a warm fire as they entered, yet they soon threw all his fleet into flames, and obliged his fort to surrender at discretion. The conquerors found there a large quantity of warlike stores, and effects to a considerable value.

Questions for Examination.

1. Who was sent out to the relief of Minorca?
2, 3. What was the conduct of admiral Byng?
4. What was the consequence?
5. What afterwards followed?
6. What treatment did Byng experience?
7. What was the result of the court-martial?
8, 9. Relate the manner of Byng's execution?
10. In what manner were the contending powers opposed to each other?
11. In what quarter did success first attend the British arms? From whose conduct?
12, 13. What were the first operations?
14—16. Relate the terrible situation of the prisoners confined in the Black Hole at Calcutta.
17, 18. What are the particulars of the success which attended colonel Clive and admiral Watson?

SECTION X.

Pelham his place and life resigns;
Clive, erst unheard of in the nation,
Saves India, brightest star that shines
In our commercial constellation.—*Dibdin.*

1. (A. D. 1757.) COLONEL CLIVE proceeded to take revenge for the cruelty practiced upon the English. About the beginning of December he arrived at Balasore, in the kingdom of Bengal. He met with little opposition either to the fleet or army, till they came before Calcutta, which seemed resolved to stand a regular siege. As soon as the admiral, with two ships, arrived before the town, he received a furious fire from all the batteries, which he soon returned with still greater execution, and in less than two hours obliged them to abandon their fortifications. By these means the English took possession of the two strongest settlements on the banks of the Ganges; but that of Geriah they demolished to the ground.

2. Soon after these successes, Hoogly, a city of great trade, was reduced, with as little difficulty as the former, and all the viceroy of Bengal's storehouses and granaries were destroyed. In order to repair these losses, the barbarous prince assembled an army of ten thousand horse and

fifteen thousand foot, and professed a firm resolution of expelling the English from all their settlements in that part of the world. 3. Upon the first intelligence of his march, colonel Clive obtained a reinforcement of men from the admiral's ships, and advanced with his little army to attack these numerous forces. He attacked the enemy in three columns, and though the numbers were so disproportionate, victory soon declared in favour of the English.

4. The English, by these victories, having placed a viceroy on the throne (for the Mogul had long lost all power in India), they took care to exact such stipulations in their own favour as would secure them in possession of the country whenever they thought proper to resume their authority. They were gratified in their avarice to its extremest wish; and that wealth which they had plundered from slaves in India, they were resolved to employ in making slaves at home.

5. From the conquest of the Indians, colonel Clive turned to the humbling of the French, who had long disputed empire in that part of the world, and soon dispossessed them of all their power and all their settlements.

6. In the meantime, when conquest shone upon us from the east, it was still more splendid in the western world. But some alterations in the ministry led to those successes which had been long wished for-by the nation, and were at length obtained. The affairs of war had hitherto been directed by a ministry but ill supported by the commons, because not confided in by the people. They seemed timid and wavering, and but feebly held together, rather by their fears than their mutual confidence. 7. When any new measure was proposed which could not receive their approbation, or any new member was introduced into government whom they did not appoint, they considered it as an infringement on their respective departments, and threw up their places with disgust, with a view to resume them with greater lustre. Thus the strength of the crown was every day declining, while an aristocracy filled up every avenue to the throne, intent only on the emoluments, not the duties, of office.

8. This was at that time the general opinion of the people, and it was too loud not to reach the throne. The ministry that had hitherto hedged in the throne, were at length obliged to admit some men into a share of the government, whose activity at least would counterbalance their

timidity and irresolution. At the head of a newly introduced party was the celebrated Mr. William Pitt, from whose vigour the nation formed very great expectations, and they were not deceived.

9. But though the old ministers were obliged to admit these new members into their society, there was no legal penalty for refusing to co-operate with them; they, therefore, associated with each other, and used every art to make their new assistants obnoxious to the king, upon whom they had been in a manner forced by the people. His former ministry flattered him in all his attachments to his German dominions, while the new had long clamoured against all continental connexions, as utterly incompatible with the interest of the nation. These two opinions, carried to the extreme, might have been erroneous; but the king was naturally led to side with those who favoured his own sentiments, and to reject those who opposed them.

10. Mr. Pitt, therefore, after being a few months in office, was ordered to resign by his majesty's command; and his coadjutor, Mr. Legge, was displaced from being chancellor of the exchequer. But this blow to his ambition was but of short continuance; the whole nation, almost to a man, seemed to rise up in his defence; and Mr. Pitt and Mr. Legge being restored to their former employments,—the one secretary of state, and the other chancellor of the exchequer,—began to act with vigour.

11. The consequence of the former ill-conducted counsels still seemed to continue in America. The generals sent over to manage the operations of the war loudly accused the timidity and delays of the natives, whose duty it was to unite in their own defence. The natives, on the other hand, as warmly expostulated against the pride, avarice, and incapacity of those sent over to command them. 12. General Shirley, who had been appointed to the supreme command there, had been for some time recalled, and replaced by lord Loudon; and this nobleman also soon after returning to England, three several commanders were put at the head of separate operations. General Amherst commanded that designed against the island of Cape-Breton; the other was consigned to general Abercrombie, against Crown Point and Ticonderoga; and the third, still more to the southward against Fort du Quesne, commanded by brigadier-general Forbes.

13. Cape-Breton, which had been taken from the French

during the preceding war, had been returned at the treaty of Aix-la-Chapelle. It was not till the English had been put in possession of that island that they began to perceive its advantageous situation, and the convenience of its harbour for annoying the British trade with impunity. It was also a convenient port for carrying on their fishery, a branch of commerce of the utmost benefit to that nation. The wresting it, therefore, once more from the hands of the French was a measure ardently desired by the whole nation. 14. The fortress of Louisbourg, by which it was defended, had been strengthened by the assistance of art, and was still better fortified by the nature of its situation. The garrison also was numerous, the commander vigilant, and every precaution taken to oppose a landing. An account of the operations of the siege can give but little pleasure in abridgment; be it sufficient to say, that the English surmounted every obstacle with great intrepidity. Their former timidity and irresolution seemed to vanish, their natural courage and confidence returned, and the place surrendered by capitulation. The fortifications were soon after demolished, and thus rendered unfited for future protection.

Questions for Examination

1. What further successes attended Colonel Clive?
2, 3. What victory did he obtain over the viceroy of Bengal?
4. What was the consequence of these victories?
5. How did colonel Clive treat the French?
6, 7. What was the conduct of the ministry?
8. Who was at the head of the newly introduced party?
9. What was the conduct of the old ministry?
For what reasons was the king favourable to his former ministers?
10. What followed the resignation of the new ministers?
12. What generals commanded the American operations?
13 Why was Cape Breton considered an advantageous situation?
14. Relate the particulars of the capture of Louisbourg?

SECTION XI.

His country's glory fired him as he died;
Her love still sounded in his falt'ring breath.
"O bless her arms!" the falling conqueror cried:
Heav'n heard, and victory adorn'd his death.
Elegy on the death of Wolfe.—

1. (A.D. 1758.) THE expedition of Fort du Quesne was equally successful, but that against Crown Point was once more defeated. This was now the second time that the English army had attempted to penetrate into those hideous wilds by which nature had secured the French possessions

in that part of the world. Braddock fell in the attempt, a martyr to his impetuosity: too much caution was equally injurious to his successor. Abercrombie spent much time in marching to the place of action, and the enemy were thus perfectly prepared to give him a severe reception. 2. As he approached Ticonderoga, he found them deeply intrenched at the foot of the fort; and still farther secured by fallen trees with their branches pointing against him. These difficulties the English ardour attempted to surmount; but as the enemy, being secure themselves, took aim at leisure, a terrible carnage of the assailants ensued; and the general, after repeated efforts, was obliged to order a retreat. 3. The English army, however, was still superior, and it was supposed, that when the artillery were arrived, something more successful might be performed; but the general felt too sensibly the terrors of the late defeat, to remain in the neighbourhood of the triumphant enemy. He therefore withdrew his troops, and returned to his camp at Lake George, from whence he had taken his departure.

4. But though, in this respect, the English arms were unsuccessful, yet upon the whole the campaign was greatly in their favour. The taking of Fort du Quesne served to remove from their colonies the terror of the incursions of the Indians, while it interrupted that correspondence which ran along a chain of forts, with which the French had environed the English settlements in America. This, therefore, promised a fortunate campaign the next year, and vigorous measures were taken to ensure success.

5. Accordingly, on the opening of the following year, the ministry, sensible that a single effort carried on in such an extensive country could never reduce the enemy, were resolved to attack them in several parts of the empire at once. Preparations were also made, and expeditions driven forward against three different parts of North America at the same time. 6. General Amherst, the commander-in-chief, with a body of twelve thousand men, was to attack Crown Point, which had hitherto been the reproach of the English army: General Wolfe was at the opposite quarter to enter the river St. Lawrence, and undertake the siege of Quebec, the capital of the French dominions in America; while general Prideaux and sir William Johnson were to attempt a French fort near the cataract of Niagara.

7. The last-named expedition was the first that succeeded. The fort of Niagara was a place of great importance

and served to command all the communications between the northern and the western French settlements. The siege was begun with vigour, and promised an easy conquest; but general Prideaux was killed in the trenches by the bursting of a mortar, so that the whole command of the expedition devolved upon general Johnson, who omitted nothing to push forward the vigorous operations of his predecessor, to which also he added his own popularity with the soldiers under him. 8. A body of French troops, who were sensible of the importance of this fort attempted to relieve it; but Johnson attacked them with intrepidity and success; for in less than an hour their whole army was put to the rout. The garrison, soon after perceiving the fate of their countrymen, surrendered prisoners of war. The success of general Amherst was less splendid, though not less serviceable: upon arriving at the destined place, he found the forts, both of Crown Point and Ticonderoga, deserted and destroyed.

9. (A.D. 1759.) There now, therefore, remained but one grand and decisive blow to put all North America into the possession of the English; and this was the taking of Quebec, the capital of Canada, a city handsomely built, populous, and flourishing. Admiral Saunders was appointed to command the naval part of the expedition; the siege by land was committed to the conduct of general Wolfe, of whom the nation had great expectations. This young soldier, who was not thirty-five, and distinguished himself on many former occasions, particularly at the siege of Louisbourg, a part of the success of which was justly ascribed to him, who, without being indebted to family or connexions, had raised himself by merit to his present command.

10. The war in this part of the world had been hitherto carried on with extreme barbarity, and retaliating murders were continued without any one's knowing who first began. Wolfe however, disdaining to imitate an example that had been set him even by some of his associate officers, carried on the war with all the spirit of humanity which it admits of. 11. It is not our aim to enter into a minute detail of the siege of this city, which could at best only give amusement to a few; it will be sufficient to say, that when we consider the situation of a town on the side of a great river, the fortifications with which it was secured, the natural strength of the country, the great number of vessels and floating batteries the enemy had provided for the defence of the river, the numerous bodies of savages continually hover-

ing round the English army, we must own there was such a combination of difficulties as might discourage and perplex the most resolute commander. The general himself seemed perfectly sensible of the difficulty of the undertaking. After stating, in a letter to the ministers, the dangers that presented, "I know" said he, "that the affairs of Great Britain require the most vigorous measures. But then the courage of a handful of brave men should be exerted only where there is some hope of a favorable event. At present the difficulties are so various, that I am at a loss how to determine." 13. The only prospect of attempting the town with success was by landing a body of troops in the night below the town, who were to clamber up the banks of the river, and take possession of the ground on the back of the city. This attempt, however, appeared peculiarly discouraging. The stream was rapid, the shore shelving, the bank above lined with sentinels, the landing-place so narrow as to be easily missed in the dark, and the steepness of the ground such as hardly to be surmounted in the day-time. All these difficulties, however, were surmounted by the conduct of the general, and the bravery of the men. 14. Colonel How, with the light infantry and the Highlanders, ascended the woody precipices with admirable courage and activity, and dislodged a small body of troops that defended a narrow pathway up to the bank; thus, a few mounting, the general drew the rest up in order as they arrived. Monsieur de Montcalm, the French commander, was no sooner apprized that the English had gained these heights, which he had confidently deemed inaccessible, than he resolved to hazard a battle, and a spirited encounter quickly began. This was one of the most furious engagements during the war. 15. The French general was slain; the second in command shared the same fate. General Wolfe was standing on the right, where the attack was most warm; as he stood conspicuous in the front line, he had been aimed at by the enemy's marksmen, and received a shot in the wrist, which, however, did not oblige him to quit the field. Having wrapped a handkerchief round his hand, he continued giving orders without the least emotion, and advanced at the head of the grenadiers, with their bayonets fixed; but a second ball, more fatal, pierced his breast; so that, unable to proceed, he leaned on the shoulder of a soldier that was next him. 16. Now struggling in the agonies of death, and just

Death of General Wolfe.

expiring, he heard a voice cry, "They run!" Upon which he seemed for a moment to revive, and, asking who ran, was informed the French. Expressing his wonder that they ran so soon, and unable to gaze any longer, he sank in the soldier's breast, and his last words were, "I die happy!" Perhaps the loss of the English that day was greater than the conquest of Canada was advantageous. But it is the lot of mankind only to know true merit on that dreadful occasion when they are going to lose it.

Questions for Examination.

1. What was the success against Fort du Quesne?
2. What difficulties had Abercrombie to encounter?
3. To what place did he withdraw his troops?
4. What was the general success of the campaign?
5. What vigorous measures were adopted the following year?
6. By whom were the different expeditions commanded?
7, 8. What are the particulars of the expedition which first succeeded?
9. What was the next decisive blow?
    To whom was intrusted the command of the expedition against Quebec?
10. In what manner did Wolfe carry on the war?
11. What was the situation and strength of Quebec?
12. What was the opinion of the general?
13, 14. Relate the particulars and success of the siege?
15. In what manner was General Wolfe wounded?
16. Relate his heroic conduct in the agonies of death?

SECTION XII.

*Fresh laurels graced the victor's brow
On Minden's gory plains;
But what avail those laurels now?—
Imaginary gains!*—*Anon.*

1. (A.D. 1759. The surrender of Quebec was the consequence of this victory, and with it soon after the total cession of all Canada. The French, indeed, the following season, made a vigorous effort to retake the city; but by the resolution of Governor Murray, and the appearance of an English fleet under the command of Lord Colville, they were obliged to abandon the enterprise. 2. The whole province was soon after reduced by the prudence and activity of General Amherst, who obliged the French army to capitulate; and it has since remained annexed to the British empire. To these conquests, about the same time, was added the reduction of the island of Guadaloupe, under commodore More and General Hopson; an acquisition of great importance, but which was restored at the succeeding peace.

3. These successes in India and America were great, though achieved by no very extensive efforts. On the contrary, the efforts the English made in Europe, and the operations of their great ally, the king of Prussia, were astonishing, yet produced no signal advantages.

4. England was all this time happily retired from the miseries which oppressed the rest of Europe; yet, from her natural military ardour, she seemed desirous of sharing those dangers of which she was only a spectator. This passion for sharing in a continental war was not less pleasing to the king of England, from his native attachment, than from a desire of revenge upon the plunderers of his country. 5. As soon, therefore, as it was known that prince Ferdinand had put himself at the head of the Hanoverian army, to assist the king of Prussia, his Britannic majesty, in a speech to his parliament, observed that the late successes of his ally in Germany had given a happy turn to his affairs, which it would be necessary to improve. The commons concurred in his sentiments, and liberally granted supplies both for the service of the King of Prussia, and for enabling the army formed in Hanover to act vigorously in conjunction with him.

6. From sending money over into Germany, the nation began to extend their benefits; and it was soon considered that men would be a more grateful supply. Mr. Pitt, who

had at first come into popularity and power by opposing such measures, was now prevailed upon to enter into them, with even greater ardour than any of his predecessors. 7. The hopes of putting a speedy end to the war by vigorous measures, the connections with which he was obliged to co-operate, and perhaps the pleasure he found in pleasing the king, altogether incited him eagerly to push forward a continental war. However he only conspired with the general inclinations of the people at this time, who, assured by the noble efforts of their only ally, were unwilling to see him fall a sacrifice to the united ambition of his enemies.

8. In order to indulge the general inclination of assisting the king of Prussia, the duke of Marlborough was at first sent into Germany, with a small body of British forces, to join Prince Ferdinand, whose activity against the French began to be crowned with success. After some small successes gained by the allied army at Crevelt, the duke of Marlborough dying, the command devolved upon lord George Sackville, who was at that time a favourite with the British army. 9. However, a misunderstanding arose between him and the commander-in-chief, which soon had an occasion of being displayed at the battle of Minden, which was fought soon after. The cause of this secret disgust on both sides is not clearly known; it is thought that the extensive genius and the inquisitive spirit of the English general were by no means agreeable to his superior in command, who hoped to reap some pecuniary advantages the other was unwilling to permit. 10. Be this as it will, both armies advancing near the town of Minden, the French began the attack with great vigour, and a general engagement of the infantry ensued. Lord George at the head of the British and Hanoverian horse, was stationed at some distance on the right of the infantry, from which they were divided by a scanty wood that bordered on a heath. The French infantry giving ground, the prince thought that this would be a favorable opportunity to pour down the horse among them, and accordingly sent lord George orders to come on. 11. These orders were but ill-observed; and whether they were unintelligible or contradictory, still remains a point for posterity to debate upon. It is certain that lord George shortly after was recalled, tried by a court-martial, found guilty, and declared incapable of serving in any military command for the future.

12. The enemy, however, were repulsed in all ther attacks with considerable loss, and, at length, giving way, were

pursued to the very ramparts of Minden. The victory was splendid, but laurels were the only advantage reaped from the field of battle.

13. After these victories, which were greatly magnified in England, it was supposed that one reinforcement more of British troops would terminate the war in favour of the allies, and a reinforcement was quickly sent. The British army in Germany, now, therefore, amounted to above thirty thousand men, and the whole nation was flushed with the hopes of immediate conquest. But these hopes soon vanished, in finding victory and defeat successively following each other. The allies were worsted at Corbac, but retrieved their honour at Exdorf. A victory at Warbourgh followed shortly after, and another at Zironburg; but then they suffered a defeat at Compen, after which both sides went into winter-quarters. 14. The successes thus on either side might be considered as a compact, by which both engaged to lose much and gain little; for no advantage whatever followed from victory. The English at length began to open their eyes to their own interest, and found that they were waging unequal war, and loading themselves with taxes, for conquests that they could neither preserve nor enjoy.

Questions for Examination.

1, 2. What consequence followed this victory?
4. What passion operated for sharing in a continental war?
5. What observation did his majesty make to the commons? and how did they concur in his sentiments?
6, 7. What was Mr. Pitt's conduct; and what were the general inclinations of the people?
8. What English commander was first sent to Germany?
9. What caused the misunderstanding which took place between the commanders?
10, 11. How did lord G. Sackville act at the battle of Minden?
12. What was the success of it?
13. What followed these victories?
14. In what light might the events of this war be considered?

SECTION XIII.

The boast of heraldry, the pomp of pow'r,
And all that beauty, all that wealth, e'er gave,
Await alike th' inevitable hour:
The path of glory leads but to the grave.—*Gray.*

1. (A.D. 1759.) IT must be confessed, that the efforts of England at this time over every part of the globe, were amazing, and the expense of her operations greater than had ever been disbursed by any nation before. The king of

Prussia received a subsidy; a large body of her forces commanded the extensive peninsula of India; another army of twenty thousand men confirmed their conquests in North America; there were thirty thousand men employed in Germany, and several other bodies dispersed in different garrisons in various parts of the world; but all these were nothing to the force maintained at sea, which carried command wherever it came, and had totally annihilated the French power on that element. 2. The courage and conduct of the English admirals had surpassed whatever had been read in history; neither superior force nor number, nor even the terrors of the tempest, could intimidate them. Admiral Hawke gained a complete victory over an equal number of French ships, on the coast of Bretagne, in Quiberon Bay, in the midst of a tempest during the darkness of night, and, what a seaman fears more, upon a rocky shore.

3. Such was the glorious figure the British nation appeared in to all the world at this time. But while their arms prospered in every effort tending to the real interests of the nation, an event happened which for a time obscured the splendour of her victories. On the twenty-fourth of October, the king, without having complained of any previous disorder, was found by his domestics expiring in his chamber. 4. He had arisen at his usual hour, and observed to his attendants, that, as the weather was fine, he would take a walk in the garden of Kensington, where he then resided. In a few minutes after his return, being left alone, he was heard to fall down upon the floor. The noise of this bringing his attendants into the room, they lifted him into bed, where he desired, with a faint voice, that the princess Amelia might be sent for; but, before she could reach the apartment, he expired. An attempt was made to bleed him, but without effect; and afterwards the surgeons, upon opening him, discovered that the right ventricle of the heart was ruptured, and that a great quantity of blood was discharged through the aperture.

5. (Oct. 25, 1760.) GEORGE the second died in the seventy-seventh year of his age, and thirty-third of his reign, lamented by his subjects, and in the midst of victory. If any monarch was happy in the peculiar mode of his death, and the precise time of its arrival, it was he. 6. The universal enthusiasm for conquest was now beginning to subside, and sober reason to take her turn in the administration of affairs. The factions which had been nursing during his

long reign had not yet come to maturity; but threatened, with all their virulence, to afflict his successor. He was himself of no shining abilities; and while he was permitted to guide and assist his German dominions, he intrusted the care of Great Britain to his ministers at home. However, as we stand too near to be impartial judges of his merits or defects, let us state his character, as delivered by two writers of opposite opinions:

7. "On whatever side," says his panegyrist, "we look upon his character, we shall find ample matter for just and unsuspected praise. None of his predecessors on the throne of England lived to so great an age, or enjoyed longer felicity. His subjects were still improving under him in commerce and arts; and his own economy set a prudent example to the nation, which, however, they did not follow. He was in temper sudden and violent; but this, though it influenced his conduct, made no change in his behaviour, which was generally guided by reason. 8. He was plain and direct in his intentions, true to his word, steady in his favour and protection of his servants, not parting even with his ministers till compelled to it by the violence of faction. In short, through the whole of his life he appeared rather to live for the cultivation of useful virtues than splendid ones; and satisfied with being good, left others their unenvied greatness."

9. Such is the picture given by his friends, but there are others who reverse the medal. "As to the extent of his understanding, or the splendour of his virtue, we rather wish for opportunities of praise than undertake the task ourselves. His public character was marked with a predilection for his native country, and to that he sacrificed all other considerations. 10. He was not only unlearned himself, but he despised learning in others; and though genius might have flourished in his reign, yet he neither promoted it by his influence nor example. His frugality bordered upon avarice; and he hoarded not for his subjects, but himself."

Which of these two characters is true, or whether they may not in part be both so, I will not pretend to decide. If his favourers are numerous, so are they who oppose him. Let posterity, therefore, decide the contest.

Questions for Examination.

1. What astonishing efforts did Britain make to carry on the war?
2. In what manner was the courage of the English admirals shown?
3. What important event obscured the lustre of these victories?
4. What circumstances preceded the king's death? What was the cause of his death?
5. What was his age, and how long did he reign?
6. What was the situation of the country at that time?
7, 8. What is the character of the king as given by his friends?
9, 10. What as given by his enemies?

CONTEMPORARY SOVEREIGNS.

Popes.

	A. D.
Benedict XIII	1724
Clement XII	1738
Benedict XIV	1740
Clement XIII	1758

Emperors of Germany.

Charles VI	1711
Charles VII	1740
Francis Stephen	1745

Emperors and Empresses of Russia.

Peter II	1727
Anne	1730
John	1740
Elizabeth	1741

King of France.

Louis XV	1715

Kings of Spain.

Philip V (restored)	1724
Ferdinand VI	1745

Emperors of the Turks.

	A. D.
Achmet III	1703
Mahomet V	1730
Osman II	1754
Mustapha III	1757

Kings of Portugal.

John V	1707
Joseph	1750

Kings of Denmark.

Frederick IV	1699
Christian VI	1730
Frederick V	1746

Kings of Sweden.

Frederick	1720
Adolphus	1750

Kings of Prussia.

Frederick II	1713
Frederick III	1740

EMINENT PERSONS.

William Pitt, earl of Chatham; Admiral Hawke; General Wolfe; Alexander Pope; James Thomson;* Dr. Young; John, lord Carteret; Philip, earl of Hardwick; Henry Pelham, H. lord Hyde and Cornbury; Horatio, lord Walpole; George Booth, earl of Warrington; J. Hamilton, earl of Abercorn, &c., &c., &c.

CHAPTER XXXVI.

GEORGE III

Born 1738. Died 1820. Began to reign 1760. Reigned 59 years.

SECTION I.

> Hail, monarch! born the pledge of happier days,
> To guard our freedom and our glories raise,
> Given to the world to spread religion's sway,
> And pour o'er many a land the mental day.—*Mickle.*

1. (October 25, 1760.) THOUGH the health of George II. had been long declining, his death was totally unexpected, and the ministry, being unprepared for such an event, felt not a little embarrassed when they first waited on their new sovereign. George III., who succeeded, was the son of Frederick, prince of Wales, and Augusta, princess of Saxe-Gotha. In consequence of the premature death of his

---

*The encouragement given to literary exertion during the reign of queen Anne, was altogether withdrawn by her successors. Pope and Swift, indeed, still continued to be patronised by their former friends, but rising merit was entirely neglected. Frederick, prince of Wales, during his brief career, was an ostentatious rather than a generous patron of letters; but after his death, even the semblance of encouragement was laid aside. The ministry had even the incredible meanness to deprive poor Thomson of a miserable pittance settled on him by Frederick. After enduring great distress, this poet at length obtained a small place, through the interest of lord Lyttleton, but he did not live to enjoy its advantages; to the disgrace of the nation and its rulers, he died in difficulties and debt.

father who died without ascending the throne, his education had devolved upon his mother, by whom he was brought up in the strictest privacy. She had unfortunately quarrelled with the late king, and the prince, though now in his twenty-second year, had been consequently such a stranger to the court of his grandfather, that he was unacquainted even with the persons of the ministers. 2. His first address to the council was gracious and conciliatory: the only remarkable occurrence that distinguished the opening of the new reign was the elevation of the earl of Bute to the office of privy councillor. 3. The parliament was assembled in November and the king's first speech gave universal satisfaction to the country. The civil list was fixed at the annual sum of 800,000*l* and liberal supplies were voted for the maintenance of the war in which the country was engaged. The king, in return for this instance of affection on the part of the people assented to a bill for further securing the independence of the judges, by providing that their offices should not be vacated on the demise of the crown.

4. (A.D. 1761.) The act of settlement prohibiting the sovereigns of Britain from intermarrying with Roman Catholics, his majesty was precluded from seeking a consort in the great families of Europe; he therefore selected as his bride a daughter of the house of Mecklenburgh Strelitz, a small principality in the north of Germany; the marriage was celebrated on the 8th of September, and on the 22nd of the same month the ceremony of the coronation was performed with great pomp and magnificence.

5. The war, which had been carried on with great spirit and success under the auspices of Mr. Pitt, continued to be supported with unabated vigour; prince Ferdinand, at the head of the allies, pursued his victorious career in Germany; and Belleisle was captured by a British force under the command of Admiral Keppell and general Hodgson. The French court, terrified at these losses, made an abortive attempt to obtain peace; but having failed in this, a successful application for assistance was made to the king of Spain, and a secret treaty called the Family Compact, was made between the two powers. 6. This transaction, though carefully concealed, did not escape the penetration of Mr. Pitt; he warned his colleagues of the insidious designs of Spain, and urged them to send out a fleet to intercept the Spanish flota, or strike some other decisive blow before the hostile projects of that court were ripe for execution. This proposal

was very coolly received by the other members of the cabinet; they were not in possession of all the information which their colleague had obtained, and they were besides jealous of the influence which Mr. Pitt's superior popularity conferred. The project was finally rejected, and Mr. Pitt immediately resigned. As a mark of gratitude, however, for his eminent public services, a pension of 3000*l.* a year was settled on him for three lives, and his wife was created baroness Chatham.

7. The retirement of this popular minister was generally attributed to the secret influence of the earl of Bute, who was supposed to have obtained complete ascendency over the mind of his royal master. The suspicion created general displeasure among the people; on the lord mayor's day, when his majesty and suite proceeded to dine in the city, the king and queen were received with coldness and silence, the earl of Bute was grossly insulted, but Mr. Pitt was welcomed with the loudest acclamations.

8. In a few months the wisdom of Mr. Pitt's anticipations was fully established; the hostile designs of Spain could no longer be concealed, and when the British ambassador remonstrated, he received nothing but evasive answers, or flat refusals to all his demands. He was in consequence recalled; and in a short time after, a declaration of war was published against Spain.

9. A new parliament being assembled, the consideration of a provision for the queen, in the event of her surviving his majesty, was recommended from the throne. An annuity of 100,000*l.* was settled on her for life, together with the palace of Somerset house (afterwards exchanged for Buckingham house), and the lodge and lands of Richmond park.

10. (A.D. 1762.) No change of importance had hitherto been made in the cabinet, except the appointment of the earl of Bute to the office of secretary of state; but a more important alteration had long been meditated, one that involved a most complete revolution in the domestic policy of England. Since the accession of the house of Brunswick, the administration of the public affairs had been principally confided to some of the great families, by whose exertions that race of sovereigns had been placed upon the throne. Their power had been considerably strengthened by the suppression of the two rebellions in 1715 and 1745, and the two former kings, more attached to their German

dominions than to their British kingdoms, surrendered the government of these countries to their ministers without reluctance. The new sovereign of Britain was entirely free from German predilections; in the court of his mother he had been taught to dislike the politics of his grandfather, and he had no longer any reason to dread dangers from the change, for the claims of the young pretender had long since sunk into total insignificance. Unfortunately, the Earl of Bute, to whom the management of such an important change was confided, did not possess abilities equal to the task. His domestic virtues, his refined taste, and generous liberality had made him deservedly beloved in private life; but his reserved habits, his coldness of manner, and his total ignorance of state affairs, made his public career odious to the people, painful to himself, and injurious to the popularity of his sovereign.

11. It was resolved to get rid of the Pelham family, which had so long been at the head of affairs; the duke of Newcastle was made so uneasy in his situation, that he resigned his post as first lord of the treasury, and was succeeded by the earl of Bute; the greater part of the ministers imitated the duke's example; and even the duke of Devonshire, whose exertions in behalf of the Hanoverian succession had been rewarded by the place of lord chamberlain, found it necessary to resign his situation. A furious paper-war ensued, and party spirit, which had slept during the triumphant administration of Mr. Pitt, was revived, and raged with unparalleled fury. National prejudices contributed to fan the flame; the earl of Bute was a Scotchman, and the old jealousy between the natives of the northern and southern divisions of the country was made a formidable engine of party hostility.

12. The war was carried on with equal vigour and success by the new administration. The French and Spaniards having in vain endeavoured to detach the Portuguese from their alliance with England, sent an army to invade the country; but an English body of auxiliaries was immediately despatched to Portugal, and the progress of the invaders was soon checked. At first, indeed, the bigoted Portuguese refused to unite cordially with their heretical allies; but when count de la Lippe was appointed to the command of their armies, he entered cordially into the views of the English general, and the Spaniards were defeated in two decisive engagements. Spain suffered still more

severely in other quarters of the globe; Havana, with plunder to the amount of three millions sterling, was taken by the earl of Albemarle and Admiral Pococke; the city of Manilla surrendered to general Draper and admiral Cornish; it was ransomed for the stipulated sum of one million, but the Spaniards violated their engagements, and the ransom was never paid. Two valuable treasure-ships, containing property to the amount of two millions sterling, were about the same time captured by British cruisers. (August 12, 1762.) While the waggons that conveyed the treasure taken from the Spanish vessels to the Tower were passing in front of the palace, the cannon in the park announced the birth of a prince of Wales, and this coincidence not a little increased the public joy at this happy event.

13. While the arms of England were thus triumphant in various quarters of the globe, the king of Prussia, her principal, and, indeed, her almost only ally, after a series of brilliant exploits, which have immortalized his name, seemed to have been brought to the very brink of ruin by the junction of the Russians with his inveterate enemies. At the very moment, however, that his destruction seemed certain, he was rescued by one of those sudden revolutions which baffle all human calculation. Elizabeth, empress of Russia, dying, was succeeded by her nephew, Peter III., who was an enthusiastic admirer of the Prussian king; he not only concluded a peace with Frederick, but even joined his arms to those of that monarch, and began to act hostilely against his former allies. Peter was, however, soon dethroned by his subjects; Catharine II., his consort, then became empress of Russia; she withdrew her forces from those of the king of Prussia, and resolved to maintain a strict neutrality. Frederic was not slow in availing himself of these favourable circumstances, and soon amply retrieved his former losses.

14. All parties were now seriously anxious for the restoration of peace. France was deprived of her colonial possessions, and saw her commerce on the brink of ruin; Spain had suffered still more severely; the Austrians and Prussians were wearied of campaigns, which left the armies at their close nearly in the same situation they occupied at the commencement; and England, notwithstanding her triumphs, felt that a continuation of such exertions would soon exhaust her resources. The seven years' war was terminated by a general peace, by which England was permitted to re-

tain Canada and several other conquests, receiving also from Spain, Florida, in exchange for the Havana. 15. Though the terms of the peace were very favourable to the interests of the English, yet the nation, intoxicated by success, regretted the termination of the war. The articles had been signed several months before the city of London could be prevailed upon to present a tardy and reluctant address of congratulation; and on the day of its presentation, the lord-mayor (Beckford) refused to attend, and the bells of the different churches rung muffled peals during the procession.

Questions for Examination.

1. By whom was George II. succeeded?
2. Did anything remarkable occur at the first meeting of the privy council?
3. What proceedings took place in parliament?
4. To whom did George III. unite himself in marriage?
5. Did any circumstances tend to show hostile dispositions in the Spanish court?
6. Under what circumstances did Mr. Pitt resign his office?
7. What were the consequences of his resignation?
8. Were Mr. Pitt's suspicions of the Spanish court well founded?
9. What dowry was settled on the queen?
10. What great change took place in the administration?
11. Did any evil consequences result from the change of ministry?
12. How was the war conducted? what triumphs did the English obtain?
13. By what means was the king of Prussia rescued from his difficulties?
14. Why were all parties anxious to terminate the war?
15. Was the peace popular in England?

SECTION II.

Like smoke emitted from Vesuvius' top
  (Dread harbinger of the volcano's powers),
So breathe the fires of discontent, nor stop
  Till all around is wrapt in burning showers.—Brown.

1. (A. D. 1763.) TRANQUILLITY might naturally have been expected at the conclusion of a glorious war, but this was prevented by the domestic dissensions which party spirit produced. The earl of Bute's unpopularity still continued, but his influence was apparently unabated; for notwithstanding the most vigorous efforts of the opposition, he prevailed upon parliament to impose a tax upon cider, which, without producing any great revenue, gave infinite dissatisfaction to the nation. Immediately after this triumph, his lordship, to the great surprise of every one, resigned his post, and retired into private life. 2. He was succeeded by Mr. George Grenville. The press soon teemed with the most virulent libels from the partisans of the several factions that divided the country. In these productions the person

of the sovereign was not always spared, until at length the ministry was roused by the appearance of No. 45 of the North Briton, a periodical paper conducted by Mr. Wilkes, the member for Aylesbury, in which it was stated that the king had uttered a deliberate falsehood in his speech to parliament. This was an offence which could not be passed over, and a general warrant was issued for the arrest of the author, printers and publishers of that paper. Mr. Wilkes was arrested and sent to the Tower; several innocent persons were taken into custody, and the ministry found that, in their eagerness to punish a delinquent, they had unfortunately raised a great constitutional question, which must of necessity be decided against them.

3. The printers taken up under the warrant, brought actions against the messengers by whom they had been arrested, and recovered heavy damages. Mr. Wilkes, also, having been brought by habeas corpus before the court of common pleas, was liberated, the judges being unanimously of opinion, that privilege of parliament extended to the cause of writing a libel. The house of commons gave a different decision. They voted that No. 45 of the North Briton was a false, scandalous, and seditious libel, and that the author of such was not protected by privilege of parliament. Soon after, Mr. Wilkes fought a duel with Mr. Martin, whom he had libelled, and was severely wounded; he had scarcely recovered from its effects when he thought fit to retire to France. (A.D. 1764.) During his absence, he was expelled the house of commons, and driven to an outlawry in the court of king's bench for not appearing to stand his trial. The only advantage that resulted from this struggle, was the declaration of the illegality of general warrants by a resolution of both houses of parliament.

4. (A. D. 1765.) The immense expenditure incurred during the late war had involved the country in considerable difficulties, and it was considered only just that the American colonies, whose interests had been most regarded in the treaty of peace, should bear their proportion of the public burdens; accordingly, a bill for imposing stamp duties on all mercantile transactions in the colonies was introduced by Mr. Grenville, and passed into a law with but little opposition. The Americans had been for some time previously very indignant at the treatment they had received from the mother country; their profitable trade with the Spanish colonies had been destroyed by new fiscal regula-

tions; the Indians had harassed their back settlements, and no royal forces were sent to check the progress of the barbarians; when, therefore, news arrived that taxes were about to be imposed on the colonies by a parliament in which they were not represented, public indignation knew no bounds, and the colonial legislatures sent remonstrances couched in very strong language to the parliament and the throne. 5. The progress of these dissensions was, however, arrested by the downfall of the Grenville administration. The minister having omitted the name of the king's mother in the bill for providing a council of regency in case of any emergency, so displeased his majesty, that he was compelled to send in his resignation. A new ministry was formed, principally by the exertions of the duke of Cumberland, at the head of which was placed the marquis of Rockingham, a nobleman conspicuous for his public, and private virtues, but not distinguished by super-eminent abilities.

6. (A.D. 1766.) The chief business of the new ministry was to undo all that their predecessors had done; the stamp act, which had excited so much dissatisfaction in America, and the cider tax, which was equally unpopular in England, were both repealed, and these judicious measures were followed by a brief interval of tranquillity.*

7. (A. D. 1767.) The Rockingham administration was so weakened by the death of the duke of Cumberland, that it was broken up, and a new cabinet formed under the auspices of Mr. Pitt, who was created earl of Chatham, and the duke of Grafton was placed at its head, as first lord of the treasury. The attention of government was first directed to the affairs of the East India company, which had been thrown into confusion by the avarice and rapacity of their servants. Lord Clive was sent out to India, with full powers to remedy these evils, and under his administration the company soon recovered its former prosperity, and laid the foundations of future greatness. 8. The unfortunate design of taxing America was again revived; an act was passed for granting duties on all glass, paper, painters' colours, and tea imported into the British colonies; which the Americans resisted by petitions, remonstrances, and agreements not to use British manufactures until the obnoxious duties were repealed. An act was also passed enjoining the colonies to provide his majesty's troops with necessaries in their quarters; the colonial house of assembly in the state of New York peremptorily refused obedience, and another act was

* The old Pretender died at Rome in this year, at the age of 76.

passed restraining the assembly from making laws until they had complied with the terms of the former statute.

9. (A.D. 1768.) The natural date of the parliament having nearly expired, it was dissolved, and writs issued for the election of a new one. Wilkes embraced the opportunity of returning from exile which a change of ministry afforded; he offered himself a candidate for Middlesex, and was elected by an overwhelming majority. He then surrendered himself to the court of king's bench, and procured the reversal of his outlawry; he was, however, sentenced to pay a fine of a thousand pounds, and to be imprisoned for twenty-two months. As he was esteemed a martyr in the cause of liberty, a subscription was opened for paying his fine, supporting him while in prison, and compounding his debts, which amounted to more than twenty thousand pounds. 10. The disturbances in America still continued to increase, and the states of New England were particularly remarkable for their determined hostility to the new duties. Descended from the puritans and republicans who had left England after the restoration of Charles II., and sought in the wilds of America the liberty of conscience denied to them at home, the New Englanders possessed in no ordinary degree the spirit of independence, and the obstinate resolution, which had characterised the soldiers of Fairfax and Cromwell. In Boston the commissioners of customs were so severely handled, that they were forced to take refuge from the fury of the populace in fort William; and to preserve the peace of the town, it was deemed necessary to send thither two regiments of foot from Halifax, and as many from Ireland.

11. The situation of Ireland began also to give the minister considerable uneasiness. By Poyning's law, passed in the reign of Henry VII., and extended by several subsequent statutes, the legislature of that country had been made so completely dependent on the British government, that it was become a mere nullity. An unwise and unjust spirit of commercial jealousy induced the English to abuse the advantages which they had obtained, and several impolitic restrictions were imposed on Irish commerce and manufactures. These measures produced little or no advantage to the English, while they crushed the rising energies of the sister kingdom; but they were obstinately maintained, for the age was not yet sufficiently enlightened to discover that the prosperity of the one country was intimately

z

connected with that of the other. A strong party had, however, been formed in Ireland to achieve the legislative independence of their country, and they gained no small part of their object by the passing of the octennial act which limited the duration of Irish parliaments to eight years, for they had been previously dissolved only on the demise of the crown.

12. In the East Indies, the English were assailed by an enemy more formidable than any they had hitherto met in that quarter. Hyder Ally, who had raised himself from the rank of a common sepoy to that of a sovereign prince, commenced hostilities against the company's settlements, and for several years kept them in a state of incessant alarm.

13. When the new parliament met, the people imagined that Mr. Wilkes would be liberated to take his seat, and therefore assembled in great numbers in St. George's fields, round the king's bench prison, in order to conduct him to the house of commons. The Surrey justices took the alarm, and read the riot act, but the multitude, refusing to disperse, the military were called out, and unfortunately ordered to fire. One man was killed on the spot, and a great number were wounded, several mortally. It happened that a Scotch regiment had been employed in this lamentable affair, a circumstance which not a little increased the public indignation. Verdicts of wilful murder against the soldiery were returned by the different inquests, and on the subsequent trials several of the soldiers were found guilty of murder.

14. The government by no means participated in the popular feeling; not only were pardons granted to those who had been convicted, but the secretary of state, lord Weymouth, sent a letter to the justices thanking them for their spirited conduct. This document was published by Mr. Wilkes, with an indignant commentary, in which he termed the affair "a horrid massacre," and added a virulent invective against the entire conduct of the government. 15. For this publication, Mr. Wilkes was expelled the house of commons, and, with strange inconsistency, the causes assigned for his expulsion included not only his late offence, but the former acts for which he had already atoned by undergoing judicial punishment. This complication of charge afforded just grounds of complaint, and not a little tended to give Wilkes a decided superiority over his opponents. (A.D. 1769.) The freeholders unanimously re-elected him, but

the house considered the election void, and issued a new writ. The same proceedings were twice repeated; until at length colonel Luttrel was prevailed upon to offer himself as candidate. Wilkes was once more returned by an immense majority, the votes for him being 1143, while those for his opponent amounted only to 269; the house of commons, notwithstanding, declared that Luttrel was and ought to be the sitting member.

16. This was considered, with some show of justice, a fatal blow to the liberties of the subject; petitions and remonstrances of the most daring nature poured in from all parts of the kingdom: the press teemed with the most virulent attacks on all constituted authorities; some went so far as to deny the legality of the present parliament, and the obligation of the people to obey its laws. An anonymous writer, named Junius, was particularly distinguished by the fierce severity of his attacks on the ministry, and by the superior brilliancy of his style, which still preserves his celebrated letters from the oblivion into which party productions usually fall. Meantime the disputes with the colonists continued to be maintained with unabated zeal; and the Irish parliament showed such a determination to throw off the yoke, that it was found necessary to elude their demands by a prorogation.

Questions for Examination.

1. How was the tranquillity of the country disturbed?
2. What circumstances took place respecting No. 45 of the North Briton?
3. How did the affair terminate?
4. What circumstances led to disunion between England and the American colonies?
5. How was the Grenville ministry overthrown?
6. By what means was tranquillity restored?
7. What was the first measure of the Grafton administration?
8. By what act was the discontent of the Americans revived?
9. How did Wilkes behave on the change of ministry?
10. In what manner did the Americans conduct themselves?
11. Was any important change made in the Irish legislature?
12. Did any new power appear in the East Indies?
13. What unfortunate event took place in St. George's fields?
14. How was Wilkes involved in a new contest with government?
15. What was the decision of the house of commons respecting the Middlesex election?
16. Did this decision produce any unpleasant results?

SECTION III.

*No self-subjecting force of soul is theirs,
That public toils as noblest honour bears.—Sterling.*

1. (A.D. 1770.) THE health of the earl of Chatham had been long in such a state as to prevent him from exerting his energies for the benefit of his country; he had the mortification to find that his influence was lost in the cabinet, and his popularity forgotten by the nation; he therefore resigned his office, and his example was imitated by the duke of Grafton. Lord North succeeded the latter as first lord of the treasury, and some trifling changes were made in the inferior departments of government.

2. Foreign nations seemed to have lost all respect for a country whose councils were subject to such sudden vicissitudes, and the subjects of the realm were no longer willing to pay that respect to the laws which is necessary to the well-being of a state. The new ministry seemed ill calculated to retrieve the honour of the country; they permitted France to acquire the island of Corsica without venturing to interfere, and tamely submitted to an insult offered by Spain to the British flag in the affair of the Falkland islands. The spirit of the nation however forced the ministry to make some exertions in the latter instance, and the matter was finally adjusted by a convention.

3. (A.D. 1771.) The debates in parliament had been hitherto printed surreptitiously, as their publication was deemed a breach of privilege. The interest felt by the public in the debates on the Middlesex election induced the printers to act more daringly than before, and at length a formal complaint was made in the house, and a messenger was sent into the city to arrest the most notorious of the offenders. One printer, having been seized by the messenger, sent for a constable, who carried both before the lord Mayor, Mr. Crosby. That gentleman, with the aldermen, Wilkes and Oliver, not only discharged the printer, but threatened to send the messenger to prison unless he found bail to answer for his appearance on a charge of illegal arrest. The house of commons received the news of these proceedings with the most violent indignation; the lord mayor and Oliver were sent to the Tower, and Wilkes was summoned to appear at the bar of the house. But an unexpected difficulty was soon raised; Wilkes refused to appear unless permitted to take his place for Middlesex,

and the house at length compromised its dignity, by ordering him to attend on the 8th of April, and then adjourning to the 9th. Since this event no attempt has been made to check the publication of the parliamentary debates, which now constitute the most important, as well as the most interesting feature in the periodical press.

4. (A.D. 1772.) The marriage of the king's brothers, the dukes of Cumberland and Gloucester, with subjects of the realm, led to the enactment of the royal marriage act, which prohibited any of the descendants of George II. from marrying before the age of twenty-five without the consent of the king in council. An act was also passed to abrogate the law by which felons, who refused to plead, were pressed to death; it was enacted that, for the future, those who did not plead should be held guilty of the crimes laid to their charge.

5. The continent of Europe was the scene of an atrocious act of injustice committed by three crowned heads; the first dismemberment of Poland was effected by an iniquitous confederacy between the Emperor of Germany, the empress of Russia, and the king of Prussia; they left the unfortunate monarch of the country little more than a nominal sovereignty, and even of this he was subsequently deprived by the royal robbers, and the name of Poland blotted from the list of nations. 6. About the same time the king of Sweden, in violation of the most solemn obligations, abrogated the free constitution of his country, and made himself despotic. 7. In Denmark, on the other hand, the royal power was overthrown by a vile faction, who deprived the king of his authority, murdered his ministers, and drove his queen, Matilda, sister to the king of England, into exile, where grief soon terminated her sufferings.

8. The planters in the island of St. Vincent had grossly ill-treated the Caribs, or native inhabitants, who had been allowed to possess their lands in quiet while the colony remained under the dominion of the French. A civil war ensued, and the planters, notwithstanding all their advantages, were worsted. Application for assistance against the rebellious savages, as they thought fit to designate men who refused to submit tamely to open robbery, was made to the British parliament; but the opposition was so strong, that the advocates of the planters were forced to yield, and peace was subsequently restored on equitable conditions.

9. (A.D. 1773.) Ireland and Scotland were, about this

time, drained of a large portion of their peasantry, driven to emigration by the cruel rapacity of the landlords; the exiles sought an asylum in America, and supplied that country, at the moment it was about to commence its great struggle for independence, with a hardy population, animated by the most bitter feelings of resentment against the country which they had been forced to abandon.

10. The voyages of discovery undertaken during the early part of this reign were very creditable to the administration by which they were sent out. Captain Phipps made an ineffectual effort to discover a north-west passage to the East Indies; Byron, Wallis, Carteret, and Cook successively navigated the globe, and discovered several new islands in the Pacific Ocean. The last-named navigator was killed, during his third voyage, at Owhyhee, in an unfortunate dispute with the natives.

11. The determination of the Americans to use no articles on which a duty was levied by the British parliament was still obstinately maintained, and the presence of the British troops in Boston kept alive those feelings of animosity which more conciliatory conduct might have extinguished. In resisting a violent act of aggression, a party of the military were compelled to fire on the populace, of whom three were killed and five dangerously wounded. The townsmen assembled on the following night, and were with much difficulty prevented from proceeding to extremities; but on the day that the unfortunate victims were interred, most of the shops in Boston were closed, the bells of all the churches in the town and neighbourhood rung muffled peals; and the funerals were escorted by all the citizens, of every rank, in mournful procession. Captain Preston, who had commanded the party, was tried for murder; and it is highly creditable to the American character, that his defence was intrusted to Adams and Quincy, the most violent advocates of freedom; and that a jury composed of townsmen acquitted the prisoner without hesitation.

12. These proceedings were naturally considered by the provincial governors as strong evidences of a rebellious spirit, and in themselves almost acts of treason; they consequently, in their public and private letters, described them in no measured terms. Mr. Hutchinson, the governor of Massachusetts, and his lieutenant, Mr. Oliver, had written several letters, in which they severely condemned the American leaders, called for the adoption of the most vigor-

ous measures, and even recommended the "taking off" of the most active opponents of government. Of these letters Dr. Franklin obtained possession, and he immediately laid them before the provincial assembly of Massachusetts. The perusal of these documents excited violent indignation; it was unanimously resolved, "that the tendency of the said letters was to overthrow the constitution of this government, and to introduce arbitrary power into the province;" and it was further voted, "that a petition should be immediately sent to the king, to remove Hutchinson and Oliver forever from the government of the province." The petition was immediately transmitted, and Franklin came over to England to support it in person before the privy council.

13. (A.D. 1774.) On the day appointed for hearing the petition, Mr. Wedderburne, the solicitor-general, appeared on behalf of the governor, and assailed Franklin for the treachery of publishing a private correspondence, in one of the most elaborate invectives ever uttered. Less fervid eloquence would have been sufficient to sway the determination of the council; the petition was declared to be scandalous and vexatious, and Franklin was dismissed from the office which he held of postmaster-general of the colonies.

14. The refusal of the Americans to purchase tea had led to a vast accumulation of that article in the storehouses of the East India company; in order to afford them some relief, a drawback of the import duty was allowed them on all tea that should be exported; and the ministry believed that the colonists would gladly pay the small tax of three pence per pound on an article which they could only procure by smuggling, and at an enormous expense. But those who had formed such expectations had sadly miscalculated the spirit and firmness of the Americans; resolutions were adopted in the several provinces, declaring that all who aided or abetted in the landing or vending of the expected tea, should be deemed enemies of their country; and the majority of the consignees, terrified at these proceedings, sent back the cargoes. In Boston, the agents of the company were dependents on the governor, and, trusting to the protection of the military, resolved to persevere; but during the night the leading patriots, disguised as Indians, boarded the vessels, and emptied the tea-chests into the water.

15. The news of this proceeding was received by the British ministry with unmixed pleasure; they thought that Boston, the great focus of American sedition, having been

guilty of a flagrant delinqency, was now completely at their mercy, and they prepared to visit it with exemplary punishment. A bill for shutting up the port of Boston, and another for annulling the charter of Massachusetts, were passed with little opposition; and these harsh measures were soon followed by a third, of a still more dangerous tendency. It enacted, "if any person were indicted for murder or any capital offence, committed in the province ef Massachusetts, in aiding the magistracy, such person or persons might be sent by the governor to some other colony or to Great Britain for trial." It was in vain that Colonel Barré and some others, showed that this measure directly tended to sanction military outrage by the hope of impunity: it passed through both houses with overwhelming majorities and immediately received the royal assent.

16. Nothing could exceed the burst of indignation with which the first intelligence of these harsh measures was received in the New England states. They sternly refused to obey laws which deprived them of their natural and chartered rights, and made active preparations to resist their enforcement. All the other colonies, except Georgia, zealously adopted the cause of the people of Massachusetts, and agreed to discontinue their commerce with Great Britain until the obnoxious statutes should be repealed. To give greater effect to their remonstrances, an assembly of delegates from the different states was organized by Franklin and other provincial leaders, which, under the name of a congress, met in Philadelphia. The congress promised every assistance to the New Englanders, and prepared a spirited petition to be laid before his majesty soliciting a redress of grievances. They also published addresses to the British people, to the Canadians, and to the West Indian colonies, vindicating the purity of their motives, and declaring their fixed resolution not to submit to oppression.

Questions for Examination.

1. Were any changes made in the ministry?
2. Did any remarkable events occur abroad?
3. By what train of events was the right of printing the parliamentary debates established?
4. What remarkable acts of parliament were passed?
5. Did any of the European powers combine to ruin Poland?
6. What revolution took place in Sweden?
7. Did anything remarkable occur in Denmark?
8. What were the circumstances of the Carib war?
9. On what account did emigration to America increase?

10. Were any remarkable voyages of discovery undertaken?
11. What military outrage created a great sensation in Boston?
12. How was the Assembly of Massachusetts placed in open hostility to its governor?
13. How was the Massachusetts remonstrance treated by the privy council?
14. How did the Americans treat the tea exported from England?
15. What vindictive measures were sanctioned by the British parliament.
16. How did the Americans act in consequence?

SECTION IV.

The hostile storms but rage awhile,
And the tired contest ends:
But ha! how hard to reconcile
The foes who once were friends!—Whitehead.

1. (A. D. 1775.) An opportunity of retracting their steps was afforded to the British ministers by the presentation of the petition from the congress at Philadelphia; especially as a new parliament had been summoned in the room of that which had sanctioned the late severe measures of coercion. It was reported that his majesty had received the petition most graciously, and the public consequently indulged in expectations of reconciliation between the colonies and the mother country. These hopes were destined to be disappointed; the house of parliament, in their address to the king at the opening of the session, stated that "a rebellion actually existed in the province of Massachusetts," and in the usual style offered to assist in its suppression with their lives and fortunes. A few members, justly anxious to avert the hazards of war, laboured hard to change the determinations of the minister; in particular Mr. Burke proposed a plan for conciliating America, in a speech of unrivalled eloquence; these efforts were vain, and nothing now remained but an appeal to the sword. Franklin also, having been long employed in a kind of treaty with the ministers, finding them determined to persevere in their insane resolutions, broke off the conference, and sailed for America, resolved to share the fortunes and hazards of his fellow-citizens.

2. The New Englanders were determined to attack the royal forces as soon as ever they should march out of Boston, and their adherence to this resolution was soon put to the test. On the night of the eighteenth of April, a detachment was sent from Boston to seize some military stores, which the insurgents had collected at Concord. In spite of every precaution, the country was alarmed; and when the advanced guard arrived early on the following morning at Lexington they found a small body of provincials prepared

to oppose them. A brief skirmish ensued, in which the Americans were defeated with some loss, and the detachment, proceeding to Concord, destroyed all the stores that they found. But they were not permitted to return unmolested; the militia, assembling in force, furiously assailed their flanks and rear; a constant fire of rifles was maintained from every hedge and every wall which skirted the road; and had not a regiment under the command of lord Percy been sent from Boston to cover their retreat, the entire detachment would have been destroyed. It was late in the evening when the British forces arrived at last within the lines of their own fortifications, having lost 65 killed, 180 wounded, and 28 prisoners.

3. Blood having been thus drawn, the whole of the discontented colonies boldly prepared to maintain the inevitable contest. Volunteers enrolled themselves in every province, and the king's stores were everywhere seized and appropriated to the use of the insurgents. The fortresses of Ticonderoga and Crown Point were surprised by a body of militia, and the Americans thus obtained possession of 100 pieces of cannon and a proportionate quantity of ammunition. The towns and villages in the neighbourhood of Boston were garrisoned, and that city thus placed under a strict blockade.

4. General Gage, who commanded the garrison, soon received reinforcements from Great Britain, under the command of generals Howe, Burgoyne, and Clinton. He resolved therefore to commence active operations; but before committing himself to the chance of war, he issued a proclamation, offering pardon to all who should lay down their arms, except Messrs. Hancock and Adams. The Americans treated the proclamation with contempt, and soon after elected Mr. Hancock president of congress.

5. In Charlestown, a place situated in the North of Boston, is an eminence called Bunker's hill, which in some degree commands the harbour; this post the Americans resolved to occupy; and a party was sent over from Cambridge to intrench themselves on the height. This they effected with such rapidity and silence during one of the short nights of June, that the appearance of their works at daybreak was the first notice of their presence. The importance of dislodging the enemy was evident to the British generals, and a detachment under the command of Howe was sent to the peninsula in boats. A tremendous cannonade was opened

on the provincials from the ships and floating batteries in the harbour, and from Cop's-hill in Boston, but the provincials maintained their post with undaunted resolution. They reserved their fire until the royal forces had advanced within sixty yards of their line, and then poured in so close and murderous a discharge, that the assailants were broken, and fled to the water's edge. A second assault was again defeated by the well-aimed and steady fire of the provincials; but when Howe rallied his men to the third attempt, the ammunition of the Americans began to fail, and, after an obstinate resistance, they were compelled to retreat. In this fierce contest the provincials lost about 450 killed, wounded, and missing; but the victors suffered still more severely; their loss amounted to more than a thousand killed and wounded, of whom 79 were officers. The unusual number of officers that fell is attributed to the fatal aim which the provincials took with their rifles, and to the belief generally prevalent in America, that the war was odious to the great body of the English people, and only supported by the nobility and gentry, from which classes the British officers are generally selected.

6. Another effort to avert the horrors of war was made by the congress, and a second pathetic petition forwarded to his majesty. It was entrusted for presentation to Mr. Penn, a descendant of the great founder of Pennsylvania, and one of the chief proprietors in that province. But public and private remonstrances were equally ineffectual; the petition was not even honoured with an answer.

7. The Americans were far from confining their exertions to the pacific means of petition and remonstrance: with a happy unanimity, they elected George Washington, esquire, commander-in-chief of all their forces; and sent two bodies of militia, under generals Montgomery and Arnold, to drive the English from Canada. After a brief but brilliant career, Montgomery was killed in an attempt to storm Quebec; and the cruelties perpetrated by the infamous Arnold so alienated the Canadians, that no hope remained of its uniting with the revolted provinces.

8. (A. D. 1776.) Boston was closely blockaded by Washington, and the garrison was soon reduced to the greatest distress. Howe, who had succeeded Gage in the command, though a general of great ability, found himself unequal to the difficulties of his situation. The inhabitants of Boston, as well as the garrison, had to sustain the horrors of famine

during the winter: and early in the spring the Americans opened batteries on the neighbouring hills, which swept the town and harbour. Under these circumstances, the town was evacuated by the English, and Washington entering it, was hailed by the citizens as their deliverer. 9. An expedition undertaken by the British against Charlestown, in South Carolina, signally failed. The General (Clinton) was unable to second the naval operations directed by sir Peter Parker; and, after a useless exhibition of bravery, the admiral was forced to retire with the loss of a ship of war, which he burned, to prevent its falling into the hands of the enemy.

10. The Americans, and the greater part of their leaders, had hitherto entertained hopes of peacefully accommodating their disputes with England; but the intelligence that the British minister had hired a body of German mercenaries for their subjugation, wrought so powerfully on their excited feelings, that they determined to renounce their allegiance, (July 4th, 1776.) On the motion of Richard Henry Lee, member for Virginia, the congress published their declaration of Independence, and elected the colonies into free and sovereign states. At the very time that this resolution was adopted, a British fleet was hovering round their coast, a British army was preparing to invade their territories, and symptoms of discouragement and disaffection were perceptible in their own soldiery. Still the congress refused to despair, and prepared to support with spirit the independence which they had so courageously asserted.

11. General Howe did not long remain idle at Halifax, whither he had retired after the evacuation of Boston; he sailed for New York, and being there joined by his brother, lord Howe, with a considerable fleet, he made himself master of that city and Long Island. Following up his triumphs, he expelled the provincial army from the Jerseys and compelled them to take refuge beyond the Delaware. This rapid success raised the hopes of the British to the highest pitch; the immediate conquest of America was looked upon as absolutely certain, and little seemed wanting to complete so desirable a consummation. 12. But they soon found that Washington, though defeated, was not subdued, and that his knowledge of the country in a great degree compensated for his inferiority of numbers. Crossing the Delaware in the middle of December, he attacked a body of Hessians at Trenton, and made 900 prisoners; and

then while lord Cornwallis was advancing to recover Trenton, the indefatigable Americans suddenly appeared in his lordship's rear, and destroyed or captured the greater part of a detachment under colonel Mawhood.

13. A very extraordinary incident took place, about this time, in the East Indies. The council of Madras had plunged the company into an unjustifiable war with the rajah of Tanjore, whom they attacked and took prisoner. Lord Pigot was sent out as a governor, with positive orders to restore the rajah, but he had scarcely effected this object, when he was seized and thrown into prison by certain members of the council. This indignity worked so bitterly on his feelings that he sickened and died, leaving behind him a higher character for honour and integrity than most of those who have made fortunes in the East. His persecutors were subsequently brought to trial and punished, but not with severity proportioned to their deserts.

14. (A.D. 1777.) The caution of Washington prevented any decisive engagement in the early part of the new campaign; but the march of Howe towards Philadelphia induced the American general to hazard a battle. The armies met near the Brandywine river, and after a long and fierce battle the English obtained a decisive victory. Philadelphia was immediately surrendered, and occupied by the English forces: a second attempt made by Washington to retrieve his losses was defeated; and by the aid of the fleet, Howe reduced the fortifications which the Americans had constructed on the banks of the Delaware, and opened free communication with his supplies.

15. But the successes of the English in the southern states were more than counterbalanced by the disaster they experienced in the northern. Early in the year, general Burgoyne, with an army of 7000 men, and a large body of Indians, received orders to advance from Canada into the state of New York, and co-operate with a body of troops which Howe was to send to his assistance. This plan, if successful, would cut off the New England States from the rest of the union, and expose them to be overrun and conquered in detail. Burgoyne's part in this expedition was executed with equal skill and intrepidity; he marched boldly through the country, bearing down all opposition. But the Americans soon assembled an army in his front, and as he had advanced to a distance from his supplies, his situation soon became very hazardous. The operations of

the army, whose assistance he expected, were miserably conducted; sir Henry Clinton did not leave New York till October, and even then, instead of hastening forward to his destination, he employed his troops in burning the unresisting towns and villages, and in devastating the country. Whether this tardiness is to be ascribed to the weakness of the general, or to the insufficiency of the orders sent out by the ministry, is not easily ascertained, but, from whatever cause, it proved the ruin of the entire expedition. On the 14th of October, general Vaughan, with the van of Clinton's army, could have rescued Burgoyne from all his difficulties; but Vaughan stopped to plunder and burn the little town of Æsopus; and before he was again prepared to advance, Burgoyne and his army were prisoners of war to the American army under the command of general Gates.

16. Burgoyne, depending on the advance of the army from New York, had allowed himself to be cooped up in Saratoga; his provisions were exhausted, his ammunition beginning to fail, his troops dispirited, and his lines incapable of long defence. He therefore surrendered on the condition that his troops, after having laid down their arms should be sent home, provided that they should not serve again in America during the present contest. Burgoyne returned to England on his parole only to experience greater mortifications; the leaders of administration threw all the blame of a failure, attributable solely to themselves, on the unfortunate general; he was refused admittance into the presence of the sovereign, denied the justice of a court martial, and subjected to a series of petty persecutions infinitely more disgraceful to the ministry than to their victim. 17. General Gates, after his victory, advanced to check the outrages committed by Clinton's soldiers; sir Henry retreated to New York before the victorious army; and the American general was consequently enabled to send such a reinforcement to Washington's army, as made it once more a match for that of Howe, and sufficient to protect the province of Pensylvania from the ravages of the enemy.

Questions for Examination.

1. How were the hopes of the friends of peace disappointed?
2. What were the circumstances of the affair at Lexington?
3. Did the Americans begin the war vigorously?
4. How was the proclamation of general Gage treated?
5. What were the circumstances of the battle of Bunker's hill?

6. Were any efforts made to restore peace?
7. How did the invasion of Canada terminate?
8. Why was Boston evacuated by the British?
9. Did the expedition against Charleston succeed?
10. Under what circumstances did the Americans publish the declaration of independence?
11. What successes did general Howe obtain?
12. Was Washington dispirited by his losses?
13. Did any remarkable circumstance occur in the East Indies?
14. Where was Washington defeated?
15. What led to the surrender of Burgoyne's army?
16. How was Burgoyne treated?
17. How did Gates use his victory?

SECTION V

Shall Chatham die, and be forgot? Oh no!
Warm from its source let grateful sorrow flow;
His matchless ardour fired each fear-struck mind.
His genius soared when Britons droop'd and pined.—*Garrick*.

1. (A. D. 1778. The event of which ministers had been vainly warned from the commencement of the unfortunate contest into which they had rashly precipitated the country, at length took place. France acknowledged the independence of the United States, and entered into a close alliance with the revolted colonies. Before the news of this treaty could reach America, lord North introduced two conciliatory bills into the British parliament, granting the provincials every thing that they had demanded before their declaration of independence. In the debates that ensued, the minister found some of his former supporters more virulent antagonists than the opposition—they taunted him for deserting the high principles of prerogative and British supremacy which he had hitherto maintained, and complained bitterly of the deception by which he had gained their support. The bills, however, passed the lower house, but their progress through the upper was marked by an incident that must not be carelessly passed over. It was known that the duke of Richmond was of opinion that peace should be purchased even by acknowledging the independence of America, and that he intended to propound these sentiments during the discussion. 2. The venerable earl of Chatham, sinking under the weight of years and bodily infirmities, attended in his place for the purpose of protesting against the dismemberment of an empire to whose greatness he had so largely contributed, and deprecated such a proceeding with great warmth and eloquence. The duke of Richmond having answered this speech, the earl rose to reply; but the powers of nature were exhausted; he fell on the floor of the

house in the attempt to utter his sentiments, and being removed to his favourite country-seat, expired in a short time after. 3. The parliament paid merited honour to the memory of the most successful and able minister that England had hitherto produced; the sum of twenty thousand pounds was granted for the payment of his debts, a pension of four thousand pounds settled on his heirs; his remains were interred with great pomp in Westminster Abbey, and a monument erected to his memory at the public expense.

4. Commissioners had been sent out to propose measures of reconciliation to the Americans when it was too late. Of course, their mission signally failed; the congress would not even listen to terms unless the recognition of their independence formed a preliminary article, and the commissioners, having made an unsuccessful attempt to bribe some of the American deputies, were dismissed with mingled contempt and indignation.

5. The first hostile collision between France and England took place at sea; admiral Keppel attacked a French squadron under the command of D'Orvilliers, but being badly supported by sir Hugh Palliser, the second in command, obtained no decisive success. Advantage was taken of this circumstance by the ministry to crush Keppel, who had been long their political opponent, and, at their instigation, Palliser preferred a charge of misconduct against his commander. But the verdict of the court-martial disappointed their expectations; Keppel was honourably acquitted, and Palliser, being subsequently brought to trial for disobedience to orders, was partially condemned; and, but for the interposition of the entire power of the ministry would have been subjected to a more ignominious verdict.*

6. (A.D. 1779) The Americans, having now obtained so powerful an ally as France, fondly hoped that the war would be terminated in a single campaign. Great, therefore, was

---

*This year a bold adventurer of the name of Paul Jones kept all the western coast of the island in alarm. He landed at Whitehaven, where he burned a ship in the harbour, and even attempted to burn the town. He afterwards landed in Scotland, and plundered the house of the earl of Selkirk He sometime after fought a bloody battle with captain Pearson, of the Serapis, whom he compelled to submit; and so shattered was his own ship in the engagement, that he had no sooner quitted her, in order to take possession of his prize, than she went to the bottom. Captain Farmer, too, of the Quebec, fought a no less desperate battle with a French ship of greatly superior force. He continued the engagement with unremitted fury, till his own ship accidentally took fire, and was blown into the air, together with himself and most of the crew.

their mortification to find the English superior during the entire year. Clinton maintained his defensive position in New York, and baffled all the attempts of Washington to force an engagement; while in the southern states, Georgia was subdued by colonel Campbell, aided by admiral Parker, and the attempts made to recover it by the American general, Lincoln, and the French admiral, D'Estaing, were signally defeated.

7. But the honour of England was not similarly maintained in other quarters: several islands of the West Indies were captured by the French; and the united fleets of France and Spain, for the latter country was now united to the enemies of Britain, swept the channel, and insulted the coasts with impunity. Lord Sandwich, the first lord of the admiralty, was a man notoriously unfit for his situation; but his colleagues, with the blind obstinacy which characterised all their measures, determined to retain him in office; even though they were aware, that, by his neglect, Plymouth was left in such a defenceless state, that its dockyards and arsenal were only saved from destruction by the ignorance of the admirals of the combined fleet.

8. In Ireland an important revolution commenced, which, though it terminated bloodlessly, threatened at one period to have caused a separation between the two oountries. The greater part of the army necessary for the defence of that country had been withdrawn to assist in the subjugation of America; and when the French and Spanish fleets menaced the island with invasion, there were no preparations made for its defence. The people, left to themselves, showed spirit worthy of the crisis. Companies of volunteers were embodied in every town and district; arms were at first cheerfully supplied by the government; officers were chosen by election; and the patriotic earl of Charlemont appointed commander-in-chief of the independent companies. When England recovered her wonted superiority by sea, the fear of invasion was removed, but the volunteers retained their arms and preserved their organization. They had learned the secret of their strength, and were determined to effect the regeneration of their country, by establishing the independence of her parliament and the freedom of her commerce. This was a new and unexpected difficulty to the ministry; but, pursuing consistently their steady course of narrow and illiberal policy, they refused to make any concession, and thus brought Ireland to the very brink of a revolution.

2A

9. (1780.) Holland was soon added to the enemies of England. Mr. Laurens, who had been president of congress, was taken by a British cruiser, and the papers found in his possession fully proved the existence of a treaty between the Dutch and the Americans. War was therefore declared, and thus was England engaged with a fourth enemy without a single ally. About the same time the northern powers of Europe joined in a confederation called the armed neutrality, which was aimed against the maritime claims of England. Its avowed design was to protect the trade of neutral vessels with the several belligerent powers.

10. But the spirit of the English nation sunk not in the apparently unequal contest. Admiral Rodney captured a Spanish convoy, defeated the enemy's fleet, though forced to engage under very disadvantageous circumstances, and relieved Gibraltar, which the Spaniards had begun to besiege. Sailing thence to the West Indies, he dispersed a French fleet far superior to his own. In America, South Carolina was subdued by sir Henry Clinton; and the American general Arnold, believing the independent cause almost hopeless, abandoned his country's cause, and entered into the royal service. The acquisition of this worthless deserter cost the life of one of Britain's best and bravest officers. Major André, adjutant-general of the royal army, having been sent to conduct the negotiation with Arnold, was seized within the American lines, and hanged as a spy, by a rigid interpretation of the laws of war.

11. The ministry had hitherto found the parliament well disposed to support their measures; but the number of petitions presented from the counties and leading towns against the administration, soon raised up a formidable opposition. (April 7th.) At length Mr. Dunning moved his celebrated resolution, "that the influence of the crown has increased, is increasing, and ought to be diminished," which was carried by a majority of twenty-eight votes; but a second resolution, designed to give effect to the former, was rejected by a majority of fifty-one, and the ministry soon after recovered their wonted superiority.

12. Some of the penal laws against the Roman catholics were wisely repealed by the parliament; but in consequence of the exertions of some misguided bigots, these measures were followed by the most formidable riots that ever dis-

graced the metropolis. (June 2.) An immense multitude assembled in St. George's-fields, to petition for a repeal of the laws that had been passed in favour of the Roman catholics, and, after adopting several resolutions, proceeded in large parties to the avenues leading to the house of commons, where they insulted several of the members. Lord George Gordon, a visionary enthusiast, came out and made a violent harangue to the multitude, informing them that their petition had been rejected. The irritated mob at once proceeded to acts of violence; they destroyed all the Romish chapels in and about town; they burned the prisons of Newgate, the King's Bench, and the Fleet, together with several private houses; they even threatened the bank, which was preserved with difficulty. At length the military were called out, and the rioters dispersed, though not until two hundred and twenty of their number had been killed or mortally wounded.

13. (1781.) The campaign which decided the question of American independence seemed at its commencement to promise a far different termination: Washington's army was so distressed that 1500 troops deserted his lines; but though they had thus shown their resentment, they refused to listen to any offers from the British generals, and the emissaries sent to seduce them were given up and hanged. Congress, however, exerted itself so successfully, that the distresses of the army were finally relieved, and Washington enabled to commence decisive operations. He at first designed to besiege New York, but, being baffled by the superior forces of sir Henry Clinton, he suddenly resolved to march into the southern states, and overpower lord Cornwallis before Clinton's army could move to his assistance. 14. This decisive operation was crowned with complete success; lord Cornwallis was attacked in Yorktown, by the combined armies of France and America; his lordship made a gallant defence, but two redoubts in his front were carried by storm, his works ruined, his lines swept by the fire of the enemy's batteries, and the effective strength of his garrison diminished by sickness. Under these circumstances, nothing remained but to propose terms of capitulation. He accordingly surrendered to general Lincoln with the same formalities that he had prescribed to that officer eighteen months before at Charleston; and it is remarkable, as a second coincidence, that the

articles were drawn up by lieutenant-colonel Laurens, whose father was still detained as a close prisoner in the Tower of London.

15. These losses were in some degree compensated by the success of our arms in the East Indies, where sir Eyre Coote defeated Hyder Ally, and restored the company's ascendancy. In the West Indies, the island of St. Eustatius was taken from the Dutch, but subsequently re-captured by the French. A desperate engagement also took place off the Dogger Bank between an English squadron, commanded by admiral Parker, and a Dutch squadron, under admiral Zoutman. After a fierce battle, which lasted three hours, the victory remained undecided, and both returned to their respective harbours.

Questions for Examination.

1. What measure did the British ministry propose?
2. Is there anything remarkable in the circumstances of lord Chatham's death?
3. What honours were paid to his memory?
4. How were lord North's commissioners treated by the Americans?
5. In what disgraceful manner was admiral Keppel treated?
6. Did the results of the campaign answer the expectations of the Americans?
7. How was the English navy neglected?
8. What important events took place in Ireland?
9. By what new enemies was England assailed?
10. Did the British obtain any triumphs?
11. What remarkable resolution was carried in parliament?
12. Did any formidable riots occur in London?
13. How was Washington baffled in the beginning of the last campaign?
14. What great triumphs did the Americans obtain?
15. Did the English obtain any successes?

SECTION VI.

For thee, sweet peace, abundance leads along
Her joyous train, and bards awake to song.
Bland's Anthology.

1. (A.D. 1782.) THE American war was now virtually at an end; all rational hopes of reducing the country again under the subjection of Great Britain were abandoned by the great majority of the nation; but the ministry at least manifested the virtue of perseverance, and declared their resolution to carry on " a war of posts." The nation at large was opposed to his insane project; and parliament, yielding to the voice of the people, gradually withdrew its support from the administration. At length, on the motion of general Conway, the house of commons voted " that

whoever advised his majesty to the continuation of the American war, should be considered as a public enemy." This of course led to the resignation of lord North; and a new ministry was formed under the auspices of Mr. Fox and the marquis of Rockingham.

2. Negotiations for peace were immediately commenced, nor were any of the belligerent powers disinclined to an accommodation. The United States, having secured their independence, had nothing to gain by a continuance of the war; the navy of France, after being severely crippled during the contest, was at its close almost annihilated by a victory which admiral Rodney gained over count de Grasse, in the West Indies, on the 12th of April; and the Spaniards, after having besieged Gibraltar, and wasted before its walls an incredible quantity of blood and treasure, had the mortification to find all their efforts fail, their grand attack signally defeated, and the floating batteries, which they had deemed irresistible, burned to the water's edge, by a tremendous storm of hot balls and shells poured on them by the gallant garrison.

3. Wilkes took advantage of the altered spirit of the times, and procured the removal of all the resolutions concerning the Middlesex election from the journals of the house of Commons; after which this celebrated demagogue sunk into complete insignificance. In Ireland, the parliament, roused by the fervid eloquence of Mr. Grattan, obtained from the new ministry the concession of their legislative independence. Immediately after which, the Irish house of commons voted a sum of £50,000 to purchase an estate for Mr. Grattan, as a reward for the services which he had rendered his country.

4. But while the new administration was exerting itself for the reformation of abuses at home and the establishment of peace abroad, it was suddenly dissolved by the death of the marquis of Rockingham. The earl of Shelbourne was appointed premier, which so displeased Mr. Fox and his friends that they immediately resigned. The noble lord did not long retain his place. Mr. Fox, to the utter astonishment of the entire nation, entered into a coalition with lord North, whom he had so long and so bitterly opposed. Their united parliamentary influence was irresistible; and they forced themselves into the royal councils in spite of the secret dislike of the king and the open disgust of the nation.

5. (A. D. 1783.) The success of the coalition was of short

duration. Immediately after concluding the peace with France and America, Mr. Fox introduced a bill for regulating the government of India, which his influence carried through the house of Commons, notwithstanding the most vigorous efforts of the company and its servants. But in the lords the opposition was more effectual, the king himself avowed his hostility to the measure, and it was finally rejected by a considerable majority. The ministry, appearing unwilling to resign, were summarily dismissed, and a new administration formed, of which Mr. William Pitt, the second son of the earl of Chatham, was the most conspicuous member.

6. (A. D. 1784.) Parliament at its meeting exhibited the unusual spectacle of ministers in a complete minority. To carry on the public business under such circumstances was, of course, impossible, and no sooner were the supplies voted than the parliament was dissolved. The coalition had given such general offence to the nation, that the new ministry obtained a decisive majority in the new house of Commons. Mr. Pitt's India Bill, which was less violent, but also less effective, than that of Mr. Fox, was passed triumphantly; and an act for restoring the Scotch estates forfeited in 1745, went through both houses without opposition, and received the royal assent.

7. (A. D. 1785.) Mr. Pitt, pursuant to the promises he had so often made, brought forward his motion for a reform in parliament. His plans were very judicious and well arranged, but they were rejected by a considerable majority, not, as was generally suspected, without his tacit consent.

8. (1786.) The south-western coast of New Holland affording several favourable spots for colonization, it was resolved to transport convicts thither, and give them an opportunity of retrieving their characters and reforming their manners in another hemisphere. About the same time a maniac, named Margaret Nicholson, made an effort to assassinate the king as he was alighting from his carriage. She was immediately seized; and, her insanity being fully proved, she was sent to Bethlehem hospital, where she remained safely guarded but unmolested.

9. (1787.) Mr. Sheridan, aided by Mr. Burke, Mr. Fox, and several others, brought forward a motion for the impeachment of Warren Hastings, late governor-general of India, for high crimes and misdemeanours in the execution of his office, which passed with but little opposition. The

consequent trial before the house of lords lingered out during the seven succeeding years, and ended in the acquittal of the accused.

10. A strong party in Holland, secretly supported by the French court, violently opposed their stadtholder, the prince of Orange, and disregarded the remonstrance made by England in his favour. The dispute would probably have rekindled a general war, had not the king of Prussia, enraged at an insult offered to his sister, sent a large army into Holland, which soon restored the authority of the stadtholder, and crushed the powers of his opponents.

11. (1788.) While the nation was enjoying profound repose, and silently repairing the losses incurred in the American war, the country was suddenly astounded by the news that his majesty had been attacked by a severe illness, which incapacitated him for discharging the duties of government. Mr. Fox insisted that the regency of right belonged to the prince of Wales; Mr. Pitt as vehemently asserted that parliament alone could provide for such an emergency. (1789.) After some very warm debates, it was finally resolved that the prince of Wales should be declared regent, subject, however, to certain restrictions, and the custody of the king's person should be intrusted to the queen, assisted by a council. The parliament of Ireland came to a very different decision: they decreed the regency of their country to the prince of Wales, without any restrictions whatsoever. This difference between the two parliaments would probably have led to fatal consequences but for the unexpected recovery of the king. His majesty's restoration to health diffused universal joy through the kingdom, and was celebrated by more universal and splendid illuminations than any previously known.

12. (1790.) A dispute took place between England and Spain about the possession of Nootka Sound, on the northwest coast of America, where the English had planted a small colony, which the Spaniards had seized, and made the settlers prisoners. An armament was prepared with astonishing rapidity, but at the expence of three million sterling: Spain, however, was unprepared for war, and all disputes were finally adjusted by an equitable convention.

13. While the country was thus respected abroad, and enjoying profound peace at home, events were occurring in a neighbouring nation which soon involved England in a long, expensive, but not inglorious war; and produced a de-

cisive change in the aspect of Europe, all whose effects are probably not yet developed.

Questions for Examination.

1. How was the American war finally terminated?
2. Why were all parties inclined for peace?
3. What circumstance showed the altered spirit of the times?
4. How was the ministry broken up?
5. Did the coalition ministry long continue?
6. How was Mr. Pitt's power strengthened?
7. What important motion made by Mr. Pitt was defeated?
8. Was any attempt made on the king's life?
9. Is there any thing remarkable in the trial of Warren Hastings?
10. What disturbances took place in Holland?
11. To what disputes did his majesty's illness give rise?
12. What arrangements were made respecting Nootka Sound?
13. What was the state of the country at this time?

SECTION VII.

Religion—freedom—vengeance—what you will,
A word's enough to raise mankind to kill ;
Some factious phrase by cunning caught and spread,
That guilt may reign, and wolves and worms be fed.—Byron.

1. No event of equal importance with the French revolution is recorded in history, and there is no subject which has given rise to such diversity of opinion. Its causes, its consequences, even the simple facts that occurred in its progress, are to this hour matters of keen and violent debate, nor can an impartial narrative be expected while many of the actors are still alive, and while the impulse then given continues to be felt in every part of Europe. It is undeniable that the form of government established in France sadly required amelioration; the privileges of the nobles were tyrannical and oppressive, and they were exercised with strict severity; the conduct of the clergy was far from being in accordance with the principles of that holy religion which they professed; the prodigality of the court was extreme; the criminal laws were unjustly constituted, and worse administered; the government placed in the hands of nobles equally ignorant and indolent; nor was there a single office, civil or military, open to the most superior merits, unless aided by the possession of high birth and titled name. These were evils poorly compensated by the private virtues of the hapless sovereign, who came to the throne of France at the moment when the accumulated evils of centuries had nearly reached their consummation. 2. While the higher classes were sunk in luxury and sloth, the lower ranks, in a state

of ignorance and degradation, and goaded on by misery, were ready to second every movement, and to join in every excess. In the middle classes, the elements of strife were even more thickly sown; they were irritated at the contempt shown them by their haughty superiors, they were indignant at seeing the doors of preferment closed against the exertions of honourable ambition, and their minds were debauched by the perusal of the speculative treatises on "the rights of man," which, despite of every restriction, daily issued from the press, and which, with very few exceptions, advocated principles subversive of all religion, and consequently of all good government.

3. The American war precipitated a revolution, which probably could not have been much longer delayed. The French soldiers, while fighting in the cause of American freedom, naturally imbibed the principles of their allies, and diffused them over the country on their return home; the royal exchequer, which had been nearly exhausted by the profligate extravagance of the former reign, was totally ruined by an expensive war, and the country was on the very eve of a national bankruptcy. When a variety of expedients, most of which made matters worse, had been tried in vain, the king determined to convoke the states-general, which had not been assembled since 1614, and they accordingly met at Versailles on the 5th of May, 1789.

4. After some angry debates, it was determined that the three orders of the clergy, the nobles, and the commons, should meet in one body, an arrangement which threw all the power into the hands of the popular party. They assumed the name of the national assembly, and immediately commenced a total change in the constitution of their country. Feudal privileges and titles were abolished; local division set aside; and the country distributed into departments instead of provinces, for the purpose of adopting a uniform system of taxation; monastic institutions were suppressed, and the English system of trial by jury substituted for the administration of justice by the old provincial parliaments.

5. Such an extensive alteration naturally disgusted the court and the nobility. Unable to conceal their hostility to the new measures, they exposed themselves to popular indignation, and, dreading the consequences, the Count d'Artois (afterwards Charles X.), the prince of Condé, and several others, emigrated. But this flight aggravated the jealousy

of the people; the Parisian mob stormed the fortress of the Bastile, the state prison of France, and levelled it with the ground; they next formed a national guard, composed entirely of citizens, at the head of which was placed M. de la Fayette; and at length a furious mob advanced to Versailles, and brought the king and royal family in triumph to the capital.

6. (1791.) The progress of the revolution in France was anxiously watched by two powerful parties in England, who viewed it with very different feelings. While one party looked upon it as the triumph of liberty, the administration and a large portion of the aristocracy regarded it as the triumph of anarchy over all legitimate authority. Nor were such feelings confined to the higher classes: the populace shared largely in the hatred to the new politics of France. A dinner to celebrate the capture of the Bastile was adjourned in London through dread of popular resentment; but in Birmingham a festive meeting to commemorate the same event was dispersed by a furious mob, which subsequently proceeded to destroy the dissenting chapels, and the houses of all who were supposed favourable to the French revolution.

7. (1792.) The principal powers on the continent having entered into a treaty to check the progress of the French revolution, it was obvious that war could not long be delayed; but the interference of the monarchs precipitated the events which they wished to prevent. The duke of Brunswick, as commander-in-chief of the allied armies, issued an ill-judged and sanguinary manifesto, which, with some suspicious circumstances in the conduct of the king and queen, so exasperated the French, that all the power of the state was thrown into the hands of the jacobins, as the most violent republicans were called. The consequences were dreadful: the palace of the king was stormed, his guards massacred, himself and family confined as close prisoners, and royalty finally abolished in France. Ere yet the world recovered from its astonishment at these events; it learned, with equal surprise and indignation, that the unfortunate king had been brought to trial by his subjects, and condemned to death by a majority of votes. This iniquitous sentence was executed on the 21st January, 1793.

8. While France was thus distracted, England was quietly enjoying the blessings of peace, and the parliament engaged in the advancement of measures equally salutary

The Duke of York at the surrender of Valenciennes.

and judicious. Several taxes that were pressed on commerce and industry were repealed; a bill introduced by Mr. Fox to make juries in cases of libel judges of law as well as fact, was passed; some further concessions were made to the Roman catholics; but Mr. Wilberforce's motion for the abolition of the slave-trade was lost by a considerable majority. 9. In the East Indies, Tippoo Saib (son of Hyder Ally), who seems to have inherited his father's hostility to England along with his dominions, was completely subdued by lord Cornwallis, and forced to purchase peace by the cession of a large portion of his dominions, and the payment of an enormous sum, for the performance of which his sons were given as hostages.

10. (1793.) The atrocities committed by the French jacobins completed the alienation of the British people from the cause of the new revolution; and the ministry, now certain of popular support, adopted several measures which left their hostility no longer doubtful. The national convention immediately declared war against the king of Great Britain and the stadtholder of Holland, intimating by this artful phraseology that the people of these countries had an interest distinct from their respective sovereigns. 11. It is certain that this declaration of war, if not directly provoked, was by no means unacceptable to the British ministry, and the great body of the aristocracy by which it was supported. Immediately after its appearance, the duke

of York was sent to join the allied armies in the invasion of France; but the invaders, though at first successful, having taken Valenciennes, soon suffered some severe checks; and at the end of the second campaign were totally defeated by the republicans. The fortified harbour of Toulon having been surrendered to the English, the French government made the most strenuous efforts for its recovery. These proved for a time abortive, until the direction of the siege was intrusted to Napoleon Bonaparte, who now for the first time appeared on that scene where he afterwards played so conspicuous a part. By his exertions the English were compelled to evacuate the town, leaving the greater portion of the citizens exposed to the sanguinary vengeance of the irritated republicans.

12. (1794.) To compensate for this ill success by land, the British navy established its wonted pre-eminence in a victory gained by earl Howe over the French fleet in the West Indies; and several of the colonies belonging to France were about the same time conquered with little trouble. 13. The domestic occurrences of this period, though not very numerous, were not deficient in importance; Messrs. Hardy, Horne Tooke, and others, were brought to trial at the Old Bailey on a charge of high-treason, and acquited, after a patient investigation, which lasted several days. That they desired to effect a great change in the constitution of the country was acknowledged by the prisoners themselves; but it was clearly proved that they wished to obtain reform only by legal and constitutional means, and that they were opposed to violence and insurrectionary movements. The ministers succeeded better with similar prosecutions in Ireland and Scotland, where several persons were found guilty of sedition, and sentenced to several degrees of punishment.

14. (1795.) The ill success of the war induced many of the continental sovereigns to make peace with the French republic. The grand-duke of Tuscany set the example, and was followed by the king of Spain, the Swiss cantons, and the regent of Sweden. The king of Prussia only waited until he had received the English subsidy, and then signed a treaty with the power he had been paid to oppose. The people of Holland expelled the stadtholder, and, erecting in their country what they called a Batavian republic, became virtually a province of France. In short, England had scarcely an ally remaining but Austria, and the con-

tinued friendship of that power was never a matter of certainty. 15. The English navy obtained some triumphs, especially a brilliant victory under lord Bridport, at Port l'Orient; but an expedition undertaken by the French emigrants, under the auspices of the British ministry, was signally defeated.

16. Symptoms of discontent, almost amounting to disaffection, began to be manifested in various parts of the empire; the successes of the war had been few and of little value, but had they been still more decisive they would not have compensated for the distress occasioned by unprecedented taxation. The people of London suffered severely from the interruption of commerce; and some of the lower class, irritated by their protracted misery, assailed the king's carriage when his majesty went in state to the house of lords. This outrage served, however, to strengthen the administration; for the parliament, indignant at the outrage offered to the sovereign, sanctioned several bills for the suppression of sedition,—bills perhaps rendered neccessary by the peculiar circumstances of the period, but which greatly diminished the limits of British freedom. 17. The prince of Wales, in order to procure the payment of his debts, married his cousin, the princess Caroline of Brunswick. We must once again refer to this unfortunate union; it is sufficient to say here, that a daughter was born in the beginning of the following year, soon after which the parents were finally separated.

18. (1796.) The Dutch and Spaniards, having joined their forces to those of the French, were now become enemies of Great Britain; and this country, from being an accessory, was now a principal in the war. Several of the Dutch settlements in the East Indies were subdued, but England lost the island of Corsica, which had been formally placed under British protection a few years previously. The Austrians were almost driven out of Italy by the French under Napoleon Bonaparte, whose brilliant career began now to excite the attention of Europe. A fruitless effort to terminate the war by negotiation was made by the British ministry. It failed because probably it never was intended to succeed.

19. (1796.) The enormous expenses which Great Britain had to sustain were found to have exhausted the resources of the country so much, that at length the bank stopped payment; and an issue of paper-money was of course the consequence. Two alarming mutinies broke out in the

navy; that at Spithead was settled by giving the seamen additional pay, but that at the Nore was not quelled without bloodshed, and the execution of some of the ringleaders. 20. But England still maintained her naval renown; a brilliant victory was gained by Sir John Jarvis over the Spanish fleet, of Cape St. Vincent, and an equally glorious triumph was obtained over the Dutch by admiral Duncan, at Camperdown. 21. Our ally had not equal fortune: Austria was everywhere defeated, and to escape total ruin was obliged to submit to the terms of peace, which Bonaparte dictated at Campo Formio.

Questions for Examination.

1. What was the state of France at the commencement of the revolution?
2. In what dangerous circumstances were the different orders of society?
3. How did the American war precipitate a revolution?
4. What triumphs were gained by the popular party at the meeting of the states-general?
5. Did these alterations produce any important results?
6. In what manner was the French revolution regarded in England?
7. What consequences were produced by the duke of Brunswick's proclamation?
8. What was the state of England at this time?
9. Were any important advantages gained in the East Indies?
10. How did the war commence?
11. What reverses did the English experience?
12. By what naval triumphs were these compensated?
13. Did any important trials occur at this time?
14. How did the allies of England behave?
15. Where was lord Bridport victorious?
16. How did the people of England show their discontent?
17. What royal marriage was contracted at this time?
18. In what manner was the war conducted?
19. Did any dangerous events occur in England?
20. How did the English navy behave?
21. Where was peace made between France and Austria?

SECTION III.

O Frantic thirst of glory and of fame!—*Mickle.*

1. (A. D. 1798.) The restoration of the legislative independence of Ireland in 1782 was far from satisfying the expectations formed by a considerable party in that country. Reform in parliament, and a repeal of the remnant of the penal laws against the Roman catholics, were rather demanded as a right than craved as a boon; and when the government refused to make concessions, the majority remained sullen and discontented, while a few wilder spirits

meditated a total separation from England, and the establishment of an Irish republic after the example of France. The lower classes were easily induced to adopt schemes that flattered their national pride; and though government, having received timely information, arrested the principal leaders, disaffection was too extensive to be thus checked, and several counties broke out into open insurrection. After a sanguinary struggle, disgraced by several atrocities on both sides, the revolters were everywhere defeated; and on the surrender of a small body of French who had been sent to aid the insurgents, peace was finally restored by the judicious and merciful measures of lord Cornwallis.

2. In the meantime, Napoleon, with a large fleet and army, proceeded to Egypt, and on his voyage obtained possession of Malta by the treachery of the knights. The career of the French invader was sufficiently triumphant in Egypt, but his hopes of permanent success were sadly blighted by the loss of his fleet, over which admiral Nelson obtained one of the most complete victories recorded in the annals of war. 3. This brilliant triumph was obtained in Aboukir Bay, one of the mouths of the Nile, on the first of August; nine sail of the line were taken; two more and a frigate either burnt or blown up during the action, and only two escaped, which, however, were subsequently captured. Soon after, Bonaparte was repulsed before Acre' chiefly by the heroic exertions of Sir Sidney Smith; and having at the same time received news from France that seemed to open safer and brighter objects, he secretly returned home, and soon effected a revolution, by which he placed himself at the head of the government, with the title of first consul.

4. The first measure taken by Napoleon after his elevation, was to send a letter to the king of England offering peace. This was instantly rejected; for a new and powerful coalition had been formed against France, from which the most splendid success was anticipated. But this coalition soon fell to pieces; the Russian emperor withdrew his forces; the duke of York was forced to quit Holland with his army on finding the population indisposed to second his efforts; and the French, under the new government, displayed even more energies.

5. In the East Indies the English waged a successful war against their old enemy Tippoo Saib; his capital was taken by storm, himself slain, and all his treasures divided among the conquerors. Since that period the entire peninsula of

India has been virtually subjected to the authority of the English.

6. (A. D. 1800.) Austria had again commenced war against France, and was maintaining it with characteristic obstinacy, when Napoleon brought it to a sudden close by one of those master-strokes of genius which baffle ordinary calculation. He led his army across the Alps into Italy in despite of the most appalling difficulties, and obtained a complete victory at Marengo. A subsidy from England induced the Austrian emperor to continue his resistance; but the battle of Hohenlinden placed him completely at the mercy of the conqueror, and he was forced to solicit terms of peace.

7. The question of a legislative union with England, which had been previously negatived in the Irish house of commons, was finally carried by the ministry. It was determined that from the 1st of January, 1801, there should be but one imperial parliament for the British Islands, in which Ireland should be represented by four spiritual peers, taken in rotation every session, twenty-eight temporal peers chosen for life, and one hundred commoners elected in the usual manner.

8. (1801.) Paul, emperor of Russia, not satisfied with deserting the alliance of England, became her bitter enemy, and persuaded the other northern powers to revive the hostile confederation, called the armed neutrality. After negotiation had been tried ineffectually, a fleet was sent against Copenhagen, under the command of admiral Parker, assisted by lord Nelson. After having passed the Sound with little difficulty, Nelson attacked, and almost annihilated the formidable lines of the Danish defence; but some of his own ships having grounded in a situation exposed to the fire of the hostile batteries, he took advantage of his previous success to offer terms of accommodation, which were immediately accepted. It is probable that the war might have been again renewed, had not intelligence been received of the deposition of the emperor Paul, who had been the head of the confederacy. His son and successor, Alexander, was anxious to be on good terms with Great Britain; and the minor states found themselves obliged to imitate his example.

9. An expedition, under the command of Sir Ralph Abercrombie, was equally successful in expelling the French from Egypt; but that distinguished officer fell in the arms of

victory. The French, having been defeated at Alexandria, offered terms when general Hutchison was preparing to besiege them in Cairo, and evacuated the country pursuant to the articles of capitulation. 10. Before the news of this success arrived in England, the country had been threatened with an invasion. Troops were collected along the coasts of France and Holland, and vessels prepared for their transportation in the harbours along the channel. Lord Nelson was sent with a flotilla to attack Boulogne, the enemy's principal rendezvous, but failed after two brilliant efforts. The bravery, however, displayed by the British sailors, and the manifest superiority of England by sea, convinced Napoleon that the enterprise was hopeless, and the project was soon laid aside.

11. Both the belligerent powers were now heartily tired of a war, which exhausted their resources, and conferred advantages on neither. In deference to the general wish, a change of ministry was effected in England; Mr. Addington (afterwards lord Sidmouth) became premier in place of Mr. Pitt, and negotiations instantly commenced. (1802.) The terms were soon arranged, and a peace was concluded at Amiens, which cannot be better described than by the words of an eminent statesmen, "it was a peace at which everybody rejoiced, but of which nobody could be proud."

12. From the moment in which the treaty of peace was signed, jealousies and discontents daily arose in France and England, which threatened to produce fresh hostilities at no very distant period. Bonaparte, having been appointed first consul for life, used every exertion to enlarge dominions of which he was in now all but name the sovereign; he aggrandized France by the annexation of Piedmont to its territories, and had given even greater offence by invading Switzerland. On the other hand, the first consul complained that England still retained possession of Malta, which, by the terms of the late treaty, should have been restored to the knights, and remonstrated against the virulent libels on his character, which were published in the English newspapers, as he believed, with the connivance of government. (A.D. 1803.) These mutual bickerings soon produced more angry demonstrations. Lord Whitworth, the English ambassador, having been treated with unmerited indignity, withdrew from France, and war was soon after proclaimed.

13. A short time previous to the recommencement of hostilities, a conspiracy for the subversion of the government

was detected in England. It was formed by a colonel Despard, who fancied that government had treated him with unjust neglect; his associates were desperate men of the lowest ranks, and nothing could be more wild or inadequate than the means by which they proposed to execute their insane projects. 14. The execution of the principal conspirators restored public confidence; but in a few months the alarm was again renewed by the account of an insurrection having broken out in Dublin. The leader of the revolt was Robert Emmet, a young man of the most amiable qualities, but a wild and visionary enthusiast. The insurgents were badly armed and worse disciplined; they were consequently subdued with little difficulty, but not before lord Kilwarden and his nephew had been murdered by the infatuated mob.

15. Napoleon recommenced the war with great vigour; his troops overran Hanover, and compelled the princes in the north of Germany to close their ports against the English. On the other hand, the British navy blockaded the mouths of the principal rivers from which British traders were excluded; and they captured several French colonies. The English having made prizes of many French merchant-ships and treated their crews as prisoners, Bonaparte seized on all the English visitors who were travelling in France and detained them as hostages. 16. About the same time, the French army, which had been employed to suppress the revolt of the negroes in St. Domingo, being cut off from all supplies by the British cruisers, was forced to surrender, and the island has since remained an independent state, under the name of Hayti. The threats of invading Britain were repeated; but after a vain display of force on both sides, no efforts were made to put the threats in execution.

Questions for Examination.

1. What calamitous event occurred in Ireland?
2. Whither did Napoleon lead his new armament?
3. How was the progress of the French in Egypt checked?
4. What was Napoleon's first attempt when appointed consul?
5. Did the English obtain any triumph in the East Indies?
6. Where was the power of Austria overthrown?
7. What important change was made in the government of Ireland?
8. How did England escape the dangers threatened by the armed neutrality?
9. By whom were the French driven from Egypt?
10. What events were produced by the threats of invasion?
11. How was a peace effected?
12. Did the peace promise to be permament?

13. What conspiracy was discovered in England ?
14. Was there not a new attempt at insurrection in Ireland ?
15. How did the war commence !
16. Of what island were the French deprived ?

SECTION IX.

*Aye, at the hour of utmost need
Thy statesmen fall, thy warriors bleed;
The vigorous mind, the valiant hand,
Desert at once the mourning land.—Cook.*

1. (A.D.) 1804). THE administration of Mr. Addington having failed to give satisfaction to the nation, he resigned, and was succeeded by Mr. Pitt, who immediately devoted all his energies to the formation of a new coalition, against France. In this labour he was not a little assisted by the general indignation which was excited by the unprincipled murder of the duke of Enghien. This unfortunate young prince was seized by the emissaries of Bonaparte in a neutral territory, dragged to the castle of Vincennes, subjected to the mockery of a trial before a military tribunal, and shot in the ditch of the castle by torch-light. Immediately after the perpetration of this crime, Bonaparte was proclaimed emperor of the French and king of Italy; but the assumption of the latter title gave great offence to Austria, whose claims on Italy were thus contemptuously disregarded.

2. One ally, however, was ensured to France by an act of questionable policy on the part of England. Spain having entered into a treaty with Napoleon, the British minister determined to intercept the treasure-ships from South America, without waiting for the formality of a declaration of war. Three of these vessels were intercepted by the British squadron, two were taken, but the third unfortunately blew up, and the greater part of the crew perished. The Spanish court, on hearing the news, immediately proclaimed itself the enemy of Great Britain.

3. (A.D. 1805). The naval triumphs of England were consummated by the almost total annihilation of the hostile fleets. The French ships of war in Toulon, having baffled the vigilance of the blockading squadron, effected a junction with the Spanish fleet at Cadiz, and sailed for the West Indies. Hither they were pursued by lord Nelson; but having heard of his approach, the allied admirals returned to Europe. Nelson soon followed, and, after several disappointments, had at length the satisfaction to discover the

French, under Villeneuve, and the Spaniards, under Gravina, on the morning of October 21st, drawn up in a double line of battle off Cape Trafalgar. The British navy attacked in two columns, the windward line being led by Nelson, in the Victory, the leeward by admiral Collingwood. After a terrible engagement, which lasted three hours, the English obtained a decisive victory. Nineteen sail of the line, with Villeneuve, and two other flag-officers, were captured; the remainder, under admiral Gravina, fled, but several of them were subsequently taken by a squadron under sir R Strachan. 4. This victory was dearly purchased by the death of Lord Nelson, who had long been the pride of the English navy. He was mortally wounded by a musket-ball in the middle of the action, and died a little before its close. 5. The grief of his country was shown by the honours paid to his memory; his brother was raised to the peerage; a liberal pension settled on his widow; his remains were deposited in St. Paul's cathedral, accompanied by a procession more splendid and magnificent than England had ever witnessed on a similar occasion, and a monument erected at the public expense as a lasting testimony of national gratitude. Rewards were also voted to the companions of his victory; admiral Collingwood was raised to the peerage, and a liberal provision was made for the wounded, and for the families of the slain.

6. The triumphs of France by land amply compensated for her losses by sea. The Austrians were everywhere defeated; the archduke Charles was driven from Italy by Massena; Ulm was surrendered to Napoleon by general Mack, under circumstances that led to strong suspicions of treachery; and, finally, Vienna itself submitted to the conqueror. The junction of the Russians gave a temporary confidence to the Austrian emperor; but his hopes proved fallacious; on the 2nd of December, Napoleon totally defeated the allied armies at Austerlitz, and Austria was necessarily compelled to submit to whatever terms the conqueror thought fit to dictate.

7. (A.D. 1806.) The failure of a coalition which he had taken so much pains to form, and the mortification of seeing his colleague, lord Melville, impeached by the house of commons, preyed on Mr Pitt's health, and, to use a common but expressive phrase, broke his heart. He was honoured with a public funeral, and a monument erected to his memory at the national expense. A new administration was formed under the auspices of lord Grenville and Mr. Fox, one of whose first measures was the final abolition of the slave-trade. Mr. Fox did not long survive his great political rival; he died in the course of the same year.

8. During the late struggle the conduct of the king of Prussia had been marked by singular indecision. Scarcely, however, had Austria been crushed, than, to the great astonishment of the world, it was announced, that Prussia, in a moment of chivalrous enthusiasm, had determined singly to cope with the victorious arms of France. The war was decided in a single campaign; the Prussians were irretrievably ruined at the battle of Jena; fortress after fortress surrendered to Napoleon, and the unfortunate king, stripped of the greater part of his dominions, had now no hope but in the assistance of Russia. 9. (A.D. 1807.) Even this last hope failed, an indecisive battle being fought at Eylau; but the Russians having failed in an attempt to relieve Dantzic, and suffered a total defeat at Friedland, solicited terms of peace. A treaty was concluded at Tilsit, by which the Prussian king was stripped of half his dominions, and had the further mortification to learn that the remainder was spared only in deference to the wishes of the young emperor of Russia.

10. This decisive success enabled Bonaparte to execute the projects which he had so long formed against the com-

merce of England. By the celebrated Berlin decrees, all the continental ports were closed against British manufactures, and Denmark, though long in alliance with England, was forced to comply with the imperious mandate. This led to the adoption of measures by the British government, which could only be justified by the most stern necessity.

11. An expedition, under the command of admiral lord Gambier, and general the earl of Cathcart, was sent to compel the surrender of the Danish fleet, in order that it might be retained as a deposite by England until the conclusion of the war, as Napoleon notoriously designed to have employed it in restoring the navy of France. The demand was peremptorily refused; but the English having bombarded Copenhagen for three days successively, his Danish majesty, to save his capital from total destruction, agreed to the proposed terms; and the whole fleet, consisting of eighteen ships of the line, fifteen frigates, and thirty-one smaller vessels, was given up, together with an immense quantity of naval stores.

12. But the other foreign expeditions undertaken by the English were unusually unsuccessful; Buenos Ayres, after its capture by sir Home Popham, was recovered by the inhabitants, and an armament sent out for its recovery under general Whitelocke failed signally and disgracefully: a fleet under admiral Duckworth forced the passage of the Dardanelles, but, being unable to make an impression on Constantinople, was compelled to retire with loss: Alexandria, in Egypt, was captured by general Fraser, but he was soon compelled to evacuate his conquest; and an expedition undertaken to assist the king of Sweden had an equally inefficient termination.

13. The Grenville administration, which had been very popular at the outset, had now declined considerably in public favour; and it probably had never possessed the full confidence of the king. The ministers having brought forward some measures of concession to the Roman catholics, which his majesty disapproved, were compelled to resign, and Mr. Pitt's friends were recalled to the cabinet.

14. Portugal was now the only part of the continent open to Great Britain, and Napoleon determined that her manufactures should be excluded from this country also. The prince-regent of Portugal, alarmed by the appearance of a powerful French army on his frontiers, promised obedience to the demands of the French emperor; but finding

that every compliance was insufficient to conciliate the invaders, and that the annihilation of his kingdom was intended, he embarked on board the English fleet, and was conveyed to the Brazilian settlements in South America. Immediately after his departure, the French occupied Lisbon without opposition.

Questions for Examination.

1. How did Napoleon excite the resentment of the European monarchs?
2. Why did the Spaniards support the French with all their might?
3. What great naval victory did the English obtain?
4. By what event was the joy for this victory diminished?
5. In what manner did the English nation show its respect for Nelson and his companions?
6. Did the French gain any advantage on land?
7. Why was there a change made in the British ministry?
8. What success had the Prussians in their war against France?
9. By what events was a peace precipitated?
10. What use did Napoleon make of his victory?
11. How did the English act under these circumstances?
12. In what expeditions were the English successful?
13. What circumstances brought about a change in the British ministry?
14. What remarkable events took place in Portugal?

SECTION X.

First from his trance the heroic Spaniard woke,
His chains he broke,
And, casting off his neck the treacherous yoke,
He called on England.—*Southey.*

1. (A. D. 1808.) THE unprincipled occupation of Portugal was followed by a series of transactions still more iniquitous in Spain, which, though at first apparently successful, blighted for ever the character of Napoleon, and contributed not a little to his final overthrow. Seldom have the annals of any country presented such a picture of vice and imbecility as was displayed by the court of Spain at the period which now occupies our attention; the king was a weak and irresolute monarch, destitute of abilities for managing the affairs of state, even in the most tranquil times; and, consequently, wholly unfit to rule at a period when all Europe was convulsed by the consequences of the French revolution. His prime minister, and the virtual ruler of Spain, was Godoy, whom the illicit attachment of the queen had raised from the rank of a private gentleman to guide the national councils, under the proud title of the Prince of the Peace. But Godoy was by no means fitted to discharge the duties of the station to which he had been raised. Possessing neither talent nor principle, he pursued a selfish and

vacillating course of policy, which wasted the resources of Spain, and made the country contemptible in the eyes of all the surrounding nations. 2. Godoy was of course unpopular; the nobility despised him as an upstart; the people regarded him as the author of all the calamities by which they were oppressed; and, at length, reports having been circulated that he intended to remove the royal family to South America, a furious insurrection broke out, which terminated in stripping Godoy of all his authority. Deprived of his only reliance, the imbecile Charles resigned the crown to his son Ferdinand, prince of Asturias, who was at once proclaimed king, to the universal delight of the people. 3. When Napoleon received intelligence of this revolution, he immediately proceeded to Bayonne, in order to be nearer the scene of action, and directed the numerous army, which he maintained in Spain, to occupy Madrid. By means of some obscure intrigues, Charles was induced to withdraw his abdication, and claim the assistance of the French emperor against his rebellious son; while at the same time assurances were privately conveyed to Ferdinand that Napoleon was attached to his cause, and would, if an appeal was made, certainly decide in his favour. 4. By such representations the entire Spanish royal family was induced to cross the frontier; and no sooner were they in the power of the French emperor, than they were severally compelled to abdicate their claims to the crown, which Napoleon was determined to transfer to his brother Joseph.

5. When the iniquitous transactions at Bayonne became known, they filled the mind of every Spaniard with feelings of the deepest indignation; one sentiment seemed to pervade the entire nation,—a determination to maintain the independence of their country, and submit to none but their legitimate sovereign. The French were able to suppress the insurrection at Madrid after a fearful massacre, which is the deepest stain on the character of Murat, by whom the garrison was commanded; but in the provinces, provisional juntos were formed, armies levied, and every preparation made for a vigorous resistance to the usurpers. The garrison of Gibraltar, and the British fleets in the Mediterranean, lent their assistance to the efforts of the patriots, and by their aid the important city of Cadiz was secured, and the French fleet, which lay in the harbour, forced to surrender. 6. The armies of France also met some severe checks; Dupont, with a force of 15,000 men, was forced

to surrender to the patriot general Castanos; Moncey was compelled to retreat from Valencia; and, lastly, a Spanish army, which had been employed by Bonaparte in the north of Germany, revolted, and was conveyed by a British squadron to the peninsula.

7. The flame of insurrection soon spread to Portugal; and though the French generals in that unhappy country endeavoured to suppress the revolt by cruelly massacring all suspected of having shared in the efforts for the liberation of their country, this detestable policy only engendered a more determined spirit of resistance, and a fiercer thirst for vengeance.

8. The news of the events in the peninsula was received in England with the greatest enthusiasm. The Spanish deputies were welcomed with the utmost warmth; all the Spanish prisoners released, clothed, armed, and sent to aid the efforts of their countrymen; munitions of war were supplied to the patriots from the British arsenals; public aids and private subscriptions were liberally contributed for the supply of their exhausted resources; and a well-appointed army under the command of sir Arthur Wellesley, sent to assist in the liberation of Portugal.

9. On the first of August the British troops landed in Mondego Bay, and soon commenced active operations. On the seventeenth, the French were defeated at Rolica; but on the twenty-first, a still more decisive battle was fought at Vimiera, and the English were completely victorious. 10. Unfortunately at this important moment, sir Arthur Wellesley was superseded in his command by sir Harry Burrard, who gave immediate orders to stop the pursuit, thus sacrificing all the fruits of this brilliant victory. On the following morning, sir Hew Dalrymple arrived to take the supreme command, and he entered into negotiations with the French commander. 11. A convention for the evacuation of Portugal was concluded at Cintra, on terms so favourable to the French that they excited universal dissatisfaction. One article provided for the security of the Russian fleet then lying in the Tagus; but this the English admiral, sir Charles Cotton, peremptorily refused to ratify; and the ships were surrendered to him on the condition of being restored in six months after the conclusion of peace with Russia.

12. Portugal being now free from the invader, sir John Moore, who had been appointed to the command of the British army, was directed to advance into northern Spain,

Death of Sir John Moore.

and aid the exertions of the patriots. The instructions sent to the gallant general had been prepared on the faith of the representations made by the Spanish deputies in London; it was not discovered, until too late, that these were wholly unworthy of credit. 13. The resolute spirit of hostility to the French in the lower ranks of the Spaniards was indubitable; but the upper ranks, at the same time ignorant and conceited, were slow to make any exertion, and thought more of securing for themselves some petty authority than joining in efforts for the liberation of their country. Like all weak and vain-glorious men, they were great boasters; they told of countless armies and exhaustless resources; but when the moment of trial arrived, their armies were found to be an undisciplined rabble, and even sometimes to have existed only on paper; their magazines were discovered to be empty, and their boasted preparations to have consisted in doing nothing. Even before sir John Moore had entered Spain, the principal forces with which he had been destined to co-operate were defeated and dispersed, in a great degree by the sheer incapacity of their generals. When sir John Moore found that all the expectations which he had been led to form were utterly groundless, he resolved to return to Portugal; the British minister to the Spanish junta, however, prevailed on him to change his resolution and to hazard an advance into the heart of the country. 14. In the mean time Napoleon himself had arrived to take the direction of the invading army, and the promptitude of his movements soon left the British general no other choice but retreat. The sufferings of the army during this retrograde movement transcend the power of description; discipline was for the most part at an end, and the country they had come to protect was treated by the famished soldiers, as if it had belonged to an enemy. 15. (A.D. 1809.) At length, when they reached Corunna, the enemy was found to have pursued them so close that nothing but a victory or a convention could secure their embarkation. Sir John Moore at once decided to risk the chances of battle: he obtained a victory so glorious as to shade the calamities of the retreat; but unfortunately the success of the army was purchased by the life of its gallant commander.

16. (A.D. 1809.) Taking advantage of the withdrawing of the French troops from Germany to recruit the armies in Spain, the emperor of Austria again determined to encounter the hazards of war, and endeavour to retrieve his former fortunes. But the same fatality which had hitherto attended the military operations of this power, still counteracted its efforts. Napoleon, in a brief but decisive campaign, made himself master of Vienna; and though his army met a severe check at Asperne, he soon after obtained a decisive victory at Wagram, which prostrated the Austrian empire at his feet.

17. But while this contest remained as yet doubtful, the English were fast retrieving their tarnished honour in the peninsula. Sir Arthur Wellesley was sent again to the scenes of his former glory, and succeeded in expelling the French from Oporto, and several other acquisitions which they had made in Portugal after the retreat of Sir John Moore. He even advanced into Spain, and obtained a brilliant victory at Talavera; but being unsupported by the Spanish authorities, he was obliged to relinquish his conquests, and terminate the campaign without obtaining any decisive advantage. For the skill and bravery, however, which had been displayed at Talavera, Sir Arthur Wellesley was elevated to the peerage, with the title of viscount Wellington.

18. To create a diversion in favour of Austria, an expedition was sent to the coast of Holland, under the command of the earl of Chatham and sir Richard Strachan. The fortress of Flushing and the island of Walcheren, were subdued; but the unhealthiness of the climate forced the conquerors to evacuate these acquisitions after the sacrifice

of many valuable lives. It must be confessed that the unfortunate enterprise was badly conceived and badly executed; the armament did not reach the coast of Holland until Austria had been irretrievably ruined; and the main objects of the expedition, the destruction of the French fleet in the Scheldt, and the occupation of Antwerp, were scarcely attempted.

19. There were, however, some gallant exploits performed during the year by the British navy, which contributed to maintain the national courage. A French squadron lying in Basque Roads was attacked by lords Gambier and Cochrane; four ships of the line and three frigates were burned, and several others disabled. Lord Collingwood destroyed, in the bay of Rossa, three sail of the line, two frigates, and twenty transports; Sir James Saumarez captured a Russian convoy in the Baltic; and several important islands were wrested from the French in the West Indies.

20. At home the attention of the public was directed, in no ordinary degree, to a parliamentary investigation into the conduct of his royal highness the duke of York, as commander-in-chief. After a laborious inquiry, the royal duke was acquitted by a great majority, but he deemed it right to resign his situation immediately after. On the 25th of October, a jubilee was celebrated with great splendor through the kingdom on account of his majesty's having entered the fiftieth year of his reign.

Questions for Examination.

1. What was the condition of Spain at this time?
2. What were the consequences of Godoy's proceedings?
3. How did Napoleon act under these circumstances?
4. In what manner were the Spanish king and prince treated by their ally?
5. Did the Spanish people show their indignation?
6. Were any triumphs obtained by the Spanish patriots?
7. What was the situation of Portugal at this time?
8. How was the intelligence of these events received in England?
9. In what manner did sir A. Wellesley commence his victorious career in the peninsula?
10. How were the fruits of his victory lost?
11. What was the convention of Cintra?
12. To what expedition was sir John Moore appointed?
13. With what difficulties had he to struggle?
14. How was he compelled to retreat?
15. By what means was the embarkation of the army secured?
16. What success had the Austrians in their new war against France?
17. For what victory was sir Arthur Wellesley raised to the peerage?
18. In what unfortunate expedition did the English engage?
19. Was this loss compensated by any victories?
20. What delicate investigation took place in England?

SECTION XI.

*United let each Briton join,
Courageously advance;
We'll battle every vain design,
And check the pride of France.*—E. *Thompson.*

1. (A.D. 1810.) THE peace with Austria enabled Napoleon to send forth armies into the peninsula, and the patriots sustained a series of reverses which seemed to have decided the fate of Spain. But it was not in the regular field of battle that the hostilities of the Spaniards were most to be dreaded; their bands of guerillas, that cut off all stragglers, intercepted convoys, and harassed every march, were more formidable than any regular army that could be assembled. The presence of the British in Portugal was justly deemed the principal impediment to the tranquillity of the French in Spain; and Napoleon therefore despatched Massena with overwhelming forces to expel the British from the entire peninsula. The French ruler deemed himself at this time secure on the side of Germany, for he had married the archduchess Maria Louisa, the daughter of the emperor of Austria, having previously divorced Josephine, the faithful companion of all his fortunes.

2. On the approach of Massena, lord Wellington determined to act on the defensive, and resisted every temptation to abandon this cautious line of policy. He retreated leisurely before the enemy until attacked at Busaco, when he turned on his pursuers, and inflicted on them a severe defeat. His lordship then continued his retreat to the impregnable lines of Torres Vedras, where he determined to remain until famine should compel Massena to retire. Nothing could exceed the astonishment of the French marshal, who firmly believed that the British were retreating to their ships, when he found them halted in a position which it would have been madness to attack: he was at once reduced to inactivity, and forced to spend the rest of the campaign in watching the English lines.

3. While the war thus lingered, the death of the princess Amelia, the favourite daughter of the king, spread a gloom over the royal family, and brought on a return of that malady by which his majesty had been previously attacked. The remainder of his life was spent in a state of mental imbecility, and the government of the country was thenceforth intrusted to the prince of Wales, who acted as regent.

4. A little before this event, a strange revolution took place in Sweden, the king was deposed, and his family excluded

from the throne; his uncle was elected in his stead, and as he was childless, the succession was settled on Charles John Bernadotte, one of Napoleon's generals.

5. (A.D. 1811.) The ability displayed by lord Wellington in selecting the lines of Torres Vedras, and the patience with which he waited the progress of events in that formidable position, received at length their merited reward. Hunger and disease made more havoc in the French army than the sword, and Massena soon found that nothing but instant retreat could save him from destruction. In this retrograde movement the French marshal fully maintained his former character for talent; but in every other respect his conduct merits the universal reprobation of posterity. Every crime to which lust and rapine could prompt an unprincipled soldiery, was committed with impunity; the claims of age or sex afforded no protection from murderous outrage; mangled corpses and smoking ruins marked the tract by which these ruffian-warriors retreated from the land where their hopes had been baffled and their pride tamed.

6. After this success, the campaign lingered without any very decisive operation. An attempt was made to recover Badajoz, which the Spaniards had surrendered to the French under very disgraceful circumstances. Soult advanced to relieve the place, and was engaged by general Beresford at Albuera. The battle was fierce and bloody; the English purchased their victory at a very dear rate, and their losses were so great that they were unable to continue the siege which they had undertaken. Massena, to recover his lost fame, attacked the English at Fuentes d'Honore, but met with a severe repulse; he was soon after recalled, and Marmont appointed in his stead. 7. The management of the Spanish armies continued to be intrusted to men, for the most part, ignorant of the first rudiments of their profession. They were frequently defeated in the course of the campaign; but they were incapable of being instructed even by adversity. The English, under general Graham, obtained a brilliant victory at Barossa; but the obstinacy and ignorance of their allies prevented them from reaping the fruit of their success.

8. (A.D. 1812.) The restrictions which had been imposed on the prince-regent being removed, it was expected that some important changes would be made in the administration: none, however, took place at that time; but a sad event in the middle of the year produced a new modification

in the ministry. The premier, Mr. Percival, was assassinated in the lobby of the house of commons by a merchant named Bellingham, who fancied that his just claims had been neglected by government. The murderer was tried at the Old Bailey, and executed; but he seemed to feel little remorse for the horrid crime which he had committed. Lord Liverpool was appointed first lord of the treasury, and Mr. Vansittart chancellor of the exchequer, in the room of the deceased minister.

9. Marmont was even a more unsuccessful rival of lord Wellington than his predecessor Massena; the important fortresses of Ciudad Rodrigo and Badajoz were besieged and stormed before the French marshal could move to their relief, and the forts erected to secure the fords of the Douro were taken almost in his presence. The two armies were several days within sight of each other near Salamanca, without coming to a general engagement: the forces were nearly equal, and the leaders anxiously waited to take advantage of any blunder that might be made by their opponents. At length Marmont made an injudicious movement to his left, in hopes to cut off the British from Ciudad Rodrigo; his line was thus necessarily weakened, and Wellington instantly seized the opportunity to make his attack. The consequence was the total rout of the French, with the loss of fourteen thousand men, killed, wounded, and prisoners. The number of killed and wounded, on the part of the victors scarcely exceeded five thousand.

10. Naturally expecting that the intelligence of this glorious victory would stimulate the Spaniards to more vigorous exertions, and relying on the promise of the British ministry to create a powerful diversion by sending an expedition from Sicily to the south-eastern coast of Spain, Wellington, who had been lately created an earl, resolved to advance into the centre of Spain, and drive the enemy from the capital. This brilliant and hazardous enterprise succeeded; the English were received with enthusiasm in Madrid, and joy was diffused throughout the entire peninsula. 11. But the hopes which were thus inspired proved delusive; the Spaniards made no exertion to second the efforts for their liberation; Ballasteros, one fo their generals, refused to receive any instructions from a foreigner; the force sent from Sicily was, by some blunder of the British ministry, late in time and miserable in amount; the French were, therefore, enabled to threaten Wellington with armies three times

Constitution and Guerrière.

more numerous than his own. Under these circumstances the English general resolved to transfer the scene of his operations to the north of Spain; but having failed in an attack on Burgos, he was compelled to retire to the frontiers of Portugal. During the retreat, the British soldiers sullied their laurels by several outrages, which were severely reprehended by Wellington, and measures taken for their prevention in future.

12. In the meantime the ambition of Napoleon had hurried him into a war with Russia, which, though successful in the outset, ended in lamentable ruin. The French army advanced in spite of every resistance to Moscow, the ancient capital of the kingdom; but there their triumphs ended. The Russians set fire to the city; the invaders, deprived of quarters, were forced to retreat; a severe winter set in, cold and famine destroyed them by thousands, and only a miserable relic of the finest army which had ever been assembled in Europe escaped across the frontiers.

13. Some unfortunate disputes between the governments of Great Britain and the United States led to a war between two countries, which similarity of language and ancient connexion ought to have kept forever in amity. The Americans unsuccessfully invaded Canada, but at sea their frigates obtained some signal triumphs over British vessels,

The first of this series of victories was the capture of the British frigate Guerrière, by the American frigate Constitution, commanded by captain Hull.

14. (A. D. 1813.) The Spanish Cortes became at length convinced of the necessity of giving the command of their armies to the British general, and a complete change in the fortunes of the war followed this judicious measure. By a series of brilliant operations, the French were driven from their several positions on the Ebro and the Douro, compelled to abandon the capital, and at length reduced to the alternative of abandoning the country, or fighting a pitched battle to preserve their conquests. Joseph adopted the latter course, and drew up his forces near Vittoria, which had been made the French depot in the northern provinces. In this position he was attacked by lord Wellington, on the 21st of June, and after a severe contest utterly overthrown. The artillery, baggage, and military chest of the fugitives, fell into the hands of the victors; and so complete was the rout, that the remnants of the defeated army scarcely deemed themselves safe until they had escaped beyond the frontier. Before pursuing them into France, it was necessary to reduce the fortresses of St. Sebastian and Pampeluna, which were immediately invested. The former, after a frightful loss, was taken by storm: the latter surrendered sometime after by capitulation.

15. The reverses of the French in the north of Europe were equally signal. Prussia and Sweden joined their armies to Russia; Austria subsequently joined the alliance, and their united forces obtained a decisive victory over those of the French emperor at Leipsic. The retreat of the defeated army was disastrous in the extreme; the Germans everywhere joined the pursuers, and, after suffering the most severe calamities, Napoleon's army was driven across the Rhine; and it became evident that the next campaign would commence with the invasion of France both on her eastern and western frontier.

Questions for Examination.

1. How was Bonaparte enabled to give his undivided attention to the affairs of the peninsula?
2. In what manner did Wellington act?
3. What remarkable event took place at this time in England?
4. Did any revolution take place in Sweden?
5. How did Massena conduct his retreat from Torres Vedras?
6. Were there any other remarkable events in the campaign?

7. How did the Spanish government behave ?
8. What event caused a change of ministry in England ?
9. What great victory did Wellington gain over Marmont ?
10. How did Wellington endeavour to improve his triumph ?
11. By what circumstances were Wellington's hopes frustrated ?
12. In what new war did Bonaparte engage ?
13. What new enemy assailed the English ?
14. What great victory did Wellington gain over Joseph Bonaparte ?
15. Did Napoleon meet any other reverses ?

SECTION XII.

Oh, more or less than man—in high or low,
Battling with nations, flying from the field ;
Now making monarch's necks thy footstool, now
More than thy meanest soldier taught to yield.—Byron.

1. (A. D. 1813.) THE operations of the allied armies in the south-eastern provinces of Spain were singularly ill conducted. Sir John Murray, to whose guidance they were intrusted, proved totally unfit for his situation. He precipitately commenced the siege of Tarragona, and then abandoned his works and guns with still more disgraceful rapidity; after which he returned to a state of inactivity. 2. But the vigour of Wellington more than atoned for these deficiencies; he crossed the Bidassoa in October, and on the 10th of November defeated Soult's army on the Nivelle. 3. (A.D. 1814.) Winter did not interrupt the operations of the armies. Soult, continually pushed by the British forces, assumed a strong position at Orthes, from which he was driven with severe loss, and Bordeaux was consequently exposed to the invading army. In the meantime the duke d'Angoulême, the representative of the ancient line of French monarchs, had arrived in Wellington's camp; to him the inhabitants of Bordeaux opened their gates, and received with the utmost enthusiasm the descendant of their former kings. Wellington, pursuing his victorious career, again defeated Soult at Toulouse; but while preparing to follow up his victory, news arrived from Paris that Napoleon had abdicated, and the war was at an end.

4. In January, 1814, the allied armies had crossed the Rhine, and advanced into the heart of France ; negotiations for peace were indeed commenced at Chatillon, but the insincerity which marked the conduct of the French commissioners prevented them from coming to any conclusion. Napoleon's great object was to recover Holland, which had achieved its independence after the battle of Leipsic, by the aid of England, and had recalled the stadtholder to his ancient dominions. The French emperor had strong hopes

that one great victory would restore him to his former preeminence. 5. Never in his proudest and most palmy days did Napoleon display more energy and ability than in this his time of difficulty; but he had beaten his enemies into the art of conquering. While he was manœuvring in their rear, the Prussians and Austrians made a rush on Paris, which fell almost without resistance. On the 6th of April, Bonaparte signed the instrument of abdication, and Louis XVIII. was recalled from exile to ascend the throne of his ancestors. The fallen emperor received the island of Elba as an independent sovereignty; the duchies of Parma and Placentia were settled on his wife and son.

6. The return of peace was celebrated with general rejoicings throughout England; and the metropolis was illuminated during three successive nights. Immediately after, the emperor of Russia, the king of Prussia, and a numerous train of other distinguished foreigners came over to England, and met a most magnificent reception. After a short but gratifying visit, they returned to the continent, leaving behind a favourable impression of their urbanity, and of the respect they shewed for the institutions of this country.

7. The American war was soon after terminated; the triumphs and losses on both sides were nearly balanced by land, but the superiority of English courage and discipline at sea was made clearly manifest in every engagement in which ships of equal force on both sides were opposed to each other. The treaty of peace was not signed before December, 1814.

8. (A. D. 1815.) A congress of ambassadors from the leading powers of Europe had assembled at Vienna to settle the state of the continent, when they were astounded by intelligence which threatened to render all their deliberations useless. Bonaparte, wearied of his exile, and invited by numerous partisans in France, sailed from Elba, and, having escaped the vigilance of the cruisers, landed once more in the country which had so long acknowledged his sway. 9. The army everywhere declared in his favour; no effectual resistance was attempted; Louis, with a few friends escaped beyond the Belgian frontier; and in an incredibly short time Bonaparte once more ascended the imperial throne. The allied sovereigns took immediate measures to dethrone a usurper whom experience had shewn to be the common disturber of nations, and a violator of the faith of treaties; and preparations were made for a second invasion of France.

Battle of Waterloo.

10. The English and Prussians began rapidly to concentrate their forces in the newly formed kingdom of Belgium, when Bonaparte, trusting to that activity which had before produced so many triumphs, determined to become the assailant, and rapidly advanced against the Prussians. After a severe contest, Blucher was forced to retire from Ligny; but he accomplished his retreat in good order, and left no trophy to the enemy but the field of battle. This caused a corresponding movement in the English forces, which had advanced to Quatre-bras, and fought a furious but indecisive battle with the enemy. Wellington halted his troops on the memorable plains of Waterloo, and rode across the country to Blucher, in order to concert a plan for their mutual operations.

11. On the 18th of June was fought the memorable battle which may be said to have decided the fate of Europe. Napoleon, believing the Prussians completely broken, hoped, by forcing the British lines, to open a passage to Brussels, and then overwhelm the allies in detail: the object of the duke of Wellington was to maintain his ground until the arrival of the Prussians should give him a decided superiority over his opponents. The efforts of the French to force the British positions were met with most undaunted firmness; the fire of an immense park of artillery, the

charges of the cuirassiers, the attacks of immense columns, failed to break any of the squares which the English had formed; and at length, when night approached, the heads of the Prussian columns were seen advancing to share in the combat. Napoleon assembled his guards for one last and desperate effort; but instead of heading them himself, he gave the command to marshal Ney. The English wings, which had rather declined from the field at the commencement of the flight, had, after the defeat of the former charges gradually come forward, until they formed a concave front to the French. They now poured a dreadful storm of musketry on the heads of the advancing columns; the imperial guards were unable to deploy into line under the heavy fire; they made the attempt and fell into confusion. At this moment the duke of Wellington gave the word to charge, the soldiers rushed forward with resistless impetuosity; some battalions, which Ney had rallied, were broken in an instant; it was no longer a battle, but a rout. The Prussians, who were comparatively fresh, continued the pursuit, and the army of Napoleon was virtually annihilated.

12. The victorious armies now advanced towards Paris without meeting any serious obstacle. On the 22d of June, Napoleon once more abdicated the throne, and fled to the sea-coast, in hopes of making his escape to America. But finding that it was impossible to baffle the vigilance of the English cruisers, he surrendered himself to captain Maitland of the Bellerophon, and was conveyed, with his retinue to an English harbour. When the allies were informed of this event, they decided that he should be sent as a prisoner to the Island of St. Helena, in the Southern Atlantic, and there detained under the strictest observation. In this little island the illustrious exile died on the 5th of May, 1821.

13. Louis XVIII. was restored to his throne without opposition: a few of Napoleon's most zealous partisans, of whom the chief were marshal Ney and colonel Labédoyere, suffered the penalties of treason; but the greater part of the delinquents escaped with impunity. The long wars which had distracted western and central Europe were now terminated, and a tranquillity promising to be of long duration, was established.

Questions for Examination.

1. How were operations conducted in the south of Spain?
2. Did Wellington obtain any success in France?
3. Was not the victory of Toulouse followed up?

4. What operations were undertaken at the north-east side of France?
5. How was the war terminated?
6. In what manner was the return of peace celebrated in England?
7. How was the American war terminated?
8. By what news was the congress of Vienna disturbed?
9. Did Napoleon again become master of France?
10. How was the war recommenced?
11. What particulars of the battle of Waterloo are mentioned?
12. What became of Bonaparte?
13. How was the war finally ended?

SECTION XIII.

*The deeds of those chiefs who fell covered with glory,
Still beam on our record of triumphs and tears :
While the memory of Nelson and Waterloo's story
Are blended by fame with the fall of Algiers.—Fitzgerald.*

1. (A.D. 1816.) It had been hoped, rather than expected, that the exertions made by the people in the different European nations to overthrow the power of Napoleon, would have been rewarded by the sovereigns conceding to them free constitutions. But the monarchs terrified at the evils which the French revolution had produced, were firmly resolved to extend rather than abridge the royal authority.

2. The restored king of Spain, whose slavish weakness had been the first cause of his own imprisonment and his kingdom's degradation, treated with the greatest ingratitude those whose blood had been shed like water to effect his restoration. The inquisition was revived, and every despotic custom, which made the government of Spain infamous, and the country miserable, were re-established in full force. The Spaniards, who entertained liberal opinions, and who had been the most zealous opponents of the French power, were bitterly persecuted, and either brought to the scaffold or driven into exile.

3. This aspect of affairs by no means contributed to allay the dissatisfaction, which pervaded Britain at the termination of the war. The channels of trade, which were only opened by a long course of warfare, were suddenly closed; the manufacturers had no demand for their goods, the prices of agricultural produce were seriously diminished, and all the evils which attend a sudden transition from war to peace were felt the most sensibly on account of the tremendous addition which the expenditure requisite to support such unparalleled exertions had made to the national debt.

4. The marriage of the princess Charlotte of Wales, with Leopold, prince of Saxe-Cobourg, and that of the duke of Gloucester, with his cousin the princess Mary, for a time

averted the gloom which seemed fast spreading over the nation; and a brilliant victory obtained by lord Exmouth over the Algerines, diverted public attention from intestine calamities. 5. Though Algiers was defended by a thousand pieces of cannon, it could not resist the intrepidity of British seamen; its defences were destroyed, its fleet burned in the harbour; and at length, to save it from total destruction, the dey offered terms of peace. He was pardoned on the conditions of liberating the Christian slaves, more than a thousand of whom were received on board the British fleet; of abolishing slavery forever in his dominions; and making reparation to the powers who had been the more immediate objects of his barbarous aggressions.

6. (A. D. 1817.) But even naval glory, always the most pleasing to Englishmen, failed to allay the discontent that pervaded the lower ranks of society; alarming riots occurred in many parts of the kingdom, and meetings were held in the metropolis, where the most threatening discourses were pronounced. The parliament in the crisis passed laws to increase the powers of government, especially the suspension of the Habeas Corpus Act, and several of the popular leaders were arrested. Some were brought to trial in London, and acquitted; but in Derby several were found guilty, and suffered the penalties of high-treason, which had not been inflicted for seventy years before. These vigorous measures, followed by a revival of commerce, and an improved harvest, restored public tranquillity; but the gloom which hung over the nation was not dispelled, and a new event served to deepen it still further. 7. The princess Charlotte of Wales, the pride and darling of England, died, with her child, who would have been heir apparent to the throne. Never was grief more universal—never was a nation's sorrow so deeply felt, and so generally manifested. The day of the funeral was voluntarily observed as a day of fasting and humiliation throughout the three kingdoms; and a stranger, witnessing the affliction on every countenance, might have supposed that every family in the realm had been deprived of one of its most beloved members.

8. (A. D. 1818.) To supply the chasm which this lamentable event had occasioned in the succession to the crown, several of the royal family formed matrimonial alliances. The dukes of Cambridge, Kent, and Clarence, and the princess Elizabeth were united to branches of different princely families in Germany, and such an increase was made in

their revenues by parliament as might enable them to support the additional expenses which they necessarily incurred. These arrangements had not been long concluded, when the royal family suffered a second loss by the death of queen Charlotte, who expired at Kew, on the 17th of November, in the seventy-fifth year of her age.

9. (A. D. 1819.) The extensive colonies which Spain had recently possessed in South America, wearied by the tyranny to which they had been subjected, threw off the yoke, and commenced a successful struggle for independence. The king of Spain, however, imagined that their subjugation was still possible, and assembled an army at Cadiz, in the isle of Leon, to form an expedition against the revolted provinces. But the soldiers who had been thus collected to crush the rising freedom of America, disappointed the hopes of their despotic sovereign. 10. *They unanimously refused to embark; and directing their attention to the miserable condition of their own country, they demanded the establishment of a free constitution, which Ferdinand was compelled to concede. Similar revolutions subsequently took place in Portugal, Naples, and Piedmont; but in the two latter countries the old despotic governments were restored by the Austrians, who have ever been strongly opposed to liberal institutions.

11. The public mind in England continued to be agitated by projects for effecting reform in parliament, and other changes in the constitution. Public meetings, attended by immense multitudes, were held in different parts of the country. One in particular, at Manchester, was attended with lamentable consequences. The magistrates having determined to arrest the leaders, especially Mr. Hunt, sent a party of yeomanry to aid the officers of police; unfortunately, in passing through the immense assembly, some confusion took place, which led to a serious affray; several of the multitude were killed, and a still greater number wounded by the sabres of the yeomanry, or severely crushed. Hunt and his friends were taken into custody on a charge of high treason; but this was soon abandoned, and they were ordered to find bail on a charge of sedition. 12. This event produced great diversity of opinion, and very angry debates within and without the walls of parliament; but the sentiments of government were expressed unequivocally in

---

* These events did not take place until the following year; but are placed here to preserve the continuity of the narrative.

a letter of thanks addressed to the magistrates and yeomanry of Manchester, for their prompt and spirited conduct. At the following assizes the grand jury threw out the bills charging the yeomanry with murder; but Hunt and his associates, being found guilty of sedition, were sentenced to different periods of imprisonment. Sir Francis Burdett, also, who had denounced the conduct of the magistrates and the ministry in very severe terms, in a letter addressed to his constituents, was brought to trial, and found guilty of a libel on his majesty's government. Finally, parliament was assembled in the end of the year, and six restrictive acts passed for the prevention of seditious meetings, for prohibiting training and arming, for checking blasphemous and seditious writings, and to impose a tax on cheap periodical publications.

13. (A. D. 1820.) On the 23rd of January his royal highness the duke of Kent died at Sidmouth, in the 53rd year of his age, leaving behind him an only daughter, the princess Victoria Augusta, now the presumptive inheritor of the British throne. On the 29th of the same month, George III died at Windsor Castle, at the advanced age

Windsor Castle.

of eighty-one, after a reign of fifty-nine years seven months and three days; the longest and most memorable in the annals of England. We are still too near the time in which this event occurred, and too much swayed by the opinions and prejudices resulting from personal feelings, to draw an impartial character of this venerable sovereign. But whatever diversity of opinion there may be respecting the politics of the monarch, none can deny the virtues of the man.

Amiable, merciful, benevolent, he was an affectionate husband, a tender father, and a faithful friend; no prouder epitaph needs to be inscribed upon his tomb.*

Questions for Examination.

1. In what manner were the hopes of the people of Europe disappointed?
2. How did the restored king of Spain behave?
3. What was the state of England after the war?
4. By what circumstances were the hopes of the people raised?
5. What victory was obtained at Algiers?
6. How did the government endeavour to check the progress of sedition?
7. What fatal event filled the nation with sadness?
8. Did any other remarkable circumstance occur in the royal family?
9. What colonies revolted against the parent state?
10. How was a constitution established in Spain?
11. What unfortunate circumstance took place at Manchester?
12. What were the consequences of this event?
13. What deaths took place in the royal family?

CONTEMPORARY SOVEREIGNS.

Popes.	A. D.	*Emperors and Empresses of Russia.*	A. D.
Clement XIV.	1769	Peter III.	1762
Pius VI.	1775	Catharine II.	1763
Pius VII.	1800	Paul I.	1797
		Alexander.	1801
Emperors of Germany.			
Joseph II.	1765	*Sovereigns of France.*	
Leopold.	1790	Louis XVI.	1774
Francis II.	1792	Republic.	1793
Assumed the title of emperor of Austria.	1804	Napoleon, consul.	1799
		emperor.	1804
		Louis XVIII.	1814
Emperors of the Turks.			
		Kings of Spain.	
Mustapha III.	1757	Charles III.	1759
Achmet IV	1774	Charles IV.	1788
Selim III.	1789	Ferdinand VII.	1808
Mahmoud II.	1808		

* The following lines form part of a poetic tribute to the memory of George III. from the pen of the Rev. George Croley. Some may consider them too laudatory; but the world is so accustomed to hearing flattery poured at the feet of kings, that it would misunderstand a candid acknowledgement of their virtues, unless made in the grave style of history:

Raise we his monument! what giant pile
Shall honour him to far posterity?
His monument shall be his ocean-isle,
The voice of his redeeming thunders be
His epitaph upon the silver sea.
And million spirits from whose neck he bore
The fetter and made soul and body free;
And unborn millions, from earth's farthest shore,
Shall bless the Christian king till the last sun is o'er.

Queen and King of Portugal.		Divided between Russia,	A. D.
	A. D.	Prussia, and Germany..	1793
Maria	1777		
John VI...			

Kings of Prussia.

Kings of Denmark.

Frederick II.	1740	Christian VII.	1756
Frederick III.	1786	Frederick VI.	1808
Frederick IV.	1797		

Kings of Sweden.

Kings of Poland.

		Gustavus III.	1772
		Gustavus IV.	1792
Stanislaus	1786	Charles XIII.	1809
Augustus IV.	1786	Charles XIV.	1818

During this long reign, a very large number of persons distinguished themselves in the literary, clerical, political, naval, military, and mercantile worlds.

CHAPTER XXXVII.

GEORGE IV.

Born 1762. Died 1830. Began to reign 1820. Reigned 10 years.

SECTION I.

No sirs—my regal claim, my rightful crown,
The honour'd title of your sovereign's wife,
No bribe shall e'er induce me to lay down,
Nor force extort it, save but with my life.—Eltham.

1. (A. D. 1820.) THE accession of a monarch, who had been actually in the possession of sovereign power for so many previous years, produced no important political changes. George IV. was publicly proclaimed on the 31st of January in London and Westminster, and matters went on for some time in their ordinary course. On the 23rd of February, the metropolis was astounded by intelligence of a plot being discovered for the assassination of his majesty's ministers. 2. The Cato-street conspiracy, as it was called, from the little street near the Edgeware road, where the conspirators used to assemble, was planned by Thistlewood, who had been before acquitted on a charge of treason, and by some other men of desperate fortunes. Their design was to obtain, on some pretence, admission to lord Harrowby's, when the ministers were assembled at a

cabinet dinner, and there murder the entire party. 3. But all their plans were betrayed to government by a spy, and a strong body of police, accompanied by a detachment of the guards, burst into their rendezvous at the moment that they were preparing for the execution of their designs. After some resistance, in which Smithers, a police officer, was killed, they were overpowered, and the greater part made prisoners. Thistlewood made his escape, but was subsequently taken at a house in Moorfields. Such was the poverty and misery of these wretched madmen, who proposed to subvert a powerful government, that, when they were searched, not even a shilling was found among the whole party. They were soon after brought to trial: Thistlewood and four others were executed, some more transported, and government, satisfied with these examples, gave up the prosecution against the rest. 4. Preparations were now commenced for the coronation of his majesty, when they were suddenly suspended by an event which excited more public interest and more angry feelings than any other that had occurred for a long period. This was the return of queen Caroline to England, and her subsequent trial before the house of lords—matters over which the historian would willingly cast a veil, but which are far too important to be omitted.

5. We have already mentioned the formal separation between the prince of Wales and his consort, soon after their marriage; some years after, her conduct was made the subject of a secret investigation, which, after a long and disgusting inquiry, terminated in her acquittal. After being subject to such an indignity, the unfortunate princess quitted England, and spent her time in travelling, especially in visiting the most celebrated spots on the coasts of the Mediterranean. She visited Jerusalem, and several other towns of Palestine, and afterwards took up her residence in that part of Italy which is subject to the Austrian emperor. Reports very injurious to her character began to be circulated, and a secret commission of eminent lawyers was sent out to Milan to investigate their truth.

6. On the king's accession to the throne, the evidence collected by the Milan commission was made the pretext for omitting the queen's name in the liturgy, and at the same time the honours due to her rank were refused by foreign powers. Deeply irritated at these results, she de-

termined to return to England, though aware that her landing would be the signal for the commencement of a rigorous prosecution, and although she had been offered an annuity of fifty thousand pounds on condition of her remaining abroad. 7. She landed at Dover on the fifth of June, and was received with the greatest enthusiasm by the populace. Equal honours were paid to her along the road to the metropolis, and her reception in London was still more gratifying.

8. On the very day of the queen's arrival in London, a message was sent to both houses of parliament, requesting that her conduct should be made the subject of investigation, and that the evidence collected at Milan should be taken into consideration. Some delay was occasioned by a useless effort of the house of commons to effect a compromise; this having failed, "a bill of pains and penalties," to deprive the queen of her rights and dignities, and to divorce her from her husband, was introduced into the lords. 9. The trial soon commenced, and lasted forty-five days, after which the bill was read a second time by a majority of twenty-eight; but on the third reading, the ministers could only command a majority of nine, and the bill was therefore abandoned.

10. During these proceedings the agitations of the public mind knew no bounds; cavalcade after cavalcade was seen proceeding out to Hammersmith, where the queen resided, with addresses containing the warmest expressions of affection for herself, and hatred of her opponents; the press teemed with virulent libels on all who were conspicuous in either party: disunion even reached the domestic circle, and the question of the queen's guilt or innocence was debated furiously in every society and in every family within the British seas. The abandonment of the bill was hailed by the queen's friends as a complete acquittal, and their delight was testified by a pretty general illumination, though it must be confessed that many who exhibited this outward sign of joy were forced to the display through dread of popular violence.

11. (A. D. 1821.) The heats and animosities produced by the queen's trial continued to rage with unabated fury through the remainder of the life of that unhappy lady; it was even supposed that the rejection of her claim to participate in the coronation would have led to some serious commotion. But that august ceremony was performed without interruption: the queen, indeed, presented herself

at the doors of Westminster Abbey, and was refused admittance, but no serious display of popular displeasure followed. 12. This last event produced a fatal effect on her health, which had been long declining; and her death, which followed soon after, was generally attributed to a broken heart. The fatality which attended this unfortunate woman seemed to follow her very remains. Her funeral was a scene of outrage and violence. It had been intended that the procession should not pass through the metropolis; but the populace attacked the military escort, and, after some loss of life, succeeded in forcing away the hearse; the funeral array then passed through the city to Whitechapel, where the corpse was restored to the constituted authorities, and then allowed to pass quietly to Harwich, whence it was transferred to Brunswick, to repose with the ashes of her illustrious ancestors.

13. Immediately after the coronation, his majesty paid a visit to Dublin, and was received by the Irish people with a burst of loyal affection such as was probably never before witnessed. After a short visit, he embarked at Kingstown in the presence of a countless multitude, who rent the air with acclamations, and with blessings on the head of the first English sovereign who had visited Ireland without hostile intentions. Shortly after his return, the king made an excursion to Hanover, the cradle of his race; and after a brief stay, returned to England.

14. Great distress was experienced throughout the British island by the depreciation of agricultural produce, and consequent difficulty of paying rents. In Ireland, the mutual discontents of the land-holders and the peasantry led to several outrages on the part of the latter, perfectly disgraceful to a civilized country. By a little vigorous exertion, however, these violences were repressed, and comparative tranquillity restored. The distress of the lower classes, which indeed almost exceeded credibility, was relieved by a general and generous subscription in England, which arrested the progress of a pestilential disease, produced by famine and distress.

Questions for Examination.

1. By what event were the minds of the people disturbed at the commencement of the new reign?
2. What were the designs of the Cato street conspirators?
3. How were the plans of the conspirators defeated?
4. What event caused the coronation to be postponed?

5. How did the queen become exposed to suspicion?
6. On what occasion were the effects of these suspicions manifested?
7. How was the queen received in England?
8. What measures were taken by the ministry?
9. How did the queen's trial terminate?
10. What effect did this lamentable occurrence produce in the country?
11. Was the ceremony of the coronation disturbed?
12. Did any remarkable circumstances attend the queen's death and burial?
13. How was the king received in Ireland?
14. Was any distress experienced in the country?

SECTION II.

O! heard they but the avenging call
Their brethren's murder gave,
Dissension ne'er their ranks had mown,
Nor patriot valour, desperate grown,
Sought refuge in the grave.—*Scott.*

1. A TIME of profound peace furnishes but few incidents worthy of being recorded by the historian; during such a period a nation is silently employed in improving its resources and repairing the injuries which had been inflicted by war on its finances. The unparalleled contest in which England had been so long engaged, imposed on her rulers a task of no ordinary difficulty; the immense debt which had been accumulated, required a large taxation to pay its interest; and though many exertions have been made to relieve the country from such pressure, no extensive reduction can reasonably be expected for a very long period. (1822.) 2. After the termination of the parliamentary session, the king proceeded to visit the Scottish capital, and was received by his northern subjects with the utmost enthusiasm. The festivities were, however, soon interrupted by the melancholy news of the death of the marquis of Londonderry, the secretary for foreign affairs, who had committed suicide in a fit of temporary insanity. After an interval of more than a month, Mr. Canning was appointed his successor, and received the seals of office at a time when a minister possessing his talents and energy was most wanting to the country.

3. The European sovereigns had entered into a league to check the progress of revolution, and chose to call their union the holy alliance. A congress was held at Verona, and a resolution taken to subvert the constitution, and restore despotism in Spain. The duke of Wellington, on the part of England, refused to sanction the design, the execution of which was intrusted to the king of France. (1823.) 4. Early in the following year, the duke of Angoulême, at the head of a powerful army, entered Spain, and soon compelled

the constitutionalists, wholly unprepared for resistance, to unqualified submission. Ferdinand, restored to the exercise of despotic power, persecuted all whom he suspected of liberal principles with extreme severity, and revived all the cruel institutions by which the government of Spain has been so long disgraced, with even more than ordinary rigour.

5. The feelings of the great majority of the English people were powerfully excited by this outrage on the liberties of a neighbouring nation; but the ministers had determined to maintain a strict neutrality, though they severely condemned the principles and conduct of the French government. But while despotism was thus re-establishing its iron reign in Europe, freedom had obtained signal triumphs in America; the revolted colonies of Spain had now completed their emancipation, and their independence was acknowledged by England and several other European powers.

6. A sanguinary struggle for the liberation of Greece from the Turkish yoke had commenced some time previously, but had long produced no result but terrific massacres. The principal members of the holy alliance viewed the insurrection of the Greeks with secret dislike; but the sympathies of the greater part of the people of Europe were awakened in their favour, and several volunteers from England and other countries tendered their assistance to the insurgents. (1824.) 7. Lord Byron, whose poetry had created a powerful feeling in favour of the Greeks, proceeded to aid them by his personal exertions, but unfortunately fell a victim to a fever at Missolonghi, in Western Greece.

8. The British colonies in Africa and India were severely harassed by the assaults of barbarous enemies; in the former, the governor, sir C. M'Carthy, was defeated and cruelly murdered by the Ashantees; but his death was subsequently avenged, and these savage warriors forced to submission. 9. In Hindostan, the Burmese were totally defeated, their strongest fortifications captured, and their territories placed at the mercy of the British troops; they were consequently forced to solicit peace, which was granted on terms that tend greatly to increase the security of the British possessions in the East.

10. From the time that the union between England and Ireland had been effected, attempts were annually made for the repeal of the remaining restrictive laws against the Roman catholics; repeated failures by no means diminished

the hopes of the Catholic leaders and their friends; and in Ireland they formed a permanent association for the furtherance of their objects. (1825.) The members of the Catholic Association were not always very measured in their language or temperate in their attacks on government, and it was judged expedient to suppress meetings which seemed pregnant with danger. 11. A bill for extending the law in Ireland against illegal societies was introduced into parliament, and as it was expected that catholic emancipation would immediately follow, it passed with but little opposition. This hope was, however, doomed to be disappointed: the catholic question was indeed carried in the lower house, but it was lost in the lords, principally on account of the exertions made by his royal highness the duke of York.

12. Speculations and joint-stock companies of every description had lately multiplied so fast, that the nation seemed infected with a species of insanity; but the bubbles soon burst, and a terrible reaction ensued. The confusion of the money market, and the commercial embarrassments thus created, did not entirely disappear for the next two or three years.

13. (A. D. 1826.) The state of Portugal, the oldest ally of England, began now to attract the attention of the public. On the death of John VI., the succession devolved on Don Pedro, who resided in Brazil; he, however, satisfied with the imperial crown which he had acquired in South America, abdicated the Portuguese throne in favour of his daughter Donna Maria, and, to prevent any domestic commotion, betrothed her to his brother Don Miguel. Before taking this decisive step, he prepared a constitution, securing the blessings of civil and religious liberty to the Portuguese, who, unfortunately, could neither appreciate the one nor the other. 14. A strong party resolved to make Don Miguel absolute king, and, under the secret sanction of the Spanish government, began to assemble forces on the frontiers. Under these circumstances, application was made to England for assistance; and an expedition was sent out with a promptitude that excited the admiration of Europe. To preserve the continuity of the narrative, we must complete the account of the transactions in Portugal, before we again return to the affairs of England. 15. In September, 1827, Don Miguel was appointed regent by his brother, and immediately proceeded to assume the reins of power. In the

following year, after the departure of the English troops, he usurped the crown in defiance of the claims of his niece, and immediately after abrogated the constitution and proclaimed himself absolute. The young queen of Portugal had, in the mean time, arrived in England; but finding her friends not sufficiently strong to overthrow the usurper, she returned to her father's court at Rio Janeiro.

Questions for Examination.

1. By what circumstances had the English ministers been long embarrassed?
2. What event caused a change in the ministry?
3. For what purpose was the holy alliance formed?
4. How was the Spanish constitution overthrown?
5. What revolutions occurred in South America?
6. Did any European nation make a fierce struggle for freedom?
7. What remarkable English nobleman died while aiding the Greeks?
8. Did any wars take place in the British colonies?
9. How did the Burmese war terminate?
10. What remarkable circumstance occurred in Ireland?
11. Did parliament adopt any measure in consequence?
12. What pecuniary embarrassments occurred in England?
13. How was public attention directed to the affairs of Portugal?
14. In what manner did the English government behave?
15. What was the final termination of the struggle in Portugal?

SECTION III.

We cannot walk, or sit, or ride, or travel,
But death is by to seize us when he lists.—Scott.

1. (A. D. 1827.) DEATH and disease, among the great and noble of the land, produced some important changes in the councils of Great Britain. On the 5th of January, his royal highness the duke of York died, sincerely and generally lamented, more especially by the army; for his conduct ever since his restoration to the office of commander-in-chief, had deservedly procured for him the endearing appellation of "the soldier's friend." 2. On the 17th of February, the earl of Liverpool, prime minister of England, was seized with a fit of apoplexy, which terminated his political existence, though his natural life was prolonged to the close of the succeeding year. He was succeeded by Mr. Canning, whose commanding eloquence and enlightened views had made him almost irresistible in the house of commons. 3. But the additional fatigues imposed upon the highly-gifted statesman, and the fierce opposition he had to encounter, proved too much for a constitution already enfeebled by neglected disease; he died on the 8th of August, in the

fifty-eighth year of his age. 4. Mr. F. Robinson, having been elevated to the peerage, by the title of lord Goderich, was next appointed premier; but his administration was loose and unsettled, and the cabinet which he had formed soon fell to pieces. The duke of Wellington was then called by his majesty to preside over the councils of Britain, and, aided by Mr. Peel, he succeeded in forming a ministry promising more firmness and stability than that which it succeeded.

5. The atrocities which marked the warfare between the Greeks and Turks were so shocking to humanity, that the sovereigns of Europe felt themselves bound to interfere, and a treaty for the pacification of Greece was signed, in London, on the 6th of July, 1827, by the representatives of England, France, and Russia. 6. In consequence of this, the allied fleets in the Mediterranean prepared to force the combatants to consent to an armistice, and blockaded the Turkish fleet in the harbour of Navarino. Ibrahim Pacha, the Turkish commander in the Morea, paying but little attention to the remonstrances of the allied admirals, the united fleets sailed into the harbour, on the 20th of October, under the command of sir Edward Codrington, to intimidate him into submission. 7. A shot fired by a Turkish vessel was the signal for a general engagement, which lasted four hours. It terminated in the almost utter annihilation of the Turkish fleet, with comparatively little loss to the allied squadrons. The independence of Greece was virtually achieved by this brilliant victory, and was further secured by the arrival of a small military force from France; the Turkish government, however, refused submission, and war was commenced against Russia. 8. The events of this war, though not properly belonging to English history, demand a brief notice. In the first campaign the Turks made an obstinate resistance, and gained some advantages over their opponents; but in the following year (1829), the Russian arms were everywhere successful; the passages of the Balkan were forced; Adrianople, the second city in the empire, was captured, and the sultan forced to consent to terms of peace, dictated almost at the gates of Constantinople. 9. The demands of Russia were, however, less exorbitant than might have been expected under the circumstances; but there is reason to believe that this moderation was inspired by a dread of provoking the jealousy and resentment of England.

10. (A. D. 1828.) After the resignation of lord Goderich, Mr. Huskisson and some other friends of the late Mr. Canning, had joined the duke of Wellington's administration, but they soon found that little harmony could exist in such a coalition. At length Mr. Huskisson, having voted against ministers, tendered his resignation, which to his great surprise and mortification was accepted, nor could all his subsequent efforts alter the inflexible spirit of the duke of Wellington. The time of the house of commons was wasted in the discussion of this and similar petty disputes, but one act of the session made an important change in the forms of the constitution. The test and corporation acts, which required the receiving of the sacrament of the Lord's supper, according to the rites of the church of England, as a necessary qualification for office, were repealed after a brief parliamentary struggle; and the hopes of the Roman catholics, for the repeal of the laws by which they were excluded from parliament, were greatly raised by this event. A motion in their favour was made by sir Francis Burdett, and carried by a majority of six; but it terminated ineffectively, as a similar motion was negatived in the house of peers.

11. The country continued to be agitated by the catholic question during the remainder of the year; on the one hand, Brunswick clubs were formed by the advocates of protestant ascendency, to resist all further concession; on the other side, the catholic leaders and their friends strenuously exerted themselves to render the cause of emancipation popular. In Ireland, the agitation was so violent that there was reason to apprehend a civil war: the most intemperate harangues were made at Brunswick meetings and in the Catholic Association; it was manifest that nothing but promptitude and decision on the part of government could avert the effusion of blood.

12. (A. D. 1829.) The commencement of the ensuing session of parliament was expected by all parties with the utmost anxiety; and it was not without surprise, that both parties found catholic emancipation recommended in the speech from the throne. A bill to give effect to this recommendation passed both houses by triumphant majorities, though not without encountering a vigorous opposition, and received the royal assent on the 13th of April.

13. From the date of this important change in the constitution, to the close of the reign, nothing of great importance occurred in England; but in France the dissatisfaction

of the people with their rulers became daily more manifest. An expedition was undertaken against Algiers, probably with the hope of diverting the attention of the French people from politics, to what had been so long their favourite passion,—military glory. (A.D. 1830.) The expedition was eminently successful; Algiers was captured, and the entire presidency subjected to the power of France; but the discontents of the French people continued to rage with as much violence as ever.

14. The illness of the king in the commencement of the year 1830 threw a damp on public affairs, and, as its fatal tendency became more apparent, speculations were rife on the probable political conduct of his successor. After a tedious sickness, which he sustained with great fortitude and resignation, George IV died at Windsor Castle, on the 25th of June. The reasons already assigned for omitting a sketch of the character of George III. are in the present instance still more forcibly applicable; we shall only say of him as a distinguished writer has said of Henry IV. of France,

> Oh! be his failings covered by his tomb,
> And guardian laurels o'er his ashes bloom.

Questions for Examination.

1. What death occurred in the royal family?
2. By what circumstance was Mr. Canning placed at the head of the mi-[nistry?]
3. What is supposed to have caused Mr. Canning's death?
4. What changes took place in consequence of Mr. Canning's death?
5. In what manner did the European sovereigns endeavour to effect the pacification of Greece?
6. What caused the battle of Navarino?
7. What were the consequences of the battle?
8. How did the Russian war with Turkey terminate?
9. Why was Russia moderate in her demands?
10. What remarkable circumstance occurred in the parliamentary session [of 1828?]
11. Was the British nation disturbed by the agitation of any important [question?]
12. How was the catholic question finally settled?
13. Did the French government engage in any important expedition?
14. When did George IV. die?

CONTEMPORARY SOVEREIGNS.

Popes.	A.D.	King and Electorate of Bohemia.	A.D.	King of Hanover.	A.D.
Leo XII.	1823	Francis II.	1792	George IV. king of Great Britain.	
Emperor of Austria.		*King of Denmark.*		*King of Naples and Sicily.*	
Francis II.	1792	Frederick VI.	1808	Ferdinand IV. rest.	1824
King of Bavaria.		*King of France.*		Francis Janiver Joseph	1825
Louis Charles Augustus	1825	Charles X.	1824		

King of the Nether-	King of Prussia. A.D.	King of Spain. A.D.
lands. A.D.	Frederick IV......1797	Ferdinand VII....1808
William I........1813	*Emperor of Russia.	King of Sweden and Norway.
King of Poland.	Nicholas I.........1825	Charles XIV.......1818
Nicholas 1. see Russia.	King of Sardinia.	Grand Seignior of Turkey.
Queen of Portugal.	Charles Felix......1821	Mahmoud II......1808
Donna Maria da	King of Saxony.	King of Wirtemburg.
Gloria...........1826	Anthony Clement, 1827	Frederic William..1816

CHAPTER XXXVIII.
WILLIAM IV.

Born 1765. Began to reign 1830. Died June 20, 1837.

SECTION I.

*The love of liberty with life is given,
And life itself the inferior gift of heaven.—Dryden.*

1. RARELY has the accession of a new sovereign afforded such general satisfaction as was manifested by all classes when the duke of Clarence ascended the throne, with the title of William IV. Unlike his predecessors, his habits were economical and his manners familiar; he exhibited himself to his people, conversed with them, and shared in their tastes and amusements; within a few weeks he attained an unprecedented degree of popularity, and was reverenced by his subjects as a father, and loved by them as a friend. 2. No change was made in the ministry; but as his majesty was connected by marriage with some of the leading whigs, it was generally believed that the policy which rigidly excluded that party from office during the two preceding reigns, would not be maintained in full force. The hopes of a coalition between the Wellington administration and the whigs were, however, soon dispelled; the opposition to the ministry, which had been almost nominal during the preceding sessions, was more than usually violent in the debate on the address; and though the formal business of both houses was hurried through with all possible despatch, the whigs were pledged to a virtual declaration of war against the cabinet before the prorogation of parliament.

3. The parliament was dissolved on the 24th of July; but before it could be again convened, a revolution in a neigh-

bouring country produced important effects on the public mind, and in some degree convulsed all Europe. Charles X, in defiance of the wishes and feelings of the great majority of the French people, was eager to restore the royal and sacerdotal power to the eminence which both possessed before the revolution. He found in prince Polignac a minister able and willing to second his projects, and he placed him at the head of the cabinet. Polignac thought that, by gratifying the national vanity of the French, and indulging their passion for military glory, he might be able to divert their attention from domestic exploits: previously to dissolving the chamber of deputies, he therefore proclaimed war against the dey of Algiers, who had committed several outrages on the subjects of France. But the expectations of the prince were miserably disappointed. His cabinet was assailed with a ferocity and violence to which the annals of constitutional warfare furnish no parallel; and as the actions of its members afforded no opportunity for crimination, their opponents made amends by attacking their presumed designs and intentions. When the chamber of deputies met, an address, hostile to the ministry, was carried by a large majority. 4. The king instantly prorogued the chambers; and when the reduction of Algiers had, as he fondly hoped, gratified the nation and restored his popularity, he once more hazarded the perilous experiment of a dissolution. The new chamber of deputies was still more hostile than the preceding. Polignac and his colleagues saw that they could not hope to retain their power by constitutional means, and in an evil hour they prepared three ordinances by which the French charter was virtually annihilated. The first dissolved the chambers before they assembled, the second disfranchised the great body of electors, and the third imposed a rigid censorship on the press.

5. When these ordinances first appeared on Monday, the 28th of July, they excited astonishment rather than indignation; a number of persons, however, connected with the journals of Paris, assembled, and issued a manifesto, in which they declared their resolution to resist, by all the means in their power, the enforcement of the ordinance imposing restrictions on the press. Several of the daily journals were not published on the following morning, and the printers and compositors engaged in their preparation, being left without employment, formed a body of active rioters. They were joined by the workmen from several manufac-

tories, the proprietors of which had agreed to suspend their business during the crisis, thus throwing into the streets an insurrectionary force, whose ferocity was more formidable than military discipline. Some disturbances took place at the offices of two journals, the proprietors of which persisted in publishing appeals to the populace; but they seemed to be of so little importance, that Charles went to enjoy his favourite amusement of hunting, and his ministers, with similar infatuation, neglected to strengthen the garrison of Paris.

6. In the evening of Tuesday, the appearance of the military to reinforce the police became the signal for the commencement of a contest. Several lives were lost, but the soldiers succeeded in dispersing the riotous mobs; and when they returned to their barracks, Marshal Marmont, the military commander of Paris, wrote a letter to the king, congratulating him on the restoration of tranquillity; and the ministers prepared their last ordinance, declaring the capital to be in a state of siege.

7. But the apparent triumph of the royalists was delusive; scarcely were the troops withdrawn when all the lamps in Paris were broken, and the citizens, protected by darkness, made energetic preparations for the struggle of the ensuing day; barricades were erected, arms were procured from the shops, the theatres, and the police-stations, and the arsenal and powder magazine were seized by the populace. When the morning of Wednesday dawned, Marmont beheld with alarm the tri-coloured flag, the banner of insurrection, waving from the towers of the cathedral, and the preparations made on all sides for an obstinate struggle. He instantly wrote to the king, recommending conciliatory measures; but receiving no answer, he prepared to act on his previous instructions. Dividing his troops into four columns, he directed them to move in different directions, and made circuits through the principal streets occupied by the insurgents. A series of sanguinary conflicts took place, in all of which the royalists were worsted; the troops of the line manifested the greatest reluctance to fire upon their countrymen; some of them disobeyed orders, and others went over to the insurgents. When evening closed, the soldiers had been beaten at every point, and they returned to their barracks wearied and disappointed. No provision was made for their refreshment after the toils of the day, while all the houses in Paris were freely opened to the insurgents, and the citizens vied

with each other in supplying them with everything that they needed.

8. The struggle was renewed with great fury on the morning of the third day; Marmont and the ministers, now convinced of their danger, proposed a suspension of arms; but before anything decisive could be effected, two regiments of the line unfixed their bayonets, and went over to the insurgents in a body. The populace reinforced by these rushed through the gap thus opened; carried the Louvre by storm, and opened from this position a terrible fire on the column of the royal army. Under this new attack the soldiers reeled; their assailants saw them waver, and charging with resistless impetuosity, drove them to a precipitate retreat. Marmont and his staff escaped with great difficulty, his scattered detachments were taken or cut to pieces; before three o'clock Paris was tranquil, and the victory of the people complete.

9. The members of the chamber of deputies, who happened to be at Paris, met at the house of M. Lafitte, and organized a provisional government; and on the following Friday they proclaimed the duke of Orleans lieutenant-general of the kingdom. On the 3rd of August the chambers met, pursuant to the original writs of convocation, and the national representatives raised the duke of Orleans to the throne, under the title of Louis Philippe I., king of the French. Charles X. was dismissed to exile with contemptuous humanity; but the efforts of the new government to protect the obnoxious ministers almost produced a new civil war. Four of these unfortunate men, arrested by individual zeal, were brought to trial; an infuriated mob clamoured for their blood, but their judges had the firmness to sentence them to perpetual imprisonment; and soon after their removal to their destined place of confinement, public tranquillity was restored.

10. The revolution of Paris was closely followed by that of Brussels. The union of Belgium with Holland by the treaty of Vienna was an arrangement which contained no elements of stability, for the Belgians and the Dutch were aliens to each other in language, religion and blood. The arbitrary measures of the king of Holland's prime minister provoked a formidable riot in Brussels, on the night of the 25th of August, which the indecision, cowardice, and stupidity of the Dutch authorities fostered into a revolutionary war. The prince of Orange made some efforts to mediate between the contending parties, but he only exposed himself

to the suspicions of both; and, after a brief struggle, Belgium was severed from the dominions of the house of Nassau.

11. Several insurrectionary movements took place in Germany; the duke of Brunswick was deposed, and replaced by his brother; the king of Saxony was forced to resign in favour of his nephew, and the elector of Hesse was compelled to grant a constitutional charter to his subjects. Poland next became the theatre of war; its Russian governor, the archduke Constantine, was expelled, and the independence of the country proclaimed; but after a long and sanguinary struggle, the gallant Poles were forced to yield to the gigantic power of Russia.

12. In England, the rural districts, especially Kent and the northern counties, exhibited alarming signs of popular discontent; but the agitation in Ireland was of a still more dangerous character, and seemed to threaten the dismemberment of the empire. Great anxiety was felt for the opening of parliament, and the development of the line of policy which the ministers would adopt at such a crisis. It was with surprise that the people learned from the premier, on the very first night of the session, that not only he was unprepared to bring forward any measure of reform, but that he would strenuously oppose any change in parliamentary representation. 13. The unpopularity which the duke of Wellington seemed almost to have courted by this declaration, was studiously aggravated by the acts of his opponents; and when the king had accepted the invitation of the Lord Mayor to dine with the citizens on the 9th of November, a letter was sent to the duke of Wellington by a city magistrate, warning him that he would be insulted, perhaps injured, by the mob, if he did not come protected by a military escort. The ministers in alarm resolved to put a stop to the entire proceedings; and on the 8th of November, to the great astonishment of the public, it was announced, not only that the king's visit would be postponed, but that there would be neither the usual civic procession in honour of the new Lord Mayor, nor the dinner in the Guild-hall, for which great preparations had been made, in consequence, as was alleged, of some seditious conspiracy. The first effect of the announcement was a general panic; the funds fell four per cent. in one day, and the whole country was filled with anxiety and alarm. But when it was discovered that no serious grounds existed for the apprehensions which had

been excited, all who had a share in exciting it were assailed with a tempest of indignant ridicule, which even a stronger cabinet than that of the duke of Wellington could not have resisted. 14. When the ministerial measure for the arrangement for the civil list was introduced, Sir Henry Parnell moved a resolution which implied that the ministers no longer possessed the confidence of parliament. After a calm debate, marked by unusual moderation on both sides, the resolution was carried in a full house by a majority of twenty-nine votes; the duke of Wellington and his colleagues instantly resigned, and earl Grey received his majesty's commands to form a new administration.

15. Earl Grey's ministry was formed of the leaders of the old whig party and the friends of the late Mr. Canning; the most remarkable appointment was that of Mr. Brougham to the office of Lord Chancellor, as a very few days before his elevation he had declared "no change that may take place in the administration can by any possibility affect me." His immediate acceptance of a peerage and office consequently excited surprise, and provoked harsh comments. Parliament adjourned for a short time to give the new ministers an opportunity for maturing their plans, which were stated by the premier to include economy and retrenchment at home, non-interference in the affairs of foreign states, and a reform in the commons' house of parliament.

16. Great anxiety was felt about the nature of the reform which the ministers would propose. Their measure was developed to the house of commons by lord John Russel, on the 1st of March, 1831, and it was found to include a greater amount of change than had been anticipated either by friends or enemies. All boroughs not containing two thousand inhabitants were totally disfranchised, those that had less than four thousand were restricted to returning one member, and the rights of representation of which these were deprived were given to large manufacturing towns, four districts of the metropolis, and to divisions of the large counties. Similar changes were proposed in the representation of Scotland and Ireland.

17. A measure which involved so important a change in the constitution, was one which naturally provoked protracted discussions. The debate on its introduction lasted seven nights; the second reading of the bill was only carried by a majority of one. The ministers were subsequently defeated on two divisions, and were compelled either to resign

their situations or dissolve their parliament. His majesty carried his resolution into effect to support the cabinet by dissolving the parliament in person, and an appeal was then made to the people, on the most important constitutional question that had been raised since the accession of the house of Hanover.

18. The event of the elections more than answered the expectations of the most ardent reformer. When the new parliament met, it appeared that fully two-thirds of the representatives were pledged to support the minister. The progress of the Reform Bill through the house of commons though slow was certain, and on the 22nd of September it was sent up to the lords. Its fate in the upper house was very different; it was rejected on a second reading by a majority of forty-one. This decision produced violent and even dangerous excitement; but the promptitude with which the house of commons, on the motion of lord Ebrington, pledged itself to the support of the ministers and their measure, calmed the agitation in the metropolis and the greater part of the country. Serious riots, however, took place at Derby and Nottingham, which were not quelled until considerable mischief had been perpetrated; Bristol suffered still more severely from the excesses of an infuriate mob, and the disturbances were not suppressed until an immense quantity of public and private property had been wantonly destroyed.

19. In the midst of this political excitement the country was visited by a pestilential disease called the Asiatic cholera, which proved very destructive, though its ravages were not so great in England as in some parts of the continent. This must, under Providence, be attributed to the judicious measures adopted by the government, and to the zealous exertions of all the gentlemen connected with the medical profession throughout the empire. In Ireland, agrarian insurrections were added to the horrors of pestilence the peasants, driven to desperation by famine and oppression on the one hand, and stimulated by the violent harangues of itinerent demagogues on the other, committed several atrocious outrages, which could not be restrained by the ordinary operations of constitutional law. France and Italy were also disturbed by insurrectionary movements, which were, however, soon suppressed; and the revolution of Belgium was completed, by its being formed into a monarchy under prince Leopold of Saxe Coburg, whose chief recommendation was his connection with the royal family of England.

20. These circumstances induced the ministers to convene parliament for the third time within the year; the Reform Bill was again introduced, and, after the second reading, had been carried by a decisive majority; the houses adjourned till the commencement of the following year. When they re-assembled, the Reform Bill was carried steadily through its remaining stages in the lower house, and once more brought into the house of peers, where its fate was regarded with great anxiety. Several of its former opponents, called waverers, had resolved to vote for the second reading, with the hope that the measure might be greatly modified in committee, and by their aid the bill pased this important stage by a majority of nine. But the ministers had no reason to boast of this success; more than twenty of those who had supported the second reading were pledged to resist the most important clauses, and, by their aid, a motion for instruction to the committee on the bill, which virtually took all control over the measure out of the hands of its proposers, was carried by a majority of thirty-five. Lord Grey, in conjunction with his colleagues, proposed to the king a new creation of peers, his majesty refused his assent to so extreme a measure, and all the members of the cabinet instantly resigned. The king then applied to the duke of Wellington to form a new administration, and his grace undertook the task under circumstances of greater difficulty than had yet been encountered by a British statesman. Opposed by the bulk of the nation and by a large majority of the house of commons, the duke soon discovered that it would be out of his power to form a ministry; he therefore resigned the commission, and advised the king to recall his former advisers. Lord Grey returned to power, having secured the success of the Reform Bill by a compromise with its opponents. It was agreed that the ministers should not create peers, but that the leaders of the opposition should secede from the house until the Reform Bill became the law of the land. Under these circumstances the measure was passed without any impediment through its remaining stages, and on the 7th of June it received the royal assent.

Questions for Examination.

1. How was the accession of William IV. received?
2. What was the state of parties at the commencement of the new reign?
3. With what design did the French ministers declare war against Algiers?

4. What ordinances were issued by Polignac?
5. How were they received in Paris?
6. When did the contest between the citizens of Paris and the royal troops begin?
7. In what condition was the royal cause after the second day's struggle in Paris?
8. How was the contest in Paris terminated?
9. Was any change made in the government of France?
10 Did the French Revolution produce any effect in Belgium?
11. Were there any insurrectionary movements in any other parts of the continent?
12. What remarkable declaration was made by the duke of Wellington?
13. Why was the king's visit to the city postponed?
14. How was the Wellington administration dissolved?
15. On what principle was lord Grey's ministry constructed?
16. What was the general nature of the Reform Bill?
17. How was it received on its first introduction into the house of commons?
18. What was the fate of the Reform Bill in the new parliament?
19. In what condition were Great Britain and the continent at this crisis?
20. How was the Reform Bill ultimately carried?

SECTION II.

The palace sounds with wail,
The courtly dames are pale,
A widow o'er the purple bows, and weeps its splendour dim;
And we who clasp the boon,
A king for freedom won,
Do feel eternity rise up between our thanks and him.—Anon.

1. (A.D. 1833–7.) THE revolution in France, the excitement attending the agitation of the Reform Bill in England, the difficulty which impeded the arrangement of the affairs of Belgium, and the war in Poland, threatened consequences fatal to the peace of Europe; it was only by slow degrees that the agitated waves were stilled, and appearances more than once seemed to threaten a renewal of the storm. Louis was zealously supported by the middle classes in France, but he was exposed to the plots of the Carlists and republicans, who were equally hostile to the continuance of a government so adverse to their favourite schemes. A Carlist insurrection in the south of France, and a republican riot at the funeral of General Lamarque in Paris, threatened to involve the nation in the perils of a civil war; but the republicans were unable to withstand the firmness of the national guard, and the capture of the duchess of Berri put an end to the war in the south of France.

2. Don Pedro had resigned the crown of Portugal when he was chosen emperor of Brazil; but when he was deposed by his South American subjects, he resolved to support his

daughter's claims to the throne of Portugal. Having secretly organized a considerable force of English and French adventurers, he effected a landing near Oporto, and took possession of that city. He expected an insurrection, but none took place; and he was closely besieged in the city by the usurper Miguel. A desultory war ensued, distinguished by no remarkable events, until Miguel's fleet was captured by Admiral Napier with a very inferior force; after which Lisbon was surprised by the constitutional forces, and the usurper driven into exile. Don Pedro's death, which soon followed his victory, did no injury to the constitutional cause, and his daughter, Don Maria da Gloria, remains in undisturbed possession of the crown of Portugal.

3. The influence of Russia was exercised in resisting the progress of liberal opinion in Germany, but was more alarmingly displayed in the east of Europe. Mahommed Ali, the pacha of Egypt, threw off his allegiance to the sultan, and sent his son Ibrahim to invade Syria. The superior discipline of the Egyptian troops rendered their victories easy, and Ibrahim might have advanced to the suburbs of Constantinople, and perhaps have taken that city, had not the sultan sought protection from the Czar. A Russian armament delivered the Ottoman empire from the impending peril, but the acceptance of such aid rendered the sultan a dependent on the court of St. Petersburg.

4. Such was the state of Europe when the British parliament was dissolved, and a new election held pursuant to the provisions of the Reform Bill. In England and Scotland the ministers had very large majorities; but in Ireland a new party mustered in considerable force, consisting of members pledged to support the repeal of the union. 5. One of the earliest measures which engaged the attention of the reformed parliament, was a coercion bill for suppressing the agrarian disturbances in Ireland, and checking the political agitation by which these tumults were in some measure encouraged. The bill passed the lords without difficulty; but in the lower house it encountered so fierce an opposition, that the ministers were compelled to abandon some of the most obnoxious clauses. With the coercion bill a measure for the regulation of the Irish church was very closely connected. The Irish church stands in the unpopular predicament of possessing a wealthy national establishment, while the great majority of the people belong not merely to a different, but to a hostile faith; impediments have consequently been of-

fered to the collection of its revenues, and there has scarcely been any popular disturbance in Ireland during the greater part of a century, which has not been more or less remotely connected with the tithe-question. Under these circumstances, the conservative party generally supported the claims of the church in their full efficiency ; the moderate reformers proposed, that after provision had been made for all necessary ecclesiastical uses, the surplus should be applied to some object of public utility, such as national education ; and a third party, stronger in zeal than numbers, regarded the property of the church as a fund that might be seized for the purposes of the state. The ministers steered a middle course between the extreme parties, and of course gave perfect satisfaction to neither ; they abolished ten bishoprics, but they abandoned the clause for applying the surplus to purposes not purely ecclesiastical, in order to facilitate the passage of the bill through the house of lords. The motion was rendered more agreeable to the Irish clergy, than it would otherwise have been, by the grant of a million sterling as a loan, in lieu of the arrears of tithes which they were unable to collect.

6. The renewal of the charter of the bank of England, led to some important discussions on the financial state of the country; but much more important was the change made in the constitution of the East India Company. While that body was secured in its political rights over the vast empire which it had acquired in Hindostan, it was deprived of its exclusive privileges of commerce, and the trade with India and China was freely opened to all the subjects of the British crown. Equally great was the change made in the constitution of the British West India colonies by the total abolition of negro slavery ; the service of the negro was changed into a compulsory apprenticeship for a limited time, and a compensation of twenty millions sterling was granted to the proprietors of the slaves.

7. Notwithstanding the importance and value of these changes, the reform parliament was far from satisfying the expectations which had been rather too sanguinely formed by the people. Some dissatisfaction was expressed at the limited amount of the reductions of taxation, the continuance of the corn laws, and of military flogging, and the impressment of seamen. It was also suspected that the cabinet was itself divided on more than one question of public policy.

8. In the United States some discussion arose, in which

the interests of England as a commercial country, were materially involved. The tariff sanctioned by Congress, imposing heavy duties on the import of manufactured goods, was strenuously opposed by the Southern states, especially the Carolinas, and an appeal to arms was threatened. With some difficulty a compromise was effected, but the attack thus made on the permanence of the union is still felt in America. The hostility of the American president to the banking system induced him to withdraw the public deposits from the bank of the United states, and a violent shock was thus given to commercial credit, which produced injurious results on both sides of the Atlantic.

9. The agitation in Ireland for the repeal of the union was continued during the recess; and soon after the meeting of parliament, Mr. O'Connell introduced the subject into the house of commons. His motion was rejected by a majority of five hundred and twenty against fifty-eight, but at the same time parliament pledged itself "to remove all just cause of complaint to promote all well considered measures of improvement." But on the nature of these measures the cabinet was divided; and the majority having evinced a disposition to appropriate the surplus ecclesiastical revenues to secular purposes of general utility, the earl of Ripon, the duke of Richmond, Mr. Stanley, and sir James Graham, resigned their offices. Their places were soon supplied; but the changes were very distasteful to the house of lords, and the new Irish tithe bill was rejected by a decided majority.

10. Another Irish question led to further changes in the ministry. In the discussion on the renewal of the coercion bill, it appeared that some members had agreed to certain compromises with its opponents of which their colleagues were ignorant. The disclosure of these negotiations led to the resignation of lords Althorp and Grey, the former of whom, however, returned to office when lord Melbourne was appointed premier. These ministerial dissensions and the opposite views of the majorities in the house of lords and commons greatly impeded the progress of legislation; almost the only important measure of the session was a bill for the reform of the poor-laws, which, though it effected very great changes, was not much connected with party politics.

11. The anomalous position of the government gave general dissatisfaction; the cabinet was assailed with equal violence by the conservatives and the extreme section of the

reformers, and the king soon began to show that he was by no means satisfied with the conduct of his ministers, especially the lord chancellor, who, during a tour in Scotland, had made some inconsistent and extraordinary speeches at various public meetings. On the death of earl Spencer, lord Althorp was obliged to vacate his office of chancellor of the exchequer, and the king took this opportunity of dismissing the Melbourne administration. Sir Robert Peel was appointed premier; but, as he was absent on the continent, the duke of Wellington undertook the management of public affairs till his return.

12. After Sir Robert Peel's return, and the formation of his cabinet the parliament was dissolved, and a new election brought the strength of parties to a very severe test. In England the partisans of Sir Robert Peel's administration had a small majority; but in Ireland, an unfortunate affray at Rathcormack, arising from an attempt to enforce the payment of tithes, so exasperated the catholic population, that the ministerial candidates were almost everywhere unsuccessful. When the parliament assembled, the ministers were beaten at the very outset in the choice of a speaker; Mr. Abercromby, the opposition candidate, having been preferred to the ministerial candidate, Sir Charles Sutton, by a majority of ten. Several other motions were decided against the ministers, but none that involved a necessity for resignation, until lord John Russell proposed a resolution, that any measure introduced regarding Irish tithes should be founded on the principle of appropriating the surplus revenue to purposes of general utility. The motion was carried by a majority of twenty-three; Sir Robert Peel and his colleagues immediately resigned, and the Melbourne cabinet was restored, with the remarkable exception of lord Brougham, whose place, as chancellor, was supplied by lord Cottenham.

13. A bill for reforming the corporations of England, founded on the report of commissioners appointed to investigate the condition of these bodies, was immediately introduced by the Melbourne administration, and passed without difficulty through the house of commons. Some important changes were made in the measure during its progress through the house of lords, but the ministers deemed it better to accept these modifications than to risk the loss of the bill. A law for regulating the marriages of dissenters was also passed by both houses; but the ministerial measures for regulating the Irish church were again rejected by the house of lords.

14. The state of Canada began to occupy a large share of public attention during the latter part of the session; the colonial house of assembly opposed the measures of government, and went to the extreme of withholding the supplies. Commissioners were sent to arrange these differences; but the Canadians of French descent made claims, not only inconsistent with the continuance of British dominion, but with the fair claims to protection of the British emigrants who had settled in the country, and their demands were consequently rejected.

15. During the struggle between the nicely balanced parties in England, the aspect of continental affairs was favourable to the continuance of peace. An attempt was made on the life of the king of the French, and various plots were formed by enthusiastic republicans to effect a revolution; but the friends of order rallied round the throne, and the only result of these attacks was to increase the strength of the government. Spain was distracted by the horrors of a disputed succession. A little before the death of Ferdinand VII., the Salic law, which had been introduced by the Bourbon dynasty, was set aside in favour of that monarch's infant daughter; and she succeeded to the throne after her father's decease, (1833). Don Carlos and his partisans protested against this arrangement, and they took advantage of the unpopularity of the regent to kindle the flames of civil war. To prevent the necessity of again returning to this subject, we may mention here that this war still continues; that the queen regent, though aided by a British auxiliary legion, has failed to establish her authority over the northern provinces, and that so completely disorganized is the entire condition of society in the peninsula, that there is no present prospect of its being speedily restored to a state of order and settled government. Though the civil war in Portugal has not been renewed, the country continues to be distracted by contests between rival parties, whose struggles are too often decided by open force, rather than constitutional means.

16. The commencement of the parliamentary session in 1836, showed that the differences between the majority of the lords and the majority of the commons were far from being reconciled. They were at issue principally on the line of policy that ought to be pursued towards Ireland, and on the measures for regulating the established church in England and Ireland. It was proposed that the Irish corporations should be reformed according to the plan which, in the pre-

ceding year, had been adopted for similar bodies in England, and a bill embodying this principle received the sanction of the lower house; the lords, however, insisted that the state of society in Ireland was such that municipal institutions were not adapted to that country, and resolved that the corporations should be altogether abolished: to this amendment the commons refused to agree, and the bill was consequently lost. A similar fate awaited the Irish tithe bill; the lords rejected the appropriation clause, and the commons would not accept the measure without it. Laws, however, were passed for the commutation of tithes in England, for the registration of births, deaths, and marriages, and for regulating episcopal sees, the opposing parties having each yielded a little to ensure unanimity.

17. In Upper Canada the refractory house of assembly was dissolved, and at the new election a majority of members favourable to the British government was returned. But in Lower Canada the demands of the French party were not only renewed but increased: and the governor, after a vain effort to conciliate the house of assembly, put an end to the session.

18. In America the progress of the contest between President Jackson and the Bank of the United States, greatly embarrassed all commercial transactions. In spite of all legislative prohibitions, the country was inundated by an over issue of paper money; and the government, to check the evil, decreed that specie alone should be received in payment for public lands. The small notes were immediately depreciated, several banks failed, and many of the leading merchants and traders were unable to discharge their engagements. The crisis was sensibly felt in England, where it greatly checked the speculation in railroads, which were beginning to be carried on to a perilous extent; the manufacturing districts suffered most severely from the temporary pressure; but the crisis was soon over, and trade again flowed in its accustomed channels.

19. The parliamentary session of 1837 produced few measures of importance; on Irish measures the houses maintained their opposite opinions, and of course nothing was done; in matters of ecclesiastical policy the result was precisely the same; the only matter in which there was any appearance of unanimity, was in the adoption of resolutions for administering the government of Lower Canada in opposition to the refractory house of assembly. A gloom was

thrown over these and other discussions by the increasing illness of the king, whose disease at an early period prognosticated its fatal termination. His majesty died on the morning of the 20th of June, sincerely regretted by every class of his subjects. During his reign of nearly seven years, the nation enjoyed tranquillity both at home and abroad; it was the only reign in the annals of England during which there was no execution for treason and no foreign war.

Questions for Examination.

1. What was the condition of France after the Revolution?
2. Did any civil war arise in Portugal?
3. How was Turkey forced into dependence on Russia?
4. What was the state of parties in the first reformed parliament?
5. To what measure of domestic policy was the attention of parliament directed?
6. What change was made in the East and West India colonies?
7. Did the reformed parliament satisfy expectations?
8. To what danger was the American union exposed?
9. On what question was lord Grey's cabinet divided?
10. What circumstances led to further change in the ministry?
11. On what occasion was the Melbourne cabinet dissolved?
12. How was sir Robert Peel compelled to resign?
13. With what measure did the Melbourne ministry succeed?
14. In what condition was Canada?
15. Can you state the circumstances of the civil war in Spain?
16. On what subjects were the majorities of the lords and commons at variance?
17. What was the progress of Canadian discontent?
18. What commercial crisis occurred in America?
19. Why was the session of 1837 unproductive of important events?

CHAPTER XXXIX.

VICTORIA.

Born 1819. Began to reign 1837.

SECTION I.

They decked her courtly halls;
They reined her hundred steeds;
They shouted at her palace gate—
A noble queen succeeds.—*Anon.*

1. VICTORIA, the only daughter of Edward, duke of Kent, succeeded her late uncle, and her accession to the throne was hailed with more than ordinary enthusiasm. All parties vied with each other in testifying their affectionate allegiance

to their youthful sovereign, called, at the early age of eighteen, to rule over the destinies of a mighty empire. The formal business of parliament was completed with all possible despatch, and, at the close of the session, parliament was dissolved. Although there was a keen trial of strength between the rival political parties, the elections were unusually tranquil; and, at their close, it appeared that the triumphs of the opposing parties were nearly balanced. Public attention was next directed to the preparation made for entertaining her majesty at a civic banquet on the 9th of November. they were on a scale of unrivalled magnificence, and her majesty's procession to the Guild-hall was one of the most pleasing pageants ever displayed in England. No change was made in the cabinet; and when parliament assembled towards the close of the year, it appeared that the ministers retained their majority in the house of commons, and that the opposition to them in the house of lords had become more moderate.

2. The state of Lower Canada was one of the most pressing subjects for the consideration of the legislature; the opponents of the government had taken up arms, and raised the standard of rebellion. But it soon appeared that their measures were ill-concerted; after a brief struggle most of the leaders abandoned their followers, and sought shelter in the United States. Immediately after the re-assembling of parliament in January, 1838, measures were introduced for the temporary government of Canada, its constitution having been suspended by the revolt; and the earl of Durham was appointed governor of all the British colonies in North America, with power, as lord commissioner, to arrange the differences between her majesty's government and her discontented subjects. The result of his mission was that the two provinces were consolidated into one, under a joint political administration; by which wise policy, party interests were dissolved, and tranquillity soon restored. Beyond the Canadian question, the parliamentary session was chiefly occupied with various measures of Irish policy, particularly the introduction of a Poor-law into that country; there were, however, a few enactments of general interest which obtained the sanction of the legislature; the parliamentary qualification was extended, arrest for debt on mesne process was abolished, and the administering of oaths in courts of justice dispensed with in respect to Quakers, Moravians, and others.

3. The 28th of June of this year (1838) witnessed the

coronation of the young queen, which took place amidst universal rejoicing; many foreign princes and ambassadors were present, who also took great interest in the imposing ceremony. Soon after parliament was prorogued by the queen in person. The internal energies of the kingdom were now developing themselves in the construction of vast works of public benefit, among which the completion of several important railways was the most conspicuous.

4. The foreign policy of the country, however, was disgraced by a proceeding which ended in the most lamentable results. Under the erroneous impression that Russia contemplated some aggressive movement against the stability of the British Indian empire through the instrumentality of Persia, an Anglo-Indian army was marched into the wild and distant country of Afghanistan. Sir John Keane was appointed to the command of the expedition, and proceeded with vast resources of men and means into the heart of the country. Candahar was occupied; and no difficulty was opposed to his career until his arrival at the fort of Ghuznee. This strong position he at once stormed and took; and the way being thus opened to Cabul, he hastened on to the capital. Dost Mohammed, the reigning prince, was deposed, and Shah Soojah, a monarch more friendly to British interests, was substituted in his place. Sir John Keane having left a strong force in Cabul with Macnaughten and Burnes, as the chief officers of the mission, hastily returned to India, and from thence to England, where, in honour of his brilliant successes, he was raised to the peerage.

5. Difficulties now began to manifest themselves in connexion with China, which ended in an open rupture with that empire. The West Indian colonies also broke out into insubordination, particularly Jamaica, in consequence of the interference of the legislature in the subject of West India slavery. The difficulties, however, were eventually compromised, and tranquillity restored.

6. The internal state of the kingdom was somewhat disturbed by Chartism, the grand desideratum put forward by the working classes as a remedy for their supposed wrongs: it required, 1st, universal suffrage; 2nd, vote by ballot; 3rd, annual parliaments; 4th, paid members; and 5th, no property qualification. The Chartists broke out into open riot towards the close of the year 1839, at Newport, Monmouthshire. Frost, Williams, and Jones, the fomentors of these disturbances, were captured, tried, and sentenced to death;

Sir Robert Peel.

but their sentence was ultimately commuted to transportation for life.

7. The first great event of the new year (1840) was the marriage of her majesty with Prince Albert, of Saxe-Coburg Gotha, which was solemnized in St. James' Chapel, on February 10th. The day was celebrated throughout the kingdom by a general holiday and great rejoicing. The chief points of interest connected with the foreign policy were the advance of an expedition against China, to obtain indemnity for the past, and better security for British commerce for the future: and the successes of the navy on the coast of Syria, in support of the power of the sultan of Turkey, against his rebellious pacha, Mohammed Ali.

8. The following year brought with it a cessation of hostilities in China, by the occupation of Canton, which was ransomed by the payment of six millions of dollars to the British by way of indemnity for the expenses of the war. The pacification of the Levant was also a matter of congratulation. The government, however, did not seem to possess the confidence of the country; and although the parliament was dissolved and an appeal made to the people, yet lord Melbourne was forced to resign. Sir Robert Peel came into office as leader of the new administration.

9. The success of the British arms, in the beginning of

the year, were now more than counterbalanced by the sad disasters which befell their army in Afghanistan. A fierce rebellion broke out on November 2nd at Cabul; Burnes and MacNaughten, the British ministers, with other civil and miltary officers, were successively murdered, and the whole country rose in arms under the treacherous Akbar Khan, the son of the deposed king Dost Mohammed, who determined on the massacre of the whole British force. Pusillanimity and indecision in the councils of the general-in-chief, led to an immediate evacuation of the country; 4,500 fighting men, together with about 12,000 camp followers, besides women and children, set forward, through ice and snow, on their lamentable retreat; and no sooner had they cleared out of their cantonments, than the blood-thirsty Afghans began to plunder the baggage and fire upon the soldiery; they continued without ceasing their revengeful assaults upon the bewildered and desponding multitude, till there was nothing left to plunder, and none left to kill. Out of a host of about 26,000 human beings, only a few hundreds were rescued from death by captivity. The ladies and the wounded had been given up to the enemy early in the march, and Dr. Brydon was the only officer who made good his retreat. In the following year, however, on the appointment of lord Ellenborough to the governor-generalship of India, in the place of lord Auckland, the British national character was repaired, the honour of their arms retrieved, and the unfortunate prisoners rescued. General Pollock was despatched into Afghanistan with an invading army; he advanced on Cabul with all possible rapidity; while on the other side general Nott, who had held out at Candahar during the recent difficulties, brought his forces also to bear on the capital. Victory everywhere attended the British arms; and the British officers and ladies, who had been taken prisoners, were also rescued, at Bameean, on the road to Turkistan. The late disgraces having now been so gloriously redeemed, it was determined to evacuate a country which ought never to have been entered. The fortifications and other works of Cabul having been destroyed, the British troops set forward on their return home, and, after a march of about ten weeks, arrived safely on the banks of the Sutledge, December 17th, 1842.

10. The war in China had broken out afresh, in consequence of the continued differences between the English and Chinese authorities; but it was renewed with so much vigour on the part of the British government, that the haughty Chinese were

compelled to solicit the establishment of peace. A treaty was entered into by sir Henry Pottinger, on August 29th, 1842, off Nankin, by which lasting peace and friendship were to exist between the two nations. China was to pay twenty-one millions dollars, several of her ports were to be thrown open to the British merchants, and the island of Hong-Kong to be ceded in perpetuity to the British empire, with other important commercial advantages.

11. At home a few slight disturbances arose in the manufacturing districts from commercial depression; the repeal of the corn-laws had become a great source of political agitation; and questions of Irish policy continued to absorb much of the attention of government. Wales, usually so tranquil, now exhibited scenes of popular violence, originating in the oppressive system of Turnpike-tolls. Government appointed a commission in October, 1843, to enquire into the operation of the turnpike laws, which ended in an amelioration of the burden and the cessation of all outrage.

12. The Afghan war had no sooner been terminated, than the treacherous conduct of the Ameers of Scinde towards the British troops in their late difficulties in Afghanistan, and their subsequent attempt to break off their engagements with the British Indian government, brought down upon them an armed British force, under Sir Charles Napier. A desperate battle was fought near Hydrabad, which resulted in the discomfiture of the Ameers, and the annexation of their country to the British possessions. The Mahrattas also displayed similar treachery; but they met a severe chatisement in the battles of Maharajpoor, and of Punniar, in the neighbourhood of Gwalior, which forced them to submit to the demands of the Indian government. These great actions closed the year 1843. In the next year circumstances occurred in the government of the British Indian empire, which led to the recall of lord Ellenborough, who was succeeded by Sir Henry Hardinge as governor-general of India. It was not long after Sir Henry's arrival, before his military skill was called into active exercise. The Sikh chiefs were making formidable preparations for invading the British territories; the attempt had been some time anticipated; but it was the desire of government to act on the defensive, rather than on the offensive; so that no great advances were made to check their crossing the Sutledge, which separated us from the Punjaub. The day at length arrived, when these lawless soldiers crossed

the river, and bade defiance to the British Indian armies. The first encounter took place at Moodkee, on December 14, 1845; the struggle was most desperate, but victory decided in favour of the British. The terrible battles of Ferozeshah, Aliwal, and Sobraon, followed in quick succession, the Sikhs incurring great losses in each engagement: in the last battle, the most terrific carnage took place; men were mowed down by hundreds; and hundreds upon hundreds were drowned in attempting to cross the Sutledge. The success of the British was complete; but it was not achieved without an immense sacrifice of officers and men; in the battle of Sobraon the Sikhs lost 10,000 men in killed and wounded, and the British 2383. The British army immediately marched upon Lahore, and entered the capital without opposition; the remaining Sikhs submitted: a treaty was concluded, and indemnities were to be paid to the British government. Thus closed one of the most eventful and fearful struggles that ever called into action the strength and valour of the Anglo-Indian army, February 10th, 1846.

13. During these martial proceedings abroad, affairs at home were assuming a more cheerful aspect; domestic tranquillity was restored, commerce greatly improved, and the revenue sustained by the imposition of an income-tax. The duties on articles imported from abroad were considerably reduced and great advances made in the principles of free-trade. The repeal of the corn-laws now continued to be a matter of universal discussion, which was considerably promoted by the formation of an anti-corn-law league, provided with immense funds for the dissemination of its principles throughout the country by means of lecturers. The moral and intellectual welfare of the working-classes was also a matter of consideration with the government. Annual grants of money were allowed by parliament to provide for the education of the people; and a committee of the privy council was appointed to manage their disbursement, under the appellation of the Committee of council on Education.

14. In Ireland, political disquietude was on the decline; many measures were passed by the legislature to improve its position and ameliorate the condition of the people; means of academical instruction were also considerably extended by grants from parliament. The failure of the potato crop, however, in 1845, and the deficiency of the harvest, carried extreme misery and want through the whole of Ireland.

To this failure may be ascribed the hasty settlement of the corn-law question. The universal cry for food quickened the government into an unflinching consideration of the subject; and consequently a measure was brought before parliament for the repeal of the corn-laws. After great discussion, this important bill was passed; Sir Robert Peel and his colleagues immediately resigned; and soon after, the anti-corn-law league was dissolved. The formation of a new ministry devolved on lord John Russel. The failure of the potato crop again in 1846, combined with a deficient harvest throughout Europe, produced great and general distress; and in the west of Scotland, but especially in Ireland, occasioned intense suffering; in the latter country, multitudes perished from famine and disease. Every effort, however, was made by public munificence and private liberality to arrest the progress of these calamities; and, by the goodness of the Almighty, a most bountiful harvest following the year of scarcity, the nation was once more blessed with plenty and abundance.

Questions for Examination.

1. How was the accession of Victoria received?
2. What subjects occupied the attention of her first parliament?
3. When did the coronation of the queen take place?
4. What events led to the occupation of Afghanistan by an Anglo-Indian army?
5. What was the state of feeling in China, and the West Indies, at this period?
6. What demand of the Chartists disturbed the public peace?
7. What were the chief events of the year 1840?
8. How were the differences with China settled?
9. What disasters befell the British army in Afghanistan? and how were they retrieved?
10. On what terms was peace finally established with China?
11. How were matters at home proceeding at this period, particularly in Wales?
12. What serious engagements occurred on the Indian frontier with treacherous allies, immediately after the Afghan war?
13. What important measures were effected by Sir Robert Peel's government? and by what means was the repeal of the corn-laws promoted?
14. What was the state of Ireland at this period? What important political measure was hastened on by the failure of the harvest?

SECTION II.

*The stately homes of England,
How beautiful they stand!
Amidst their tall ancestral trees,
O'er all the pleasant land.—Mrs. Hemans.*

1. THE opulent dwellers in what Mrs. Hemans styles "the stately homes of England,"—the nobility and gentry, as well as the wealthy middle class,—experienced a new call upon their wonted liberality in the year 1847, when another deficient harvest, and the utter failure of the potato crop, created a recurrence of the sad scenes of famine and destitution in Ireland and the west of Scotland. Benevolent persons in the United States of America also contributed liberally to the relief of the suffering poor in Ireland, by sending over cargoes of provisions from their own abundant harvests. Numbers, nevertheless, perished from famine and its attendant diseases.

2. The Orleans dynasty was not of long continuance. All Louis Philippe's energies had been devoted to the aggrandizement of his family; many stringent measures against the liberties of the French people had gradually weakened their affection. Dreading an outbreak, he fortified Paris under a pretence of safety against a foreign foe; but in reality to secure himself against insurrection. The king issued an ordinance declaring the Reform banquets, which were held at various places in France, illegal; and the attempt to suppress one in Paris, in February, 1848, led to an insurrection. Some of the troops joined the people; the palace was attacked, and the king fled in disguise.

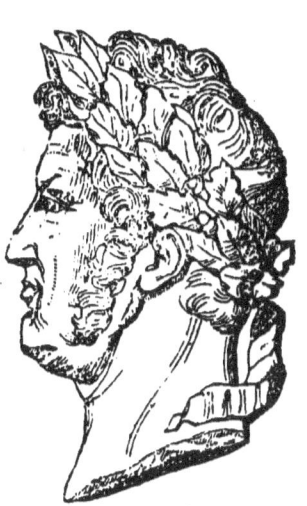
Louis Philippe.

A republic was declared, and a provisional government formed. After various changes, Louis Napoleon, nephew of the Emperor Napoleon, was made President of the Republic for four years. Louis Philippe and his family retired to England, where that monarch soon after died.

3. The nation suffered a great loss in the death of Sir Robert Peel. He was thrown from his horse in St. James' Park, and so injured that he survived but a few hours. His loss

was much regretted; and to him the nation is indebted for many improvements in their commercial and domestic policy. His death occurred July 2nd, 1850.

4. In 1851, the fairy palace, erected in Hyde Park, was opened to the public. It was, in every respect, a triumph; and people flocked to the "Great Exhibition" from all parts of the globe. The contents of the mammoth fabric were of wonderful variety. It contained colossal statuary, and the miniature needle; the fur dress of the Greenlander, and the silken robe of Persia; the Damascus blade, and the stone hatchet used in the islands of the Pacific; the golden altar of extraordinary value from Spain, and the rude idols from Australia. In this "Crystal Palace," productions from every part of the globe were collected; and amongst these, the fruits of native industry occupied an honourable position. The building was in the form of a Gothic cathedral, and some of the tallest elms in the park were sheltered under its roof.

5. The electric telegraph between France and England was completed. This new and important invention was now in general use, both in England and the continent of Europe.

Duke of Wellington.

6. Arthur, duke of Wellington, died suddenly at Walmer Castle, December 14th, 1852. He was one of England's greatest generals, and, although he had fought many battles,

yet he never experienced a defeat. Deep and sincere was the lamentation of the English people at his decease. He was buried in St. Paul's cathedral with much solemnity, and all classes vied in paying honours to this truly noble and great man.

7. After repeated defeat, and resignation, lord John Russell's weak administration retired from office in February, 1852, and was succeeded by a conservative government.

8. On the 7th of November, 1852, a *senatus consultum* was issued by Napoleon to the French nation, proposing the re-establishment of the empire. The people having by an immense majority, expressed their desire for the change, the empire was proclaimed on the 2nd of December.

9. The financial measures of lord Derby's administration met with considerable opposition; and a hostile vote in the house of commons led to the resignation of ministers. They retired in December, 1852, after a short tenure of office of nearly ten months' duration. A coalition cabinet, composed of Whig, Peelite and Radical legislators, under the premiership of lord Aberdeen, succeeded to power. As many of the new ministers were not only men of recognized ability, but had, at various periods, held office, great expectations were formed respecting them.

10. For many years a dispute had raged at Constantinople between the Latin and Greek churches, with reference to the guardianship of the holy places in Jerusalem. France espoused the cause of the Latin, and Russia that of the Greek church. In November, 1852, the czar Nicholas first put forward that claim to a protectorate of the Greek Christians in Turkey, which lord John Russell afterwards so injudiciously admitted. The preposterous demand was based upon a forced interpretation of certain passages in the treaty of Kainardji, concluded between Russia and Turkey in 1771. The rather acrimonious discussion that took place between France and Russia, respecting the key of the church of Bethlehem, brought the matter fully before the public. In the course of the dispute, both parties threatened hostile measures; and, while the Russian army on the Pruth was reinforced, and put in readiness for an advance, the French fleet in the Mediterranean approached the Bosphorus. Early in 1853, a favourable change occurred; and as the rival powers seemed willing to make reasonable concessions, hopes were entertained of an amicable solution of the difficulty. These were suddenly dispelled by the arrival at Constantinople, in February, 1853, of Prince Menschikoff, on an extraordinary mission. The real

nature of his mysterious errand did not transpire until May, when his demands were found to be altogether incompatible with the dignity of the sultan as an independent sovereign.

11. These demands were of course rejected; and, in spite of the anxiety of the sultan and his ministers to make every reasonable concession, the Russian troops crossed the Pruth early in July, and proceeded to occupy the principalities of Moldavia and Wallachia. After this act of aggression, various attempts were made to settle the matter by negotiation, but they all failed; and on the 5th of October, the Porte formally declared war. On the 14th, the combined fleets of France and England passed the Dardanelles, at the request of the sultan.

Battle of Sinope.

12. The Turks rushed to the rescue of the principalities, and, under the judicious guidance of Omar Pasha, gained many brilliant victories. The Russians, defeated on land, determined to strike a blow at the Turkish navy, and committed the unparalleled outrage at Sinope, which at once excited the

indignation of Europe. The Turkish fleet, riding in fancied security, almost within sight of the armaments of the western powers, was ruthlessly attacked by an overwhelming force, and destroyed. This wanton assault by the stronger on the weaker state, showed that nothing but the most vigorous measures could bring Russia to submission.

13. The English government displayed an unfortunate repugnance to resist force by force, but events hurried them on; and, in March, 1854, a royal message was communicated to both houses of parliament, proclaiming war against Russia. Even after this, English ministers clung to diplomacy, and talked loudly of pacific measures, while they pretended to be preparing for an energetic prosecution of the contest.

14. The emperor Napoleon III., having been duly recognized by foreign powers, looked out for a partner to share his throne. Instead of seeking an alliance with a royal house, he selected Eugenie de Montejo, countess of Téba, for his bride. The marriage was solemnized in January, 1853; and the romantic manner in which the whole affair had been arranged, rendered it particularly interesting to the French people. During this eventful year, a fusion between two branches of the Bourbon family was effected, and the duke of Bordeaux acknowledged by all, except the duchess of Orleans, as the rightful heir to the French throne.

15. The queen of Portugal died on the 15th of November, 1853, and was succeeded by her eldest son, under the title of Don Pedro V. Several ministerial changes occurred in Spain, in which country the despotic interference of the queen-mother, Christina, produced discontent and led to rebellion. In February, an attempt was made upon the life of the emperor of Austria, but the assassin was disarmed and captured before he could effect his purpose, and soon afterwards suffered the extreme penalty of the law.

16. A fire broke out in Windsor Castle, March 19th, 1853, but it was happily extinguished before much damage had been done to that noble residence, endeared to the country by so many associations.

17. The year 1854 was, in many respects, a memorable one. While the much-despised Turks were gaining renown in expelling the Russians from the principalities, France and England were engaged in making preparations to take part in the contest. Lord Raglan was appointed to command the English army, which reached Gallipoli in the spring. The Turks pursued their victorious career on the banks of the Danube; the

Russians, having been defeated in many desperate attempts, abandoned the siege of Silistria, and virtually withdrew from the contest in that direction. In the meantime the allied fleets had not been altogether idle. The Russians violated the laws of honourable warfare by firing upon a flag of truce; and soon after the commission of this outrage, the allied squadrons bombarded Odessa. The attack lasted the whole day, April 22d. All the batteries erected for the defence of this commercial city were silenced—some of them having been materially damaged, and others entirely destroyed.

18. The crowning event of the year was the expedition, composed of French, Turkish, and English soldiers, which sailed from the Turkish shores in the autumn. Its departure had been delayed by the terrible ravages of the cholera amongst the troops, and from the destruction of stores, caused by a disastrous fire which broke out in a mysterious manner at Varna. The Russians did not attempt to dispute the landing of the expeditionary force; but retreated to a strong position on the Alma, from whence they were driven, with great slaughter, by the French, English, and Turkish armies, on the 20th of September. Although the Russians fought obstinately at first, they were so awed by the determined manner in which the English troops carried the heights—for their men advanced up to the terrible batteries—that they fled in utter confusion, from a position which their commander had just before boasted he could hold against any assailant for several days. There can be little doubt that, if the allied army had possessed a proper cavalry force, or its leaders had known the real condition of the enemy, the Russians might have been completely subdued, and Sebastopol gained, without further trouble. But the expedition was, in too many respects, a "leap in the dark"; hence, its numerous failures, and the disappointment and suffering that ensued.

19. The first bombardment commenced October 17th, but the results were unsatisfactory. In the meantime the Russian government sent large reinforcements to their army in the Crimea, determined, if possible, to expel the allies. The battle of Balaklava was fought October 25th, when the English cavalry made that celebrated charge, so disastrous and yet so glorious. The Russians quailed before their band of heroes, who rode gallantly forward to almost certain destruction.

20. The occupation, by the Austrians, of the Danubian principalities, released a large portion of the Russian army,

which was at once dispatched to the relief of Sebastopol. Having been harangued by the grand duke, excited by military and religious ceremonies, and well primed with intoxicating beverages, these troops advanced in overwhelming numbers upon the English lines. In the dense fog of a November morning, they swarmed through the valley of Inkerman, surprised, and carried the English outposts, and commenced the battle with every advantage. But for seven hours, on that terrible 5th of November, the small band of English soldiers maintained their ground against their numerous assailants. It was truly a soldier's battle. The general determination was victory or death. At length, General Bosquet arrived at the scene of the struggle, with the gallant French allies, and, from that moment the issue was no longer doubtful. The Russians were driven into Sebastopol with fearful loss, and that victory terminated the first campaign. The Muscovite hordes, naturally enough, felt unwilling to face men who would not yield an inch of ground, but fought even against hope.

21. A violent storm committed sad havoc amongst the shipping, riding at anchor outside the little harbour at Balaklava, in which the *Prince Resolute*, and several other noble vessels, foundered. The catastrophe of the 14th November will long occupy a prominent place in the annals of disasters at sea.

22. Lord Aberdeen's government did not realize the high expectations that had been formed respecting it. In home legislation it was particularly unfortunate; and its feeble direction of the war created alarm and disquietude. Lord John Russell's loudly-heralded reform bill proved a failure; and this minister's attempt to repeal the parliamentary oaths was defeated by a majority of five.

23. On the 20th of June, 1854, the Queen opened the Crystal Palace, at Sydenham, with great solemnity. She was attended by her ministers and foreign ambassadors, and about forty thousand persons were present at the ceremony.

24. Towards the close of 1853, the cholera again manifested itself in the north of England. It reached the metropolis early in the following year, and committed fearful ravages. But the visitation of 1853 and 1854 was not so fatal in its effects as that of 1849 had been.

25. In the midsummer of 1854, Madrid became the theatre of an insurrection. The flight of the queen-mother, Christina, the dismissal of her favourites, and the formation of

a constitutional government under Espartero, had the effect of quelling the storm, and saved the young queen's throne.

26. The year 1855 opened gloomily enough. The sad condition of the army in the Crimea excited general indignation; so terrible were the evils of mismanagement, that hundreds of brave soldiers perished from the effects of exposure. Mr. Roebuck brought forward a motion for inquiry, which on the 29th of January, was carried by a majority of 157. Thus fell the Aberdeen administration, just two years after it had obtained power. After some delay lord Palmerston succeeded in forming a second coalition; but a slight difficulty having occurred respecting the Sebastopol committee, the Peelites soon after seceded, and left lord Palmerston sole master.

27. On the 3rd of March, the public were surprised by the announcement of the sudden death of the real author of the war, the emperor Nicholas. The adhesion of Sardinia to the western alliance, and the visit of the emperor Napoleon and his empress to England, and their enthusiastic reception, in some degree restored public confidence. During the summer, Victoria returned the visit, and was received at Paris with general rejoicing.

28. It was supposed by many that the death of the Czar would ensure the restoration of peace; and the conferences, re-opened at Vienna during the year 1855, were watched with considerable interest. Although the English plenipotentiary, lord John Russell, made the most disgraceful sacrifices, and actually abandoned every point which he had been sent out to maintain, the arrogance of Russia was such that she would make no concessions. Lord John Russell's vacillation raised a storm in the country, and he was afterwards compelled to resign his post as minister of the crown.

29. Meanwhile the war was waged with renewed vigour. The second bombardment of Sebastopol commenced on the 9th of April; and several expeditions were organized in the Crimea, most of which were completely successful. After the third bombardment, which opened on the 6th of June, the French gained possession of the Mamelon, whilst the English won the Quarries. On the 18th (the anniversary of Waterloo), the French assailed the Malakoff—and the English the Redan; but the gallantry and devotion of the troops were not rewarded with success. The failure preyed on lord Raglan's mind; and he was soon after attacked by disease, which carried him off on the 28th of June. His mild and gracious behaviour at the council-board and in the private circle, as

well as his coolness in the field of battle, won the admiration of all. He will ever be remembered as the good lord Raglan. His gentle nature shone like a star amid the elements of strife and contention. But he was not the man for the emergencies in which he was called to act a leading part.

30. On the 16th of August the Russians crossed the Tchernaya, and made a desperate effort to relieve the doomed fortress of Sebastopol, but were repulsed by the French and Sardinians with great loss. This was their last effort. The French gained possession of the Malakoff on the 8th of September, on which occasion the English again failed in an attack upon the Redan ; but on the following day, the Russians evacuated the southern portion of Sebastopol. Thus, within twelve months of the landing of the allied armies in the Crimea, the " standing menace" had been wrested from the foe; and the fleet which committed the outrage at Sinope, totally destroyed.

31. While these events were in progress in Europe, war had been waged in the Asiatic dominions of the sultan. General Williams was sent by the English government to the Turkish army, and, by his efforts, order and discipline were established. On the 29th of September, the garrison of Kars, under the direction of this gallant British officer, repulsed the Russians, who assaulted it with immensely superior forces. But no succour reached the heroic garrison; and, although the Turks endured their sufferings with great constancy, and fought like lions whenever the enemy appeared, they were finally compelled to surrender, and Kars fell on the 28th of November. An expedition despatched from the Crimea, in October, to the entrance of the Bug and the Dnieper, obtained signal success. Kinburn was captured, and a French and English force established there. Some naval operations in the sea of Azoff were in every respect successful; and, with these, the campaign of 1855 closed.

32. This triumph led to the revival of negotiations. Austria proposed an ultimatum, which was eventually accepted by Russia, and conferences were opened at Paris early in the year. Russia, having learned wisdom from adversity, made certain concessions ; and, on the 30th of March, 1856, the treaty of Paris was signed, which restored tranquillity to Europe.

33. Meantime, Great Britain became involved in a serious dispute with China. It arose out of a trifling incident. A Chinese lorcha (a small vessel) was fired upon by the Chinese

for some infraction of their police regulations. She was said to have borne the British flag, and the act of the Chinese authorities was resented as a national insult, though it has never been proved that she was under English colors. The commissioner, Yeh, was called upon for reparation, which he refused. This led to actual hostilities, during which the naval force of the United States became involved; and France also took part in the conflict by sending out a strong armament. Great Britain deputed lord Elgin as ambassador to negotiate a settlement of the difficulties, and he was accompanied by a large force to support his pretensions. France also despatched thither an ambassador; and Mr. William B. Reed was sent out on the part of the United States. The English bombarded and took Canton. Yeh was made prisoner, but the Emperor showed no disposition to yield. The real object of all these operations was to compel the Chinese to open their ports to foreign nations, on a more liberal policy than hitherto.

Questions for Examination.

1. What is said of the famine?
2. Of the French revolution?
3. Of Sir Robert Peel?
4. Of the Crystal Palace?
5. Of the telegraph?
6. Of the duke of Wellington?
7. Of lord John Russell's administration?
8. Of Louis Napoleon?
9. Of lord Derby's administration?
10. Describe the origin of the war between Russia and the allied powers?
11. What countries did the Russians invade?
12. What followed?
13. What was done by England?
14. By the emperor Louis Napoleon?
15. What transpired in Portugal?
16. What happened at Windsor?
17. What were the first military events of 1854? [of the Alma.
18. What expedition was undertaken by the allies? Describe the battle
19. What is said of the first bombardment? Of the Russians? Of
20. Of the Austrians? Of Inkerman? [Balaklava?
21. Of the storm of November 14th?
22. Of lord Aberdeen's government?
23. Of the Crystal Palace?
24. Of the cholera?
25. What took place in Spain?
26. What were the early events of 1855?
27. What is said of the Czar?
28. Of the attempts to make peace?
29. Of the military operations in the Crimea? Of lord Raglan?
30. Of operations in the Crimea?
31. What military operations took place in Asia?
32. How was the treaty of peace accomplished, and when was it signed?
33. What is said of the war with China?

The New Houses of Parliament.

SECTION III.

*He is come to ope the testament
Of bleeding war.—Shakspeare.*

1. THE war with Russia had greatly increased the burden of taxation in Great Britain, and had impaired its military strength. But it was soon followed by another war which was not less expensive, and impaired far more seriously the military strength of the empire. We refer, of course, to the destructive war which was kindled by the mutiny of the sepoys in India. This is so serious an affair, that we shall give its incidents more particularly than in ordinary cases.

2. In the spring of 1856, lord Dalhousie ceased to be governor-general of India, and was succeeded by viscount Canning.

3. Secured from all apprehensions of foreign enemies, and ruling an apparently prosperous and happy people, lord Canning entered upon the government of India with fairer prospects than any governor-general since the first conquest of that country. Not many months, however, elapsed before a naval and military expedition was on its way from Bombay to Bushire, and war was publicly declared against the Shah-in-Shah. After two or three slight actions, in which the Persians were immediately put to flight, the "king of kings" was constrained to sue for peace, and to accept the easy conditions which were imposed upon him. The British troops were recalled to India, and arrived only in time to encounter the most imminent peril that ever menaced the Eastern empire of Britain.

4. It had long been notorious that the Mohammedans of Upper India were discontented with their subordinate position, and that their idle and sensual habits rendered them insolent and fractious. This feeling of unquiet was not a little embittered by the decision arrived at with regard to the titular dignity of the king of Delhi. The court of directors had authorized lord Dalhousie, on the death of the heir-apparent in 1849, to "terminate the dynasty of Timour, whenever the reigning king should die." But as these instructions had been issued with great reluctance, the governor-general had recourse to a compromise, and agreed to recognize the king's grandson as heir-apparent, on condition that he quitted the fortress at Delhi for the royal palace at the Kootub. The royal family had no choice but to submit, though the humiliation to which they were about to be subjected rankled in their

bosoms, and in those of the Delhi Mohammedans generally. They were too sensible, however, of their weakness, to attempt any opposition to the powerful British government, until an opportunity presented itself in a quarter where, perhaps, it was least expected.

5. From the time when lord Hastings created the Nawab of Oude an independent king, and freed him from his allegiance to his rightful suzerain, the king of Delhi, there had been a feud between those two houses, inflamed by their difference in religious matters—the one being a bigoted Soonnee, the other as fanatical a Sheeah. But the dethronement of Wajid Ally Shah, and the annexation of his kingdom, gave deep offence to a large portion of the Bengal army, who were natives of Oude, and drew togther in one common cause the Mohammedans of both sects. Still it was clear that, from their numerical inferiority, the Mohammedans alone could not hope to break the English yoke from off their necks, so long as the Hindoo soldiery remained true to their salt. Unfortunately circumstances occurred to remove this obstacle. From various causes, which it would be tedious to enumerate, a suspicion had seized the credulous and childish mind of the Hindoos that their religion, and, above all, their caste, were in danger. It had been sedulously spread abroad that the British government, relying on its power, had resolved to compel all its subjects to embrace the Christian religion; and, to render this the more easy, had devised a means for defiling the whole of their Hindoo sepoys. This notable device was no other than to issue cartridges greased with pigs and bullock's fat for the Enfield rifles, the ends of which must be bitten off before they could be used. Thus every Hindoo soldier would become unclean and an outcast, and have no other resource than to join the religion of his deceitful masters. Mohammedan emissaries carefully fanned the latent sparks of disaffection, and presently the smouldering fire burst forth into a fierce, devouring conflagration.

6. The first symptoms of a mutinous spirit manifested themselves in the 19th and 34th regiments, both of which were disbanded, and one man of the 34th hanged for wounding the adjutant and serjeant-major. Their example was followed by the 3rd Oude irregular infantry, stationed at Lucknow, who where compelled by Sir Henry Lawrence to lay down their arms, and their ringleaders were punished. On the 6th of May, eighty-five men of the 3rd light cavalry at Meerut refused to use the new cartridges, and other symptoms of discontent

were evinced, but disregarded. On the 10th the troops broke out into open mutiny, killed many of the officers and other Europeans (men, women, and children), at the station, and finally went off to Delhi. This course was dictated by the fact that there was in the neighbourhood, at the time, ample means for cutting the mutineers off, but for the culpable inactivity of general Hewitt, commander of the station.

7. On the 11th of May, the mutineers from Meerut entered Delhi, and were instantly joined by the native troops there, who proclaimed the titular king of Delhi to be emperor of Tuolia, massacred all the European residents they could find, and even plundered the stores and dwellings of wealthy natives. A handful of determined men, however, under the command of lieutenant Willoughby, succeeded in blowing up the arsenal, and thus prevented an immense amount of ammunition from falling into the hands of the mutineers. It has been observed by the author of an article in the *Edinburgh Review*, referring to the mutinous occupation of the Monghol capital on the morning of the 11th of May, that, "If all the movements of the revolt had been pre-arranged, there could have been no better stroke of tactics than this: Delhi is the chief city of Mohammedan India; the 'imperial city,' the 'city of the Mogul'; it had been the home of those mighty emperors who had ruled so long in Hindostan—of Sir Shah, of Akbar, and of Aurungzebe; and was still the residence of their fallen successors, the titular kings of Delhi, whom fifty years ago, our armies had rescued from the grasp of the Mahrattas. Beyond the palace-walls these remnants of royalty had no power; they had no territory, no revenue, no authority. In *our* eyes they were simply pensioners and puppets. Virtually, indeed, the Mogul was extinct. *But not so in the minds of the people of India*. Empty as was the sovereignty of the Mogul, it was still a living fact in the minds of the Hindoos and Mohammedans, especially in Upper India."

8. The rebellion now spread rapidly through the presidency of Bengal, as well as in other parts of India. At Umballah, the rebels, between the 26th of March and the 1st of May, kindled fifteen incendiary fires, by which an immense amount of ammunition, government stores, and private property were destroyed, but the garrison was saved from destruction by the timely arrival of a reinforcement of European troops from Kussowlee. The whole kingdom of Oude, with the exception of Lucknow, its capital, was soon in the hands of the insurgents. Benares and Allahabad witnessed the revolt of many

regiments and were saved from capture only by a frightful expense of bloodshed and havoc. Similar outbreaks took place at Juanpore, Sultanpore, Agra, Bareilly, and other stations.

9. The mutiny had now become very widely extended; and the situation of the British posts, still holding to their fidelity, was becoming daily more perilous.

10. At Lucknow, sir Henry Lawrence attacked and defeated a numerous body of insurgents, but, was soon afterwards himself besieged in his residency. Here he bravely held out against overwhelming numbers until the beginning of July, when he was mortally wounded in a sally, and the heroic little band compelled to retire into a smaller fort.

11. At Cawnpore a terrible disaster befell the British arms. Sir Hugh Wheeler, a veteran officer of approved bravery, had entrenched himself in the barracks with a force of less than 300 fighting men, and upward of 500 women and children, the wives and families of officers and civilians, and of the Queen's 32nd regiment then besieged at Lucknow. The insurgents were commanded by Nena Sahib, or rather, Dhandoo Pant, Rajah of Bhitoor, the adopted son of the late Peishwah Bajee Rao. This man, under the mask of kindly feeling toward the English nurtured a deadly hatred against the government which had refused to acknowledge his claims as the Peishwah's successor. He had long been addicted to the most revolting sensuality, and had lost all control over his passions. Wearied and enraged by the desperate resistance of this handful of brave men, he offered them a safe passage to Allahabad if they would give up their guns and treasure. The place, indeed, was no longer tenable; and the survivors, diminished in number, were exhausted by constant vigils and want of food. In an evil moment, then, they accepted the terms of their perfidious enemy, marched down to the river, and embarked on board the boats which had been prepared for them. Suddenly a masked battery opened a fire upon them, and crowds of horse and foot soldiers lined either bank. Many were shot dead, still more were drowned, and about 150 taken prisoners: four only escaped, by swimming. The men were instantly put to death in cold blood; the women and children were spared for a few days longer.

12. All this time the main body of the rebels, frequently strengthened by fresh arrivals, had their head quarters at Delhi. On the lower plateau that commands that city was encamped a British force burning for revenge, but too weak

to venture upon an assault. On every occasion, however, they repulsed the repeated sorties of the enemy, and drove them with great slaughter, within the walls. A strange mortality deprived them of their commanders at brief intervals. Gen. Anson died of cholera at Kurnaul, on his way down from the hills. His successor, sir Henry Barnard, was carried off by the same disease before the walls of Delhi. The third was general Reid, whose health also failed him, and compelled him to resign the command to Brigadier Wilson.

13. No sooner had the sad tidings of the massacre at Delhi reached Calcutta, than the governor-general instantly dispatched a vessel to Ceylon to intercept the troops proceeding to China in support of lord Elgin's mission. At the sametime he telegraphed to Madras and Bombay for all the European troops that could be spared; and on the death of general Anson, appointed sir Patrick Grant commander-in-chief of the forces in India, pending the confirmation of the appointment by the home government. Large reinforcements were also drawn from Mauritius and the Cape; and as the mutiny assumed still more formidable dimensions, the European residents in Madras and Calcutta were enrolled into voluntary corps of horse and foot militia.

14. Never, perhaps, did greater excitement prevail in England than when the first intelligence arrived of the revolt of the Bengal army, and of the fiendish atrocities perpetrated by soldiers whose loyalty had become proverbial. As each successive mail brought the narrative of additional horrors, indignation at such unparalleled treachery and brutality almost surpassed the natural feelings of sympathy for those who had suffered such cruel wrongs. The government was urged on all sides to send out immense armies of retribution, and to pause at no amount of expenditure necessary to recover the lost position. Volunteers from all ranks and classes of society spontaneously came forward to tender their services, and, through the initiation of the lord Mayor of London, whose brother, colonel Finnis, was one of the first victims of the mutiny, a relief fund was instituted for the aid of the many hundreds so suddenly reduced to destitution.

15. By the middle of October, upwards of £150,000 were subscribed for this purpose, and the fountain of charity still gave no signs of drying up. It was in the latter end of June that the news of the Meerut revolt and massacre was first received by the ministry, and within three months, more than 30,000 excellent troops had left the British shores, and regi-

General Havelock defeating Nena Sahib on the Banks of the Ganges.

ment after regiment continued to be dispatched in the same direction.

16. Within forty-eight hours of the notification of general Anson's death, sir Colin Campbell was on his way to the East to assume the chief command; and a steady fixed determination was evinced throughout the British Island to reconquer the revolted provinces at any cost of blood or treasure. But before Sir Colin could reach his destination, the tide had already turned, and the victories of British troops had begun to supersede the massacre of defenceless women and children.

17. Gen. Havelock, taking the command at Allahabad of the 78th Highlanders, the Queen's 64th, the 1st Madras fusiliers, and Ferozepore regiment of Sikhs had set out in the hope of arriving at Cawnpore in time to release sir Hugh Wheeler and his devoted comrades. After marching 126 miles, fighting four actions, and capturing a number of guns of heavy calibre, in eight days, and in the worst season of an Indian climate, he was yet too late to avert the terrible catastrophe. The day before he entered Cawnpore, Nena Sahib foully murdered the women and children, who alone survived at the Cawnpore garrison, and caused them to be flung, the dead and the dying, into a well of the courtyard of the assembly rooms.

18. The indefatigable Havelock followed the treacherous Mahratta to Bhitoor, which he captured and dismantled. Then collecting some boats, he crossed the Ganges, and, thrice forcing the enemy from strong positions, arrived within a day's march of Lucknow. But encumbered with his sick and wounded,—cholera having broken out in his little camp,—he was compelled to retrace his steps towards the river.

19. On the banks of the Ganges, for the eighth time, he defeated the enemy, and captured his guns; and a few days afterward, the 15th of August, he marched out from Cawnpore, and again drove them from Bhitoor. His approach had enabled the garrison of Lucknow to sally forth and secure many head of cattle; and, a little later, having undermined a house, they blew up over a hundred of the insurgents and disabled their two heaviest guns. Thus relieved, they informed general Havelock that they could hold their own until he received the reinforcements that were coming up from Calcutta. They would have arrived at Cawnpore some

weeks sooner than they actually did, had not general Lloyd proved unequal to the occasion at Dinapore.

20. Until the 25th of July, three regiments of native infantry stationed at that place had continued faithful; but circumstances having occurred to create suspicion, the general was advised to disarm them. Instead of doing so, he merely ordered them to give up their percussion caps before a certain hour; by which time they were making the best of their way to the river Soane. When it was too late to be of service, the 10th and a battery of artillery were sent in pursuit, but failed to inflict much loss. Subsequently a detachment under captain Dunbar was dispatched to relieve Arrah, a civil station closely invested by the Dinapore mutineers. Marching without taking proper precautions, these troops fell into an ambush, and were driven back to their boats, with the loss of 150 killed and wounded. The glory of relieving Arrah was reserved for major Eyre, of the Bengal artillery, who, with three guns and 150 men of the 5th fusiliers, dispersed the insurgents, captured Jugdeespore, and restored the communication between Calcutta and the upper provinces.

21. With rare exceptions, the native chiefs preserved their engagements with the British government during this critical period. The contingent forces, indeed, of Scandiah and Holkar joined the mutineers, but those princes do not appear to have been in any way accessory to the movement. The Sikh states, and especially the rajahs of Jheend and Puttiala, rendered signal service; and both the Nepaulese government and the Maharajah Goolab Sing of Cashmere (who died on the 2nd of August) sent considerable bodies of auxiliary troops to the aid of the British. Still more significant is the fact that the villagers, almost invariably, exhibited more sympathy for the British than for their own countrymen. It is true that they oftentimes plundered unarmed fugitives, but they showed still less mercy to the rebel sepoys when not in sufficient force to protect themselves. It thus appears evident that the revolt of the Bengal army was actually a mutiny, and not a popular insurrection.

22. Meanwhile the mutterings of disaffection began to be heard also in the Bombay presidency. The 27th N. I. broke out into open mutiny at Kolapore, and, shortly afterwards, the 21st N. I. conspired at Kurrachee to massacre the European inhabitants; but their projected villany being discovered, they were promptly disarmed, and the ringleaders justly punished.

The Joudpore legion was not more faithful to its colours than other contingent forces; and the trifling successes which attended their first movements, encouraged the enemies of the British government throughout Rajpootana to take up arms and join their ranks.

23. The Madras troops, with the exception of the 8th light cavalry, exhibited a rare and honourable example of fidelity amid such wide-spread treachery and rebellion. But on the north-east-frontier of Bengal, the Assamese, displayed a restlessness that boded no good; and their vicinity to the Burmese on the one hand, and to the Santhals on the other, rendered it necessary to adopt energetic measures to keep them in awe.

24. Unhappily, the governor-general of India, lord Canning, too rarely manifested the decision of character demanded in such an emergency. Of personal courage there was no want, but he was deficient in quickness of conception and in moral hardihood. His councillors were even more timid than himself. And thus the mutineers were encouraged, and the European residents in Calcutta, in the same proportion, disheartened, by the habitual vacillation of the government.

25. At one time, during the advent of the great Mohammedan festival of the Mohurrum, a panic prevailed throughout all classes of the Christian inhabitants; and was only allayed by the unexpected arrival of Lord Elgin, with the *Shannon* and the *Pearl*.

26. At a later period, lord Canning converted this feeling of distrust into one of disgust and indignation, by appointing a lieutenant-governor of the central provinces, with two Mohammedan assistants, to supersede martial law, and to tie the hands of the military leaders upon whose promptness and resolution depended the safety both of individuals and the state. In pursance of the same impolitic line of conduct, an act was passed by the legislature rendering it a misdemeanor to possess arms or ammunition, without first obtaining a license to that effect. As his lordship had previously returned an ungracious answer to a petition of the European community praying that the native population might be disarmed, it was felt that this was at least an intimation that the European settlers were no more trustworthy than the people of the country.

27. While these dissensions reigned at the Presidency, sir James Outram, who had succeeded general Lloyd at Dinapore, hastily collected what forces he could muster, and pushed

on to reinforce general Havelock at Cawnpore. With characteristic magnaminity, however, he first disclaimed all intention of plucking the nobly-earned laurels from the grasp of his junior officer, and intimated his desire to accompany him solely in his civil capacity of chief commissioner of Oude. His march upward from Allahabad, however, was much impeded by the heavy rains, and at one point a small body of the enemy attempted to harass his flank; but being vigorously attacked by a detachment under major Eyre, they were destroyed almost to a man. It was thus the 19th of September before general Havelock was in a position to cross the Ganges for a third time, and to advance with an efficient force to relieve the long-beleaguered garrison at Lucknow.

28. On that day the army of relief crossed the river by a bridge of boats, and encamped on the other side. General Havelock's force consisted of about 2000 European infantry, the Sikh regiment of Ferozepore, three batteries of field artillery, and a handful of volunteer cavalry. The rebels mustered about 40,000 strong, but their numerical superiority only served to enhance the prowess of their conquerors. The first engagement took place on the 21st of September, at the village of Mongarwar, and resulted in the total defeat of the mutineers. Five-field pieces and two guns in position were taken; two of the former being captured by the volunteer cavalry, led on to the charge by general Outram in person.

29. From this point the army pushed on by forced marches without encountering any organized opposition, until it arrived before the city of Lucknow. Skirting the suburbs of that one stately capital, General Havelock forced his way through every obstacle, and by the evening of the 25th, had relieved the heroic garrison.

30. The relief was opportune. Two mines had already been driven under the chief works, and, in a few hours more, would have been loaded and sprung. The besieged would thus have been at the mercy of those who knew no mercy.

31. The city, however, had still to be subdued. From several advantageous positions, the enemy continued to fire upon the fort, and were only finally dislodged after a series of determined assaults.

32. In these operations the loss of the British was very severe. General Neil, the brave and energetic saviour of Benares, and the inexorable avenger of the massacre of Cawnpore, was among the slain. With him fell major Cooper, in

command of the artillery, and many other gallant spirits. Even now much remained to be done. Taking courage from their overwhelming numbers, the enemy soon closed again around the army of deliverance, and cut off their communications with Cawnpore. Encumbered with not less than 1000 women and children, and sick or wounded men, it would have been hazardous, if not impossible, to have attempted a retrograde march across a difficult country, harassed on all sides by an active and desperate enemy. Under these circumstances, sir James Outram, who had now assumed the chief command, determined on remaining at Lucknow, and awaiting the arrival of reinforcements. His position, indeed, was critical, but events in another quarter were in the meantime operating in his favour.

33. Until the latter end of August, the British troops before Delhi are rather to be considered as an army of observation, than as a besieging force. Their inferiority in numbers and artillery was barely counterbalanced by their superior discipline, courage, and physical strength. These advantages enabled them, indeed, to maintain their ground, but not to assume the offensive.

34. Toward the close of August, however, a reinforcement of European and Sikh troops, under brigadier Nicholson, arrived from the Punjab, and, on the 25th of that month, the rebels were defeated at Nujuffghur, with great slaughter and the loss of thirteen guns. A few days later, a heavy siege-train was received from Ferozepore, and breaching batteries were constructed on the north side of the city. The siege may be said to have commenced on the 7th of September; and, by the evening of the 13th, the engineers reported two practicable breaches,—one near the Cashmere, the other near the Water bastion. Arrangements were, therefore, at once made for an assault to take place at daybreak on the following morning.

35. The first column, commanded by brigadier Nicholson, advanced under a tremendous fire, and applying their scaling-ladders, carried the Cashmere bastion, and established themselves in the main-guard. Almost simultaneously, the second column, under brigadier Jones, stormed the Water bastion, and effected a junction with their comrades inside the walls.

36. A third column, under colonel Campbell, awaited the blowing open of the Cashmere gate to join in the assault. They had not long to wait. Lieutenant Salkeld and Home, of the engineers, accompanied by three sergeants carrying

the powder-bags, walked up to the gateway in broad daylight, and, while exposed to a heavy fire of musketry, coolly fastened the bags to the iron spikes of the gate. In the performance of this heroic exploit, lieutenant Salkeld was severely wounded, and two of the sergeants killed upon the spot; but the train was lighted, and the gate blown open with a tremendous crash.

37. As the smoke cleared away, the storming party sprang through the ruins with a British cheer; and, the three columns uniting, made themselves master of the whole line of works, from the Water bastion to the Cabul gate; and before nightfall were in possession of Skinner's house, the Church, the College, and the adjacent grounds. This brilliant success, however, was not achieved without great loss of life.

38. Of the European soldiery, eight officers and 162 rank and file were killed, with fifty-two officers and 510 rank and file wounded; of the sepoys, 413 were placed *hors de combat*, of whom 103 were slain outright. The total number of casualties thus amounted to 1145, or one-third of the entire assaulting force. Among the mortally wounded was brigadier Nicholson, whose death was justly deplored as a national calamity.

39. Simultaneously with these main attacks, a diversion was made by a fourth column, consisting of Sikhs, Ghoorkas, and Cashmerians, on the suburbs of Kishengunge and Pahareepore. But, in spite of their most strenuous efforts, these troops failed to overcome the desperate resistance offered by the enemy; and, in the end, were compelled to retreat, though not ingloriously.

40. The day following, the assault was consumed in shelling the palace and in battering the magazine. A breach was effected; and, at daylight on the 16th, a storming party dashed forward with such impetuosity that the rebel artillerymen dropped their lighted port-fires and fled, leaving undischarged six guns of large calibre commanding the breach and loaded with grape. On the 17th, the British troops became masters of the Bank, formerly the palace of the Begum Sumroo, and, shortly afterward, of the Jumma Musjid, or principal mosque. Heavy guns were now brought to play upon the palace and the bridge of boats; and by the evening of the 20th, the rebels entirely evacuated the city and its suburbs. Then was seen the extent of the damage sustained by the former capital of the Moghul dynasty. Whole streets had been laid in ruins; dead bodies tainted the air in all

directions; the inhabitants, reduced to beggary, were crouching, terror-stricken, in obscure lurking places. But the British soldier is merciful in victory, as he is irresistible in battle. To armed rebels, no mercy was shown; but women and children, and the defenceless citizens, were spared and protected.

41. The venerable descendant of Timour—venerable only by reason of his gray hairs and extreme old age—had fled, with his principal Begum, two sons, and a grandson, to the tomb of his ancestor, Hoomayoon, son of the mighty Baber. Here he was discovered and seized by Captain Hodson, of the 2nd European fusiliers. His own life and that of his queen were respected; but the princes were led out and shot, and their dead bodies publicly exposed at the Kotwalee, or mayor's court.

42. Gen. Wilson, whose health failed him in the hour of victory, now resigned the command to brigadier Penny, C.B., a veteran of approved gallantry. Colonel Burn, whose father so gallantly defended Delhi against Jeswunt Rao Holkar in 1803, was appointed military commandant within the city, and measures were successfully taken to re-establish order, and to afford protection to well-disposed and peaceful citizens. Two moveable columns, consisting each of 1600 infantry, 500 cavalry, three troops of horse artillery, and 18 guns, were told off, and ordered to follow up the retreating enemy without delay. One of these, commanded by Colonel Greathed, of the 84th, came up with a rebel force strongly posted near Bolundshuhur, and, after a spirited engagement, utterly discomfited them, with the loss of two guns, a vast quantity of ammunition, and 100 men.

43. On the same day the other column overtook the mutineers at Muttra, and inflicted severe chastisement. The security of Agra was thus assured, and a direct road laid open into Oude. Reinforcements from England were at the same time arriving at Calcutta, and each successive day fresh troops were rapidly pushed up the country. The tide had turned. The mutineers had lost their opportunity.

44. Since June, 1857, a large body of Europeans, including many women and children, had been held beleaguered in the residency at Lucknow. Towards the close of September, general Havelock attempted to relieve them. He had penetrated through the enemy's numerous forces to the residency just in time to prevent its fall. His force not being sufficient to protect the retreat of the women and children to

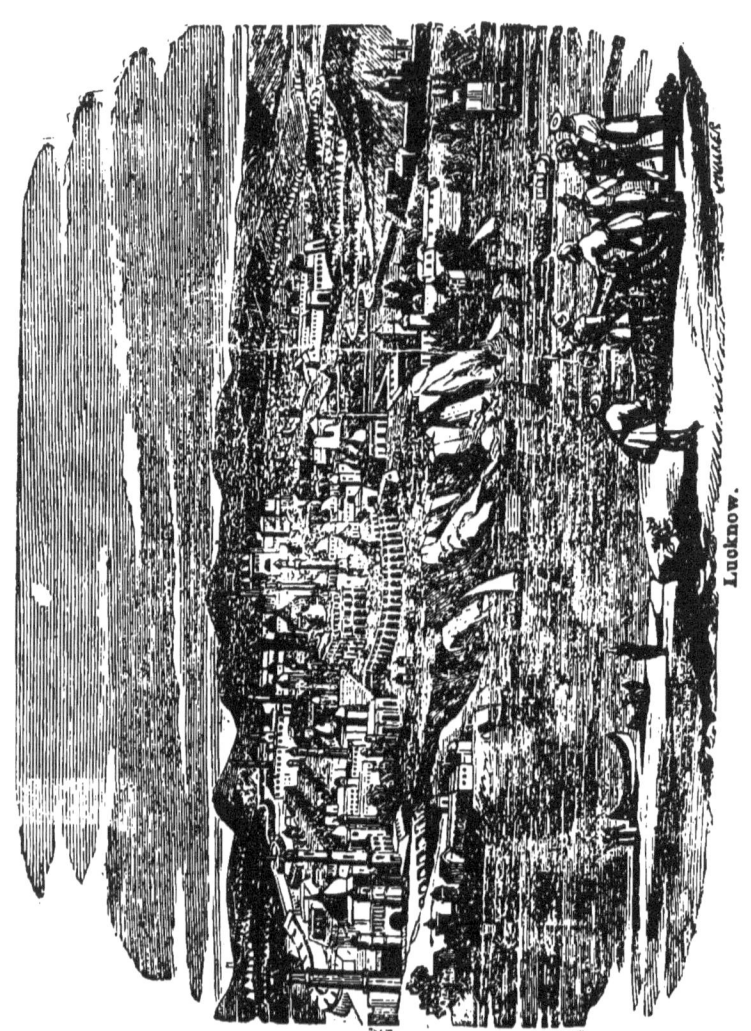
Lucknow.

Cawnpore, he remained at the residency, the garrison of which was strengthened by a portion of the troops, the rest falling back upon Cawnpore.

45. Lucknow was held by 50,000 rebels, who pressed the siege of the residency with great vigour, and the position of the defenders was extremely critical.

46. Sir Colin Campbell, the commander-in-chief, left Cawnpore with a strong force, on the 9th of November, to relieve Lucknow. He succeeded, by a well-conceived stratagem, on the 12th, in bringing away the garrison, with the women and children, and marched for Cawnpore.

47. On the third day after leaving Lucknow, general Havelock died from the effects of dysentery, brought on by excessive fatigue and anxiety.

48. In December, Cawnpore was attacked by 25,000 rebels with 50 guns, and Sir Colin Campbell was summoned from the neighbourhood of Lucknow for its defence. He arrived in season to save the place, after a severe action with the enemy.

49. Sir Colin remained at Cawnpore, collecting a large force for the final siege of Lucknow. During the time which was thus occupied, several actions of minor importance took place; but it was not till the 17th of March that Lucknow was recovered, after a short but active siege. After its fall, the kingdom of Oude, of which it was the capital, was speedily restored to obedience and comparative tranquillity.

50. Since the fall of Lucknow, the war has assumed a guerilla character in various parts of India; and no other event of equal importance has transpired.

Questions for Examination.

1. What is said of the war with Russia? Of the Sepoy mutiny?
2. Of lords Dalhousie and Canning?
3. Of the Persian war?
4. Of the Mohammedans of Upper India? Of the king of Delhi?
5. Of the Mohammedans and Hindoos? Of the greased cartridges?
6. What took place in Oude? In Lucknow? At Meerut?
7. At Delhi? What was said by a writer in the Edinburgh Review?
8. What is said of the spread of the rebellion?
9. Of the situation of the British posts?
10. What took place at Lucknow?
11. At Cawnpore? What is said of Nena Sahib?
12. What was occurring at Delhi?
13. At Calcutta?
14. In England?
15. What force was sent out to India?
16. Who was appointed commander-in-chief?
17. What was done by general Havelock? By Nena Sahib?

18. By Havelock at Bhitoor?
19. On the banks of the Ganges?
20. What took place at Arrah?
21. What is said of the native chiefs?
22. What took place in the Bombay presidency?
23. What is said of the Madras troops? Of the Assamese?
24. What is said of lord Canning?
25. Of the Mohurrum?
26. Of lord Canning's measures respecting the central provinces?
27. Of Sir James Outram? Of Havelock?
28. Of the battle of Mungarwar?
29. Of Havelock at Lucknow?
30. Of the relief?
31. Of the city?
32. Of the losses? Of Outram?
33. Of the British troops before Delhi?
34. What events followed?
35. What was done by Nicholson? By Jones?
36. By Campbell? B. Salkeld and Home?
37. By the storming party?
38. What is said of the losses?
39. What was done in the suburbs of Delhi?
40. What was done on the 16th of September? The 17th?
41. What is said of the king of Delhi?
42. Of generals Wilson and Penny? Of Greathed?
43. What events followed?
44. What took place at Lucknow?
45. What is said of the siege?
46. Of Sir Colin Campbell?
47. Of general Havelock?
48. What took place at Cawnpore?
49. At Lucknow?
50. After the fall of Lucknow?

CHAPTER XL.

SKETCH OF THE PROGRESS OF LITERATURE, SCIENCE, AND THE ARTS, DURING THE PRESENT CENTURY.

> Calmly they show us mankind victorious
> O'er all that's aimless, blind, and base;
> Their presence has made our nature glorious,
> Unveiling our night's illumined face.—*Sterling.*

1. In the middle of the last century, science, and literature in England were fast losing all traces of originality; invention was discouraged, research undervalued, and the examination of nature proscribed. It seemed to be generally established, that the treasures accumulated in the preceding age were quite sufficient for all national purposes, and that the only duty which authors had to perform was to reproduce what had been thus accumulated, in a more elegant shape, adorned with all the graces of polished style. Tameness and monotony naturally result from a slavish adherence to established rules, and every branch of literature felt this blighting influence. History, perhaps, was in some degree an exception; for Hume, Robertson, but more especially Gibbon, exhibited a spirit of original investigation which found no parallel amongst their contemporaries. 2. The American war first broke the chains that had thus fettered the public mind; passions were excited, party zeal kindled; and, in the keen encounters of rival statesmen, an example was set of bidding defiance to all arbitrary rules. Parliamentary eloquence was the first result of the change, and the principal cause of its further extension. While Burke, Fox, Sheridan, and, at a latter period, Pitt, spoke as their peculiar habits of thought prompted them, not as the rhetoric of the schools taught, Cowper and Burns made vigorous efforts for the emancipation of poetry, and substituted the suggestions of nature for the dictates of art. Their success, however, would scarcely have been decisive, had not the American war been followed by a still more terrible convulsion. 3. The French revolution shook everything that had been morally as well as politically established in Europe to the very foundation. There was no principal, however sacred,—no institution, however sanctioned by long experience,—no rule of conduct however tried and proved,—that was not rudely questioned and fiercely assailed. Hopes were entertained by some, that a new era of social happiness was about to dawn upon the world; others feared that society was about

to be rent in sunder, and every sign of civilization destroyed. It is not our purpose to say anything of the political effects produced by the French revolution: its literary consequences, as has been the case with every period of great excitement, were decidedly beneficial. A total change was wrought in every branch of literature, a change which demanded from every writer, vigorous thought instead of eloquent expression.

4. Crabbe, the poet of rustic life in England, derived his impulse from the American war; but it is to the struggle with France that we owe Coleridge, Wordsworth, and Southey,—men alike in their devotion to nature, but different in their modes of testifying that homage, because each has followed the bent of his own mode of thought. The enthusiasm with which these eminent poets hailed the dawn of freedom in France, embittered their disappointment when they saw the evil uses to which the name of liberty was perverted; they became vehement opponents of the political developement of the French revolution, but they clung fondly to its intellectual principles, and maintained the right of genius to explore untravelled paths, though its course might not be that pointed out by critics. Their example was followed by Montgomery, Byron, Scott, and Campbell; and by a host of other writers whose works have enriched modern literature. The female mind also felt the influence of this mighty revolution, and some of the noblest productions in modern poetry have been written by ladies. We may mention the names of Miss Joanna Bailie and Mrs. Hemans.

5. There was, however, one species of poetry, the drama, which had little or no share in the success which we have described; in fact, it was almost destroyed by that very means. It is at the moment when a nation is wakening into intellectual life, that the drama most flourishes; men are then eager to receive instruction, and the theatre affords it in the most pleasing as well as the most forcible form. But as civilization advances, other and more efficient means of instruction are provided; the drama loses its influence over the improved generation, just as the picture-books of childhood cease to be valued in youth; it sinks into a mere means of entertainment, and its strength is lost with its high purpose. The periodical press now holds the position that the stage did in the time of queen Elizabeth. That the drama might advance, it would be necessary for civilization to retrograde, and that would be far too high a price to pay even for another Shakspeare.

6. The great extension and excellence of our periodical press, both literary and political, is one of the most striking characteristics of the age. Not merely the reviews and magazines, but even the common newspapers, display literary merits of a very high order. Men of the most eminent abilities and exalted stations contribute to our journals; and they consequently hold a high rank in the literature of the age. Reviews, especially, have risen into unexampled eminence, and have maintained their stations by a succession of articles that tend at once to improve the taste and enlarge the understanding. Some of the periodicals have a circulation which, in a past age, would not have been credited. This is owing to the more general diffusion of education among all classes.

7. The importance of affording useful instruction to every class of the community, is now universally acknowledged; and the progress of education has become so rapid, that there is every prospect that its blessings will soon become universal. And not only is the quantity of instruction increased, but its quality is greatly improved, as might easily be shown by a comparison of our present school-books with those of the last century. It is no exaggeration to state, that the elements of a really useful education may be more easily obtained by the poor of the present day, than by the richest of past generations.

8. History, which used to be a mere repetition of what had been previously narrated by others, has called criticism to its aid. Instead of a slavish adherence to authority, we now see writers carefully examine facts, compare evidence, and investigate the motives which might have led original authors to conceal or disguise the truth. Lingard, Hallam, Turner, Southey, and sir James Mackintosh, have been especially conspicuous for their critical sagacity, in eliciting the truth from conflicting statements; but notwithstanding their exertions, the English school of historical criticism may still be regarded as in its infancy.

9. Perhaps we may ascribe this deficiency in our histories to the unexampled progress and popularity of romantic literature, owing chiefly to the labours of Sir Walter Scott, who was among the first to unite in works of fiction the highest flights of imagination with the realities of life. Novels and romances have ceased to be dangerous and absurd, though they were both in a period not very remote. Historical romances are to this age what the historical plays of Shaks-

peare were to a former period,—vivid pictures of our ancestors; representing them, if not exactly as they thought and acted, yet so nearly what they might have been, that they become to us a kind of acquaintance, and seem brought within the sphere of our personal knowledge.

10. Periodical criticism supplies the place of what used to be termed general literature; hence formal works on mental and moral philosophy and the *belles lettres* are rare. Blair and lord Kames were the guides of our fathers in matters of taste: we have rejected their authority, and defer more to the principles maintained by the leading reviews. These principles, however, are scattered in different essays over a multitude of volumes, and no one has yet appeared of sufficient authority to be entrusted with the task of collecting them into a new code. 11. Reid, Stewart, and Brown, were the last great writers on metaphysics. Their fame will probably long remain uneclipsed, for the science of mind seems to have lost its hold on public attention, as indeed have almost all merely speculative studies. What is chiefly desired in the present day, is something practical and immediately useful.

12. Political economy and statistics have occupied the position which was once held by metaphysics. Adam Smith was in some measure the founder of the former science, from his investigating the nature and causes of a nation's wealth. Since his day, the subject has engaged the attention of several eminent writers, especially Ricardo, Malthus, and Macculloch. The cultivation of statistics must be the source of all future improvement in the science of political economy, because it is to the table of the statistician that the economist must look for his facts; and all speculations not founded upon facts, though they may be admired and applauded when first propounded, will, in the end, assuredly be forgotten.

13. The abstract sciences have made great progress in England during the last few years; principally owing to the great exertions of Airy, Ivory, Peacock, and Hamilton, who have greatly extended the domain of mathematical calculation. In the mixed and applied sciences, also, much has been done, though no very conspicuous discovery can be mentioned. 14. Astronomy owes much to the great impulse it has received from the discovery of a new planet by Sir William Herschell; and it has not been less benefitted by the labours of his son and successor, Sir John Herschell, whose investigations into the nature of the displacements

observed among the fixed stars, have led to many, and will lead to more important results. The science of optics has become almost wholly new from the improvements effected by Sir David Brewster and Dr. Young. But above all, dynamics have been enriched by a series of discoveries, amounting to a complete revolution in our knowledge of motive powers. It will be sufficient to mention one of these, —the application of steam to machinery.

15. Chemistry, electricity, and electro-magnetism, may be almost regarded as new sciences, in consequence of the numerous discoveries of Davy, Dalton, and Farraday. It would be impossible to enumerate all the practical advantages that have resulted from the improvements in chemical science; but we may mention the use of gas to light our cities and public buildings, and the invention of the safety-lamp, by which the dangers to be dreaded from the explosion of the fire-damp in mines have been in a great degree averted.

16. The progress of maritime and inland discovery was very great during the early part of the reign of George III. It has since made less advance, because the first navigators left little for their successors to explore. The interior of Africa has, however, at length been penetrated by the Landers, and Burnes has found a practicable route from the British possessions in Northern India to Central Asia. The value of these researches has been fully proved by the fact that many of the places discovered in the reign of George III. by Cook, Wallis, Carteret, Vancouver, &c., have already become colonies, or valuable depots of British commerce.

17. Only one speculative science, it seems, has enjoyed popularity,—we mean geology. Perhaps part of its success is owing to its connection with the practical science of mineralogy. Geology makes us acquainted with so many singular facts tending to prove that the world was once tenanted by a race of beings different from those now found in it, that we cannot be surprised at the delight with which it is studied. Indeed, a much less agreeable subject might become popular, if recommended by men of such ability as Conybeare, Smith, Buckland, Sedgwick, Mantell, and Lyell.

18. Physiology, anatomy, and natural history, have received very remarkable improvements. Hunter's example has stimulated many to exert themselves in the same field of science; and the result has been a perceptible increase of

the average duration of human life. The investigation of the nervous system by Sir Charles Bell, is among the most recent and brilliant of the additions that have been made to the medical science.

19. Statiscal science may almost be regarded as the creation of this age. The word "statistics" was invented in the middle of the last century by a German professor, to express a summary view of the physical, moral, and social condition of states. He justly remarked, that a numerical statement of the extent, density of population, imports, exports, revenues, &c., of a country, more perfectly explained its social condition than general statements, however graphic or however accurate. When such statements began to be collected and exhibited in a popular form, it was soon discovered that the political and economical sciences were likely to gain the position of physical sciences; that is to say, they were about to obtain records of observation, which would test the accuracy of recognized principles and lead to the discovery of new modes of action. But the great object of this new science is to lead to the knowledge of human nature; that is, to ascertain the general course of operation of man's mental and moral faculties, and to furnish us with a correct standard of judgment, by enabling us to determine the average amount of the past, as a guide to the average probabilities of the future. This science is yet in its infancy, but has already produced the most beneficial effects. The accuracy of the tables of life have rendered the calculations of rates of insurance a matter of much greater certainty than they were heretofore; the system of keeping the public accounts has been simplified and improved and, finally, the experimental sciences of medicine and political economy, have been fixed upon a firmer foundation than could be anticipated in the last century. Even in private life this science is likely to prove of immense advantage, by directing the attention to the collection and registration of facts, and thus preventing the formation of hasty judgments and erroneous conclusions.

20. Political economy, though an older science than statistics, must be regarded as intimately connected with that branch of knowledge. Its object is to ascertain the laws which regulate the distribution of wealth, and the relation of demand and supply in the production and consumption of both natural and artificial commodities. Such a science is consequently of the highest importance to a commercial and

manufacturing community; and the increased attention paid to it of late years, has led to a removal of many severe restrictions, which, under a false notion of protection, were imposed on British trade. At first, political economy was regarded with great suspicion, being looked upon as one of those idle speculations, which, under the false designation of social sciences, were broached in France during the frenzy of the revolution, at the close of the last century. But its importance is now so fully recognized, that professorships of the new science have been established in the principal universities.

21. Even in this slight sketch it would be unpardonable not to mention the great, the almost miraculous increase of machinery in our manufactories; an increase consequent upon the cultivation of the sciences and their practical application. The use of steamboats, of locomotive engines, and of countless machines for superseding manual labour, has placed Britain far in advance of all other manufacturing countries, and proportionably increased the comforts of every class of the community.

22. Great as the progress of British industry, arts, and sciences was, under the three preceding reigns, it has recently received a new impulse by the formation of the British Association for the promotion of science, which promises to produce the most beneficial results. The meetings of this society are held annually at some one or other of the great towns of the empire. Its objects are, to give a strong impulse and more systematic direction to scientific enquiry; to promote the intercourse of those who cultivate science in the different parts of the British empire, with each other, and with foreign philosophers; to obtain a more general attention to the objects of science, and a removal of any disadvantages of a public kind which might impede its progress. The Association has had a meeting in each of the following places: York, Oxford, Cambridge, Edinburgh, Dublin, Bristol, and Liverpool. It is divided into seven sections: 1, Mathematics and Physics; 2, Chemistry and Mineralogy; 3, Zoology and Botany; 4, Anatomy and Physiology; 5, Geology; 6, Statistics; and 7, Mechanical Science. In all these departments, but especially the last two, the greatest benefits have resulted from bringing practical men into immediate contact with the theoretical cultivators of science. Magnetical observatories have been established in consequence in various parts

of the empire, and several series of observations have been made to determine the direction and intensity of the magnetic force. The attention of the Association has also been directed to experiments tending to illustrate the nature of the connection between electricity and magnetism; and since its formation, meteorology has been so extended as to become a new science. The attention of the statistical section has been recently directed to the state of public education, and to the condition of the working classes, both in the manufacturing and agricultural districts. It is to be hoped that these investigations will point out the evils which require to be remedied, and the means by which society in Great Britain may be elevated and improved.

23. Turning from the useful to the elegant arts, we must first remark the great revival of architectural taste during the last two reigns, especially as displayed in the many improvements of the metropolis. Inconvenient and narrow passages have been removed to make room for Regent Street, one of the finest lines of communication in Europe; the Regent's Park and the new squares in Pimlico, occupy spaces which were recently unsightly wastes; and the Strand, from being an inconvenient thoroughfare, has been widened into a street which, for its beauty, combined with its adaptation to business, has few if any rivals. The erection of those two magnificent structures, Waterloo and London Bridges, has led to the opening of new lines of communication, which promise to be equally ornamental and useful. Recent calamities have also given an impulse to architectural skill. The destruction of both houses of Parliament and the Royal Exchange by fire, have rendered the erection of new edifices necessary; and judging from the excellence of the designs which have been tendered for the erection of new houses for the legislature, there is every reason to believe that the new building will be worthy of an enlightened age and nation.

24. Though painting and sculpture have not been unpatronized, it must be confessed that they have not advanced with the same rapidity and steadiness as the other arts, though England possesses professors of both who deserve to be ranked among the ornaments of their country. Many causes may be assigned for this inferiority, but the principal is the discontinuance of the use of pictures and statues for religious purposes since the time of the Reformation. Notwithstanding this disadvantage, however, the English school of art has recently made such great advances, that it bids fair at no distant day

to rank as the first in Europe. The National Gallery, which has been recently completed in Trafalgar Square, will probably be found one of the best aids to the encouragement of excellence in statuary and painting, and to the formation of the public taste for appreciating the beauties of art.

25. The great additions made to the British Museum, and the freedom with which its treasures are opened to the public, must tend greatly to inspire a taste for contemplating the wonders of nature and art. The department of Natural History must be taken in connection with the Zoological Gardens, which have been recently established, not only in the metropolis, but in various parts of the empire; thus viewed, it is unrivalled in the world. The Elgin marbles contain specimens of Athenian sculpture belonging to an age when that art had attained the summit of its glory, and, though unfortunately mutilated, they furnish models to the young aspirants, which cannot be studied without the most advantageous results. In the gallery of Egyptian antiquities, the historical student has an opportunity of seeing the advances made in civilization by a powerful nation three thousand years ago, and for consulting the strongest evidences of the truth of Biblical history.

26. In this rapid view of literature, science, and the arts, space has only allowed the mention of a few leading features; but there is one circumstance more, too important to be omitted,—the growing and marked connection between religion and every department in which human intelligence is exercised. The discoveries of the traveller are combined with the labours of the missionary; the studies of the naturalist are directed to elucidate the wonders of creative power; our best poets have dedicated no small portion of their works to celebrating the praises of their God ; and in other departments of literature few traces can be found of the levity, the profaneness, and the sneers at things sacred, which so often sullied the writings of the past generation. It is now deeply felt and strongly enforced, that all researches, whether mental or material, directly tend to give new proofs of the power, the wisdom, and the beneficence of that Almighty Being who has called into existence, and so wonderfully adapted to each other, the universe of matter and the universe of mind.

27. But it is not in reference to England alone that this beneficial change in the character of our national literature demands our thankfulness and admiration. The language of

England girdles the globe; it is spoken in every climate and every quarter of the earth; her colonies are laying the foundations of future states; the descendants of her colonies have already become one of the foremost nations in rank and influence. England has thus obtained great influence in the future progress of civilization, and on her is thrown the responsibility of moulding the character of countless generations. While we thus perceive that she has been called by the dispensation of Providence to fulfil a higher destiny, we should at the same time feel how important is the trust, and earnestly desire that its performance should be such as to promote the honour of God and the welfare of mankind establishing everywhere the principles announced at the advent of our blessed Redeemer, "Peace on earth, good will toward men."

Questions for Examination.

1. In what state was British literature about the middle of the last century?
2. By what political event was a change effected?
3. What consequences resulted from the French revolution?
4. Were those effects exhibited in our poetical literature?
5. How did the drama fail to share in the general improvement?
6. What circumstances connected with the periodical press are peculiarly characteristic of the present age?
7. Has much been effected for the causes of national education?
8. Are histories, written in the present day, remarkable for anything that was rare in the last century?
9. What branch of literature has flourished to the probable injury of history?
10. Why are works on general literature rare?
11. Have metaphysics received much attention?
12. What advantages may result from the cultivation of political economy and statistics?
13. Have any advances been made in the mathematical sciences?
14. What improvements have been effected in the physical sciences?
15. Have any sciences been so much improved that they may almost be regarded as new?
16. What advantages have resulted from the progress of maritime and inland discovery?
17. Why has geology become popular?
18. Did the medical sciences share in the general improvement?
19. What are the nature and objects of statistical science?
20. In what condition is the new science of Political Economy?
21. What great inventions have been made in the useful arts?
22. What is the design of the British Association?
23. Have any improvements been made in architecture?
24. What are the present state and future prospects of painting and sculpture?
25. What benefits result from the British Museum?
26. Is there any circumstance peculiarly gratifying in the view of modern literature?
27. What is there peculiarly important in the present condition of England?

CHAPTER XLI.

THE BRITISH CONSTITUTION.

1. EVERY government is instituted to secure the general happiness of the community; and especially to protect the person and property of every individual. Constitutions are established to secure the good administration of the government, by giving the people some direct or indirect control over their rulers, and also a share in the formation of the laws. 2. The British constitution differs from most others in its formation. It was formed very gradually. Checks against the abuses of power were not devised until the evils were actually felt, and consequently its details, though sometimes cumbrous, and perhaps inconsistent, are the results of long experience, and have been rendered, by old habits, exactly suited to the peculiar circumstances of the nation.

3. The government established in England by the Norman conqueror was a feudal despotism. The land was divided into fiefs, which were for the most part given to the Norman lords or barons, who were invested with absolute power over the lives and fortunes of their vassals. There were no written limitations to the power of the king over the barons; but Henry I. eager to secure partisans in his usurpation of the crown from his brother Robert, granted a charter of privileges to his nobility, which contained also a few stipulations in favour of the great body of the people.

4. The conditions of this charter were flagrantly violated; until at length, in the reign of John, the barons, with a powerful body of their adherents, appeared in arms against the king, and forced him to sign Magna Charta, the great foundation of English liberty. Though this charter was principally designed to protect the nobles from the encroachments of royal power, it contained some important provisions in favour of general liberty; a clear proof of the growing power of the commons.

5. When the importance of commerce began to be understood, it was found necessary to secure the trading towns and communities from the exactions of their powerful neighbours; for in the middle ages piracy and highway robbery were deemed honourable professions by most of the feudal nobles in Europe. To protect trade, charters of incorporations were

granted to several cities and towns, by which they were released from dependence on a feudal lord, and permitted to enjoy a government of their own choosing. A gradual change took place through the country in consequence of the adventurous and reckless spirit of the Norman barons. Some sold their fiefs to raise money for joining the crusades; others wasted them by piecemeal to support their riot and dissipation; and thus from various causes a body of small landholders began to be formed, independent of the great barons, and looking to the crown for protection against them. 6. When the earl of Leicester took up arms to restrain the capricious tyranny of Henry III. he summoned a parliament to sanction his designs; and, that the voice of the nation might be more clearly expressed, he invited the counties to elect knights of the shire, and the cities and towns to send deputies, to aid in these consultations. This appears to have been the first attempt to form a house of commons; but the origin and early progress of that branch of the legislature is involved in great, not to say hopeless, obscurity.

7. The commons were generally courted by the king as a counterbalance to the power of the nobility. Until the civil wars between the rival houses of York and Lancaster, having thinned the ranks of the barons, extinguishing many noble houses, and almost annihilating the influence of the rest, the royal power became supreme, and so continued during the reigns of the four sovereigns of the house of Tudor. 8. But the commons during this period had been silently collecting their strength, and, on the accession of James I. they insisted on their privileges with a pertinacity which led to a long struggle between the king and the parliament. In this contest the majority of the house of lords, which had been reinforced by the elevation to the peerage of some of the heads of the old English families, espoused the cause of the commons. At length Charles I. was coerced into granting the petition of right, which secured many valuable constitutional privileges to the people. But passions had been excited in the struggle which brought on a civil war, that ended in the overthrow of the monarchy.

9. During the reign of Charles II. the celebrated habeas corpus was passed, by which personal liberty is secured to the subject; but the perfection of the British constitution was completed in 1688, when James II. was hurled from the throne for his arbitrary principles, the right of parliament to regulate the succession to the crown established, and the

liberties of the people secured by the Bill of Rights and the Act of Settlement. 10. After that period no important change was made in the constitution until the passing of the recent Reform Bill, by which the decayed and deserted boroughs have lost their right of sending members to parliament, and the privilege has been transferred to the larger counties and more important towns.

11. The legislative power of England is placed in the parliament, which consists of three parts,—the king, (or queen,) the lords and the commons.

12. The crown of England is hereditary, but parliament has a right to alter the line of succession. After the abdication of James II., the right of succession was limited to protestants, and on the impending failure of protestant heirs to Charles I., the settlement was extended to the protestant line of James I., viz. to the princess Sophia of Hanover, and the heirs of her body, being protestants. The present reigning family is descended from the princess Sophia, and holds the throne in right of her parliamentary title.

13. The duties of the sovereign are described in the coronation oath. They are, first, to govern according to law; secondly, to execute judgments in mercy; and thirdly, to maintain the established religion. 14. The prerogatives of the king, by which is meant those privileges which belong to him in consequence of his high station and dignity, are either direct or incidental. The chief of his direct prerogatives are, the power of making war and peace; of sending and receiving ambassadors; of pardoning offences; of conferring honours and titles of dignity; of appointing judges and subordinate magistrates; of giving or revoking commissions in the army or navy; and of rejecting bills proffered to him by the other branches of the legislature. He is the head of the national church, and nominates to vacant bishoprics and other ecclesiastical preferments.

15. But the king can only exercise his prerogatives through ministers, who are responsible to the nation for every act emanating from royal authority. Hence arises the aphorism that the "king can do no wrong," his ministers being alone answerable.

16. The incidental prerogatives of the king are various. A few alone need be mentioned: no costs can be recovered against him; his debt shall be preferred before that of a subject; no suit or action can be brought against him, but any

person having a claim in point of property on the king must petition him in chancery.

17. There are certain privileges also conceded to the royal family; the queen retains her title and dignity even after the death of her husband; she has authority to buy and sell in her own name, and to remove any suit in which she is concerned to whatever court she pleases, without any of the usual legal formalities. The king's eldest son is by his birth prince of Wales, and, by creation, duke of Cornwall and earl of Chester. All the king's children receive the title of "royal highness."

18. The house of lords is sometimes called the upper house of parliament. Its members are either temporal peers, whose dignities are hereditary, or spiritual peers, who sit only for life. The Scottish representative peers sit only for one parliament, the Irish representative peers sit for life. A peer may vote by proxy; but each peer can hold the proxy for one absent peer only. The house of lords can alone originate any bills that affect the rights or privileges of the peerage, and the commons are not permitted to make any alteration in them. Peers can be tried by the house of lords only; and this house constitutes the court in which officers of state are tried on impeachment by the house of commons; it is also the last court of appeal from inferior jurisdictions. Each peer may enter his protest on the journals when a vote passes contrary to his sentiments, and assign the reasons of his dissent in writing. When sitting in judgment, his verdict is given "on his honor." The same form is observed in his answers on bills in chancery, but in civil and criminal cases he must be sworn.

19. The house of lords (A.D. 1836) consists of—

Princes of the blood royal (all dukes)	4	Peers of Scotland	16
Other dukes*	21	Peers of Ireland	28
Marquesses	19	English bishops	26
Earls	110	Irish bishops	4
Viscounts	18	Making in all	426
Barons	180		

---

* *The origin and other particulars relative to the different classes of the nobility.*—DUKE.—This title was unknown in England till the reign of Edward III., who, in 1335, created his son, Edward the Black prince, duke of Cornwall (as before mentioned).
MARQUIS.—Richard II., in 1385, conferred the title of marquis on Robert de Vere, earl of Oxford, by making him Marquis of Dublin. This is supposed to be the origin of the title in England.
EARL.—This is a very ancient title, having been in use among our Saxon ancestors. In those times it was an official dignity, haivng a

20. The house of commons consists of members chosen by counties, cities, boroughs, and universities. The members for counties, commonly called knights of the shire, must possess a real estate of £600 a year, and members for cities or boroughs of £300 a year. The sons of peers and members for the universities are not required to produce these qualifications.

21. Aliens, clergymen, judges, returning officers in their respective jurisdictions, officers of the excise, &c., those who hold pensions of limited duration, contractors with government, and some others exposed to external influence, are uneligible to parliament.

22. The right of voting for members of parliament is given by the late reform act to leaseholders in counties seized of lands or tenements worth ten pounds a year, to tenants at will, farming lands at a rent of fifty pounds a year, and to holders in fee simple of lands or tenements of the yearly value of forty shillings. In cities and boroughs the right of voting is given to resident householders whose tenements are worth an annual rent of £10, but the rights of freemen in the old constituency are preserved for the term of their natural lives.

23. The house of commons contains—

English county members.	143 ⎫		Irish county members....	64 ⎫
Universities.............	4 ⎬ 471		Universities.............	2 ⎬ 105
Cities and boroughs......	324 ⎭		Cities and boroughs......	39 ⎭
Welsh county members..	15 ⎫ 29			
Cities and boroughs......	14 ⎭		Making in all.....	658
Scotch county members..	30 ⎫ 53			
Cities and boroughs......	23 ⎭			

24. In order to understand the manner in which the public business is transacted in parliament, we insert a brief account of the usual forms, and an explanation of the terms generally used. Discussions generally arise on a motion

---

jurisdiction over the place from which the title took its name. Soon after the Norman conquest, we find that William created several earls, allotting to each the third penny arising from the pleas in their respective districts. That grant, has, however, long since ceased, and in lieu of it the earls now receive a small annuity from the exchequer.

VISCOUNT.—The title of viscount is of much more recent date: the first we read of being John Beaumont, who was created viscount Beaumont by Henry VI. in the year 1439.

BARON.—In English history we often find the word Baron used to denominate the whole collective body of the nobility. When, after the Norman conquest, the Saxon title of *Thane* was disused, that of baron succeeded, and being the lowest title among the nobles, was very generally applied as the term *lord* is now; with which indeed, it appears to be synonymous.

being made by a member, seconded by another and then put from the chair in the shape of a question. On each of these every member is entitled to be heard once; but he may rise again to explain, and the member who originates a motion is allowed to reply.

25. Committees are, first, those of the whole house, which may be to consider of certain resolutions in respect to the nature of which considerable latitude prevails; or the house resolves itself into such committee to consider the details of a bill, the principle of which is never discussed unless on its several readings; or there may be committees for financial purposes as those of "supply," or "ways and means." Secondly, there are select committees, chosen by ballot or otherwise, for some specific purpose,—the numbers composing such bodies seldom exceed twenty or thirty members; occasionally these are declared committees of secrecy. Thirdly, election committees, which are strictly judicial tribunals, and whose duty it is to try the merits of controverted elections,—these are always chosen by ballot. Fourthly, committees on private bills.

26. When the whole house is in committee, the speaker vacates the chair, some other member is called on to preside, and he sits in the seat of the senior clerk. The mace is then placed under the table. For committees of supply and ways and means, there is a chairman, who receives a salary.

27. The prorogation of parliament is an act of the crown; but either house may adjourn its sittings to the next or any future day, as of course it may adjourn any debate. Motions of adjournment may be made at any time, and repeated at the pleasure of any member.

28. When a motion has been made upon which the house happens to be unwilling to come to a vote, there are formal modes of avoiding a decision, among which are passing "to the other orders," or moving "the previous question." The former means, that the house should—casting aside and taking no further notice of the matter then before it—proceed to the other business appointed for that day; the latter, that a vote be previously taken as to the expediency of their coming to any decision on the question raised. If "the previous question" be decided in the negative, the motion on which it bears is only gotten rid of for the time, whereas a direct negative to the motion itself would be a proscription of it for the remainder of the session, as well as a denial of its principle.

29. With respect to a bill, moving that it be "read this day six months" is a mode of throwing it out without coming to an express declaration against the principle of the measure.

30. An acceptance of "the Chiltern hundreds" is a form which has now no other meaning than that the member accepting resigns his seat. By an express act of parliament, no office having emolument attached, can be conferred by the crown on a member of the house of commons without his thereby vacating his seat, and it is only thus that a member can rid himself of the duties which any body of constituents may impose even without his consent. The crown, therefore, as an accommodation to the house at large, is always ready to confer on any member "the stewardship of his majesty's Chiltern hundreds," which office, when it has served his purpose, he immediately resigns.

31. The King, we have already said, is the fountain of executive justice. Law, whether criminal or civil, however, is administered by the judges, who, with the exception of the lord chancellor, hold their places during good behaviour. No man can be tried for any offence until the grand jurors of his country have decided that there is reasonable ground for the accusation. He is then given in charge to a jury of his equals, and their verdict is final. No man can be tried twice for the same offence; and when a person is convicted by a jury, there is no appeal but to the mercy of the king.

32. The administration of civil law could not be described within our narrow limits. It must suffice therefore to state, that the civil and common law courts are open to every suitor; and that justice is freely administered to all, whatever may be their rank or station.

Questions for Examination.

1. What is the use of a constitution?
2. Whence arises the peculiar excellence of the British constitution?
3. By whom was the first charter granted to the English people?
4. What circumstances led to the concession of Magna Charta?
5. Why were corporations established?
6. What was the origin of the house of commons?
7. Did the kings favour the house of commons?
8. When did the authority of the king come into collision with th authority of parliament?
9. What led to the revolution of 1688?
10. What change was made by the Reform Bill?
11. Into what branches is the British legislature divided?
12. How is the inheritance of the crown regulated?
13. Where are the king's duties prescribed?

14. What are the king's direct prerogatives?
15. How are these prerogatives exercised?
16. What are the king's incidental prerogatives?
17. Are any privileges conceded to the royal family?
18. Can you describe the privileges of the peerage?
19. How are the members of the house of lords classed?
20. What are the qualifications for a member of parliament?
21. Are any persons excluded from the lower house of parliament?
22. How is the right of voting for members of parliament regulated?
23. How are the members of the house of commons classed?
24. In what manner do discussions arise?
25. Can you describe the committees of the house of commons?
26. What form is used on going into committee?
27. How does prorogation of parliament differ from adjournment?
28. How does the house avoid coming to a decision?
29. How may a bill be rejected without prejudice to the principle it involves?
30. What is meant by accepting the Chiltern hundreds?
31. How is the criminal law administered?
32. Has due provision been made for the administration of common and civil law?

APPENDIX.

The following Tables are extracted from a very ingenious and valuable Engraving, entitled "HISTORY MADE EASY, or a GENEALOGICAL CHART OF THE KINGS OF ENGLAND," *by* E. REYNARD; *to which we beg to refer the reader for further useful information.*

MONARCHS BEFORE THE CONQUEST.

	No.	MONARCHS.	Began to Reign. A.D.	Reign'd Years.
Anglo-Saxons.	1	Egbert*	827	10
	2	Ethelwolf	838	20
	3	Ethelbald	857	3
	4	Ethelbert	860	6
	5	Ethelred I. †	866	5
	6	Alfred ‡	872	29
	7	Edward the Elder	901	24
	8	Athelstan	925	15
	9	Edmund I. §	940	6
	10	Edred	946	9
	11	Edway	955	4
	12	Edgar	959	16
	13	Edward II	975	3
	14	Ethelred II. ‖	978	37
	15	Edmund Ironside II	1016	1
Saxons. Danes.	16	Sweyn	1014	3
	17	Canute	1017	19
	18	Harold I	1036	3
	19	Hardicanute	1039	2
	20	Edward III, or the Confessor	1041	25
	21	Harold II., son of Godwin, earl of Kent.	1066	1

* Egbert descended from Cerdic, the first king of Wessex, a Saxon General, who in the year A. D. 495, arrived in Britain. It is said in the Saxon annals, that he was descended from Woden, the root of the Saxon families; and by his conquest which he made in Britain, he may be considered as one of the first founders of the English monarchy. The kings of England descend from him in the male line to Edward the Confessor, and in the female line to the illustrious princess who now sits upon the throne.

† Killed in battle against the Danes, in 871.

‡ Introduced trial by jury, divided England into shires and hundreds, and founded the University of Oxford.

§ Was killed by Leolf, a notorious robber.

‖ In 1014, Sweyn, king of Denmark, made himself master of England, and was crowned king; and Ethelred fled into Normandy. On the death of Sweyn, which happened in 1015, the crown was contested by Edmund Ironside (the lawful successor of Ethelred), and Canute, the descendant of Sweyn, who at length agreed to divide the kingdom among them; but Edmund, being murdered shortly after this treaty was entered into; Canute (surnamed the Great) was declared king of all England in 1017.

MONARCHS SINCE THE CONQUEST.

		MONARCHS.	Began to Reign	To whom married.	When married.	Reigned Years
House of Norman.	House of Blois.	1 William I.*	1066	Matilda of Flanders	1053	21
		2 William II	1087	(Never married)	—	13
		3 Henry I	1100	Matilda of Scotland	1100	35
		4 Stephen†	1135	Matilda of Bologne	1135	19
Plantagenet Race.		5 Henry II.‡	1155	Eleanor of Guienne	1151	34
		6 Richard I	1189	Berenguella of Navarre	1191	10
		7 John	1199	Earl Montague's daugh.	1185	17
				Avisa of Gloucester	1189	—
				Isabella of Angouleme	1200	—
		8 Henry III	1216	Eleanor of Provence	1236	56
		9 Edward I	1272	Eleanor of Castile	1253	35
				Mary of France	1299	—
		10 Edward II	1307	Isabella of France	1308	19
		11 Edward III	1327	Philipa of Hainault	1328	50
		12 Richard II	1377	Ann of Luxemburgh	1332	22
				Isabella of France	1396	—
House of Lancaster.	House of York.	13 Henry IV.§	1399	Mary Bohun	1397	13
				Joanna of Navarre	1403	—
		14 Henry V	1413	Catharine of France	1420	10
		15 Henry VI	1422	Margaret of Anjou	1444	38
		16 Edward IV.‖	1461	Elizabeth Woodville	1465	22
		17 Edward V	1483	(Never married)	—	—
		18 Richard III	1483	Ann Nevill	1471	2
House of Tudor.		19 Henry VII.¶	1485	Elizabeth of York	1486	23
		20 Henry VIII	1509	Catharine of Arragon	1509	37
				A. Boleyn; J. Seymour	1536	—
				A. of Cleves, C. Howard	1540	—
				Catharine Parr	1543	—
		21 Edward VI	1546	(Died young)	—	6
		22 Mary I	1553	Philip, king of Spain	1554	5
		23 Elizabeth	1558	Never married)	—	44
Race of Stuart.		24 James I.**	1603	Ann of Denmark	1589	22
		25 Charles I	1625	Henrietta of France	1625	24
		26 Charles II	1661	Catharine of Portugal	1662	24
		27 James II	1685	A. Hyde, 1660; M. Mod	1673	4
		28 Will. III & Mary II	1689	Mary, daugh. of Jas. II	1683	13
		29 Anne	1702	Geo. prince of Denmark	1683	12
House of Brunswick.		30 George I.††	1714	Sophia of Zell	1681	12
		31 George II	1727	Wilhelmina of Anspach	1705	33
		32 George III	1760	Charlotte of Meck Strel	1761	60
		33 George IV	1820	Caroline of Brunswick	1795	10
		34 William IV	1830	Adelaide of Saxe Mein	1818	7
		35 Victoria	1837	Albert of Saxe Gotha	1840	—

* Son of Robert, Duke of Normandy.
† Son of Adela and Count of Blois; hence the house of Blois.
‡ Son of Matilda and Geoffrey Plantagenet; hence the Plantagenet race.
§ Son of John of Gaunt, duke of Lancaster; hence the h. of Lancaster.
‖ Son of Richard, duke of York, lineally descended from Lionel, duke of Clarence, the second son of Edward the Third; hence the house of York.
¶ Was the son of Margaret and Edward Tudor. Margaret was a lineal descendant from John of Gaunt, duke of Lancaster; Edmund Tudor was the son of Owen Tudor, who married the widow of Henry V; hence the house of Tudor.
** Son of Mary, queen of Scots, and Henry Stuart, Lord Darnley; hence the race of Stuarts.
†† Elector of Hanover; hence the race of Brunswick.

DIVISION OF ENGLAND.

At the time of the Roman invasion.

England, including Wales, was, at the invasion of the Romans, divided into the following seventeen states.

Called by the Romans   Consisting of

1. THE DAMMONII . . Cornwall and Devon.
2. DUROTRIGES . . . . . Dorsetshire.
3. BELGÆ . . . . Somersetshire, Wilts, and parts of Hants.
4. ATTREBATII . . . . . . Berkshire.
5. REGNI . . . . Surrey, Sussex, and remaining part of Hants.
6. CANTII . . . . Kent.
7. DOBUNI . . . . Gloucester and Oxfordshire.
8. CATTIEUCHLANI . . Bucks, Bedford, and Hearts.
9. TRINOBANTES . . . . Essex and Middlesex.
10. ICENI . . . . Suffolk, Norfolk Huntingdon, and Cambridge.
11. CORITANI . . . . Northampton, Leister, Rutland, Lincoln, Nottingham, and Derby.
12. CORNAVI . . . . Warwick, Worcester, Stafford, Chester, and Shropshire.
13. THE SILURES . . . . Radnor, Brecon, Glamorgan, Monmouth, and Hereford,
14. DEMETÆ . . . . Pembroke, Cardigan, and Caermarthen.
15. ORDOVICES . . . . . . Montgomery, Merioneth, Caernarvon, Flint, and Denbigh.
16. THE BRIGANTES . . York, Durham, Lancashire, Westmoreland, and Cumberland.
17. OTTADINI . . . . Northumberland to the Tweed.

KINGS OF ENGLAND.

From the invasion of Julius Cæsar to the departure of the Romans.

ANNO A.C.	A.D.	A.D.
1. Cassivelaunus 83	6. Marius 15	12. Alectus 232
2. Theomantius......50	7 Coilus............175	13. Asclepiodorus..262
3. Cymbeline......24	8. Lucius..........207	14. Coilus II.......289
A.D.	9. Severus (cm)....211	15. Const'ntius(em)310
4. Guiderius........45	10. Bassianus......218	16. Const'nt'ne(em)329
5. Arviragus........73	11. Carausius......225	

From the departure of the Romans till the introduction of the Saxons by Vortigern.

A.D.	A.D.	A.D
Octavius..........383	Gratian............431	Constantius........446
Maximinianus.....391	Constantine I......446	Vortigern.........450

INTRODUCTION OF CHRISTIANITY.

According to Bede, and other authentic historians, the kingdoms of the Heptarchy embraced Christianity in about the following order:

	A.D.		A.D.
Kent	593	Wessex	636
East Saxons	604	Mercia	669
Northumberland	628	South Saxons	686
East Anglia	636		

	Began.	Ended.	Capital.
The kingdom of Kent	457	823	Canterbury.
East Saxons, or Essex	527	746	London.
Northumberland	547	792	York
East Anglia	575	783	Dunwich.
West Saxons, or Wessex	519	1066	Winchester.
Mercia	582	847	Leicester.
South Saxons	490	600	Chichester.

THE BRITISH MINISTRY.

September, 1841.

		Salary.
Sir ROBERT PEEL Bart	First Lord of the Treasury	£5,000
Lord LYNDHURST	Lord High Chancellor	14,000
Lord WHARNCLIFFE	Lord President of the Council	2,000
Duke of BUCCLEUCH	Lord Privy Seal	2,000
Sir JAMES R. G. GRAHAM	Secretary of State—*Home Dep.*	5,000
Earl of ABERDEEN	Secretary of State—*Foreign Dep.*	5,000
Lord STANLEY	Secretary of State—*Colonial Dep.*	5,000
Rt. Hon. HENRY GOULBOURN	Chancellor of the Exchequer	5,000
Earl of HADDINGTON	First Lord of the Admiralty	4,500
Sir EDWARD KNATCHBULL	Paymaster-General	2,500
Earl of RIPON	President of Board of Control	2,000
Rt. Hon. W. E. GLADSTONE	President of the Board of Trade	
Sir THOMAS FREEMANTLE	Secretary at War	2,580
Duke of WELLINGTON	Commander of the Forces	

REVENUE.

The total income of the year ending January 5, 1844, was......£50,071,943

END.

*DA32.7
G624
1866
children's

*DA32.7
G624
1866
children's

In the Soudan.

BY ANNA T. SADLIER.

Soldiers, ... sounding,
 Where... awake:
Yonder ... city
 Holds your long-desired stake.
See in dusky, orient columns
 Heathen foes come on apace.
Soldiers, ye were wont to meet them,
 Sternly, face to face.

Soldiers, see, the night clouds creeping,
 Slowly o'er the desert waste;
Stars are gleaming, darkness falling;
 Soldiers, hasten ye, O haste!
Nearer come those Moslem legions,
 Swartly, dark-browed, sworn to slay:
Soon the amber, tropic morning
 Shows them in their dread array.

Soldiers, whence this shadow settling
 O'er your faces gray and chill,
Gone the flush of kindling ardor,
 High hearts now forever still.
Soldiers, see, the day nigh breaking,
 Rise, O rise, your weapons take,
God, can this be death that checks them,
 Can it be such hearts could break?

Soldiers, yesterday departing,
 Ye have left home, country, all,
Tell us not the desert gave you
 Nameless graves—a common pall.
Gallant hearts, the foe is coming,
 See th' advancing lines, the fire,
Reck ye not of fearful charges,
 Forlorn hopes and vengeance dire.

Silent yet, white faces gazing
 Upwards to these alien stars;
Lips set coldly, pulses nerveless—
 Warriors of many wars.
See, your useless swords are lying
 Where your hands relaxed their hold.
Oh, what fiery courage bade ye
 Gird them on in days of old.

Soldiers, in your homes of mourning,
 Eyes grown wan with tears are pressed
On the lines whose deadly import
 Few who read have fully guessed:
War lists, with the dead and missing.
 Brides and mothers, wherefore ...
Far, where desert sands are burn...
 Heroes lie in glorious sleep!

Soldiers, see, the Nile's strange ...
 Flows hard by your place of r...
Death, whom ye have ...
 Holds you each his ...
Never more sh... ttle
 Rouse ye, ... trumpet calls;
Soldiers, the ... sounding
 On your d... ars coldly falls.

MUSIC AND THE DRAMA.

*DA32.7
G624
1866
children's

bring down the budget as soon as possible. On being ____ Mr. Gagnon to name a day as ____ he would make an effort to present the ____ next. It is not probable that he will be able to do this, however, as he complains that the ordinary duties of his office take up every moment of his time. While on this topic it may be mentioned that the Conservatives confidently expect a surplus for the present fiscal year, owing to the increased subsidy from the Federal Government granted them last year.

MONTREAL ELECTORAL DIVISION.

The House next went into committee upon Mr. Taillon's motion with respect to the West and Centre divisions of Montreal. There was no opposition, Mr. McShane stating he was not prepared to discuss the question at the moment, but would reserve his remarks for a later stage. In consequence, the bill was reported and ordered to be read a third time to-day, after which the House adjourned. When the bill comes up for its third reading Mr. McShane will move, if he can get the concurrence of the House, that the bill be recommitted to the committee of the whole to enable him to move an amendment that the representation of Montreal be increased to seven members in the manner laid down in his speech of Wednesday.

THE DEFICIT.

It is impossible to gather from the statement presented by the Treasurer an exact idea of the amount of the deficit between the revenue and normal expenditure of the province for the last fiscal year, because loans and other moneys received and spent on capital account are placed together with the receipts and disbursements on revenue account. There will be much dispute as to which account many items should be charged, but even the ministry admit a deficit ranging from two hundred to two hundred and fifty thousand dollars. Among the rank and file the amount is variously stated all the way up to $800,000, and there are rumors of cooked accounts. If the accounts be indisputable the deficit cannot reach a larger sum than $500,000, if so much. However, the budget debate will clear up the whole mystery, and until then it is impossible for any one to insist upon a particular figure.

NOTES.

The Corporation of the Protestant Insane Asylum of Montreal have sent to the ministry a petition asking that the Leduc farm be granted them for the site of the proposed asylum, and in addition the sum of $20,000.

The Public Accounts Committee met yesterday morning, and elected Mr. Garneau ____man.

*DA32.7
G624
1866
children's

THE "AWETO."

The oddest insect in existence—so odd that unless it were vouched for and explained scientifically would be considered a hoax—is the aweto. It is not easy to decide whether it ought to be classed under the fauna or flora of New Zealand, for it is as much vegetable as animal, and in final stage, it is a vegetable and nothing else. This is the vegetable caterpillar, called by naturalists *Hipialis virescens*. It is a perfect caterpillar, and a fine one also, growing to three and a half inches. Until it is full grown it conducts itself very much like any other insect, except that it is never found anywhere but in the neighborhood of the Rata tree, a large scarlet-flowered myrtle, and that it habitually buries itself a few inches under ground. Then, when the Aweto is fully grown, it undergoes a wonderful change. For some inexplicable reason, the spore of a vegetable fungus, the *Sphæria Robertsii*, fixes itself directly on its neck, takes root, [...] diminutive bulrush, [...] without leaves, and w[...]

DA32.7
G624
1866
children's

www.ingramcontent.com/pod-product-compliance
Lightning Source LLC
Chambersburg PA
CBHW051156300426
44116CB00006B/335